Not For Tourists Guide to

NEW YORK CITY

ot For Tourists, Inc

Skyhorse Publishing

designed by:
Not For Tourists, Inc
NFTTM—**Not For Tourists**TM **Guide to New York City**
www.notfortourists.com

Printed in China
Print ISBN: 978-1-5107-4415-8
Ebook ISBN: 978-1-5107-4420-2
ISSN 2162-6103
Copyright © 2018 by Not For Tourists, Inc.
20th Edition

Every effort has been made to ensure that the information in this book is as up-to-date as possible at press time. However, many details are liable to change—as we have learned.
Not For Tourists cannot accept responsibility for any consequences arising from the use of this book.

Not For Tourists does not solicit individuals, organizations, or businesses for listings inclusion in our guides, nor do we accept payment for inclusion into the editorial portion of our book; the advertising sections, however, are exempt from this policy. We always welcome communications from anyone regarding ANYTHING having to do with our books; please visit us on our website at www. notfortourists.com for appropriate contact information.

"New York is the concentrate of art and commerce and sport and religion and entertainment and finance, bringing to a single compact arena the gladiator, the evangelist, the promoter, the actor, the trader and the merchant." —E. B. White

Dear NFT User:

We released our first book, the NFT Guide to Manhattan, in May 2000 after two grueling years of research and development in which we pounded the pavement so hard that our feet still hurt. Looking back on those heady first days it's hard to fathom that over a decade later, we'd be working on our nineteenth edition of the guide. That's 19—a number so high copy editors cry when they see it written out.

But even after 20 editions it always warms each of our cold, crusty, curmudgeonly hearts when we come across someone on the street consulting their little black book. Whether you're navigating your way through this "concrete jungle where dreams are made of" (as Alicia once sang) using our specially formulated maps that at least one optometrist has ensured us is at least 30 percent less strain-inducing than it once was, or just quietly taking in the full force of our collective genius as we distill the best bar on the block down to a haiku-like three- to ten-word blurb, trust us, we always feel a flush of pride when we see people out in public reading a NFT guide.

That's because like the best house-cured meat along Arthur Avenue, the finest crust on a Staten Island pizza pie, or the most transcendent Brooklyn mayonnaise, this little black guide is, at its core, an artisanal product. With NFT, the blurbs you get are all house made, never processed, especially via some faceless algorithm—because, let's face it, our servers could never handle it anyway. Like that roomy boutique on that sketchy block down by the waterfront, NFT is carefully curated to offer you the best of what a neighborhood has to offer. And if a trendy, stinky, or otherwise unfun place isn't worth your or anyone else's time, we feel free to exclude it, because at NFT we pride ourselves in not only being "well edited" but actually "best edited."

Anyway, as we like to say, wrap your furry paws around this superior guide of all things New York City and get ready to scout the holes in the wall so holey the Department of Buildings should have long since shut them down, bars so divey you'll need a scuba tank to get there, and shops so indispensable they're still working for Lehman Brothers years after the collapse. Of course if and when you come across something we missed, please send us a note at www.notfortourists.com, because at its core, NFT is a family, and we wouldn't be who we are without you. So if you're new to us, welcome! And if you're coming back, thanks for continuing to trust us enough to show us around in public…

Table of Contents

Subway Map/Bus Map
foldout, last page

Map 1 · **Financial District**

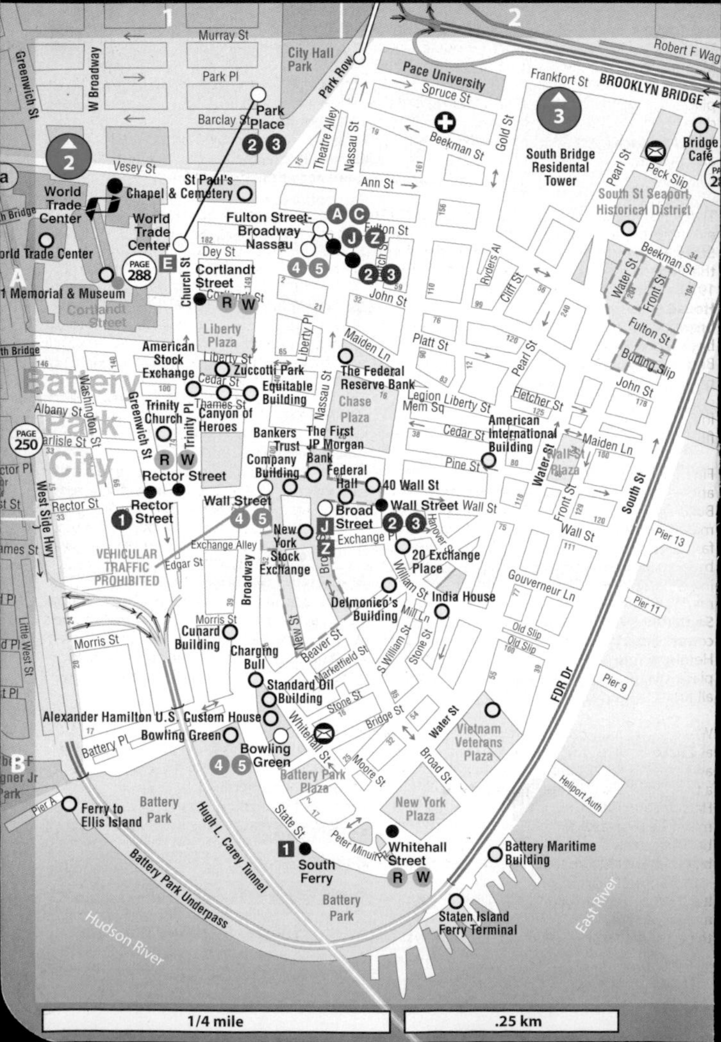

Murray St

City Hall Park

Park Pl

Park Row

Pace University

Frankfort St

BROOKLYN BRIDGE

Robert F Wag

2

Greenwich St

W Broadway

Barclay St

Spruce St

Beekman St

Gold St

3

South Bridge Residental Tower

Bridge Café

2

Peck Slip

Vesey St

Park Place

2 3

St Paul's Chapel & Cemetery

Ann St

Pearl St

South St Seaport Historical District

World Trade Center

2

Beekman St

World Trade Center

Fulton Street Broadway Nassau

A C

Rector St

J Z

John St

Cliff St

Ryders Al

Water St

Front St

Fulton St

Dey St

E

Cortlandt Street

4 5

2 3

PAGE 288

Church St

R W

John St

Platt St

Pearl St

Maiden Ln

Liberty Pl

American Stock Exchange

Liberty Plaza

Liberty St

Cedar St

Zuccotti Park

Equitable Building

The Federal Reserve Bank

Chase Plaza

Legion Mem Sq

Liberty St

American International Building

Battery Park City

PAGE 250

Albany St

Trinity Church

Thames St

Canyon of Heroes

Nassau St

Maiden Ln

Cedar St

Wall St Plaza

Pine St

Carlisle St

Rector Pl

Greenwich St

Trinity Pl

Bankers Trust Company Building

The First JP Morgan Bank

Federal Hall

40 Wall St

West Side Hwy

Rector Street

R

Thames St

Wall Street

4 5

New York Stock Exchange

J

Wall Street

2 3

Wall St

Front St

South St

Rector Street

1

Broadway

Exchange Alley

Edgar St

Broad Street

Exchange Pl

William St

20 Exchange Place

Pier 13

VEHICULAR TRAFFIC PROHIBITED

Morris St

Cunard Building

Broadway

Delmonico's Building

India House

Gouverneur Ln

Old Slip

Pier 11

Little West St

Charging Bull

Beaver St

William St

Standard Oil Building

Stone St

Old Slip

Morris St

Pl

Battery Pl

Alexander Hamilton U.S. Custom House

Bowling Green

Whitehall St

S William St

Bridge St

Water St

Vietnam Veterans Plaza

Pier 9

Heliport Auth

Ferry to Ellis Island

Battery Park

Bowling Green

4 5

Beaver St

Moore St

Broad St

New York Plaza

Battery Park Plaza

FDR Dr

East River

Hugh L. Carey Tunnel

State St

Peter Minuit

South Ferry

1

Whitehall St

R W

Whitehall Street

Battery Maritime Building

Battery Park Underpass

Battery Park

Staten Island Ferry Terminal

Hudson River

1/4 mile	.25 km

Neighborhood Overview

This is where it all began. Site of the original Dutch settlement on Manhattan Island, the Financial District contains more historical markers than any other part of the city. If you're looking for a place to start, check out **St. Paul's Chapel and Cemetery**, which dates back to 1766, **Trinity Church**, whose spire was once the tallest point in Manhattan, and **Federal Hall**, site of the first capitol of the United States. You can also head to Battery Park to take the **ferry** to the Statue of Liberty, and, far more interestingly, to Ellis Island where you can explore the history of immigration in the United States.

That's just the beginning. The importance of New York as a financial and commercial center is evident on practically every street. To take it in, check out, in no particular order, the **New York Stock Exchange**, the NYSE Amex Equities (formerly known as the **American Stock Exchange**), the **Federal Reserve Bank**, the first **JP Morgan Bank** (still visibly scarred from a bombing in 1920), John D. Rockefeller's **Standard Oil Building**, and the **Alexander Hamilton US Custom House** (now the National Museum of the American Indian). The architecture of the chocolate brown federal-style **India House** and stunning maritime themed interior of the **Cunard Building** both represent distinct eras of New York's commercial past. Rivaling Grand Central and Brooklyn Bridge as Manhattan's most gorgeous gateway, the **Battery Maritime Building** is the departure point for the summer ferry to Governor's Island, where you can stroll around fortifications built during the Revolutionary War. Last but not least, the **Charging Bull** statue at **Bowling Green**, initially installed as a piece of guerrilla art, has become the ultimate symbol for New York's financial strength, and beloved by photo-snapping tourists from all over the world.

Financial growth led to the creation of the modern skyscraper, and many famous examples soar above these streets. Notable buildings include **40 Wall Street** (now known as the "Trump Building"), art deco gems **20 Exchange Place** and the **American International Building**, the massive **Equitable Building**, and the **Bankers Trust Company Building**. Of course, the most famous structure is the one that's missing—the World Trade Center Towers, which were destroyed by a terrorist attack on September 11, 2001. That said, the **World Trade Center** has been reborn in an inspiring if slightly schizophrenic monument to both its tragic past and hopeful future. Two mammoth pools mark the footprint of the original towers and the gut wrenching **National September 11 Memorial & Museum** literally digs deep to tell the definitive story of that day and commemorate those lives lost. Looking up, One World Trade Center, the city's (and Western Hemisphere's) tallest skyscraper, towers over the site. As soon as its ceremonial spire was put in place, the 1,776-foot-high landmark restored Lower Manhattan's visual and psychic balance; now all that's left is to rent out all that vacant space.

When you're ready for a break from all that history and architecture, take in some people watching at **Zuccotti Park** (onetime hub for the Occupy Wall Street protest) or reflect in the relative peace and quiet of the **Vietnam Veterans Plaza**. The best way to chill out might be by simply grabbing a beer on board the free **Staten Island Ferry** and checking out the awesome views of New York Harbor commuters get to enjoy every day. The tourists will all be at **South Street Seaport**, which might be best avoided unless you like crowded cobblestoned shopping malls. As far as kicking back in quaint downtown is concerned, Stone Street and Front Street are perfect spots to grab a bite and a drink after a day of wandering around. We'll see you there!

It ain't the village by any stretch, but Front Street has some good options like wine bar **Bin 220** and **Fresh Salt**. Old stalwarts like the **The Paris Cafe** and the **Bridge Cafe** capture the history of the area. The semi-secret Blue Bar at **India House** is a NFT favorite—you can thank us later.

O Landmarks

- **20 Exchange Place** •
  20 Exchange Pl [William St]
  Cool facade with bronze depictions of various modes of transport.
- **40 Wall St** • 40 Wall St [William St]
  Tallest building in the world for a day in 1930. Oh and Trump owns it.
- **70 Pine Street** • 70 Pine St [Pearl St]
  Great Art Deco skyscraper.
- **8 Spruce Street** • 8 Spruce St [William St]
  76-story Gehry masterpiece overlooking the Brooklyn Bridge. Sublime.
- **Alexander Hamilton U.S. Custom House** •
  1 Bowling Green [State St]
  Stately Cass Gilbert building; check out the oval staircases.
- **American Stock Exchange** •
  86 Trinity Pl [Thames St]
  212-306-1000
  New York's other stock exchange.
- **Bankers Trust Company Building** •
  14 Wall St [Nassau St]
  More neck-craning excitement from the NYC skyline!
- **Battery Maritime Building** •
  10 South St [Broad St]
  Ready-to-be-converted riverfront building.
- **Bowling Green** • Broadway & State St
  Watch the tourists take pics of the bull. New York's first park.
- **Canyon of Heroes** •
  Broadway b/n Bowling Green & City Hall Park
  Markers in the sidewalk remember those honored with a ticker tape parade.
- **Charging Bull** • Bowling Green Park
  Rub his cojones for luck.
- **Cunard Building** • 25 Broadway [Morris St]
  Former Cunard headquarters, former post office, currently a locked building with great ceiling mosaics.
- **Delmonico's** • 56 Beaver St [S William St]
  212-509-1144
  Once the site of THE restaurant in New York.
- **Equitable Building** • 120 Broadway [Cedar St]
  Its massiveness gave momentum to zoning laws for skyscraper
- **Federal Hall** • 26 Wall St [Broad St]
  212-825-6888
  Where George the First was inaugurated.
- **Federal Reserve Bank of New York** •
  33 Liberty St [William St]
  212-720-6130
  Where *Die Hard 3* took place.

- **Ferry to Ellis Island** • Pier A & Battery Park
  The main building features beautiful domed ceilings and Guastavino tiled arches.
- **The First JP Morgan Bank** •
  23 Wall St [Broad St]
  Still visibly scarred from an anarchist bombing in 1920.
- **The Oculus Greenwich St** • Dey St [Dey St]
  646-370-3337 • $$
  Yes, it's a shopping mall but it's the most beautiful one ever made.
- **India House Club** • 1 Hanover Sq [Stone St]
  212-269-2323
  Members-only club in historic, nautical-themed house.
- **National September 11 Memorial & Museum** • Greenwich St [Cortlandt St]
  212-312-8800
  Awe-inspiring tribute to those lost, surrounded by rebirth.
- **New York Stock Exchange** •
  20 Broad St [Exchange Pl]
  212-656-5168
  Where *Wall Street* took place.
- **The Oculus** • Greenwich St [Dey St]
  212-284-9982
  Yes, it's a shopping mall, but it's the most beautiful one ever made.
- **One World Trade Center** • Vesey St [West St]
  At 1,776 feet, the tallest building in the Western Hemisphere.
- **South Street Seaport** • 12 Fulton St [South St]
  212-732-7678
  Mall with historic ships as backdrop.
- **St. Paul's Chapel & Cemetery** •
  Broadway & Fulton St
  212-233-4164
  Old-time NYC church and cemetery.
- **Standard Oil Building** •
  26 Broadway [Morris St]
  Sweeping wall of a building overlooking Bowling Green.
- **Staten Island Ferry** • 1 Whitehall St [Stone St]
  Grab a tall boy on board and enjoy the view.
- **Vietnam Veterans Memorial Plaza** •
  55 Water St [Coenties Slip]
  212-471-9496
  A nice quiet spot to contemplate our faded dreams of empire.
- **World Trade Center** • Church St & Vesey St
  Inspiring (if schizophrenic) monument to tragic past and hopeful future.
- **Zuccotti Park** • Trinity Pl & Cedar St
  Birthplace of Occupy Wall Street, ca. 2011.

Our Stone Street favorite is **Adrienne's Pizza Bar**, and on Front Street it's the New Zealand goodness of **Nelson Blue**. You can eat cheaply at **Sophie's**, **Financier Patisserie**, **Zaitzeff**, and greasy spoon **Pearl Street Diner** while you wait for financial success and a table at **Mark Joseph**.

Coffee

- **Cosi** • 55 Broad St [Beaver St]
  212-344-5000
  Starbucks-lite with fire roasted sandwiches.
- **FIKA** • 66 Pearl St [Broad St]
  646-837-6588
  Great coffeehouse run by friendly Swedes.
- **Financier Patisserie** • 35 Cedar St [Liberty St]
  212-952-3838
  Trés bien croissants.
- **Jack's Stir Brew Coffee** •
  222 Front St [Peck Slip]
  212-227-7631
  Excellent little coffeehouse, especially for these parts.

Farmers Markets

- **Bowling Green Greenmarket** •
  Broadway & Battery Pl
  Tues & Thurs 8 am–5 pm, Year Round
- **PATH Greenmarket** • Barclay St & W Broadway
  Tues & Thurs 8 am–6 pm, April–Dec
- **Staten Island Ferry Whitehall Terminal Greenmarket** • 4 South St [Whitehall St]
  Tues & Fri 8 am–7 pm, Year Round

Nightlife

- **Bin 220** • 220 Front St [Beekman St]
  212-374-9463
  Escape the tourists at this excellent little wine bar.
- **The Dead Rabbit** • 30 Water St [Broad St]
  646-422-7906
  Fancy cocktails in an old-timey, Irish-American atmosphere.
- **Fresh Salt** • 146 Beekman St [Front St]
  212-962-0053
  Where architects go for happy hour.
- **Harry's Cafe & Steak** • 1 Hanover Sq [Pearl St]
  212-785-9200
  The vintage French wine flows like a river. Or at least it used to.
- **India House Club** • 1 Hanover Sq [Stone St]
  212-269-2323
  Secret bar to the left up the stairs. You're welcome.

- **Jeremy's Ale House** • 228 Front St [Peck Slip]
  212-964-3537
  Weekend nights are at your own risk.
- **Killarney Rose** • 127 Pearl St [Hanover St]
  212-422-1486
  Irish pub where you can pregame for the Staten Island Ferry.
- **Liquid Assets** • 55 Church St [Fulton St]
  212-693-2001
  Plush seating and soft lighting.
- **Paris Café** • 119 South St [Peck Slip]
  212-240-9797
  Good, historic bar but used to be better. Best very late.
- **Ulysses Folk House** • 95 Pearl St [Hanover Sq]
  212-482-0400
  Slightly hipper downtown bar.
- **Vintry** • 57 Stone St [Mill Ln]
  212-480-9800
  Fine wine and whiskey for sophisticated grape and grain lovers.
- **Whitehorse Tavern** •
  25 Bridge St [Whitehall St]
  212-668-9046
  Downtown dive. Not to be confused with the one in the West Village.

🍴 Restaurants

- **Acqua at Peck Slip** • 21 Peck Slip [Water St]
212-349-4433 • $$$
Italian straight off the boat. Nice one.
- **Adrienne's Pizzabar** •
54 Stone St [S William St]
212-248-3838 • $$
Delectable rectangular pies from a NYC pizza master.
- **Barbalu** • 225-227 Front St [Beekman St]
646-918-6565 • $$$
Elegant Italian from Sandy survivors/former Barbarini owners.
- **Bareburger** • 155 William St [Ann St]
646-657-0388 • $$
Good local burger chain serving up exotic meats.
- **Battery Gardens** •
1 Battery Pl
212-809-5508 • $$$$$
Panoramic views of NY harbor with a wood-burning fireplace.
- **The Capital Grille** • 120 Broadway [Pine St]
212-374-1811 • $$$$$
High-end chain perfect for someone else's expense account.
- **Cosi** • 55 Broad St [Beaver St]
212-344-5000 • $
Sandwiches for the masses.
- **Cowgirl Sea-Horse** • 259 Front St [Dover St]
212-608-7873 • $$
Surf shack serving up home "beach baskets."
- **Delmonico's** • 56 Beaver St [S William St]
212-509-1144 • $$$
Classic NYC spot. Since 1837.
- **Dig Inn Seasonal Market** •
80 Pine St [Pearl St]
212-785-1110 • $
Excellent farm-fresh meat and veggie buffet, surprisingly inexpensive.
- **Dorlan's Tavern** • 213 Front St [Beekman St]
212-779-2222 • $$$
At least ten raw oyster options. We're there.

- **Eataly NYC Downtown** • 101 Liberty St
[Church St] 212-897-2895 • $$$
Bustling WTC version of Batali/Bastianich brainchild.
- **El Luchador** • 87 South St [John St]
646-398-7499 • $$
Great taqueria w/ outdoor seating.
- **Felice 15** • 15 Gold St [Platt St]
212-785-5950 • $$$
Nice contemporary Italian with good appetizers.
- **Financier Patisserie** • 62 Stone St [Mill Ln]
212-344-5600 • $$
Have your cake and a light meal, too.
- **GRK Fresh Greek** • 111 Fulton St [Ann St]
212-385-2010 • $$$
Good quick Greek for lunch.
- **Grotto Pizzeria** • 69 New St [Beaver St]
212-809-6990 • $$
More quick, tasty Italian. Less nudity than that other grotto.
- **The Growler** • 55 Stone St [Mill Ln]
917-409-0251 • $$
Pub grub, craft beer, and a dog-friendly patio.
- **Harry's Cafe & Steak** • 1 Hanover Sq [Pearl St]
212-785-9200 • $$$$
When the market is flush so is Harry.
- **Luke's Lobster** • 26 S William St [Broad St]
212-747-1700 • $$
Fresh-from-the sea lobster rolls, without sticker shock.
- **Mark Joseph Steakhouse** •
261 Water St [Peck Slip]
212-277-0020 • $$$$
Luger's wannabe: damn close, actually, and they take plastic.
- **Melt Shop** • 110 Fulton St [Dutch St]
646-741-7910 • $$
"Shop" tots and fried chicken grilled cheese sandwiches. Ah.
- **Neapolitan Express** • 40 Wall St [Williams St]
844-697-5423 • $$
Mission-driven pizza; 900-degree ovens with zero emissions.

Gourmet markets **Jubilee** and **Zeytuna** keep Financial District dwellers fed. Pick up some wine from **Downtown Cellars** or **Pasanella**, then grab a coffee at **Fika**.

- **Paris Café** • 119 South St [Peck Slip]
212-240-9797 • $$$
Good burgers and seafood, a bit pricey though.
- **Pearl Street Diner** • 212 Pearl St [Platt St]
212-344-6620 • $
Greasy spoon hidden among the skyscrapers.
- **Sophie's Cuban** • 73 New St [Beaver St]
212-809-7755 • $
Great cheap Cuban/Caribbean.
- **Sophie's Cuban** • 76 Fulton St [Gold St]
212-608-6769 • $
Great cheap Cuban/Caribbean.
- **Suteishi** • 24 Peck Slip [Front St]
212-766-2344 • $$$
Hip seaport sushi. Get the Orange/Red Dragon split.
- **Trading Post** • 170 John St [South St]
Super-cool bi-level American, with oysters and drinks.
- **Trinity Place** • 115 Broadway [Cedar St]
212-964-0939 • $$$$
Good drinks and American-Irish cuisine in bank vault space.
- **Ulysses Folk House** • 95 Pearl St [Hanover Sq]
212-482-0400 • $$$
Highlight: the buffet spread.
- **Wall Street Bath & Spa** • 88 Fulton St [Gold St]
212-766-8600 • $$
Pre- and post- rub and tub grub.
- **Zaytuna** • 59 Maiden Ln [William St]
212-742-2436 • $$
Gourmet take-out. NFT fave.

🛍 Shopping

- **Bowne & Co Stationers** •
211 Water St [Beekman St]
212-748-8651
Old fashioned presses make prints, maps & cards.
- **Century 21** • 22 Cortlandt St [Broadway]
212-227-9092
Where most New Yorkers buy their underwear.
- **Dick's Cut Rate Hardware** • 9 Gold St [Platt St]
212-425-1070
Not a sex shop.
- **Drago Shoe Repair** • 123 Fulton St [Dutch St]
212-947-8496
When your sole needs fixin'.
- **Jubilee Marketplace** • 99 John St [Cliff St]
212-233-0808
Godsend for Financial District dwellers.
- **La Petite Cave** • 83 Maiden Ln [Liberty St]
212-514-9817
Friendly owner with well curated wine selection.
- **Northern Grade** • 203 Front St [Fulton St]
212-406-0300
Stylish, all-American made clothing and accessory brands
- **Pasanella and Son Vintners** •
115 South St [Peck Slip]
212-233-8383
Great wine shop. Movies screenings in the back tasting room!
- **Zeytuna** • 59 Maiden Ln [William St]
212-742-2436
Excellent gourmet store—fish, meat, cheese counters. Yum.

Map 2 • TriBeCa

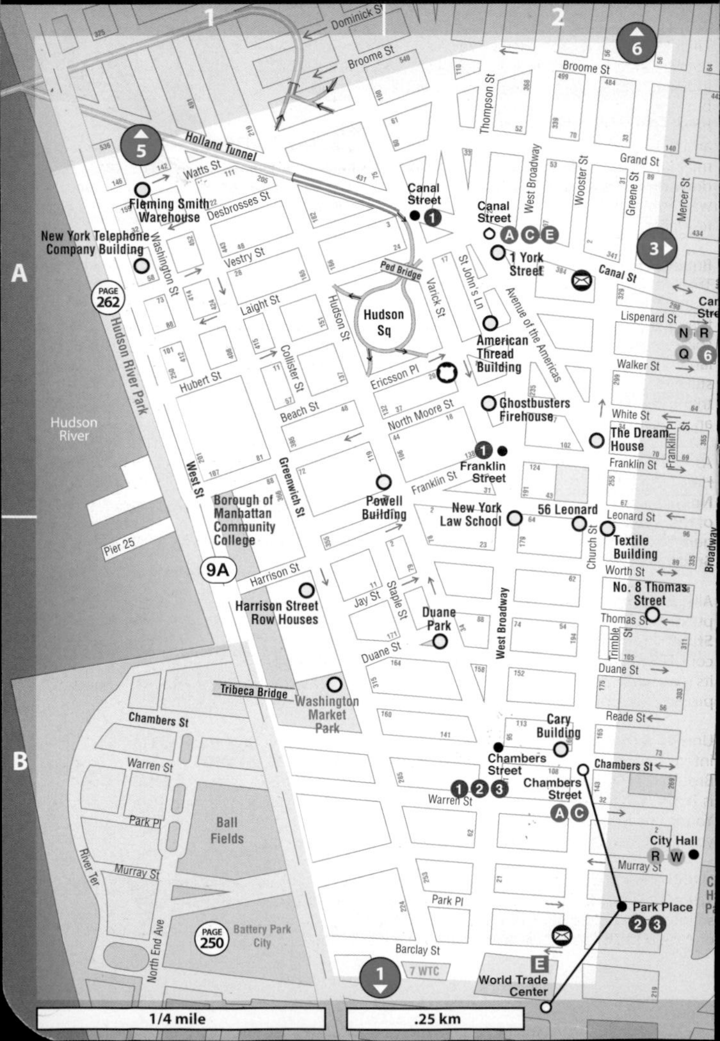

N

1

2

Dominick St

Broome St

648

Broome St

499

464

140

6

▲
6

Holland Tunnel

Watts St

5
▲

208

437

Fleming Smith
Warehouse

Desbrosses St

New York Telephone
Company Building

Washington St

Vestry St

Canal
Street
1

Canal
Street
A C E

1 York
Street

Thompson St

West Broadway

Wooster St

Greene St

Mercer St

434

Grand St

3 ▶

Canal St

✉

PAGE
262

Laight St

Hudson River Park

Collister St

Hudson St

Ped Bridge

Varick St

St John's Ln

Hudson
Sq

Avenue of the Americas

Lispenard St

N R
Q 6

Canal
Stre

341

Hubert St

Beach St

Ericsson Pl

American
Thread
Building

North Moore St

Walker St

White St

84

The Dream
House

Franklin St

102

9A

Hudson
River

West St

Greenwich St

Borough of
Manhattan
Community
College

Pier 25

Harrison St

Harrison Street
Row Houses

Powell
Building

Franklin
Street
1

Franklin St
211

New York
Law School
64

124

56 Leonard

Church St

Leonard St

Textile
Building

Worth St

No. 8 Thomas
Street

Thomas St

Staple St

Jay St

Duane
Park

Duane St
164

West Broadway

24

152

Trimble Pl

Duane St

73

Reade St

Tribeca Bridge

Washington
Market Park

760

141

Cary
Building

113

108

Chambers St

Chambers St

Chambers St
Row

Chambers Street
1 2 3

Chambers
Street
A C

City Hall
R W

Murray St

Park Place
2 3

✉

E
World Trade
Center

7 WTC

1
▼

Chambers St

Warren St

Park Pl

Murray St

River Ter

North End Ave

Battery Park
City

PAGE
250

Warren St
62

Park Pl

Barclay St

Ball
Fields

1/4 mile	.25 km

Neighborhood Overview

Map 2

Thinking of moving to TriBeCa? Well, then, congratulations—you've clearly made your first $10 million! And, if you already live there…well, you're not reading a guidebook anyway…but maybe your assistant is. As for the rest of us, we'll just have to be content with walking around the neighborhood and choosing which fabulous converted loft building we'd live in when WE make our first $10 million. Such is life in one of New York's prime neighborhoods—minutes away from downtown, the West Village, SoHo, and Chinatown, decent subway access, a few minutes' walk to either the Battery Park City promenade or Hudson River Park, excellent restaurants, a few killer bars—if you can afford it, of course.

But even if you can't, there's no question that walking around is our favorite pastime in the Triangle Below Canal Street (Canal Street being the north side of the triangle, Broadway being the east side of the triangle, and the West Side Highway being the west side of the triangle). On your walk, you'll pass one of the city's oldest parks (**Washington Market Park**), some ancient row houses (the **Harrison Street Row Houses**) and our favorite TriBeCa landmark, the **Ghostbusters Firehouse** (you'll know it when you see it, trust us). A great starting point for seeing TriBeCa is its nexus, lovely little **Duane Park**. It's a quaint little triangle surrounded on all sides by gorgeous factory buildings converted into lofts you'd give an arm and a leg to live in.

As for the buildings themselves, there are a several worth noting, including Henry J. Hardenbergh's **Textile Building**, Carrère and Hastings' **Powell Building**, which now houses Nobu, Ralph Walker's massive **New York Telephone Company Building**, the rounded front of the **American Thread Building**, the Venetian mash-up of **No. 8 Thomas Street**, cast-iron gem the **Cary Building**, and, the "pièce de résistance," Stephen Decatur Smith's **Fleming Smith Warehouse** on Washington Street.

Although most of the new construction (especially along Broadway) fits into the boring/puerile category, one new building to check out is Enrique Norten's postmodern **One York Street**; his insertion of a glass tower in the middle of two 19th-century buildings is pretty cool. **New York Law School's** new building at 185 West Broadway shines brightly at night as its law students burn the candle at both ends. Meanwhile, Herzog & de Meuron's **56 Leonard** project set records for residential sales.

Unfortunately, we just don't get to TriBeCa as much at night any more, as two of its most interesting cultural hotspots—the Knitting Factory and Roulette—have long since moved to Brooklyn. However, one of the coolest long-running sound and light installations in the world is here, at 275 Church Street, just steps from the swanky **TriBeCa Grand Hotel**. La Monte Young and Marian Zazeela's **Dream House** is a special place to chill out and get in touch with your inner being in the midst of all this residential poshness.

Nightlife is quieter here than in other neighborhoods, but upscale drinks can be found at **TriBeCa Grand** and **Bubble Lounge** and **Nancy Whiskey** and **Puffy's** are classic dives. Old school hangout **Walker's** is a New York classic and should not be missed; otherwise, check out the **Flea Theatre**'s calendar or wait for the **TriBeCa Film Festival**.

Map 2

8 9 10
5 6 7
2 3 4
1

TriBeCa

○ Landmarks

- **56 Leonard** • 56 Leonard St [Church St]
  Knee-buckling 60-story glass Jenga palace.
- **American Thread Building** •
  260 W Broadway [Beach St]
  Check out cool rounded front; watch out for
  tunnel traffic.
- **Cary Building** • 105 Chambers St [Church St]
  Cast-iron goodness on Chambers. We like it.
- **Dream House** • 275 Church St [White St]
  212-925-8270
  Cool sound + light installation by La Monte
  Young and Marian Zazeela. Closed during
  summer.
- **Duane Park** • Duane St & Hudson St
  One of the nicest spots in all of New York.
- **Fleming Smith Warehouse** •
  451 Washington St [Watts St]
  TriBeCa's most sublimely beautiful structure.
  Believe it.
- **Ghostbusters Firehouse** •
  14 N Moore St [Varick St]
  Are you the gatekeeper?
- **Harrison Street Row Houses** •
  Harrison St & Greenwich St
  Nice collection of preserved Federalist
  architecture.
- **New York Law School** •
  185 W Broadway [Leonard St]
  212-431-2100
  New York Law's new main building burns
  brightly on cold TriBeCa nights.
- **New York Telephone Company Building** •
  140 West St [Vestry St]
  Massive Art Deco gem still looms over
  now-fashionable TriBeCa.
- **No. 8 Thomas Street** •
  8 Thomas St [Broadway]
  Bizarre Venetian townhouse in the middle of
  downtown. Really.
- **One York Street** • 1 York St [Canal St]
  Enrique Norten's postmodern offering is pretty
  damned good.
- **Powell Building** • 105 Hudson St [Franklin St]
  Carrere & Hastings gem w/ Nobu on the
  ground floor.
- **Textile Building** • 66 Leonard St [Church St]
  Henry J. Hardenbergh goodness in TriBeCa.
- **Washington Market Park** •
  310 Greenwich St [Chambers St]
  One of the city's oldest marketplaces.

☕ Coffee

- **Everyman Espresso** • 301 West Broadway
  [Canal St]
  Third-wave/pourovers in stylish digs.
- **Kaffe 1668 South** • 275 Greenwich St [Murray St]
  212-693-3750
  Excellent coffee in a really cool space.
- **La Colombe Torrefaction** •
  319 Church St [Lipsenard St]
  212-343-1515
  New York's first outpost of top-notch Philly
  roasters.
- **Le Pain Quotidien** •
  81 W Broadway [Warren St]
  646-652-8186
  Excellent coffee and pastries. Thanks Belgium.
- **Square Diner** • 33 Leonard St [W Broadway]
  212-925-7188
  Old-school diner coffee.

⭕ Farmers Markets

- **Tribeca Greenmarket** •
  Greenwich St b/n Chambers & Duane
  Wed 8 am–3 pm Apr–Dec; Sat 8 am–3 pm Year
  Round

8 9 10
5 6 7
2 3 4
1

Nightlife is quieter here than in other neighborhoods, but upscale drinks can be found at **TriBeCa Grand** and **Bubble Lounge** and **Nancy Whiskey** and **Puffy's** are classic dives. Old school hangout **Walker's** is a New York classic and should not be missed; otherwise, check out the **Flea Theatre**'s calendar or wait for the **TriBeCa Film Festival**.

🍸 Nightlife

- **Anotheroom** • 249 W Broadway [N Moore St]
212-226-1418
Cosy, cute, and narrow
- **B Flat** • 277 Church St [White St]
212-219-2970
Stylish Japanese basement cocktail den.
- **The Bennett** • 134 West Broadway [Duane St]
212-784-6650
Artisanal cocktails and comfort food inspired eats.
- **Brandy Library** • 25 N Moore St [W Broadway]
212-226-5545
Refined but cozy with lots of free tasting events
- **Kenn's Broome Street Bar** •
363 W Broadway [Broome St]
212-784-6650
Real low-key for this part of town.
- **Distilled** • 211 West Broadway [Franklin St]
212-601-9514
Good cocktails and grub in pleasant communal setting.
- **Evening Bar** • 85 West Broadway [Chambers St]
Creative cocktails from PDT alum alongside Carmellini small plates.
- **Lucky Strike** • 59 Grand St [W Broadway]
212-941-0772
Hipsters, locals, ex-smoky. Recommended.
- **Macao** • 311 Church St [Walker St]
212-431-8642
Expensive but exquisite cocktails inspired by 1930s Chinese opium dens.
- **Nancy Whiskey Pub** •
1 Lispenard St [W Broadway]
212-226-9943
Good dive. As if there were any other kind.
- **Patriot Saloon** • 110 Chambers St [Church St]
212-748-1162
So trashy it's good; suddenly an august downtown institution

- **Puffy's Tavern** • 81 Hudson St [Harrison St]
212-227-3912
Suits, old timers, and hipsters. Top TriBeCa watering hole.
- **Racines** • 94 Chambers St [t Church St]
212-227-3400
French wine bar and food, one of our TriBeCa favorites.
- **Smith & Mills** • 71 N Moore St [Greenwich St]
212-226-2515
Upscale cool cocktails. Limited seating.
- **Soho Grand Hotel** •
310 W Broadway [Canal St]
212-965-3000
Swank sophistication.
- **Terroir** • 24 Harrison St [Greenwich St]
212-625-9463
Happening wine bar with funky list and tasty eats.
- **Toad Hall** • 57 Grand St [W Broadway]
212-431-8145
Laid back vibe with SoHo locals.
- **The Roxy Hotel** • 2 6th Ave [White St]
212-519-6600
Posh drinks in an uber-cool space; service is another matter.
- **Tribeca Tavern & Café** •
247 W Broadway [Beach St]
212-941-7671
Good enough for us
- **Walker's** • 16 N Moore St [W Broadway]
212-941-0142
Where old and new Tribeca neighbors mix.
- **Ward III** • 111 Reade St [W Broadway]
212-240-9194
Fantastic cocktail den. Awesome drinks, no attitude.
- **Warren 77** • 77 Warren St [Greenwich St]
212-227-8994
Do you believe in miracles? A classy sports bar in NYC.

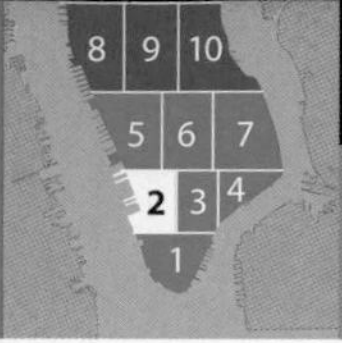

Map 2

8 9 10
5 6 7
2 3 4
1

TriBeCa

🍴 Restaurants

- **'wichcraft** • 397 Greenwich St [Beach St]
212-780-0577 • $$
Sandwiches, soups, and sweets from one of those TV chefs.
- **American Cut** • 363 Greenwich St [Franklin St]
212-226-4736 • $$$$$
Forgione + steak = a perfect pairing.
- **Benares** • 45 Murray St [Church St]
212-766-4900 • $$
Decent Indian option, very good naan.
- **Bouley** • 163 Duane St [W Broadway]
212-964-2525 • $$$$$
Absolute top NYC dining. Love the apples in the foyer.
- **Bubby's** • 120 Hudson St [N Moore St]
212-219-0666 • $$
Great atmosphere — good home-style eats and homemade pies.
- **Cafe Clementine** •
227 West Broadway [White St]
212-965-0909 • $$
Fresh, satisfying soups, salads, and sandwiches in a tiny space.
- **China Blue** • 135 Watts St [Washington St]
212-431-0111 • $$$$
Hip Chinese in deserted northwest corner of TriBeCa.
- **Church Lounge** •
2 Ave of the Americas [White St]
212-519-6600 • $$$
Sunday buffet brunch is great.
- **City Hall** • 131 Duane St [Church St]
212-227-7777 • $$$$$
Bright, expensive, lots of suits, but still cool.
- **Cupping Room Café** •
359 W Broadway [Broome St]
212-925-2898 • $$$
Keeps the mimosas flowing at brunch.
- **Da Mikele** • 275 Church St [White St]
212-925-8800 • $$$
Solid Italian w/ good pies.

- **Distilled** • 211 West Broadway [Franklin St]
212-601-9514 • $$$$
Creative comfort cuisine in post-modern public house.
- **Edward's** • 136 W Broadway [Duane St]
212-233-6436 • $$
Middle-of-the-road, kid's menu, mostly locals, sometimes great.
- **Estancia 460** • 460 Greenwich St [Watts St]
212-431-5093 • $$
Louche Argentines and brilliant french toast. Formerly Sosa Borella.
- **Félix** • 340 W Broadway [Grand St]
212-431-0021 • $$$
Buzzing Brazilian with French overtones, see and be seen.
- **Gotan** • 130 Franklin St [Varick St]
212-431-5200 • $$
Serious sandwiches, serious espresso, settle in for some mood lighting.
- **Grandaisy Bakery** •
250 W Broadway [Beach St]
212-334-9435 •
Breads and pizzas by the one and only.
- **The Greek** • 458 Greenwich St [Desbrosses St]
646-476-3941 • $$$$
Bang-on Greek miles from Astoria.
- **Jungsik** • 2 Harrison St [Hudson St]
212-219-0900 • $$$$
White tablecloth multi-star Korean.
- **Khe-Yo** • 157 Duane St [W Broadway]
212-587-1089 • $$
Laotian goodness for the TriBeCa set Reasonable prices.
- **Kori** • 253 Church St [Leonard St]
212-334-0908 • $$$
Korean. Hip space. It's TriBeCa.
- **Landmarc** • 179 W Broadway [Leonard St]
212-343-3883 • $$$$$
Modern, posh, great steaks and wines; and, of course, pricey.

If you've got cash, Tribeca's got you covered. **Nobu** has top-shelf sushi, **Odeon** has the cool factor, **Landmarc** has killer steaks, **Il Giglio** has white-tablecloth-Italian, and **Bouley** is a top NYC dining experience. Otherwise, we go for the far-above-average pub grub at **Walker's** or cabbie favorite **Pakistan Tea House**.

- **Little Park** • 85 West Broadway [Chambers St]
212-220-4110 • $$$
Nicely appointed farm-to-table from Andrew Carmellini.
- **Locanda Verde** •
377 Greenwich St [N Moore St]
212-925-3797 • $$$$
Top-shelf Italian in ever-hip TriBeCa.
- **Lucky Strike** • 59 Grand St [W Broadway]
212-941-0772 • $$
Good bar in front, reliable food in back.
- **Lupe's East LA Kitchen** •
110 Ave of the Americas [Watts St]
212-966-1326 • $
Tex-Mex. Quaint. Eat here.
- **Marc Forgione** • 134 Reade St [Hudson St]
212-941-9401 • $$$$$
Top-end TriBeCa perfection. Go. If you can.
- **Nobu** • 195 Broadway
212-219-0500 • $$$$$
Designer Japanese. When we have 100 titles, we'll go here.
- **The Odeon** • 145 W Broadway [Thomas St]
212-233-0507 • $$$
We can't agree about this one, so go and make your own decision.
- **Racines** • 94 Chambers St [Church St]
212-227-3400 • $$$
French all the way--great wines, food, bar scene
- **Roc** • 190 Duane St [Greenwich St]
212-625-3333 • $$$
Lovely Italian, good for weekend brunch.
- **Rosa Mexicano** • 41 Murray St [Church St]
212-849-2885 • $$$$
Yes, it's expensive, but it's still better than most NYC Mexican.

- **Salaam Bombay** •
319 Greenwich St [Duane St]
212-226-9400 • $$
Indian; excellent lunch buffet.
- **Saluggi's** • 325 Church St [Lispenard St]
212-226-7900 • $$
Brussels sprout, bacon, caramelized onion pie: get it.
- **Sophie's Cuban** • 96 Chambers St [Church St]
212-608-9900 • $$
Great cheap Cuban/Caribbean.
- **Square Diner** • 33 Leonard St [W Broadway]
212-925-7188 • $
Classic neighborhood diner.
- **Thalassa** • 179 Franklin St [Hudson St]
212-941-7661 • $$$
Greek. But it's cheaper and better in Astoria.
- **Tribeca Grill** • 375 Greenwich St [Franklin St]
212-941-3900 • $$$$$
Are you looking at me?
- **Tribeca Tavern & Café** •
247 W Broadway [Beach St]
212-941-7671 •
Great brew selection...and is that "November Rain" I hear?
- **Viet Café** • 345 Greenwich St [Jay St]
212-431-5888 • $$$
Glossy out of a magazine.
- **Walker's** • 16 N Moore St [W Broadway]
212-941-0142 • $$
Surprisingly good food for a pub!
- **Tutto** • 77 Hudson St [Harrison St]
212-233-3287 • $$$
Neighborhood Japanese.

Map 2

8 9 10
5 6 7
2 3 4
1

TriBeCa

Shopping

- **Amish Market** • 53 Park Pl [W Broadway]
  212-608-3863
  Lots prepared foods. Do they deliver by horse and buggy?
- **Arcade Bakery** • 220 Church St [Thomas St]
  212-227-7895
  French-trained, small-batch bakery.
- **Babesta Cribz** • 56 Warren St [W Broadway]
  646-290-5508
  Stuff for hipster babies and their parents.
- **Balloon Saloon** • 133 W Broadway [Duane St]
  212-227-3838
  We love the name.
- **Boffi Soho** • 31 Greene St [Grand St]
  212-431-8282
  High-end kitchen and bath design.
- **Danny's Cycles** • 75 Varick St [Watts St]
  212-334-8000
  Bike messenger mecca; formerly Canal Street Bicycles.
- **Duane Park Patisserie** •
  179 Duane St [Staple St]
  212-274-8447
  Yummy!

- **Grandaisy Bakery** •
  250 W Broadway [Beach St]
  212-334-9435
  Breads and pizzas by the one and only.
- **Issey Miyake** • 119 Hudson St [N Moore St]
  212-226-0100
  Flagship store of this designer.
- **Korin** • 57 Warren St [W Broadway]
  212-587-7021
  Supplier to Japanese chefs and restaurants.
- **Let There Be Neon** • 38 White St [Church St]
  212-226-4883
  Neon gallery and store.
- **MarieBelle's Fine Treats & Chocolates** •
  484 Broome St [Wooster St]
  212-925-6999
  Top NYC chocolatier. Killer hot chocolate.
- **The Mysterious Bookshop** • 58 Warren St [W Broadway]
  212-587-1011
  Specialty—mystery books.

Hit up **Grandaisy Bakery** and **Duane Park Patisserie** for baked goods and **MarieBelle** for chocolate. We like **Selima Optique** for cool specs, **Steven Alan** for trendy threads, **Korin** for cutlery, and **Tent & Trails** for plotting NYC escapes.

- **Oliver Peoples** • 366 W Broadway [Watts St]
212-925-5400
Look as good as you see, and vice-versa.
- **Selima Optique** • 59 Wooster St [Broome St]
212-343-9490
Funky eyewear for the vintage inclined.
- **SoHo Art Materials** • 3 Wooster St [Crosby St]
212-431-3938
A painter's candy store.
- **Steven Alan** • 103 Franklin St [Church St]
212-343-0692
Trendy designer clothing and accessories.
One-of-a-kind stuff.
- **Tribeca Wine Merchants** •
40 Hudson St [Duane St]
212-393-1400
High quality for a high rollers neighborhood.

- **Urban Archaeology** •
158 Franklin St [W Broadway]
212-371-4646
Retro fixtures.
- **What Goes Around Comes Around** •
351 W Broadway [Broome St]
212-343-1225
LARGE, excellent collection of men's, women's, and children's vintage.
- **Whole Foods** • 270 Greenwich St [Murray St]
212-349-6555
Tribeca natural market outpost means strollers and celebrities.
- **Zucker's Bagels and Smoked Fish** •
146 Chambers St [W Broadway]
212-608-5844
Damn good, fresh, hand-rolled bagels and hearty schmears.

Map 3 · **City Hall / Chinatown**

Neighborhood Overview

Map 3

Chinatown. Home of the NFT offices from 1998 until 2010, we truly have a love-hate relationship with this neighborhood. On one hand you have one of the highest concentrations of great (and cheap!) food in all of New York, one of the city's most interesting and diverse parks in **Columbus Park**, lots of history, and a daytime hustle-and-bustle that is probably only matched by midtown Manhattan.

On the other hand…it's quite possibly New York's grimiest neighborhood, there is almost no nightlife, and peace and quiet is, of course, nonexistent during daylight hours. But hey—if you want peace and quiet, what are you doing in the middle of New York City anyway?

Our advice is to just get in there and mix it up with the locals, many of whom live in the huge **Confucius Towers** complex at the base of the Manhattan Bridge. And mixing it up is something that New Yorkers have been doing in this area for hundreds of years, starting with the incredibly dangerous "Five Points" area north of Collect Pond (the setting for Scorcese's seething *Gangs of New York*). Both the Five Points and Collect Pond are gone (the area itself is now **Columbus Park**), but little **Doyers Street** (aka "Bloody Angle") was the scene of Chinese gang wars for over 50 years.

Today, though, you can stroll around like the most clueless tourist and have absolutely no problems at all—gang wars have been replaced with street and shop commerce, from the tourist vendors of Mott Street to the **produce market** in the shadow of the Manhattan Bridge, with all of Canal Street's wall of tourists and locals connecting the two. The mass of humanity is sometimes overwhelming.

Fortunately, there are some cool places to try and hide away for a few moments, including the **Eastern States Buddhist Temple** and Maya Lin's new **Museum of Chinese in America**. The best "living museum," however, is without a doubt **Columbus Park**, which has an incredible range of activities—from early-morning tai chi to afternoon mah-jongg—happening within its borders throughout the day. In summer, a stop at classic **Chinatown Ice Cream Factory** will also cool your jets momentarily.

Columbus Park also serves as the northeast border of the City Hall area. There are several standout examples of civic architecture, including **City Hall** itself, the **Tweed Courthouse**, the **US Courthouse**, the condo-ized **Woolworth Building**, the sublime **Hall of Records/Surrogate Court** building, and, one of our favorite buildings in all of New York, McKim, Mead, & White's masterful **Municipal Building**, complete with a wedding-cake top and the Brooklyn Bridge stop of the 4-5-6 trains underneath.

From the Municipal Building, a walk over the **Brooklyn Bridge** is almost a *de rigueur* activity; if you'd rather stay in Manhattan, though, check out the **African Burial Ground** or watch police procedurals being filmed from **Foley Square**. Or head back east a bit to discover another bit of New York City history, an ancient **Jewish Burial Ground** on St. James Place.

No matter what you do here don't forget to EAT. It's worth the traffic, the smells, the lines, and the general rudeness of people. Believe it.

Map 3

City Hall / Chinatown

O Landmarks

- **87 Lafayette St** • 87 Lafayette St [White St]
Ex-firehouse designed in Chateau style by
Napoleon LeBrun.
- **African Burial Ground** •
290 Broadway [Duane St]
212-637-2019
Colonial burial ground for 20,000+
African-American slaves.
- **Brooklyn Bridge** • Chambers St & Centre St
The granddaddy of them all. Walking toward
Manhattan at sunset is as good as it gets.
- **Centre Marketplace** • Centre St & Broome St
Another great street we can't afford to live on.
- **Chatham Towers** • 170 Park Row [Worth St]
1960s poured-concrete apartment buildings
overlooking Chatham Square. Nice windows.
- **Chinatown Arcade** • 48 Bowery [Canal St]
Hidden dirty hallway connecting Elizabeth to
the Bowery.
- **Chinatown Fair** • 8 Mott St [Bowery]
551-697-5549
Sneak out of the office to play Ms. Pac Man
here.
- **Chinatown Ice Cream Factory** •
65 Bayard St [Mott St]
212-608-4170
The best ice cream (ginger, black sesame,
mango, red bean, et al.), ever.
- **Chinatown Visitors Kiosk** •
Walker St & Baxter St
Good meeting point. Just look out for the
dragon.
- **City Hall** • 260 Broadway [Park Pl]
212-788-3000
Built in 1811, the diminutive seat of
government.
- **Columbus Park Playground** •
67 Mulberry St [Bayard St]
212-408-0100
Former Five Points hub now operates as prime
Chinatown hangout.
- **Confucius Plaza** • Bowery & Division St
Confucius say: live here!
- **Criminal Courthouse** •
100 Centre St [Leonard St]
212-374-4423
Imposing.
- **Doyers Street (Bloody Angle)** •
Doyers St [Chatham Sq]
Rare curvy street in Manhattan; film scouts
love it.
- **Eldridge Street Synagogue** • 12 Eldridge St
[Division St]
212-219-0888
The first large-scale building by Eastern Euro
immigrants in NY.
- **Foley Square** • Worth St & Centre St
Now with bizarre black obelisk. Guiliani hated
it.
- **Lighting District** • Bowery [Broome]
Light up your life with products from these
fine purveyors…
- **Municipal Building** • Chambers St & Park Row
Wonderful McKim, Mead & White masterpiece.
- **Museum of Chinese in America** •
215 Centre St [Howard St]
212-619-4785
Beautiful new home designed by Maya Lin.
- **Not For Tourists** • 2 E Broadway [Chatham Sq]
212-965-8650
NFT headquarters from 1998 to 2010.
- **Old New York Life Insurance Company** •
346 Broadway [Leonard St]
Great narrow McKim, Mead & White with
hand-wound clock and cool internal stairwells.
- **Old Police Headquarters** •
240 Centre St [Grand St]
A beautiful building in the center of the not so
beautiful Little Italy/Chinatown area.
- **Shearith Israel Cemetery** •
55 St James Pl [Oliver St]
Oldest Jewish cemetery in New York.
- **Super-Cool Cast Iron** • Crosby St & Grand St
We want to live on the top floor of this
building.
- **Surrogate's Courthouse** •
31 Chambers St [Elk St]
Great lobby and zodiac-themed mosaics.
- **Thurgood Marshall US Courthouse** •
40 Centre St [Pearl St]
Cass Gilbert masterpiece from 1935.
- **Tweed Courthouse** •
52 Chambers St [Broadway]
Great interior dome, but will we ever see it?
- **Woolworth Building** • 233 Broadway [Park Pl]
A Cass Gilbert classic. Stunning lobby.

Think Kansas is boring at night? You haven't been to Chinatown at 10 pm on a Monday. That said, you can shoot pool at the tiki-themed **Tropical 128**. There's also sprawling **Fontana's** (the site of several NFT parties), and dancing at **Santos Party House**.

 Coffee

- **Ferrara Café** • 195 Grand St [Mulberry St]
  212-226-6150
  The best of the Little Italy cafés.
- **Kung Fu Tea** • 234 Canal St [Centre St]
  212-334-3536
  Milky bubble tea for your afternoon sugar shot.
- **Saturdays Surf** • 31 Crosby St [Grand St]
  212-966-7875
  Small espresso bar with laid-back surfer vibe.

 Farmers Markets

- **City Hall Park Greenmarket** •
  276 Canyon of Heroes
  Tues & Fri 8 am–5 pm, Jun–Dec

 Nightlife

- **Apotheke** • 9 Doyers St [Bowery]
  212-406-0400
  Flaming expensive Euro-cocktails in a (supposedly) former opium den.
- **Capitale** • 130 Bowery [Grand St]
  212-334-5500
  Formerly the Bowery Savings Bank. Cool space.
- **Experimental Intermedia** •
  224 Centre St [Grand St]
  212-431-5127
  Experimental art/performance art shows involving a variety of artistic media.
- **M1-5 Bar** • 52 Walker St [Broadway]
  212-965-1701
  DJ bar that hosts lots of private events.
- **Randolph Beer** • 343 Broome St [Elizabeth St]
  212-334-3706
  Lots of wood and even more beer.
- **Tropical 128** • 128 Elizabeth St [Broome St]
  212-925-8219
  Polynesian theme, billiards, and lots of dudes.

Map 3

8 9 10
5 6 7
2 **3** 4
1

City Hall / Chinatown

Restaurants

- **88 Palace** • 88 E Broadway [Forsyth St]
212-941-8886 • $$
Dim sum madness under the Manhattan Bridge.
- **Aux Epices** • 121 Baxter St [Canal St]
212-274-8585 • $$
Sweet little Malaysian spot doling out gourmet plates.
- **Banh Mi Saigon** • 198 Grand St [Mulberry St]
212-941-1541 • $
The best Vietnamese sandwiches. Ever.
- **Big Wong King** • 67 Mott St [Bayard St]
212-964-0540 • $
If you're gonna be a king, that's the kind of king to be.
- **Billy's Bakery** • 75 Franklin St [Broadway]
212-647-9958 • $
Yummiest treats this side of homemade.
- **Bo Ky** • 80 Bayard St [Mott St]
212-406-2292 • $
Chinese/Vietnamese hybrid. Killer soups.
- **Breakroom** • 83 Baxter St [White St]
212-227-2802 • $$
If you need a burger or a taco in Chinatown, this is the place.
- **Buddha Bodai** • 5 Mott St [Worth St]
212-566-8388 • $$
Veg heads dig this place.
- **Chee Cheong Fun Food Cart** •
195 Hester St • $
Try a pork steamed rice roll ("chee cheong fun") for breakfast. • **Cong Ly** • 124 Heser St [Chrystie St]
212-343-1111 • $
Most interesting pho in the city. Plus grilled pork!

- **Despana** • 408 Broome St [Centre St]
212-219-5050 • $
Excellent Spanish take-out/gourmet grocery, complete w/ bull.
- **Dim Sum Go Go** • 5 E Broadway [Catherine St]
212-732-0797 • $$
New, hip, inventive dim sum; essentially, post-modern Chinese.
- **Ferrara Café** • 195 Grand St [Mulberry St]
212-226-6150 • $
Classic Little Italy patisserie.
- **Food Sing 88** • 2 E Broadway [Chatham Sq]
212-219-8223 • $
Outstanding beef soup with hand-pulled noodles.
- **Fried Dumpling** • 106 Mosco St [Mulberry St]
212-693-1060 • $
Five for a buck.
- **Fuleen Seafood** • 11 Division St [Catherine St]
212-941-6888 • $$$
Chinatown gem; amazing lunch specials.
- **Golden Unicorn** •
18 E Broadway [Catherine St]
212-941-0911 • $$
Dim sum—great for medium-sized groups.
- **Great NY Noodletown** •
28 Bowery [Bayard St]
212-349-0923 • $
Cheap Chinese soups and BBQ and deep-fried squid. At 2 am.
- **Jing Fong Restaurant** •
20 Elizabeth St [Canal St]
212-964-5256 • $$
Large Hong Kong-style dim sum house.
- **J.J. Noodle** • 19 Henry St [Catherine St]
212-571-2440 • $
Killer shrimp wonton soup. Very cheap.
- **Joe's Shanghai** • 9 Pell St [Bowery]
212-233-8888 • $$
Crab Soup Dumpling Mecca. Worth the wait.
- **La Mela Ristorante** •
167 Mulberry St [Grand St]
212-431-9493 • $$$
Family-style Italian dining.
- **Le Pain Quotidien** • 100 Grand St [Mercer St]
212-625-9009 • $$
Excellent breads. Communal table. Euro vibe.

First stop: the crab soup dumplings at **Joe's Shanghai**. Second stop: the salt-and-pepper squid at **Pho Viet Huong**. On from there, classic Thai at **Pongsri Thai**, dim sum at **Mandarin Court**, **88 Palace**, or **Dim Sum Go Go**. In a hurry? Get a kebab at street cart **Xinjiang**. Too much Asian? Head to SoHo gem **Despaña** for Spanish sandwiches.

8	9	10
5	6	7
2	**3**	4
1		

- **Luna Pizza** • 225 Park Row [Pearl St]
  212-385 8118 • $
  Pizza-maker back; go for the grandma pie.
- **Mandarin Court** • 61 Mott St [Bayard St]
  212 608-3838 • $$
  Consistently good and frenetic dim sum.
- **Margherita NYC** • 107 Grand St [Mulberry St]
  212-226 8391 • $$
  Very good pizza returns to the heart of Little Italy.
- **Mei Li Wah Bakery** •
  64 Bayard St [Elizabeth St]
  212-966-7866 • $
  Sweet pastries, savory buns, tea, and noodles.
- **New Malaysia** • 46 Bowery [Canal St]
  212-964-0284 • $$
  A hidden gem that's literally hidden. Try the specials.
- **Nha Trang** • 87 Baxter St [White St]
  212-233-5948 • $$
  Excellent Vietnamese. Pho beef satee is good.
- **Nha Trang Centre** • 148 Centre St [Walker St]
  212 941-9292 • $
  No-frills Vietnamese.
- **Nice Green Bo** • 66 Bayard St [Mott St]
  212-625-2359 • $
  Amazing Shanghainese. Nice alternative to Joe's.
- **Nyonya** • 199 Grand St [Mulberry St]
  212-334-3669 • $$
  Malaysian when you're sick of Chinese.
- **OK 218 Restaurant** •
  218 Grand St [Elizabeth St]
  212-226-8039 • $
  Perfect name for this average Chinese spot.
- **Pho Pasteur** • 85 Baxter St [White St]
  212-608-3656 • $
  Excellent soup. Pho sure.
- **Piacere** • 351 Broome St [Elizabeth St]
  212-219-4080 • $$$
  Decent 'za, especially for Little Italy. Go figure.
- **Ping's** • 22 Mott St [Mosco St]
  212 602-9988 • $$
  Eclectic Asian seafood. And we mean "eclectic."

- **Pongsri Thai** • 106 Bayard St [Baxter St]
  212-349-3132 • $$
  Ever wonder where district attorneys go for cheap, tasty Thai?
- **Sanur Restaurant** • 18 Doyers St [Bowery]
  212-267-0088 • $
  Amazing, super cheap Malaysian.
- **Sau Voi Corp** • 101 Lafayette St [Walker St]
  212-226-8184 • $
  Great banh mi. And Vietnamese music tapes too!
- **Shanghai Cuisine** •
  14 Elizabeth St [Bayard St]
  212-964-5640 • $
  Great soup dumplings return to Manhattan's Chinatown.
- **Shanghai Asian Manor** •
  21 Mott St [Mosco St]
  212-766-6311 • $$
  You can't have too many soup dumplings or scallion pancakes.

- **Smile To Go** • 22 Howard St [Crosby St]
  646-863-3893 • $
  Deliciously fresh veggies, small sandwiches, and baked goods, tiny space.
- **Sofia's of Little Italy** •
  143 Mulberry St [Grand St]
  212-219-9799 • $$$
  A cut above the other tourist traps around here.
- **Super Taste** • 26 Eldridge St [Canal St]
  212-625-1198 • $
  Beginners: Try the spicy beef noodle soup.
- **Taiwan Pork Chop House** •
  3 Doyers St [Bowery]
  212-791-7007 • $
  Fried chicken leg and spicy wontons are excellent.
- **Tasty Hand-Pulled Noodles Inc.** •
  1 Doyers St [Bowery]
  212-791-1817 • $
  Stop by for a bowl on your post office run.
- **Vegetarian Dim Sum House** •
  24 Pell St [Mott St]
  212-577-7176 • $
  Cheap lunches for those who don't eat animals. Tip: Snow pea dumplings.
- **Wah Fung** • 79 Chrystie St [Hester St]
  212-925-5175 • $
  Succulent BBQ pig for stunningly cheap prices.
- **Wah Mei Fast Food** • 190 Hester St [Baxter St]
  212-925-6428 • $
  Linoleum floors, fluorescent lights, and an amazing pork chop over rice.
- **Wo Hop** • 17 Mott St [Mosco St]
  212-962-8617 • $
  Chinatown mainstay. Best when drunk.
- **Xi'an Famous Foods** • 45 Bayard St [Mott St]
  $
  Hand pulled noodles and tasty lamb burgers.

🛍 Shopping

- **Aji Ichiban** • 37 Mott St [Pell St]
  212-233-7650
  Load up on free samples from the huge selection of Asian candies and snacks.
- **Alleva** • 188 Grand St [Mulberry St]
  212-226-7990
  Killer Italian import shop.
- **Bangkok Center Grocery** •
  104 Mosco St [Mulberry St]
  212-349-1979
  Curries, fish sauce, and other Thai products.
- **Catherine Meat Market** •
  21 Catherine St [Henry St]
  212-693-0494
  Fresh pig deliveries every Tuesday!
- **Chinatown Arcade** • 8 Motte St
  Bizarre indoor mall/passageway. Check it out.
- **Chinatown Ice Cream Factory** •
  65 Bayard St [Mott St]
  212-608-4170
  Take home a quart of mango. Oddest flavors in NYC.
- **Civil Service Book Shop** •
  34 Carmine St
  212-226-9506
  Specialty—civil services.
- **Clic** • 255 Centre St [Broome St]
  212-966-2766
  Art books and an art gallery.
- **Di Palo Fine Foods** • 200 Grand St [Mott St]
  212-226-1033
  Delicacies from across Italy. Excellent cheese.
- **Downtown Music Gallery** •
  13 Monroe St [Catherine St]
  212-473-0043
  Independent labels and artists.
- **Fay Da Bakery** • 83 Mott St [Canal St]
  212-791-3884
  Chinese pastry and boba like nobody's business.

City Hall / Chinatown

Map 3

Rule Number One: Stay away from tourist trap Canal Street, unless you're in the market for poorly made knockoffs whose proceeds probably help fund all manner of badness. Do hit **New Beef King** for homemade jerky, **Di Palo Fine Foods** for Italian imports, **K & M Camera** for shutterbug stuff, and **papabubble** to watch candy-making magic happen.

- **Forsyth Outdoor Produce Market** •
  Forsyth St & Division St
  Cheapest veggies and fruit in Manhattan.
  Long lines.
- **Fountain Pen Hospital** •
  10 Warren St [Broadway]
  212-964-0580
  They don't take Medicaid.
- **Harney & Sons** • 433 Broome St [Crosby St]
  212-933-4853
  Awe-inspiring tea selection. Sampling encouraged.
- **K & M Camera** • 368 Broadway [White St]
  212-523-0954
  Good all-around camera store, open Saturdays!
- **Lendy Electric** • 176 Grand St [Baxter St]
  212-431-3698
  Great bastion of the electrical supply world.
- **Lung Moon Bakery** • 83 Mulberry St [Canal St]
  212-349-4945
  Chinese bakery.
- **Madewell** • 486 Broadway [Broome St]
  212-226-6954
  Always-packed, casually cool J.Crew offshoot.
- **Muji Soho** • 455 Broadway [Grand St]
  212-334-2002
  Why is Japanese design so functional and cute?
- **New York City Store** •
  1 Centre St [Chambers St]
  212-669-7452
  Great NYC books and schwag you can't get anywhere else.
- **New York Mart** • 128 Mott St [Grand St]
  212-680-0178
  Solid Chinatown grocery, lots of produce, roast duck to-go.
- **No 6** • 6 Centre Market Pl [Grand St]
  212-226-5759
  Notable selection of carefully selected original American and European vintage.

- **Ocean Star Seafood Market** •
  239 Grand St [Chrystie St]
  212-274-0990
  Cantonese market with fresh fish and veggies.
- **OMG** • 408 Broadway [Walker St]
  212-966-6620
  Inexpensive jeans, t-shirts, and casual urban basics.
- **Opening Ceremony** •
  35 Howard St [Crosby St]
  212-219-2688
  Expensive hipster threads for tiny bodies.
- **papabubble** • 380 Broome St [Mulberry St]
  212-966-2599
  Candy labratory. Willy Wonka would be proud.
- **Piemonte Ravioli** • 190 Grand St [Mulberry St]
  212-226-0475
  Old-school and homemade.
- **Putnam Rolling Ladder Co.** •
  32 Howard St [Crosby St]
  212-226-5147
  If your apartment can accommodate one of these, we're jealous.
- **Sun's Organic Tea Shop** •
  79 Bayard St [Mott St]
  212-566-3260
  Inexpensive loose leaf teas, knowledgeable staff.
- **Western Spirit** • 392 Broadway [Walker St]
  212-343-1476
  Belt buckles, bolo ties, Navajo turquoise Jewelry and Texan kitsch.
- **Yellow Rat Bastard** •
  483 Broadway [Broome St]
  212-925-4377
  Filled with young street clothes and skate gear.
- **Yunhong Chopsticks Shop** •
  50 Mott St [Bayard St]
  212-566-8828
  Super-cute chopstick shop in C-town.

Map 4 • **Lower East Side**

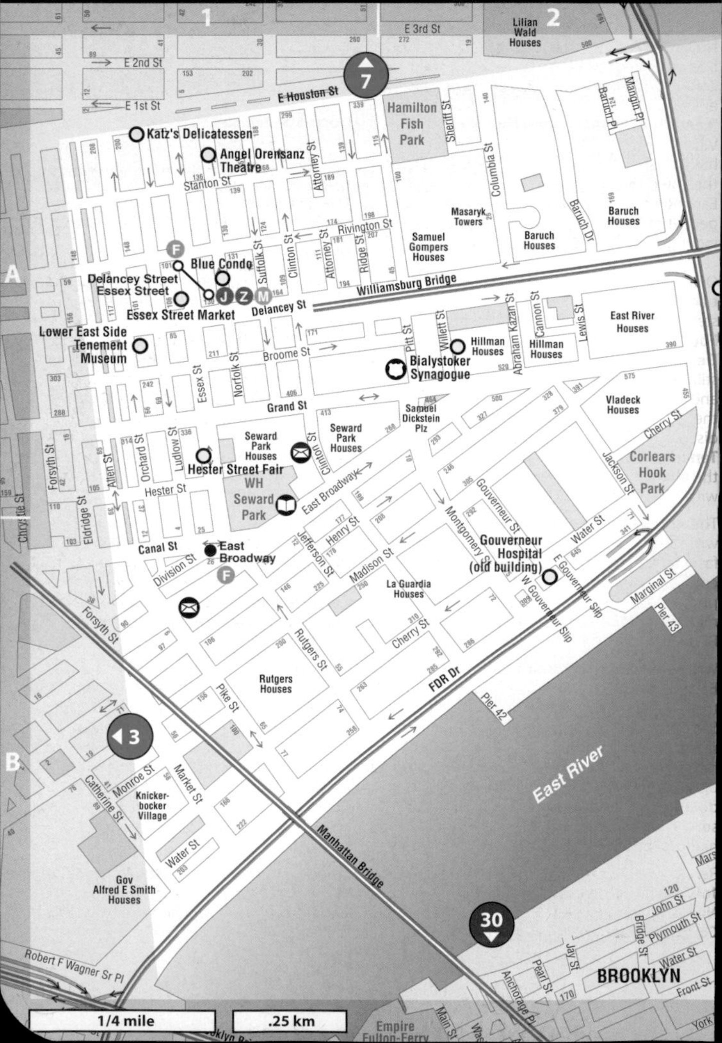

1
2

E 3rd St

Lilian Wald Houses

E Houston St

7

E 2nd St

E 1st St

Hamilton Fish Park

Katz's Delicatessen

Angel Orensanz Theatre

Stanton St

Masaryk Towers

Rivington St

Samuel Gompers Houses

Baruch Houses

A

F Blue Condo

Delancey Street
Essex Street

J Z M

Essex Street Market

Delancey St

Williamsburg Bridge

East River Houses

Lower East Side Tenement Museum

Broome St

Hillman Houses

Hillman Houses

Bialystoker Synagogue

Vladeck Houses

Grand St

Samuel Dickstein Plz

Corlears Hook Park

Seward Park Houses

Hester Street Fair

WH Seward Park

Seward Park Houses

Canal St

East Broadway

Gouverneur Hospital (old building)

B

Division St

F

La Guardia Houses

3

Forsyth St

Rutgers Houses

FDR Dr

Pier 42

East River

Knicker-bocker Village

Water St

Gov Alfred E Smith Houses

Manhattan Bridge

30

BROOKLYN

Robert F Wagner Sr Pl

| 1/4 mile |
| .25 km |

Empire Fulton Ferry

Neighborhood Overview

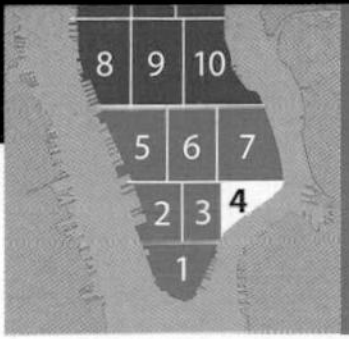

Map 4

Now characterized by bars and nightclubs and the high-heeled, cologne-drenched crowds that flock to them, the Lower East Side has traditionally been known as the epicenter of immigrant cultures. At one time the term "Lower East Side" applied to what's now called the East Village as well, but starting in the latter part of the 20th century, the two neighborhoods have commonly been referred to separately, with Houston Street as the dividing line. While the Lower East Side has the grittier reputation, with its sprawl of housing projects along the East River, and shared border with Chinatown on the southern and western edges, gentrification is quickly sweeping across the landscape; one of the more obvious signs is the incongruous **Blue Condo** rising above Norfolk Street.

Of all the groups who settled here, the area is perhaps most known for its Jewish roots, and traces can still be found if you look hard enough. A number of historic synagogues still stand, including **Bialystoker Synagogue** on Willett Street, and the **Angel Orensanz Foundation**, which has been converted into an art gallery. The venerable **Katz's Delicatessen** on Houston Street is an obvious starting point for any culinary tour, and if you still have room after all that pastrami, head to **Russ & Daughters** for bagels, smoked fish, and old world appetizing. If a light snack is what you're after, **Kossar's Bialys** is still one of the best deals in town. Once your belly is full, walk along the tenement buildings and discount clothing stores along Orchard Street until you reach the **Lower East Side Tenement Museum**. There you can tour restored apartments of actual people who lived in the area long ago, and thank your lucky stars that at least you don't share your tiny studio with a half dozen relatives.

The overlapping of Jewish, Puerto Rican and Chinese cultures, as well as the changes wrought by the neighborhood's rising attractiveness to developers make any walking tour fascinating. Along Clinton Street, old school Latino businesses stand side-by-side with cutting-edge eateries. On Broome Street, pungent Chinese vegetable markets encounter pricey boutiques. Art center **ABC No Rio**, which grew out of downtown's squatter movement and punk rock scene is located a couple blocks from the swanky **Hotel on Rivington**. You get the picture.

When you're done with history, you can always do some more eating. Check out the stalls at **Essex Street Market**—established in the 1930s to replace the pushcarts that once clogged these streets—for gourmet groceries, meats, and produce. If you're passing by on a Saturday, **Hester Street Fair** will give you a taste of the city's booming foodie scene with its many artisanal delights. And then there's the infamous nightlife, a slice of party heaven (or hell) clustered around Orchard, Clinton, Ludlow, Rivington, and Stanton Streets. If you're not up for impressing bouncers at **Libation** or downing vodka shots at **Mehanata**, do what we do and catch a show. **Mercury Lounge** is one of our favorite venues, and there's always something going on at **Cake Shop** or **Arlene's Grocery**. This is best attempted on a week night, of course. Don't say we didn't warn you.

Ready for a night out on the Lower East Side? Chug some cut-rate PBRs at **Welcome to the Johnsons** then head to **Arlene's Grocery** for rock n' roll karaoke. Or check out burlesque at **Nurse Bettie**, then get cozy on a couch at **The Back Room**. Or sample beers at **Spitzer's Corner** then catch a show at **Cake Shop** or **Fat Baby**. Go!

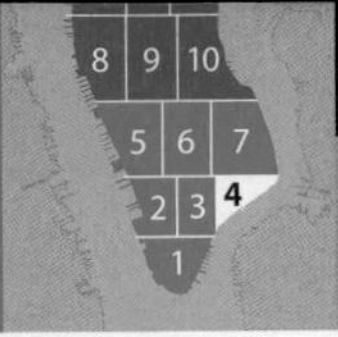

Map 4

8 9 10
5 6 7
2 3 4
1

Lower East Side

O Landmarks

- **Angel Orensanz Foundation for the Arts** •
172 Norfolk St [Stanton St]
212-529-7194
Performance space in ex-synagogue. Amazing.
- **Bialystoker Synagogue** •
7 Bialystoker Pl [Grand St]
212-475-0165
The oldest building in NY to currently house a
synagogue. Once a stop on the Underground
Railroad.
- **Blue Condo** • 105 Norfolk St [Delancey St]
Bernard Tschumi's odd masterpiece.
- **East River Park** • East River Park at Broome St
212-533-0656
The park the FDR Drive built.
- **Gouverneur Hospital** •
621 Water St [Gouverneur St]
One of the oldest hospital buildings in the
world.
- **Katz's Delicatessen** •
205 E Houston St [Ludlow St]
212-254-2246
Classic New York pastrami; I'll have what she's
having!
- **Lower East Side Tenement Museum** •
108 Orchard St [Broome St]
212-982-8420
Great illustration of turn-of-the-century (20th,
that is) life.

O Coffee

- **Caffe Vita** • 124 Ludlow St [Rivington St]
212-260-8482
Seattle coffee ballers' first outpost east of the
Mississippi.
- **El Rey Coffee Bar & Luncheonette** • 100
Stanton St [Ludlow St]
212-260-3950
Third-wave coffee and good grub, too.
- **Kopitiam** • 151 E Broadway
646-894-7081
The Malaysian-style white coffee garners raves.
- **Ludlow Coffee Supply** • 176 Ludlow St
[Houston St] Quality coffee, above-average
food, and a barber component.
- **Roasting Plant** • 81 Orchard St [Broome St]
212-775-7755
Custom-ground coffee. Theatrical.

Farmers Markets

- **Hester Street Fair** • Hester St [Essex St]
Fancy street grub and artisanal snacks every
Saturday from April–Oct.
- **Lower East Side Youthmarket** •
Grand Ave b/n Pitt St & Abraham Pl
Sundays, July–Nov, 8 am–4 pm.

Nightlife

- **169 Bar** • 169 E Broadway [Rutgers St]
646-833-7199
Sometimes good, sometimes not.
- **Arlene's Grocery** • 95 Stanton St [Ludlow St]
212-358-1633
Cheap live tunes.
- **Bacaro** • 136 Division St [Ludlow St]
212-941-5060
Wine and pretty snacks from Venice.
- **The Back Room** • 102 Norfolk St [Delancey St]
212-228-5098
The secret room is behind a bookcase.
- **The Bars at the Hotel on Rivington** •
107 Rivington St [Ludlow St]
212-475-2600
Groovy baby.

Map 4

Ready for a night out on the Lower East Side? Chug some cut-rate PBRs at **Welcome to the Johnsons** then head to **Arlene's Grocery** for rock n' roll karaoke. Or check out burlesque at **Nurse Bettie**, then get cozy on a couch at **The Back Room**. Or sample beers at **Spitzer's Corner** then catch a show at **Cake Shop** or **Fat Baby**. Go!

- **Chloe 81** • 81 Ludlow St [Broome St]
  212-677-0067
  Another secret bar you won't get into.
- **Clandestino** • 35 Canal St [Ludlow St]
  212-475-5505
  Inviting bar off the beaten track.
- **Clockwork Bar** • 21 Essex St [Hester St]
  212-677-4545
  Much needed punk rock dive in an increasingly chic nabe.
- **The Delancey** • 168 Delancey St [Clinton St]
  212-254-9920
  Overrated, but the roof is cool if you can get up there.
- **Donnybrook** • 35 Clinton St [Stanton St]
  212-228-7733
  Upscale yet rustic pub for the professional crowd.
- **Eastwood** • 200 Clinton St [Clinton St]
  212-233-0124
  Drinks and eclectic grub + brunch.
- **Genuine Liquorette** • 191 Grand St [Mulberry St]
  Big-time cocktails in sculpted setting never lacking for whimsy.
- **Libation** • 137 Ludlow St [Rivington St]
  212-529-2153
  If you like this place, please leave New York.
- **Local 138** • 138 Ludlow St [Rivington St]
  212-477-0280
  Great happy hour. No douchebags most of the time.
- **Los Feliz** • 109 Ludlow St [Delancey St]
  212-228-8383
  Taqueria/tequileria full of revolutionary splendor and a hidden subterranean labyrinth.
- **The Magician** • 118 Rivington St [Essex St]
  212-673-7851
  Hipster haven. The NFT cartographer loves it.
- **Mehanata** • 113 Ludlow St [Delancey St]
  212-625-0981
  Keep an eye out for DJ Eugene Hutz.
- **Mercury Lounge** • 217 E Houston St [Essex St]
  212-260-4700
  Rock venue with occasional top-notch acts.

- **Mr. Purple** • 180 Orchard St [Stanton St]
  212-237-1790
  Crafty cocktails and a stunning 15th floor view of Manhattan.
- **Nitecap** • 151 Rivington St [Essex St]
  212-466-3361
  Expansive, creative cocktail menu, fun theme.
- **Nurse Bettie** • 106 Norfolk St [Rivington St]
  212-477-7515
  Cozy cocktails and burlesque. Recommended on weeknights.
- **Parkside Lounge** •
  317 E Houston St [Attorney St]
  212-673-6270
  Good basic bar, live acts in the back.
- **Pianos** • 158 Ludlow St [Stanton St]
  212-505-3733
  Painful scene with decent live tunes.
- **Set L.E.S.** • 127 Ludlow St [Rivington St]
  212-982-8225
  Drinks with above-average gastropub grub.
- **The Skinny** • 174 Orchard St [Stanton St]
  212-228-3668
  Shimmy through sweating crowds in this appropriately named dive bar.
- **The Slipper Room** • 167 Orchard St [Stanton St]
  212-253-7246
  Striptease for the arty crowd.
- **The Ten Bells** • 247 Broome St [Ludlow St]
  212 228 4450
  Organic wine bar with candlelit Euro-vibe. Nice!
- **Verlaine** • 110 Rivington St [Essex St]
  212-614-2494
  Mellow, French-Vietnamese motif with deceptively sweet cocktails.
- **Welcome to the Johnsons** •
  123 Rivington St [Essex St]
  212-420-9911
  Great decor, but too crowded mostly.

Map 4

Lower East Side

🍴Restaurants

- **Bacaro** • 136 Division St [Ludlow St]
  212-941-5060 • $$
  Venetian snack bar.
- **Barrio Chino** • 253 Broome St [Orchard St]
  212-228-6710 • $$
  Started as a tequila bar, but now more of a restaurant.
- **Benson's NYC** • 181 Essex St [Houston St]
  929-376-5574 • $$$
  Great bacon and beer selection. What else is needed?
- **Cafe Katja** • 79 Orchard St [Broome St]
  212-219-9545 • $$$
  The LES Euro zone welcomes Austria into the fold.
- **Cheeky Sandwiches** • 35 Orchard St [Hester St]
  646-504-8132 • $
  New Orleans po' boys dressed. The real deal.
- **Clinton Street Baking Co.** •
  4 Clinton St [E Houston St]
  646-602-6263 • $$
  Homemade buttermilk everything. LES laid back. Top 5 bacon.
- **Cocoron 61** • 16 Delancey St [Allen St]
  212-925-5220 • $$$
  Japanese Soba specialists.
- **Congee Village** • 100 Allen St [Delancey St]
  212-941-1818 • $$
  Porridge never tasted so good.
- **Contra** • 138 Orchard St [Rivington St]
  212-466-4633 • $$$$
  Inventive set menus highlighting seasonal ingredients.
- **Creperie** • 135 Ludlow St [Rivington St]
  212-979-5521 • $
  A hole-in-the-wall that serves sweet and savory crepes.
- **Dimes** • 49 Canal St [Orchard St]
  212-925-1300 • $$$
  California-to-table cuisine; young creative vibe.
- **Dirt Candy** • 86 Allen St [Broome St]
  212-228-7732 • $$$
  Haute-vegetarian that's fun for all.
- **Dirty French** • 180 Ludlow St [E Houston St]
  212-254-3000 • $$$$
  Hip French inside the hipper-than-thou Ludlow Hotel.
- **Eastwood** • 221 East Broadway [Clinton St]
  212-233-0124 • $$$
  Fish 'n chips, Scotch eggs, and, of course, kale.
- **El Castillo de Jagua** •
  113 Rivington St [Essex St]
  212-982-6412 • $
  Great cheap Dominican.
- **El Sombrero** • 108 Stanton St [Ludlow St]
  212-254-4188 • $$
  Cheap margaritas. Dates back to earlier days of the LES.
- **Essex** • 119 Rivington St
  212-533-9616 • $$$
  Great space, OK food.
- **The Fat Radish** • 17 Orchard St [Canal St]
  212-300-4053 • $$$
  Modern British eats with a hip, industrial backdrop.
- **Gaia Italian Cafe** •
  251 E Houston St [Norfolk St]
  646-350-3977 • $$
  Super cheap BYOB Italian with superb food and strict rules.
- **Grey Lady** • 77 Delancey St [Allen St]
  646-580-5239 • $$$
  Oysters, noshes and goodness for pre-Bowery Ballroom sustenance.
- **il laboratorio del gelato** •
  188 Ludlow St [E Houston St]
  212-343-9922 • $
  Mind-bogglingly incredible artisanal gelato.

Map 4

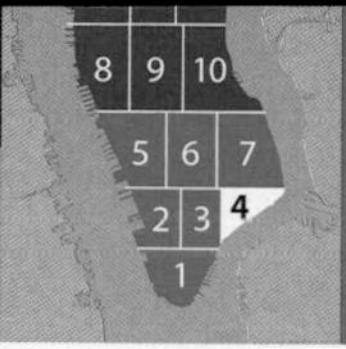

Sliders at the **Meatball Shop** and brunch at **Clinton Street Baking Co.** keep 'em lined up, but if you're with a group, just get a big table at **Congee Village**. We love **Tiny's Giant Sandwich Shop** and **Nonna's L.E.S. Pizza** for a quick bite, and **Shopsin's** when we just need some good old fashioned mac n' cheese pancakes.

- **Katz's Delicatessen** •
  205 E Houston St [Ludlow St]
  212-254-2246 • $$
  Classic New York pastrami; I'll have what she's having!
- **Kossar's Bialys** • 367 Grand St [Essex St]
  212-473-4810 • $
  Where NFT gets their morning bialys and bagels.
- **Kottu House** • 250 Broome St [Ludlow St]
  646-781-9222 • $$
  Spicy Sri Lankan goodness, good veg options too.
- **Kuma Inn** • 113 Ludlow St [Delancey St]
  212-353-8866 • $$
  Spicy Southeast Asian tapas.
- **La Contenta** • 102 Norfolk St [Delancey St]
  212-432-4180 • $$$
  We're contented with the fish tacos and margaritas, gracias.
- **Lam Zhou Handmade Noodle** •
  40 Bowery
  212-566-6933 • $
  Noodles hand-pulled before your eyes, no frills, little English.
- **LES Enfants de Boheme** •
  177 Henry St [Jefferson St]
  646-476-4843 • $$$
  French goodness deep in the heart of the LES.
- **The Meatball Shop** • 84 Stanton St [Allen St]
  212-982-8895 • $$
  Amazing balls in many different varieties.
- **Mission Chinese** •
  171 East Broadway [Essex St]
  212-529-8800 • $$$
  Always packed Chinese hipster spot is worth the hype.
- **Nakamura** • 172 Delancey St [Attorney St]
  212-614-1810 • $
  Internationally renowned ramen.

- **Pig and Khao** • 68 Clinton St [Rivington St]
  212-920-4485 • $$$$
  Filipino fusion that's all good — short rib, pork belly, chicharron, ahhh.
- **Russ & Daughters Cafe** •
  127 Orchard St [Rivington St]
  212-475-4881 • $$$
  Cheery café serving up fish noshes from popular retail store.
- **Set L.E.S.** • 127 Ludlow St [Rivington St]
  212-982-8225 • $$$
  Go for the sliders and the clams casino…and drinks, of course.
- **Shopsin's** • 120 Essex St [Rivington St]
  212-924-5160 • $
  Kenny's back! Get your Blisters on My Sisters in the Essex St Market.
- **Souvlaki GR** • 116 Stanton St [Essex St]
  212-777-0116 • $$
  Perfect Greek sandwiches to transport you away to the islands.
- **Speedy Romeo** • 63 Clinton St [Rivington St]
  212-529-6300 • $$$
  Pizza with inventive toppings; St. Louis style via Brooklyn.
- **The Stanton Social** •
  99 Stanton St [Ludlow St]
  212-995-0099 • $$$
  Cocktails and unique small plates for trendy thirty-somethings.
- **Sticky Rice** • 85 Orchard St [Broome St]
  212-274-8208 • $$
  Thai treats, Asian BBQ, BYOB, and Wi Fi?!
- **Sweet Chick** • 178 Ludlow St [Houston St]
  646-657-0233 • $$$
  Your basic chicken 'n waffle hangover solution.

• **Tiny's Giant Sandwich Shop** •
129 Rivington St [Norfolk St]
212-228-4919 • $
Great art work on the walls, complements
delicious sandwiches in your belly.
• **Wildair** • 142 Orchard St [Rivington St]
646-964-5624 • $$$
Cozy wine bar with inventive dishes.

🛍 Shopping

• **Babeland** • 94 Rivington St [Ludlow St]
212-375-1701
Sex toys without the creepy vibe.
• **Bike Works** • 106 Ridge St [Rivington St]
212-388-1077
Friendly, small place for repairs; consistently
top rated.
• **Bluestockings** • 172 Allen St [Stanton St]
212-777-6028
Specialty—political/left wing.
• **Boba Guys** • 23 Clinton St [Stanton St]
Artisanal bubble tea.
• **Chari & Co.** • 175 Stanton St [Clinton St]
212-475-0102
Cozy Japanese bike shop with down-to-earth
staff.
• **Dah Bike Shop** • 134 Division St [Ludlow St]
212-925-0155
BMX experts. Totally rad!
• **Doughnut Plant** • 379 Grand St [Norfolk St]
212-505-3700
Great, weird, recommended.
• **Economy Candy** • 108 Rivington St [Essex St]
212-254-1531
Floor-to-ceiling candy madness.
• **Edith Machinist** •
104 Rivington St [Ludlow St]
212-979-9992
Where to buy your vintage boots and bags.
• **Erin McKenna's Babycakes NYC** •
248 Broome St [Ludlow St]
855-462-2292
Awfully good vegan, gluten-free pastries, and
cupcake tops!
• **Essex Street Market** •
120 Essex St [Rivington St]
212-312-3603
Classic public market with a great combo of
old-school and fresh-faced vendors.

Lower East Side

Map 4

We buy our gear at **Ludlow Guitars**, retro glasses at **Moscot**, jewelry at **Wendy Mink**, groceries at **Essex Street Market**, and uhhh…just browse at **Babeland**. **Bluestockings** is worth a look for activist lit, **Economy Candy** has everything, and if you're hungry, hit **Kossar's Bialys**, and **Doughnut Plant**.

- **Frank's Bike Shop** • 533 Grand St [Jackson St]
  212-533-6332
  Sales, repairs, and rentals.
- **il laboratorio del gelato** •
  188 Ludlow St [E Houston St]
  212-343-9922
  Mind-bogglingly incredible artisanal gelato.
- **Joy's Flower Pot** • 40 Hester St [Essex St]
  212-777-7701
  Flowers, succulents, cacti, air plants, and too-cute terrariums.
- **Kossar's Bialys** • 367 Grand St [Essex St]
  212-473-4010
  Oldest bialy bakery in the US. The absolute sh**.
- **Labor Skate Shop** • 46 Canal St [Orchard St]
  646-351-6792
  Hip skate kids roll on in to hang and pick up a cool board.
- **Melt Bakery** • 132 Orchard St [Rivington St]
  646-535-6358
  Surprising, tasty, seasonal ice cream sandwiches.
- **Moishe's Bakery** • 504 Grand St [E Broadway]
  212-673-5832
  Best babka, challah, hamantaschen, and rugalach.
- **Moscot** • 108 Orchard St [Delancey St]
  212-477-3796
  Glasses like your grandfather used to wear.

- **Petee's Pie** • 61 Delancey St [Allen St]
  212-966-2526
  Pie engineers with "best of" pedigree.
- **Roni-Sue's Chocolates** •
  148 Forsyth St [Rivington St]
  212-260-0421
  Chocolate-covered bacon and other sweets sold from inside Essex Market.
- **Russ & Daughters** •
  179 E Houston St [Orchard St]
  212-475-4880
  Fab Jewish soul food—lox, herring, sable, etc
- **Saxelby Cheesemongers** •
  120 Essex St [Rivington St]
  212-220-0204
  All-American and artisinal.
- **September Wines & Spirits** •
  100 Stanton St [Ludlow St]
  212-388-0770
  Wines from a varity of family-operated vineyards. Free tastings!
- **Top Hops** • 94 Orchard St [Delancey St]
  212-254-4677
  Sip a beer while you shop for more beer.
- **xCubicle** • 48 Wall St
  917-338-0645
  Game system and smartphone repair.
- **Zarin Fabrics** • 69 Orchard St
  212-925-6112
  Major destination in the fabric district.

Map 5 · West Village

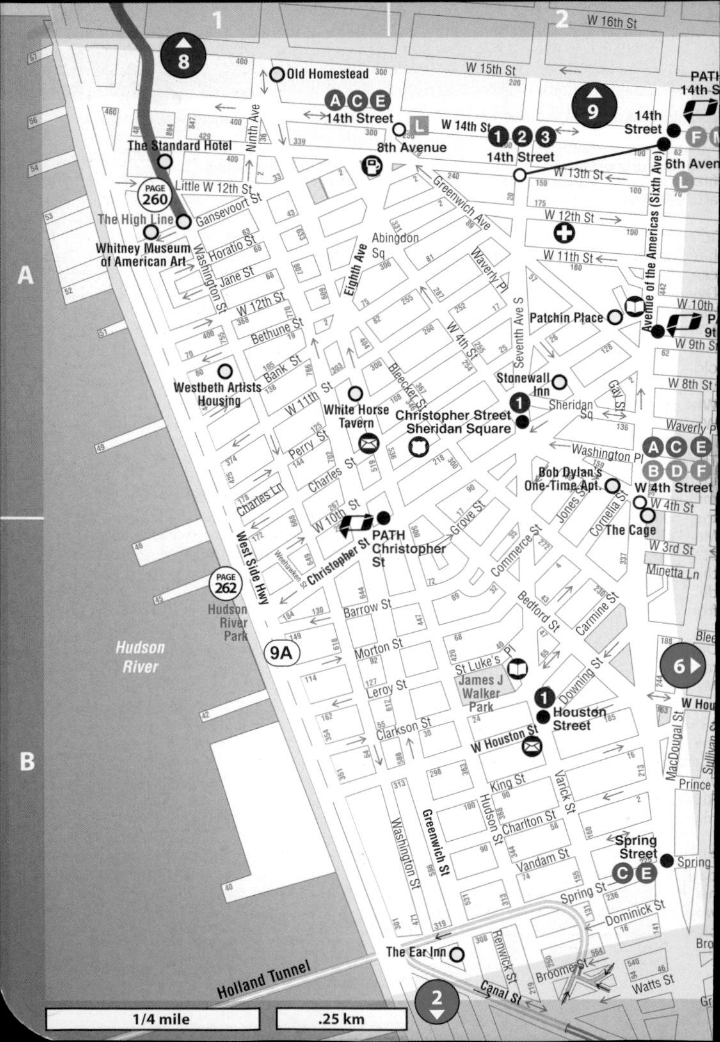

W 16th St
W 16th St

PATH
14th St

8

Old Homestead

A C E
14th Street
8th Avenue

1 2 3
14th Street

9

14th Street

The Standard Hotel

Ninth Ave

Little W 12th St

Gansevoort St

The High Line
PAGE 260

Whitney Museum of American Art

Washington St

Horatio St

Jane St

W 12th St

Bethune St

Bank St

Westbeth Artists Housing

W 11th St

Perry St

Charles St

Charles Ln

White Horse Tavern

Greenwich Ave

W 13th St

W 12th St

W 11th St

Abingdon Sq

Eighth Ave

Waverly Pl

Greenwich St

Seventh Ave S

W 4th St

Bleecker St

W 13th St

Avenue of the Americas (Sixth Ave)

6th Ave
L

Patchin Place

W 10th St
9th

W 9th St

W 8th St

Stonewall Inn

Sheridan Sq

Christopher Street
Sheridan Square

1

Waverly Pl

A C E
B D F
W 4th Street

Bob Dylan's One-Time Apt.

The Cage

W 3rd St

West Side Hwy

Christopher St

PATH
Christopher St

Grove St

Commerce St

Bedford St

Jones St

Cornelia St

Minetta Ln

Barrow St

9A

Hudson River Park

PAGE 262

Hudson River

Morton St

Leroy St

Clarkson St

St Luke's Pl

James J Walker Park

Houston St

1
Houston Street

W Houston St

Downing St

Carmine St

6

W Ho

MacDougal St

King St

Charlton St

Vandam St

Greenwich St

Hudson St

Varick St

Spring St

Spring Street
C E

Spring

Dominick St

The Ear Inn

Renwick St

Holland Tunnel

Canal St

Broome St

Watts St

2

Ble

| 1/4 mile | .25 km |

Ah, the West Village. This is the idyllic neighborhood of Jane Jacobs, the district of odd-angled streets designed to disorient grid-seasoned New Yorkers. Bordered by collegiate Greenwich Village to the east, millionaire stronghold Tribeca to the South, and factory-turned-gallery heaven Chelsea to the North, this neighborhood has quaint beauty, a thriving restaurant scene, and top-notch shopping, making it the ultimate address for the very, very rich. But its draw goes deeper than finding the boots or the cheeseburger that will change your life, because of all the famous artists, musicians, and writers who once lived, worked, drank, strolled, and starved here.

To catch a glimpse of more Bohemian times, head to the **White Horse Tavern** (1880), which has the dubious honor of being the place where Dylan Thomas drank himself to death. You can see where Edgar Allen Poe was treated at **Northern Dispensary** (1831), and visit Bob Dylan's old apartment at **161 West 4th Street**. Charming, gated **Patchin Place** (1849) was once home to writers Theodore Dreiser, e.e. Cummings, and Djuna Barnes. Thelonious Monk, Miles Davis, and every other jazz great under the sun played at **Village Vanguard** (1935). Poet Edna St. Vincent Millay helped found **Cherry Lane Theater** (1924), which remains the oldest continuously operating off-Broadway theater. Absent is Gertrude Vanderbilt Whitney's Studio Club on West 8th Street, which moved uptown in the 1950s. In 2015 the **Whitney Museum of American Art** returned to its West Village roots with a new building at Washington and Gansevoort Streets right next to the High Line.

The atmosphere of artistic creativity and non-conformity that permeated this neighborhood in the early 20th century (and still does, to some extent) gave rise to the gay rights movement, sparked by the 1969 riots at **Stonewall Inn**. The West Village has also been the scene of vehement preservation efforts. **The Ear Inn** (1817), one of the oldest bars in Manhattan, was an early example of the New York City Landmarks Preservation Commission acting to protect a historic building. The **Jefferson Market Courthouse** (1877), now part of the New York Public Library, was also saved by the outcry of the community when faced with demolition. Since 1969 much of the area has been preserved as a historic district that runs from 14th Street to West 4th or St. Luke's Place, and from Washington St. to University Place.

Despite all that architectural preservation, perhaps no area has seen as dramatic change in recent years as the blocks between 14th, Gansevoort, and Hudson Streets, also known as the Meatpacking District. The slaughterhouses, meat markets, hookers, and johns have been displaced by highest of high-end shops, nightclubs, and glittering hotels, paving the way for a different kind of meat market entirely. The Standard Hotel, one of the most visible signs of the area's resurgence, straddles **The High Line**, converted from a railway to a green public space that runs all the way up to 34th Street. It's worth a stroll, if only to remind yourself that you're (literally) above all the luxury below. Continue your walk along ever-popular **Hudson River Park**, before hitting one of the West Village's fine bars and restaurants and having more fun than you can afford.

Along Sixth Avenue at West 4th Street is **The Cage**, one of the city's most heralded outdoor basketball courts. The level of play is high and the competition intense; not your typical neighborhood pick-up game, several NBA players have tested their chops here. When you've worked up an appetite watching from the sidelines, hit up the **Old Homestead**, New York's oldest steakhouse; the only thing better than the wood paneling and leather banquettes is that nifty retro neon out front.

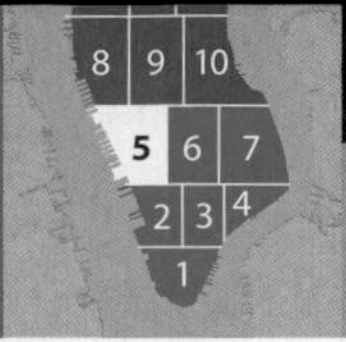

Map 5
8 9 10
5 6 7
2 3 4
1

West Village

O Landmarks

- **Bob Dylan's One-Time Apartment •**
161 W 4th St [Cornelia St]
Bob Dylan lived here in the '60s.
- **The Cage (Basketball Court) •**
6th Ave & W 4th St
Where everybody's got game…
- **The Ear Inn •** 326 Spring St [Greenwich St]
212-226-9060
Second-oldest bar in New York; great space.
- **The High Line •**
Gansevoort to 34th St b/n 10th & 11th Ave
212-500-6035
Stunning elevated park; a testament to human creativity.
- **Hudson River Park •** Battery Pl to 59th St
212-627-2020
Bicycle and walking paths; tennis, batting cages, dog runs!
- **Jefferson Market •** 425 6th Ave [W 10th St]
212-243-4334
Now a library.
- **Old Homestead Steakhouse •**
56 9th Ave [W 14th St]
212-242-9040
Said to be NY's oldest steakhouse, circa 1868.
- **Patchin Place •**
W 10th St b/n 6th Ave & Greenwich Ave
Tiny gated enclave, once home to E.E. Cummings.
- **The Standard •** 848 Washington St [W 12th St]
212-645-4646
Hip Meatpacking District hotel straddling the High Line.
- **The Stonewall Inn •**
53 Christopher St [7th Ave S]
212-488-2705
Uprising here in 1969 launched the gay rights movement.
- **Westbeth Artists Housing •**
55 Bethune St [Washington St]
Cool multifunctional arts center.
- **White Horse Tavern •**
567 Hudson St [W 11th St]
212-989-3956
Another old, cool bar. Dylan Thomas drank here (too much).
- **Whitney Museum of American Art •**
99 Gansevoort St [10th Ave]
212-570-3600
Always has something to talk about, like the controversial Biennial.

🖥 Coffee

- **Joe the Art of Coffee •** 141 Waverly Pl [Gay St]
212-924-6750
Excellent espresso.
- **Toby's Estate •** 44 Charles St [7th Ave S]
646-590-1924 Australian artisanal coffee powerhouse.

🍎 Farmers Markets

- **Abingdon Square Greenmarket •**
W 12th St & Hudson St
Sat 8 am–2 pm, year round

🍸 Nightlife

- **Art Bar •** 52 8th Ave [W 4th St]
212-727-0244
Great spaces, cool crowd.
- **Arthur's Tavern •** 57 Grove St [Bleecker St]
212-675-6879
Featuring great jazz and blues since 1937.
- **Automatic Slims •** 733 Washington St [Bank St]
212-645-8660
LOUD. Yes, that loud.
- **Barrow's Pub •** 463 Hudson St [Barrow St]
212-741-9349
Low-key, old man bar.
- **Blind Tiger Ale House •**
281 Bleecker St [Jones St]
212-462-4682
Beer heaven. Good food. Good vibe.
- **Blue Ribbon Bar •** 34 Downing St [Bedford St]
212-691-0404
Haute wine bar from the Bromberg brothers' epicurean empire.
- **Boom Boom Room •**
848 Washington St [W 13th St]
212-645-4646
Chic beautiful things drink at the top of the Standard Hotel.
- **Brass Monkey •** 55 Little W 12th St [10th Ave]
212-675-6686
Lots of beers, big wood tables, low light, and multiple levels.
- **Cielo •** 18 Little W 12th St [9th Ave]
212-645-5700
Too much 'tude.

West Village

So many bars, so little time. The **Ear Inn** and **White Horse Tavern** are classics while **Employees Only** and **Little Branch** have speakeasy cocktails covered. Check out live jazz at **Village Vanguard**, world music at **SOB's**, cabaret at **Marie's Crisis** and **The Duplex** and movies at **IFC** or revival house **Film Forum**.

- **City Winery** • 155 Varick St [Vandam St]
  212-608-0555
  Adult yupsters sip pinot while David Byrne plays a live set.
- **Cornelia Street Cafe** • 79 Cornelia St [W 4th St]
  212-989-9319
  Cozy live music.
- **Cubbyhole** • 281 W 12th St [W 4th St]
  212-243-9041
  Homey atmosphere and friendly crowd at this lesbian bar mainstay.
- **Daddy-O** • 44 Bedford St [Leroy St]
  212-414-8884
  Good for a first date or after-work drinks.
- **The Duplex** • 61 Christopher St [7th Ave S]
  212-255-5438
  Everything's still fun.
- **The Ear Inn** • 326 Spring St [Greenwich St]
  212-226-9060
  Second oldest bar in NYC. A great place.
- **Employees Only** • 510 Hudson St [W 10th St]
  212-242-3021
  Classy cocktails for big bucks.
- **Fiddlesticks Pub & Grill** •
  56 Greenwich Ave [Perry St]
  212-463-0516
  Good Irish fare, depressing environs.
- **The Four-Faced Liar** • 165 W 4th St [Cornelia St]
  212-206-8959
  A spirited neighborhood bar with wonderfully friendly bartenders.
- **Henrietta Hudson** • 438 Hudson St [Morton St]
  212-924-3347
  Good lesbian vibe.
- **The Hog Pit** • 37 B West 26th Street
  212-213-4871
  Sweet potato fries and BBQ Ribs make city folk squeal in this dive bar.
- **Hogs & Heifers Saloon** •
  859 Washington St [W 13th St]
  212-929-0655
  Girls on the bar, flaming shots, and bartenders with megaphones, oh my!
- **Hudson Bar and Books** •
  636 Hudson St [Horatio St]
  212-229-2642
  Like *Cheers* for a hipper, more sophisticated crowd.
- **Injera** • 11 Abingdon Sq [8th Ave]
  212-206-9330
  Ethiopian wine bar with solid food to match.

- **Johnny's Bar** • 90 Greenwich Ave [W 12th St]
  212-741-5279
  Occassional celeb sightings at this popular dive.
- **Kettle of Fish** • 59 Christopher St [7th Ave S]
  212-414-2278
  Cozy couches and darts.
- **Little Branch** • 22 7th Ave S [W 12th St]
  212-929-4360
  Clever cocktails in an intimate, cavernous setting.
- **Marie's Crisis** • 59 Grove St [7th Ave S]
  212-243-9323
  Showtunes only! And no, Billy Joel doesn't count.
- **Off The Wagon** • 109 MacDougal St [Minetta Ln]
  212-533-4487
  College bar at it's finest. It possible.
- **The Other Room** • 143 Perry St [Washington St]
  212-645-9758
  Surprisingly decent beer selection with great, low-key vibe.
- **Pieces** • 8 Christopher St [Gay St]
  212-929-9291
  Favorite local gay dive, newly renovated, cheap drinks.
- **Plunge** • 18 9th Ave [W 13th St]
  212-206-6700
  The Gansevoort's rooftop bar for pretty people.
- **The Rusty Knot** • 425 West St [W 11th St]
  212-645-5668
  Who knew rich kids loved nautical themed bars?
- **Smalls Jazz Club** • 183 W 10th St [W 4th St]
  212-252-5091
  Classic New York jazz scene; all night for $20.
- **SOB's** • 204 Varick St [W Houston St]
  212-243-4940
  World music venue with salsa lessons on Mondays.
- **Soho Cigar Bar** • 32 Watts St [Sullivan St]
  212-941-1781
  Smoker-friendly lounge.
- **Standard Biergarten** •
  848 Washington St [W 13th St]
  212-645-4100
  Gallons of beer, pretzels, and partying young ones.

Map 5

West Village

- **The Stonewall Inn** •
  53 Christopher St [7th Ave S]
  212-488-2705
  From the L to the GB and T, this is where it all
  began.
- **Paul's Casablanca** • 305 Spring St [Renwick St]
  212-620-5220
  A sexy Moroccan hot spot or an ode to Pier 1
  Imports?
- **Turks & Frogs** • 323 W 11th St [Greenwich St]
  212-691-8875
  Wine bar off the beaten track.
- **The Upholstery Store** •
  713 Washington St [11th St]
  212-352-2300
  Very cozy, decent wine, atmosphere may lead to
  napping.
- **Village Vanguard** • 178 7th Ave S [Perry St]
  212-255-4037
  Classic NYC jazz venue. Not to be missed.
- **Vin Sur Vingt** • 201 W 11th St [Greenwich St]
  212-924-4442
  Bold wine choices and French small plates in a
  cozy space.
- **Vol de Nuit** • 148 W 4th St [6th Ave]
  212-982-3388
  Belgian beers, cool vibe.
- **White Horse Tavern** •
  567 Hudson St [W 11th St]
  212-989-3956
  Another NYC classic.
- **Wilfie and Nell** • 228 W 4th St [W 10th St]
  212-242-2990
  Cool space, good food; too bad someone told
  the i-bankers.
- **Wogie's** • 39 Greenwich Ave [Charles St]
  212-229-2171
  Philly-caliber cheesesteaks & 700-level Phans.

🍴 Restaurants

- **A Salt & Battery** • 112 Greenwich Ave [Jane St]
  212-691-2713 • $$
  If you can eat it, they can fry it.
- **Agave** • 140 7th Ave S [Charles St]
  212-989-2100 • $$$
  Surprisingly good Southwest-Mex.
- **Aquagrill** • 210 Spring St [Sullivan St]
  212-274-0505 • $$$$$
  NFT's favorite straight-up seafood restaurant.
  Great feel.
- **Bar Sardine** • 183 W 10th St [7th Ave S]
  646-360-3705 • $$$
  Gabriel Stulman gastropub; inventive and open
  late.
- **Bar Six** • 502 6th Ave [W 13th St]
  212-691-1363 • $$$
  Pretty much a perfect French bistro.
- **Barbuto** • 775 Washington St [12th St]
  212-924-9700 • $$$$
  Jonathan Waxman's oven-roasted chicken
  masterpiece.
- **Benny's Burritos** • 113 Greenwich Ave [Jane St]
  212-633-9210 • $$
  An NYC Mexican institution.
- **Black Tap** • 529 Broome St [Sullivan St]
  917-639-3089 • $$
  Soho burger spot with the buzzy milkshakes.
- **Bleeker Street Pizza** • 69 7th Ave S [Bleeker St]
  212-924-4466 • $
  A couple pepperonis above the average
  grab-a-slice pizza place.
- **Bobo** • 181 W 10th St [7th Ave]
  212-488-2626 • $$$$
  Hip eats, if you can find the unmarked basement
  entrance.
- **Bonsignour** • 35 Jane St [8th Ave]
  212-229-9700 • $$
  Over-priced but tasty café, celeb-sighting likely.

Taïm has some of the best falafel on the planet, and for a cheap breakfast that even celebs appreciate, **La Bonbonniere** can't be beat. Impress dates by locating the unmarked basement door of **Bobo**. Try **En Brasserie** for Japanese izakaya and **Keste** for pizza. For a splurge check out **Spice Market**.

- **Bosie Tea Parlor** • 10 Morton St [Bleecker St]
  212-352-9900 • $$
  Fine teas, tasty little sandwiches, proper tea service, lovely staff.
- **Bubby's** •
  High Line 73 Gansevoort St [Washington St]
  212-206-6200
  Comfort food masters' High Line outpost.
- **Buvette** • 42 Grove St [Bleecker St]
  • $$$
  French all the way, grâce à Dieu.
- **Café Altro Paradiso** • 234 Spring St [6th Ave]
  646-952-0828 • $$$$
  Fancified basic Italian in stylish setting.
- **Café Cluny** • 284 W 12th St [W 4th St]
  212-255-6900 • $$$$
  The Odeon's younger cousin in the West Village, also French.
- **Caliente Cab Co** • 61 7th Ave S [Bleecker St]
  212-243-8517 • $$
  Cheesy spot the kids would probably like.
- **Casa** • 72 Bedford St [Commerce St]
  212-366-9410 • $$$
  Triple B's: Beautiful Brazilian brunch.
- **Casa la Femme** • 140 Charles St [Washington St]
  212-505-0005 • $$$$
  A Fantastic Culinary Experience on the West Village.
- **Charlie Bird** • 5 King St [6th Ave]
  212-235-7133 • $$ $$
  Italo-comfort cuisine/paean to NYC.
- **Coppelia** • 201 W 14th St [7th Ave]
  212-858-5001 • $$$
  Fancy-ish diner with a Cuban twist. Always open.
- **Corner Bistro** • 331 W 4th St [Jane St]
  212-242-9502 • $
  Top NYC burgers. Perfect at 3 am.

- **Cowgirl** • 519 Hudson St [W 10th St]
  212-633-1133 • $$
  Good chicken fried steak.
- **Deb's Catering** • 3 Madison St
  212-964-1300 • $
  Get cheap but interesting food for lunch from their "salad bar."
- **Decoy** • 529 Hudson St [Charles St]
  212-691-9700 • $$$$
  If they're elevating Peking duck why is the place subterranean?
- **Do Hwa** • 55 Carmine St [Bedford St]
  212-414-1224 • $$$$
  Hot off the barbie Korean with friends.
- **Employees Only** • 510 Hudson St [W 10th St]
  212-242-3021 • $$$$
  Deco-decorated eatery with a damn good bar.
- **EN Japanese Brasserie** •
  435 Hudson St [Leroy St]
  212-647-9196 • $$$$
  Amazing izakaya not to be missed.
- **Extra Virgin** • 259 West 4th [Perry St]
  212-691-9359 • $$$
  Brunch, dinner, and a little bit of everything. Pure New York.
- **Fedora** • 239 W 4th St [10th St]
  646-449-9336 • $$$
  Subterranean cocktail-forward coziness and inventive shareable dishes.
- **Fiddlesticks Pub & Grill** •
  56 Greenwich Ave [Perry St]
  212-463-0516 • $$
  This pub's authentic Irish fare is nothing to fiddle around with.
- **galanga** • 149 W 4th St [6th Ave]
  212-228-4267 • $$
  Creative Thai that's spicy and delish.

Map 5

- **Gottino** · 52 Greenwich Ave [Perry St]
  212-633-2590 · $$$
  The Italian small plate trend fulfills its potential here.
- **Gradisca** · 126 W 13th St [Ave of the Americas]
  212-691-4886 · $$$$
  Romantic Italian loyal to the regular customers.
- **Hector's** · 44 Little W 12th St [Washington St]
  212-206-7592 · $$
  Unfancy burgers under the fancy High Line.
- **High Street on Hudson** ·
  637 Hudson St [Horatio St]
  917-388-3944 · $$$
  All-day bread-forward haute farm-to-table Philly import.
- **Houseman** · 508 Greenwich St [Spring St]
  212-641-0654 · $$$
  Rustic, elegant, ever-changing menus in Hudson Square.
- **I Sodi** · 105 Christopher St [Bleecker St]
  212-414-5774 · $$$
  Tuscan through and through.
- **Injera** · 11 Abingdon Sq [8th Ave]
  212-206-9330 · $$$$
  Solid Ethiopian with bonus Ethiopian wine bar to match.
- **Jeffrey's Grocery** ·
  172 Waverly Pl [Christopher St]
  646-398-7630 · $$$
  All-day affair with emphasis on oysters.
- **Joe's Pizza** · 7 Carmine St [Bleecker St]
  212-366-1182 · $
  Excellent slices.
- **John's Pizzeria** · 278 Bleecker St [Jones St]
  212-243-1680 · $$
  Quintessential NY pizza.
- **Joseph Leonard** · 170 Waverly Pl [Grove St]
  646-429-8383 · $$$
  Top-notch NYC dining experience. Worth the splurge and wait.
- **Kesté Pizza & Vino** · 271 Bleecker St [Jones St]
  212-243-1500 · $$$
  So authentic, it's the headquarters for the APN (look it up).
- **La Bonbonniere** · 28 8th Ave [Jane St]
  212-741-9266 · $
  Best cheap breakfast in the city.

- **La Nacional** · 239 W 14th St [8th Ave]
  212-243-9308 · $$$
  Hidden Spanish social club serving traditional tapas.
- **La Sirene** · 558 Broome St [Varick St]
  212-925-3061 · $$$
  Gourmet French that's BYOB? We're in heaven.
- **Le Gigot** · 18 Cornelia St [Bleecker St]
  212-627-3737 · $$$$
  Classic cuisine Française, complete with Parisian price tag.
- **Little Owl** · 90 Bedford St [Barrow St]
  212-741-4695 · $$$$
  Fun, intimate bistro.
- **Malatesta Trattoria** ·
  649 Washington St [Christopher St]
  212-741-1207 · $$
  Authentic Italiano in cozy surroundings—e delizioso gnocchi!
- **Mah Ze Dahr** · 28 Greenwich Ave [Charles St]
  212-498-9810
  Deluxe baked goods with a neighborhood vibe.
- **Mary's Fish Camp** · 64 Charles St [W 4th St]
  646-486-2185 · $$$
  Amy Sedaris used to wait tables here for fun. Killer food!
- **Mas (farmhouse)** · 39 Downing St [Bedford St]
  212-255-1790 · $$$$
  Sneak away to the South of France.
- **Mighty Quinn's** · 75 Greenwich Ave [11th St]
  646-524-7889 · $$$
  Highly regarded "Texalina" hybrid barbecue mini-chain.
- **Moustache** · 90 Bedford St [Grove St]
  212-229-2220 · $$
  Excellent sit-down falafel.
- **No 28** · 28 Carmine St [Bleecker St]
  212-463-9653 · $$
  Finally, real Napoli pizza for reasonable prices.
- **Old Homestead Steakhouse** ·
  56 9th Ave [W 14th St]
  212-242-9040 · $$$$$
  Said to be NY's oldest steakhouse, circa 1868.

West Village

Map 5

Foodies, hit **Murray's Cheese**, **Myers of Keswick**, **Ottomanelli & Sons**, **Citarella**, **Faiccos**, and **Murray's Bagels**. Sip java at **Joe The Art of Coffee**, browse for books at **Three Lives & Company**, or go ahead and blow your bonus at **Jeffrey**, **Alexander McQueen**, and **Stella McCartney**.

- **One If By Land, TIBS** • 17 Barrow St [Bleecker St]
212-228-0822 • $$$$$
Exudes romance.
- **The Original Sandwich Shoppe** •
58 Greenwich Ave [Perry St]
212-255-2237 • $$
Sandwiches and baked goods worth slapping someone over.
- **Palma** • 28 Cornelia St [W 4th St]
212-691-2223 • $$
Italian restaurant with cooks who have Italian accents.
- **Pearl Oyster Bar** • 18 Cornelia St [W 4th St]
212-691-8211 • $$$
For all your lobster roll cravings. NFT fave.
- **Perla Cafe** • 234 W 4th St [10th St]
212-933-1824 • $$$
Neighborhood-y Italian cafe/bistro from Gabriel Stulman.
- **Perry Street** • 176 Perry St [Washington St]
212-352-1900 • $$$$$
Satisfyingly simplified New French from Jean-Georges Vongerichten.
- **Philip Marie** • 569 Hudson St [W 11th St]
212-242-6200 • $$$
Romantic—and with great steak!
- **Piccolo Angolo** • 621 Hudson St [Jane St]
212-229-9177 • $$
The lobster cannelloni is famous. The service is colorful.
- **Pinto** • 118 Christopher St [Bedford St]
212-366-3433 • $$
Fun, fusion-y Thai; good takeout option.
- **Potjanee** • 48 Carmine St [Bedford St]
212-627-7745 • $$
Reliable Thai takeout.
- **Ramen-Ya** • 181 W 4th St [Jones St]
212-989-5440 • $$$
Pork & chicken broth plus small plates and rice bowls.
- **RedFarm** • 529 Hudson St [Charles St]
212-792-9700 • $$$
Farm-fresh dim sum. Home of the Pac Man dumpling.

- **Rosemary's** • 18 Greenwich Ave [W 10th St]
212-647-1818 • $$$
Greenmarket Italian from a garden (with chickens!) on the roof.
- **Sanpanino** • 494 Hudson St [Christopher St]
212-645-7228 • $
Mouthwatering Italian sandwiches. We love #14.
- **Santina** • 820 Washington St [Gansevoort St]
212-254-3000 • $$$$
Swanky Italian focusing on vegetables and seafood.
- **Slowly Shirley** • 121 W 10th St [Greenwich Ave]
212-243-2827
Subterranean mixological excellence from NYC cocktail veterans.
- **Snack Taverna** • 63 Bedford St [Morton St]
212-929-3499 • $$$
Greek for hipsters. More upscale than its sister restaurant on Thompson.
- **Souen** • 210 Ave of the Americas [Prince St]
212-807-7421 • $$$
High-end vegetarian.
- **Spain** • 113 W 13th St [Ave of the Americas]
212-929-9580 • $$
Old-school joint with free tapas while you drink.
- **The Spotted Pig** • 314 W 11th St [Greenwich St]
212-620-0393 • $$$$
We finally got in. All great except for pig ears.
- **Taim** • 222 Waverly Pl [Perry St]
212-691-1287 • $$
Gourmet falafel with mind-blowing housemade sauces.
- **Tartine** • 253 W 11th St [W 4th St]
212-229-2611 • $$$
BYOB + Solid French = NFT pick.

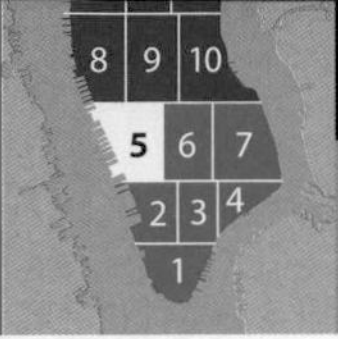

Map 5

West Village

- **Tea & Sympathy** •
  108 Greenwich Ave [W 13th St]
  212-989-9735 • $$$
  Eccentric English. Cult favorite.
- **Tortilla Flats** • 767 Washington St [W 12th St]
  212-243-1053 • $$
  Free shot of tequila on your b-day? Like, totally awesome.
- **Trattoria Spaghetto** •
  232 Bleecker St [Carmine St]
  212-255-6752 • $$$
  Pasta restaurant with very original name.
- **Two Boots** • 201 W 11th St [Greenwich Ave]
  212-633-9096 • $
  Cajun pizza.
- **Untitled** • 99 Gansevoort St [Washington St]
  212-570-3670 • $$$$
  Haute-farm-to-table at the Whitney.
- **Via Carota** • 51 Grove St [7th Ave S]
  $$$$
  All-day Tuscan cuisine, done to perfection.
- **Wallse** • 344 W 11th St [Washington St]
  212-352-2300 • $$$$
  Top-notch Austrian cuisine keeps the West Villagers coming back.
- **The Waverly Inn** • 16 Bank St [Waverly Pl]
  917-828-1154 • $$$
  Hip, revamped café-cum-speakeasy. Good luck getting in.
- **Waverly Restaurant** •
  385 Ave of the Americas [Waverly Pl]
  212-675-3181 • $$
  Great old-school diner with classy waiters.
- **Westville** • 210 W 10th St [Bleecker St]
  212-741-7971 • $$
  Trendy organic belly timber served with a fresh market flair.
- **Whole Green Inc** • 35 7th Ave [W 13th St]
  212-337-3400 • $
  Best bang-for-your-buck juice bar in these parts.
- **Wood and Ales** • 234 W 14th St [7th Ave]
  212-206-0430 • $$
  Friendly, wood-paneled sports bar & grill.

🛍 Shopping

- **Alexander McQueen** •
  747 Madison Ave [E 65th St]
  212-645-1797
  Brit bad boy designs.
- **Bleecker Street Records** •
  188 W 4th St [Barrow St]
  212-255-7899
  Classic Village record shop. Great selection.
- **C.O. Bigelow Chemists** • 414 6th Ave [W 9th St]
  212-533-2700
  Classic village pharmacy. Do try and patronize it.
- **Casa Magazines** • 22 8th Ave [W 12th St]
  212-645-1197
  Seemingly every magazine ever, among the last of its kind.
- **Citarella** • 424 6th Ave [W 9th St]
  212-874-0383
  Wealthy foodies love this place.
- **The End of History** • 548 Hudson St [Perry St]
  212-647-7598
  Very cool shop specializing in antique glass.
- **Faicco's Italian Specialties** •
  260 Bleecker St [Cornelia St]
  212-243-1974
  Proscuitto bread, homemade sausage, huge heros, pork heaven.
- **Flight 001** • 96 Greenwich Ave [Jane St]
  212-989-0001
  Cute hipster travel shop. And they sell NFT!
- **Grom** • 233 Bleecker St [6th Ave]
  212-206-1738
  This gelato is so good and so expensive.

West Village

Map 5

Foodies, hit **Murray's Cheese**, **Myers of Keswick**, **Ottomanelli & Sons**, **Citarella**, **Faiccos**, and **Murray's Bagels**. Sip java at **Joe The Art of Coffee**, browse for books at **Three Lives & Company**, or go ahead and blow your bonus at **Jeffrey**, **Alexander McQueen**, and **Stella McCartney**.

- **Health & Harmony** • 470 Hudson St [Barrow St]
  212-691-3036
  Small health food store with good selection and decent prices.
- **House of Oldies** • 35 Carmine St [Bleecker St]
  212-243-0500
  Everything on vinyl.
- **Jacques Torres** • 350 Hudson St [Charlton St]
  212-414-2462
  Tastebud bliss brought to you by the Master of Chocolate.
- **Jeffrey** • 449 W 14th St [Washington St]
  212-206-1272
  Avant-garde (and wildly expensive) mini-department store.
- **The Leather Man** •
  111 Christopher St [Bedford St]
  212-243-5339
  No, you won't look like James Dean. But it'll help.
- **Milk & Cookies** • 19 Commerce St [7th Ave]
  212-243-1640
  Cookies will rise again and this place will blow up.
- **Murray's Cheese** • 254 Bleecker St [Leroy St]
  212-243-3289
  We love cheese, and so does Murray's.
- **Music Inn** • 169 W 4th St [Jones St]
  212-243-5715
  Bursting with beautiful drums & stringed world instruments, they do repairs.
- **Myers of Keswick** • 634 Hudson St [Horatio St]
  212-691-4194
  Killer English sausages, pasties, etc. And "Bounty!"

- **O. Ottomanelli & Sons** •
  285 Bleecker St [Jones St]
  212-675-4217
  High quality meats and the friendliest butchers in town.
- **popbar** • 5 Carmine St [Ave of the Americas]
  212-255-4874
  Gelato on a stick.
- **Scott Jordan Furniture** •
  137 Varick St [Spring St]
  212-620-4682
  Solid hardwood furniture. Super-cool and mostly unaffordable.
- **Stella McCartney** • 112 Greene St [Prince St]
  212-255-1556
  Hip, animal-friendly fashion.
- **Suprema Provisions** • 305 Bleecker St
  [7th Ave S] 646-964-4994
  Super-shmancy gourmet Italian food market and wine bar/small plate powerhouse.
- **Te Company** • 163 W 10th St [7th Ave S]
  High-end tea store.
- **Three Lives & Company** •
  154 W 10th St [Waverly Pl]
  212-741-2069
  Classic Village bookshop. Thank God.
- **Vitra** • 100 Gansevoort St
  212-463-5700
  Sleek and modern home furnishings. Super-cool.
- **Waterfront Bike Shop** •
  391 West St [Christopher St]
  212-414-2453
  Sales, service, repairs, and rentals.

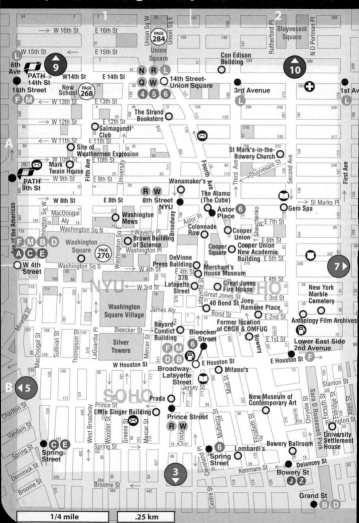

Map 6 · Washington Sq / NYU / NoHo / SoHo

Neighborhood Overview

Map 6

Simply put, this is still the center of the universe. It all radiates from the corner of Broadway and Houston, which serves as the intersection for four of New York City's most exciting neighborhoods: Greenwich Village, Soho, NoHo, and NoLiTa. While the area is far from bucolic—green space is limited to a few patches of grass in **Washington Square Park**— it has everything one could possibly want in terms of culture. Architecture, art galleries, movie theaters, live music, shopping, restaurants, old New York, new New York, and every other kind of New York are all here for the taking. If you're new to the city and ready to dive in and explore, start here.

One of this area's highlights is the sheer number of buildings from every period of New York City's development. Just walk the streets and you'll traverse over two hundred years of architectural history. Start with the somewhat-hidden former stables at **Washington Mews** for a taste of 18th-century New York. Other ancient (for New York) buildings include **St. Marks Church in-the-Bowery** (1799), **Colonnade Row** (1830s), the **Old Merchant's House** (1832), **Grace Church** (1846) and the **Cooper Union Building** (1859). The stunning white terra cotta exterior of Louis Sullivan's **Bayard-Condict Building** (1899), and Ernest Flagg's **Great Jones Fire House** (1899) and **Little Singer Building** (1904) hearken back to New York at the turn of the 20th century. In the early 20th century Daniel Burnham (**Wanamaker's**, 1904/1907) and Henry J Hardenbergh (**376 Lafayette St**, 1888, and the **Con Edison Building**, 1914) added their contributions to the area. Our ultimate favorite is the little-known **DeVinne Press Building** (1885) by Babb, Cook & Willard (and not just because **Astor Wines** is there). Starting in the 21st century, modern (or should we say postmodern?) architecture has run rampant along the Bowery, transforming the once derelict district. Notable examples include Thom Mayne's **Cooper Union New Academic Building** (2009), Kazuyo Sejima and Ryue Nishizawa's brilliant **New Museum of Contemporary Art** (2007), and Herzog & de Mauron's bizarre **40 Bond** (2007).

Unlike these buildings, some historical places of interest seem hidden in plain sight. Our favorite of these is the lovely **New York City Marble Cemetery**, tucked away on Second Street between The Bowery and Second Avenue. NYU's **Brown Building** was the site of the horrific Triangle Shirtwaist Fire, while **18 West 11th Street** was the site of the Weathermen explosion. A plaque at the **Mark Twain House** on West 4th Street commemorates his time as a Greenwich Villager. And, while you can't rock out at **CBGB** anymore, you can still visit the site (now a John Varvatos store), right around the corner from where Joey Ramone lived on East 2nd Street, also known as **Joey Ramone Place**.

Just as there's no shortage of history, the cultural options here can make your head spin. A few of our favorites include the **Salmagundi Club** for art, the Astor Center for food and cooking events, and **Anthology Film Archives** for experimental film. The **Bowery Ballroom** is one of the best venues in NYC to catch up-and-coming musical acts. Browsing **The Strand**'s 18 miles of books is a must, as is checking out the critics' picks at **Other Music**, which has outlasted practically every other record store in this 'hood.

For all the history and culture here, signs of the area's down-and-out heyday in the 1970s and 1980s are few and far between. **Milano's** still serves up divey goodness, as it's been doing since the 1800s. Skate punks still hang out at **The Alamo** (give it a spin), even while fancy glass towers rise around it. You can still get your punk rock and goth gear at **Trash & Vaudeville**, and browse the magazine racks at **Gem Spa**. Much of the rest of St. Mark's Place along here now resembles a cross between a strip mall and Little Tokyo, which stretches along 9th Street as well. If you're ready for a break from all this excitement, grab some ramen, then get a cocktail at **Angel's Share** (one flight up and behind a Japanese restaurant) or explore the sake list at **Decibel** while feeling like you've left the Village far behind.

Map 6

Washington Sq / NYU / NoHo / SoHo

O Landmarks

- **376 Lafayette St** •
376 Lafayette St [Great Jones St]
Henry Hardenbergh's NoHo masterpiece, circa 1888.
- **40 Bond** • 40 Bond St [Bowery]
Uber-futuristic condo projects by Herzog & de Meuron et al.
- **The Alamo (The Cube)** • 4th Ave & Astor Pl
Give it a spin sometime.
- **Bayard-Condict Building** •
65 Bleecker St [Crosby St]
Louis Sullivan's only New York building.
- **Brown Building of Science** •
23-29 Washington Pl [Greene St]
Site of the Triangle Shirtwaist Fire.
- **Colonnade Row** • 428 Lafayette St [Astor Pl]
Remains of a very different era.
- **Con Edison Building** • 145 E 14th St [Irving Pl]
Cool top.
- **Cooper Union** • 30 Cooper Sq [Bowery]
212-353-4100
Great brownstone-covered building.
- **Cooper Union New Academic Building** •
41 Cooper Sq [E 6th St]
Supercool, futuristic, and eco-friendly architecture.
- **DeVinne Press Building** •
399 Lafayette St [E 4th St]
Killer 1885 brick-and-glass masterpiece by Babb, Cook & Willard.
- **Former location of CBGB & OMFUG** •
315 Bowery [Bleecker St]
Now houses high-end retail. Ew.
- **Great Jones Firehouse** •
Bowery & Great Jones St
The coolest firehouse in NYC.
- **Joey Ramone Place** • Bowery & E 2nd St
It's Joey Ramone's place. Period.
- **Little Singer Building** •
561 Broadway [Prince St]
A fine building by Ernest Flagg.
- **Mark Twain House** • 14 W 10th St [5th Ave]
Mark Twain lived here. It's also NYC's most haunted portal.
- **The Merchant's House Museum** •
29 E 4th St [Lafayette St]
212-777-1089
The merchant is now dead.

- **New Museum** • 235 Bowery [Prince St]
212-219-1222
Brilliant white stacked cubes houses contemporary art and killer bookstore. Yah.
- **The New School** • 66 W 12th St [5th Ave]
212-229-5600
Legendary progressive university located in and around Greenwich Village.
- **New York City Marble Cemetery** •
74 E 2nd St [1st Ave]
212-228-6401
Cool, but generally closed. But you can still see in.
- **New York University** •
70 Washington Sq S [LaGuardia Pl]
212-998-1212
One of the city's largest private employers.
- **Salmagundi Club** • 47 5th Ave [E 12th St]
212-255-7740
Cool building.
- **Site of the Weathermen Explosion** •
18 W 11th St [5th Ave]
Townhouse where the Weathermen's plans to destroy Columbia's library went awry.
- **St. Mark's Church In The Bowery** •
131 E 10th St [3rd Ave]
212-674-6377
Old church with lots of community ties.
- **Union Square Clock/Metronome** •
52 E 14th St [Broadway]
Get lost in time while looking South in Union Square.
- **University Settlement** •
184 Eldridge St [Rivington St]
212-453-0242
Providing a haven for lower east siders of all ages since 1886.
- **Wanamaker's** • E 8th St & Broadway
Former classiest department store in the city is now a Kmart. Ugh.
- **Washington Mews** •
University Pl (entrance) [5th Ave]
Where horses and servants used to live. Now coveted NYU space.
- **Washington Square Park** •
W 4th St & Washington Square W
From Potter's field to counterculture mecca and everything in between.

For better or worse, this area is why New York is called the city that never sleeps. For dives, we like **Scratcher**, **Milano's**, and **Blue & Gold**. For cocktails, check out **Mayahuel** or **Angel's Share**. Catch a reading at **KGB**, an indie film at **Angelika Film Center** or **Sunshine Cinema**, or live music at **Joe's Pub** or **Le Poisson Rouge** or **Bowery Ballroom**. We guarantee you won't be bored.

☕ Coffee

- **Atlas Café** • 73 2nd Ave [E 4th St]
  212-539-0966
  Middle Eastern eats, juice, and vegan stuffs.
- **Café Gitane** • 242 Mott St [Prince St]
  212-334-9552
  Worth the wait. Delicious food, beautiful people.
- **Caffe Reggio** • 119 MacDougal St [W 3rd St]
  212-475-9557
  A New York classic. Check out the custom coffee cups.
- **Coffee Project New York** •
  239 E 5th St [2nd Ave]
  Home of the deconstructed latte.
- **Gimme! Coffee** • 228 Mott St [Prince St]
  212-226-4011
  Amazing cappuccinos from the Ithaca experts.
- **Ground Support Cafe** •
  399 W Broadway [Spring St]
  212-219-8722
  Serving up the almighty coffee from Intelligentsia.
- **Joe The Art of Coffee** • 9 E 13th St [5th Ave]
  212-924-3300
  Joe really knows his joe. Collegiate coffee house. NYU hangout.
- **Hi Collar** • 214 E 10th St [2nd Ave]
  212-777-7018
  Japanese coffee shop by day/sake bar by night.

- **La Colombe Torrefaction** •
  400 Lafayette St [E 4th St]
  212-677-5834
  Philly's Stumptown expands toward the East Village.
- **La Colombe Torrefaction** •
  270 Lafayette St [Prince St]
  212-625-1717
  Philly's Stumptown.
- **Mudspot** • 307 E 9th St [2nd Ave]
  212-529-8766
  The Mudtruck's stationary shop.
- **Porto Rico Importing Co** •
  201 Bleecker St [MacDougal St]
  212-477-5421
  Beans by the barrel full.
- **Think Coffee** • 248 Mercer St [W 3rd St]
  212-228-6226
- **Third Rail Coffee** • 159 2nd Ave [10th St]
  Quality coffee and baked goods.
- **V Bar** • 225 Sullivan St [W 3rd Ave]
  212-253-5740
  Cozy spot. Morning = café. Night = wine bar.

🌽 Farmers Markets

- **Saint Mark's Church Greenmarket** •
  E 10th St & 2nd Ave
  Tues 8 am–7 pm Jun–Dec

🌑 Nightlife

- **8th Street Wine Cellar** •
28 W 8th St [MacDougal St]
212-260-9463
Classy and calm. Luckily NYU kids don't drink wine.
- **Amelie Wine Bar** • 22 W 8th St [Macdougal St]
212-533-2962
French wine bar with delish foie gras, escargot, etc. Bon ap'!
- **Amsterdam Billiards Club** •
110 E 11th St [4th Ave]
212-995-0333
Expensive and more posh than most pool halls.
- **Angel's Share** • 8 Stuyvesant St [E 9th St]
212-777-5415
Semi-hidden cocktail spot. Bring someone special.
- **Attaboy** • 134 Eldridge St [Delancey St]
Milk & Honey torchbearers carry on mixological tradition.
- **Bar Goto** • 245 Eldridge St [Houston St]
212-475-4411
Crafted cocktails and Japanese bar comfort food.
- **Bar Next Door** • 129 MacDougal St [W 3rd St]
212-529-5945
For serious jazz enthusiasts with a penchant for wine and crispy pizza.
- **Bar Veloce** • 175 2nd Ave [E 11th St]
212-260-3200
Sip grappa on a first date. Also in Chelsea.
- **Beauty Bar** • 231 E 14th St [3rd Ave]
212-539-1389
Just a little off the top, dahling?
- **Black & White** • 86 E 10th St [4th Ave]
212-253-0246
Amazing rockin' DJs on weeknights; beware Bridge and Tunnel infiltration on weekends.
- **Blue & Gold Tavern** • 79 E 7th St [1st Ave]
212-473-8918
Another fine East Village dive.

- **Blue Note** • 131 W 3rd St [MacDougal St]
212-475-8592
Classic jazz venue. Pricey.
- **Boiler Room** • 86 E 4th St [2nd Ave]
212-254-7536
Longtime comfortable, welcoming, no-nonsense gay dive.
- **Botanica Bar** • 47 E Houston St [Mulberry St]
212-343-7251
Good bar, but we still miss the Knitting Factory.
- **Bowery Ballroom** • 6 Delancey St [Bowery]
212-533-2111
Great space that attracts great bands.
- **The Box** • 189 Chrystie St [Rivington St]
212-982-9301
Burlesque and bottle service for the filthy rich.
- **Burp Castle** • 41 E 7th St [2nd Ave]
212-982-4576
Belgian ales and hushed voices.
- **Carroll Place** • 157 Bleecker St [Thompson St]
212-260-1700
Multi-level brunch, dinner, wine bar, live music destination.
- **Central Bar** • 109 E 9th St [4th Ave]
212-529-5333
Student-filled yet spicy dance party.
- **The Cock** • 93 2nd Ave [5th Ave]
In spot formerly known as The Hole; so there's that.
- **Comedy Cellar** •
117 MacDougal St [Minetta Ln]
212-254-3480
Big names make surprise appearances.
- **Corkbuzz** • 13 E 13th St [5th Ave]
646-873-6071
Outstanding wine selection in a classy setting.
- **Fanelli's Cafe** • 94 Prince St [Mercer St]
212-226-9412
Old-time SoHo haunt. Nice tiles.
- **The Fat Black Pussycat** •
130 W 3rd St [MacDougal St]
212-533-4790
Average rock venue.

McSorley's Old Ale House has been in operation 1854, and has a great old-school barroom atmosphere; weekend nights are insane. For a great beer selection, seek out Peculier Pub in Greenwich Village or if you're on the other side of Broadway Jimmy's 43 or Burp Castle, the latter of which is great for Belgian beer and quiet conversation.

- **Home Sweet Home** •
  131 Chrystie St [Broome St]
  212-226-5709
  Non-descript taxidermy hang out.
- **The Immigrant** • 341 E 9th St [1st Ave]
  646-308-1724
  Wine and snacks in a cozy tenement.
- **Jadis Wine Bar** • 42 Rivington St [Eldridge St]
  212-254-1675
  Perfect date spot for poor NFT employees.
- **Joe's Pub** • 425 Lafayette St [Astor Pl]
  212-967-7555
  Excellent range of acts in intimate space.
- **KGB Bar** • 85 E 4th St [2nd Ave]
  212-505-3360
  Former CP HQ. Meet your comrades. Readings, too.
- **Le Poisson Rouge** •
  158 Bleecker St [Sullivan St]
  212-505-3474
  Seductive and strangely fun eclectic live music.
- **Lobby Bar** • 335 Bowery [E 2nd St]
  212-505-9100
  Great spot for a night cap.
- **Loreley Beer Garden** • 7 Rivington St [Bowery]
  212-253-7077
  Tons of beer, individual pitchers optional.
- **Mad River Bar & Grill** •
  1442 3rd Ave [E 82nd St]
  212-988-1832
  Miss college? Start chugging cheap beer here.
- **Marshall Stack** • 66 Rivington St [Allen St]
  212-228-4667
  Winner for best bar that seemed like it would be awful.
- **Mayahuel** • 304 E 6th Ave [2nd Ave]
  212-253-5888
  Tequila and mezcal den with awesome old Mexico decor.

- **McSorley's Old Ale House** •
  15 E 7th St [3rd Ave]
  212-474-9148
  Lights or darks?
- **Milano's** • 51 E Houston St [Mott St]
  212-226-8844
  Grungy, narrow, awesome, narrow, grungy.
- **Mother Ruin** • 18 Spring St [Elizabeth St]
  212-219-0942
  Handcrafted cocktails and small plates.
- **Peasant** • 194 Elizabeth St [Spring St]
  212-965-9511
  For ambience, head down to the dark cave of wine.
- **Peculier Pub** • 145 Bleecker St [LaGuardia Pl]
  212-353-1327
  Large beer selection. NYU hangout.
- **Pegu Club** • 77 W Houston St [Wooster St]
  212-473-7348
  There's a reason the classic cocktails are famous.
- **Reservoir** • 70 University Pl [E 10th St]
  212-475-0770
  Surprisingly good food, lots of sports.
- **Rockwood Music Hall** •
  196 Allen St [E Houston St]
  212-477-4155
  Live music nightly.
- **Sake Bar Decibel** • 240 E 9th St [2nd Ave]
  212-979-2733
  Hip, underground sake bar.
- **Spring Lounge** • 48 Spring St [Mulberry St]
  212-965-1774
  Divey goodness since the 1920s.

- **Scratcher** • 209 E 5th St [Bowery]
212-477-0030
Low-key port for you and your Guinness.
- **Sly Fox** • 140 2nd Ave [St Marks Pl]
212 – 614-3283
Bring your own space heater.
- **Spring Street Lounge** •
48 Spring St [Mulberry St]
212-965-1774
All-ESPN-watchin' post-college moochers.
- **Standings** • 43 E 7th St [2nd Ave]
212-420-0671
Hardest working (and smallest) sports bar in
New York.
- **Sweet & Vicious** • 5 Spring St [Bowery]
212-334-7915
Great outdoor space.
- **Swift Hibernian Lounge** •
34 E 4th St [Bowery]
212-260-3600
Irish bar that tries more than most.
- **Terra Blues** • 149 Bleecker St [Thompson St]
212-777-7776
Live blues. If you're into that.
- **Tom & Jerry's** • 288 Elizabeth St [E Houston St]
212-260-5045
Low key and friendly place for a drink.
- **The Uncommons** •
230 Thompson St [W 3rd St]
646-543-9215
Board game cafe in former Village Chess spot.
- **V Bar** • 225 Sullivan St [W 3rd Ave]
212-253-5740
Sleepy coffeeshop by day, laidback bar by
night.
- **Von** • 3 Bleecker St [Bowery]
212-473-3039
Great vibe. Great bar.
- **Webster Hall** • 125 E 11th St [4th Ave]
212-353-1600
Feel the music through the floor.

🍴 Restaurants

- **12 Chairs** • 56 MacDougal St [King St]
212-254-8640 • $
Rough around the edges. Fantabulous blintzes
and pierogies.
- **ACME** • 9 Great Jones St [Lafayette St]
212-203-2121 • $$$$
Nordic hotspot for the chic and loaded.
- **Alidoro** • 105 Sullivan St [Prince St]
212-334-5179 • $$
High-end Italian sandwiches.
- **Alta** • 64 W 10th St [Ave of the Americas]
212-505-7777 • $$$
Unique tapas. Good date place.
- **Amelie Wine Bar** • 22 W 8th St [Macdougal St]
212-533-2962 • $$$
French wine bar with delish foie gras, escargot,
etc. Bon ap'!
- **Misirizzi** • 36 E 4th St [Bowery]
212-375-0100 • $$$$
Quaint, lovely Italian place with excellent
service.
- **Artichoke Basille's Pizza** •
328 E 14th St [2nd Ave]
212-228-2004 • $$
Stand in line for amazing Sicilian slices.
- **Artichoke Basille's Pizza** •
111 MacDougal St [Minetta Ln]
646-278-6100 • $$
Gut-busting artichoke slices.
- **Arturo's** • 106 W Houston St [Thompson St]
212-677-3820 • $$
Classic NYC pizza joint with live jazz. NFT
favorite.
- **Aurora Soho** • 510 Broome St [Watts St]
212-334-9020 • $$$
Hip Williamsburg Italian opens on the big
island.
- **Awash** • 338 E 6th St [2nd Ave]
212-982-9589 • $$
Ethiopian. It's ok to eat with your hands.
- **B Bar & Grill** • 40 E 4th St [Bowery]
212-475-2220 • $$
Bordering on cheesy.
- **B&H Dairy** • 127 2nd Ave [St Mark's Pl]
212-505-8065 • $
Eat mushroom barley soup and homemade
challah at the counter.

It's probably unfair for one neighborhood to claim all the glory, but this one's tops for restaurants too, from wallet-busting upscale (**Babbo** and **Strip House**), to awesome street carts (**NY Dosas** in Washington Square Park). We like **Frank** for Italian, **Zabb Elee** for Thai, **Num Pang** for sandwiches, and **Ssam Bar** for everything. Out late? **Veselka** and **Blue Ribbon** have your back.

- **Babbo** • 110 Waverly Pl [MacDougal St]
  212-777-0303 • $$$$
  Super Mario: Go for the pasta tasting menu.
- **Balthazar** • 80 Spring St [Crosby St]
  212-965-1414 • $$$$$
  Simultaneously pretentious and amazing.
- **Bar Primi** • 325 Bowery [E 2nd St]
  212-220-9100 • $$$$
  Pasta-forward Italian with daily specials.
- **Ben's Pizza** • 123 MacDougal St [W 3rd St]
  212-677-0976 • $
  Top NYC slices; unusual cheese taste.
- **Blue Hill** • 75 Washington Pl [MacDougal St]
  212-539-1776 • $$$$$
  Wonderful food in an unexpected location.
- **Blue Ribbon Brasserie** •
  97 Sullivan St [Spring St]
  212-274-0404 • $$$$$
  Open 'til 4am. Everything's great.
- **Blue Ribbon Sushi** • 119 Sullivan St [Prince St]
  212-786-0808 • $$$$$
  Great sushi.
- **Bohemian Restaurant** •
  57 Great Jones St [Broadway]
  $$$$$
  Haute Japanese referral-only speakeasy cuisine.
- **Bowery Meat Company** • 9 E 1st St [Bowery]
  212-460-5255 • $$$$
  Young creative steakhouse treatment, meat ecumenical.
- **Bruno** • 204 E 13th St [3rd Ave]
  212-598-3080 • $$$
  Inspired, schizoid-chic pizzeria.
- **By Chloe** • 185 Bleecker St [Macdougal St] • $$
  Sleek vegan fast casual from Food Network winner.
- **Café Gitane** • 242 Mott St [Prince St]
  212-334-9552 • $$
  Can be busy, but worth the wait. Delicious food, beautiful people.

- **Café Habana** • 17 Prince St [Elizabeth St]
  212-625-2001 • $$$
  Grilled corn + beautiful staff – amazing Cuban joint.
- **Café Bakko** • 81 St Marks Pl [1st Ave]
  212-982-9166 • $
  Kebabolicious.
- **Calexico Carne Asada** • Prince St & Wooster St
  $
  Taco truck run by hipsters. Tasty!
- **Carroll Place** • 157 Bleecker St [Thompson St]
  212-260-1700 • $$$
  Brunch. And wood-fired rosemary wings. And brunch. Again.
- **Cha-An Japanese Tea House** •
  230 E 9th St [Stuyvesant St]
  212-220-0030 • $$
  Japanese tea ceremonies Fridays and Sundays. Must reserve.
- **Chick-fil-A Express** •
  5 University Pl [Washington Sq N] • $
  Boneless chicken delights tucked away in NYU's Weinstein Hall.
- **ChikaLicious** • 203 E 10th St [2nd Ave]
  212-995-9511 • $$
  Dessert for dinner? We vote yes.
- **Claudette** • 24 5th Ave [9th St]
  212-868-2424 • $$$
  Seasonal Provençal comfort cuisine.
- **Cocoron 37** • 37 Kenmare St [Elizabeth St]
  212-900-0800 • $$$
  Soba for you, me, and the jerk talking on his cell phone.
- **Cones** • 272 Bleecker St [Morton St]
  212-414-1795 • $
  Putting butterfat to use in flavors you never imagined.

- **Cozy Soup 'n' Burger** •
  739 Broadway [Astor Pl]
  212-477-5566 • $
  Big cheap greasy burgers; i.e., Heaven.
- **Cuba** • 222 Thompson St [W 3rd St]
  212-420-7878 • $$
  Authentic Cuban, bar, live music, etc.
- **Dos Toros Taqueria** • 137 4th Ave [E 13th St]
  212-677-7300 • $
  Solid Mission-style burritos.
- **Downtown Bakery** • 69 1st Ave [E 4th St]
  212-254-1757 • $
  Authentic hole-in-the-wall Mexican. Awesome
  breakfast sandwiches.
- **Duane Park** • 308 Bowery [Hudson St]
  212-732-5555 • $$$$$
  Underrated New American.
- **El Idolo** • 244 E 14th St [8th Ave]
  $
  Almost East LA worthy tamales and cemitas.
- **Epistrophy** • 200 Mott St [Spring St]
  212-966-0904 • $$
  Genuine Italian coffee spot with light dishes
  and heavenly pasta.
- **Estela** • 47 E Houston St [Mulberry St]
  212-219-7693 • $$$
  Shareable diverting/diverse dishes and great
  wine program.
- **Famous Ben's Pizza** •
  177 Spring St [Thompson St]
  212-966-4494 • $
  Good slice pizza.
- **Frank** • 88 2nd Ave [E 5th St]
  212-420-0106 • $$
  Good food, great breakfast.
- **Freemans** • Freeman Alley [Rivington St]
  212-420-0012 • $$$
  Taxidermy-filled hideaway with fab cocktails
  and delicious, rustic fare.

- **Freud** • 506 Laguardia Pl [Bleecker St]
  212-777-0327 • $$$
  Upscale Austrian from Edi & the Wolf folks.
- **Goemon** • 29 Kenmare St [Elizabeth St]
  212-226-1262 • $$$
  Cocoron's inventive soup-curry hybrid sister
  restaurant.
- **Gotham Bar & Grill** • 12 E 12th St [5th Ave]
  212-620-4020 • $$$$$
  Excellent New American—one of the best.
- **Great Jones Café** • 54 Great Jones St [Bowery]
  212-674-9304 • $$$
  Classic soul food. Sort of.
- **Il Buco** • 47 Bond St [Bowery]
  212-533-1932 • $$$$$
  Lovely Italian food. Great wines by the glass.
  Uber-hip scene.
- **Il Mulino** • 86 W 3rd St [Thompson St]
  212-673-3783 • $$$$
  Fine Italian dining at fine Italian dining prices.
- **Indochine** • 430 Lafayette St [Astor Pl]
  212-505-5111 • $$$
  You can do better.
- **Jane** • 100 W Houston St [Thompson St]
  212-254-7000 • $$$
  Good all-around; perfect location for pre-post
  Angelica movie.
- **Japonica** • 90 University Pl [E 12th St]
  212-243-7752 • $$$
  Madonna went here once.
- **John's of 12th Street** • 302 E 12th St [2nd Ave]
  212-475-9531 • $$
  Classic Italian. Get the rollatini.
- **Jules Bistro** • 65 St Marks Pl [1st Ave]
  212-477-5560 • $$$
  Small French bistro with live unimposing jazz.

There is no shortage of top-notch pizza around these parts. **Lombardi's** was the first pizzeria in the US, and still puts its coal oven to good use. For an upscale pie, try the exquisite creations at Mario Batali's **Otto**. For great pizza along with live jazz, check out **Arturo's** on Houston Street. And you can get great slices at **Artichoke Basille's Pizza**.

- **Kenka** • 25 St Marks Pl [2nd Ave]
  212-254-6363 • $
  Step into rural Japan for a dirt cheap feast of traditional grub. Don't expect sushi.
- **Khyber Pass** • 34 St Marks Pl [Second Ave]
  212-473-0989 • $
  Good Afghani.
- **Korilla BBQ** • 23 3rd Ave [St Marks Pl]
  646-823-9423 • $
  Addictive Korean BBQ burritos, tacos at their food truck.
- **La Esquina** • 114 Kenmare St [Cleveland Pl]
  646-613-7100 • $
  Taqueria trifecta: taco stand, corner cantina, and secret subterranean abode.
- **Lahore Deli** • 132 Crosby St [E Houston St]
  212-965-1777 • $
  Indo-Pak deli popular with cabbies.
- **Le Turtle** • 177 Chrystie St [Rivington St]
  646-918-7189 • $$$
  Stylish, vegetable-forward French cuisine.
- **Little Poland** • 200 2nd Ave [E 12th St]
  212-777-9728 • $$
  Best breakfast special in the city.
- **Lombardi's** • 32 Spring St [Mott St]
  212-941-7994 • $$$
  Said to be the first pizzeria in the US, circa 1905.
- **Love Mamak** • 174 2nd Ave [11th St]
  212-254 5370 • $$$
  Viet-Thai-Malay mashup goodness.
- **Lucien** • 14 E 1st Ave
  212-260-6481 • $$$
  Solid brasserie, small and cozy.
- **Maman** • 211 West Broadway [Franklin St]
  646-882-8682 • $$$
  High-end all-day café channeling the South of France.
- **Manousheh** • 193 Bleecker St [Macdougal St]
  347-991-5778 • $
  Lebanese-style flatbreads for the win.
- **Max Brenner Chocolate by the Bald Man** •
  841 Broadway [E 13th St]
  212-380-0030 • $$
  For tourists who like chocolate for dinner.

- **Mercer Kitchen** • 99 Prince St [Mercer St]
  212-966-5454 • $$$$
  Psuedo-famous New American with a French accent.
- **Mighty Quinn's** • 103 2nd Ave [E 7th St]
  212 677-3733 • $$
  Wood smoked meats with a Texas and Carolina twang.
- **Mile End Deli** • 53 Bond St [Bowery]
  212-529-2990 • $$
  Upscale Jewish deli with Canadian inspiration.
- **Miss Lily's** • 132 W Houston St [Sullivan St]
  646 588-5375 • $$$
  Jamaican plates with a dub beat from a resident DJ.
- **Momofuku Ko** • 8 Extra Pl [E 1st St]
  $$$
  Spectacular tasting menu. Online reservations only.
- **Momofuku Noodle Bar** •
  171 1st Ave [E 10th St]
  212-777-7773 • $$$$
  Because who can get into M. Ko?
- **Momofuku Ssam Bar** •
  207 2nd Ave [E 13th St]
  212-254-2296 • $$
  Pork. Pork. Other stuff. Pork. Yum.
- **Motorino** • 349 E 12th St [1st Ave]
  212-777-2644 • $
  Excellent pies via Napoli via Brooklyn.
- **Nix** • 72 University Pl [11th St]
  212 498 0203 • $$$$
  Four-star vegetarian/vegan cuisine.
- **Nomad** • 78 2nd Ave [E 4th St]
  212-253-5410 • $$
  Funky North African food and funkier atmosphere.
- **Num Pang** • 28 E 12th St [University Pl]
  212-255-3271 • $
  Tasty Cambodian sandwiches.
- **NY Dosas** • Washington Sq S at Thompson St
  $
  Cheap and yummy Indian lunch cart.
- **Olive's** • 191 Prince St [Wooster St]
  212-941-0111 • $
  Killer soups/sandwiches. A top take-out option.

- **Otafuku** • 220 E 9th St [Stuyvesant St]
646-998-3438 • $$
Blink-and-you'll-miss-it counter has the best
Japanese street food.
- **Otto** • 1 5th Ave [Washington Mews]
212-995-9559 • $$$$
Batali's lardo, and everyone's beautiful.
- **Parm** • 248 Mulberry St [Prince St]
212-993-7189 • $$
Chicken, eggplant, and meatball hero heaven
is only an hour wait away.
- **Paul's Da Burger Joint** •
131 2nd Ave [St Marks Pl]
212-529-3097 • $
Burger heaven.
- **Pasquale Jones** • 187 Mulberry St • $$$
Pizza-pasta-farm-to-table haute comfort
cuisine.
- **Peep** • 177 Prince St [Sullivan St]
212-254-7337 • $$
Stylin' Thai. See-through bathroom mirrors.
- **Pepe Rosso** • 149 Sullivan St [W Houston St]
212-677-4555 • $
Italy on a budget. Fast.
- **Prune** • 54 E 1st St [1st Ave]
212-677-6221 • $$$
Get there early for brunch if you don't want to
wait. Like, 8 am.
- **Rai Rai Ken** • 218 E 10th St [2nd Ave]
212-477-7030 • $
Tiny and tasty ramen shop.
- **Raoul's** • 180 Prince St [Sullivan St]
212-966-3518 • $$$$
A Soho institution. You may like the steak frites
more than your date.
- **Red Bamboo Soul Café** •
140 W 4th St [Ave of the Americas]
212-260-1212 • $$
Vegetarian soul food. Killer lunch special.
- **Rice to Riches** • 37 Spring St [Mott St]
212-274-0008 • $
24 kinds of rice pudding in a bright fishbowl.

- **Rosario's Pizza** • 173 Orchard St [Stanton St]
212-777-9813 • $
Top drunken slice in the LES.
- **Ruby's** • 219 Mulberry St [Spring St]
212-925-5755 • $$
Down under delights for the downtown scene.
- **S'mac** • 345 E 12th St [1st Ave]
212-358-7912 • $$
Classic comfort cuisine achieves more cheesy
goodness.
- **Sacred Chow** • 227 Sullivan St [W 3rd St]
212-337-0863 • $$
Heavenly vegan tapas. The brownie is a
wheat-free revelation.
- **Sadelle's** • 463 West Broadway [Houston St]
212-254-3000 • $$$
Jewish deli by day/fancy candlelit Eastern
European by night.
- **Saigon Shack** •
114 MacDougal St [Bleecker St]
212-228-0588 • $$
Modern Vietnamese on a NYU-friendly budget.
- **Sammy's Roumanian** •
157 Chrystie St [Delancey St]
212-673-0330 • $$$
An experience not to be missed. Chopped liver
which will instantly kill you.
- **Saxon + Parole** • 316 Bowery [Bleecker St]
212-254-0350 • $$$
Nice choice for a night out along the New
Bowery.
- **Senza Gluten** • 206 Sullivan St [Bleecker St]
212-475-7775 • $$$
Elegantly crafted gluten-free Italian (!).
- **Shuko** • 47 E 12th St [Broadway]
212-228-6088 • $$$$$
Stylish, scrumptious, 'spensive sushi tasting
menus.
- **The Smile** • 26 Bond St [Lafayette St]
646-329-5836 • $$$
Mediterranean-inflected bistro fare; breakfast
& lunch, too.

This 'hood is definitely over-represented when it comes to general buzz. **Biang!** is a *muy autentico* Flushing export serving up Chinese dishes from unfamiliar regions. **Sadelle's** is an all-day joint elevating traditional deli food higher than an 80-pound bat mitzvah. And if you're burned out on the umpteenth iteration of pad thai, try the inventive menu at **Uncle Boons**.

- **Soba-ya** • 229 E 9th St [3rd Ave]
212-533-6966 • $$$
Japanese noodle perfection to the highest level.
- **Spice Thai** • 39 E 13th St [University Pl]
212-982-3758 • $$
Trendy Thai. Always packed.
- **Strip House** • 13 E 12th St [5th Ave]
212-328-0000 • $$$$$
Super downtown steakhouse. NFT favorite.
- **Taj Restaurant** • 310 E 6th St [2nd Ave]
212-505-8056 • $$
Rich sauces, fresh naan, live music half underground.
- **Tomoe Sushi** •
172 Thompson St [W Houston St]
212-777-9346 • $$$$
Good sushi, long line.
- **Tuck Shop** • 68 E 1st St [1st Ave]
212-979-5200 • $
Savory Australian pies, vegemite, and lamingtons.
- **Ukrainian East Village Restaurant** •
140 2nd Ave [E 9th St]
212-614-3283 • $
Pierogies, borscht, blintzes, goulash. Comfort food.
- **Uncle Boons** • 7 Spring St [Bowery]
646 370 6650 • $$$
Best Thai on the block...of any block in Manhattan. Killer crab-fried rice.
- **Upstate Craft Beer & Oyster Bar** • 95 1st Ave [6th St]
212-460-5293 • $$$
Curated fresh seafood, craft beer, and oysters.
- **Vanessa's Dumplings** •
220 E 14th St [3rd Ave]
212-529-1329 • $
Sesame pancake sandwiches are to die for.
- **Veselka** • 144 2nd Ave [E 9th St]
212-228-9682 • $
Pierogies absorb beer. At 4 am that's all you need to know.

- **Vic's** • 31 Great Jones St [Lafayette St]
212-253-5700 • $$$$
Italo-New American comfort food.
- **Yakitori Taisho** • 5 St Marks Pl [3rd Ave]
212-228-5086 • $
Skewered chicken and pan-fried noodles washed down with Asahi.

○ Shopping

- **Alabaster Bookshop** • 122 4th Ave [E 12th St]
212-982-3550
Quintessential overstuffed used book shop.
- **Apple Store (SoHo)** •
103 Prince St [Greene St]
212-226-3126
Don't come looking for produce.
- **Astor Wines & Spirits** •
399 Lafayette St [E 4th St]
212-674-7500
NFT fav. The king of all NYC liquor stores.
- **Balenciaga** • 148 Mercer St [Prince St]
212-206-0872
Gorgeous, super high-end clothes and accessories.
- **Bfold** • 224 E 13th St [3rd Ave]
212-529-7247
Folding bikes.
- **Bicycle Habitat** • 244 Lafayette St [Spring St]
212-431-3315
Full-time mechanics and sales, too.
- **Black Seed** • 170 Elizabeth St [Spring St]
212-730-1950
For your Montreal bagel fix; let the debate begin.
- **Blick Art Materials** • 1 Bond St [Lafayette St]
212-533-2444
Huge, super organized, recommended.

Map 6

Washington Sq / NYU / NoHo / SoHo

- **Bonnie Slotnick Cookbooks** •
28 E 2nd St [2nd Ave]
212-989-8962
Specializing in cookbooks; great out-of-print finds.
- **Chess Forum** • 219 Thompson St [W 3rd St]
212-475-2369
Ornate, themed, and traditional chess sets, play 'til midnight.
- **Dashwood Books** • 33 Bond St [Lafayette Ave]
212-387-8520
Photography.
- **Dominique Ansel Bakery** •
189 Spring St [Sullivan St]
212-219-2773
Home of the Cronut.
- **Dual Specialty Store** • 91 1st Ave [E 6th St]
212-979-6045
Indian grocery store stocked with every spice imaginable.
- **Forbidden Planet** • 832 Broadway [E 13th St]
212-473-1576
Let your inner sci-fi/fantasy nerd run wild.
- **The Frye Company** • 113 Spring St [Mercer St]
212-226-3793
Flagship store for the revered boot brand.
- **Gem Spa** • 131 2nd Ave [St Marks Pl]
212-995-1866
Magazine stand that serves fantastic egg creams.
- **Global Table** • 107 Sullivan St [Spring St]
212-431-5839
Quietly elegant tableware.
- **H&M** • 515 Broadway [Spring St]
855-466-7467
Cheap, hip clothes raining from the ceiling.

- **Honest Chops** • 319 E 9th St [2nd Ave]
212-388-0762
Upscale halal whole animal butchery
- **John Derian** • 6 E 2nd St [Bowery]
212-677-3917
Whimsical découpage plates and curios for the home.
- **Kiehl's** • 109 3rd Ave [E 13th St]
212-677-3171
Great creams, lotions, and unguents; laughably good service.
- **Laduree Soho** • 398 West Broadway [Spring St] 646-392-7868
International macaron experts.
- **Lighting by Gregory** •
158 Bowery [Delancey St]
212-226-1276
Bowery lighting mecca. Good ceiling fans.
- **Lighting Studio II** • 150 Bowery [Broome St]
212-219-3361
Dazzling explosion of chandeliers; a walk-through is a must.
- **Marc Jacobs** • 113 Prince St
212-343-1490
Salivate over clothing you can't afford.
- **The Market NYC** • 159 Bleecker St [Sullivan St]
Hip, unique designs by local designers. Open Saturdays & Sundays.
- **McNally Jackson** • 52 Prince St [Mulberry St]
212-274-1160
General Interest books.
- **Milk & Hops** • 779 Broadway [9th St]
212-995-5588
Great craft beer selection and artisanal cheeses.
- **MoMA Design Store** • 81 Spring St [Crosby St]
646-613-1367
Cutting-edge, minimalist, ergonomic, offbeat, and funky everything.

Map 6

Outside SoHo's glorified mall, the city's most eclectic shopping waits. Sample lotions at **Kiehl's**, and browse for housewares at **John Derian**, designer shoes at **Coclico**, trendy threads at **Odin**, books at **The Strand**, music at **Other Music**, old prints at **Pageant Print Shop**, and cool gifts at **MoMA Design Store**. The selections at **Astor Wines & Spirits** and **New Beer Distributors** remind us why we live here.

- **NYC Velo** • 64 2nd Ave [E 4th St]
  212-253-7771
  This shop has a special place in our heart. Good clothing!
- **Pageant Print Shop** • 69 E 4th St [2nd Ave]
  212-674-5296
  Just prints, really. But really great prints.
- **Pino's Prime Meats** •
  149 Sullivan St [Prince St]
  212-475-8134
  Old-world Italian butcher. Pino's tips are priceless.
- **Prada** • 575 Broadway [Prince St]
  212-334-8888
  Rem Koolhaas-designed store that you can only afford to look at.
- **Raffetto's** • 144 W Houston St [MacDougal St]
  212-777-1261
  Take-home Italian foods. Ravioli like mamma used to make.
- **REI** • 295 Lafayette St [E Houston St]
  212-680-1938
  Outdoor gear superstore in the Puck Building.
- **Stereo Exchange** •
  627 Broadway [Bleecker St]
  212-505-1111
  Just-under-obscenely-priced audiophile equipment. Good for male depression.
- **Strand Book Store** • 828 Broadway [E 12th St]
  212-473-1452
  Used mecca; world's messiest and best bookstore.
- **Sullivan Street Tea & Spice Company** •
  208 Sullivan St [Bleecker St]
  212-387-8702
  Worldly herbs, spices, salts, and teas.
- **Sunrise Sunrise Mart** • 494 Broome St [W Broadway]
  212-219-0033
  Japanese specialties and an affordable lunch counter in back.

- **T2 Tea** • 67 Prince St [Crosby St]
  212-219-1956
  Super colorful Aussie tea shop with pots and accessories.
- **Taschen** • 107 Greene St [Prince St]
  212-226-2212
  God (and the Devil's) gift to publishing.
- **Tokio 7** • 83 E 7th St [1st Ave]
  212-353-8443
  Designer consignment. Great for lucky finds.
- **Trader Joe's** • 142 E 14th St [Irving Pl]
  212-529-4612
  Legendary bargain food chain with legendary long lines.
- **Trash & Vaudeville** • 4 St Marks Pl [3rd Ave]
  212-982-3590
  Decades-old NYC HQ for punk and goth gear.
- **Uniqlo** • 546 Broadway [Spring St]
  917-237-8811
  Cashmere, cashmere, and more cashmere—in every color!
- **Warby Parker** •
  161 Ave of the Americas [Spring St]
  646-517-5223
  Where everyone shops for their $95 retro eyeglasses.
- **Whole Foods** • 4 Union Sq E [University Pl]
  212-673-5388
  Always natural. Always crowded. Tons of NYU kids.
- **Whole Foods** • 95 E Houston St [2nd Ave]
  212-420-1320
  Beautiful produce for beautiful people. Surprisingly uncrowded.

It's no longer the city's Bohemia—we hear that's somewhere in Philly. But if you're dead-set on staying in Manhattan, the East Village is downtown's most livable neighborhood. Blame that on all the well-worn tenements and their (relatively) affordable small studios and "junior" one-bedrooms, some of them rent stabilized. In these apartments dwell old timers, NYU kids, and everyone in between, making for awesome people watching, day or night. A stroll through **Tompkins Square Park** on any warm weekend pretty much sums it up. Cute pooches and their oh so hip owners convene at the dog run while bongo drums echo over near Avenue B. Little kids shriek at the playground while crusty punks and gritty old men occupy the benches on the Southwestern side. Just a typical slice of life in the East Village, and a sweet life it is if you can swing the rent.

Before the crowds young professionals lived here, and before the artists, musicians, and squatters that preceded them, this area was home to waves of German, Irish, Italian, Jewish, Ukrainian, and Polish immigrants. A few historical sites remain from those times. One of our favorites is **Saint Brigid's Church** (1848), which was built by Irish immigrants. The church was saved by the developer's cudgel in just the nick of time, and restored thanks to a generous anonymous donor, the whole episode a miracle befitting the Roman Catholic church's namesake. Another holdout, **Russian and Turkish Baths** (1892) still offers old-world plaza treatments. One more significant marker from the neighborhood's past is the **General Slocum Monument**, which commemorates the tragic sinking of the General Slocum steamship in the East River in 1904. The deadliest single disaster in the city's history until 9/11, over 1,000 lives were lost, mainly German women and children from a neighborhood church that chartered the boat for a day trip to Long Island.

In the 1960s, Puerto Rican immigrants flooded into Alphabet City, another name for the blocks between Avenue A and Avenue D. Avenue C, also known as Loisaida Avenue, retains some of this character today, even while bars and restaurants catering to more recent arrivals open shop. The loveliest aspects of this area are the many community gardens, planted on once-blighted lots and maintained by volunteers. We particularly like the always-tranquil **6BC Botanical Garden** on 6th Street between Avenue B and Avenue C. The best times to visit are Saturday and Sunday afternoons from May through October.

The term "East Village" came into use in the 1960s, when artists, musicians, writers, performers, intellectuals, and political radicals flocked to the neighborhood. A hugely influential art scene sprang up from the 1960s through the 1980s, but unfortunately, many of those galleries and performance spaces fell victim to skyrocketing rents in the 1990s and early 2000s. A few institutions have survived, though—you can still catch a poetry slam at the **Nuyorican Poet's Café**, or dance the night away like it's still 1984 at **The Pyramid Club**. One of our favorite summer events, the Charlie Parker Jazz Festival, takes place in **Tompkins Square Park**, right across the street from the **Charlie Parker House**. When you visit the park be sure to pass by the **Joe Strummer Mural**, a neighborhood landmark honoring one of the icons of punk rock. For live rock n' roll (or any kind of music scene), you're better off heading to the Lower East Side. But if you've come for the awesome bars, restaurants, and shopping that make this the neighborhood you'll never want to leave, read on.

O Landmarks

- **6BC Botanical Garden** •
624 E 6th St [Avenue C]
Early Alphabet City community garden, now permanent park.
- **Charlie Parker Residence** •
151 Avenue B [E 10th St]
The Bird lived here. Great festival every summer in Tompkins Square.
- **General Slocum Monument** •
Tompkins Sq Park [Avenue A]
Memorial to one of the worst disasters in NYC history.
- **International Bar** • 120 1st Ave [E 7th St]
212-777-1643
RIP…but wait! It's back from the dead!
- **Joe Strummer Mural** •
112 Avenue A [E 7th St]
Ha, you think it's funny…turning rebellion into money?
- **Nuyorican Poets Café** •
236 E 3rd St [Avenue C]
212-780-9386
Where mediocre poets die of humiliation.
- **The Pyramid Club** • 101 Avenue A [E 7th St]
212-228-4888
Classic '80s and '90s club.
- **Russian and Turkish Baths** •
268 E 10th St [1st Ave]
212-674-9250
Sweat away all your urban stress.
- **St. Brigid Roman Catholic Church** •
119 Avenue B [E 8th St]
Historic Irish church spared demolition, still standing on Tompkins Square.
- **Tompkins Square Park** • E 9th St & Ave A
212-387-7685
Home to many.

Coffee

- **Abraco** • 86 E 7th St [1st Ave]
212-388-9731
Sip an amazing espresso by the window.
- **Ciao for Now** • 523 E 12th St [Avenue A]
212-677-2616
Neighborhood fave for coffee and pastries.
- **Ninth Street Espresso** •
700 E 9th St [Avenue C]
212-358-9225
Absolutely fantastic coffee drinks. Cool Portland vibe.

Farmers Markets

- **Lower East Side Girls Club Farmers Market** •
Avenue C & E 9th St
212-982-1633
Wed 12 pm–7 pm, Jul 9–Oct 8
- **Tompkins Square Greenmarket** •
Ave A & E 7th St
Sun 8 am–6 pm, year round

Map 7

Dive bars are an East Village specialty, and some of the finest specimens in the city are right here: try **Manitoba's**, **Lucy's**, **7B**, **International Bar**, and **Coal Yard**. This hood rules for cocktails too: check out **Summit Bar**, **Elsa**, or **Louis 649** if you can't bear the wait at **Death and Company**. **Drop Off Service** has our favorite happy hour this side of the East River. Cheers!

🍸 Nightlife

- **11th Street Bar** • 510 E 11th St [Avenue A]
212-982-3929
Darts, Irish, excellent.
- **2A** • 25 Avenue A [E 2nd St]
212-505-2466
Great upstairs space.
- **7B (Horseshoe Bar)** • 108 Avenue B [E 7th St]
212-677-6742
Godfather II shot here. What can be bad?
- **Ace Bar** • 531 E 5th St [Ave A]
212-979-8476
Darts, pinball, pool, and even skee ball!
- **Alphabet Citiy Beer Co.** • 96 Ave C [6th St]
646-422-7103
Tons of rotating craft beers on tap; great to-go offerings.
- **Amor y Amargo** • 443 E 6th St [Ave A]
212-614-6818
Cruel bitters bar.
- **B Side** • 204 Ave B [13th St]
212-475-4600
Jukebox, games, and shot-and-a-beer specials.
- **Blind Barber** • 339 E 10th St [Ave B]
212-228-2123
Consider how many licenses they need; the mind simply reels.
- **Bua** • 122 St Marks Pl [1st Ave]
212-979-6276
Neighborhood bar during the week, mobs of pretty people on the weekend.
- **Cherry Tavern** • 441 E 6th St [1st Ave]
212-777-1448
Get the Tijuana Special.
- **Coal Yard** • 102 1st Ave [E 6th St]
212-677-4595
Awesome dive bar that draws a fascinating cross section of locals.
- **d.b.a.** • 41 1st Ave [E 2nd St]
212-475-5097
Awesome beer list and outdoor patio. NFT fave.
- **Death and Company** •
433 E 6th St [Avenue A]
212-388-0882
Classy cocktails served Prohibition style. No password required.

- **Doc Holliday's** • 141 Ave A [9th St]
212-979-0312
Longtime dive in it through thick and thin; respect.
- **Drop Off Service** • 211 Avenue A [E 13th St]
212-260-2914
Awesome half-off everything happy hour 'til 8 pm.
- **Fat Buddha** • 212 Ave A [13th St]
212-598-0500
Asian-fusion cocktails and food.
- **Good Beer** • 422 E 9th St [1st Ave]
212-677-4836
Ridiculous microbrew selection. Is this heaven?
- **Josie's Bar** • 520 E 6th St [Ave A]
212-228-9532
Pleasantly woody tavern trending toward dive (not a bad thing).
- **Karma Lounge** • 51 1st Ave [E 3rd St]
212-677-3160
Hookah lounge, party like it's 2002; make Bloomberg weep.
- **Lois** • 98 Ave C [7th St] 212-475-1400
Sleek, charming bar featuring wine on tap (and good food).
- **Lucy's** • 135 Avenue A [St Marks Pl]
212-673-3824
Classic dive. Say hi to Lucy.
- **Maiden Lane** • 162 Avenue B [E 10th St]
646-755-8911
Cozy high top tables and muscular cocktails.
- **Mama's Bar** • 34 Avenue B [E 3rd St]
212-777-5729
Laid-back respite from the Avenue B craziness, with food from Mama's next door.
- **Manitoba's** • 99 Avenue B [E 6th St]
212-982-2511
Punk scene.
- **Mona's** • 224 Avenue B [E 13th St]
212-353-3780
Depressing. Recommended.

Map 7

8 9 10

5 6 7

2 3 4

1

East Village

- **Niagra** • 112 Avenue A [E 7th St]
212-420-9517
Neighborhood rocker watering hole.
- **Nublu** • 62 Ave C [E 5th St]
646-546-5206
Sexy lounge with world music, nice ambience, and outdoor porch.
- **Nuyorican Poets Café** •
236 E 3rd St [Avenue C]
212-780-9386
Where mediocre poets die of humiliation.
- **Otto's Shrunken Head** •
538 E 14th St [Avenue A]
212-228-2240
Not your grandma's tiki bar.
- **PDT** • 113 St Marks Pl [Avenue A]
212-614-0386
Enter through a phone booth in a hot dog joint. No joke.
- **The Phoenix** • 447 E 13th St [1st Ave]
212-477-9979
Gay dive bar with great jukebox.
- **Planet Rose** • 219 Avenue A [E 13th St]
212-353-9500
Karaokeeeeeee.
- **Pouring Ribbons** • 225 Avenue B [E 14th St]
917-656-6788
Creative, challenging cocktails.
- **Proletariat** • 102 St Marks Pl [1st Ave]
Beer library/deep dive into the brewing arts.
- **The Pyramid Club** • 101 Avenue A [E 7th St]
212-228-4888
Classic '80s and '90s club.
- **Sidewalk** • 94 Avenue A [E 6th Ave]
212-473-7373
Classic open mic.
- **Sophie's** • 507 E 5th St [Avenue A]
212-228-5680
More crowded counterpart to Joe's.
- **St Dymphnas** • 118 St Marks Pl [1st Ave]
212-254-6636
Homey Irish drinks and food.

- **The Summit Bar** • 133 Avenue C [E 8th St]
347-465-7911
Clean classic cocktails.
- **Ten Degrees Bar** • 121 St Marks Pl [1st Ave]
212-358-8600
Cozy wine bar with live jazz on Wednesdays.
- **The Wayland** • 709 E 9th St [Ave C]
212-777-7022
Tiny bar, small snacks, lovely cocktails.
- **WCOU Radio (Tile Bar)** • 115 1st Ave [E 7th St]
212-254-6171
East Village survivor. Low key and great.
- **Zum Schneider** • 107 Avenue C [E 7th St]
212-598-1098
Get weisse, man. Prost.

Restaurants

- **Arepa Factory** • 147 Ave A [9th St]
646-490-6828 • $$
Assembly-line arepa joint w/ vegan and veg options galore.
- **Babu Ji** • 22 E 13th St [E 11th St]
212-951-1082 • $$$
Stylish, young. creative Indian via Australia.
22 E 13th St
- **Big Arc Chicken** • 233 1st Ave [E 14th St]
212-477-0091 • $
Cheap Middle Eastern food complete with Arabic TV.
- **Big Gay Ice Cream Shop** •
125 E 7th St [Avenue A]
212-533-9333 • $
Imaginative swirled soft serve treats. Try a salty pimp.
- **Black Iron Burger** • 540 E 5th St [Ave B]
646-439-0276 • $
Burgers with horseradish cheese and awesome onion rings.

Residents here are spoiled rotten when it comes to food. Just head to 7th Street between First and A: sandwiches at **Porchetta**, lobster rolls at **Luke's Lobster**, arepas at **Caracas Arepa Bar**, and delicious Greek fare at **Pylos**. **7A**'s always open, **Banjara** holds it down in Little India, and if you still have room, check out **Puddin'** for—take a wild guess.

- **Bobwhite Counter** • 94 Ave C [6th St]
  212-228-2972 • $$$
  Three words: Fried Chicken Supper.
- **The Brindle Room** • 277 E 10th St [Ave A]
  212-529-9702 • $$$
  Gastropublicly comfortable cuisine with sought-after burgers.
- **Buenos Aires** • 513 E 6th St [Ave A]
  212-228-2775 • $
  Superior Argentine food: steaks, wine, friendly atmosphere.
- **Café Mogador** • 101 St Marks Pl [1st Ave]
  212-677-2226 • $$
  Perfect place for hummus and a latte.
- **Caravan of Dreams** • 405 E 6th St [1st Ave]
  212-254-1613 • $
  Organic vegan cuisine.
- **Crif Dogs** • 113 St Marks Pl [Ave A]
  212-614-2728 • $
  Kick-ass wieners.
- **Desnuda** • 122 E 7th St [Ave A]
  212-254-3515 • $$
  For wine and ceviche lovers only.
- **Donostia** • 155 Ave B [10th St]
  646-256-9773 • $$$
  Tapas, pinchos, conservas—hang a while like they do in Spain.
- **Dumpling Man** • 100 St Marks Pl [1st Ave]
  212-505-2121 • $
  Constantly rotating dumpling roster; good but not great.
- **Edi & the Wolf** • 102 Ave C [E 7th St]
  212-598-1040 • $$$
  Fantastic Austrian food, excellent variety, rustic atmosphere.
- **Esperanto** • 145 Ave C [E 9th St]
  212-505-6559 • $$
  Bistro has live Brazilian music, choice summer spot.
- **Fat Buddha** • 212 Ave A [13th St]
  212-598-0500 • $$$
  Go for Korean-fusion early, stay to party (or not).
- **Flinders Lane** • 162 Ave A [10th St]
  212-228-6900 • $$$$
  Eclectic Australian just north of Tompkins Square Park.
- **Gruppo** • 98 Ave B [E 11th St]
  212-995-2100 • $$
  Pizza and pasta in a casual setting.

- **Hearth** • 403 E 12th St [1st Ave]
  646-602-1300 • $$$
  Rich, feast-like farm-to-table Italian.
- **Il Posto Accanto** • 190 E 2nd St [Ave B]
  212-228-3562 • $$$
  Tiny, rustic Italian enoteca.
- **Jeepney** • 201 1st Ave [E 12th St]
  212-533-4121 • $$
  Shabby chic Filipino gastropub.
- **Kafana** • 116 Ave C [7th St]
  212-353-8000 • $$$
  Serbian sausages and spirits for sunny Sundays.
- **Kingsley** • 190 Ave B [12th St]
  212-674-4500 • $$$
  Inventive, upscale, farm-fresh New American.
- **Lavagna** • 545 E 5th St [Ave A]
  212-979-1005 • $$$
  We hear it's great....
- **Lil' Frankie's Pizza** • 19 1st Ave [E 1st St]
  212-420-4900 • $$
  Cheap, good pizzas and Italian.
- **Luke's Lobster** • 93 E 7th St [1st Ave]
  212-387-8487 • $$
  Fresh-from-the-sea lobster rolls, without sticker shock.
- **Luzzo's** • 211 1st Ave [E 13th St]
  212-473-7447 • $$
  Real coal oven. Top ten worthy.
- **Mala Project** • 122 1st Ave [7th St]
  212-353-8880 • $$
  Dry pot Sichuan spiciness, handsome, authentic, and welcoming.
- **Marcha Cocina** • 111 Ave C [7th St]
  646-781-9147 • $$$
  Tasty tapas, brunch, and, of course, sangria via Washington Heights.
- **Milon** • 93 1st Ave [E 6th St]
  212-228-4896 • $
  Cheap Indian. Unbelievable decor.
- **Mother of Pearl** • 95 Ave A [6th St]
  212-614-6818 • $$$
  Post-modern Polynesian; bright, airy, with cocktails.

Map 7

8 9 10
5 6 7
2 3 4
1

East Village

- **Noreetuh** • 128 1st Ave [St Marks Pl]
646-892-3050 • $$$
Modern Hawaiian cuisine.
- **Odessa** • 119 Ave A [St Marks Pl]
212-253-1470 • $
Diner. Awesome deep-fried meat pierogies.
- **Panna II Indian Restaurant** •
93 1st Ave [E 6th St]
212-598-4610 • $
Another psycho-decor Indian. Whatever.
- **Pardon My French** • 103 Ave B [E 7th St]
212-358-9683 • $$
Great French spread. Nice music a plus.
- **Poco** • 33 Ave B [E 3rd St]
212-228-4461 • $$$
Warning: Home of the all-u-can drink $20 brunch.
- **Punjabi Grocery & Deli** • 114 E 1st Ave [1st Ave]
212-533-3356 • $
Deli, grocery, and cabbie-worthy Indian eats.•
- **Pylos** • 128 E 7th St [Ave A]
212-473-0220 • $$
Delicious Greek, cool hanging-pot ceiling.
- **Ray's Candy Store** • 113 Avenue A [E 7th St]
212-505-7609 • $
Avenue A's Belgian fries-and-ice cream institution.
- **Root & Bone** • 200 E 3rd St [Ave B]
646-682-7080 • $$$
Southern all the way, just like Mamma Rooney used to make it.
- **Royale** • 157 Loisaida Ave [E 10th St]
646-394-9224 • $$
Perfect burgers with stellar fixin's, and a deal to boot.
- **Sidewalk** • 94 Avenue A [E 6th St]
212-473-7373 • $$
Do not eat here.
- **Sigiri** • 91 1st Ave [E 6th St]
212-614-9333 • $$
Excellent BYOB Sri Lankan above a great beer shop.
- **St Dymphna's** • 118 St Marks Pl [1st Ave]
212-254-6636 • $
A great Irish pub doesn't need shamrocks.

- **Superiority Burger** • 430 E 9th St [Ave A]
212-256-1192 • $
Vegetarian burger/fast food joint.
- **Supper** • 156 E 2nd St [Ave A]
212-477-7600 • $$$
Spaghetti con limone is yummy. Great brunch. Otherworldly atmosphere.
- **Takahachi** • 85 Ave A [E 6th St]
212-505-6524 • $$$
Super-good Japanese and sushi. A mainstay.
- **Timna** • 109 St Marks Pl [Ave A]
646-964-5181 • $$$
Modern Israeli cuisine; eye-opening Mediterranean.
- **Tree** • 190 1st Ave [E 11th St]
212-358-7171 • $$$
Cozy vibe with good French food and prixe fixe.
- **Tuome** • 536 E 5th St [Ave B]
646-833-7811 • $$$$
Farm-to-table New American; we recommend the "Pig Out" for two.
- **Virginia's** • 647 E 11th St [Ave C]
212-658-0182 • $$$$
Eclectic options and good burgers at the bar.
- **Westville East** • 173 Ave A [E 11th St]
212-677-2933 • $$
Trendy organic belly timber served with a fresh market flair.
- **Xe May** • 96 St Marks Pl [1st Ave]
212-388-1688 • $
Killer bánh mì served with a smile.
- **Yuca Bar** • 111 Ave A [E 7th St]
212-982-9533 • $$$
Amazing Latin-style brunch, less amazing Latin-style dinner.
- **Zum Schneider** • 107 Avenue C [E 7th St]
212-598-1098 • $$
Finally some downtown wurst.

We can't decide if we like **Abraço** or **Ninth Street Espresso** better—we'll take both! Browse vintage oddities at **Obscura Antiques**, used tomes at **Mast Books**, and jewelry at **The Shape of Lies**. Cute boutiques? 9th Street between First and Second. Late-night bodega taco fix? **Zaragoza**.

Shopping

- **11th Street Flea Market** • 1st Ave & E 11th St
  Stuff you didn't even know you needed!
- **Alphabets** • 64 Avenue A [E 5th St]
  212-475-7250
  Fun miscellany store.
- **Big Gay Ice Cream Shop** •
  125 E 7th St [Avenue A]
  212-533-9333
  Imaginative swirled soft serve treats. Try a salty pimp.
- **Black Seed** • 176 1st Ave [11th St]
  646-484-5718
  For your Montreal bagel fix; let the debate begin.
- **Butter Lane** • 123 E 7th St [Avenue A]
  212-677-2880
  Riding the cupcake trend…
- **East Village Books** • 99 St Marks Pl [1st Ave]
  212-477-8647
  Messy pile of used stuff.
- **East Village Wines** • 138 1st Ave [St Marks Pl]
  212-677-7070
  Classic EV liquor store. With booze!
- **Enchantments** • 424 E 9th St [Avenue A]
  212-228-4394
  Witchy apothecary, custom carved candles, and all things occult.
- **Exit 9** • 51 Avenue A [E 3rd St]
  212-228-0145
  Always fun and changeable hipster gifts. First place to sell NP!!
- **Fly Dove NYC** • 197 E 7th St [Avenue B]
  212-300-4407
  Women's clothing boutique.
- **Gringer & Sons** • 29 1st Ave [E 2nd St]
  212-475-0600
  Kitchen appliances for every price range.

- **Lancelotti Housewares** •
  66 Avenue A [E 5th St]
  212-475-6851
  Fun designer housewares, not too expensive.
- **Mast Books** • 72 Avenue A [E 4th St]
  646-370-1114
  Small but excellent selection.
- **Mr. Throwback** • 437 E 9th St [Avenue A]
  646-410-0310
  Vintage NBA jerseys, Starter jackets, Nintendo, and toys for dudes.
- **No Relation Vintage** • 204 1st Ave [E 13th St]
  212-228-5201
  Cheap vintage basics for patient sifters.
- **Obscura Antiques & Oddities** •
  207 Avenue A [E 13th St]
  212-505-9251
  Kitschy & Arbitrary Americana. Pricey, but sociologically fascinating.
- **Ray's Candy Store** • 113 Avenue A [E 7th St]
  212-505-7609
  Avenue A's Belgian fries-and-ice cream institution.
- **Saifee Hardware & Garden** •
  114 1st Ave [E 7th St]
  212-979-6396
  Classic East Village hardware store. It has everything.
- **The Shape of Lies** • 127 E 7th St [Avenue A]
  212-533-5920
  Vintage and locally-made jewelry.
- **Sunny and Annie's** • 94 Ave B [6th St]
  212-677-3131
  This bodega's PHO Real sandwich is worth the wait.
- **Zaragoza Mexican Deli and Grocery** •
  215 Avenue A [E 13th St]
  212-780-9204
  Bodega with burritos.

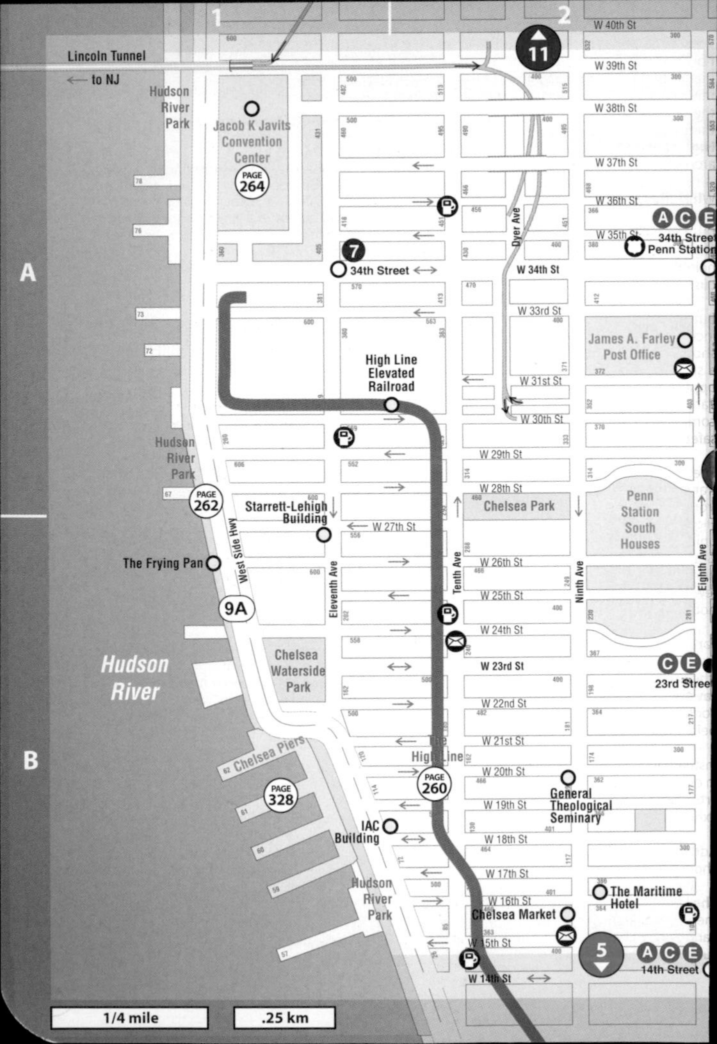

Map 8 · Chelsea

Lincoln Tunnel
← to NJ

Hudson River Park

Jacob K Javits Convention Center
PAGE 264

W 40th St
W 39th St
W 38th St
W 37th St
W 36th St
W 35th St — 34th Street
Penn Station

Dyer Ave

A C E

34th Street ←
7

W 34th St
W 33rd St
W 31st St

James A. Farley Post Office

High Line Elevated Railroad

W 30th St
W 29th St

W 28th St — Chelsea Park

Penn Station South Houses

Starrett-Lehigh Building

← W 27th St

W 26th St

The Frying Pan

9A

West Side Hwy

Eleventh Ave

W 25th St

W 24th St

Tenth Ave

Ninth Ave

Eighth Ave

C E
23rd Street

W 23rd St

Hudson River

Chelsea Waterside Park

W 22nd St
W 21st St

High Line
PAGE 260

W 20th St

General Theological Seminary

Chelsea Piers
PAGE 328

IAC Building

W 19th St
W 18th St
W 17th St

The Maritime Hotel

Hudson River Park

W 16th St

Chelsea Market

W 15th St

5
14th Street

A C E

W 14th St

1/4 mile   .25 km

Neighborhood Overview

Map 8

Located due south of Midtown's gazillion office buildings and due north of the West Village and the Financial District, Chelsea is a magnet for the young, the beautiful, and the wealthy. A polished mix of quaint, restored townhouses and sparkling new condos in the sky combine to create a unique and appealing neighborhood that deftly bridges the transition from downtown to Midtown. With the opening of the long-awaited **High Line** in 2009, luxury marched west towards the river, with multiple shiny new buildings clustered around the new ribbon of green that cuts through the heart of the neighborhood.

While the neighborhood is diverse and welcoming to all, it would be dishonest to pretend that it isn't best known as the epicenter of all things gay. A substantial, muscle-bound gay population spawned the term "Chelsea boy," used either derisively or admiringly depending on one's taste. Several of the city's best gay bars, book stores, and social service organizations are located within the borders of this neighborhood. And while the gyms aren't exclusively gay, they know who their best and most loyal customers are.

But even if you're not a gay male, the charms of Chelsea are many and unmistakable: a thriving, inclusive nightlife with something for everyone, great dining for almost any budget, and great shopping for...middle budgets and upwards (though the odd deal can certainly be found tucked into a side street or a more modest storefront on one of the avenues). On top of that, there are ample opportunities for recreation here—aside from the aforementioned High Line, there's the Hudson River Park (which, unsurprisingly, is alongside the body of water bearing the same name), massive sports complex Chelsea Piers, brilliant **Chelsea Market**, with its wonderfully diverse food vendors, and the safety-first, divided bike lanes on 8th and 9th Avenues.

The architecture of the neighborhood is some of New York's most noteworthy. Frank Gehry's translucent, Iceberg/schooner hybrid **InterActiveCorp Building** is regrettably too short to be seen from vantage points that aren't near its location at the intersection of 18th Street and the West Side Highway. But it's a leading candidate for coolest building in Chelsea and one of the loveliest, most unique buildings erected in Manhattan in recent years. A few blocks away lies the gorgeous, Neo-Gothic campus of the **General Theological Seminary**, the oldest Episcopal theological school. Just north of there, the historic **London Terrace** luxury apartment complex fills an entire city block. Up a few blocks more, the **Starrett-Lehigh Building** is an art deco freight warehouse and factory that now houses several high-profile media and fashion companies.

Farther uptown, on 8th Avenue between 31st and 33rd Streets, the **James A. Farley Post Office** stands in proud, marble magnificence across the street from the grotesquely ugly Madison Square Garden (the unworthy replacement for the demolished Penn Station). A couple blocks west of there is the **Javits Center**, the biggest exhibition hall in the city and another architectural lowlight. As a New Yorker, the best reason you'll ever have for going there is a jobs fair or an industry expo—the latter being preferable because there's likely to be free food or booze.

Instead of heading up into the 30s, take a walk through west Chelsea in the 20s and you'll find yourself in one of the great visual art districts of the world. Over 300 galleries show the newest work of the best artists working today. Despite the occasional dud, you have a better-than-even chance of encountering exhilarating, high-quality work. Now and then, you might even find something you can afford to buy!

Add in some of the best people-watching in the city, and you'll know why so many other New Yorkers choose to pay a small fortune every month to live in a shoebox here.

The Half King is perfectly positioned for a drink *apres-gallery*. **The Kitchen**'s list of performances over the years is legendary, and rock shows still happen at the **Hammerstein** and **Highline** Ballrooms. Various gay crowds have their home bars here: **Gym** (hunks!) and **The Eagle** (leather-daddies and cubs) are two of the best.

Map 8

Chelsea

14 15
11 12 13
8 9 10
5 6 7

○ Landmarks

• **100 Eleventh Avenue** •
100 11th Ave [W 19th St]
Jean Nouvel's West Side condo/window frame depot.
• **Chelsea Market** • 75 9th Ave [W 16th St]
212-652-2110
Foodies flock here. So should you.
• **Chelsea Piers** • W 23rd St & Hudson River Park
212-336-6666
28-acre waterfront sports mecca.
• **Frying Pan** • 12th Ave & W 26th St
212-989-6363
Old ship makes for amazing party digs.
• **General Theological Seminary** •
440 W 21st St [9th Ave]
212-243-5150
Oldest seminary of the Episcopal Church; nice campus.
• **IAC Building** • 555 W 18th St [West Side Hwy]
Gehry finally comes to NYC. And kicks ass.
• **Jacob K. Javits Convention Center** •
655 W 34th St [11th Ave]
212-216-2000
Glass-sheathed behemoth hosting various and sundry cons.
• **James A. Farley Post Office** •
421 8th Ave [W 31st St]
212-330-3296
Another McKim, Mead & White masterpiece. Slated to become Moynihan Station.
• **The Maritime Hotel** • 363 W 16th St [9th Ave]
212-242-4300
Ahoy! Porthole office building now uber-cool hotel.
• **Starrett-Lehigh Building** •
601 W 26th St [11th Ave]
One of the coolest factories/warehouses ever built.

☕ Coffee

• **Billy's Bakery** • 184 9th Ave [W 21st St]
212-647-9956
Mindblowingly good cakes to go with your coffee.
• **Blue Bottle Coffee** • 450 W 15th St [10th Ave]
Cult coffee that's more lab than shop.
• **Joe The Art of Coffee** •
405 W 23rd St [9th Ave]
212-206-0669
Joe really knows his joe.
• **Ninth Street Espresso** •
75 9th Ave [W 15th St]
212-228-2930
Gourmet coffee counter inside Chelsea Market.

🍸 Nightlife

• **Billymark's West** • 332 9th Ave [W 29th St]
212-629-0118
Down and dirty dive.
• **Death Ave Brewing Company** •
315 10th Ave [28th St]
212-695-8080
Good space, beer, cocktails, and Greek-inspired grub.
• **The Distinguished Wakamba Cocktail Lounge** • 543 8th Ave [W 37th St]
212-244-9045
Plastic palm trees and provocatively-clad barmaids.
• **The Eagle** • 554 W 28th St [11th Ave]
646-473-1866
Get your leather on (or off).
• **Flight 151** • 151 8th Ave [W 17th St]
212-229-1868
Prepare for takeoff on Mondays with $4 Margaritas.
• **Gallow Green** • 542 W 27th St [11th Ave]
212-564-1662
Lush rooftop garden, crisp cocktails, and a macabre train car.
• **Gym Sports Bar** • 167 8th Ave [W 19th St]
212-337-2439
Where the boys go to watch the game…and each other.
• **The Half King** • 505 W 23rd St [10th Ave]
212-462-4300
Always the perfect drinking choice in Chelsea. Amazing brunch.

Chelsea

Map 8

Try **Spice** for some tasty Thai. **Grand Sichuan** is one of our favorite spots for Chinese in all of New York. Across the street, check out **Co.**'s stellar pizzas. Got a bonus? Indulge at **Buddakan, Del Posto,** or **Morimoto.** For diner food, there's always the **Skylight.**

- **Hammerstein Ballroom** •
311 W 34th St [8th Ave]
212-279-7740
Lofty rock venue.
- **The Heath** • 542 W 27th St [11th Ave]
212-564-1662
Classy cocktails, live jazz, train cars, 1930s supper club vibe.
- **Highline Ballroom** • 431 W 16th St [10th Ave]
212-414-5994
New venue for rock, folk, dance, whatever.
- **The Kitchen** • 512 W 19th St [10th Ave]
212-255-5793
The kind of place Jesse Helms would have hated.
- **The Molly Wee Pub** • 402 8th Ave [W 30th St]
212-967-2627
You may just need a pint after a trip to Penn Station.
- **The Park** • 118 10th Ave [W 17th St]
212-352-3313
Good patio. We're split on this one.
- **Tippler** • 425 W 15th St [10th Ave]
212-206-0000
Perfectly mixed cocktails in a dark room under Chelsea Market.
- **Upright Citizen's Brigade Theatre** •
307 W 26th St [8th Ave]
212-366-9176
See smart, new comics and sometimes famous ones too.
- **Westside Tavern** • 360 W 23rd St [9th Ave]
212-366-3738
Local mixture.

🍽 Restaurants

Artichoke Basille's Pizza •
114 10th Ave [17th St]
212-792-9200 • $$
Perfect pies under the High Line, open till pretty late, too.

Blossom • 187 9th Ave [W 21st St]
212-627-1144 • $$$
$20 entrees. Did we mention it's 100% vegan and Kosher?

- **Bottino** • 246 10th Ave [W 24th St]
212-206-6766 • $$$
Good, clean Italian. A good post-gallery spot.
- **Bowery Eats** • 88 10th Ave [W 16th St]
212-376-4984 • $
Sandwiches in a sea of kitchen supplies.
- **Buddakan** • 75 9th Ave [W 16th St]
212-989-6699 • $$$$$
NYC branch of Stephen Starr's insanely popular Philadelphia behemoth.
- **Clyde Frazier's Wine & Dine** •
485 10th Ave [W 37th St]
212-842-1110 • $$$
Sleek and over the top food and design, just like Clyde.
- **Cookshop** • 156 10th Ave [W 20th St]
212-924-4440 • $
Loft-like, local ingredient-focused eatery.
- **Cull & Pistol** • 75 9th Ave [15th St]
646-568-1223 • $$$$
Sit down oysters and shellfish inside Chelsea Market.
- **Death Ave Brewing Company** •
315 10th Ave [28th St]
212-695-8080 • $$$
Your very basic pub grub, but it's necessary.
- **Del Posto** • 85 10th Ave [W 15th St]
212-497-8090 • $$$$$
Marble-lined, multi-level temple to the Italian food gods.
- **Dickson's Farmstand Meats** •
75 9th Ave [W 15th St]
212-242-2630 • $
Great sandwiches at lunch time like sloppy joe and meatball.
- **El Quinto Pino** • 401 W 24th St [9th Ave]
212-206-6900 • $$
Tiny, table-free tapas joint from owners of Tia Pol.
- **Flight 151** • 151 8th Ave [W 17th St]
212-229-1868 • $$
Prepare for takeoff on Mondays with $4 Margaritas.

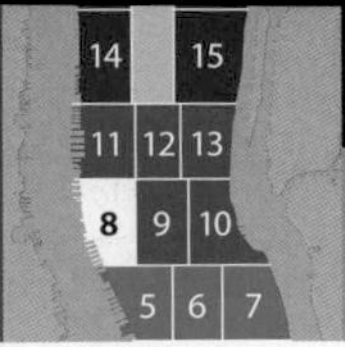

Map 8

14 15
11 12 13
8 9 10
5 6 7

Chelsea

- **Friedman's Lunch** • 75 9th Ave [W 16th St]
212-929-7100 • $
Super-delish brunch/lunch spot inside
bustling Chelsea Market.
- **Grand Sichuan** • 229 9th Ave [W 24th St]
212-620-5200 • $$
Some of the best Chinese in NYC.
Recommended.
- **La Sirena** • 88 9th Ave [17th St]
212-977-6096 • $$$$
Batali-Bastianich fine dining Italian in Maritime
Hotel.
- **Le Grainne Cafe** • 183 9th Ave [21st St]
646-486-3000 • $$$
All-day cute French brunch/lunch/dinner w/
savory crepes.
- **Los Tacos No.1** • 75 9th Ave [9th Ave]
212-246-0343 • $$
Chelsea Market's yummy taco option.
- **Meatball Shop** • 200 9th Ave [W 22nd St]
212-257-4363 • $
Fancy Italian balls in pork, chicken, and beef
form.
- **Momofuku Nishi** • 232 8th Ave [W 22nd St]
646-518-1919 • $$$
David Chang channeling Marco Polo; hijinks
ensue.
- **Rail Line Diner** • 400 W 23rd St [9th Ave]
212-924-3709 • $$
Not cheap as far as diners go, but generous
portions.
- **Morimoto** • 88 10th Ave [W 16th St]
212-989-8883 • $$$$
Stephen Starr's couture Japanese temple. Iron
Chef-prepared cuisine.
- **Ovest Pizzoteca** • 513 W 27th St [10th Ave]
212-967-4392 • $$$
Decent 'za under the High Line.
- **Pepe Giallo** • 195 10th Ave [W 25th St]
212-242-6055 • $$
Takeout Italian.
- **Pomodoro** • 518 9th Ave [W 39th St]
212-239-7019 • $$
Takes "fast food" Italian to the next level;
superb foccacia.

- **Porteno Restaurant** • 299 10th Ave [27th St]
212-695-9694 • $$$$
Modern Argentine; above and beyond steak
and red wine.
- **The Red Cat** • 227 10th Ave [W 23rd St]
212-242-1122 • $$$$
Hip and expensive.
- **Salinas** • 136 9th Ave [19th St]
212-776-1990 • $$$$
Good Spanish w/ a nice back garden.
- **Sergimmo Salumeria** •
456 9th Ave [W 35th St]
212-967-4212 • $
Serious sandwiches stuffed with
mouthwatering Italian meats.
- **Skylight Diner** • 402 W 34th St [9th Ave]
212-244-0395 • $
24-hour diner. If you must.
- **Sullivan Street Bakery** •
236 9th Ave [W 24th St]
212-929-5900 • $
Artisan breads, foodie approved. NFT
approved. God approved.
- **Tia Pol** • 205 10th Ave [W 22nd St]
212-675-8805 • $$
Very good, very popular (crowded) tapas joint.
- **Tick Tock Diner** • 481 8th Ave [W 34th St]
212-268-8444 • $
Midtown outpost of "Eat Heavy" Clifton, NJ
roadside diner.
- **Tipsy Parson** • 156 9th Ave [W 19th St]
212-620-4545 • $$$
Scrumptious Southern and comfy brunch
spot.
- **Txikito** • 240 9th Ave [W 24th St]
212-242-4730 • $$$
Unique gourmet Basque cooking.
- **Wisefish Poke** • 263 W 19th St [8th Ave]
212-367-7653 • $$
Fast-casual Hawaiian poke bowls.

Chelsea

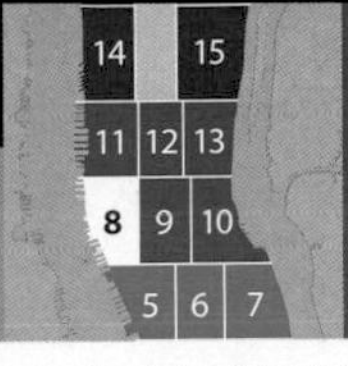

14	15	
11	12	13
8	9	10
5	6	7

Map 8

B&H Photo remains a go-to electronics store (closed Saturdays) and **Printed Matter**'s selection of artists' books is probably the best in the world. For food, simply hit brilliant **Chelsea Market** to get Italian imports (**Buon Italia**), wine (**Chelsea Wine Vault**), dairy (**Ronnybrook Farm**), fish (**The Lobster Place**), cheese (**Lucy's Whey**) and bread (**Amy's Bread**).

🛍 Shopping

- **192 Books** • 192 10th Ave [W 21st St]
  Reads like a library—with a premium on art books and literature.
- **Amy's Bread** • 75 9th Ave [W 15th St]
  212-462-4338
  Perfect breads.
- **Aperture Bookstore** •
  547 W 27th St [10th Ave]
  212 505 5555
  We love Aperture. Say hi for us.
- **Apple Store (Chelsea)** •
  401 W 14th St [9th Ave]
  212-444-3400
  Less crowded than the other locations.
- **Artists & Fleas** • 75 9th Ave [15th St]
  Market for quirky jewelry, accessories, vintage, housewares.
- **B&H Photo** • 420 9th Ave [W 33rd St]
  212-444-6615
  Where everyone in North America buys their cameras and film. Closed Saturdays.
- **Billy's Bakery** • 184 9th Ave [W 21st St]
  212-647-9956
  Yummiest treats this side of homemade.
- **Buon Italia** • 75 9th Ave [W 16th St]
  212 633 9090
  Italian import mecca—get the 24 month prosciutto.
- **Chelsea Market Baskets** •
  75 9th Ave [W 16th St]
  212-727-1111
  Gift baskets for all occasions.

- **Chelsea Wine Vault** • 75 9th Ave [W 16th St]
  212-462-4244
  Excellent shop inside the Chelsea Market.
- **City Bicycles** • 307 W 38th St [Eighth Ave]
  212-563-3373
  Sales and rentals.
- **Enoch's Bike Shop** • 480 10th Ave [37th St]
  212-582-0620
  Sales, rentals and repairs.
- **Esposito's Pork Store** •
  500 9th Ave
  212-279-3298
  Authentic 1890 butcher shop.
- **Fat Witch Bakery** • 75 9th Ave [W 16th St]
  888-419-4824
  Excellent chocolate brownies.
- **L'Arte del Gelato** • 75 9th Ave [W 16th St]
  212-366-0570
  Gelato to make you sing an aria. Or just pig out.
- **The Lobster Place** • 75 9th Ave [W 16th St]
  212-255-5672
  Fresh fish and Maine lobster, if you can afford it.
- **Milk & Hops** • 166 9th Ave [20th St]
  212-989-1999
  Great craft beer selection and artisanal cheeses.
- **Printed Matter** • 231 11th Ave
  212-925-0325
  Astounding selection of artist's books; highly recommended.

Map 9 · **Flatiron / Lower Midtown**

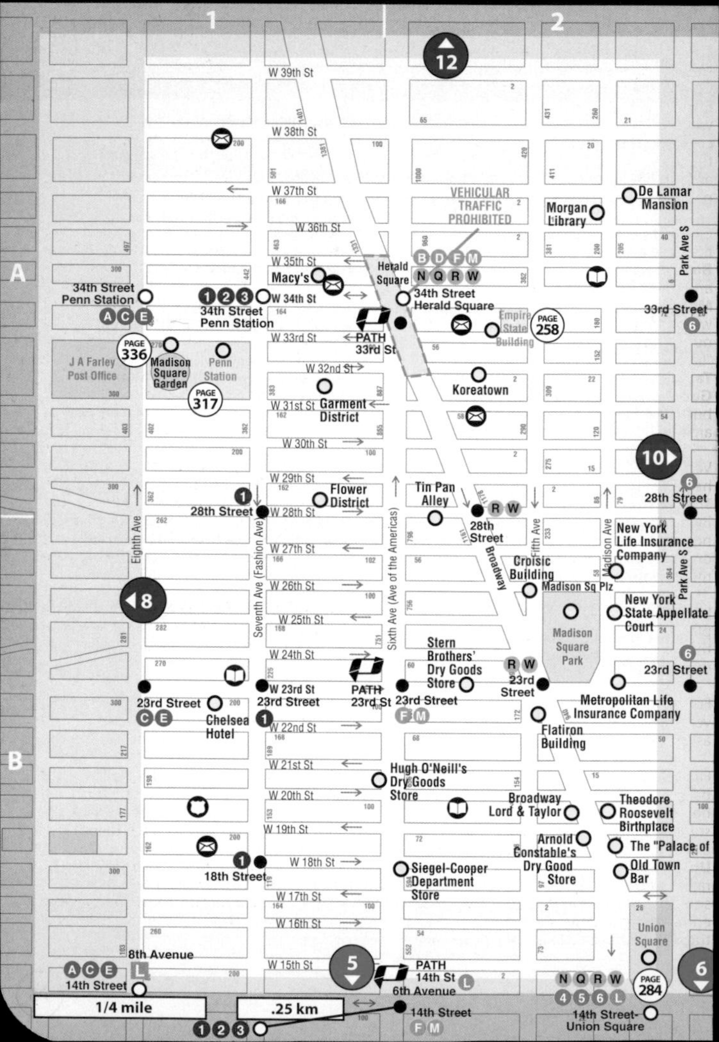

W 39th St

W 38th St

W 37th St

W 36th St

12

VEHICULAR
TRAFFIC
PROHIBITED

W 35th St

Herald Square

Macy's

B D F M
N Q R W

**34th Street
Herald Square**

Morgan
Library

De Lamar
Mansion

Park Ave S

A

34th Street
Penn Station

1 2 3
A C E

W 34th St

34th Street
Penn Station

PATH
33rd St

PAGE
258

Empire
State
Building

33rd Street

6

PAGE
336

Madison
Square
Garden

J A Farley
Post Office

Penn
Station

PAGE
317

W 33rd St

W 32nd St

W 31st St

Garment
District

Koreatown

W 30th St

W 29th St

Flower
District

Tin Pan
Alley

R W

1

28th Street

W 28th St

28th
Street

Seventh Ave/Fashion Ave

W 27th St

Eighth Ave

Sixth Ave (Ave of the Americas)

Broadway

Seventh Ave

Madison Ave

28th Street

6

New York
Life Insurance
Company

10

Croisic
Building

Madison Sq Plz

8

W 26th St

W 25th St

Stern
Brothers'
Dry Goods
Store

New York
State Appellate
Court

Madison
Square
Park

Park Ave S

W 24th St

PATH
23rd St

R W

23rd
Street

23rd Street

6

B

23rd Street

C E

Chelsea
Hotel

1

W 23rd St

F M

W 22nd St

W 21st St

Metropolitan Life
Insurance Company

Flatiron
Building

Hugh O'Neill's
Dry Goods
Store

W 20th St

Broadway
Lord & Taylor

Theodore
Roosevelt
Birthplace

The "Palace of"
Old Town
Bar

W 19th St

1

18th Street

W 18th St

Siegel-Cooper
Department
Store

Arnold
Constable's
Dry Good
Store

W 17th St

W 16th St

Union
Square

A C E L

8th Avenue
14th Street

5

PATH
14th St

6th Avenue

L

N Q R W
4 5 6 L

PAGE
284

6

14th Street

1 2 3

14th Street

F M

14th Street-
Union Square

1/4 mile

.25 km

Neighborhood Overview

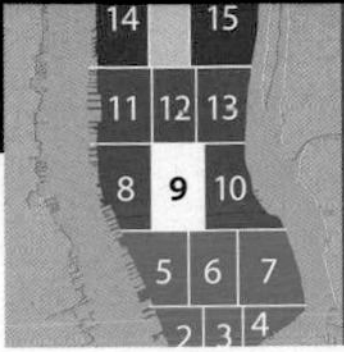

Map 9

The amazing variety of people, places and things that typifies New York cannot be better experienced than in this area. Containing some of the most tourist-heavy areas—the **Empire State Building** and **Macy's** at Herald Square—you will also find the hip, expensive, and fabulously exclusive communities of Gramercy (to the east) and Chelsea (to the west). Flatiron is also the home to the lesser-known "Silicon Alley," after the many start ups in the area. In this incredibly diverse and unassuming neighborhood you will see moms pushing strollers, hipsters in low-slung pants, and wealthy elderly women walking their perfectly groomed poodles.

One of the most obvious draws of the area is the impressive architecture. You certainly can't miss the amazing sight of the towering **Empire State Building** or the aptly-named **Flatiron Building**. But also not to miss is the less-obvious **Chelsea Hotel**, a favorite of many musicians and artists from Bob Dylan to Sid Vicious. Early 20th century additions to the area include the **MetLife Tower**, the **New York Life Building**, and the **New York State Appellate Court**, all of which are ranged on the east side of **Madison Square Park**. Equally impressive are the myriad number of current and former cast-iron department store buildings that make up the historic "Ladies' Mile" area, including the **Arnold Constable Dry Goods Store**, the **Broadway Lord & Taylor**, the **Croisic Building**, the **Hugh O'Neill Dry Goods Store**, the **Stern Brothers' Dry Goods Store**, and, our all-time favorite, the **Siegel-Cooper Department Store**. We can't help but mention that this area was also the scene of one of the greatest crimes *against* architecture—namely, the destruction of McKim, Mead & White's original Penn Station in 1963.

Venture to the **Garment District** and you will be surrounded by the shops and people that helped make New York City the fashion leader of the world in the late 1800's and early 1900's. The nearby **Flower District** was once several blocks filled with lush greenery of every variety. By the 2010s however, high rent and massive competition squeezed most retailers out, and it's now less than a block in size and can easily be missed. Luckily **Koreatown** is still going strong on 32nd Street (between Fifth and Broadway). Stroll through here on a Friday night to find the restaurants and bars packed to the brim.

Look down as you walk on 28th Street between Fifth Avenue and Broadway and you will see a plaque in the sidewalk dedicated to **Tin Pan Alley**. If you're a music buff you'll want to take in the historical significance of this area, dated back to 1885 when a group of songwriters and music publishers got together to lobby for copyright laws.

For a piece of Presidential history, visit the **Birthplace of Theodore Roosevelt**. A recreated version of the brownstone President Roosevelt was born in on October 27th, 1858 now serves as a museum dedicated to the 26th President.

Finding a small patch of fresh green grass in Manhattan is almost as challenging as finding a parking spot, but in this area you have not one, but two parks. **Madison Square Park** is a beautifully manicured park where you can be sure to catch hundreds of sunbathers on any summer Saturday. It is also home to the long lines of the **Shake Shack**. If you can afford to wait an hour or two, you'll be treated to one of the best hamburgers of all-time. Farther south, **Union Square** is one of the more famous parks in Manhattan, having had several historic rallies and riots as well as being a main subway hub; it is busier than most parks. If you can squeeze yourself into a spot on one of the overflowing park benches, you'll be treated to some entertaining people watching. It's also worth noting for the dog lovers out there, that both of these parks have sizable dog parks.

Map 9

Flatiron / Lower Midtown

O Landmarks

- **The "Palace of Trade"** • 885 Broadway [E 19th St]
  The mansard roof to end all mansard roofs.
- **Croisic Building** • 220 5th Ave [E 26th St]
  Just another outstanding NYC building. Circa 1912.
- **De Lamar Mansion** • 233 Madison Ave [E 37th St] Dutch sea captain's mansion now inhabited by Polish diplomats.
- **Empire State Building** • 350 5th Ave [W 33rd St] 212-736-3100. View unlike any other (except maybe Top of the Rock).
- **Flatiron Building** • 175 5th Ave [W 22nd St]
  A lesson for all architects: design for the actual space.
- **Flower District** • W 28th St b/n 6th & 7th Aves
  Lots of flowers by day, lots of nothing by night.
- **Garment District** • 34th to 40th St b/n 6th to 9th Ave.
  Clothing racks by day, nothing by night. Gritty, grimy.
- **Hotel Chelsea** • 222 W 23rd St [7th Ave]
  The scene of many, many crimes.
- **Hugh O'Neill's Dry Goods Store** • 655 6th Ave [W 20th St]
  Brilliant cast-iron from Mortimer Merritt.
- **Koreatown** • W 32nd St b/n Broadway & 5th Ave
  Korean restaurants, bars, and shops. Bustling on the weekends.
- **Lord & Taylor Building** • 901 Broadway [E 20th St]
  Incredible detail on former Lord & Taylor outlet.
- **Macy's** • 151 W 34th St [7th Ave] 212-695-4400
  13 floors of wall-to-wall tourists! Sound like fun?
- **Madison Square Garden** • 4 Penn Plaza [W 31st St] 212-465-6741
  MSG's one thing in Chinatown; in Midtown it's something different.
- **Madison Square Park** • E 23rd St & Broadway 212-538-1884. One of the most underrated parks in the city. Lots of great weird sculpture.
- **Metropolitan Life Insurance Co** • 1 Madison Ave [E 23rd St]
  Cool top, recently refurbished.
- **The Morgan Library & Museum** • 225 Madison Ave [E 37th St] 212-685-0008
  See cool stuff the dead rich dude collected.
- **New York Life Insurance Company** • 51 Madison Ave [E 26th St]
  The gold roof? Your insurance premiums at work.
- **New York State Appellate Court** • Madison Ave & E 25th St
  Insanely ornate 1899 courthouse; where new lawyers get sworn in.
- **Old Town Bar** • 45 E 18th St [Broadway] 212-529-6732. Classic NY pub housed in former speak-easy.
- **Penn Station** • 8th Ave & W 32nd St
  Well, the old one was a landmark, anyway…
- **Siegel-Cooper Co. Department Store** • 616 6th Ave [W 18th St]
  Beaux-Arts retail madness. Now a f***in' Bed, Bath & Beyond.
- **Stern Brothers' Dry Goods Store** • 32 W 23rd St [6th Ave]
  Awesome ornate cast-iron; now houses Home Depot. Whatever.
- **Theodore Roosevelt Birthplace** • 28 E 20th St [Broadway] 212-260-1616. Recreation of childhood home of only president born in NYC.
- **Tin Pan Alley** • W 28th St b/n 6th Ave & Broadway
  Where American popular music climbed out of the crib.
- **Union Square** • E 14th St & University Pl
  Famous park for protests and rallies. Now bordered by chain stores.

Coffee

- **Café Grumpy** • 224 W 20th St [7th Ave] 212-255-5511
  Best coffee on the island.
- **Culture Espresso** • 72 W 38th St [6th Ave] 212-302-0200
  Amazing coffee right near Bryant Park.
- **Gregorys Coffee** • 874 6th Ave [W 31st St] 646-476-3838
  Take a break from Macy's or Koreatown with a latte.
- **Ports Coffee** • 251 W 23rd St [8th Ave] 646-290-6151
  A friendly crew of baristas helps feed your caffeine addiction.
- **Spoon** • 40 E 33rd St 646-230-7000
  Serving up Stumptown beans—coffee of the gods.
- **Stumptown Coffee** • 18 W 29th St [Broadway] 347-414-7805
  The real deal straight outta Portland.
- **Toby's Estate** • 160 5th Ave [21st St] 646-559-0161
  Australian artisanal coffee powerhouse.

Flatiron / Lower Midtown

Map 9

11 12 13
8 9 10
5 6 7
2 3 4

Whether you prefer celebrity sighting at **Raines Law Room**, dress-code mandatory joints like **230 Fifth**, or classic NYC watering holes like **Old Town Bar** and **Peter McManus**, you have options. NFT cabaret experts state unequivocally that the **Metropolitan Room** is the best cabaret club in the city.

Farmers Markets

• **Union Square Greenmarket** •
E 17th St & Broadway
NYC's best greenmarket.
Mon, Wed, Fri & Sat 8 am–6 pm, year round.

Nightlife

• **230 Fifth** • 230 5th Ave [E 26th St]
212-725-4300
Dress code and overpriced drinks. Best view of NYC makes it worthwhile.
• **Ace Hotel Lobby Bar** • 20 W 29th St [Broadway]
212-679-2222
Amazing cocktails in an amazing space.
• **Anthony Anderson's Mixtape Comedy Show** • 208 W 23rd St [7th Ave]
212-367-9000
Entertainment for the people, by the people.
• **The Archive** • 12 E 36th St [Madison Ave]
212-213-0093
Relaxed, subdued; solid cocktails.
• **Barracuda** • 275 W 22nd St [8th Ave]
212-645-8613
Neighborhood fave, low-key gay bar.
• **Belgian Beer Cafe** • 220 5th Ave [W 26th St]
212-575-2337
Belgian fare and brews, plus growlers to go.
• **Birreria** • 200 5th Ave [W 23rd St]
212-937-8910
Retractable-roof beer garden atop Eataly.
• **Flatiron Lounge** • 37 W 19th St [6th Ave]
212-727-7741
We like it. Especially if someone else is paying.
• **The Ginger Man** • 11 E 36th St [Madison Ave]
212-532-3740
Where button-down midtown types loosen up over bitter beers.
• **Gotham Comedy Club** • 208 W 23rd St [7th Ave]. 212-367-9000
In a new, shiny location.• **Hotel Metro Rooftop Bar** • 45 W 35th St [6th Ave]
212-279-3535
Fresh air + beer 14 floors above Manhattan.
• **Jazz Gallery** • 1160 Broadway [W 27th St]
646-494-3625
Not-for-profit jazz venue.

• **Lillie's** • 13 E 17th St [5th Ave]
212-337-1970
Perfect for anyone with an Irish-Victorian fetish.
• **Maysville** • 17 W 26th St [Broadway]
646-490-8240
Whiskey-forward bar and full service restaurant.
• **Midtown Live** • 251 W 30th St [8th Ave]
212-695-8970
Rock club with good happy hour specials.
• **Old Town Bar** • 45 E 18th St [Broadway]
212-529-6732
Excellent old-NY pub.
• **Park Bar** • 15 E 15th St [Fifth Ave]
212-367-9085
Good date spot; small enough to encourage a little conversation.
• **Peter McManus** • 152 7th Ave [W 19th St]
212-929-9691
Refreshingly basic. Gorgeous old phone booths.
• **The Raines Law Room** • 24 E 39th St
Cocktails worth your time. And money.
• **Rattle N Hum** • 14 E 33rd St [Madison Ave]
212-481-1586
40 beers on tap!
• **Rogue Bar** • 757 6th Ave [W 25th St]
212-242-6434
Big sports bar.
• **Society Billiards + Bar** • 10 E 21st St [5th Ave]
212-420-1000
Well-appointed, classy pool hall.
• **Stout** • 133 W 33rd St [7th Ave]
212-629-6191
Huge Midtown pub.
• **Taj Lounge** • 48 W 21st St [5th Ave]
212-620-3033
Indian lux lounge. Lots of private events.
• **Tir Na Nog** • 254 W 31st St
212-630-0249
Penn Station hangout.
• **Triple Crown Restaurant & Ale House** • 330 7th Ave [W 29th St]
212-736-1575
Typical Midtown bar. Expensive, insipid. But, hey, we hear the bartenders are nice.

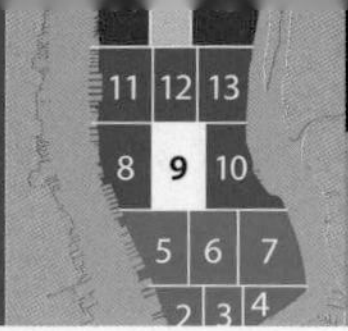

Flatiron / Lower Midtown

Map 9

11 12 13
8 9 10
5 6 7
2 3 4

🍴 Restaurants

- **ABC Kitchen** • 35 E 18th St [Broadway]
  212-475-5829 • $$$$
  Fancy farm-to-table. In a carpet store.
- **Alidoro** • 18 E 39th St [Madison Ave]
  646-692-4330 • $$
  High-end Italian sandwiches.
- **Basta Pasta** • 37 W 17th St [5th Ave]
  212-366-0888 • $$$
  Pac-rim Italian. Hmmm.
- **BCD Tofu House** • 5 W 32nd St [5th Ave]
  212-967-1900 • $$$
  California-based Korean tofu chain.
- **Ben's NY Kosher** • 209 W 38th St [7th Ave]
  212-398-2367 • $$
  Deli standards, Middle Eastern and Kosher
  Chinese.
- **Blaggard's Pub** • 8 W 38th St [5th Ave]
  212-382-2611 • $$
  Smells like last night's vomit. Overpriced, awful
  service.
- **Blue Water Grill** • 31 Union Sq W [E 16th St]
  212-675-9500 • $$$$$
  Seafood. We're torn on this one.
- **BonChon Chicken** • 325 5th Ave [33rd Ave]
  212-686-8282 • $$
  Fast-casual Korean fried chicken powerhouse.
- **BonChon Chicken** • 207 W 38th St [7th Ave]
  212-221-3339 • $$
  Times Square location of Korean fried chicken
  powerhouse.
- **Boqueria** • 53 W 19th St [6th Ave]
  212-255-4160 • $$$
  Cheese stuffed dates wrapped in bacon? We're
  there.
- **The Breslin** • 16 W 29th St [Broadway]
  212-679-1939 • $$$
  Meet. Wait. Meat. Lamb burgers is a culinary
  gem.
- **BRGR** • 287 7th Ave [W 26th St]
  212-488-7500 • $
  Good FRFR.
- **Burger & Lobster** • 39 W 19th St [6th Ave]
  646-833-7532 • $$$
  London-based burger-lobster joint; menu
  boiled down to essentials.

- **BXL Zoute** • 50 W 22nd St [6th Ave]
  646-692-9282 • $$$
  Belgian cuisine with requisite beer-mussels
  specials.
- **Cafeteria** • 119 7th Ave [W 17th St]
  212-414-1717 • $$$
  Comfort food, open all night.
- **Chandni Restaurant** • 11 W 29th St
  [Broadway] • 212-686-4456 • $
  Cabbies love this Indian-Pakistani place. Open
  'til 4 am.
- **Chick-fil-A** • 1000 6th Ave [W 37th St]
  212-704-9920 • $
  Legendary fried chicken sandwiches; closed
  Sunday.
- **Cho Dang Gol** • 55 W 35th St [6th Ave]
  212-695-8222 • $$$
  There's usually a line for good reason at this
  homey Korean.
- **Chop't** • 24 E 17th St [Union Square W]
  646-336-5523 • $
  Salads for office drones.
- **The City Bakery** • 3 W 18th St [5th Ave]
  212-366-1414 • $$
  Stellar baked goods.
- **The Clocktower** • 5 Madison Ave [E 24th St]
  212-413-4300 • $$$$
  Superstar-filled roster brings Britishy elegance
  to sleek hotel restaurant.
- **Coffee Shop** • 29 Union Sq W [E 16th St]
  212-243-7969 • $$
  Diner with a samba skew.
- **Cosme** • 35 E 21st St [Broadway]
  212-913-9659 • $$$$
  Locally sourced haute Mexican from one of
  Mexico's top chefs.
- **Craft** • 43 E 19th St [Broadway]
  212-780-0880 • $$$$$
  Outstanding. A top-end place worth the $$$$.
- **Don's Bogam** • 17 E 32nd St [Madison Ave]
  212-683-2200 • $$$
  Korean BBQ heaven.
- **Eataly** • 200 5th Ave [W 23rd St]
  212-229-2560 • $$$
  Try to get a seat somewhere. Go ahead, we
  dare you.

Flatiron / Lower Midtown

Map 9

Impress a date with the size of your wallet at **Gramercy Tavern**, **Eleven Madison Park** and NFT-fave **Craft**, or impress them with your wit and conversation over tapas at **Boqueria**. Otherwise, hit **City Bakery** for their pretzel croissants, **Eisenberg's** for egg creams, or **Kang Suh** for all-night Korean BBQ.

- **Eisenberg's Sandwich Shop** •
174 5th Ave [W 22nd St] • 212-675-5096 • $$
Old-school corned beef and pastrami.
- **Eleven Madison Park** • 11 Madison Ave [E 24th St] • 212 889-0905 • $$$$$
Where the elite meet to greet.
- **Elmo** • 156 7th Ave [W 19th St]
212 337-8000 • $$
Lounge downstairs, dine upstairs at this swanky Chelsea venue.
- **Evergreen Shanghai Restaurant** • 10 E 38th St [5th Ave] • 212-448-1199 • $
Their scallion pancakes are worth the wait, and they know it.
- **Giorgio's of Gramercy** • 27 E 21st St [Broadway] • 212-477-0007 • $$$$$
Cozy Italian.
- **Go! Go! Curry!** • 273 W 38th St [8th Ave]
212-730-5555 • $
Japanese deep fried fast food.
- **Gramercy Tavern** • 42 E 20th St [Broadway]
212-477 0777 • $$$$$
Expensive, but good, New American.
- **Hanbat** • 53 W 35th St [6th Ave]
212-629-5588 • $$
The Bi Bim Bab is amazing. Open all night!
- **Hangawi** • 12 E 32nd St [5th Ave]
212-213-0077 • $$$
Serene, top-end vegetarian Korean.
- **Hanjan** • 36 W 26th St [6th Ave]
212-206-7226 • $$$
Sophisticated Korean-Chinese food and cocktails.
- **Her Name Is Han** • 17 E 31st St [Madison Ave]
212-779-9990 • $$$
Korean soul food for homesick students, and the rest of us.
- **Hill Country** • 30 W 26th St [Broadway]
212-255-4544 • $$$
Good ol' Texas 'cue; go for the wet brisket.
- **Home's Kitchen** • 22 E 21st St [Broadway]
212-475-5049 • $$
Hands down, best fried rice.
- **ilili** • 236 5th Ave [W 27th St]
212-683-2929 • $$$
Hearty Lebanese food in a fancy setting.
- **Johny's Luncheonette** • 124 W 25th St [6th Ave] • 212-243-6230 • $
Sit at the counter and get an egg and cheese on a roll.

- **Kunjip** • 32 W 32nd St [Broadway]
212-216-9487 • $$
The best Korean food in Manhattan; try the bo saam!
- **La Vie en Szechuan** • 14 E 33rd St [Madison Ave] • 212-683-2779 • $$
Spiced up Chinese in an unlikely neighborhood.
- **Lan Sheng** • 128 W 36th St
212-575 8899 • $$
Szechuan fare that once earned a Michelin star.
- **Le Coq Rico** • 30 E 20th St [Park Ave S]
212 267-7426 • $$$
Chicken-forward bistro via Paris from veteran chef Antoine Westermann.
- **Le Zie** • 172 7th Ave [W 20th St]
212-206-8686 • $$$
Venetian. That means it's Italian.
- **The Liberty** • 29 W 35th St [5th Ave]
212-967-4000 • $$$
New American tavern with not a statue in sight.
- **Mandoo Bar** • 2 W 32nd St [W 31st St]
212-279-3075 • $
Mandoo these dumplings taste good!
- **Marta** • 29 E 29th St [Madison Ave]
212-651-3800 • $$$
Wood-fired pizzas and Italian seasonal entrees.
- **Mendy's Kosher Deli** • 61 E 34th St [Park Ave]
212-576-1010 • $$
Pastrami, matzoh ball soup, and knishes.
- **Momoya** • 185 7th Ave [W 21 St]
212-989-4466 • $$$
Nice selection of unique sushi.
- **New Wonjo** • 23 W 32nd St [Broadway]
212-695 5815 • $$$
Can you ever have enough 24/7 Korean BBQ restaurants?
- **The NoMad Restaurant** •
1170 Broadway [E 28th St]
347-472-5660 • $$$$
Elegant comfort cuisine in the NoMad Hotel.
- **Nuchas Empanadas** •
97 W 32nd St [Broadway] • 212-912-0035 • $
Flawless, juicy Argentine turnovers from a kiosk and truck.
- **Olympic Pita** •
58 W 38th St [6th Ave] • 212-869-7482 • $
Scrumptious shawarma.

Map 9

Flatiron / Lower Midtown

- **Periyali** • 35 W 20th St [5th Ave]
  212-463-7890 • $$$$
  Upscale Greek. Pretty damned great.
- **Ravagh** • 11 E 30th St [Madison Ave]
  212-696-0300 • $
  All your kebab needs.
- **Rosa Mexicano** • 9 E 18th St [5th Ave]
  212-629-9000 • $$$
  New Union Square outpost of Manhattan Mexi
  chain.
- **Rye House** • 11 W 17th St [5th Ave]
  212-255-7260 • $$$
  Small plates and agreat selection of spirits.
- **Sala One Nine** •
  35 W 19th St [6th Ave] • 212-229-2300 • $$
  Garlic on everything, bring breathmint. Must
  try: Filet Mignon sandwich.
- **Shake Shack** • 11 Madison Ave [E 23rd St]
  212-889-6600 • $
  Enjoy homemade shakes 'n burgers in the
  park. On a 2-hour line.
- **Simit Sarayi** • 435 5th Ave [E 39th St]
  212-683-4100 • $$
  International Turkish chain brings its bagels to
  NYC.
- **Socarrat** • 259 W 19th St [8th Ave]
  212-462-1000 • $$$
  Authentic paella feast, sit next to the
  Spaniards at the communal table.
- **Soju Haus** • 315 5th Ave [E 32nd St]
  212-213-2177 • $$$
  Wash down Korean food with namesake
  booze.
- **Szechuan Gourmet** • 21 W 39th St [6th Ave]
  212-921-0233 • $$
  Amazing Chinese in this part of the city?
  Believe it.
- **Tarallucci E Vino** • 15 E 18th St [5th Ave]
  212-228-5400 • $$
  Espresso in the morning, wine after work.
  Delicious and versatile.
- **Teisui** • 246 5th Ave [28th St]
  917-388-3596 • $$$$$
  High-concept, high-end Japanese tasting
  menus.
- **Tocqueville** • 1 E 15th St [5th Ave]
  212-647-1515 • $$$$$
  Lovely everything—and you can actually hear
  each other speak!

- **Toledo** • 6 E 36th St [5th Ave]
  212-696-5036 • $$$$
  Classy Spanish.
- **Triple Crown Restaurant & Ale House** •
  330 7th Ave [W 29th St] • 212-736-1575 • $$
  Pub grub that will make you shrug.
- **Waldy's Wood Fired Pizza** •
  800 6th Ave [W 27th St] • 212-213-5042 • $$
  Where former Beacon chef fires up gourmet
  penne and pie.
- **Wined Up** • 913 Broadway [E 20th St]
  212-673-6333 • $$$
  Impress a date here. Cozy, quiet, best wine
  selection.
- **Woorijip** • 12 W 32nd St [5th Ave]
  212-244-1115 • $
  Cheap Korean buffet, hot and cold, great
  variety.
- **Zero Otto Nove Trattoria** •
  15 W 21st St [5th Ave] • 212-242-0899 • $$$
  Arthur Avenue pizza import; highly
  recommended.

🛍 Shopping

- **30th Street Guitars** • 234 W 27th St
  212-868-2660
  Ax heaven. Seriously.
- **ABC Carpet & Home** •
  888 Broadway [E 19th St]
  212-473-3000
  A NYC institution for chic, even exotic, home
  decor and design.
- **Abracadabra** • 19 W 21st St [5th Ave]
  212-627-5194
  Magic, masks, costumes—presto!
- **Academy Records** • 12 W 18th St [5th Ave]
  212-242-3000
  Top jazz/classical mecca.
- **Adorama** • 42 W 18th St [5th Ave]
  212-741-0052
  Good camera alternative to B&H. Still closed
  Saturdays, though.
- **Ariston Flowers** • 110 W 17th St [6th Ave]
  212-929-4226
  Excellent florist with orchids as well.

Need sporting goods? **Paragon** is the paragon of sporting goods stores. Food heaven is found at **Eataly**—just bring your credit card. **30th Street Guitars** and **Rogue Music** will rock your world. **Idlewild** is one of New York's finest bookshops, specializing in travel and literature.

- **Barnes & Noble** • 33 E 17th St [Broadway]
212-253-0810
Chain bookstore.
- **Beecher's Cheese** • 900 Broadway [E 20th St]
212-466-3340
Handmade cheese by the block or in gourmet grilled sandwiches.
- **Books of Wonder** • 18 W 18th St [5th Ave]
212-989-3270
Top NYC children's bookstore, always has signed copies around too.
- **Bottlerocket Wine & Spirit** •
5 W 19th St [5th Ave]
212-929-2323
Free tastings every Thursday, Friday, and Saturday!
- **Breads Bakery** • 18 E 16th St [Union Square W] 212-633-2253
Artisanal bakers and babka specialists.
- **Chelsea Bicycles** • 130 W 26th St [Sixth Ave]
212-727-7278
Sales, service, and rentals.
- **The Container Store** • 629 6th Ave [W 19th St]
212-366-4200
Organize your closet...and your life!
- **Danny's Cycles** •
546 6th Ave [W 14th St]
212-255-5100
Sales, service, repairs, and rentals.
- **Design Within Reach** •
903 Broadway [E 20th St]
212-477-1155
"Within reach" is relative, but the stuff is definitely cool.
- **Eataly** • 200 5th Ave [W 23rd St]
212-229-2560
Over the top (in a good way) Italian culinary superstore.
- **Fishs Eddy** • 889 Broadway [E 19th St]
212-420-9020
Bizarre dishes to complete your cool abode.
- **Flying Tiger** • 920 Broadway [E 21st St]
212-777-1239
The Stew Leonard's of quirky Danish design.
- **Idlewild Books** • 12 W 19th St [5th Ave]
212-414-8888
One of the best travel + literature bookstores on the planet.

- **Jazz Record Center** • 170 7th Ave S
212-675-4480
All that jazz!
- **Luthier Music** • 49 W 24th St [6th Ave]
212-397-6038
One of the best for classical and flamenco guitars.
- **M&J Trimmings** • 1008 6th Ave [W 38th St]
212-391-6200
For your DIY sewing projects.
- **Macy's** • 151 W 34th St [7th Ave]
212-695-4400
Love the wooden escalators.
- **Muji Chelsea** • 16 W 19th St [5th Ave]
212-414-9024
Beautiful Japanese aesthetic applied to daily living.
- **NYC Racquet Sports** • 157 W 35th St [7th Ave]
212-695-5353
Serious tennis supplies.
- **Paragon Sporting Goods** •
867 Broadway [E 18th St]
212-255-8889
Top NYC sporting goods store, plus tennis permits!
- **The Pennsy** • 2 Penn Plaza [7th Ave]
NYC food luminaries populate high-end food court.
- **Rogue Music** • 220 W 30th St [7th Ave]
212-629-5073
Used equipment you probably still can't afford.
- **Sound by Singur** • 242 W 27th St [8th Ave]
212-924-8600
High end audio and video. And we mean "high-end."
- **Tannen's Magic** • 45 W 34th St [6th Ave]
212-929-4500
Serving both professional and amateur magicians since 1925.
- **Trader Joe's** • 675 6th Ave [W 21st St]
212-255-2106
Finally some welcome relief for the 14th Street store.
- **Whole Foods** • 250 7th Ave [W 24th St]
212-924-5969
Healthy shopping of the gayborhood.

Map 10 · **Murray Hill / Gramercy**

1

2

13

E 39th St

98th

712

E 38th St

Tunnel Approach St

325

Second Ave

Tunnel Exit St

E 37th St

303

330

E 36th St

650

Queens Midtown Tunnel

The Corinthian

561

E 35th St

522

St. Vartan Park

350

Sniffen Court

Sniffen Ct

298

248

615

E 34th St

300

577

496

A

72

129

E 33rd St

33rd Street

6

E 32nd St

477

Kips Bay Plaza

NYU Medical Center

54

101

E 31st St

343

Park Ave S

Lexington Ave

133

E 30th St

350

Third Ave

Second Ave

E 29th St

240

First Ave

473

Curry Hill

E 28th St

350

28th Street

6

178

E 27th St

Bellevue Hospital Center

69th Armory

Broadway Alley

160

E 26th St

209

348

Baruch College

E 25th St

321

9

24

E 24th St

Vet Adm Medical Center

1081

25

E 23rd St

Waterside Plaza

23rd Street

6

Protestant Welfare Agencies Building

201

E 22nd St

Mayor James Harper Residence

100

E 21st St

300

Baruch Field

Marina & Skyport

Peter Cooper Village

FDR Dr

Marginal St

Asser Levy Pl

National Arts Club

Gramercy Park

244

E 20th St

The Players

Augustus St. Gaudens Playground

E 19th St

Pete's Tavern

Irving Pl

150

E 18th St

Tammany Hall / Union Sq Theater

E 17th St

Stuyvesant Town

Union Sq E

Union Square

PAGE 284

Friends Meeting House

E 16th St

146

Rutherford Pl

Stuyvesant Square

Nathan D Perlman Pl

E 16th St

Avenue C

E 16th St

4 5 6 L

N R Q W

290

E 15th St

E 15th St

14th Street–Union Square

6

3rd Avenue

L

1st Avenue

7

E 14th St

East River

1/4 mile

.25 km

Neighborhood Overview

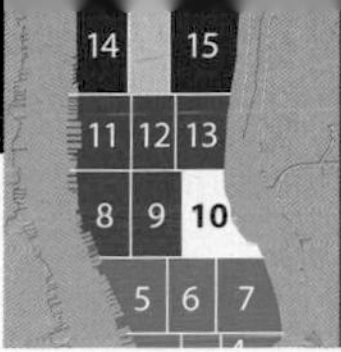

Map 10

The Murray Hill/Gramercy area of New York is one of New York's largest studies in contrast. On one hand, there are massive housing and hospital complexes that take up several city blocks; on the other hand, there are narrow alleys and small, gated parks of unparalleled beauty. Add it all together and we get (ho-hum) just another brilliant slice of New York.

Murray Hill's contrast, for instance, can be found by checking out lovely little **Sniffen Court**, one's of Manhattan's finest residential alleys, and then walking south to teeming **Kips Bay Plaza**, a set of two parallel housing towers designed by I.M. Pei. Or by watching kids play in **St. Vartan's Park**, then walking south on First Avenue to gaze at the humongous **NYU** and **Bellevue** Medical Centers (by which time, the "hill" portion of Murray Hill has evaporated). For the hill itself, head to Park Avenue and Lexington Avenue in the upper 30s—from there, you can get a sense of why this area is so-named (our unofficial guess is that Park Avenue and 38th Street is about the highest point in these parts). Then walk the side streets in the East Thirties to see some really prime real estate, as well as consulates, hotels, and lots of other stuff you can't afford.

Moving south from Murray Hill, the neighborhood changes rather dramatically in the East 20s. You first encounter **"Curry Hill"** on Lexington Avenue in the upper 20s, a fantastic strip of Indian restaurants and groceries. Two large landmarks, one old and one new, punctuate the southern end of this strip—the looming brickwork of the **69th Armory**, now home to many special events throughout the year, and then **Baruch College**'s postmodern new main building just south of there (architects like to call this type of building a "vertical campus;" what that means is a 15-minute wait for an elevator between classes). Baruch is joined in this area by two other schools of note, the **School of Visual Arts** and NYU's **Dental School**, both on East 23rd Street.

The area changes again south of 23rd Street, becoming one of New York's loveliest residential neighborhoods, Gramercy Park. The **park itself** is gated, controlled and accessed by those who actually live around it. For the rest of us, we'll just need to be content with looking in at the park through its wrought-iron gates and staring at incredible period architecture facing the park. Our favorite three examples of this architecture are the **Mayor James Harper Residence** on the west side of the park, and the **Players** and **National Arts** Clubs on the southwestern side of the park. Then stroll down hidden Irving Place, a six-block long stretch of restaurants and nightlife options which dead-ends at 14th Street. Classic watering hole **Pete's Tavern**, where writer O. Henry drank, is a must-stop on this walk.

But the aforementioned contrast is still alive and kicking down here, because a few blocks to the east of warm, intimate Gramercy are the hulking **Stuyvesant Town** and Peter Cooper Village housing complexes, which together comprise over 11,000 residential units. Controversy has marked these two huge complexes for the past several years, as longtime owner Met Life spurned a (lower) offer from a tenant's group to buy the complex, instead selling to Tishman Speyer for $5.4 billion in 2006. It was the largest single sale of American property, which, now thanks to a deflated housing market, is now undoubtedly the largest property fiasco in American history (since Tishman had to turn over the property to its creditors to avoid bankruptcy). For us: no thanks, we'll stick with our Brooklyn walk-up, and just visit.

Irish pubs abound in this neighborhood, and all of them (**Failte**, **Molly's**, **Paddy Reilly's**) have their devotees. We prefer dives like **McSwiggan's**, live music venues **Irving Plaza** or the **Jazz Standard**, and (of course!) classic watering hole **Pete's Tavern**.

Map 10

Murray Hill / Gramercy

O Landmarks

- **69th Armory** • 68 Lexington Ave [E 26th St]
  Event space, historic landmark, hookers at
  night.
- **Baruch College** • 55 Lexington Ave [E 25th St]
  646-312-1000
  Baruch's "vertical campus;" very cool unless
  you need an elevator quickly.
- **Curry Hill** • Lexington Ave & E 28th St
  Eat your way down Lexington in the 20s!
- **Gramercy Park** • E 20th St & Irving Pl
  New York's only keyed park. This is where the
  revolution will doubtlessly start.
- **Kips Bay Plaza** • 1st Ave & E 30th St
  I. M. Pei does the superblock, 1960s-style. A
  tad brutalist.
- **Mayor James Harper Residence** •
  4 Gramercy Park W [E 21st St]
  Cool wrought-iron madness from 1846.
- **MeetingHouse of the Religious Society of
  Friends** • 15 Rutherford Pl [E 16th St]
  212-475-0466
  Quaker meeting house from 1861. No guns,
  please.
- **The National Arts Club** •
  15 Gramercy Park S [E 20th St]
  212-475-3424
  One of two beautiful buildings on Gramercy
  Park South.
- **Pete's Tavern** • 129 E 18th St [Irving Pl]
  212-473-7676
  Where O. Henry hung out. And so should you,
  at least once.
- **The Players** • 16 Gramercy Park S [E 20th St]
  212-475-6116
  The other cool building on Gramercy Park
  South.
- **Protestant Welfare Agencies Building** •
  281 Park Ave S [E 22nd St]
  Looming Gothic structure circa 1894. Worth a
  look.
- **Sniffen Court** • 3rd Ave & E 36th St
  Great little space.
- **St. Vartan Park** • 1st Ave & E 35th St
  Murray Hill kid/playground nexus.
- **Stuyvesant Town** • 1st Ave & E 20th St
  Would you really want to live here? Really?
- **Tammany Hall/Union Square Theater** •
  100 E 17th St [Park Ave S]
  212-505-0700
  Once housed NYC's Democratic political
  machine.

Coffee

- **Franchia** • 12 Park Ave [E 35th St]
  212-213-1001
  Modern Korean tea and treats.
- **Irving Farm Coffee Roasters** •
  71 Irving Pl [E 19th St]
  212-995-5252
  Brilliant coffee.
- **Lady Mendl's Tea Salon** •
  56 Irving Pl [E 17th St]
  212-533-4466
  It's tea time for the ladies of Manhattan.
- **Maialino** • 2 Lexington Ave [E 21st St]
  212-777-2410
  Drip bar located in the Gramercy Park Hotel.

O Farmers Markets

- **Murray Hill Youthmarket** •
  E 33rd St & 2nd Ave
  Sat 8 am–3 pm, Jun–Nov
- **Stuyvesant Town Greenmarket** •
  14th Street Loop & Avenue A
  Sun 9:30 am–4 pm, June–Nov

Murray Hill / Gramercy

14	15
11	12	13
8	9	10
5	6	7

Map 10

Irish pubs abound in this neighborhood, and all of them (**Failte**, **Molly's**, **Paddy Reilly's**) have their devotees. We prefer dives like **McSwiggan's**, live music venues **Irving Plaza**, **Rodeo Bar**, or the **Jazz Standard**, and (of course!) classic watering hole **Pete's Tavern**.

◉ Nightlife

- **Bar Jamon** • 125 E 17th St [Irving Pl]
  212-253-2773
  Pig out at this wine bar.
- **Failte Irish Whiskey Bar** •
  531 2nd Ave [E 29th St]
  212-725-9440
  Sip Guiness by the fire. Shoot a round of pool. A favorite of Irish Ex-pats.
- **Gramercy Theater** •
  127 E 23rd St [Lexington Ave]
  212-614-6932
  Music venue.
- **Irving Plaza** • 17 Irving Pl [E 15th St]
  212-777-6800
  Staple rock venue.
- **Jazz Standard** • 116 E 27th St [Lexington Ave]
  212-576-2232
  Solid shows. BBQ upstairs!
- **Joshua Tree** • 513 3rd Ave [E 34th St]
  212-689-0058
  Murray Hill meat market.
- **McSwiggan's** • 393 2nd Ave [E 23rd St]
  212-683-3180
  One of the best dive bars on the island.
- **Mercury Bar** • 493 3rd Ave [E 33rd St]
  212-683-2645
  Lots of TVs for sports. You make the call.
- **Middle Branch** • 154 E 33rd St [Lexington Ave]
  212-213-1350 Quality cocktails in mixologically underserved neighborhood.
- **Molly's** • 287 3rd Ave [E 22nd St]
  212-889-3361
  Great Irish pub with a fireplace.

- **New York Comedy Club** •
  241 E 24th St [3rd Ave]
  212-696-5233
  ...and the bartender asks, "where did you get that!"
- **Paddy Reilly's Music Bar** •
  519 2nd Ave [E 29th St]
  212-686-1210
  Sunday night means pints of Guinness and live Irish fiddlin'.
- **Pete's Tavern** • 129 E 18th St [Irving Pl]
  212-473-7676
  Where O. Henry hung out. And so should you, at least once.
- **Plug Uglies** • 256 3rd Ave [E 20th St]
  212-780-1944
  Full length shuffle board table!
- **Rolf's** • 281 3rd Ave [E 22nd St]
  212-477-4750
  December holiday visit is a must for some German bier.
- **Rose Bar** • 2 Lexington Ave [E 21st St]
  212-920-3300
  Another classy hotel bar NFT can't afford.
- **Ted's Corner Tavern** • 523 3rd Ave [E 35th St]
  212-689-2676
  Ted sure has good taste in craft beer. Plus Mediterranean food.
- **Waterfront Ale House** •
  540 2nd Ave [E 30th St]
  212-696-4104
  Decent local vibe.

Murray Hill / Gramercy

Map 10

🍴 Restaurants

- **2nd Avenue Deli** •
162 E 33rd St [Lexington Ave]
212-689-9000 • $$
Reborn in a new location. Miracles do happen.
- **Anjappar Chettinad** •
116 Lexington Ave [E 28th St]
212-265-3663 • $$$
Southern Indian food from a global chain. And a full bar.
- **Bar Jamon** • 125 E 17th St [Irving Pl]
212-253-2773 • $
Pig out at this wine bar.
- **BLT Prime** • 111 E 22nd St [Park Ave S]
212-995-8500 • $$$$
Steakhouse with Craft-like, a-la-carte sides.
- **Blue Smoke** • 116 E 27th St [Park Ave S]
212-447-7733 • $$$$
Finger lickin' BBQ, Danny Meyer style (with downstairs jazz club).
- **The Cannibal** • 113 E 29th St [Park Ave]
212-686-5480 • $$$
Hope you like meat. And beer.
- **Chote Nawab** • 115 Lexington Ave [E 28th St]
212-679-4603 • $$
Nice Indian restaurant with lots of seafood options.
- **Clover Delicatessen** • 621 2nd Ave [E 34th St]
212-683-0227 • $
This stellar deli has one of the best signs in NYC.
- **Coppola's** • 378 3rd Ave [E 27th St]
212-679-0070 • $$
Neighborhood Italian.
- **Covina** • 127 E 27th St [Lexington Ave]
212-204-0225 • $$$
Mediterranean-esque hotel New American by way of California.
- **El Parador Café** • 325 E 34th St [2nd Ave]
212-679-6812 • $$$
NY's oldest and friendliest Mexican.
- **El Pote** • 718 2nd Ave [E 39th St]
212-889-6680 • $$$
Spanish food in all its classic, old-school glory.
- **Franchia** • 12 Park Ave [E 35th St]
212-213-1001 • $$
Modern Korean tea and treats.
- **Friend of a Farmer** • 77 Irving Pl [E 19th St]
212-477-2188 • $$
Chic country-cooking.
- **Gemini Diner** • 641 2nd Ave [E 35th St]
212-532-2143 • $$
Open 24 hours. Diner.
- **Gramercy Cafe** • 184 3rd Ave [E 17th St]
212-982-2121 • $$
Open 24 hours. Diner. You know the drill.
- **Haandi** • 113 Lexington Ave [E 28th St]
212-685-5200 • $$
Stellar Pakistani grilled meats.
- **I Trulli** • 122 E 27th St [Lexington Ave]
212-481-7372 • $$$$$
Italian. Great garden.
- **Irving Farm Coffee Roasters** •
71 Irving Pl [E 19th St]
212-995-5252 • $
Good coffee, great treats, superior service.
- **Jackson Hole** • 521 3rd Ave [E 35th St]
212-679-3264 • $$
Extremely large burgers. A post-drinkfest must.
- **Jaiya** • 396 3rd Ave [E 28th St]
212-889-1330 • $$$
Inventive, spicy Thai.
- **Joe Jr** • 167 3rd Ave [E 16th St]
212-473-5150 • $
Great diner atmosphere, fairly decent diner food.
- **L'Express** • 249 Park Ave S [E 20th St]
212-254-5858 • $$
Always-open French diner.
- **La Posada** • 364 3rd Ave [E 26th St]
212-213-4379 • $
Authentic Mexican burritos, tacos and enchiladas.
- **Le Parisien Bistrot** • 163 E 33rd St [3rd Ave]
212-889-5489 • $$$
Classic French bistro fare.

Murray Hill / Gramercy

Map 10

Everyone has their Curry Hill favorite; ours is vegetarian dosa house **Pongal**. If you're into meat, upscale burger joint **Rare** or steakhouse **BLT Prime** both make the cut. Tom Colicchio's **Riverpark** spiffs up an underserved corner of Kips Bay. And good Thai (**Jaiya**) can be found, but the sleeper pick here is **Turkish Kitchen**, our favorite Turkish in all of New York.

• **Maoz Vegetarian** • 38 Union Sq E [E 16th St]
212-260-1988 • $
Cheap and tasty falafel take-out chain from Amsterdam.

• **Mee's Noodle Shop & Grill** •
930 2nd Ave [E 30th St]
212-888-0027 • $
Noodles, General Tso's and sushi for cheap.

• **Mexico Lindo** • 459 2nd Ave [E 26th St]
212-679-3665 • $$
Famous Mexican food.

• **Murray Hill Diner** •
222 Lexington Ave [E 33rd St]
212-686-6667 • $$
Last of a vanishing breed. Simple Greek food and greasy classics.

• **Nuvita** • 102 E 22nd St [Park Ave S]
212-677-2222 • $$$$
Sophisticated Italian without the pretension.

• **O Ya** • 120 E 28th St [Lexington Ave]
212-204-0200 • $$$$$$
Hyper-expensive Japanese tasting menus via Boston.

• **Penelope** • 159 Lexington Ave [E 30th St]
212-481-3800 • $$
Gingham décor but oh, what a menu!

• **Pete's Tavern** • 129 E 18th St [Irving Pl]
212-473-7676 • $$$$
Good pub food, especially after/while drinking!

• **Pongal** • 110 Lexington Ave [E 28th St]
212-696-9458 • $$
Possibly NY's best vegetarian Indian. Sada dosa…mmmm.

• **Posto** • 310 2nd Ave [E 18th St]
212-716-1200 • $$
Savory thin-crust pizza, salads.

• **Rare Bar & Grill** •
303 Lexington Ave [E 37th St]
212-481-1999 • $$$
Should be better, given the focus. We're divided on this one.

• **Riverpark** • 450 E 29th St [1st Ave]
212-729-9790 • $$$$$
Colicchio brings his vision to underserved corner of Kips Bay.

• **Sam's Place** • 132 E 39th St [Lexington Ave]
212-599-6360 • $$
Hidden old-school Italian haunt

• **Saravana Bhavan** •
81 Lexington Ave [E 26th St]
212-679-0204 • $$
All about the dosas at this multi-national Indian vegetarian spot.

• **Sarge's Deli** • 548 3rd Ave [E 37th St]
212-679-0442 • $$
24-hour-a-day pastrami, convenient to GCT.

• **Scotty's Diner** • 336 Lexington Ave [E 39th St]
212-986-1520 • $$
When you need food, not an Instagram photo.

• **Tiffin Wallah** • 127 E 28th St [Lexington Ave]
212-685-7301 • $
Veggie lunch buffet for a few bucks.

• **Turkish Kitchen** • 386 3rd Ave [E 28th St]
212-679-6633 • $$$
Excellent Turkish, great décor, brilliant bread. NFT pick!

• **Union Square Café** • 101 E 19th St
212-243-4020 • $$$$$
Second location of first restaurant of Danny Meyer's empire.

• **Upland** • 345 Park Ave S [E 26th St]
212-686-1006 • $$$$
If San Bernardino County were on the Tyrrhenian Sea.

• **Vamos! Tacos Y Tequila** •
348 1st Ave [E 20th St]
212 358-7800 • $$$
Crappy New York service, great California cuisine.

• **Vatan** • 409 3rd Ave [E 29th St]
212-689-5666 • $$
All-you-can-eat vegetarian Indian feast.

• **Vezzo** • 178 Lexington Ave [E 31st St]
212-839-8300 • $$
From the owners of Gruppo and Posto. Delizioso.

• **The Water Club** • FDR Drive & 30th St
212-683-3333 • $$$$
Romantic, good brunch on the East River.

• **The Watering Hole** • 106 E 19th St [Park Ave S]
212-674-5783 • $$
Perfect place to watch the game.

• **Yama** • 122 E 17th St [Irving Pl]
212-475-0969 • $$
Sushi deluxe.

Map 10

Murray Hill / Gramercy

Shopping

- **City Opera Thrift Shop** •
  222 E 23rd St [3rd Ave]
  212-684-5344
  They always have something or other.
- **DaVinci Artist Supply** •
  132 W 21st St
  212-871-0220
  Discounts to student, teachers, and art
  professionals.
- **Dover Street Market** •
  160 Lexington Ave [30th St]
  646-837-7750
  Multi-floor multi-brand orgy of fashion.
- **Foods of India** • 121 Lexington Ave [E 28th St]
  212-683-4419
  Huge selection including harder to find spices.

- **Housing Works Thrift Shop** •
  157 E 23rd St [Lexington Ave]
  212-529-5955
  Our favorite thrift store.
- **Kalustyan's** • 123 Lexington Ave [E 28th St]
  212-685-3451
  International spice and specialty food market
  dating back to 1944.
- **La Delice Pastry Shop** •
  372 3rd Ave [E 27th St]
  212-532-4409
  Delectable pastries, buttery croissants, layer
  cakes.
- **Lamarca Cheese Shop** •
  161 E 22nd St [3rd Ave]
  212-673-7920
  Italian culinary goodies.

Murray Hill / Gramercy

Map 10

The constantly changing **Dover Street Market** is a boffo orgy of high-end designers. Hit either **Lamarca** or **Lamazou** cheese shops to go along with pastries from **La Delice**. Indian shops **Foods of India** and **Om Saree Palace** are always worth a look. **Jam** will have any envelope you could ever need and **Nuthouse Hardware** is New York's only 24-hour hardware store, with power tool rentals. Cool.

- **Lamazou** • 370 3rd Ave [E 27th St]
  212-532-2009
  Great selection of cheese and gourmet products.
- **Ligne Roset** • 250 Park Ave S [E 20th St]
  212-375-1036
  Modern, sleek furniture. Only for people with very good jobs.
- **Max Nass** • 118 E 28th St [Lexington Ave]
  212-679-0154
  Vintage jewelry, repairs, restringing, and restoration.
- **Nemo Tile Company** • 48 E 21st St [Broadway]
  212-505-0009
  Good tile shop for small projects.
- **Nuthouse Hardware** • 202 E 29th St [3rd Ave]
  212 545 1447
  Open 24-hours; equipment rentals, too.

- **Pookie & Sebastian** • 541 3rd Ave [E 36th St]
  212-951-7110
  Murray Hill outpost for fun, flirty, girly garb.
- **Spokesman Cycles** • 34 Irving Pl [E 16th St]
  212-995-0450
  Sales, service, repairs, and rentals.
- **Todaro Bros.** • 555 2nd Ave [E 30th St]
  212 532 0633
  Home made mozzerella, pastas, high quality groceries.
- **Vintage Thrift Shop** • 286 3rd Ave [E 22nd St]
  212-871-0777
  Vintage clothes you can actually afford.

Map 11 · **Hell's Kitchen**

W 60th St

W 59th St

PAGE 266

Time Warner Center

Columbus Circle

59th Street Columbus Circle

W 58th St

W 57th St

W 56th St

W 55th St

W 54th St

W 53rd St

14

Dewitt Clinton Park

12

W 52nd St

Daily Show Studio

W 51st St

Hudson River

PAGE 262

W 50th St

West Side Hwy

50th Street

W 49th St

W 48th St

Hudson River Park

Eleventh Ave

Tenth Ave

Ninth Ave

W 47th St

Associated Musicians of Greater New York

Restaurant Row

W 46th St

W 45th St

Intrepid Sea, Air and Space Museum

Broadway Dance Center

Eighth Ave

W 44th St

W 43rd St

42nd Street Port Authority Bus Terminal

W 42nd St

Theatre Row

Port Authority Bus Terminal

W 41st St

PAGE 320

Dyer Ave

W 40th St

8

Lincoln Tunnel

The Annex/ Hell's Kitchen Flea Market

W 39th St

Jacob K Javits Convention Center

PAGE 264

W 38th St

| 1/4 mile | .25 km |

W 37th ST

Neighborhood Overview

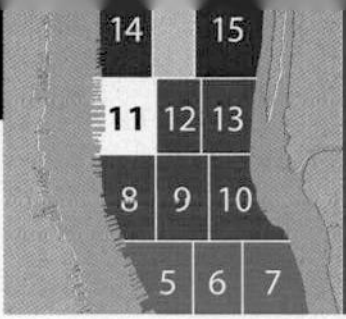

14 | 15
11 | 12 | 13
8 | 9 | 10
5 | 6 | 7

Map 11

Named for the squalor its early immigrant tenements epitomized, the scruffy patch of bodega-infused real estate between Broadway and that unlikely landing strip known as the Hudson is home to intimate theaters, niche restaurants and—along with a rising tide of gentrification—an army of toy dogs likely to stage a coup one day. The neighborhood is also characterized by an abundance of things too big and ugly to put anywhere else in Manhattan: car dealerships, cell phone towers, cruise liners, the Port Authority, and stables for those hansom cab horses, the last of which accounts for certain odors and the distinct clip-clop of every rush hour.

It's also farther west than the subways venture, harshly industrial-looking and often beset by Lincoln Tunnel traffic or gale-force nautical winds. Yes, Hell's Kitchen may seem like the edge of the civilized world, and the panoramic view of New Jersey does little to dampen this grungy impression. Yet most locals come to cherish the mellow vibe and dearth of McDonald's locations that come with living just outside Manhattan's hyperkinetic and tourist-infested core. Here you'll have no trouble hailing a cab, or getting the bartender's attention. And as for the out-of-towners—well, they only get as far in as Ninth Avenue before their legs get tired.

Hell's Kitchen may be close to Central Park, but why fight the crowds? Instead explore **Hudson River Park**, an elegantly sculpted swath of greenery running along the coast of the island. Its linearity makes for ideal bikers and joggers, but the idle will find plenty of lovely spots to spread a picnic blanket and watch lunatics paddle by in kayaks. **Dewitt Clinton Park** always has an entertaining game going on its baseball/soccer/everything field; it also boasts two popular dog runs for the bonding of canines and their owners alike. Community gardens have sprung up there and close by, thanks to green-thumbed volunteers from the area.

Two essential elements to absorb: one you find on stage, and the other you find on the end of a fork—usually in that order. The former is available at one of the countless off- and off-off-Broadway theatres lying around—you know, the type that isn't showing something along the lines of "A Musical Loosely Cobbled Together From A String Of # 1 Hit Singles". **Theatre Row** is, as the name suggests, a lineup of such venues featuring, ahem, riskier fare—though perhaps not as scandalous as the peepshows that once littered that stretch of 42nd Street. Satirical mainstay **The Daily Show** also tapes around here, if you're looking for entertainment that's as free as it is hilarious. Head up to **Restaurant Row** on 46th to sample one of the cozy eateries and candlelit nightlife nooks that cater to audiences after the curtain falls. Almost every sub-genre of food is accounted for, and authenticity is rampant—don't be surprised to find actual French people eating at a French bistro!

Mom-and-pop places have proved resilient—everything from artisanal bread to custom-made paints can be found at tiny stores run by devoted experts. You might even see an old-school coffee shop without so much as a name on a sign out front. But the best spot for browsing may be the **Hell's Kitchen Flea Market**, nestled between bus ramps on 39th Street, which offers outdoor bargain-hunting on weekends. The usual gridlock is traded for a bazaar of vintage clothing, jewelry and collectibles, most priced a bit cheaper than they were before these particular vendors moved from a Chelsea location known as The Annex.

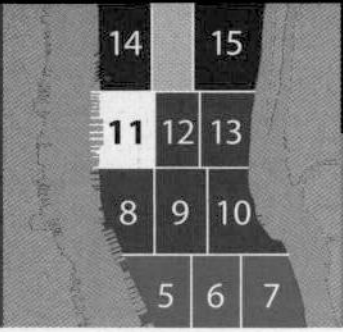

Map 11
14 15
11 12 13
8 9 10
5 6 7

Hell's Kitchen

O Landmarks

- **Broadway Dance Center** • 322 W 45th St [Broadway]
  212-582-9304
  The place for tap lessons.
- **Daily Show Studio** • 733 11th Ave [W 52nd St]
  Home of our favorite TV show. Thank you Jon Stewart.
- **Dewitt Clinton Park** • 11th Ave & W 52nd St
  Where the neighborhood mutts meet to sniff butts.
- **Hell's Kitchen Flea Market** •
  W 39th St & Dyer Ave
  212-243-5343
  Old Chelsea Annex flea market is now located here.
- **Intrepid Sea, Air and Space Museum** •
  12th Ave & W 46th St
  212-245-0072
  Holy crap! An aircraft carrier in the middle of the Hudson River!
- **Port Authority Bus Terminal** •
  625 8th Ave [W 41st St]
  212-502-2200
  Add an "S" and you've got a sporting goods chain.
- **Restaurant Row** • 8th Ave & W 46th St
  Mingle with tourists during pre-theater dinners.
- **Theatre Row** • W 42nd St b/n 9th & Dyer Aves
  Cluster of off-Broadway theatres including Playwrights Horizons.

Coffee

- **Blue Bottle Coffee** • 600 11th Ave [45th St]
  212-582-7940
  Cult coffee masters outlet at Gotham West Market.
- **Empire Coffee & Tea** • 568 9th Ave [W 41st St]
  212-268-1220
  Best coffee in these tourist filled parts.

Farmers Markets

- **57th Street Greenmarket** •
  9th Ave & W 57th St
  Wed 8 am–6 pm May-Dec; Sat 8 am–6 pm, Apr–Dec
- **Port Authority Greenmarket** •
  8th Ave & W 42nd St
  Thurs 8 am–5 pm, year round.

Hell's Kitchen

14	15
11	12	13
8	9	10
	5	6	7

Map 11

Land of contrast: Reservations are essential at **Bar Centrale**, with its speakeasy vibe and classic cocktails—and then there's an utter dive like **Rudy's Bar & Grill**, which serves each beer with a free hot dog. Elsewhere, you've got a decadent club-style concert venue and legendary smoker's roof in **Terminal 5**.

Nightlife

- **9th Avenue Saloon** • 656 9th Ave [W 46th St]
  212-307-1503
  Low-key, beer-friendly gay bar close to Midtown.
- **Bar Centrale** • 324 W 46th St [8th Ave]
  212-581-3130
  Make reservations to see Broadway stars relaxing after the show.
- **Birdland** • 315 W 44th St [8th Ave]
  212-581-3080
  Top notch jazz.
- **Blue Ruin** • 538 9th Ave [W 40th St]
  917-945-3497
  Pressed tin ceiling and lots of booze.
- **Don't Tell Mama** • 343 W 46th St [8th Ave]
  212-757-0788
  Good cabaret space.
- **Flaming Saddles** • 793 9th Ave [W 53rd St]
  212-713-0481
  Country-western, gay, bartenders dance on the bar, lots of cuties.
- **Gossip Bar & Restaurant** •
  733 9th Ave [W 50th St]
  212-265-2720
  Amazing staff, great selection, comfortable atmosphere
- **Holland Bar** • 532 9th Ave [W 40th St]
  212-502-4609
  One of the last great dives of New York
- **The House of Brews** • 302 W 51st St
  212-541-7080
  Fratty but friendly atmosphere, great beer selection.

- **Hudson Hotel Library** •
  358 W 58th St [9th Ave]
  212-554-6000
  Super-super-super pretentious.
- **Hudson Terrace** • 621 W 46th St [11th Ave]
  212-315-9400
  Rooftop space with nice views.
- **Industry** • 355 W 52nd St [9th Ave]
  646-476-2747
  Large space with great decor, hot bartenders; come with friends.
- **Laurie Beechman Theatre** •
  407 W 42nd St [9th Ave]
  212-695-6909
  Intimate basement cabaret with fabulous drag shows.
- **The Ritz** • 369 W 46th St [9th Ave]
  212 333 4177
  Three floors, two patios, no cover.
- **Rudy's Bar & Grill** • 627 9th Ave [W 44th St]
  646-707-0890
  Classic Hell's Kitchen. Recommended.
- **Swing 46** • 349 W 46th St [9th Ave]
  212-262-9554
  Good place for a drink before a show.
- **The Tank** • 312 W 36th St
  212-563-6269
  Major destination for experimental music.
- **Terminal 5** • 610 W 56th St [11th Ave]
  212-665-3832
  Ex-club space now used for mid-level indie bands
- **Valhalla** • 815 9th Ave [W 54th St]
  212-757-2747
  Warm, wooden watering hole with staggering beer selection.

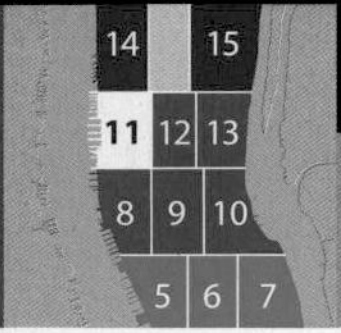

Map 11

14 15
11 12 13
8 9 10
5 6 7

Restaurants

- **2 Bros Pizza** • 542 9th Ave [W 40th St]
212-777-0600 • $
Decent pizza for a buck a slice.
- **5 Napkin Burger** • 787 9th Ave [W 45th St]
212-757-2277 • $$
Pricey burgers.
- **99 Cents Fresh Pizza** • 569 9th Ave [W 41st St]
212-268-1461 •
Yeah it's cheap, but watch out for the crazies.
- **Afghan Kebab House** •
764 9th Ave [W 51st St]
212-307-1612 • $$
Great kebabs, friendly.
- **Ariana Afghan Kebab** •
787 9th Ave [W 52nd St]
212-262-2323 • $
Afghan. Always go for the lamb.
- **Arriba Arriba Mexican Restaurant** •
762 9th Ave [W 51st St]
212-489-0810 • $$
Sangria and large Mexican lunch for $7 bucks.
- **Asiate** • 80 Columbus Cir [Broadway]
212-805-8881 • $$$$$
Highest-end Japanese/French. Bring lots of
Yen/Euro.
- **Bar Masa** • 10 Columbus Cir [Broadway]
212-823-9800 • $$$$
Brilliant and expensive. But still a lot cheaper
than Masa.
- **Burrito Box** • 885 9th Ave [W 57th St]
212-489-6889 • $
Cheap and tasty Mexican with killer guac.
- **Casellula** • 401 W 52nd St [9th Ave]
212-247-8137 • $$$
Sophisticated wine and cheese pairings.
- **Chipotle** • 620 9th Ave [W 44th St]
212-247-3275 • $
Cheap, fast, Mex-American goodness in
mall-like setting.
- **Churrascaria Plataforma** •
316 W 49th St [8th Ave]
212-245-0505 • $$$$
Brazilian Feast! Don't eat all day…then come
here.

- **Danji** • 346 W 52nd St [9th Ave]
212-586-2880 • $$$
Gourmet Korean small plates with a twist.
- **Don Giovanni Ristorante** •
358 W 44th St [9th Ave]
212-581-4939 • $$
One of the better cheap pies in the city.
- **El Centro** • 824 9th Ave [W 54th St]
646-763-6585 • $
Open late for those sudden south-of-the-
border cravings.
- **Empanada Mama** • 763 9th Ave [W 51st St]
212-698-9008 • $
No one fries them better.
- **Esca** • 402 W 43rd St [9th Ave]
212-564-7272 • $$$$$
Dave Pasternack knows fish, some of which he
catches himself.
- **etcetera etcetera** • 352 W 44th St [9th Ave]
212-399-4141 • $$$$
Beautiful bar, delicious Italian food.
- **Gazala Place** • 709 9th Ave [W 48th St]
212-245-0709 • $$
Brilliant Middle Eastern food. Share an
appetizer platter.
- **Gossip Bar & Restaurant** •
733 9th Ave [W 50th St]
212-265-2720 • $$
Irish fare, amazing staff, guilty-pleasure menu,
awesome bar.
- **Guantanamera** • 939 8th Ave [W 56th St]
212-262-5354 • $$$
Tasty Cuban. Great for lunch.
- **Hakkasan** • 311 W 43rd St [8th Ave]
212-776-1818 • $$$$
Sleek, spendy London import specializing in
Cantonese cuisine.
- **Hell's Kitchen** • 754 9th Ave [W 47th St]
212-977-1588 • $$$
Haute cuisine, Mexican style. Packed.
- **Hudson Common** • 356 W 58th St [9th Ave]
212-554-6217 • $$$$$
Lovely and pricey and goody.

The breadth and depth of deliciousness is staggering here. **Hallo Berlin** boasts German soul food, **Esca** serves top-notch splurge/splash seafood, and **Island Burgers** features about forty variations of their signature dish. Middle Eastern lovers get their fix at BYOB gem **Gazala Place** or **Hummus Kitchen**. Pre-theater pick is French stalwart **Tout Va Bien**.

Hummus Kitchen • 768 9th Ave [W 51st St]
212-333-3009 • $$
Hummus so good they named a kitchen after it.

Ippudo • 321 W 51st St [8th Ave]
212-974-2500 • $$
Famous ramen with less wait than the downtown location.

Island Burgers & Shakes •
766 9th Ave [W 51st St]
212-307-7934 • $$
Aptly named. A classic.

Joe Allen • 326 W 46th St [8th Ave]
212-581-6464 • $$$
De rigueur stargazing, open late.

Landmarc • 10 Columbus Cir [W 58th St]
212-823-6123 • $$$$
Uptown outpost of brilliant downtown steakhouse.

Luckys Famous Burgers •
370 W 52nd St [9th Ave]
(212) 247-6717 • $
Minimalist, messily-devoured takeout burgers.

Marseille • 630 9th Ave [W 44th St]
212-333-2323 • $$$$
True to the name, an expatriate's delight.

Meske • 468 W 47th St [10th Ave]
212-399-1949 • $$
Friendly and consistently good Ethiopian.

Mont Blanc • 315 W 48th St [8th Ave]
212-582-9648 • $$$
Classic fondue spot. Remember—drink wine, not water!

Morningstar • 879 9th Ave
212-246-1593 • $
French toast with ice cream at midnight, terrible coffee.

Mother Burger • 329 W 49th St [9th Ave]
212-757-8600 • $$
Decent food, with a bonus: really cheap margaritas—outdoors!

Nizza • 630 9th Ave [W 45th St]
212-956-1800 • $$
Share some fantastic antipasti: socca, tapenade, focaccette, and more.

Orso • 322 W 46th St [8th Ave]
212-489-7212 • $$$$
Popular busy Italian.

Per Se • 10 Columbus Cir [W 58th St]
212-823-9335 • $$$$$
Divine...but you practically have to sell a kidney to afford it.

Pio Pio • 604 10th Ave [W 44th St]
212-459-2929 • $$
Excellent Peruvian in great setting, especially the ceviche and chicken.

Pure Thai Cookhouse • 766 9th Ave [51st St]
212-581-0999 • $$
Tasty, affordable Thai in a classy little dining room.

Shake Shack • 691 8th Ave [W 44th St]
646-435-0135 • $$
Danny Meyer's pitch perfect burger joint.

Shorty's • 576 9th Ave [W 42nd St]
212-967-3055 • $
Philly cheese steak without the snobbery. Extra Cheez Whiz, please.

Taboon • 773 10th Ave [W 52nd St]
212 713 0271 • $$
Great bang for your buck. Middle Eastern/ Mediterranean.

Totto Ramen • 366 W 52nd St [9th Ave]
212-582-0052 • $$
Incredible ramen, just be prepared to line up.

Tout Va Bien • 311 W 51st St [8th Ave]
212-265-0190 • $$$$
Warm, homey, pre-theater, French. NFT approved.

Turkish Cuisine • 631 9th Ave [W 44th St]
212-397-9650 • $$
Turkish food, in case you were wondering. It's always good.

Uncle Nick's • 747 9th Ave [W 50th St]
212-245-7992 • $$$
Greek, noisy.

ViceVersa • 325 W 51st St [8th Ave]
212-399-9291 • $$$$
Creative yet accessible Italian cuisine with a cool, sleek vibe.

Whole Foods • 10 Columbus Cir [8th Ave]
212-823-9600 • $
By far the cheapest eats in Time Warner Center. Euros love it.

Map 11

Hell's Kitchen

🛍 Shopping

- **10th Avenue Wines & Liquors •**
  812 10th Ave [W 54th St]
  212-245-6700
  Boozehound specials and tastings.
- **Amish Market •** 731 9th Ave [W 50th St]
  212-245-2360
  Good prepared foods, unfortunately not
  delivered via horse and buggy.
- **Ample Hills Creamery •** 600 11th Ave [45th
  St] 212-582-9354
  Brooklyn artisanal ice creamologists with
  creative flavors.
- **Amy's Bread •** 672 9th Ave [W 47th St]
  212-977-2670
  Providing the heavenly smells that wake up
  Hell's Kitchen.
- **Bouchon Bakery •** 10 Columbus Cir [8th Ave]
  212-823-9366
  Heavenly pastries in a gigantic mall.
- **Cakes 'N Shapes •** 466 W 51st St [10th Ave]
  212-629-5512
  Custom cakes with photographic designs and
  creative shapes.

- **Coco and Toto •** 730 11th Ave [W 52nd St]
  212-956-5822
  Adorable pet boutique grooms, walks, and
  babysits beloved furballs.
- **Delphinium Home •** 353 W 47th St [9th Ave]
  212-333-7732
  For the "too lazy to make my own card" set.
- **Epstein's Paint Center •**
  562 W 52nd St [W 52nd St]
  212-265-3960
  Honest advice, top quality from century-old
  shop.
- **Happy Feet •** 754 10th Ave [W 51st St]
  212-757-8400
  Reliable deals on all imaginable pet supplies.
- **Hell's Kitchen Flea Market •**
  W 39th St & Dyer Ave
  212-243-5343
  Vintage treasures abound every Sat & Sun.

Amish Market is the top-end supermarket; Ninth Avenue International is amazing for Greek groceries. Sullivan Street Bakery makes bundles of heaven disguised as bread. Delphinium is the store where you can buy a non-Hallmark card, and Chelsea Garden Center, in spite of its geographic indifference, can provide the perfect flowers to go with it.

- **Janovic** • 766 10th Ave
  212-245-3241
  Top NYC paint store. Shades/blinds too.
- **Liberty Bicycles** • 846 9th Ave [W 55th St]
  212-757-2418
  This bike shop totally rocks.
- **Little Pie Company** • 424 W 43rd St [9th Ave]
  212-736-4780
  A homemade dessert equals happiness.
- **Ninth Avenue International Grocery** •
  543 9th Ave [W 40th St]
  212-279-1000
  Mediterranean/Greek specialty store.
- **Ninth Avenue Vintner** •
  669 9th Ave [W 46th St]
  212 664 9463
  Good suggestions from the staff.
- **Pan Aqua Diving** • 460 W 43rd St [10th Ave]
  212-736-3483
  SCUBA equipment and courses.

- **Poseidon Greek Bakery** •
  629 9th Ave [W 44th St]
  212-757-6173
  Old-school Greek delicacies like spanakopita.
- **Sea Breeze Fish Market** •
  541 9th Ave [W 40th St]
  212 563 7537
  Bargains on fresh seafood.
- **Sullivan Street Bakery** •
  533 W 47th St [11th Ave]
  212-265-5580
  Artisan breads, foodie approved. NFT approved. God approved.
- **Tumi** • 10 Columbus Cir [8th Ave]
  212-823-9390
  When your luggage gets lost and insurance is paying.
- **Whole Foods** • 10 Columbus Cir [8th Ave]
  212-823-9600
  "Whole Paycheck" everywhere except NYC, where it beats Food Emporium.

Map 12 • **Midtown**

Neighborhood Overview

Map 12

14 15
11 12 13
8 9 10
5 6 7

Welcome to the heart of everything—clogged arteries and all. An utter tourist hell to some, Midtown may also be where you slave away in an antiseptic glass tower for more than half your waking day. But while many avoid the area altogether, **Times Square** and its side streets possess ample virtues. If you can tolerate the slow walkers, group photos, and incessant invitations to comedy shows, you'll be rewarded with some of New York's finest art and most impressive architecture, the brightest lights this side of Tokyo, world-famous hotels and cathedrals, a pair of iconic animal statues, and of course a little animal known as Broadway.

Topping our Midtown list is **The Museum of Modern Art**. Yes, it's pricey and gets packed on the weekend, but the art will blow your mind and the sculpture garden is divine. Bargain tip: it's free on Friday evenings. If you still enjoy the smell and feel of real-live books, the main branch of the **New York Public Library** (guarded by the famous lion statues *Patience* and *Fortitude*) is spectacular. Inside, visit the Map Room and The Rose Main ReadingRoom, one of the most beautiful spaces in the world to get lost in a book. Right outside, you can bask on the lawn of beautiful **Bryant Park**, stare up at the sky, and transcend the chaos of the city. At least until a pigeon poops on you or a swarm of moviegoers tramples your mellow.

For a dose of glamour and history, stop in at the **Algonquin Hotel**, where famous writers, entertainers, and socialites used to cavort and carouse in the 1920s. To see how the ultra-rich used to (and still) live, pop into the gorgeous **Plaza Hotel**. If you have a small fortune lying around unused, we hear the Edwardian Suite is quite suitable. Gaze at the exquisite, 1908 facade of the **Alwyn Court Apartments** and decide if you would rather live behind those walls or just look at them like a fine sculpture. When it's movie time, catch it at the plush, gold-trimmed **Ziegfeld Theatre**, which boasts the biggest screen in the city.

Times Square is the dominion of tourists, but it's worth sneaking in late at night when they're back in their hotels, so you can check out the cool pedestrian plaza where the street used to be (though we kind of miss the comfy lawn chairs from the first summer they tried it). One of the area's greatest assets, of course, is the Broadway theatre scene. If you need cheap tickets to a play or musical, weave through the crowds to the **TKTS** booth. After braving the line, grab a seat on the actually-really-awesome bleachers that climb over the booth like a staircase. The real gems, though, can be found on the periphery of the square, including the striking **New York Times Building**, the exhibits at **Discovery Times Square** (brave the tourists—it's worth it!), and the rare tourist-free bar, **Jimmy's Corner**.

Midtown is home to oodles of thrilling architecture. Arguably, the most exciting is the **Hearst Tower**, a stunning masterpiece blending old and new, and the first "green" skyscraper in New York. Sprouting through the roof of the original 1928 building is an angular tower built with recycled steel, completed in 2006. Duck into the lobby to check out the one-of-a-kind water sculpture. Other architectural highlights include **Carnegie Hall**, **St. Patrick's Cathedral**, **St. Thomas Church**, **Villard House**, **Rockefeller Center**, **One Bryant Park**, and the **American Radiator Building**. And finally, don't miss the trippy **Austrian Cultural Forum**, which hosts a number of events open to the public.

For a change of pace, check out **Little Brazil**'s small strip of restaurants, bars (some with live music), and shops. Or go north a block to the famous **Diamond District**, which appeared in the 1940s when orthodox Jews transplanted here from war-torn Europe. Finally, stare up at **The Debt Clock** and wonder how this nation's permanent structural deficit will likely bankrupt your theoretical grandchildren. You may decide you need a drink after seeing how the debt-to-GDP ratio creeps inexorably ever upward; on second thought, make that a double.

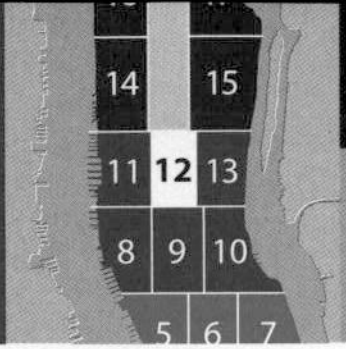

Map 12 | 14 | 15

11 | 12 | 13

8 | 9 | 10

5 | 6 | 7

Midtown

O Landmarks

- **30 Rockefeller Plaza** •
  30 Rockefeller Plaza [W 51st St]
  Tallest building at Rock Center;
  RCA = GE = Comcast.
- **Algonquin Hotel** • 59 W 44th St [6th Ave]
  212-840-6800
  Where snark was invented.
- **Alwyn Court Apartments** •
  180 W 58th St [7th Ave]
  100-year-old apartment building with
  awesomely detailed exterior.
- **American Radiator Building** •
  40 W 40th St [6th Ave]
  Massive gold-and-black Art Deco gem looms
  over Bryant Park.
- **Bryant Park** • 6th Ave & W 42nd St
  Summer movies, winter ice-skating, hook-ups
  year round.
- **Carnegie Hall** • 881 7th Ave [W 57th St]
  212-247-7800
  Stock up on free cough drops in the lobby.
- **The Debt Clock** • 6th Ave & W 44th St
  How much the US has borrowed—pennies,
  really.
- **Diamond District** •
  W 47th St b/n 5th & 6th Ave
  Big rocks abound! Center of the world's
  diamond industry.
- **Hearst Tower** • 300 W 57th St [8th Ave]
  It's green! It's mean! It's fit to be seen!
- **Little Brazil** • W 46th St b/n 5th & 6th Ave
  Small stretch of Brazilian businesses. Gisele
  not included.
- **Museum of Modern Art (MoMA)** •
  11 W 53rd St [5th Ave]
  212-708-9400
  Is there anything these Rockefellers don't do?
- **New York Public Library** •
  5th Ave & W 42nd St
  917-275-6975
  Wonderful Beaux-Arts building with stunning
  reading room.
- **New York Times Building** •
  8th Ave & W 40th St
  Renzo Piano's impressive new home for The
  Gray Lady.
- **One Bryant Park** • 1111 6th Ave [W 42nd St]
  212-764-0694
  New York's third-tallest building: sleek,
  elegant, and environmentally friendly.

- **The Plaza Hotel** • 768 5th Ave [W 58th St]
  212-759-3000
  Now anyone can be Eloise with her own Plaza
  condo.
- **Rockefeller Center** •
  45 Rockefeller Plaza [W 49th St]
  212-332-6868
  Sculpture, ice skating, and a mall!
- **St. Patrick's Cathedral** • 5th Ave & E 51st St
  212-753-2261
  NYC's classic cathedral.
- **Times Square** • 7th Ave & W 42nd St
  It looks even cooler than it does on TV!
- **TKTS** • Broadway & W 47th St
  Get cheap Broadway tix underneath the cool
  looking stairs.
- **Villard House** • 457 Madison Ave [E 51st St]
  Killer brownstone palazzos by holy fathers
  McKim, Mead & White.
- **Ziegfeld Theatre** • 141 W 54th St [6th Ave]
  212-765-7600
  Glorious 1969 movie palace. 1,100 seats and
  red carpeting.

☕ Coffee

- **Blue Bottle Coffee** •
  1 Rockefeller Ctr [5th Ave]
  Cult coffee that's more lab than shop.
- **Blue Bottle Coffee** •
  54 W 40th St [6th Ave]
  Bryant Park outpost of cult coffee masters.
- **FIKA** • 41 W 58th St [5th Ave]
  212-832-0022
  Swedish oasis in Midtown: strong coffee and
  homemade pastries.
- **Zibetto** • 1385 6th Ave [W 56th St]
  A real Italian espresso bar. Un caffe, per favore

⭕ Farmers Markets

- **Rockefeller Center Greenmarket** •
  W 50th St & Rockefeller Plaza
  Wed, Thur & Fri, 8 am–6 pm, Jul–Sept

Grab a cocktail at the elegant and laid-back **Faces & Names**, or belly up to the bar at **Jimmy's Corner** for a beer and a shot. Bowl some frames at, uh, **Frames** in Port Authority or the nearby **Bowlmor Lanes**. Other options: **Iridium** for jazz, **King Cole** for class, **Caroline's** or **HA!** for comedy, or escape it all on the patio of **Bookmarks**.

Nightlife

- **Arena** • 135 W 41st St [Broadway]
  212-278-0988
  Anything goes excess is back, albeit in midtown.
- **Blue Bar** • 59 W 44th St [6th Ave]
  212-840-6800
  If you're in the mood for a Harvey Wallbanger.
- **Bookmarks** • 299 Madison Ave [E 41st St]
  212-204-5498
  Escape the Midtown ruckus at this nifty rooftop bar.
- **The Carnegie Club** • 156 W 56th St [7th Ave]
  212-957-9676
  Drink your 50-year-old cognac with your 22-year-old date.
- **Caroline's on Broadway** •
  1626 Broadway [W 50th St]
  212-757-4100
  Laughs in Times Square. A classic.
- **Dave & Busters** • 234 W 42nd St [6th Ave]
  646-495-2015
  Another dateless Friday night.
- **Emmett O'Lunney's Irish Pub** •
  210 W 50th St [Broadway]
  212-957-5100
  Above-average Irish pub popular with the after-work crowd.
- **Faces & Names** • 159 W 54th St [7th Ave]
  212-380-9311
  Fabulous staff, elegant vibe, superb bar and very good food.
- **Flute** • 205 W 54th St [7th Ave]
  212-265-5169
  Munch on strawberries and cream with your bubbly.
- **Heartland Brewery** • 127 W 43rd St [6th Ave]
  646-366-0235
  Heartland HeartLAND HEARTLAND!
- **The House of Brews** • 302 W 51st St [8th Ave]
  212-541-7080
  Fratty but friendly atmosphere, great beer selection.
- **Iridium Jazz Club** •
  1650 Broadway [W 51st St]
  212-582-2121
  Good mainstream jazz venue. Pricey.

- **Jimmy's Corner** • 140 W 44th St [Broadway]
  212-221-9510
  This cozy joint is the best bar around here. trust us.
- **Judge Roy Bean Public House** •
  38 W 56th St [5th Ave]
  212-262-8300
  When you need a craft beer in Midtown.
- **King Cole Bar** • 2 E 55th St [5th Ave]
  212-339-6857
  Drink a red snapper and admire the gorgeous mural.
- **Paramount Bar** • 235 W 46th St [Broadway]
  212 827 4116
  Tiny, pretentious, unavoidable.
- **Point Break** • 12 W 45th St [5th Ave]
  212-391-8053
  No Swayze or Keanu. Just drunken Midtown office slaves.
- **R Lounge** • 714 7th Ave [W 48th St]
  212-261-5200
  Sip cocktails with (gulp) tourists and take in the fine view.
- **Royalton Hotel** • 44 W 44th St [5th Ave]
  212-869-4400
  Starck + Schrager = cool.
- **The Rum House** • 228 W 47th St [Broadway]
  646-490-6924
  Dive smell gone, but fun still remains.
- **Russian Vodka Room** •
  265 W 52nd St [8th Ave]
  212-307-5835
  Russian moods and cranberry vodka. Awesome.
- **Sardi's** • 234 W 44th St [7th Ave]
  212-221-8440
  Absorb the sacred DNA at the upstairs bar.
- **View Lounge** • 1535 Broadway [W 46th St]
  212-704-8900
  Down a drink on the 48th floor, then get out.
- **Whiskey Trader** • 71 W 55th St [6th Ave]
  212-582-2223
  Awesome lounge/sports bar hybrid with good drink specials.

Map 12

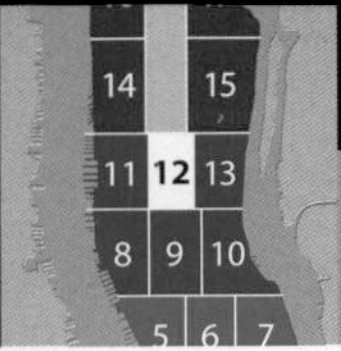

14 15
11 12 13
8 9 10
5 6 7

Midtown

🍴Restaurants

- **21 Club** • 21 W 52nd St [5th Ave]
212-582-7200 • $$$$
Old, clubby New York.
- **Akdeniz** • 19 W 46th St [5th Ave]
212-575-2307 • $$
Turkish oasis in Midtown.
- **Angelo's Pizza** • 1697 Broadway [W 53rd St]
212-245-8811 • $$
For total tourist pizza, it ain't half bad.
- **Applejack Diner** • 230 W 55th St [Broadway]
212-586-6075 •
Endless cup of coffee.
- **Aureole** • 135 W 42nd St [Madison Ave]
212-319-1660 • $$$$
Well-done but unimaginative.
- **BG** • 754 5th Ave [W 57th St]
212-872-8977 • $$$$$
Another reason to spend the whole day at
Bergdorf's.
- **Big Apple Deli** • 219 E Broadway
646-858-3111 • $
Standard deli, excellent selection, accurate
orders, not a chain.
- **Blue Fin** • 1567 Broadway [W 47th St]
212-918-1400 • $$$
Sleek, stylish seafood & sushi spot in the W
Hotel.
- **Brasserie 8 1/2** • 9 W 57th St [5th Ave]
212-829-0812 • $$$$$
A must for brunch. Lovely for cocktails and
dinner too.
- **Burger Joint** • 119 W 56th St [6th Ave]
212-708-7414 • $
Fancy hotel lobby leads to unexpected burger
dive. Awesome.
- **Cafe Zaiya** • 18 E 41st St [Madison Ave]
212-779-0600 • $$
Japanese food court that's cheap and fast.
- **Carmine's** • 200 W 44th St [7th Ave]
212-221-3800 • $$$
Pre-theater Italian standby with ungodly
portions.

- **Carnegie Deli** • 854 7th Ave [W 55th St]
212-757-2245 • $$$
Still good. Still really, really good.
- **Cold Stone Creamery** •
253 W 42nd St [8th Ave]
212-398-1882 • $
Because ice cream without trendiness ain't
worth a lick.
- **Cosmic Diner** • 888 8th Ave [W 53rd St]
212-333-5888 • $
Great food, large portions, they do take out.
- **Estiatorio Milos** • 125 W 55th St [6th Ave]
212-245-7400 • $$$$
Fancified Greek food for people with expense
accounts.
- **Faces & Names** • 159 W 54th St [7th Ave]
212-586-9311 • $$
Fabulous staff, elegant vibe, superb bar, and
very good food.
- **FIKA** • 41 W 58th St [5th Ave]
212-832-0022 • $
Great Swedish take-out sandwiches and
salads.
- **Gabriel Kreuther** • 41 W 42nd St [6th Ave]
212-257-5826 • $$$$$
Danny Meyer alum's Alsatian-inflected
four-star dining experience.
- **Haru** • 229 W 43rd St [7th Ave]
212-398-9810 • $$$$
Excellent mid-range Japanese. Loud, good.
- **Indian Accent** • 123 W 56th St [6th Ave]
212-842-8070 • $$$$
Elegant, high-end Indian cuisine; nary a steam
table in sight.
- **Joe's Shanghai** • 24 W 56th St [5th Ave]
212-333-3868 • $$
Uptown version of killer dumpling factory.
- **John's Pizzeria** • 260 W 44th St [8th Ave]
212-391-7560 • $$
A tad touristy, but fantastic pizza and a great
space.

There's something for every taste in this area. Greasy burgers tucked inside a fancy hotel at **Burger Joint**, cheap but *ah-mazing* chicken parm at **Luigi's**, street food at the halal cart at **53rd & 6th**. For high-end experiences, savor the French-American fare at **The Modern**, the seafood at **Le Bernadin**, David Chang's **Ma Peche**, or the vintage charms of **21 Club**. **Carnegie** is a standby deli, with its overstuffed sandwiches and autographed headshots on the wall.

- **La Bonne Soupe** • 48 W 55th St [5th Ave]
  212-586-7650 • $$
  Ooh la la, the best salad dressing accompanies my soupe a l'oignon.
- **Le Bernardin** • 155 W 51st St [7th Ave]
  212-554-1515 • $$$$$
  Top NYC seafood.
- **Luigi's Gourmet Pizza** •
  936 8th Ave [W 55th St]
  212-265-7159 • $$
  Best chicken parm under $20 in town.
- **Mangia** • 50 W 57th St [6th Ave]
  212-582-5882 • $
  Caterers with a café.
- **Margon** • 136 W 46th St [7th Ave]
  212-354-5013 • $
  Great Cuban sandwiches but the coffee is the real hit.
- **The Modern** • 9 W 53rd St [5th Ave]
  212-333-1220 • $$$$
  With gnocchi to die for, spend a lot and then STILL splurge on dessert.
- **Molyvos** • 871 7th Ave [W 56th St]
  212-582-7500 • $$$
  Top Greek. Someday we'll check it out w/ your credit card.
- **Nobu 57** • 40 W 57th St [5th Ave]
  212-757-3000 • $$$$$
  Uptown branch of wildly popular and renowned downtown sushi joints.
- **Norma's** • 119 W 56th St [6th Ave]
  212-708-7460 • $$$$
  Inventive and upscale brunch. Cool menus.
- **Obica Mozzarella Bar** •
  590 Madison Ave [E 57th St]
  212-355-2217 • $$
  A strange but tasty concept.
- **Oceana** • 120 W 49th St [6th Ave]
  212-759-5941 • $$$$$
  Le Bernadin Jr.
- **The Palm Restaurant** •
  250 W 50th St [8th Ave]
  212-333-7256 • $$$$
  Upscale but friendly, everything is delicious and staff is superb.
- **Park Italian Gourmet** • 60 W 45th St [6th Ave]
  212-382-0580 • $
  How is this old-school sandwich shop still here? Go today for lunch.
- **Petrossian** • 182 W 58th St [7th Ave]
  212-245-2214 • $$$$$
  The decor's not updated, but the fare is FINE.

- **Pongsri** • 244 W 48th St [Broadway]
  212-582-3392 • $$
  Great, spicy Thai.
- **Pret a Manger** • 135 W 50th St [6th Ave]
  212-409-6150 • $
  British sandwich chain.
- **Pret a Manger** • 1350 6th Ave [W 54th St]
  212-307-6100 • $
  British sandwich chain.
- **Redeye Grill** • 890 7th Ave [W 56th St]
  212-541-9000 • $$$
  Sprawling and diverse.
- **Robert** • 2 Columbus Cir [W 58th St]
  212-299-7730 • $$$$$
  Posh dining atop the Museum of Arts & Design. Someone take us, please?
- **Russian Samovar** • 256 W 52nd St [8th Ave]
  212-757-0168 • $$$
  Classic Russian food and flavored vodkas.
- **The Russian Tea Room** •
  150 W 57th St [7th Ave]
  212-581-7100 • $$$$$
  Exquisite Russian dining experience & New York icon.
- **Sofrito** • 244 W 57th St [Broadway]
  212-754-5999 • $$
  Mofongo for the gods.
- **Thalia** • 828 8th Ave [W 50th St]
  212-399-4444 • $$$
  Chic atmosphere, excellent food.
- **Tina's Cuban Cuisine** • 23 W 56th St [5th Ave]
  212-315-4313 • $$
  Straight up classics like rice, beans, roast pork and plantains.
- **Toloache** • 251 W 50th St [8th Ave]
  212-581-1818 • $$$
  Designer Mexican in Midtown.
- **Virgil's Real BBQ** • 152 W 44th St [6th Ave]
  212-921-9494 • $$$
  It's real. Hush puppies and CFS to die for.

Map 12

Midtown

Shopping

- **Apple Store (Fifth Avenue)** •
  767 5th Ave [E 59th St]
  212-336-1440
  Giant glass shrine houses all things Apple.
- **Bergdorf Goodman** • 754 5th Ave [W 57th St]
  212-753-7300
  Hands down—the best windows in the
  business.
- **Billy's Bakery** • 1 W 59th St [Central Park S]
  646-755-3237
  Yummiest treats this side of homemade.
- **Burberry** • 9 E 57th St [5th Ave]
  212-407-7100
  Signature "beige plaid" purveyor.
- **Chanel** • 15 E 57th St [5th Ave]
  212-355-0050
  Official outfitter of "ladies who lunch."
- **Drama Book Shop** • 250 W 40th St [7th Ave]
  212-944-0595
  Alas, poor Yorick…

- **Ermenegildo Zegna** • 663 5th Ave [E 57th St]
  212-421-4488
  A truly stylish and classic Italian designer.
- **Forever 21** • 1540 Broadway [W 45th St]
  212-302-0594
  Open til 1 am, lifesaver during late-night
  wardrobe emergencies.
- **Henri Bendel** • 712 5th Ave [W 56th St]
  212-247-1100
  Offbeat department store specializing in the
  unusual and harder-to-find.
- **Mets Clubhouse Shop** •
  11 W 42nd St [5th Ave]
  212-768-9534
  For Amazin' stuff!
- **MoMA Design and Book Store** •
  11 W 53rd St [5th Ave]
  212-708-9700
  Cutting-edge, minimalist, ergonomic, offbeat,
  and funky everything.
- **Muji Times Square** • 620 8th Ave [W 40th St]
  212-382-2300
  Like a Japanese IKEA, but cooler and without
  meatballs.

Midtown

Midtown is home to one of the great world shopping districts. Legendary retailers like **Bergdorf Goodman** and **Saks Fifth Avenue** are majestic retail palaces, while numerous boutiques and flagships for individual brands jostle for position. In **Times Square**, there are several touristy chains, as well as a **Forever 21** that's open until 1 a.m. and comes in handy for late-night wardrobe emergencies. For unique finds, check out **MoMA Design Store** or **Muji**, and stock up on spirits at **Park Avenue Liquor** or **Oak and Steel**.

• **Oak and Steel Fine Wines & Spirits** •
1776 Broadway [W 57th St]
212-262-7702
Excellent selection, very knowledgeable staff.

• **Park Avenue Liquor Shop** •
270 Madison Ave [E 41st St]
212-685-2442
Amazing selection of scotch. Makes us wish we had more $$$.

• **Petrossian Boutique** •
911 7th Ave [W 58th St]
212-245-2217
Caviar and other delectables. Bring the Gold Card.

• **Roberto's Winds** • 149 W 46th St [6th Ave]
212-391-1315
Saxophones, horns, clarinets, and flutes. If it blows, bring it here.

• **Saks Fifth Avenue** • 611 5th Ave [E 49th St]
212-753-4000
Fifth Avenue mainstay with lovely holiday windows and bathrooms.

• **Steinway & Sons** • 109 W 57th St [6th Ave]
212-246-1100
Cheap knockoff pianos. Just kidding.

• **The Store at Museum of Arts and Design** •
2 Columbus Cir [8th Ave]
212-299-7700
Not your average museum store.

• **Sunrise Mart** • 12 E 41st St [5th Ave]
646-380-9280
Pick up a bento box, lunch special or Japanese groceries.

• **Tiffany & Co.** • 727 5th Ave [E 56th St]
212-755-8000
Grande dame of the little blue box.

• **Uniqlo** • 666 5th Ave [W 52nd St]
877-486-4756
Japanese t shirts and more T-shirts—in every color!

Map 13 · **East Midtown**

E 61st St

Lexington Avenue/ 59th Street

15

N R W

E 60th St

ROOSEVELT ISLAND TRAMWAY

Queensboro Bridge

59th Street

4 5 6

Roosevelt Island Tram

E 59th St

E 58th St

Sutton Place

FDR Dr

E 57th St

Sutton Place

A

E 56th St

Central Synagogue

E 55th St

E 54th St

Citicorp Center

E M

Lexington Ave 53rd Street

E 53rd St

The Lever House

51st Street

Seagram Building

6

The Seven Year Itch

E 52nd St

112

St. Bartholomew's Church

General Electric Building

E 51st St

E 50th St

Waldorf Astoria

Beekman Pl

First Ave

Mitchell Pl

General D MacArthur Plaza

East River

E 49th St

E 48th St

Second Ave

Third Ave

Lexington Avenue

Park Ave

Madison Ave

E 47th St

Dag Hammarskjold Plaza

Peace Garden

E 46th St

E 45th St

United Nations Plaza

B

Vanderbilt Ave

PAGE 318

Grand Central Terminal

Depew Pl

E 44th St (Archbishop Fulton J Sheen Pl)

United Nations

PAGE 286

E 43rd St

Grand Central 42nd Street

4 5 6

7 S

Chrysler Building

Chanin Building

E 42nd St

Daily News Building

Tudor City

Tudor City Pl

Queens Midtown Tun

To Queens

Robert Moses Playground

E 41st St

E 40th St

Exit St

Entrance St

E 39th St

10

FDR Dr

E 38th St

| 1/4 mile | .25 km |

Neighborhood Overview

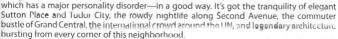
No matter how angry, late, or tired we are from dealing with the overwhelming crowds in this part of town, one glance up at Grand Central Terminal with the Chrysler Building looming in the background never fails to give us a burst of energy and a shot of civic pride. Welcome to East Midtown, which has a major personality disorder—in a good way. It's got the tranquility of elegant Sutton Place and Tudor City, the rowdy nightlife along Second Avenue, the commuter bustle of Grand Central, the international crowd around the UN, and legendary architecture bursting from every corner of this neighborhood.

The hub of this neighborhood—and arguably the city—is **Grand Central Terminal**. One of the busiest train stations in the world, this gorgeous building also houses many hidden surprises under its vaunted ceiling. Start in the main concourse where you'll see a magnificent clock above the information booth. This spot is what New Yorkers mean when they say, "Meet me at the clock." Some of these meet ups turn into dates at the deluxe and hard-to-find cocktail lounge **Campbell Apartment**. Others wisely opt for a trip into the world of old-school New York dining at the highly recommended **Oyster Bar**. Ask to sit in the Saloon for a real treat. Shopping options abound here with lots of cool shops (books, MTA souvenirs, etc.) and the best food shopping in Midtown at **Grand Central Market**.

You may have heard of a little organization called the **United Nations**. It's housed in an iconic glass building perched on the edge of the East River. We highly recommend the public tour where you get to see the General Assembly, an amazing art collection, and international diplomats scurrying about. Currently the UN headquarters is undergoing a massive $3 billion renovation. The project is estimated to be completed around the same time the UN finally ends world poverty. We can still dream, right?

Architecture nerds rave and worship at Mies van der Rohe's **Seagram Building**, argue over the value of Phillip Johnson's **Lipstick Building**, and contemplate the public art underneath **The Lever House**. One of the city's most unique places of worship is the **Central Synagogue** with vivid Moorish details. Stroll by at night for an otherworldly experience. **St. Bart's** on Park Avenue is gorgeous in a more traditional way, while the **Chrysler Building**, **Chanin Building**, and **General Electric Building** (570 Lexington) are worshiped for their Art Deco brilliance.

If you want a break from all the tall buildings, check out the **Seven Year Itch** subway grate where Marilyn Monroe's dress blows up for all the world to see. Head way east to walk down **Sutton Place** to see where lots of exclusive New Yorkers take up residence. Or stroll around Tudor City and marvel at the handsome Neo-Gothic apartments that diplomats and divas call home. It's a nice way to unwind and enjoy this unique urban enclave without having to drop $2.7 gazillion on a condo.

Not many budget drinking options around here (except **Blarney Stone**), so go highbrow at **The Brasserie** inside The Seagram Building, **Campbell Apartment** inside Grand Central, **World Bar** inside the Trump Tower, or **Sir Harry's** inside the Waldorf. If you like to drink with the suits after work, **PJ Clarke's** is your spot.

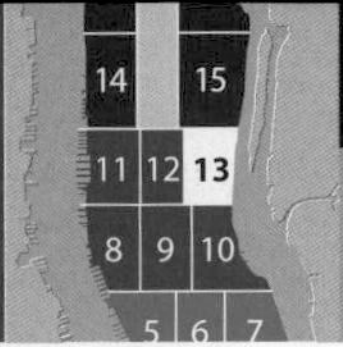

Map 13

East Midtown

O Landmarks

- **Chanin Building** •
  122 E 42nd St [Lexington Ave]
  Not the Chrysler, but still a way-cool Art Deco masterpiece.
- **Chrysler Building** •
  405 Lexington Ave [E 42nd St]
  212-682-3070
  The stuff of Art Deco dreams. Wish the Cloud Club was still there.
- **Citicorp Center** •
  153 E 53rd St [Lexington Ave]
  How does it stand up?
- **Daily News Building** •
  220 E 42nd St [2nd Ave]
  Great Caesar's ghost! An Art Deco gem.
- **General Electric Building** •
  570 Lexington Ave [51st St]
  Ornate 50-story Art Deco-Gothic tower.
- **Grand Central Terminal** •
  89 E 42nd St [Park Ave]
  212-340-2583
  Another Beaux-Arts masterpiece. Ceiling, staircases, tiles, clock, Oyster Bar, all great.
- **The Lever House** • 390 Park Ave [E 54th St]
  Great example of modernism, but even better, it's so fresh and so clean!
- **Lipstick Building** • 885 3rd Ave [E 53rd St]
  Philip Johnson does New York, deliriously (well).
- **Seagram Building** • 375 Park Ave [E 53rd St]
  Or, "how to be a modernist in 3 easy steps!"
- **The Seven Year Itch** •
  E 52nd St & Lexington Ave
  Marilyn Monroe's lucky subway grate.
- **St. Bartholomew's Church** •
  325 Park Ave [E 51st St]
  212-378-0022
  Brilliant Byzantine-style church with great dome, performances, etc.
- **Sutton Place** • Sutton Pl b/n E 57th & E 59th St
  Quiet, exclusive little lane for the rich and sometimes famous.
- **Tudor City** • Tudor City Place [E 42nd St]
  3000 apartments in "American" Tudor style. Hmmmm.
- **United Nations** • 405 E 42nd St [1st Ave]
  212-963-8687
  NYC is the capital of the planet. Just sayin'.
- **Waldorf Astoria** • 301 Park Ave [E 49th St]
  212-355-3000
  Great hotel, although the public spaces aren't up to the Plaza's.

Coffee

- **Aroma Espresso Bar** • 205 E 42nd St [3rd Ave]
  212-557-1010
  The Israeli version of Starbucks comes stateside.
- **Cosi** • 60 E 56th St [Madison Ave]
  212-588-1225
- **Ground Central** • 155 E 52nd St [3rd Ave]
  646-964-4438
  Hip coffee shop in Midtown? How times have changed.
- **Ground Central** • 800 2nd Ave [E 43rd St]
  646-484-5697
  Pour-overs and boxes to go; open weekends, too.
- **Joe The Art of Coffee** •
  44 Grand Central Terminal [Park Ave]
  212-661-8580
  Located in the Graybar passage off Lexington Ave.
- **Macchiato Espresso Bar** •
  141 E 44th St [Lexington Ave]
  212-867-6772
  Nice coffee shop for this part of town.

Farmers Markets

- **Dag Hammarskjold Plaza Greenmarket** •
  E 47th St & 2nd Ave
  Wed 8 am–4 pm, Year Round

East Midtown

Map 13

The Oyster Bar should be on any New Yorker's list of must eats.
Aquavit's Scandinavian Sunday buffet brunch is as amazing as it is
expensive. **Sakagura** is a great option for Japanese and sake, while
Sushi Yasada has the best raw fish in the city. For a classic NYC burger,
PJ Clarke's is a good bet.

Nightlife

- **Blarney Stone** • 710 3rd Ave [E 45th St]
  212 490-0457
  The only bar in purgatory.
- **The Campbell Apartment** •
  15 Vanderbilt Ave [E 42nd St]
  212-953-0409
  Awesome space, awesomely snooty!
- **Le Bateau Ivre** • 230 E 51st St [2nd Ave]
  212-583-0579
  Open 'til 4 am. French wine bar.
- **Lips** • 227 E 56th St [3rd Ave]
  212-675-7710
  Drag shows, bitchy bingo, fierce lip syncing,
  good campy fun.
- **P.J. Clarke's** • 915 3rd Ave [E 55th St]
  212-317-1616
  Old-timey midtown pub with burgers, beers,
  and bankers.
- **Sofia Wine Bar & Café** •
  242 E 50th St [2nd Ave]
  212-888-8660
  Italian wine bar, plus food goodies…
- **The World Bar** •
  845 United Nations Plaza [E 46th St]
  212-935-9361
  Expensive, classy hideaway for diplomats and
  Derek Jeter

Restaurants

- **99 Cents Fresh Pizza** • 151 E 43rd St [3rd Ave]
  212-922-0257 • $
  Fresh slice of pizza for 99 cents. Deal of the
  century.
- **Agern** • 89 E 42nd St [Park Ave]
  646-568-4018 • $$$$$
  Elegant, pedigreed local/seasonal
  contemporary Nordic cuisine.
- **Amma** • 246 E 51st St [2nd Ave]
  212 644-0330 • $$$$
  Posh Indian worth the $$$. In Midtown, no
  less.
- **Aquavit** • 65 E 55th St [Park Ave]
  212-307-7311 • $$$$$
  Stellar dining experience: top-drawer
  Scandinavian.
- **BLT Steak** • 106 E 57th St [Park Ave]
  212-752-7470 • $$$$$
  Pricey and good, not great.
- **Chola** • 232 E 58th St [3rd Ave]
  212-688-4619 • $$$$
  Pricey south Indian cuisine.
- **Cipriani Dolci** • 87 E 42nd St [Park Ave]
  212-973-0999 • $$$
  Eat with people richer than you on the West
  Balcony of Grand Central.
- **Cipriani Le Specialità** •
  110 E 42nd St [Park Ave]
  212 499-0599 • $$$
  Fancy, ya know.
- **Comfort Diner** • 214 E 45th St [3rd Ave]
  212-867-4555 • $$
  A hearty breakfast is served.
- **Cosi** • 60 E 56th St [Madison Ave]
  212-588-1225 • $
  Sandwiches for the masses.
- **Dawat** • 210 E 58th St [3rd Ave]
  212-355-7555 • $$$$
  Top-end Indian.
- **Docks Oyster Bar** • 633 3rd Ave [E 40th St]
  212-986-8080 • $$$$
  Great seafood, good atmosphere.
- **Ess-A-Bagel** • 831 3rd Ave [E 51st St]
  212-980-1010 • $
  Bagels with attitude.
- **Felidia** • 243 E 58th St [3rd Ave]
  212-758-1479 • $$$$
  Top Northern Italian.
- **The Four Seasons** • 99 E 52nd St [Park Ave]

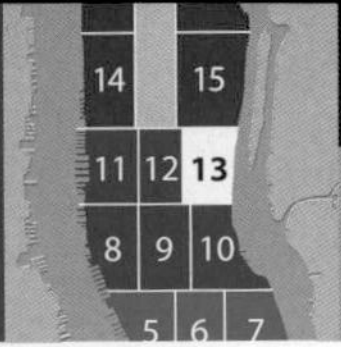

Map 13

East Midtown

212-754-9494 • $$$$$
Designer everything. Even the cotton candy.
• **Grand Central Oyster Bar** •
89 E 42nd St [Park Ave]
212-490-6650 • $$$
Classic New York seafood joint. Go for the Saloon.
• **Gulluoglu Baklava & Cafe** •
982 2nd Ave [E 52nd St]
212-813-0500 • $
Baklava airlifted from Istanbul.
• **Hide-Chan Ramen** • 248 E 52nd St [2nd Ave]
212-813-1800 • $$
This broth is porktastic.
• **La Fonda Del Sol** • 200 Park Ave
212-867-6767 • $$$$
Excellent tapas in a semi-corporate setting.
• **Le Bateau Ivre** • 230 E 51st St [2nd Ave]
212-583-0579 • $$$
French, open 'till 4 am.
• **Le Relais De Venise L'Entrecote** •
590 Lexington Ave [E 52nd St]
212-758-3989 • $$$
Good steak frites and salad via Paris.
• **Lexington Brass** •
517 Lexington Ave [E 48th St]
212-392-5976 • $$$
Gastropub grub and a stellar brunch, not bad for Midtown.
• **Little Collins** • 667 Lexington Ave [E 56th St]
212-308-1969 • $$
Excellent coffee shop with Aussie accents.
• **Momosan** • 342 Lexington Ave [40th St]
646-201-5529 • $$$
Iron Chef-caliber ramen in sleek Midtown digs.
• **Monkey Bar** • 60 E 54th St [Madison Ave]
212-288-1010 • $$$$
Graydon Carter does Midtown with old-New York menu.
• **Mr Chow** • 324 E 57th St [2nd Ave]
212-751-9030 • $$$
Decades-old upscale Chinese joint focusing on Beijing cuisine (duck!).
• **New York Luncheonette** •
135 E 50th St [Lexington Ave]
212-838-0165 • $$
Diner where Obama lunched with Bloomy.

• **Num Pang** • 140 E 41st St [Lexington Ave]
212-867-8889 • $$
Not your average Cambodian midtown office sandwich.
• **P.J. Clarke's** • 915 3rd Ave [E 55th St]
212-317-1616 • $$$
Pub grub. A fine burger.
• **Palm One Too** • 837 2nd Ave [E 45th St]
212-687-2953 • $$$$$
Steaks and chops. Go to Luger's.
• **Aretsky's Patroon** • 160 E 46th St [3rd Ave]
212-883-7373 • $$$$
An oasis of civility.
• **Pershing Square** • 90 E 42nd St [Park Ave]
212-286-9600 • $$$$
Excellent food and awesome space.
• **Rosa Mexicano** • 1063 1st Ave [E 58th St]
212-753-7407 • $$$$
Inventive Mexican. Great guac.
• **Sakagura** • 211 E 43rd St [3rd Ave]
212-953-7253 • $$$
Midtowners are very happy to have this excellent izakaya.
• **Shun Lee Palace** •
155 E 55th St [Lexington Ave]
212-371-8844 • $$$$$
Top-end Chinese.
• **Sidecar at PJ Clarke's** • 205 E 55th St [3rd Ave]
212-317-2044 • $$$$$
P. J. Clarke's quieter, more refined restaurant sibling.
• **Smith & Wollensky** • 797 3rd Ave [E 49th St]
212-753-1530 • $$$$$
Don't order the fish.
• **Soba Totto** • 211 E 43rd St [3rd Ave]
212-557-8200 • $$$
Dig into noodles next to Japanese office workers. Top lunch deals.
• **Sparks Steak House** • 210 E 46th St [3rd Ave]
212-687-4855 • $$$$$
If you can't go to Luger's.

East Midtown

The Food Emporium under bridge is actually kind of cool and the New York Transit Museum Gallery Annex and Store has fun gift ideas. Sherry Lehmann has a ridiculous selection of fancy booze you can't afford. And there's a Home Depot in a basement on 59th Street? That's just plain weird.

• **Sushi Yasuda** • 204 E 43rd St [3rd Ave]
212-972-1001 • $$$$
Best sushi in NYC. Let the debate begin…
• **Taksim** • 1030 2nd Ave [E 54th St]
212-421-3004 • $$$
All manner of Turkish delights.

🛍 Shopping

• **Amish Market** • 240 E 45th St [3rd Ave]
212-370-1761
Lots prepared foods. Do they deliver by horse and buggy?
• **Apple Store (Grand Central)** •
89 E 42nd St [Park Ave]
212-284-1800
Because Grand Central needs more people.
• **Architects & Designers Building** •
150 E 58th St [Lexington Ave]
212-644-2766
Over 200,000 sq. ft. of commercial and residential furnishings. Wow.
• **Beer Table 22** • Grand Central Terminal
[42nd St] 212-922-0008
Great craft beer to go, conveniently located in GCT
• **Buttercup Bake Shop** •
973 2nd Ave [E 52nd St]
212-350-4144
Move over Magnolia. Buttercup's all grown up.
• **Cohen & Taliaferro** •
59 E 54th St [Madison Ave]
212-751-8135
Antique maps and rare travel books. Cool!
• **Conrad's Bike Shop** •
25 Tudor City Pl [E 42nd St]
212-697-6966
Good Euro bikes. Sweet logo.
• **Crush Wine & Spirits** •
153 E 57th St [Lexington Ave]
212-980-9463
Stock up on booze to survive the walk through Midtown.
• **Food Emporium** • 401 E 59th St [1st Ave]
212-752-5897
Unique market design underneath the Queensboro Bridge.

• **Grand Central Market** •
87 E 42nd St [Park Ave]
212-878-7034
Pick up fixings for a gourmet dinner before jumping on the train.
• **Home Depot** • 980 3rd Ave [E 59th St]
212-888-1512
Mega home improvement chain comes to the city.
• **Ideal Cheese** • 942 1st Ave [E 52nd St]
888-743-1913
All cheese is ideal.
• **Innovative Audio Video** •
150 E 58th St [Lexington Ave]
212-634-4444
Quality music systems and home theaters.
• **New York Transit Museum Gallery Annex & Store** • Grand Central Terminal, Main Concourse [E 42nd St]
212-878-0106
Specialty—NYC/transit books.
• **Sherry-Lehmann Wine & Spirits** •
505 Park Ave [E 59th St]
212-838-7500
Wines and spirits for the connaisseur.
• **Sports Authority** • 845 3rd Ave [E 51st St]
212-355-9725
Sporting goods for the masses.
• **United Nations Bookshop** •
1st Ave & E 42nd St
212-963-7680
The UN's college bookstore: official reports, tchotchkes and T-shirts.
• **Urbanspace Vanderbilt** •
230 Park Ave [45th St]
646-747-0810
The ultimate foodie court.
• **Whole Foods** • 226 E 57th St [3rd Ave]
646-497-1222
"Whole Paycheck" but great, fresh food.
• **Yankees Clubhouse Shop** •
110 E 59th St [Park Ave]
212-758-7844
Any Yankee fan's paradise.

Map 14 · **Upper West Side (Lower)**

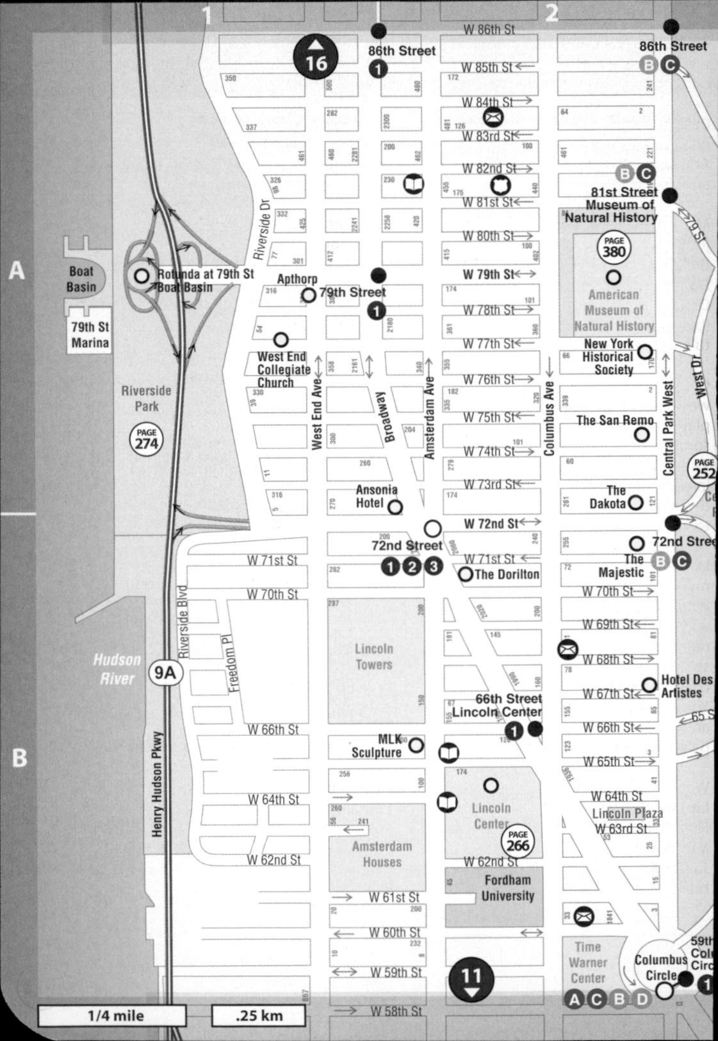

W 86th St

86th Street

16

86th Street

1

W 85th St

W 84th St

W 83rd St

W 82nd St

81st Street

Museum of
Natural History

PAGE
380

Riverside Dr

American
Museum of
Natural History

79th St
Marina

Boat
Basin

Rotunda at 79th St
Boat Basin

Apthorp

79th Street

W 79th St

W 78th St

W 77th St

New York
Historical
Society

West End
Collegiate
Church

Riverside
Park

PAGE
274

West End Ave

Broadway

Amsterdam Ave

W 76th St

W 75th St

The San Remo

W 74th St

Columbus Ave

W 73rd St

The
Dakota

PAGE
252

Ansonia
Hotel

W 72nd St

72nd Street

1 2 3

72nd Street

B C

The Dorilton

W 71st St

W 71st St

The
Majestic

W 70th St

W 70th St

Hudson
River

9A

W 69th St

W 68th St

Lincoln
Towers

Freedom Pl

Riverside Blvd

Hotel Des
Artistes

W 67th St

66th Street
Lincoln Center

1

W 66th St

MLK
Sculpture

W 66th St

W 65th St

W 64th St

W 64th St

Lincoln
Center

PAGE
266

Lincoln Plaza

W 63rd St

Henry Hudson Pkwy

Amsterdam
Houses

W 62nd St

W 62nd St

Fordham
University

W 61st St

W 60th St

W 59th St

11

W 58th St

Time
Warner
Center

Columbus
Circle

59th
Col
Circ

A C B D

A B C D

1/4 mile

.25 km

Neighborhood Overview

Map 14

18	19	20
16		17
14		15
11	12	13

Away from the bustle of midtown and downtown Manhattan, the lower part of the Upper West Side offers a decidedly different, slower pace. But by no means does this neighborhood feel sleepy. Sandwiched between two parks, this neighborhood offers great food, museums, dive bars, and beautiful Art Deco architecture, not to mention the cultural meccas of Lincoln Center and the American Museum of Natural History, all of which remind you that New York is a livable city after all.

Many of the buildings that line the streets of the Upper West Side are landmarks. **The Ansonia** (built between 1899 and 1904) was originally a hotel and is now an exclusive apartment building. It has had many famous residents including Babe Ruth and Theodore Dreiser. **The Dakota** (built from 1880–1884) is best known for being the home of John Lennon and Yoko Ono, and the place where Lennon was killed at the entrance to the building. **The Dorilton** (built in 1902), **The Majestic** (built in 1894), and **The San Remo** (completed in 1931) all attest to bygone days of elaborate building construction.

Green space surrounds this neighborhood. To the east lies Central Park, but most locals head west to the gorgeous Riverside Park. It is filled with beautiful flower gardens, wonderful playgrounds, and some great spots to sit down and relax by the water. For those looking for something more active, a path runs along the Hudson River, perfect for jogging and biking. **The Boat Basin at 79th Street** is the only facility in the city that allows year-round residency in boats. It is also used as a launch site for kayaks, canoes, and sailboats, which you can rent in the summer. The rotunda overlooks the marina and is the site of the Boat Basin café (open April to October), a great place to unwind with a beer as the sun sets over the Hudson.

Like a city unto itself, **The American Museum of Natural History** is one of the largest museums in the world. Founded in 1869, the museum contains 25 interconnected buildings with lots of famous permanent exhibits (anthropological collections, rooms on human biology and evolution, a life-sized model blue whale, and the world's largest sapphire in the world, to name a few). Be sure to check out the always popular Hayden Planetarium and its spectacular space show—it's a great spot to experience the wonders of the universe—and of course the collection of dinosaur fossils that tantalize visitors of all ages. Just south of AMNH is **The New-York Historical Society** which has a fabulous collection documenting the history of New York and the United States. Some highlights include many of James Audubon's watercolors, paintings from the Hudson River School, and materials from the Civil War and Reconstruction.

When Upper West Siders tire from museums, they join the rest of the city's cultural elite at **Lincoln Center**, probably the most famous arts and culture center in the world. Home of the Film Society of Lincoln Center, Jazz at Lincoln Center, the Lincoln Center Theater, the Metropolitan Opera, the City Opera, the City Ballet, and the New York Philharmonic, as well as Juilliard, the School of American Ballet, and the Library for the Performing Arts, this place is just bursting with artistic brilliance.

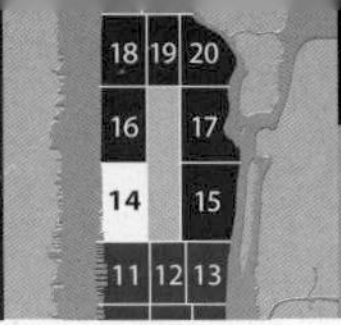

Upper West Side (Lower)

Map 14

O Landmarks

- **American Museum of Natural History** • Central Park W & W 79th St
212-769-5100
Includes an outstanding planetarium and lots and lots of stuffed animals.
- **The Ansonia** • 2109 Broadway [W 73rd St] 212-877-9800
Truly unique residence on Broadway.
- **The Apthorp** • 2201 Broadway [W 78th St] Huge, city-block-spanning condos complete with inner courtyard.
- **The Dakota** • W 72nd St & Central Park W Classic Central Park West apartment building, designed by Henry J Hardenbergh.
- **The Dorilton** • Broadway & W 71st St Understated it ain't. But damn, it's pretty.
- **Hotel Des Artistes** • 1 W 67th St [Central Park W]
$4,000,000 artist studios on CPW. Nice one.
- **Lincoln Center** • 70 Lincoln Center Plaza [W 62nd St] 212-875-5000
A rich and wonderful complex. Highly recommended—movies, theater, music, opera.
- **The Majestic** • 115 Central Park W [W 71st St] Great brick by Chanin.
- **MLK Sculpture** • 122 Amsterdam Ave [W 65th St] Massive brutalist-but-cool square monument to MLK.
- **New-York Historical Society** • 170 Central Park W [W 77th St] 212-873-3400
Oldest museum in New York City.
- **Rotunda at 79th St Boat Basin** • W 79th St [Riverside Dr] 212-496-2105
Rotunda, arcade, arches, and boats.
- **The San Remo** • Central Park West & W 74th St Emery Roth's contribution to the Upper West Side skyline.
- **West End Collegiate Church** • 368 West End Ave [W 77th St] 212-787-1566
Dutch/Flemish goodness from Robert Gibson, circa 1892.

Coffee

- **Aroma Espresso Bar** • 161 W 72nd St [Amsterdam Ave] 212-595-5700
The Israeli version of Starbucks comes stateside.
- **Box Kite Coffee** • 128 W 72nd St [Columbus Ave] 212-574-8203
Tiny. Cute. Great coffee. Very new Yorky.
- **Irving Farm Coffee Roasters** • 224 W 79th St [Broadway] 212-874-7979
Kalita brew bar, reclaimed wood, medium on the hipster scale.
- **Joe The Art of Coffee** • 514 Columbus Ave [W 85th St] 212-875-0100
Joe really knows his joe.
- **Le Pain Quotidien** • 60 W 65th St [Lincoln Sq] 212-721-4001
Excellent coffee and pastries. Thanks Belgium.
- **Plowshare Coffee** • 2730 Broadway [105th St] 212-222-0280
Sustainable Rockland County artisan roasters.

Farmers Markets

- **79th Street Greenmarket** • Columbus Ave & W 79th St Sun, 8 am–4 pm, Year Round
- **Tucker Square Greenmarket** • W 66th St & Columbus Ave Thurs & Sat 8 am–5 pm, Year Round

Upper West Side (Lower)

For a night of culture, go to Lincoln Center or see a concert at the **Beacon Theater**. For drunken revelries and beer pong, hit **Jake's Dilemma**. Was that out loud? We meant to say, With a selection of wine for everyone, seek out **Barcibo Enoteca**. And Harry and Sally set up their best friends at **Cafe Luxembourg**.

🌙 Nightlife

- **Beacon Theater** • 2124 Broadway [W 74th St]
212 465 6500
Former movie palace with beautiful neo-Grecian interior.
- **Bin 71** • 237 Columbus Ave [W 71st St]
212-362-5446
Sip wine with 30-something Upper West Siders.
- **Blondies Sports Bar** •
212 W 79th St [Amsterdam Ave]
212-362-4360
Want to catch a game? Any game? Come here.
- **Café Luxembourg** •
200 W 70th St [Amsterdam Ave]
212-873-7411
Hey, is that Tom Hanks over there?
- **The Dead Poet** •
450 Amsterdam Ave [W 82nd St]
212-595-5670
Good Irish feel. No secret society that we know of.
- **Dive 75** • 101 W 75th St [Columbus Ave]
212-362-7510
The quintessential dive bar with the friendliest staff around.
- **Dublin House** • 225 W 79th St [Broadway]
212-874-9528
Great dingy Irish pub. Recommended.
- **Fred's** • 476 Amsterdam Ave [W 83rd St]
212-579-3076
Sort of old-school. Sort of fun.

- **George Keeley** •
485 Amsterdam Ave [W 83rd St]
212-873-0251
A rotation of good draft beers and all the sports you need.
- **Hi Life Bar & Grill** •
477 Amsterdam Ave [W 83rd St]
212-787-7199
Not a bad option for this part of town.
- **Jake's Dilemma** •
430 Amsterdam Ave [W 81st St]
212-580-0556
Drink beer and pretend you're still in college.
- **Malachy's Donegal Inn** •
103 W 72nd St [Columbus Ave]
212-874-4268
Friendly Irish dive keeping it real on the Upper West Side.
- **Manhattan Cricket Club** • 226 W 79th St
[Broadway] 646-823-9252
Crafted cocktails in intimate, clubby setting; strict no-beer pong policy.
- **Prohibition** • 503 Columbus Ave [W 84th St]
212-579-3100
Cool space, music, people, etc. Sometimes.
- **Stand Up NY** • 236 W 78th St [Broadway]
212-595-0850
The frog replies, "Brooklyn—they're a dime a dozen out there!"
- **The Tangled Vine Wine Bar and Kitchen** •
434 Amsterdam Ave [W 81st St]
646-863-3896
Have an environmentally friendly wine trio at this UWS hot spot.
- **West End Hall** • 2756 Broadway (W 105th St)
212-662-7200
Indoor beer garden with pub grub and giant TVs.

18	19	20
16		17
14		15
11	12	13

Map 14

Upper West Side (Lower)

🍴 Restaurants

- **'cesca** • 164 W 75th St [Amsterdam Ave]
  212-787-6300 • $$$$
  Sunday Sauce worthy of a cameo in
  "Goodfellas."
- **Albert's Mofongo House** •
  4762 Broadway [W 61st St]
  212-569-3431 • $$$
  Exceptional food, festive drinks, and
  family-friendly events.
- **Ali Baba** • 515 Amsterdam Ave [W 85th St]
  212-787-6008 • $
  Yemenite-Israeli chef brings twist to Kosher
  takeout.
- **Amber Restaurant** •
  221 Columbus Ave [W 70th St]
  212-799-8100 • $$
  Multiple asian cuisines, all decent. Fast service.
  Comfortable seating.
- **Bar Boulud** • 1900 Broadway [W 63rd St]
  212-595-0303 • $$$
  Before the opera, stop in for the fabulous
  charcuterie plate.
- **Bettola** • 412 Amsterdam Ave [W 80th St]
  212-787-1660 • $$
  Try the wood-fired pizza at this authentic
  Italian restaurant.
- **Blondies** • 212 W 79th St [Amsterdam Ave]
  212-362-4360 • $$
  Pair wings with a salad to save your arteries.
- **Boat Basin Cafe** •
  W 79th St & Hudson River [Riverside Dr]
  212-496-5542 • $$
  Burgers, buckets of beer, and a killer view.
- **Brother Jimmy's BBQ** •
  428 Amsterdam Ave [W 80th St]
  212-501-7515 • $$
  Good ol' Southern gluttony!

- **Bustan** • 487 Amsterdam Ave [W 84th St]
  212-595-5050 • $$
  Modern Middle Eastern with a multicultural
  spin.
- **Café Lalo** • 201 W 83rd St [Amsterdam Ave]
  212-496-6031 • $$
  Packed dessert and coffee destination.
- **Café Luxembourg** •
  200 W 70th St [Amsterdam Ave]
  212-873-7411 • $$$$$
  Top-end bistro. Anyone know what
  Luxembourgian cuisine is?
- **Calle Ocho** • 45 W 81st St [Columbus Ave]
  212-873-5025 • $$$
  Pan-Latin restaurant with a bottomless sangria
  brunch.
- **Celeste** • 502 Amsterdam Ave [W 84th St]
  212-874-4559 • $$
  Cheap and tasty homemade pastas. A true
  gem.
- **Chirping Chicken** •
  355 Amsterdam Ave [W 77th St]
  212-787-6631 • $
  Grilled birds done right. No chirping.
- **Dovetail** • 103 W 77th St [Columbus Ave]
  212-362-3800 • $$$$
  Notable NYC chef brings impeccable wine list,
  indulgent prix fixe dinner.
- **Fairway Café** • 2127 Broadway [W 74th St]
  212-595-1888 • $$
  When it's all too much.
- **Fine & Shapiro** •
  138 W 72nd St [Columbus Ave]
  212-877-2721 • $$$
  Very old-school kosher deli.
- **Fishtag** • 222 W 79th St [Broadway]
  212-362-7470 • $$$
  Excellent basement seafood spot with
  Mediterranean flavors.

Map 14

For Daniel Boulud's take on seasonal French cuisine, check out **Bar Boulud** and its charcuterie bar. Or take a walk to **Telepan** where Bill Telepan serves up rock-steady seasonal tasting menus and great cocktails. But if breaking the bank isn't in the agenda, check out **Kefi** for the best Greek food around. Meanwhile, sushi snobs don't even have to leave the neighborhood with **Gari** close by.

• **Freddie & Pepper's Pizza** •
303 Amsterdam Ave [W 74th St]
212-799-2378 • $
Thin crust pizza. Has been around forever.

• **French Roast** • 2340 Broadway [W 85th St]
212-799-1533 • $$
Open 24 hours. Good croque-monsieur.

• **Gabriel's** • 11 W 60th St [Broadway]
212-956-4600 • $$$
Local draw; good all around.

• **Gari Columbus** •
370 Columbus Ave [W 78th St]
212-362-4816 • $$$$$
Why UWS sushi snobs no longer have to take the cross-town bus.

• **Good Enough to Eat** •
520 Columbus Ave
212-496-0163 • $$$
Good brunch but Sunday line starts early.

• **Gray's Papaya** • 2090 Broadway [W 71st St]
212-799-0243 • $
Open 24 hours. An institution.

• **Han Dynasty** • 215 W 85th St [Broadway]
212-858-9060 • $$$
Spicy Szechuan. Dan dan noodles, anyone?

• **Harriet's Kitchen** •
502 Amsterdam Ave [W 84th St]
212-721-0045 • $$
Reliable comfort food take-out joint.

• **Jacob's Pickles** •
509 Amsterdam Ave [W 84th St]
212-470-5566 • $$
Upmarket Southern-style menu and booze, and yes, plenty of pickles.

• **Kefi** • 222 W 79th St [W 84th St]
212-873-0200 • $$
Greek food gets an upgrade at this amazingly affordable gem.

• **La Caridad 78** • 2199 Broadway [W 78th St]
212-874-2780 • $$
Cheap Cuban paradise.

• **Land Thai Kitchen** •
450 Amsterdam Ave [W 82nd St]
212-501-8121 • $$
Standard Thai.

• **Le Pain Quotidien** •
50 W 72nd St [Central Park W]
212-712-9700 • $$
Great breads. Communal table. Euro vibe.

• **The Milling Room** •
446 Columbus Ave [82nd St]
212-595-0580 • $$$
Fancy tavern food.

• **Nanoosh** • 2012 Broadway [W 69th St]
212-362-7922 • $
Cheap, fast Middle-Eastern food. Good for before the movies.

• **Nice Matin** • 201 W 79th St [Amsterdam Ave]
212-873-6423 • $$$
Traditional French food staple with outdoor seating.

• **Nougatine** • 1 Central Park W [Columbus Cir]
212-299-3900 • $$$$$
Brilliant $24.07 prix fixe lunch!

• **Parm** • 235 Columbus Ave [W 71st St]
212-776-4921 • $$
Mini-chain frying up righteous namesake sandwiches.

• **Patsy's Pizza** • 61 W 74 St [Columbus Ave]
212-579-3000 • $$
Small city chain. Excellent thin-crust pizza. Fresh ingredients.

• **Pier i Cafe** • 500 W 70th St [West Side Hwy]
212-362-4450 • $$
In season, sip a beer, munch a burger, and take in that view.

• **RedFarm** • 2170 Broadway [W 77th St]
212-724-9700 • $$$
Creative, farm-fresh dim sum. Home of the Pac Man dumpling.

• **Rosa Mexicano** •
61 Columbus Ave [W 62nd St]
212-977-7700 • $$$$
Inventive Mexican. Great guac.

Map 14

18	19	20
16		17
14		15
11	12	13

Upper West Side (Lower)

• **Salumeria Rosi Parmacotto** •
283 Amsterdam Ave [W 73rd St]
212-877-4801 • $$
Eatery doubles as excellent salami shop.
Beware of '80s glam interior.

• **Santa Fe** • 73 W 71st St [Columbus Ave]
212-724-0822 • $$$
Calm Southwest.

• **Sarabeth's** • 423 Amsterdam Ave [W 80th St]
212-496-6280 • $$
Brunch, brunch, and brunch.

• **Schaller's Stube** • 1652 2nd Ave (E 86th St)
646-726-4355
Sausage counter from the German meat
market next door. - $

• **Shake Shack** • 366 Columbus Ave [W 77th St]
646-747-8770 • $$
Now you can get your Shack Burger year
round.

• **Sushi Yasaka** • 251 W 72nd St [West End Ave]
212-496-8460 • $$$
Assorted Japanese with tons of rolls. Try the
mini omakase.

• **Tessa** • 349 Amsterdam Ave [77th St]
212-390-1974 • $$$$
Exposed brick and steel French-Italian-
Mediterranean tavern.

🛍 Shopping

• **67 Wine** • 179 Columbus Ave [W 68th St]
212-724-6767
Top-notch selection and helpful staff. Lots of
tastings.

• **Bicycle Renaissance** •
430 Columbus Ave [W 81st St]
212-724-2350
Mountain bikes galore; convenient to Central
Park.

• **Bloomingdale's Outlet** •
2085 Broadway [W 72nd St]
212-634-3190
Multi-floor outlet version of the classic
department store.

• **Century 21** • 1972 Broadway [W 66th St]
212-518-2121
Where most New Yorkers buy their underwear.

• **Citarella** • 2135 Broadway [W 75th St]
212-874-0383
Expensive but delicious breads, meats,
cheeses, and pastries.

• **Eddie's Bicycles** •
490 Amsterdam Ave [W 83rd St]
212-580-2011
Plus rentals.

• **Fairway Market** • 2127 Broadway [W 74th St]
212-595-1888
Top-notch supermarket, but always packed.

New York's prime food shopping can be found in this neighborhood. **Zabar's** (cheeses, fish, coffee, free samples) and **Fairway** (fresh produce, breads, dry goods, total chaos) are within blocks of each other. To pair some wine with that fine food, we like **67 Wine & Spirits**. And everyone can find something to wear at the uptown outpost of **Century 21**.

- **Gracious Home** • 1992 Broadway [W 68th St]
  212-231-7800
  A side of hardware with your fancy housewares.
- **GreenFlea Market** •
  Columbus Ave & W 77th St
  212-239-3025
  Fantastic craft and antique market with local vendors. Sundays only.
- **Jonathan Adler** •
  304 Columbus Ave [W 74th St]
  212-787-0017
  Funky, fun housewares.
- **Laytner's Linen & Home** •
  2276 Broadway [W 82nd St]
  212-724-0180
  Things that'll make you want to stay home more.
- **Levain Bakery** • 351 Amsterdam Ave [77th St]
  Mega-cookie purveyors' expanded domicile.
- **Patagonia** • 426 Columbus Ave [W 81st St]
  917-441-0011
  Eco-conscious store selling fleece for your adventurous subway ride.

- **Pookie & Sebastian** •
  322 Columbus Ave [W 75th St]
  212-580-5844
  Flirty tops, girly dresses, and fly jeans—for UWS chicks.
- **Strings and Other Things** •
  1995 Broadway [W 68th St]
  212-362-0857
  Petite and lovely shop for violin, viola, and cello.
- **Toga Bikes** • 110 West End Ave [W 65th St]
  212-799-9625
  NYC's oldest bike shop.
- **Town Shop** • 2270 Broadway [W 82nd St]
  212-787-2762
  Where experts will fit you for the perfect bra.
- **Western Beef** • 75 West End Ave [W 63rd St]
  212-459-2800
  If you don't have time for Fairway and Zabar's.
- **Westsider Records** •
  233 W 72nd St [Broadway]
  212-874-1588
  Cool record store. You'll find some interesting stuff.
- **Zabar's** • 2245 Broadway [W 80th St]
  212-787-2000
  Manhattan supermarket legend. NFT's favorite.

Map 15 · **Upper East Side (Lower)**

1
2

2nd Avenue/
86th Street
Q

E 86th St

17

86th Street
4 5 6

Carl
Schurz
Park

E 85th St

The
Jeffersons
High-rise

Zion-St Marks Evangelical
Lutheran Church

E 84th St

E 83rd St

East End Ave

E 82nd St

Metropolitan
Museum
of Art
PAGE 378

E 81st St

Frank E. Campbell
Funeral Chapel

E 80th St

Parisian-style
Chimneys

New York
Society
Library

A

E 79th St

E 78th St

77th Street
6

E 77th St

Bemelmans Bar

E 76th St

PAGE
252

John
Jay
Park

E 75th St

Fifth Ave

Madison Ave

Park Ave

Lexington Avenue

Third Ave

E 74th St

E 73rd St

Second Ave

First Ave

York Ave

Bobby Wagner Walk

E 72nd St

Breakfast at Tiffany's
Apartment Building

2nd Avenue/
72th Street
Q

Weill
Medical
College
(Cornell)

Frick
Collection

Asia
Society

E 71st St

E 70th St

The Explorers
Club

E 69th St

68th Street
Hunter College

E 68th St

Memorial
Sloan Kettering
Cancer Center

Park East
Synagogue

6

E 67th St

The Manhattan House

Rockefeller
University

The Lotos
Club

E 66th St

FDR Dr

Temple
Emanu-El

E 65th St

Bernie Madoff
Apartment

E 64th St

E 63rd St

Foot Bridge

Lexington Avenue
63rd Street

F

E 62nd St

East
River

Mount Vernon
Hotel Museum
and Garden

The Metropolitan
Club

E 61st St

Lexington
Avenue/
59th Street

Roosevelt Island Tram

5th Avenue/
59th Street
N R W

E 60th St

N R W

13

59th Street
4 5 6

Roosevelt
Island Tram

Queensboro B

To Queens

Central
Park

1/4 mile | .25 km

You know the reputation of the Upper East Side: Snooty, fancy and rich. But while this historical neighborhood is home to some of the oldest wealth in New York, it's home to a lot more than you see on the CW: On the weekends, especially in the warm days, check out everyone in their flip flops and sunglasses (designer, please) heading to the most green space in Manhattan, Central Park. If you're not sunbathing or throwing a Frisbee, check out some of the most famous museums in the world, lively restaurants, shopping and brunch—oh you must be a lady/gentleman who brunches if you wander up here. Old or young, this neighborhood is changing—and especially in the summer, sans a trip to the Hamptons, there is no better place to be.

Long before **Bernie Madoff** made this neighborhood infamous, the fabulously wealthy started settling into the Upper East Side over a century ago. As a result, there are beautiful high rises up and down Park Avenue. Fifth Avenue is the home of what was dubbed "Millionaires Row" at the turn of the 19th century—the Carnegies, the Vanderbilts, the Astors, and their friends all walked the streets lined with glorious mansions, now known as Museum Mile. For a different sort of landmark head up to 85th for **The Jeffersons High Rise**…you know, that dee-luxe apartment in the sky from the classic TV show. Or walk by where Holly Golightly frolicked at the **Breakfast at Tiffany's Apartment**.

There are many historical sites to check out in one of the most historic districts in New York. Check out the **New York Society Library**, which moved to its current location on 79th Street from University Place in 1937. **Temple Emanu-El** on 65th Street is one of the oldest temples in New York City—it was founded as a result of the second wave of immigration of Jews to America. Established in 1845, the reform congregation moved to its current location in 1927, where it welcomes Jews whose families have been going for generations and those who just moved to the city.

Want to stop and see a couple of exhibits? How about some of the most famous museums in the world? **The Frick Collection**, housed in the 1914 mansion of industrialist Henry Clark Frick, includes works by Rembrandt, Degas, Goya, and many more of the art world's best-known names. (Visitor's tip: "Pay what you wish" admission every Sunday between 11 am and 1 pm.) For a look into the art of worlds past, head over to **The Met** which houses, oh, over two million pieces and can take days to see it all. One last stop? **The Asia Society and Museum**, which houses an impressive art collection and performing arts program.

If you love classic New York entertainment (and have a giant wad of cash), this your neighborhood. Step inside the Carlyle Hotel to find **Bemelmans Bar**, named for the Austrian-born artist who created Madeline children's books. It's a lovely place to stop for a drink and hear some piano during happy hour. Right next door is **Café Carlyle** which attracts stars like Judy Collins, Elaine Strich, and even Woody Allen on his clarinet.

Map 15

Upper East Side (Lower)

O Landmarks

- **Asia Society** • 725 Park Ave [E 70th St]
  212-288-6400
  Small-scale modernism.
- **Bemelmans Bar** • 35 E 76th St [Madison Ave]
  212-744-1600
  Features lovely mural by creator of Madeline
  books, Ludwig Bemelmans.
- **Bernie Madoff Apartment** •
  133 E 64th St [Park Ave]
  Madoff lived here, before he went to The Big
  House.
- **Breakfast at Tiffany's Apartment** •
  169 E 71st St [Lexington Ave]
  Where Holly Golightly and "Fred" lived in
  Breakfast at Tiffany's.
- **The Explorers Club** • 46 E 70th St [Park Ave]
  212-628-8383
  Indiana Joneses of the world hang out here.
  Some events open to the public.
- **Frank E. Campbell Funeral Chapel** •
  1076 Madison Ave [E 81st St]
  212-288-3500
  Undertaker to the famously deceased like
  Lennon and Joan Crawford.
- **The Frick Collection** • 1 E 70th St [5th Ave]
  212-288-0700
  Lots of furniture.
- **The Jeffersons High-Rise** •
  185 E 85th St [3rd Ave]
  We're movin' on up...to a dee-luxe apartment
  in the sky-hi.
- **The Lotos Club** • 5 E 66th St [5th Ave]
  212-737-7100
  Twain loved this private literary club. NFT is
  still waiting for an invite.
- **The Manhattan House** •
  200 E 66th St [3rd Ave]
  Seminal UES "white-brick" building.
- **Metropolitan Club of New York** • 1 E 60th St
  [5th Ave]
  212-838-7400
  1894 millionaire's clubhouse built by McKim,
  Mead & White.
- **Metropolitan Museum of Art** •
  1000 5th Ave [E 81st St]
  212-535-7710
  The mother of all art musuems. Check out:
  temple, roof garden, Clyfford Still room,
  baseball cards.
- **Mount Vernon Hotel Museum and Garden** •
  421 E 61st St [1st Ave]
  212-838-6878
  Nice old building.

- **New York Society Library** •
  53 E 79th St [Madison Ave]
  212-288-6900
  A subscription library that predates the public
  library (1754!).
- **Parisian-Style Chimneys** •
  E 80th St & Park Ave
  A touch of Paris on the UES.
- **Park East Synagogue** •
  163 E 67th St [3rd Ave]
  212-737-6900
  1890 Moorish-Jewish asymmetrical brilliance
  from Schneider & Herter.
- **Roosevelt Island Tram** • E 59th St & 2nd Ave
  As featured in Spider Man.
- **The Sherry-Netherland Hotel** •
  781 5th Ave [E 59th St]
  212-355-2800
  Super-cool spired tower and super-stuffy
  hotel.
- **Zion-St Mark's Evangelical Lutheran Church** •
  339 E 84th St [2nd Ave]
  212-288-0600
  Last "Germantown" church (see the General
  Slocum memorials inside).

Coffee

- **Beanocchio's** • 1413 York Ave [E 75th St]
  212-861-8060
  Nice little spot, despite the lame name.
- **Joe The Art Of Coffee** •
  1045 Lexington Ave [E 75th St]
  212-988-2500
  Joe really knows his joe.
- **Le Pain Quotidien** • 1270 1st Ave [E 68th St]
  212-988-5001
  Excellent coffee and pastries. Thanks Belgium.
- **Le Pain Quotidien** •
  833 Lexington Ave [E 64th St]
  212-755-5810
  Excellent coffee. Excellent pastries. Thanks
  Belgium.
- **Le Pain Quotidien** •
  1131 Madison Ave [E 84th St]
  212-327-4900
  Excellent coffee. Excellent pastries. Thanks
  Belgium.
- **Oren's Daily Roast** •
  985 Lexington Ave [E 71st St]
  212-717-3907
  Hip staff pours superior java at local
  mini-chain.

Upper East Side (Lower)

For a down and out dive (translation: our kind of bar) ride the **Subway Inn** or go old country Irish whiskey tasting at **Donohues**. For a little more class grab the perfect glass of wine at **Uva**. For even more class, no old money Upper East Side evening is complete without a visit to **Bemelmans Bar**.

- **Oslo** • 422 E 75th St [1st Ave]
  Coffee with attention to detail.
- **Via Quadronno** • 25 E 73rd St [Madison Ave]
  212 650 9880
  Straight up Italian espresso from Milan.
- **Viand** • 673 Madison Ave [E 61st St]
  212 751 6622
  Old-school diner complete with long counter.

🍎 Farmers Markets

- **82nd Street / St. Stephen's Greenmarket** •
  E 82nd St & York Ave
  July–Dec, Sat, 9 am–3 pm.

🍸 Nightlife

- **American Trash** • 1471 1st Ave [E 77th St]
  212-988-9008
  Punk rockin' I-Bankers unite.
- **Bailey's Corner Pub** •
  1607 York Ave [E 85th St]
  212-650-1341
  Friendly Irish local. Watch the game or play darts.
- **Baker Street** • 1152 1st Ave [E 63rd St]
  212 688 9663
  Flat screen TVs with above average bar food.
- **Bar Seine** • 37 E 64th St [Madison Ave]
  212-734-9100
  Check into this classy hotel bar for rest, relaxation and cocktails.
- **Bemelmans Bar** • 35 E 76th St [Madison Ave]
  212-744-1600
  When NFT actually has money, we drink here. Classic UES vibe.
- **Brandy's Piano Bar** • 235 E 84th St [3rd Ave]
  212-744-4949
  Good ol' rollicking time.
- **Café Carlyle** • 35 E 76th St [Madison Ave]
  212-744-1600
  Classic cabaret venue where Woody plays. Hellishly expensive.
- **Caledonia Scottish Pub** •
  1609 2nd Ave [E 83rd St]
  212-879-0402
  Put on your kilt to sip Scotch and nibble on haggis.

- **Club Macanudo** • 26 E 63rd St [Madison Ave]
  212-752-8200
  A perfect environment for smokers (and non-smokers).
- **Comic Strip Live** • 1568 2nd Ave [E 81st St]
  212-861-9386
  A rabbi walks into a bar with a frog on his shoulder…
- **Dangerfield's** • 1118 1st Ave [E 61st St]
  212-593-1650
  Hardy har har.
- **Donohue's Steak House** •
  845 Lexington Ave [E 64th St]
  212-744-0938
  Old-school Irish. Sit at the bar and drink whiskey.
- **Dorrian's** • 1616 2nd Ave [E 84th St]
  212-772-6660
  Pop your collar for the last beer of the night here.
- **Finnegan's Wake** • 1361 1st Ave [E 73rd St]
  212-737-3664
  Standard Irish pub. Therefore, pretty good.
- **Hungarian House** • 213 E 82nd St [3rd Ave]
  212 650 1974
  Party Hungarian-style. Lots of special events.
- **Iggy's** • 1452 2nd Ave [E 75th St]
  212-327-3043
  Super-friendly bartenders help cue up the cheesy karaoke action.
- **The Jeffrey** • 311 E 60th St [2nd Ave]
  212 355 2337
  Tons of craft beer, truffle potato chips and giant TVs.
- **Jones Wood Foundry** • 401 E 76th St [1st Ave]
  212-249-2700
  Chill with the European expats and cheer on their favorite 'football' squads
- **Lexington Bar & Books** •
  1020 Lexington Ave [E 73rd St]
  212-717-3902
  Proper attire required but James Bond films available upon request.
- **O'Flanagan's** • 1215 1st Ave [E 66th St]
  212-439-0660
  Unpretentious bar where recent grads and college kids mix peacefully.

Map 15

18 19 20
16 17
14 15
11 12 13

Upper East Side (Lower)

• **The Penrose** • 1590 2nd Ave [83rd St]
212-203-2751
Tasty cocktails & pub grub with a touch of
class.
• **Ryan's Daughter** • 350 E 85th St [2nd Ave]
212-628-2613
Free chips!
• **Session 73** • 1359 1st Ave [E 73rd St]
212-517-4445
Live music and yuppies.
• **The Stumble Inn** • 1454 2nd Ave [E 76th St]
212-650-0561
Thanks to the amazing specials, expect to
stumble out.
• **Subway Inn** • 1140 2nd Ave [E 60th St]
212-223-8929
Sad, bad, glare, worn-out, ugh. Totally great.
• **Trinity Pub** • 299 E 84th St [2nd Ave]
212-327-4450
Low on the UES meathead scale. Thank
goodness!

🍴 Restaurants

• **Afghan Kebab House II** •
1345 2nd Ave [E 71st St]
212-517-2776 • $$
Great kebabs.
• **Agora Turkish** • 1565 2nd Ave [E 80th St]
212-717-1220 • $$
BYO family-run Turkish with big flavors and a
small price.
• **Alice's Tea Cup Chapter II** •
156 E 64th St [Lexington Ave]
212-486-9200 • $$
Eat brunch or take tea in a fairy tale setting.
• **Andre's Cafe** • 1631 2nd Ave [E 85th St]
212-327-1105 • $$
Low-key Hungarian savories (goulash) and
sweets (strudel).
• **Antonucci** • 170 E 81st St [3rd Ave]
212-570-5100 • $$$$$
Pleasant Italian spot on quiet block for dining
al fresco.

• **Atlantic Grill** • 49 W 64th St
212-787-4663 • $$$$$
Seafood galore. Old money loves this place.
• **Barking Dog** • 1678 3rd Ave
212-831-1800 • $$
Bring Fido along for brunch.
• **Beach Cafe** • 1326 2nd Ave [E 70th St]
212-988-7299 • $$
Comfort food for brunch, dinner easy as a
beach here.
• **Beyoglu** • 1431 3rd Ave [E 81st St]
212-650-0850 • $$$
Make a meal out of meze.
• **Burger Heaven** •
804 Lexington Ave [E 62nd St]
212-838-3580 • $
'Nuff said.
• **Burger One** • 1150 Lexington Ave [W 80th St]
212-737-0095 • $
Pint-sized counter with burgers, fries, and
tacos (of course).
• **Burke Bar Café** • 1000 3rd Ave [E 59th St]
212-705-3800 • $$$$
Chef Burke's elegant, inside-Bloomingdale's
café with cheeky menu.
• **Café Boulud** • 20 E 76th St [Madison Ave]
212-772-2600 • $$$$$
Elegant, slightly more relaxed sibling of Daniel.
• **Calexico** • 1491 2nd Ave [E 78th St]
347-967-5955 • $$
Wonderful, welcoming Tex-Mex or Cali-Mex, as
the case may be.
• **Candle 79** • 154 E 79th St [Lexington Ave]
212-537-7179 • $$$$
Upscale vegetarian cuisine in luxurious
surroundings.
• **Candle Café** • 1307 3rd Ave [E 75th St]
212-472-0970 • $$$
Delicious vegetarian café ironically next door
to Le Steak.
• **Canyon Road** • 1470 1st Ave [E 77th St]
212-734-1600 • $$$
Southwest haven.

Upper East Side (Lower)

Map 15

JG Melon's burger is one of the best reasons to go above 14th Street. **Cascabel**'s counter features wallet-friendly Mexican, and for an old-time favorite, try **Cilantro**. Get your seafood any way you like it at **Atlantic Grill** or grab a lobster roll from **Luke's Lobster**. If after all that you need a giant sundae and a candy fix, try **Dylan's Candy Bar**, a magical wonderland created by Ralph Lauren's daughter, Dylan.

- **Cascabel Taqueria** • 1556 2nd Ave [E 80th St]
212-717-8226 • $
Great Mexican food at Taco Bell prices.
- **Daniel** • 60 E 65th St [Park Ave]
212-288-0033 • $$$$$
Overrated $150+ meal.
- **Donguri** • 309 E 83rd St [2nd Ave]
212-737-5656 • $$$$$
Transcendent, UES Japanese standout.
- **The East Pole** • 133 E 65th St [Lexington Ave]
212-249-2222 • $$$$
Sort of like a four-star British tavern, if you can imagine that.
- **FAT** • 1064 Madison Ave [E 81st St]
212-772-0022 • $$$
Great brunch spot—part of the Eli Zabar empire.
- **Eat Here Now** • 839 Lexington Ave [E 64th St]
212-751-0724 • $$
Clean, classic diner. Fast, friendly service.
- **EJ's Luncheonette** • 1271 3rd Ave [E 73rd St]
212-472-0600 • $$
Homey mini-chain diner.
- **Elio's** • 1621 2nd Ave [E 84th St]
212-772-2242 • $$$$$
UES Italian where schmoozing with the "who's-who" goes down.
- **Farinella** • 1132 Lexington Ave [E 79th St]
212-327-2702 • $$
4 ft long pizzas and fresh panini Napoli-style service.
- **Flex Mussels** • 174 E 82nd St [3rd Ave]
212-717-7772 • $$$
23 flavors—try the Abbey or Spaniard.
- **Heidelberg** • 1648 2nd Ave [E 86th St]
212-628-2332 • $$$
Dirndls and lederhosen serving colossal beers and sausage platters.
- **Heidi's House** • 308 E 78th St [2nd Ave]
212-249-0069 • $$$
Cozy comfort food in a happy place.
- **Hummus Kitchen** • 1613 2nd Ave [E 84th St]
212-988-0090 • $$
Hummus so good they named a Kitchen after it.
- **Indian Tandoor Oven** •
175 E 83rd St [3rd Ave]
212-628-3000 • $$
Delectable Indian specialties in cozy, color-draped surroundings.

- **Jackson Hole** • 232 E 64th St [3rd Ave]
212-371-7187 • $$
Extremely large burgers from this mini-chain.
- **Jacques Brasserie** • 204 E 85th St [3rd Ave]
212-327-2272 • $$$$
UES spot for tasty moules frites and Stella on tap.
- **JG Melon** • 1291 3rd Ave [E 73rd St]
212-650-1310 • $$
Top NYC burgers. Always crowded. Open 'till 2:30 a.m.
- **JoJo** • 160 E 64th St [Lexington Ave]
212-223-5656 • $$$$$
Charming French standout.
- **Kings' Carriage House** •
251 E 82nd St [2nd Ave]
212-734-5490 • $$$$
Romantic fine dining in a charming, old carriage house.
- **Le Pain Quotidien** •
833 Lexington Ave [E 64th St]
212-755-5810 • $$
Great breads. Communal Table. Euro vibe.
- **Le Pain Quotidien** •
1131 Madison Ave [E 84th St]
212-327-4900 • $$
Great breads. Communal Table. Euro vibe.
- **Le Veau d'Or** • 129 E 60th St [Lexington Ave]
212-838-8133 • $$$
Classic Parisian bistro with a cheap prix fixe.
- **Lexington Candy Shop** •
1226 Lexington Ave [E 83rd St]
212-288-0057 • $
Charming old-timey soda shop with twirly stools.
- **Little Vincent's Pizza** •
1399 2nd Ave [E 73rd St]
212-249-0120 • $
Unpretentious neighborhood staple in a sea of pricey restaurants.
- **Luke's Lobster** • 242 E 81st St [2nd Ave]
212-249-4241 • $$
Fresh-from-the-sea lobster rolls, without sticker shock.

Map 15

Upper East Side (Lower)

18 19 20
16 17
14 15
11 12 13

- **Maya** • 1191 1st Ave [E 65th St]
212-585-1818 • $$$$
Top-drawer Mexican.
- **Mei Jin Ramen** • 1574 2nd Ave [E 82nd St]
212-327-2800 • $$
Hard-to-find beef ramen with sweet lunch specials.
- **Neil's Coffee Shop** •
961 Lexington Ave [E 70th St]
212-628-7474 • $$
Friendly diner for Hunter students and old timers.
- **The New Amity Restaurant** •
1134 Madison Ave [E 84th St]
212-861-3255 • $$
Sometimes you just need a not-so-cheap tuna melt.
- **Nica Trattoria** • 354 E 84th St [1st Ave]
212-472-5040 • $$
Cash-only Italian with great food and lots of rules.
- **Oita Sushi** • 1317 2nd Ave [E 70th St]
212-535-0002 • $$$
Small sushi bar with creative rolls.
- **Orsay** • 1057 Lexington Ave [E 75th St]
212-517-6400 • $$$$$
Upscale brasserie popular with "about-town" uptowners.
- **Our Place** • 242 E 79th St
212-288-4888 • $$$$
Next level Chinese.
- **Pastrami Queen** •
1125 Lexington Ave [E 78th St]
212-734-1500 • $$
Meats worthy of their royal names.
- **Poke** • 343 E 85th St [2nd Ave]
212-249-0569 • $$
Good sushi. BYO Sake.
- **Serafina** • 33 E 61st St [Madison Ave]
212-702-9898 • $$
Pretty decent pizza and pasta.
- **Serendipity 3** • 225 E 60th St [3rd Ave]
212-838-3531 • $$
Home of the legendary "Frrrozen Hot Chocolate."
- **Sette Mezzo** • 969 Lexington Ave [E 70th St]
212-472-0400 • $$$$$
Oprah's fave.

- **Sushi of Gari** • 402 E 78th St [1st Ave]
212-517-5340 • $$$$$
Sure to please even the snootiest sushi snobs.
- **Tony Dragonas Cart** •
Madison Ave & E 62nd St
$
Street meat goes Greek.
- **Up Thai** • 1411 2nd Ave [E 74th St]
212-256-1199 • $$$
Thai classics on a higher level. And cocktails!
- **Uskudar** • 1405 2nd Ave [E 73rd St]
212-988-4046 • $
Delicious Turkish on the UES.
- **Uva** • 1486 2nd Ave [E 77th St]
212-472-4552 • $
Come for the wine list, food optional.
- **Vero Panini & Wine Bar** •
1483 2nd Ave [E 77th St]
212-452-3354 • $$
Try a panini or some pasta with your cocktails or wine.
- **Via Quadronno** • 25 E 73rd St [Madison Ave]
212-650-9880 • $$
This paninoteca is the cheapest lunch option around.
- **Viand** • 673 Madison Ave [E 61st St]
212-751-6622 • $$
Basic diner.

🛍 Shopping

- **Agata & Valentina** • 1505 1st Ave [E 79th St]
212-452-0690
Great gourmet market that will suck your wallet dry.
- **Agent Provocateur** •
675 Madison Ave [E 61st St]
212-840-2436
Super fabulous, slightly hardcore lingerie, get your credit cards ready.
- **Barneys New York** •
660 Madison Ave [E 61st St]
212-826-8900
Museum-quality fashion (with prices to match). Recommended.

Can't afford $600 socks on Madison Avenue? Check out **Housing Works Thrift Shop** or **BIS Designer Resale** for clothes handed down from Park Avenue. Although pricey, **Eli's** is one of the best places to buy food in the city, and **Fairway** is another great option for UES victuals. For unique wine breads try **Orwasher's** and for all your fastening needs, hit up **Tender Buttons**.

• **Bis Designer Resale** •
1134 Madison Ave [E 84th St]
212-396-2760
Where you can actually afford Gucci and Prada.

• **Bloomingdale's** • 1000 3rd Ave [E 60th St]
212-705-2000
Where your mother disappears when she's in town.

• **Butterfield Market** •
1114 Lexington Ave [E 78th St]
212-288-7800
UES gourmet grocer circa 1915.

• **Creel & Gow** • 131 E 70th St [Lexington Ave]
212-327-4281
Super fancy, arty things for rich people in a former stable.

• **Dean & Deluca** • 1150 Madison Ave [E 85th St]
212-717-0800
Divine & Expensive.

• **Dylan's Candy Bar** • 1011 3rd Ave [E 60th St]
646-735-0078
Keeping NYC pediatric dentists in business since 2001.

• **Eli's Manhattan** • 1415 3rd Ave [E 80th St]
212-717-8100
Blissful gourmet shopping experience. Just bring $$$.

• **Fairway Market** • 240 E 86th St [2nd Ave]
212-327-2008
So big. So good. So New York.

• **Garnet Wines & Liquors** •
929 Lexington Ave [E 69th St]
212-772-3211
Huge selection for people with money.

• **Housing Works Thrift Shop** •
202 E 77th St [3rd Ave]
212-772-8461
Our favorite thrift store.

• **In Vino Veritas** • 1375 1st Ave [E 73rd St]
212-288-0100
These bros know their wine.

• **Jeff's Bicycles NYC** • 1400 3rd Ave [E 79th St]
212-794-2929
Since 1977; convenient to Central Park.

• **Laduree** • 864 Madison Ave [70th St]
646-558-3157
International macaron specialists.

• **Lyric Hi-Fi & Video** •
1221 Lexington Ave [E 83rd St]
212-439-1900
Friendly, high-end stereo shop.

• **Maison Kayser** • 1294 3rd Ave [E 74th St]
212-744-3100
Spectacular baguettes straight from a Paris legend.

• **Orwashers** • 308 E 78th St [2nd Ave]
212-288-6569
Handmade wine breads. Best challah on the east side.

• **Ottomanelli Butcher Shoppe** •
1549 York Ave [E 82nd St]
212-772-7900
Old-school butcher still going strong.

• **Park East Kosher** • 1623 2nd Ave [E 84th St]
212-737-9800
Meats and smoked fish. It's all good, and it's all kosher.

• **Sprinkles Cupcake ATM** •
780 Lexington Ave [E 61st St]
24/7 cupcake and cookie vending machine, impressively not stale!

• **State News** • 1243 3rd Ave [E 72nd St]
212-879-8076
Longstanding party supply store with costumes, piñatas, and kid stuff.

• **Tender Buttons** •
143 E 62nd St [Lexington Ave]
212-758-7004
Antique, rare, and unusual buttons.

• **Two Little Red Hens** •
1652 2nd Ave [E 86th St]
212-452-0476
Lovely cases of cakes and pies flanked by kitschy hen memorabilia.

• **Ursus Books and Prints** •
50 E 78th St
212-772-8787
Specialty—art books.

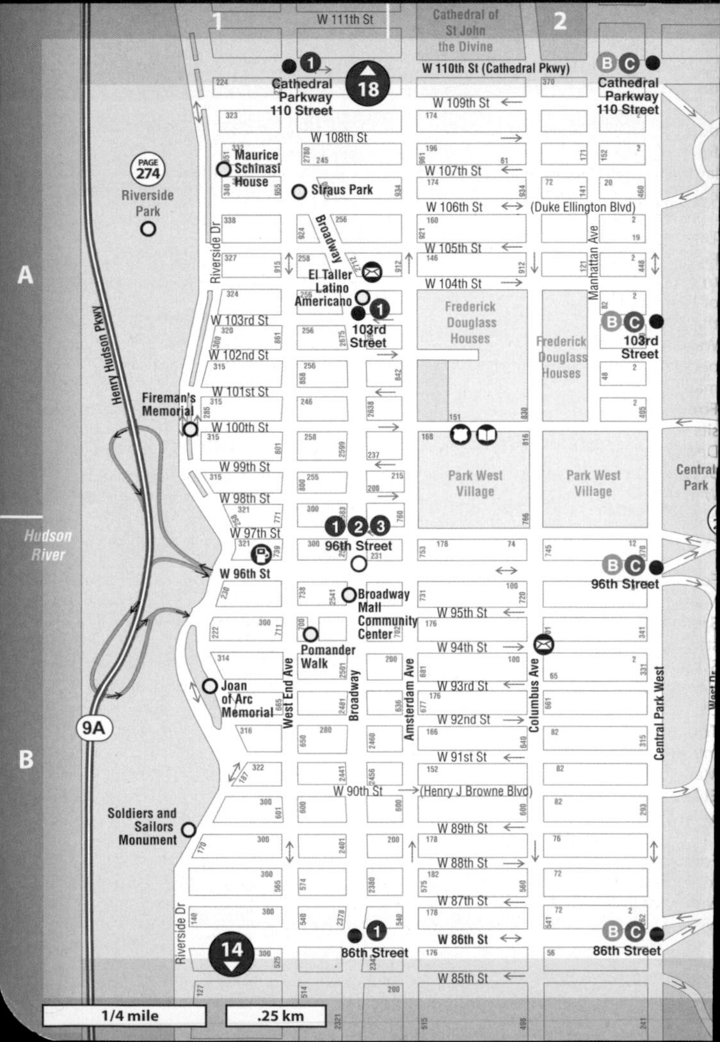

Map 16 · **Upper West Side (Upper)**

Ⓝ

W 111th St

Cathedral
of St John
the Divine

1 ▲ **2**

❶ ▲ **18**

W 110th St (Cathedral Pkwy)

224

**Cathedral
Parkway
110 Street**

370

Ⓑ Ⓒ

**Cathedral
Parkway
110 Street**

323

W 109th St

W 108th St

780

**Maurice
Schinasi
House**

245

196

W 107th St

171

162

240

174

61

72

141

20

Straus Park

934

W 106th St   (Duke Ellington Blvd)

**PAGE
274**

**Riverside
Park**

338

160

W 105th St

21

19

Broadway

256

146

912

448

327

915

W 104th St

324

**El Taller
Latino
Americano**

912

✉

Riverside Dr

**Frederick
Douglass
Houses**

❶

W 103rd St

320

256

**103rd
Street**

**Frederick
Douglass
Houses**

Ⓑ Ⓒ

**103rd
Street**

315

W 102nd St

256

48

315

W 101st St

382

**Fireman's
Memorial**

288

246

2638

830

495

315

W 100th St

258

2599

191

168

816

258

255

237

Park West
Village

215

Park West
Village

300

200

790

745

❶ ❷ ❸
96th Street

300

231

753

178

74

12

Ⓑ Ⓒ

W 96th St

321

258

96th Street

💺

738

2541

**Broadway
Mall
Community
Center**

731

186

**Joan
of Arc
Memorial**

738

222

271

W 95th St

241

**Pomander
Walk**

W 94th St

✉

314

200

W 93rd St

65

331

316

Broadway

Amsterdam Ave

677

176

Columbus Ave

West End Ave

280

2460

W 92nd St

640

315

Central Park West

850

West Dr

W 91st St

322

W 90th St   (Henry J Browne Blvd)

62
90

2441

2456

150

9A

300

600

178

293

300

178

76

**Soldiers and
Sailors
Monument**

778

W 89th St

300

500

574

2380

182

560

W 88th St

176

W 87th St

548

2279

178

W 86th St

541

515

56

Ⓑ Ⓒ

Riverside Dr

140

❶
86th Street

2348

540

86th Street

14 ▼

300

W 85th St

527

200

915

498

241

| 1/4 mile | | .25 km | |

**Hudson
River**

Neighborhood Overview

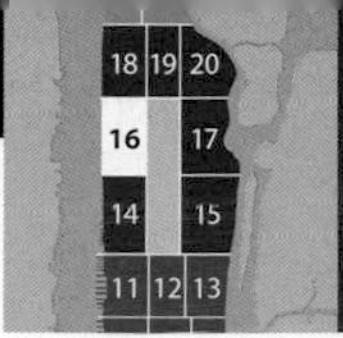

Map 16

Close to Columbia University, this neighborhood is home to much of New York's liberal intelligentsia. It is not uncommon to overhear discussions about the fate of health care reform or the latest Phillip Roth novel at the dog run, or on line for coffee at a neighborhood bakery. But the neighborhood is far from snobby. Mixed in with the college professors, theater directors, doctors, and lawyers are many families with young children, and twenty-somethings, all of whom enjoy the slower pace of life and physical beauty of Manhattan's Upper West Side.

This neighborhood is one of the greenest spaces in New York. Situated between Riverside and Central Park, there are many places to run, bike, or sit in the shade of a tree. There are few tourist attractions in this part of Central Park, but the natural beauty of the park and its recreational spaces are abundant. You can enter the reservoir from this end of the park, and enjoy a scenic view while running 1.6 miles around a dirt path. Walking west from Central Park to Riverside Park, peek into **Pomander Walk**, a tiny, pedestrian-only street of tiny houses. In Riverside Park, take the time to explore the many famous monuments. After 9/11, neighborhood residents gathered at the **Fireman's Memorial** to commemorate those that were lost. The statue of **Joan of Arc** sits within an island on Riverside Drive that is maintained by neighborhood residents. Dedicated on Memorial Day in 1902 and modeled after a Corinthian temple, the **Soldiers and Sailors Monument** commemorates those who served during the Civil War. If you're looking for some place to sit and read, **Straus Park**, a small green island between West End and Broadway, offers a quiet spot to rest amid the bustle of the street.

For a neighborhood so far from the bustling theater hub of Times Square and Museum Mile, the Upper West Side offers its fair share of cultural entertainment. **Symphony Space** is a multidisciplinary arts center. There is always a reading or concert on the main stage, and the **Leonard Nimoy Thalia** next door is always showing a classic movie. Symphony Space also occasionally hosts free marathon concerts, and is known for its fun "Wall To Wall" series. Come early to get a seat and stay as long as you want. For jazz, check out **Smoke**; many well-known musicians perform. They also have excellent food. The **Underground Lounge** hosts decent comedy nights and also occasionally has live music. The West Side Arts Coalition sponsors visual arts exhibitions at the **Broadway Mall Community Center** in a renovated Beaux-Arts building in the middle of Broadway. **El Taller Latino Americano** has live music, salsa dancing, and an occasional film, as well as Spanish classes, all very affordable.

For cheap drinks, check out **Abbey Pub** or **Broadway Dive**. For a good LGBT spot, head to **Suite**. Go Euro with the Beligum brews at **B. Cafe**. **Cleopatra's Needle** is jamming with open mike and jam sessions around the grand piano and **Smoke** is, uh, smokin' with live jazz. The **Village Pourhouse** is where the football fans and softball teams go.

Map 16

18 19 20
16 17
14 15
11 12 13

Upper West Side (Upper)

O Landmarks

- **Broadway Mall Community Center** •
W 96th St & Broadway
Beaux-Arts home of The West Side Arts
Coalition.
- **El Taller** • 2710 Broadway [W 104th St]
212-665-9460
Vibrant cultural hub for Latino art, music, and
dance.
- **Firemen's Memorial** •
W 100th St & Riverside Dr
Memorial to fallen fire fighters.
- **Joan of Arc Memorial** •
Riverside Dr & W 93rd St
Impressive statue erected in 1915.
- **Pomander Walk** • 261 W 94th St [Broadway]
Great little hideaway.
- **Riverside Park** •
Hudson River b/n 59th & 155th St
212-870-3070
330 acres of Olmsted/Moses parkland along
the Hudson River.
- **Schinasi Mansion** •
351 Riverside Dr [W 107th St]
My name is Elmer J. Fudd, I own a mansion...
- **Soldiers and Sailors Monument** •
W 89th St & Riverside Dr
It's been seen in *Law & Order*, along with
everything else in New York.
- **Straus Park** • Broadway & W 106th St
Green respite just off the craziness of
Broadway.

Coffee

- **Le Pain Quotidien** •
2463 Broadway [W 91st St]
212-769-8879
Excellent coffee and pastries. Thanks Belgium.
- **Silver Moon Bakery** •
2740 Broadway [W 105th St]
212-866-4717
Delicious morning coffee and croissant.

 Farmers Markets

- **97th Street Greenmarket** •
Columbus Ave & W 97th St

🍸 Nightlife

- **Broadway Dive** • 2662 Broadway [W 101st St]
212-865-2662
How's that for a name?
- **Buceo 95** • 201 W 95th St [Amsterdam Ave]
212-662-7010
Surprisingly affordable wine bar with delicious
tapas.
- **Cleopatra's Needle** •
2485 Broadway [W 92nd St]
212-769-6969
Solid middle eastern food and solid live jazz
performances.
- **Dive Bar** • 732 Amsterdam Ave [W 96th St]
212-749-4358
That's "dive" as in "deep"; Columbia hangout.
- **Lion's Head Tavern** •
995 Amsterdam Ave [W 109th St]
212-866-1030
Sports bar where locals and Columbia
students drink cheaply.
- **The Parlour** • 250 W 86th St [Broadway]
212-580-8923
Irish pub, two spaces, good hangout.
- **Smoke** • 2751 Broadway [W 106th St]
212-864-6662
Local jazz hangout. Sunday nights are fun.
- **Suite** • 992 Amsterdam Ave [W 109th St]
212-222-4600
Karaoke on Thursdays. Rare gay bar in the
neighborhood.
- **Tap A Keg** • 2731 Broadway [W 104th St]
212-749-1734
Cheap beer and pool tables!

Wait in line for bagels and lox at **Barney Greengrass**. Jam econo with the rice & beans at either **Flor de Mayo** or **El Malecon**. Dine on awesome Mexican at **Taqueri Y Fonda** and rich Indian at **Indus Valley**. On the go? Swing by **Roti Roll** for Indian treats, **Absolute Bagels** for freshness right out of the oven, and pastry rivaling what you'd find in Paris at **Silver Moon Bakery**.

Restaurants

Awash • 947 Amsterdam Ave [W 106th St]
212-961-1416 • $$
Tasty Ethiopian.

Ayurveda Café •
706 Amsterdam Ave [W 94th St]
212-932-2400 • $$$
Indian veggie delights for the body and soul.

Barney Greengrass •
541 Amsterdam Ave [W 86th St]
212-724-4707 • $$$
Sturgeon and eggs make the perfect NYC b-fast.

Bella Luna • 574 Columbus Ave [W 88th St]
212-877-2267 • $$$
Old fashion Italian with live jazz Tuesdays.

Blockheads •
951 Amsterdam Ave [W 106th St]
212-662-8226 • $$
Mexican, SF-style food for, well you know, blockheads.

Broadway Restaurant •
2664 Broadway [W 101st St]
212-865-7074 • $
Great breakfast and sandwiches, good place to start the day.

Carmine's • 2450 Broadway [W 91st St]
212-362-2200 • $$$
Large-portion Italian.

Cascabel Taqueria •
2799 Broadway [W 108th St]
212-665-1500 •
Great Mexican food and drinks; nice outdoor seating.

City Diner • 2441 Broadway [W 90th St]
212-877-2720 • $$
Neighborhood joint.

Crepes on Columbus •
990 Columbus Ave [W 109th St]
212-222-0259 • $$
Savory & sweet crepes in abundance.

Edgar's Café •
650 Amsterdam Ave [W 92nd St]
212-496-6126 • $$
Salads, desserts, and atmosphere.

El Malecon • 764 Amsterdam Ave [W 97th St]
212-864-5648 • $
Roast chicken and a con leche.

• **El Rey de la Caridad** •
973 Amsterdam Ave [W 108th St]
212-222-7383 • $$
Enjoy a Dominican feast. Bring your Spanish dictionary.

• **Flor de Mayo** • 484 Amsterdam Ave
212-787-3388 • $$
Cuban-Chinese-Chicken-Chow.

• **Gabriela's** • 688 Columbus Ave [W 94th St]
212-961-9600 • $$
Cheery Mexican.

• **Gennaro** • 665 Amsterdam Ave [W 92nd St]
212-665-5348 • $$$
Crowded Italian

• **Giovanni's** • 1011 Columbus Ave [W 109th St]
212-663-7000 • $$
Pretty good slice.

• **Henry's** • 2745 Broadway [W 105th St]
212-866-0600 • $$$
Friendly uptown joint.

• **Indus Valley** • 1350 Broadway [W 100th St]
212-257-4016 • $$$
Locals rave about this Indian food but it costs.

• **Jerusalem Restaurant** •
2715 Broadway [W 104th St]
212-865-2295 • $
Good Middle Eastern, friendly service, open late.

• **Kouzan** • 685 Amsterdam Ave [W 93rd St]
212-280-8099 • $$
Upscale Japanese dining with a pseudo nightclub-like atmosphere.

• **La Mirabelle** • 102 W 86th St [Columbus Ave]
212-496-0458 • $$$
New York old-timers keep coming back for classic French cuisine.

• **Malaysia Grill** • 224 W 104th St [Broadway]
212-579-1333 • $$
Inexpensive Malaysian pleasure.

• **Mermaid Inn** •
568 Amsterdam Ave [W 88th St]
212-799-7400 • $$$$
Simple seafood creations in a tasteful setting.

• **Metro Diner** • 2641 Broadway [W 100th St]
212-866-0800 • $$
Get in line for weekend brunch.

Upper West Side (Upper)

• **Momofuku Milk Bar** •
561 Columbus Ave [W 87th St]
347-577-9504 • $$
A dessert-lover's delight (try the cake truffles!).

• **Noche Mexicana** •
842 Amsterdam Ave [W 102nd St]
212-662-6900 • $$
Certainly more authentic than Blockheads up
the street.

• **Pio Pio Salon** •
702 Amsterdam Ave [W 94th St]
212-665-3000 • $$
Tasty rotisserie chicken with all the fixins.
Thanks Peru!

• **Pizzeria Sirenetta** •
568 Amsterdam Ave [W 88th St]
212-799-7401 • $$$
Rustic Italianesque pizzeria from Mermaid Inn
folks.

• **Regional** • 2607 Broadway [W 98th St]
212-666-1915 • $$$
20 regional Italian cuisines and Sunday
brunch.

• **Roti Roll Bombay Frankie** •
994 Amsterdam Ave [W 109th St]
212-666-1500 • $
Hole-in-the-wall rotis to soak up alcohol.

• **Saiguette** • 935 Columbus Ave [W 106th St]
212-866-6888 • $
Damn good Vietnamese including
scrumptious banh mi sandwiches.

• **Talia's Steakhouse** •
668 Amsterdam Ave [W 93rd St]
212-580-3770 • $$$$
Your basic everyday kosher steakhouse.

• **Taqueria Y Fonda** •
968 Amsterdam Ave [W 108th St]
212-531-0383 • $$
Amazing Mexican dive. Columbia kids love this
place.

• **Thai Market** •
960 Amsterdam Ave [W 107th St]
212-280-4575 • $$
Another favorite Thai among locals.

Upper West Side (Upper)

Map 16

Looking for a nice bottle of wine to bring to dinner? Try **Whole Foods Wine**, which is the first branch of the upscale grocery store to have one. **Barzini's** has nice fresh produce as does **Garden of Eden**. For smoked fish and prepared foods try **The Kosher Marketplace**. **Schatzie's** is the best butcher around and **Joon Fine Seafood** has fresh fish at fair prices.

Shopping

• Absolute Bagels •
2788 Broadway [W 108th St]
212-932-2052
Amazing. Home of the hard-to-find pumpernickel raisin.
• Barzini's • 2451 Broadway [W 91st St]
212-874-4992
Huge selection of cheeses. Fresh bread and produce.
• Ben & Jerry's • 2722 Broadway [W 104th St]
212-866-6737
Hippie treat trifecta: Cherry Garcia, Phish Food, and Half Baked.
• Champion Bicycles •
896 Amsterdam Ave [W 104th St]
212-662-2690
Well priced, good guys.
• Garden of Eden •
2780 Broadway [W 107th St]
212-222-7300
Produce is pretty good here.
• Gotham Wines And Liquors •
2517 Broadway [W 94th St]
212-932-0990
Friendly neighborhood favorite.
• Gothic Cabinet Craft •
2652 Broadway [W 101st St]
212-678-4368
Real wood furniture. Made in Queens!
• Health Nuts • 2611 Broadway [W 99th St]
212-678-0054
Standard health food store.
• Innovation Bike Shop •
105 W 106th St [Columbus Ave]
212-678-7130
Sales, service, rentals, and accessories.
Janovic • 2680 Broadway [W 102nd St]
212-531-2300
Top NYC paint store.
The Kosher Marketplace •
2442 Broadway [W 90th St]
212-580-6378
For all of your Kosher needs.

• Mani Marketplace •
697 Columbus Ave [W 94th St]
212-662-4392
Fantastic little grocery with jazz on the sound system.
• Michael's • 808 Columbus Ave [W 100th St]
212-865-0813
Gigantic arts and crafts store straight from suburbia.
• Mitchell's Wine & Liquor Store •
200 W 86th St [Amsterdam Ave]
212-874-2255
Worth a trip just for the gorgeous neon sign.
• Mugi Pottery •
993 Amsterdam Ave [W 109th St]
212-866-6202
Handcrafted pottery. Like in the movie *Ghost*.
• Murray's Sturgeon Shop •
2429 Broadway [W 90th St]
212-724-2650
UWS comfort food: rugelah, knishes, and, lots of sturgeon.
• New Westlane Wines & Liquor •
689 Columbus Ave [W 93rd St]
212-678-4908
Behind the bullet proof glass is a pretty good selection.
• New York Flowers & Plant Shed •
209 W 96th St [Amsterdam Ave]
212-662-4400
Makes you wish you had more (or any) garden space.
• Schatzie The Butcher •
2665 Broadway
212-410-1555
Butcher with good prime meat and poultry.
• Upper 90 Soccer & Sport •
697 Amsterdam Ave [W 94th St]
646-863-3105
Great selection of soccer apparel and accessories.
• Whole Foods • 808 Columbus Ave [W 97th St]
212-222-6160
Finally. Good fresh food north of 96th Street.
• Whole Foods Wine •
808 Columbus Ave [W 100th St]
212-222-6160
Featuring lots of NY State wines.

Map 17 · **Upper East Side / East Harlem**

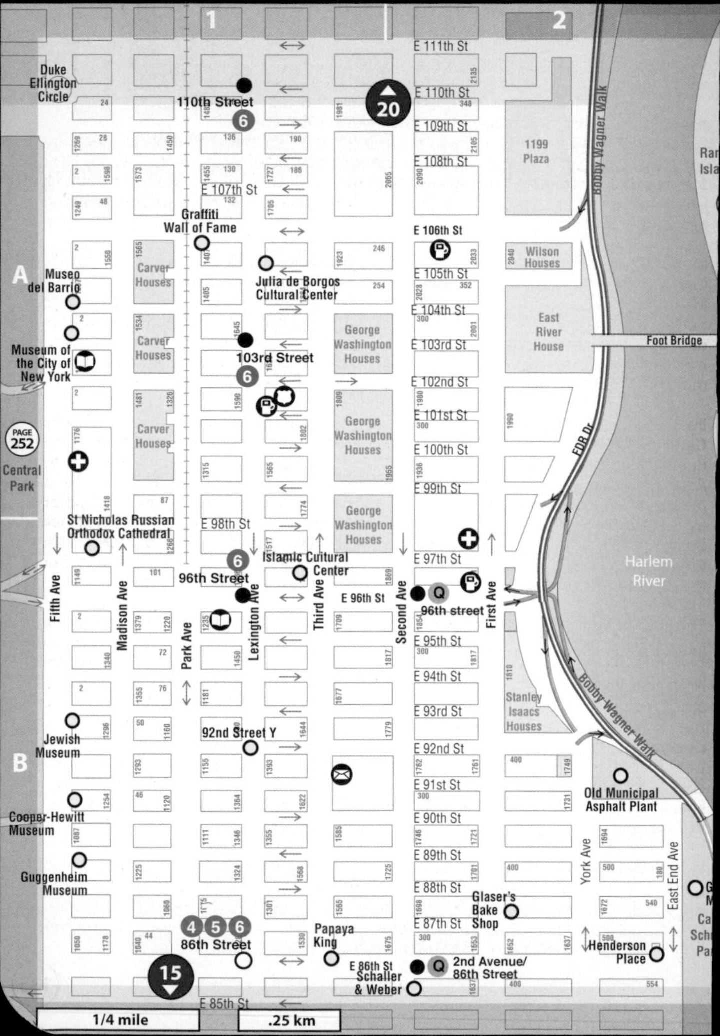

1

2

E 111th St

Duke
Ellington
Circle

24

110th Street
6

1199
Plaza

E 110th St
20

E 109th St

E 108th St

E 107th St

A

Graffiti
Wall of Fame

Museo
del Barrio

Carver
Houses

Julia de Borgos
Cultural Center

E 106th St

E 105th St

Wilson
Houses

Museum of
the City of
New York

Carver
Houses

E 104th St

E 103rd St

George
Washington
Houses

East
River
House

Foot Bridge

PAGE
252

Central
Park

103rd Street
6

Carver
Houses

E 102nd St

E 101st St

E 100th St

George
Washington
Houses

St Nicholas Russian
Orthodox Cathedral

E 99th St

E 98th St

George
Washington
Houses

Harlem
River

Islamic Cultural
Center

E 97th St

96th Street
6

E 96th St

Q
96th street

Fifth Ave

Madison Ave

Park Ave

Lexington Ave

Third Ave

E 95th St

Second Ave

First Ave

E 94th St

E 93rd St

Stanley
Isaacs
Houses

92nd Street Y

E 92nd St

B

Jewish
Museum

E 91st St

E 90th St

Old Municipal
Asphalt Plant

Cooper-Hewitt
Museum

E 89th St

E 88th St

Guggenheim
Museum

Glaser's
Bake
Shop

York Ave

East End Ave

4 5 6
86th Street

Papaya
King

E 87th St

E 86th St

Henderson
Place

15

Schaller
& Weber

E 86th St

2nd Avenue/
86th Street

Q

E 85th St

1/4 mile

.25 km

Neighborhood Overview

Map 17

18	19	20
16		17
14		15
11	12	13

Whew, finally a break from the chaos. This part of the Upper East Side is a place for families, young, old, black, white, Latino, rich, poor—it just depends what block you stumble upon. Head above 96th Street for some of the best Mexican food on the planet, or head west to Central Park, where you'll find kids and adults playing soccer, softball, and football. Get some culture at the neighborhoods museums, get some knowledge at a lecture at the **92nd Street Y**, but most importantly, get ready to be somewhere where people can actually live, work, and shop. Nothing hip or cool here, this is just a good old-fashioned New York neighborhood.

Much of this part of the Upper East Side is known as Carnegie Hill, named for the Carnegie Mansion on 91st and Fifth Avenue (it's now the **Cooper-Hewitt Design Museum**). **Gracie Mansion**, the charming Federal-style mansion in Carl Schurz Park, dates to 1799 and has served as the official residence of New York City mayors since the days of Florello La Guardia. **Henderson Place**, built in 1881 for families of "moderate means" was designed by the architectures of Lamb and Rich and with 24 units still remaining, serves as an example of original middle-class living in the Big Apple.

Ever think a Soviet battle could take place on American soil? The **Russian Orthodox Cathedral of St. Nicholas** was the site of a power struggle between czarist and Soviet Russians after its founding in 1902. Finally conflict-free, it is an amazing sight to see. **Asphalt Green**, an old municipal asphalt plant, now houses sports fields; the source of much controversy, some called it the ugliest thing they'd ever seen, but MoMA hailed it as a masterpiece of functional design. Head over to 91st Street and decide for yourself. Both visitors and native New Yorkers will learn something new at **The Museum of the City of New York**, with its vast collection of over 1.5 million objects and images telling the story of the city's past.

The Jewish Museum features works by Chagall, a video and film archive, and traveling exhibits that are always worth a peek. Head up to 104th Street and down to the Caribbean at **Museo del Barrio**, where you can find an excellent collection of Latin American art. Elsewhere, **The Guggenheim** not only houses Picasso, Chagall, Mondrian, and Kandinsky but is also a piece of art itself, with Frank Lloyd Wright's influence seen on the swirling staircase that guides visitors through. One of the best ways to see the Guggenheim is on the first Friday of every month at Art After Dark, where visitors can tour the museum and enjoy some cocktails and music along the way. Before you leave, check the schedule at the **92nd Street Y**, which frequently hosts boldface-name speakers. And the **Graffiti Wall of Fame** at 106th and Park (yes, that 106 & Park for those BET fans out there), is an awesome collection of street art at its best.

Wanna watch the game or play a few games of beer pong? You've come to the right place. Check out the cheap specials at **Rathbones**, watch the big game at **Kinsale**, or "dive" right into things at **Reif's**. Then, escape the beer-filled Upper East Side bars with a stop for a cozy drink at **Auction House**, or **ABV** and its smartly curated beer and wine lists, or even the mixology of **The Guthrie Inn**.

Map 17

18	19	20
16	17	
14	15	
11	12	13

Upper East Side / East Harlem

O Landmarks

- **92nd Street Y** •
  1395 Lexington Ave [E 92nd St]
  212-415-5500
  Community hub for film, theater, and
  interesting lectures.
- **Asphalt Green** • E 90th St & East End Ave
  212-369-8890
  Industrial architecture turned sports facility.
- **Cooper-Hewitt National Design Museum** • 2
  E 91st St [5th Ave]
  212-849-8400
  Great design shows; run by the Smithsonian.
- **El Museo del Barrio** •
  1230 5th Ave [E 104th St]
  212-831-7272
  NYC's only Latino museum.
- **Glaser's Bake Shop** • 1670 1st Ave [E 87th St]
  212-289-2562
  Best black-and-white cookies for more than a
  century.
- **Gracie Mansion** • E End Ave & 88th St
  212-570-4751
  Our own Buckingham Palace, right above the
  FDR drive.
- **Graffiti Wall of Fame** • E 106th St & Park Ave
  This street art will blow you away.
- **Guggenheim Museum** •
  1071 5th Ave [E 88th St]
  212-423-3500
  Wright's only building in NYC, but it's one of
  the best.
- **Henderson Place** • E End Ave & E 86th St
  Charming Queen Anne-style apartment
  houses circa 1881–82.
- **Islamic Cultural Center** •
  1711 3rd Ave [E 96th St]
  212-722-5234
  Enormous and extraordinary mosque. Bustling
  on Fridays.
- **The Jewish Museum** •
  1109 5th Ave [E 92nd St]
  212-423-3200
  Over 28,000 artifacts of Jewish culture and
  history.
- **Julia de Burgos Latino Cultural Center** •
  1680 Lexington Ave [E 105th St]
  212-831-4333
  Artistic and community hub of East Harlem.

- **Museum of the City of New York** •
  1220 5th Ave [E 103rd St]
  212-534-1672
  Fascinating exhibitions on life in the big city.
- **Papaya King** • 179 E 86th St [3rd Ave]
  212-369-0648
  Dishing out damn good dogs since 1932.
- **Schaller & Weber** • 1654 2nd Ave [E 86th St]
  212-879-3047
  A relic of old Yorkville with great German
  meats.
- **St. Nicholas Russian Orthodox Cathedral** •
  15 E 97th St [5th Ave]
  This UES cathedral, built in 1902, remains the
  center of Russian Orthodoxy in the US.

Coffee

- **Gracie's Diner** • 352 E 86th St [2nd Ave]
  212-879-9425
  Old-school diner. Open 24 hrs.

O Farmers Markets

- **92nd St Greenmarket** • 1st Ave & E 92nd St
  Sun 9 am–5 pm July–Nov
- **Harvest Home East Harlem Farmers Market** •
  3rd Ave & E 104th St
  212-828-3361
  Thu 8 am–4pm, Jul–Nov
- **Mount Sinai Greenmarket** •
  Madison Ave & E 99th St
  Wed 8 am–4 pm July–Nov

Nightlife

- **Auction House** • 300 E 89th St [2nd Ave]
  212-427-4458
  Stylish lounge…or at least stylish for the
  Upper East Side.
- **Biddy's Pub** • 301 E 91st St [2nd Ave]
  212-534-4785
  Skip the pretension, grab the beer at this small
  neighborhood spot.
- **The District** • 1679 3rd Ave [E 94th St]
  212-289-2005
  Upscale pub for the grown up frat boys.

Upper East Side / East Harlem

Map 17

For the signature UES meal, there's nothing like brunch at **Sarabeth's**. If you want to shell out for a good steak, head to the **Parlor Steakhouse**. Also, don't miss the the bar food at **Earl's Beer & Cheese**, *cemitas* sandwiches at **Cafe Ollin**, and Alsatian at **Cafe D'Alsace**. Between paydays, head over to **Papaya King** ("Tastier than a filet mignon") or **Shake Shack**.

- **Earl's Beer & Cheese** •
1259 Park Ave [E 97th St]
212-289-1581
Best beer selection for miles. And awesome food.
- **East End Bar and Grill** •
1604 1st Ave [E 87th St]
212-348-3783
Mellow Irish hang out.
- **Eastside Billiards** •
163 E 86th St [Lexington Ave]
212-831-7665
Go for the pool, not the atmosphere.
- **The Guthrie Inn** • 1259 Park Ave [E 97th St]
212-423-9900
Amazing cocktails from a well-known mixologist.
- **The Lexington Social** •
1634 Lexington Ave [E 104th St]
646-820-7013
Good happy hour and tapas.
- **Phil Hughes** • 1682 1st Ave [E 88th St]
212-722-9415
An honest-to-god dive bar on the UES.
- **Rathbones Pub** • 1702 2nd Ave [E 88th St]
212-369-7361
Your basic Manhattan pub.
- **Reif's Tavern** • 302 E 92nd St [2nd Ave]
212-426-0519
Dive-o-rama since 1942.
- **Third Avenue Ale House** •
1644 3rd Ave [E 92nd St]
646-559-9131
New school pub food and beer brunches.

Restaurants

- **Barking Dog** • 1678 3rd Ave [E 94th St]
212-831-1800 • $$
Woof woof. This food ain't too bad.
- **Burritos Y Mas** • 1571 Lexington Ave
[E 101st St]• $
646-918-7478
Tiny spot, big burritos, from steak to seitan.

- **Café D'Alsace** • 1695 2nd Ave [E 88th St]
212-722-5133 • $$$$
Chic Alsatian bistro with an actual beer sommelier.
- **Cafe Ollin** • 339 E 108th St [1st Ave]
212-828-3644 • $
Tiny Mexican hole cranking out awesome cemitas and more.
- **Cafe Sabarsky** • 1048 5th Ave [E 86th St]
212-288-0665 • $$$
Beautiful wood-paneled surroundings for sipping Viennese coffee.
- **Corner Bakery** • 1645 3rd Ave [E 92nd St]
212-860-0060 • $$
Brisk brunch spot with dine-in and take-out options.
- **Delizia 92 Ristorante & Pizza** •
1762 2nd Ave [E 92nd St]
212-996-3720 • $$
Great, if slightly overpriced, NYC pizza and pasta.
- **El Caribeno** • 1675 Lexington Ave [E 105th St]
212-831-3996 • $$
Dominican hang out for roast chicken and pork.
- **El Paso** • 1643 Lexington Ave [E 104th St]
212-831-9831 • $
Fantastic Mexican. Try the chilaquiles and spicy guacamole.
- **El Paso Taqueria** • 64 E 97th St [Park Ave]
212-996-1739 • $$
Finally, real Mexican food at incredibly good prices.
- **GK Triple A Diner** • 2061 2nd Ave [E 106th St]
212-410-6950 • $
Standard diner food.
- **Gracie's Diner** • 352 E 86th St [2nd Ave]
212-879-9425 • $
Diner that's open all night.

Map 17

18 19 20
16 17
14 15
11 12 13

Upper East Side / East Harlem

- **Il Salumaio** • 1731 2nd Ave [90th St]
646-852-6876 • $$
Cozy wine bar with an Italian deli counter.
- **Infirmary NYC** • 1720 2nd Ave [E 89th St]
917-388-2512 • $$$
HMO-approved Cajun food.
- **Joy Burger Bar** •
1567 Lexington Ave [E 100th St]
212-289-6222 • $
Burgers that, yes, bring joy to your mouth.
- **La Isla Restaurant** • 1883 3rd Ave [E 104th St]
212-534-0002 • $
Locals get take-out from this Puerto Rican
diner.
- **Libertador** • 1725 2nd Ave [E 89th St]
212-348-6222 • $$
Grilled meats and empanadas.
- **Little Luzzo's** • 119 E 96th St [Park Ave]
212-369-2300 • $
In the pizza wasteland of the UES, these slices
hit the spot.
- **Mansion Restaurant** •
1634 York Ave [E 87th St]
212-535-8888 • $
Don't be scared of anything on this diner's
massive menu.
- **Maz Mezcal** • 316 E 86th St [2nd Ave]
212-472-1599 • $$
Decent Mexican in a soulless area, good salsa.
- **Midnight Express Diner** • 1715 2nd Ave [E
89th St]
212-860-2320 • $
Fine for breakfast, downright amazing for 3 am
food.
- **Naruto Ramen** • 1596 3rd Ave [E 90th St]
212-289-7803 • $$
Sip Japanese soup at the cramped counter.
- **Nick's Restaurant & Pizzeria** •
1814 2nd Ave [E 94th St]
212-987-5700 • $$$
Piping hot, thin-crust, brick oven pizza (and
pasta).
- **Noglu** • 1266 Madison Ave [E 91st St]
646-895-9798 • $$$
Upscale gluten-free French import.

- **Papaya King** • 179 E 86th St [3rd Ave]
212-369-0648 • $
Dishing out damn good dogs since 1932.
- **Peri Ela** • 1361 Lexington Ave [E 90th St]
212-410-4300 • $$
Classy Turkish restaurant.
- **Pinocchio Ristorante** •
1748 1st Ave [E 91st St]
212-828-5810 • $$$$$
Itty bitty sleeper Italian with rave reviews and
loyal fans.
- **Pío Pío** • 1746 1st Ave [E 91st St]
212-426-5800 • $$
The Matador chicken combo will feed the
whole family.
- **Russ & Daughters at the Jewish Museum** •
1109 5th Ave 92nd St • $$$
Lower East Side lox masters' cafe inside the
Jewish Museum.
- **Sabor A Mexico** • 1744 1st Ave [E 90th St]
212-289-2641 • $$
Small, home-cooked, cheap, and delicious.
- **Sarabeth's** • 1295 Madison Ave [E 92nd St]
212-410-7335 • $$$
Good upper class breakfast, if you can get in.
- **Schaller's Stube** • 1652 2nd Ave [E 86th St]
646-726-4355 • $$
Sausage counter from the German meat
market next door.
- **Sfoglia** • 1402 Lexington Ave [E 92nd St]
212-831-1402 • $$$$
Exquisite and experimental Italian by 92nd
Street Y.
- **Shake Shack** • 154 E 86th St [Lexington Ave]
646-237-5035 • $
Finally, something good on 86th Street.
- **Table d'Hote** • 44 E 92nd St [Madison Ave]
212-348-8125 • $$$$
Cozy French vibe. Good Prix Fixe.
- **Uptown Lounge** • 1576 3rd Ave [E 89th St]
212-828-1388 • $$
Decent food meets incredibly potent cocktail
specials.

Feed your mind at **The Corner Bookstore** before heading over to **Eli's Vinegar Factory** for an overpriced (but delicious) bag of groceries. For German treats and meats, **Schaller & Weber** is the place. **Mister Wright** knows his wine and booze. **Wankel's** is the best for hardware. Make the kids happy at **The Children's General Store**. Of course, what you're really here for are the black-and-white cookies at **Glaser's**.

- **The Weir** • 1672 Third Ave (E 94th St)
  646-895-9581
  Cheery Irish pub with slick design & sports on TV.
- **White Castle** • 351 E 103rd St [1st Ave]
  212-876-6737 • $
  One of four in Manhattan.
- **Zebu Grill** • 305 E 92nd St [2nd Ave]
  212-426-7500 • $$$$$
  Candlelit Brazilian bistro with exposed brick and earthy wooden tables.

Shopping

- **Blacker & Kooby Stationers** •
  1390 Lexington Ave [E 92nd St]
  212-369-8308
  Good selection of stationery, pens, and art supplies.
- **Cooper-Hewitt National Design Museum Shop** • 2 E 91st St [5th Ave]
  212-849-8355
  Cool design stuff.
- **Corner Bookstore** •
  1313 Madison Ave [E 93rd St]
  212-831-3554
  Tiny, old-school shop. Great selection.
- **Danny's Cycles** • 1690 2nd Ave [E 87th St]
  212-722-2201
  Service, repair, and rentals.
- **Glaser's Bake Shop** • 1670 1st Ave [E 87th St]
  212-289-2562
  Best black-and-white cookies for more than a century.

- **Housing Works Thrift Shop** •
  1730 2nd Ave [E 90th St]
  212-722-8306
  Uptown outpost of our favorite thrift shop.
- **Kitchen Arts & Letters** •
  1435 Lexington Ave [E 93rd St]
  212-876-5550
  Fine selection of food and wine books.
- **La Tropezienne Bakery** •
  2131 1st Ave [E 110th St]
  212-860-5324
  Excellent French bakery in El Barrio.
- **Mister Wright Fine Wines & Spirits** •
  1593 3rd Ave [E 90th St]
  212-722-4564
  Good liquor store with huge selection and tastings.
- **Museum of the City of New York** •
  1220 5th Ave [E 103rd St]
  212-534-1672
  Great NYC-focused gift shop.
- **Schaller & Weber** • 1654 2nd Ave [E 86th St]
  212-879-3047
  A relic of old Yorkville with countless German meats.
- **Vinyl Wine** • 1491 Lexington Ave [E 96th St]
  646-370-4100
  Excellent hand-picked selection. And a record player.
- **Wankel's Hardware** • 1573 3rd Ave [E 88th St]
  212-369-1200
  The best hardware store around.

Map 18 • Columbia / Morningside Heights Ⓝ

Neighborhood Overview

Map 18

Squeezed between the Upper West Side and Harlem, Columbia and Morningside Heights have had a symbiotic relationship with ups and downs. In truth, any institution with a multi-billion-dollar endowment (and we're talking multi-multi-billion-dollar here) is going to get to call the shots, but like every other behemoth institution of learning in an urban environment understands, the delicate dance takes constant maintenance. For your purposes, 116th Street between Broadway and Amsterdam is the main entrance of the gorgeous main campus of Columbia. A stroll through here is almost edifying—or at the very least a pleasant escape from the chaotic city around, just watch out for the freshmen rushing to and from class.

Until the late 19th century, Morningside Heights was mostly undeveloped farmland. In 1895, **Columbia University** moved from Midtown Manhattan to 116th and Broadway, the site of a former insane asylum, and the rest is history. Over time the university was perceived as a Gibraltar of culture within a barren, dangerous part of town; that psychodrama played out in the notorious 1968 campus protests, ostensibly over plans to build a gym in Morningside Park but really over just about everything as the world around seemed to implode. Tensions eased over time, especially after Morningside Heights rents began to skyrocket in the '90s, but Morningside Park still serves as the dividing line between Columbia and basically everything else. Today, that relationship ebbs and flows as the university's plans for expansion heat up, generating both land disputes (including unseemly eminent domain fights) and of course more gentrification.

But speaking of "seeing light" (or whatever Columbia's "In lumine Tuo videbimus lumen" motto refers to; our Latin basically sucks), there's also the **Cathedral of St. John the Divine**, the world's largest Anglican church and fourth largest church in the world. An awe-inspiring display of architecture and that something else that makes people want to build stuff very high into the air, the cathedral is a beacon for procrastinators everywhere, although it dates back to the 19th century, the thing is still unfinished. The church has three distinct phases of construction that are immediately visible as you gaze up at the Gothic masterwork. The grounds are just as fun; look for the resident peacocks and sculptor Greg Wyatt's 40-foot-high *Peace Fountain* that goofs on tried-and-true allegorical representations of good and evil.

Meanwhile, there's an old corny joke that should hip you to who is actually buried in **Grant's Tomb**—or not, since it's really a mausoleum for the head of the Union Army and the 18th President of the United States (along with the 19th First Lady). The final resting place of Ulysses S. Grant, who spent the last part of his life in New York City working on a memoir (sounds familiar, no?), is actually a national memorial under the supervision of the National Park Service. Don't miss the asinine mosaic tile benches around the perimeter, someone's screwy idea of a "fun" public art project from the late 1960s.

Right across the street from Grant's Tomb is **Riverside Church**, an interdenominational house of worship with longstanding ties to the city's African American community. Martin Luther King, Jr., Nelson Mandela, and Kofi Annan have all given notable speeches at the church; Dr. King most famously denounced the Vietnam war here. The Gothic architecture is modeled after the cathedral in Chartres, France and the 392-foot-high tower—one of Upper Manhattan's most notable landmarks—is unusual in that it's actually functional, with 24 floors worth of programming space.

Since outsiders rarely head uptown, neighborhood nightlife mostly consists of grad students avoiding dissertations in beer bars (**1020Bar**), undergrads avoiding papers with heavier drinking (**The Heights Bar & Grill**), and residents avoiding that all in dives (**Paddy's**). Columbia will regularly bring in world-class operas at the **Miller Theater**.

O Landmarks

- **Cathedral Church of St. John the Divine** •
1047 Amsterdam Ave [W 112th St]
212-316-7540
Our favorite cathedral. Completely unfinished
and usually in disarray, just the way we like it.
- **Columbia University** •
2960 Broadway [W 116th St]
212-854-1754
A nice little sanctuary amid the roiling masses.
- **Grant's Tomb** • W 122nd St & Riverside Dr
212-666-1640
A totally underrated experience, interesting,
great grounds.
- **Pupin Hall** • 550 W 120th St [Broadway]
Original site of the Manhattan Project.

Coffee

- **Cafe Amrita** • 301 W 110th St [Central Park W]
212-222-0683
Study (or update your blog) while you
caffeinate.
- **Hungarian Pastry Shop** •
1030 Amsterdam Ave [W 111th St]
212-866-4230
Professors and grad students love to read here.
- **Joe Coffee** •
550 W 120th St [Broadway]
212-924-7400
Third-wave Joe mini-chain Columbia campus
outpost.
- **Max Caffe** •
1262 Amsterdam Ave [W 122nd St]
212-531-1210
Great spot to hang out. Open at 8 am.
- **Oren's Daily Roast** •
2882 Broadway [W 112th St]
212-749-8779
Hip staff pours superior java at local
mini-chain.
- **Toast** • 3157 Broadway [La Salle St]
212-662-1144
Good coffee starting at 11 am.

Farmers Markets

- **Columbia Greenmarket** •
Broadway & W 114th St
Thu & Sun 8 am–6 pm, year round.
- **Morningside Park Farmers Market** •
Manhattan Ave & W 110th St
914-923-4837
Sat, 9 am–5 pm, June–Dec

The Columbia kids have many long-standing quick favorites such as the giant slices of **Koronet Pizza** or the quick Middle Eastern food of **Amir's**. For something more relaxed, try Ethiopian at **Massawa**, brunch time at **Kitchenette**, or the dangerously delicious meat emporium of **Dinosaur BBQ**. Italian lovers get their fix at cozy **Max SoHa** and the wonderful **Pisticci**.

Nightlife

- **1020 Bar** • 1020 Amsterdam Ave [W 110th St]
  212-531-3468
  Columbia dive with super cheap beer.
- **Cafe Amrita** • 301 W 110th St [Central Park W]
  212-222-0683
  Caffeinated Columbia students, snacks, wine, beer.
- **Cotton Club** • 656 W 125th St [St Clair Pl]
  212-663-7980
  Good, fun, swingin' uptown joint.
- **The Heights Bar & Grill** •
  2867 Broadway [W 111th St]
  212-866-7035
  Hang out on the rooftop with Columbia students.

- **Alfred Lerner Hall** • 2920 Broadway [W 114th St]
  212-854-9067
  Columbia student union features coffee, conventions, and wacky parties.
- **Max Caffe** •
  1262 Amsterdam Ave [W 122nd St]
  212-531-1210
  Low-key date place. Wine, good food, and sweet patio.
- **Showman's** •
  375 W 125th St [Morningside Ave]
  212-864-8941
  Live jazz. In Harlem. That's all you need to know.
- **Solomon & Kuff** • 2331 12th Ave [W 133rd St]
  212-939-9443
  Sharp focus on rum with sustainable West Indian menu items.

Columbia / Morningside Height

Map 18

18	19	20
16		17
14		15
11	12	13

 Restaurants

- **Amir's Grill** • 2911 Broadway [W 113th St]
212-749-7500 • $
A for price. B- for quality.
- **Bettolona** • 3143 Broadway [La Salle St]
212-749-1125 • $$$
Pizza from a wood burning oven in a sleek dining room.
- **Community Food and Juice** •
2893 Broadway [W 113th St]
212-665-2800 • $$$
Columbia foodies dig this place. And so should you.
- **Dinosaur Bar-B-Que** •
700 W 125th St [Broadway]
212-694-1777 • $$$
Not just for Syracuse fans. Head WAY uptown.
- **The Heights Bar & Grill** •
2867 Broadway [W 111th St]
212-866-7035 • $$
Columbia students can't drink all the time so they eat here.
- **Hungarian Pastry Shop** •
1030 Amsterdam Ave [W 111th St]
212-866-4230 • $
Exactly what it is—and excellent.
- **Jin Ramen** • 3183 Broadway [Tiemann Pl]
646-559-2862 • $$
Kickin' ramen for Columbia crowd to slurp on.
- **Kitchenette** •
1272 Amsterdam Ave [W 123rd St]
212-531-7600 • $$
Cozy and good for everything.
- **Koronet Pizza** • 2848 Broadway [W 111th St]
212-222-1566 • $
Just one slice. Really. That's all you'll need.
- **Le Monde** • 2885 Broadway [W 112th St]
212-531-3939 • $$
French bistro pub with a nice bar.

- **Massawa** • 1239 Amsterdam Ave [W 121st St]
212-663-0505 • $$
Neighborhood Ethiopian joint.
- **Max Soha** • 1274 Amsterdam Ave [W 123rd St]
212-531-2221 • $$
The Italian genius of Max, uptown.
- **Mill Korean** • 2895 Broadway [W 113th St]
212-666-7653 • $$
Good Korean for Columbia kids.
- **Miss Mamie's Spoonbread Too** •
366 W 110th St [Manhattan Ave]
212-865-6744 • $$
Soul food spectacular.
- **Pisticci** • 125 La Salle St [Broadway]
212-932-3500 • $$
Wonderful, friendly Italian. A true gem.
- **Subsconscious** •
1213 Amsterdam Ave [W 120th St]
212-864-2722 • $
Lunch deli with quality usually reserved for Midtown.
- **Symposium** •
544 W 113th St [Amsterdam Ave]
212-865-1011 • $$
Traditional underground (literally) Greek fare.
- **Toast** • 3157 Broadway [La Salle St]
212-662-1144 • $$
Great diverse café menu.
- **Tom's Restaurant** •
2880 Broadway [W 112th St]
212-864-6137 • $
Yes. This is the Seinfeld diner. Can we go now?
- **V&T Pizzeria** •
1024 Amsterdam Ave [W 110th St]
212-666-8051 • $
Columbia pizza and pasta. Family friendly if you're into that.

Columbia / Morningside Heights

Map 18

18 19 20
16 17
14 15
11 12 13

The newly-expanded **Book Culture** is a world-class academic bookstore and **Ricky's** provides a resource for style needs. Coffee on the go at **Oren's** or sit and talk Nietzsche at **Hungarian Pastry Shop**. Groceries and free samples at the 24-hour **Westside Market**. Or everything at the massive **Fairway**. And then you have a world-class neighborhood wine store in **Vino Fino**.

🛍 Shopping

- **Amsterdam Liquor & Wine •**
  1356 Amsterdam Ave [W 126th St]
  212-222-1334
  Stock up on your way to that beer pong party.
- **Appletree Market •**
  1225 Amsterdam Ave [W 120th St]
  212-865-8840
  One of the better grocery options for Columbia kids.
- **Book Culture •**
  536 W 112th St [Amsterdam Ave]
  212-865-1588
  Excellent bookstore servicing Columbia/Barnard students.
- **Book Culture •** 2915 Broadway [W 114th St]
  646-403-3000
  Offshoot of the original location that Columbia students love.
- **C-Town •** 560 W 125th St [Old Broadway]
  212-662-2388
  No-frills market way cheaper than your local bodega.
- **Clinton Supply Co. •**
  1256 Amsterdam Ave [W 122nd St]
  212-222-8245
  Random hardware stuff for your new dorm or apartment.
- **Fairway Market •** 2328 12th Ave [W 133rd St]
  212-234-3883
  So big. So good. So New York.
- **Franklin & Lennon Paint Co. •**
  537 W 125th St [Broadway]
  212-864-2460
  Long-standing outlet with biggest selection of paint and supplies.
- **Hartley Pharmacy •**
  1219 Amsterdam Ave [W 120th St]
  212-749-8481
  Mom-and-pop pharmacy with staff that knows you personally.
- **Mondel Chocolates •**
  2913 Broadway [W 114th St]
  212-864-2111
  Mom-and-pop candy shop with great chocolates.
- **Samad's Gourmet •**
  2867 Broadway [W 111th St]
  212-749-7555
  Hard to find Middle Eastern and world delicacies.
- **Sea & Sea Fish Market •**
  310 St Nicholas Ave [W 125th St]
  212-222-7427
  Fish and more fish. They'll fry it up for you!
- **University Hardware •**
  2905 Broadway [W 113th St]
  212-662-2150
  Where the smart kids get their hammers.
- **Vino Fino •**
  1252 Amsterdam Ave [W 122nd St]
  212-222-0388
  Lots of tastings and friendly owners.
- **Westside Market •**
  2840 Broadway [W 110th St]
  212-222-3367
  Bordering on gourmet shopping for Columbia U.

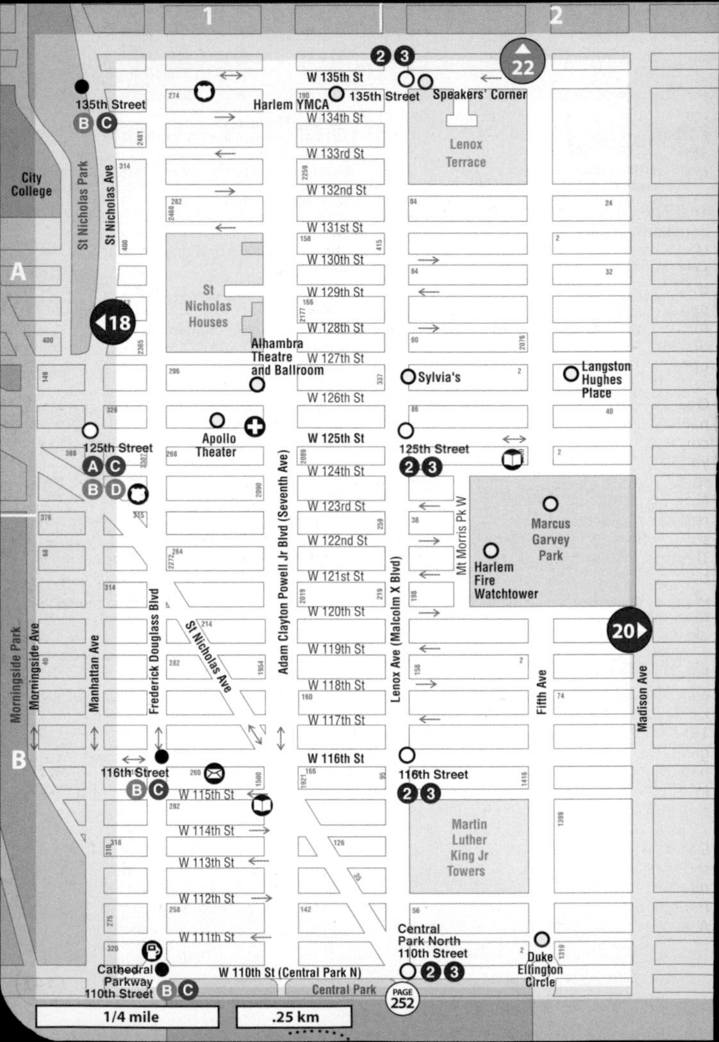

Map 19 • Harlem (Lower)

1

2

N

City College

St Nicholas Park

135th Street

B C

274

2481

314

St Nicholas Ave

400

A

St Nicholas Houses

St Nicholas Houses

2365

282

2640

158

415

St Nicholas Ave

148

296

328

380

Morningside Ave

58

Manhattan Ave

264

376

Frederick Douglass Blvd

565

282

714

1954

St Nicholas Ave

Morningside Park

B

318

275

320

2 3

W 135th St

135th Street

Harlem YMCA

W 134th St

W 133rd St

W 132nd St

W 131st St

W 130th St

W 129th St

W 128th St

Alhambra Theatre and Ballroom

W 127th St

W 126th St

125th Street

A C

B D

Apollo Theater

Adam Clayton Powell Jr Blvd (Seventh Ave)

W 125th St

W 124th St

W 123rd St

W 122nd St

W 121st St

W 120th St

W 119th St

W 118th St

W 117th St

W 116th St

116th Street

B C

W 115th St

W 114th St

W 113th St

W 112th St

W 111th St

Cathedral Parkway 110th Street

B C

W 110th St (Central Park N)

Speakers' Corner

22

Lenox Terrace

84

168

84

86

527

Sylvia's

Langston Hughes Place

40

268

2389

Mt Morris Pk W

258

2310

38

198

Lenox Ave (Malcolm X Blvd)

158

2

2

180

1921

166

80

18

125th Street

2 3

Marcus Garvey Park

Harlem Fire Watchtower

Fifth Ave

74

Madison Ave

20

116th Street

2 3

Martin Luther King Jr Towers

250

282

126

142

258

56

Central Park North 110th Street

2 3

1416

1398

1310

2

Duke Ellington Circle

Central Park

PAGE 252

1/4 mile   .25 km

Neighborhood Overview

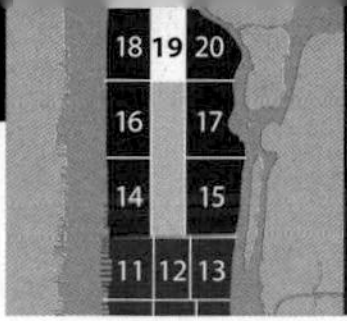

Map 19

New Yorkers below 96th Street rarely venture above the park for more than a chicken-and-waffles feast or an amateur night ticket. Well, the joke's on them. Harlem is a thriving neighborhood in every sense of the word—great community spirit, great street life, great architecture, great arts and culture…pretty much great everything. The lifeline of this neighborhood is 125th Street, a thoroughfare known for the **Apollo Theater**, a zillion stores, and players strutting their stuff.

That said, Harlem has been evolving for some time now—brownstones sell for upward of a million dollars, but row-houses with shattered windows and planked doors remain; the Upper West Side it's not. Bill Clinton made national headlines when he found some reasonably priced office space up on 125th Street; he still maintains his personal office there. But even as American Apparel wrangles itself a spot across from the Apollo, the nabe retains a sense of gritty pride. 125th Street is packed with vendors selling everything from fur vests to coco helado. A random TV in the wall next door to the Apollo plays Soul Train on repeat. Storefront churches fill Sunday mornings with Gospel ballads. Just journey uptown to check it out, and hit the ATM—125th can still be a cash-only kind of street.

Over the years, a mind-boggling number of writers, artists, and civil rights leaders made names for themselves in Harlem, and the community is proud of its past. At the northeast corner of Central Park, a statue of jazz great **Duke Ellington** sitting at his piano welcomes you to the neighborhood. Dedicated in 1997, this relatively recent memorial was surprisingly the first to be dedicated to an African American in New York City. Within the Morris Historical District lies **Marcus Garvey Park**, renamed for the famous black nationalist leader in 1973. If you're into literary history, visit Langston Hughes Place, the street where the poet lived; look for the ivy-covered building halfway down the block. Then check out his first residence at the still-operating **Harlem YMCA**. The facilities became an oasis for black visitors and artists during the Harlem Renaissance, when many of New York's hotels, theaters, and restaurants were segregated. The list of short-term residents is impressive, with Hughes, Ralph Ellison, Claude McKay, and James Baldwin all once calling the 135th Street location home.

Food, music, and entertainment happily collide in Harlem. The **Apollo Theater** is easily the area's most notable landmark, with everyone from Ella Fitzgerald to the Jackson Five kicking off their careers on that stage. The Amateur Night show has been running since 1934 and still happens on Wednesdays—just prepare for a line. Even more musical greats—Billie Holiday, Bessie Smith—haunted the **Alhambra Theatre and Ballroom**. If it had been around, we like to think they all would have chowed at **Sylvia's**, a soul food institution that has dished out piping hot fried chicken, waffles, and mashed potatoes since 1962.

Dive bars, underground jazz, and live music spectacles mesh for a diverse scene. Catch a show at the landmark **Apollo Theater** (Harlem residents, bring proof of address for a discount); sip fancy cocktails at **67 Orange Street**; or watch indie movies (many about Harlem) at **Maysles Cinema**, part of the documentary film center founded by filmmaker Albert Maysles.

Map 19

18	19	20
16		17
14		15
11	12	13

Harlem (Lower)

O Landmarks

- **Alhambra Ballroom** •
  2116 Adam Clayton Powell Blvd [W 121st St]
  212-222-6940
  Last Harlem dance hall.
- **Apollo Theater** •
  253 W 125th St [Frederick Douglass Blvd]
  212-531-5300
  The one and the only.
- **Duke Ellington Circle** •
  5th Ave & Central Park N
  Nice monument to a jazz great.
- **Harlem Fire Watchtower** •
  Marcus Garvey Park
  It's tall.
- **Harlem YMCA** • 180 W 135th St [7th Ave]
  212-912-2100
  Sidney Poitier, James Earl Jones, and Eartha
  Kitt have performed in this Y's "Little Theatre."
- **Langston Hughes Place** •
  20 E 127th St [5th Ave]
  212-534-5992
  Where the prolific poet lived and worked
  1947–1967.
- **Marcus Garvey Park** •
  E 120th St & Madison Ave
  Appealingly mountainous park.
- **Speaker's Corner** • Lenox Ave & W 135th St
  Famous soapbox for civil rights leaders,
  including Marcus Garvey.
- **Sylvia's** • 328 Malcolm X Blvd [W 127th St]
  212-996-0660
  This restaurant is worth the trip.

Coffee

- **Lenox Coffee** • 60 W 129th St [Lenox Ave]
  646-833-7839
  Classy café with lots of lattes and laptops.
- **Starbucks** • 77 W 125th St [Lenox Ave]
  917-492-2454
  Use the bathroom. Then head to the closest
  indie shop.

Farmers Markets

- **Harlem Harvest Madison Ave
  Farmers' Market** • Madison Ave & E 112th St
  212-348-2733
  Sat 8 am–4 pm, Jul–Nov
- **Harlem State Office
  Building Farmers' Market** •
  163 W 125th St [Adam Clayton Powell Jr Blvd]
  917-515-8046
  Tues 8 am–5:30 pm & Sat 8 am–4 pm, Jul–Nov.

Harlem (Lower)

Map 19

Harlem dining is increasingly global and Marcus Samuelsson's **Red Rooster** has brought a lot of foot traffic to 125th Street, but don't stop there. Kick off the morning at **Il Caffe Latte** with steaming lattes and breakfast wraps. Settle in at **Patisserie des Ambassades** for French-Senegalese entrees. And head to **Amy Ruth's** or **Sylvia's** when home-style cooking beckons.

🍸 Nightlife

- **67 Orange Street •**
2082 Frederick Douglass Blvd [W 113th St]
212-662-2030
Classy cocktail bar with speakeasy style.
- **Apollo Theater •**
253 W 125th St [Frederick Douglass Blvd]
212-531-5300
The one and the only.
- **Bier International •**
2099 Frederick Douglass Blvd [W 113th St]
212-280-0944
Tons of top foreign brews on tap, so bring freunds.
- **Ginny's Supper Club •**
310 Lenox Ave [W 126th St]
212-421-3821
Hopping jazz club under Red Rooster.
- **Harlem Tavern •**
2153 Frederick Douglass Blvd [W 116th St]
212-866-4500
Hybrid duties: Beer garden, sport bar, and pub food.
- **Just Lorraine's Place •**
2247 Adam Clayton Powell Jr Blvd [W 132nd St]
212-234-0720
Friendly watering hole that locals love.
- **Moca Bar & Lounge •**
2210 Frederick Douglass Blvd [W 119th St]
212-665-8081
Serving up hip hop, classics, and R&B.
- **Shrine •**
2271 Adam Clayton Powell Jr Blvd [W 134th St]
212-690-7807
Drink for cheap while Harlem and Columbia bands play.
- **W XYZ Bar •**
2296 Frederick Douglass Blvd [W 124th St]
212-749-4000
Drinkin' and mixin' inside the Harlem Aloft Hotel.

🍴 Restaurants

- **Africa Kine Restaurant •**
2267 7th Ave [133rd St]
212-666-9400 • $$
Highly regarded Senegalese restaurant.
- **Amy Ruth's •** 113 W 116th St [Lenox Ave]
212-280-8779 • $$
Soul food, incredible fried chicken.
- **Billie's Black •**
271 W 119th St [St Nicholas Ave]
212-280 2248 • $$
Good food = live entertainment.
- **Boulevard Bistro •**
239 Malcolm X Blvd
212-678-6200 • $$$
Modern Southern food for modern Harlem.
- **Chaiwali •**
274 Lenox Ave [124th St]
646-688-5414 • $$$
Inspired Indian that manages to be both elegant and homespun.
- **The Cecil •**
210 W 118th St [Adam Clayton Powell Jr Blvd]
212-866-1262 • $$$$
Upscale mash up of modern Asian fare and soul food.
- **Chez Lucienne •**
308 Lenox Ave
212-289-5550 • $$
Cozy little French bistro. Authentic and affordable!
- **Corner Social •** 321 Lenox Ave [W 126th St]
212-510-8552 • $$$
A solid backup when the Rooster is packed across the street.
- **Harlem BBQ •**
2367 Frederick Douglass Blvd [W 127th St]
212-222-1922 • $$
Football-sized frozen cocktails and entire $6 chickens to-go.

Map 19

Harlem (Lower)

18	19	20
16		17
14		15
11	12	13

- **Harlem Shake** • 100 W 124th St [Lenox Ave]
646-508-5657 • $$
Shakes and burger joint with throwback look.
- **IHOP** •
2294 Adam Clayton Powell Jr Blvd [W 135th St]
212-234-4747 • $$
Pancakes with unlimited swill coffee, just like in college.
- **Il Caffe Latte** •
189 Malcolm X Blvd [W 119th St]
212-222-2241 • $
Fresh sandwiches, massive $3 lattes and a stellar Latin wrap.
- **Jacob Restaurant** •
373 Malcolm X Blvd [W 129th St]
212-866-3663 • $
Soul food and salad by the pound for cheap.
- **Le Baobab** • 120 W 116th St [Lenox Ave]
212-864-4700 • $
Satisfying Senegalese complete with TV in French.
- **Lido** •
2168 Frederick Douglass Blvd [W 117th St]
646-490-8575 • $$$
Sophisticated Northern Italian with requisite exposed brick atmosphere.
- **LoLo's Seafood Shack** •
303 W 116th St [Frederick Douglass Blvd]
646-649-3356 • $$
Spicy Caribbean steampots and fritters in a ramshackle backyard.
- **Manna's** •
2353 Frederick Douglass Blvd [W 125th St]
212-749-9084 • $$
Pile a buffet plate with everything from oxtail to collard greens.
- **Melba's** •
300 W 114th St [Frederick Douglass Blvd]
212-864-7777 • $$$
Upscale soul food.
- **Minton's** •
206 W 118th St [Adam Clayton Powell Jr Blvd]
212-243-2222 • $$$$
The famous jazz club reborn with haute-soul food.

- **Patisserie Des Ambassades** •
2200 Frederick Douglass Blvd [W 119th St]
212-666-0078 • $
Great breakfast pastries. Senegalese food too.
- **Red Rooster** •
310 Lenox Ave
212-792-9001 • $$$
The latest uptown craze from chef star Marcus Samuelsson.
- **Seasoned Vegan** •
55 St Nicholas Ave [W 113th St]
212-222-0092 • $$
"Chicken nuggets", "po' boys," and "crawfish." Plus raw food.
- **Shrine** •
2271 Adam Clayton Powell Jr Blvd [W 134th St]
212-690-7807 • $$
Atmosphere first, foodstuffs second. Local bands play.
- **Sylvia's** • 328 Malcolm X Blvd [W 127th St]
212-996-0660 • $$$
An institution. Not overrated.
- **Zoma** •
2084 Frederick Douglass Blvd [W 113th St]
212-662-0620 • $$
Tasty Ethiopian in a tasteful setting.

🛍 Shopping

- **467 Lenox Liquors** •
467 Lenox Ave [W 133rd St]
212-234-7722
Standard liquor store, sans bullet-proof glass.
- **Adja Khady Food** •
251 W 116th St [Frederick Douglass]
646-645-7505
Friendly West African culinary supplies and community hang out.
- **Atmos** •
203 W 125th St [Adam Clayton Powell Jr Blvd]
212-666-2242
Palace of popular urban streetwear.

Harlem (Lower)

With everything from **Champs** to **M.A.C. Makeup**, 125th Street anchors Harlem shopping. **H&M** stocks the same trendy threads as everywhere else, without the long lines. Street vendors fill any other gaps. Everything you want is here, guaranteed. And when you want to take the plunge and indulge any and all dashiki-wearing fantasies, check out the open-air **Malcolm Shabazz Harlem Market.**

Map 19

B.O.R.N. Boutique •
52 W 125th St [Malcolm X Blvd]
212-722-3706
Upscale vintage for stylish Harlemites.

The Brownstone •
24 E 125th St [Madison Ave]
212-996-7980
Clothing boutique featuring local designers.

Champs • 208 W 125th St [7th Ave]
212-280-0296
Sports, street shoes, and wear. For losers too.

Dr. Jay's •
256 W 125th St [Frederick Douglass Blvd]
212-665-7795
Urban fashions is just what the doctor ordered.

Grandma's Place • 84 W 120th St [Lenox Ave]
212-360-6776
Harlem toy store. Your grandkid will probably love it.

H&M • 125 W 125th St [Lenox Ave]
855-466-7467
Sort-of-hip, disposable fashion.

Harlem Underground •
20 E 125th St [5th Ave]
212-987-9385
Embroidered Harlem t-shirts.

Hats by Bunn • 2283 7th Ave [W 134th St]
212-694-3590
Cool caps.

Jimmy Jazz • 132 W 125th St [Lenox Ave]
212-665-4198
Urban designers with a range of sizes.

Levain Bakery •
2167 Frederick Douglass Blvd [117th St]
646-455-0952
Bodacious, weighty super-mega cookies.

MAC • 202 W 125th St [7th Ave]
212-665-0676
Beauty products in many colors and shades.

Malcolm Shabazz Harlem Market •
52 W 116th St [Lenox Ave]
212-987-8131
An open-air market for all your daishiki needs.

Paragon Department Store •
488 Lenox Ave [W 135th St]
212-926-9470
It's like a compulsive hoarder decided to sell everything.

Settepani • 196 Lenox Ave [W 120th St]
917-492-4806
Lovely baked goods.

Trunk Show Consignment •
275 W 113th St [8th Ave]
212-662-0009
Cool designer fashions recycled, but just bring a fat wad of cash.

United Hardware •
2160 Frederick Douglass Blvd [W 117th St]
212-666-7778
Good for basic tools; that's about all.

Map 20 · El Barrio / East Harlem

1

2 Major Deegan Expwy

87

E 135th St

E 134th St

Bruckner Blvd

Lincoln Ave

Alexander Ave

E 132nd St

Abraham Lincoln Housing

Abraham Lincoln Housing

Willis Ave

THE BRONX
PAGE 242

E 132nd St

E 131st St

Third Ave Bridge

Harlem River

E 130th St

E 129th St

Harlem River Dr

A

E 128th St

Willis Ave Bridge

E 127th St

Keith Haring "Crack is Wack" Mural

Metro North Harlem 125th St

E 126th St

4 5 6 125th Street

Robert F Kennedy Bri

E 125th St (Dr Martin Luther King Jr Blvd)

Harlem Fire Watchtower

E 124th St

Paladino Ave

Marcus Garvey Park

E 123rd St

Taino Towers

Sen R Wagner Sr Houses

Sen R Wagner Sr Houses

Ronald McNair Pl

E 122nd St

E 121st St

Harlem Courthouse

Sylvan Pl

119

E 120th St

E 119th St

Second Ave

First Ave

E 118th St

Fifth Ave

Madison Ave

Park Ave

Lexington Ave

Third Ave

E 117th St

Pleasant Ave

Religious Street Shrine: Virgen del Carmen

6 116th Street

E 116th St

Pete Pascale Pl

Church of Our Lady of Mt Carmel

B

E 115th St

Danny's Club & Fashion

Sen R Taft Houses

Sen R Taft Houses

JW Johnson Housing

JW Johnson Housing

Jefferson Houses

Jefferson Houses

E 114th St

FDR Dr

Robt Wagner

Jefferson Park

E 112th St

La Marqueta

E 111th St

6 110th Street

E 110th St

Duke Ellington Circle

17

1/4 mile   .25 km

Neighborhood Overview

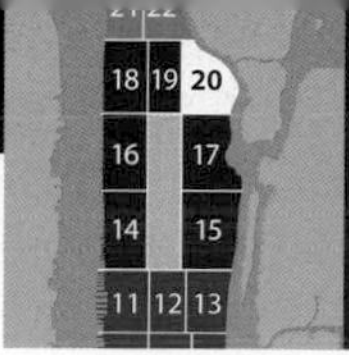

18 19 20
16   17
14   15
11 12 13

Map 20

El Barrio, also known as Spanish Harlem or East Harlem (just don't call it "SpaHa"), is a neighborhood that is alive with history and culture—Puerto Rican, African American, Mexican, Italian, Dominican and increasingly Asian...it's really one of the most diverse neighborhoods in the city. It's not uncommon to find people playing congas on the street or riding tricked-out bicycles with Puerto Rican tunes blasting from their radios. You can feel a real sense of community in the bodegas and on the streets as residents chat up their neighbors and warmly greet one another with "Papi" or "Mami." In the summer locals crowd into **Thomas Jefferson Park** and the abundant community gardens provide locals with the perfect chill out spots. Exploring this neighborhood is highly recommended.

But it's not all pretty. East Harlem has been through some tough times in the past few decades to say the least. And unfortunately, to a lot of New Yorkers, it is still a place to avoid. **Keith Haring's "Crack is Wack" Mural** is a symbol of the urban decay in the 1970s and '80s when drugs, poverty, and violence ravaged the neighborhood. Burnt-out buildings were the norm and social problems skyrocketed. Today concrete housing projects dominate the landscape (some very unique like **Taino Towers**) with a few vacant lots here and there, but crime is way down and rents are creeping up.

In recent years the neighborhood has rapidly changed with new condos sprouting up everywhere (some even with doormen), a growing Mexican population moving in (check out 116th Street between Second and Third for amazing food and groceries), and even a touch of suburbia with the gigantic **Costco** that opened in 2009.

Before the Puerto Rican migration, Italians used to call East Harlem home. In the 1930s there were tens of thousands of immigrants from Southern Italy living here. The Italian legacy has almost entirely disappeared with the last of the great bakeries closing a few years ago. Today there are only a few remnants left including the gorgeous **Church of Our Lady of Mount Carmel** (the first Italian church in New York), the **Virgen del Carmen Shrine**, and restaurants like **Rao's** and **Patsy's Pizza**.

Underneath the Metro-North viaduct is another remnant of the old neighborhood, the historic public market **La Marqueta**. Established by Mayor LaGuardia in 1936, this place was the hub of shopping activity for decades with over 500 vendors. Now it only has a few businesses left selling Puerto Rican delicacies like bacalao. But it is slowly being revived by the city with new vendors selling everything from baked goods to garden supplies. In the meantime, locals pack the public plaza (that looks more like a cage) between 115th & 116th Street on Saturdays in the summer for live music and dancing.

To see the neighborhood in full party mode, head here for the second weekend in June when the Puerto Rican Day Parade is in full swing. On Sunday the parade strolls down Fifth Avenue, but on Saturday Third Avenue and 116th Street come alive for a full-on Puerto Rican party—live music, barbecues on the sidewalk, and lots of Nuyorican pride.

Camaradas is your one-stop hot spot for drinks and live entertainment from old-school DJs to Latin grooves. **Mojitos** has a friendly bar to knock back a few drinks. **The Duck** is an uptown country dive that's as weird as it sounds; requisite women-dancing-on-bar vibe.

Map 20

El Barrio / East Harlem

O Landmarks

- **Church of Our Lady of Mt Carmel** •
  448 E 116th St [Pleasant Ave]
  212-534-0681
  The first Italian parish in NYC.
- **Danny's Club & Fashion** • 1st Ave & E 114th St
  Funky neighborhood fashion shop going
  strong for 30+ years.
- **Harlem Courthouse** •
  170 E 121st St [Lexington Ave]
  One of the most impressive buildings in
  Manhattan.
- **Keith Haring "Crack is Wack" Mural** •
  2nd Ave & E 127th St
  Keith was right.
- **La Marqueta** • 1590 Park Ave [E 115th St]
  212-312-3603
  This public market used to be bustling; not so
  much anymore.
- **Religious Street Shrine: Virgen del Carmen** •
  240 E 117th St
  Shrine built by Italians in memory of soldiers
  who died in WW II.
- **Taino Towers** • 3rd Ave & E 123rd St
  Unique low-income housing development
  opened in 1979.
- **Thomas Jefferson Park** •
  2180 1st Ave [E 112th St]
  212-860-1383
  Green space with a giant pool and bbqs in the
  summer.

Coffee

- **Love Cafe** • 283 Pleasant Ave [E 115th St]
  212-369-6916
  Super friendly indie shop almost too good to
  be true.
- **Lion Lion** • 332 E 116th St [1st Ave]
  917-262-0517
  Cocktails await behind the black curtain.

El Barrio / East Harlem

Patsy's pizza really is the "original" New York thin-crust pizza. The slices from the take-out window are the best in NYC. Unless you know the Mayor, **Rao's** is another New York restaurant you'll never see the inside of. 116th Street is a budget culinary wonderland. Try **Taco Mix**, **Sandy**, or **El Nuevo Caridad**.

Farmers Markets

- **La Marqueta** • Park Ave & E 115th St
  Sat 8 am–8 pm, July–Nov

Nightlife

- **Amor Cubano** • 2018 3rd Ave [E 111th St]
  212-990-1220
  The house band always has this place grooving.
- **Camaradas El Barrio** •
  2241 1st Ave [E 115th St]
  212-348-2703
  Eclectic live music and tasty bar food. Great vibe.
- **The Duck** • 2171 2nd Ave [E 112th St]
  212-831-0000
  Uptown country dive. Weird as it sounds.
- **Mojitos** • 227 E 116th St [3rd Ave]
  212-828-8635
  Good Mexican happy hour destination.

Map 20

El Barrio / East Harlem

Restaurants

- **A Taste of Seafood** •
2530 Frederick Douglas Blvd
212-866-0275 • $
Fried fish sandwiches on white bread. Lord,
have mercy!
- **Amor Cubano** • 2018 3rd Ave [E 111th St]
212-996-1220 • $$
Good Cuban food. Great live music.
- **Camaradas El Barrio** •
2241 1st Ave [E 115th St]
212-348-2703 • $$
Spanish/Puerto Rican/tapas/music. Nice!
- **Charlie's Place** •
1960 Madison Ave [E 125th St]
212-410-0277 • $$
Harlem's first sushi bar.
- **Cuchifritos** • 168 E 116th St [Lexington Ave]
212-876-4846 • $
Puerto Rican fried treats.
- **El Nuevo Caridad** • 2257 2nd Ave [E 116th St]
212-860-8187 • $
Dominican baseball stars approve of this
chicken.
- **El Tapatio Mexican Restaurant** •
209 E 116th St [3rd Ave]
212-876-3055 • $$
Tiny but good.
- **Harley's Smokeshack** •
355 E 116th St [1st Ave]
212-828-6723 • $$$
They smoke it, so you can eat it—turkey wings
to meatballs.
- **IHOP** • 2082 Lexington Ave [E 125th St]
212-860-0844 • $$
Pancakes and carafes of coffee, plus a 24-hour
window.
- **Kahlua's Café** • 2117 3rd Ave [E 116th St]
212-348-0311 • $$
Awesome Mexi-grub. Tiny, loud, and fun.

- **Kiosk** • 80 E 116th St [Park Ave]
212-348-9010 • $$
Tiny Moroccan joint with live entertainment
sometimes.
- **Makana** • 2245 1st Ave [E 115th St]
212-996-3534 • $$
A great little Hawaiian-Japanese BBQ takes
Manhattan.
- **Mojitos** • 227 E 116th St [3rd Ave]
212-828-8635 • $$
Live music Thursday, Friday, and Saturday.
- **Patsy's Pizzeria** • 2287 1st Ave [E 118th St]
212-534-9783 • $$
The original thin-crust pizza. Best take-out
slices in NY.
- **Pee Dee Steakhouse** •
2006 3rd Ave [E 110th St]
212-996-3300 • $
Grilled meats for cheap.
- **Polash** • 2179 3rd Ave [E 119th St]
212-410-0276 • $$
Surprisingly solid uptown Indian Restaurant.
- **Quesadillas Doña Maty** •
228 E 116th St [2nd Ave]
646-789-6237 • $
Friendly Mexican joint grilling quesadillas on
the sidewalk.
- **Rao's** • 455 E 114th St [1st Ave]
212-722-6709 • $$$$$
An Italian institution, but you'll never get in.
- **Ricardo Steak House** •
2145 2nd Ave [E 110th St]
212-289-5895 • $$
Steak, bar, outside patio with upscale vibe and
valet parking.
- **Sandy Restaurant** • 2261 2nd Ave [E 116th St]
212-348-8654 • $
Neighborhood Dominican joint. Try the lechon
asado.
- **Taco Mix** • 234 E 116 St [3rd Ave]
212-289-2963 • $
The best tacos in El Barrio. Go for the al pastor.

El Barrio / East Harlem

21	22	
18	19	20
16		17
14		15
11	12	13

Map 20

Casablanca Meat Market is always packed, and for good reason with excellent homemade sausages. For do-it-yourself projects **The Demolition Depot** is a gold mine (but where do they get this stuff?). Latin music fans swear by **Casa Latina Music Store**. There's even a touch of suburbia in East Harlem with **Costco**.

Shopping

- **Bosie Bakery** • 2132 2nd Avenue [E 110th St]
646-490-5403
French pastry connection.
- **Capri Bakery** • 186 E 116th St [3rd Ave]
212-410-1876
Spanish El Barrio bakery.
- **Casa Latina Music Shop** •
151 E 116th St [Lexington Ave]
212-427-6062
El Barrio's oldest record store.
- **Casablanca Meat Market** •
125 E 110th St [Park Ave]
212-534-7350
The line out the door every Saturday says it all.
- **Costco** • 517 E 117 St [Pleasant Ave]
212-896-5873
Giving Long Islanders another reason to drive into the city.
- **The Demolition Depot** •
216 E 125th St [3rd Ave]
212-860-1138
Amazing selection of architectural salvage.
- **Don Paco Lopez Panaderia** •
2129 3rd Ave [E 116th St]
212-876-0700
Mexican bakery famous for Three Kings Day cake.
- **Eagle Tile & Home Centers** •
2254 2nd Ave [E 115th St]
212-423-0333
Update the tile in your kitchen or bathroom.
- **Goodwill Thrift Store** •
2231 3rd Ave [E 122nd St]
212-410-0973
A few floors of used stuff (some of it pretty good).

- **Heavy Metal Bike Shop** • 2016 3rd Ave [E 110th St]
212-410-1144
Pedal to the metal for repairs and parts.
- **Hot Bread Kitchen** • 1590 Park Ave [115th St]
212-369-3331
Community-minded multinational baked goods.
- **La Marqueta** • 1590 Park Ave [E 115th St]
212-312-3603
A couple Puerto Rican food stalls. Still waiting to be revived.
- **Lora Decorators** • 204 E 120th St
212-534-1025
Well Known by Madison Avenue clientele, Reupholster your sidewalk/dumpster chair.
- **Mi Mexico Lindo Bakery** •
2267 2nd Ave [E 116th St]
212-996-5223
Grab a tray at this old-school bakery.
- **Raices Dominican Cigars** •
2250 1st Ave [E 116th St]
212-410-6824
Hand rolled cigars. With a smoking room!
- **Raskin Carpets** • 2246 3rd Ave [E 122nd St]
212-369-1100
Long time East Harlem store has Santa at Xmas.
- **V&M American Outlet** •
2226 3rd Ave [E 121st St]
212-987-6459
Everything for your apartment
- **V.I.M.** • 2239 3rd Ave [E 122nd St]
212-369-5033
Street wear—jeans, sneakers, tops—for all.
- **Young Fish Market** • 2004 3rd Ave [E 110th St]
212-876-3427
Get it fresh or fried.

Map 21 • **Manhattanville / Hamilton Heights**

Map 21 • Manhattanville / Hamilton Heights

W 160th St
W 159th St
W 158th St
W 157th St
157th Street
W 156th St
W 155th St
W 154th St
W 153rd St
W 152nd St
W 151st St
W 150th St
W 149th St
W 148th St
W 147th St
W 146th St
W 145th St
145th Street
W 144th St
W 143rd St
W 142nd St
W 141st St
W 140th St
W 139th St
W 138th St
137th Street
City College
W 137th St
W 136th St
W 135th St
W 134th St

EDW M Morgan
Riverside Dr
Henry Hudson Pkwy
Riverside Dr
Broadway
Amsterdam Ave
Convent Ave
Hamilton Pl
Hamilton Ter
St Nicholas Ave
St Nicholas Pl
Edgecombe Ave
Jackie Robinson Park
Bradhurst Ave
Harlem River Dr
St Nicholas Ter
12th Ave

Hudson River
Riverside Park
PAGE 274
North River Water Pollution Control Plant & Riverbank State Park
Ped Bridge
Ped Bridge

Audubon Terrace
American Academy of Arts and Letters
Hispanic Society Museum
Trinity Church Cemetery's Graveyard of Heroes
Trinity Cemetery
Church of the Intercession
Church of the Crucifixion
Bailey House
145th Street
Hamilton Heights Historic District
Hamilton Grange National Memorial
City College
155th Street
Macombs Dam Br
135th Street

9
23
22
18

1/4 mile   .25 km

Neighborhood Overview

Map 21

Hamilton Heights doesn't quite feel like Manhattan. Wedged between the Hudson River to the west and St. Nicholas Park to the east, this neighborhood of hilly parks, museums, and beautiful old brownstones offers a pleasant respite from the concrete and steel of the rest of the island. Columbia University's continuing expansion threatens to throw gentrification into double-time, but even in the face of rising rents, Alexander Hamilton's former country estate retains almost a bucolic feel.

Counting landmark buildings in Hamilton Heights is like keeping track of nuns in Rome. The number is staggering, but none are as striking as **City College**'s white and brick Neo-Gothic buildings; turrets, towers, and gargoyles practically litter the historic campus. For classic New York, mosey up to the **Hamilton Heights Historic District**, just north of City College, where stunning homes line the streets where Alexander Hamilton's original home sat; **Hamilton Grange National Memorial** has since been moved to nearby St Nicholas Park. The **Bailey House**, the home of P.T. Barnum's partner James Bailey, is one of the coolest residences in all of Manhattan, and probably the only one built on a circus fortune. For crazy concrete church design, nothing beats the **Church of the Crucifixion**.

Sure, the authorities built Riverbank State Park to appease residents after the city dumped a sewage plant along the river, but it's a great neighborhood resource and includes a roller skating rink, running track, and a soccer field. Skip the gym fees, and swim laps at the nice indoor pool. The **Trinity Cemetery Graveyard of Heroes** feels almost otherworldly, with lovely rolling paths that feel out of place in Upper Manhattan. Several Astors, Charles Dickens' son, and John James Audubon are all buried here, as is three-term mayor Ed Koch. St. Nicholas Park is worth a visit just for its spacious lawns, but don't miss Hamilton Grange. The National Park Service restored the building after moving it to the park in 2009.

In a city where museums charge in excess of $20 just to elbow strangers for a glimpse of a Botticelli, the **Hispanic Society of America** Museum and Library is miraculous. Admission is free to the museum and reference library, which showcases the arts and cultures of Spain, Portugal, and Latin America. Browse the society's prints, paintings and artifacts, but linger in **Audubon Terrace**. The square-city block plot was named for the famous naturalist, John James Audubon, who once farmed in Washington Heights. The land became a cultural center in 1904 and also houses the **American Academy of Arts and Letters**. Years of neglect left the terrace looking drab, but a a recent glass structure addition linking the Academy of Arts and Letters and the Hispanic Society signals a welcome rejuvenation.

Harlem Public serves up good food and great drinks and is a welcome addition to a somewhat sparse nightlife scene.

Meander up Broadway for your pick of taquerias and Dominican eats. **Picante** boasts some of the nabe's best sit-down Mexican. Cheap Middle Eastern can be found at **Queen Sheeba**. **Trufa** provides a bistro option.

Map 21

25
24
23
21 22
18 19 20

Manhattanville / Hamilton Height

⭕ Landmarks

- **American Academy of Arts & Letters** •
  633 W 155th St [Riverside Dr]
  212-368-5900
  New glass structure links it to the Hispanic
  Society.
- **Audubon Terrace** • Broadway & W 155th St
  Pleasant, if lonely, Beaux Arts complex. What's
  it doing here?
- **Bailey House** • 10 St Nicholas Pl [W 150th St]
  Romanesque revival mansion from PT
  Barnum's partner James Bailey.
- **City College** • 160 Convent Ave [W 130th St]
  212-650-7000
  Peaceful gothic campus.
- **The Episcopal Church Of The Crucifixion** •
  459 W 149th St [Convent Ave]
  212-281-0900
  Whacked-out concrete church by Costas
  Machlouzarides, circa 1967.
- **Hamilton Grange National Memorial** •
  414 W 141st St [St Nicholas Ave]
  Alexander Hamilton's house, twice relocated
  and now facing the wrong way. Damn those
  Jeffersonians!
- **Hamilton Heights Historic District** •
  W 140th & W 145th St b/n Amsterdam &
  St Nicholas Ave
  192 houses, apartments, and churches on the
  National Registry of Historic Places. Who
  knew?
- **Hispanic Society Museum** •
  613 W 155th St [Broadway]
  212-926-2234
  Free museum (Tues–Sat) with Spanish
  masterpieces.
- **Trinity Church Cemetery Graveyard of
  Heroes** • 3699 Broadway [W 153rd St]
  Hilly, almost countryish cemetery.

☕ Coffee

- **Café One** • 1619 Amsterdam Ave [W 139th St]
  212-690-0060
  Free wifi, quality pastries, and reliable java.
- **The Chipped Cup** • 3610 Broadway [149th St]
  212-368-8881
  Fair trade, third wave, and fancy pastries.
- **Manhattanville Coffee** •
  142 Edgecombe Ave [142nd St]
  646-781-9900
  Quality cups and small bites.

🍎 Farmers Markets

- **Grass Roots Farmers Market** •
  Edgecombe Ave & W 145th St
  212-234-9607
  Tues & Sat 9 am–4 pm, Jul–Nov

🍸 Nightlife

- **The Grange** •
  1635 Amsterdam Ave [W 141st St]
  212-491-1635
  Crafted cocktails, great beers, and young
  creative menu.
- **Harlem Public** • 3612 Broadway [W 149th St]
  212-939-9404
  Good food, good drinks, exciting addition to
  neighborhood.

Manhattanville / Hamilton Heights

Map 21

Check out **B-Jays USA** for every sneaker under the sun, **Felix Supply Hardware** for stocking up on basics, and **V.I.M.** for duds and kicks; when someone says they're the best jeans and sneaker store in America, you should probably pay attention.

Restaurants

- **Ecuatoriana Restaurant** •
1685 Amsterdam Ave [W 143rd St]
212-491-4626 • $$
Legit Ecuadorian fare, sans guinea pig.
- **Famous Fish Market** •
684 St Nicholas Ave [W 145th St]
212-491-8323 • $
Deep fried and from the sea.
- **Jesus' Taco** • 501 W 145th St [Amsterdam Ave]
212-234-3330 • $
Tacos and burgers.
- **Jimbo's Hamburger Palace** •
528 W 145th St [Amsterdam Ave]
212-926-0338 • $
Cheap, fast, easy burgers.
- **La Flor De Broadway** • 3395 Broadway
[138th St]
212-281-1556 • $
Solid pan Carribean food and excellent Cuban
sandwiches.
- **La Oaxaquena Restaurant** •
1969 Amsterdam Ave [W 157th St]
212-283-7752 • $
One of the best in a parade of taquerias.
- **Olga's Pizza** • 3409 Broadway [W 138th St]
212-234-7878 • $
Bare-bones pies, whole or by the slice.
- **Oso** • 1618 Amsterdam Ave [140th St]
646-858-3139 • $$$
Stylish Mexican.
- **Picante** • 3424 Broadway [W 139th St]
212-234-6479 • $$
Arguably Manhattanville's best Mexican, plus
affordable margs.
- **Queen Sheeba** •
317 W 141st St [Frederick Douglass Blvd]
212-862-6149 • $
Cafeteria-style Middle Eastern that's friendly
on the wallet.
- **Subsconcious** •
1213 Amsterdam Ave [W 140th St]
212-690-0080 • $
Standard sandwiches and full blown salad bar.
- **Trufa** • 3431 Broadway [W 140th St]
212-281-6165 • $$
Bistro featuring pastas and New American
entrees.

Shopping

- **Bronx Spirits Liquors** •
3375 Broadway [W 137th St]
212-926-2888
For wine, sometimes reliable is all you need.
- **Foot Locker** • 3549 Broadway [W 146th St]
212-491-0927
Get your sneakers from a fake referee.
- **Junior Bicycle Shop** •
1826 Amsterdam Ave [W 150th St]
212-690-6511
Repairs.
- **Sister's Uptown Bookstore and Cultural
Center** • 1942 Amsterdam Ave [W 156th St]
212-862-3680
Books and events celebrating black women,
amazing staff.
- **Unity Liquors** •
704 St Nicholas Ave [W 146th St]
212-491-7821
Right by the subway, where all liquor stores
should be.
- **V.I.M.** • 508 W 145th St [Amsterdam Ave]
212-491-1143
Street wear—jeans, sneakers, tops—for all.

Map 22 • Harlem (Upper)

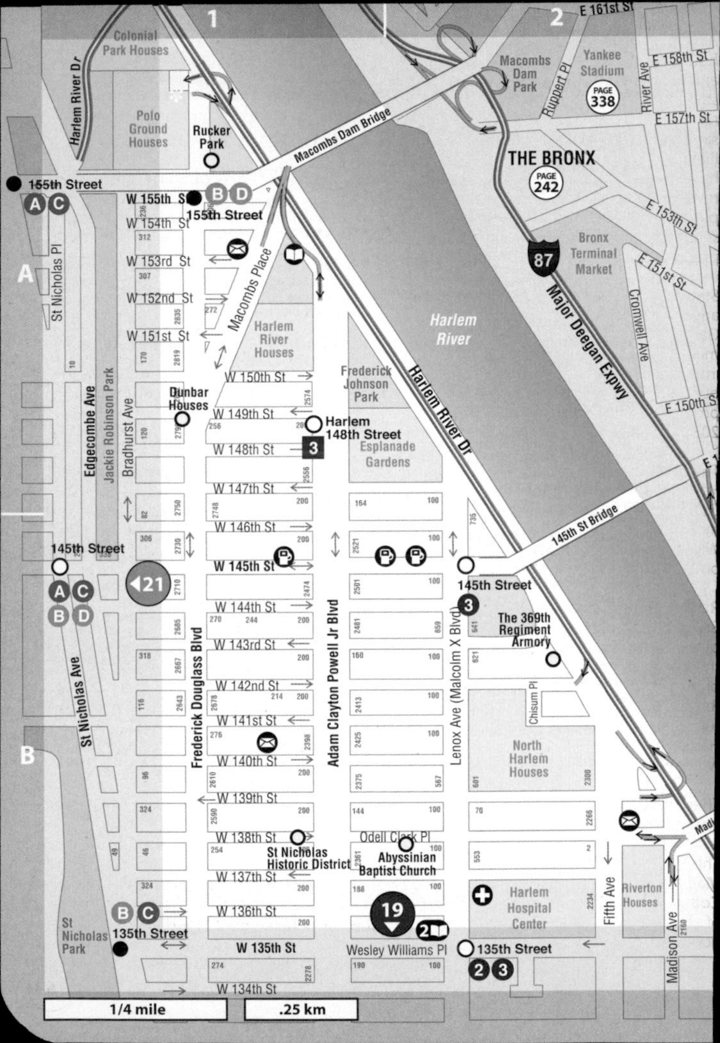

THE BRONX

PAGE 242

PAGE 338

Yankee Stadium

Bronx Terminal Market

87

Colonial Park Houses

Polo Ground Houses

Rucker Park

Macombs Dam Park

Macombs Dam Bridge

Ruppert Pl

Major Deegan Expwy

Harlem River Dr

E 161st St
E 158th St
E 157th St
River Ave
E 153rd St
E 151st St
Cromwell Ave
E 150th St

155th Street
W 155th St
155th Street
W 154th St
W 153rd St
W 152nd St
W 151st St
W 150th St

A C
B D

Edgecombe Ave
Bradhurst Ave
Jackie Robinson Park
St Nicholas Pl
Macombs Pl

Harlem River Houses

Frederick Johnson Park

Harlem River

Harlem River Dr

Dunbar Houses

Harlem 148th Street
3

W 149th St
W 148th St
W 147th St
W 146th St
W 145th St

Esplanade Gardens

145th Street

A C
B D

21

145th Street
3

The 369th Regiment Armory

W 144th St
W 143rd St
W 142nd St
W 141st St
W 140th St
W 139th St
W 138th St

Frederick Douglass Blvd
Adam Clayton Powell Jr Blvd
Lenox Ave (Malcolm X Blvd)
St Nicholas Ave
Chisum Pl

145th St Bridge

North Harlem Houses

Fifth Ave
Madison Ave

Riverton Houses

St Nicholas Historic District
Odell Clark Pl

Abyssinian Baptist Church

19

Harlem Hospital Center

B C

135th Street

St Nicholas Park

W 137th St
W 136th St
W 135th St
W 134th St

Wesley Williams Pl

2

135th Street
2 3

Neighborhood Overview

At first glance, upper Harlem lacks character. Generic buffets and 99-cent stores line Lenox, one of the 'habe's anchor streets. 145th Street sprawls with suburban gas stations and an entrance to the 145th Street Bridge. High rises dot the uptown skyline. But this 20-block triangle sandwiched between St. Nicholas to the west and the Harlem River to the east is the lifeline of black culture in New York. Everyone from starving artists to self-made millionaires have called upper Harlem home, and a visit to the **Schomburg Center for Research** reveals the neighborhood's significant impact. Not surprisingly, gentrification is a sensitive point of controversy. But for now, the culture remains intact. Old churches maintain a sense of community. Heavenly soul food attracts locals and tourists. Historic districts preserve the look and feel. Upper Harlem has it all—you just have to dig a little.

Start at 135th Street and Lenox, or "Speaker's Corner," an intersection where back in the day anyone shouted their concerns and critiques of current events. Most famously, Marcus Garvey presented his views on race at this corner. The Harlem Hellfighters, an all-black military unit that fought in World War I and World War II, housed their headquarters at the imposing **369th Regiment Armory**. The building still operates as a sustainment brigade, but an obelisk outside honors the soldiers. Long before the Hellfighters, Ethiopian traders protested segregation policies by founding the **Abyssinian Baptist Church** in 1808. After 203 years, the congregation only moved once, in 1923, to its striking Neo-Gothic building.

The Rockefeller family built the **Dunbar Houses** in 1926 to provide affordable housing in Harlem. The complex attracted writers, artists, musicians, and poets, including W.E.B. DuBois, the first African-American to graduate from Harvard. Similarly ambitious residents moved in to the **St. Nicholas Historic District**, sometimes called "Strivers' Row," Stanford White designed the houses, where many upwardly mobile residents lived. Note the original "Walk your Horses" signs (there aren't any carriage rides in the neighborhood).

Rucker Park is home to famously intense pickup games. Kareem Abdul-Jabbar, Kobe Bryant, and hundreds of exceedingly talented locals have dribbled on those courts. Swing by to try your hand or just enjoy the show. The **Schomburg Center** focuses on preserving the history of people of African descent worldwide. The center's dizzying array of artifacts, prints, images and manuscripts includes more than 100,000 items. The **Countee Cullen Regional Branch Library** also has an excellent African American reference section; at the turn of the century, Madame C.J. Walker lived at this same address—the "richest woman in Harlem" earned her fortune by selling hair care products specifically for African-American women.

There isn't a lot of nightlife above 135th Street but stalwart **Londel's Supper Club** has classic jazz on Fridays and Saturdays with no cover.

The parade of routine delis on Lenox hides some of Manhattan's tastiest eats. **Miss Maude's Spoonbread** dishes out calorically foolish comfort food. Do not miss **Charles' Country Pan Fried Chicken** to chow down on mindblowing hot birds. If you want a taste of the sea, hit up the window service at **O'Fishole Seafood** for fried fishy take-out goodness.

Map 22

Harlem (Upper)

⊙ Landmarks

- **The 369th Regiment Armory** •
  2366 5th Ave [W 142nd St]
  Home of the Harlem Hellfighters.
- **Abyssinian Baptist Church** •
  132 Odell Clark Pl [Lenox Ave]
  212-862-7474
  NY's oldest black congregation.
- **The Dunbar Houses** •
  W 149th St & Frederick Douglass Blvd
  Historic, multi-family apartment buildings
  from the 1920s.
- **Holcombe Rucker Park** •
  Frederick Douglass Blvd & W 155th St
  Famous basketball court that birthed the likes
  of Kareem Abdul-Jabbar and more.
- **St. Nicholas Historic District** •
  202 W 138th St [7th Ave]
  Beautiful neo-Georgian townhouses.

☕ Coffee

- **Dunkin' Donuts** • 110 W 145th St [Lenox Ave]
  212-234-3440
  Decent coffee served in gigantic Styrofoam
  cups.
- **Dunkin' Donuts** •
  2730 Frederick Douglass Blvd [W 145th St]
  212-862-0635
  Decent coffee served in gigantic Styrofoam
  cups.
- **Starbucks** •
  301 W 145th St [Frederick Douglass Blvd]
  212-690-7835
  One of the few coffee spots around here.

🍎 Farmers Markets

- **Harlem Hospital Greenmarket** •
  104 E 126th St
  Thu 8 am–5 pm Jul–Nov

Wandering Lenox and 145th Streets will unearth everything from cheap, expansive supermarkets like **Pathmark** to niche sneaker shops like **Sneaker Q**. **Make My Cake** has sugary cupcakes, cheesecakes and regular cakes.

Nightlife

• **Harlem Nights** •
2361 7th Ave [138th St]
646-820-4603
Handsome, crafty bar with much live music.
• **Londel's** •
2620 Frederick Douglass Blvd [W 140th St]
212-234-6114
Great live music on Friday & Saturdays.

Restaurants

• **Charles' Country Pan Fried Chicken** •
2461 Frederick Douglass Blvd [W 151st St]
212-281-1800 • $
The fried chicken they serve in heaven.
• **Grini's Grill** • 100 W 143rd St [Lenox Ave]
212-694-6274 • $
This "tapas bar" actually serves heaping plates of meat and rice.
• **Londel's** •
2620 Frederick Douglass Blvd [W 140th St]
212-234-6114 • $$$
Good Southern with live music on the weekend.
• **Mama Tina's Pizza** •
2649 Frederick Douglass Blvd [W 141st St]
212-360-2020 • $
Decent pizza for late-night nangs.
• **People's Choice** •
2733 Frederick Douglass Blvd [W 145th St]
212-281-3830 • $$
Jerk chicken and oxtail stews worth a taste.

Shopping

• **B. Oyama** • 2312 Adam Clayton Powell Jr Blvd
212-234-5128
Fashion for men.
• **Backin Robbins** •
2730 Frederick Douglass Blvd [W 145th St]
212-862-0635
Do they still have 31 flavors?
• **Luis Liquor** • 108 W 145th St [Lenox Ave]
212-694-6619
Perfect grab-and-go shop near the subway.
• **Make My Cake** •
2380 7th Ave [W 139th St]
212-234-2344
Freshly baked cakes from a Southern family recipe.
• **The Schomburg Shop** •
515 Malcolm X Blvd [W 135th St]
212-491-2206
Shop specializing in Black history and culture.
• **Sneaker Q** • 693 Lenox Ave [142nd St]
212-491-9179
Get your kicks at this Lenox storefront.

Map 23 · **Washington Heights**

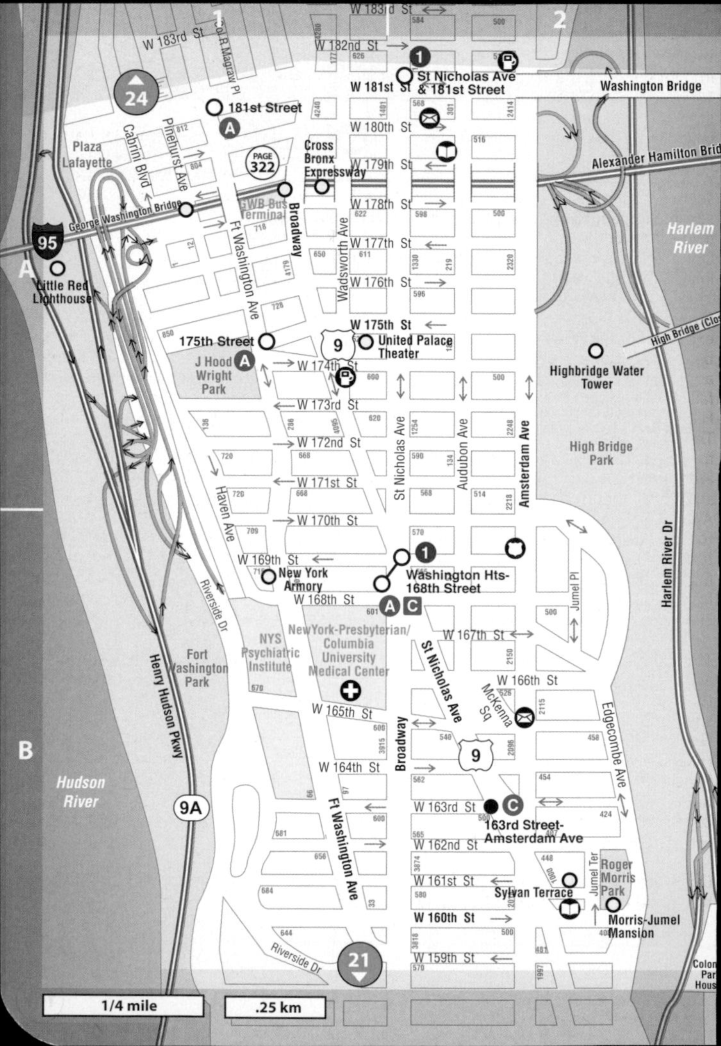

W 183rd St

W 182nd St

1 St Nicholas Ave & 181st Street

W 181st St

Washington Bridge

24

181st Street
A

W 180th St

Alexander Hamilton Brid

Plaza
Lafayette

Cabrini Blvd

Pinehurst Ave

Cross
Bronx
Expressway

W 179th St

W 178th St

PAGE
322

Broadway

W 177th St

Harlem
River

GWB Bus
Terminal

George Washington Bridge

Ft Washington Ave

Wadsworth Ave

W 176th St

95

W 175th St

9

United Palace
Theater

Highbridge Water
Tower

A

Little Red
Lighthouse

175th Street
A

W 174th St

J Hood
Wright
Park

W 173rd St

High Bridge
Park

W 172nd St

St Nicholas Ave

Audubon Ave

Amsterdam Ave

Haven Ave

W 171st St

W 170th St

W 169th St

1

New York
Armory

Washington Hts-
168th Street
A **C**

W 168th St

Harlem River Dr

NewYork-Presbyterian/
Columbia
University
Medical Center

W 167th St

Riverside Dr

NYS
Psychiatric
Institute

St Nicholas Ave

Jumel Pl

W 166th St

McKenna
Sq

Fort
Washington
Park

W 165th St

B

Broadway

9

Edgecombe Ave

Hudson
River

W 164th St

9A

W 163rd St
C

163rd Street-
Amsterdam Ave

Henry Hudson Pkwy

Ft Washington Ave

W 162nd St

W 161st St

Jumel Ter

Roger
Morris
Park

Sylvan Terrace

W 160th St

Morris-Jumel
Mansion

Riverside Dr

21

W 159th St

Colo
House

1/4 mile   .25 km

Neighborhood Overview

Washington Heights is a veritable United Nations of immigrant stories. Irish settlers moved up north in the 1900s. After World War I, European Jews called this hilly stretch of Manhattan home. Now, the 'hood swings to an undeniable merengue beat. The largely Dominican sliver of northern Manhattan probably claims more authenticity than any Punta Cana all-inclusive. Street vendors whip up delectable chimichurris, a sort of Dominican hamburger. Broadway houses a seemingly limitless number of chicken-and-rice eateries. English almost feels like a second language. As with all of Manhattan, this swath of delis and polluxial root change in the future. Hipsters searching for cheap rent keep hiking uptown, and higher end Dominican fusion eateries are breaking into the restaurant scene. It looks like everyone knows that all you have to do is take the A train even farther than Harlem.

Some of Manhattan's most storied buildings live far uptown, and The Heights are no exception. Most notable is the **Morris-Jumel Mansion**, a hilltop home that looks like it belongs in Gone With the Wind, not Gotham. British Colonel Roger Morris built the abode in 1765, but George Washington famously stationed his headquarters here in the fall of 1776. After the Revolutionary War, Morris left the estate, which stretched up from Harlem. If that's not impressive enough, note that Washington also took John Adams, Thomas Jefferson, and John Quincy Adams to dine there in 1790. The museum is open for visits, but beware: There have been rumors of hauntings. For a less ghostly architecture tour, check out the two-block historic district of **Sylvan Terrace**. This stretch of wooden row-houses line the skinny street leading up to the mansion. Although the turn-of-the-century homes underwent a few incarnations—from wooden to faux brick to stucco—they are now largely restored to their original facades. Another turn of the century creation, the **New York Armory**, had a similar rebirth. The armory first served as a training center for the National Guard in 1909. It rose to fame as a center for track and field competitions until the 1980s, when it became a homeless shelter. Now, the armory has been restored and functions as a track and field center.

This skinny expanse of Manhattan boasts some of the country's top transportation accomplishments. Construction began in 1948 for the **Cross-Bronx Expressway**, one of the country's first highways to forge through such a densely populated urban area; suffice it to say, "first" does not necessary mean "best." Heading west into Fort Lee, NJ, the **George Washington Bridge** is the only 14-lane suspension crossing in the country. Hikers, bikers, and skaters can skip the pricey tolls and enjoy views of Palisades Interstate Park in New Jersey. The best part about the bridge: **The Little Red Lighthouse** that rests underneath. The charmingly out-of-place tower only operated between 1921 and 1948, but it earned fame from the 1942 children's book The Little Red Lighthouse and the Great Gray Bridge, by Hildegarde Swift and Lynd Ward.

Duck into **Coogan's** or **Le Chéile** for a pint. When the live music itch strikes, the shabby but grand **United Palace** hosts a bevy of artists.

Map 23

Washington Heights

O Landmarks

- **The Armory** •
  216 Fort Washington Ave [W 169th St]
  212-923-1803
  World class running facility houses Track &
  Field Hall of Fame.
- **Cross Bronx Expressway** •
  Cross Bronx Expressway [Ittner Pl]
  Worst. Highway. Ever.
- **George Washington Bridge** •
  W 178th St [Henry Hudson Pkwy]
  Try to see it when it's lit up. Drive down from
  Riverdale on the Henry Hudson at night and
  you'll understand.
- **George Washington Bridge Bus Station** •
  4211 Broadway [178th St]
  800-221-9903
  Nervi's bus masterpiece connecting
  Washington Heights with the world.
- **High Bridge Water Tower** • Highbridge Park
  Defunct but cool water tower; tours inside are
  worth the hassle.
- **The Little Red Lighthouse** •
  Fort Washington Park [W 178th St]
  Enter from 181st Street. It's there, really!
- **Morris-Jumel Mansion** •
  65 Jumel Terrace [W 162nd St]
  212-923-8008
  The oldest building in New York, at least until
  someone changes it again.
- **Sylvan Terrace** •
  b/n Jumel Ter & St Nicholas Ave
  The most un-Manhattanlike place in all the
  world.
- **United Palace Theater** •
  4140 Broadway [W 175th St]
  212-568-6700
  Movie theater, then church, now rock venue.
  Gorgeous inside.

Coffee

- **Dunkin' Donuts** •
  1416 St Nicholas Ave [W 181st St]
  212-928-1900
  Decent coffee served in gigantic Styrofoam
  cups.
- **Jou Jou** • 603 W 168th St [Broadway]
  212-781-2222
  Open 24 hours!
- **Starbucks** •
  803 W 181st St [Ft Washington Ave]
  212-927-4272
  Fuel up and take a break from 181st.

Dominican eats dominate the food scene up here; **Margot Restaurant** is easily one of the best. Hit up **Malecon** for unsurpassed roast chicken. When variety beckons **Sushi Yu** dishes up a tasty alternative and **Saggio** is a pleasant Italian trattoria. And good luck choosing from the massive **Hudson View** menu (though we're sorry to report that there is not much of a view).

Farmers Markets

• **175th Street Greenmarket** •
Broadway & W 175th St
Thurs, 8 am–4 pm, June–Nov

Nightlife

• **Coogan's** • 4015 Broadway [W 169th St]
212-928-1234
Join doctors, professors, and off-duty cops for a cold one.
• **Le Chéile** • 839 W 181st St [Cabrini Blvd]
212-740-3111
Nice-looking Irish bar with good beer & food.

Map 23

25
24
23
21 22
18 19 20
16 17

Map 23

Washington Heights

Restaurants

- **181 Cabrini** • 854 W 181st St [Cabrini Blvd]
212-923-2233 • $$
Seasonal American bistro.
- **Antika** • 3924 Broadway [W 165th St]
212-781-9100 • $$
It's all about the grandma-style pizza.
- **Aqua Marina** • 4060 Broadway [W 171st St]
212-928-0070 • $
OK Uptown Italian.
- **Carrot Top Pastries** •
3931 Broadway [W 165th St]
212-927-4800 • $
Baked goods and coffee too!
- **Coogan's** • 4015 Broadway [W 169th St]
212-928-1234 • $$
Where med students and cops go.
- **Dallas BBQ** • 3956 Broadway [W 166th St]
212-568-3700 • $$
When you can't get to Virgil's.
- **El Conde** • 4139 Broadway [W 175th St]
212-781-3231 • $$$
Big slabs of MEAT.
- **El Galicia** • 4083 Broadway [W 172nd St]
212-568-0163 • $$
A humble taste of the Spanish sea. And tapas.
- **Empire Szechuan Noodle House** •
4041 Broadway [W 170th St]
212-568-1600 • $$
Take a guess at what they serve.
- **Flaco's Pizza** • 3876 Broadway [W 162nd St]
212-923-3733 • $
Chowing on this cheap, delish pizza won't
keep you flaco.
- **Hudson View Restaurant** •
770 W 181st St [Fort Washington Ave]
212-781-0303 • $$
Ch- ch- ch- choices.
- **Malecon** • 4141 Broadway [W 175th St]
212-927-3812 • $
Fabulous roast chicken.
- **Manolo Tapas** • 4165 Broadway [W 176th St]
212-923-9100 • $$$
Uptown portal to Spain with rustic cuisine and
ambiance.
- **Marcha Cocina** • 4055 Broadway [W 171st]
212-928-8272 • $$$
Tasty trifecta of tapas, brunch, and cocktails.
- **Parrilla Latin Bistro** •
3920 Broadway [W 164th St]
212-543-9500 • $$
Argentine with cool-ass grill.
- **Saggio Restaurant** •
827 W 181st St [Cabrini Blvd]
212-795-3080 • $$$
Every good neighborhood needs a solid Italian
trattoria.
- **Silver Palace Chinese Restaurant** •
3846 Broadway [W 160th St]
212-927-8300 • $$
Standard storefront Chinese fare.
- **Sushi Yu II** • 825 W 181st St [Pinehurst Ave]
212-781-5255 • $
Raw fish for when you need to take a plantain
break.
- **University Deli** • 601 W 168th St [Broadway]
212-568-3838 • $
Standard deli fare, with a large doctor
clientele.

Washington Heights

Map 23

Broadway's chaos anchors this nabe's shopping options. Stroll the street for a mind-boggling number of hardware stores, check out oodles of vendors at **La Plaza de las Americas**, and score free delivery on groceries at **Liberato**. Find a decent selection of wine and liquor at **Columbia Wine**. For a taste of Russia, check out **Moscow on the Hudson**. It's all here.

 Shopping

- **3841 Hardware** • 3879 Broadway [W 160th St]
  212-927-2240
  No name required at this classic, Broadway tool supply shop.
- **Baskin-Robbins** •
  728 W 181st St [Colonel Robert Magaw Pl]
  212-923-9239
  31 flavors and other frozen treats.
- **Bravo Supermarket** •
  1331 St Nicholas Ave [W 177th St]
  212-927-1331
  Clean and well-supplied.
- **Carrot Top Pastries** •
  3931 Broadway [W 165th St]
  212-927-4800
  Top carrot cake, muffins, chocolate cake, rugalach, and more.
- **The Children's Place** •
  600 W 181st St [St Nicholas Ave]
  212-923-7244
  Cute clothes for little ones.
- **Columbia Wine** • 4038 Broadway [169th St]
  212-543-2633
  Well-appointed, non-plexiglass wine & liquor store.
- **Fort Washington Bakery & Deli** •
  808 W 181st St [Fort Washington Ave]
  212-795-1891
  Damn good looking cookies.
- **Goodwill Thrift Store** •
  512 W 181st St [Amsterdam Ave]
  212-923-7910
  Everything and anything for cheaper.
- **La Bella Nails & Spa** •
  4033 Broadway [W 169th St]
  212-927-2023
  Time for that bi-weekly pedicure.

- **La Plaza de Las Americas** •
  Broadway & W 175th St
  Outdoor street vendor market.
- **Liberato Grocery** •
  3900 Broadway [W 163rd St]
  212-927-0250
  Get your fruits and veggies delivered—free!
- **Modell's** • 606 W 181st St [St Nicholas Ave]
  212-568-3000
  Lots and lots of sporting goods.
- **Moscow on the Hudson** •
  801 W 181st St [Fort Washington Ave]
  212-740-7397
  Comrades, this place is Russian culinary heaven.
- **Nunez Hardware** •
  4147 Broadway [W 175th St]
  212-927-8518
  Scavenge for tools at this old-school, stocked-to-bursting shop.
- **Spoiled Brats** • 4 Bennett Ave [W 181st St]
  212-543-2202
  Because your pet can never have enough toys.
- **Total Beauty Supplies** •
  650 W 181st St [Wadsworth Ave]
  212-923-6139
  Bad hair days are over.
- **Vargas Liquor Store** •
  114 Audubon Ave [W 171st St]
  212-781-5195
  Convenient for paper-bag-drinking in Highbridge Park, if that's your thing.
- **Victor's Bike Repair** •
  4125 Broadway [174th St]
  212-740-5137
  Sales, service, repairs, and rentals.

Map 24 · **Fort George / Fort Tryon**

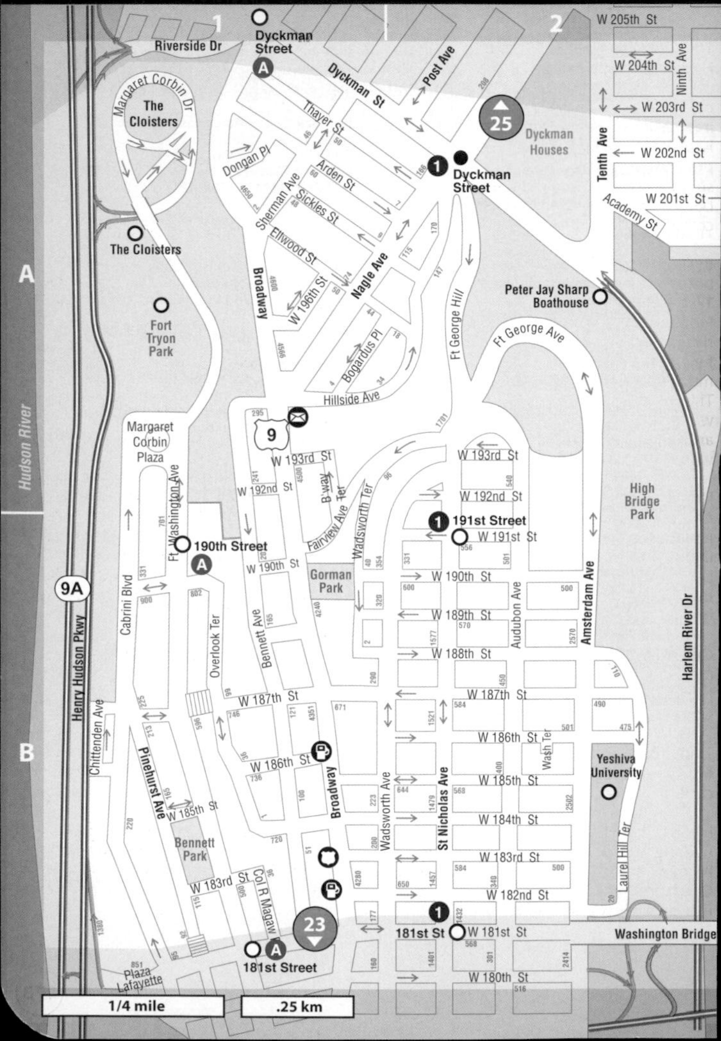

Riverside Dr

Dyckman
Street

Ⓐ

W 205th St

W 204th St

Ninth Ave

W 203rd St

Tenth Ave

W 202nd St

W 201st St

Academy St

Dyckman St

Post Ave

Margaret Corbin Dr

The
Cloisters

Thayer St

Arden St

Sherman Ave

Sickles St

Ellwood St

Dongan Pl

▲
25

Dyckman
Houses

❶
Dyckman
Street

The Cloisters

Broadway

W 196th St

Nagle Ave

Fort
Tryon
Park

Bogardus Pl

Peter Jay Sharp
Boathouse ○

Ft George Hill

Ft George Ave

Hillside Ave

Hudson River

Margaret
Corbin
Plaza

✉
9

W 193rd St

W 192nd St

High
Bridge
Park

Ft Washington Ave

W 192nd St

W 193rd St

B-way

Fairview Ave Ter

Wadsworth Ter

9A

❶
190th Street
Ⓐ

W 190th St

Gorman
Park

❶
191st Street
W 191st St

Amsterdam Ave

Cabrini Blvd

Bennett Ave

W 189th St

W 188th St

Audubon Ave

Overlook Ter

W 187th St

W 187th St

Wash Ter

Chittenden Ave

W 186th St

Broadway

W 185th St

Wadsworth Ave

St Nicholas Ave

W 186th St

W 185th St

Yeshiva
University ○

Pinehurst Ave

W 183rd St

Co. R Magaw Pl

W 184th St

W 183rd St

Laurel Hill Ter

Bennett
Park

23
▼

Ⓐ
181st Street

❶
181st St   W 181st St

Harlem River Dr

Washington Bridge

Plaza
Lafayette

W 180th St

Henry Hudson Pkwy

1/4 mile	.25 km

Neighborhood Overview

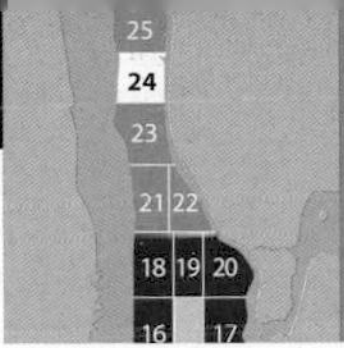

Map 24

The Fort George/Fort Tryon area is also known locally as Hudson Heights, mostly for the benefit of realtors showing off this area's huge upside (literally!). Fort George is the name of the last fort of its kind, built in 1776 at the intersection of Audubon Avenue and 192nd Street. The area is diverse: The neighborhoods surrounding Fort Tryon Park and Yeshiva University are predominantly Jewish, while east of Broadway tends to be more Latin and Caribbean. The streets are some of the steepest on the island, and provide pleasant views (and a lower-body workout). Residents appreciate the quiet streets and better values and best of all, the commute to Lower Manhattan is just a half-hour.

Built in 1935 by Frederick Law Olmsted, Jr. (the son of one of the master architects behind both Central and Prospect Parks) on land donated to the city by John D. Rockefeller, **Fort Tryon Park** is the 67-acre chunk of green high up on the bluff above the Hudson River. From here, the Hudson is stunning: the pristine Palisades on the New Jersey side of the river were also made possible by Rockefeller philanthropy, in an effort to protect the view for future generations. In 1995 Bette Midler's New York Restoration Project assisted on a much-needed renovation of the park. If you are feeling cultural, pay a visit to **The Cloisters**. The complex, an extension of the Metropolitan Museum of Art, is a fully formed Medieval wonderland, with elements from four French cloisters, stained-glass windows, tapestries, and gardens. Don't miss the Medieval Festival that takes place every year in Fort Tryon Park when reenactors reimagine life in the Middle Ages. Warderere!

Down at the edge of the Harlem River stands the **Peter Jay Sharp Boathouse**. The first new community boathouse in New York City in years, it opened in 2004 and offers rowing lessons to members of the community. To reach the boathouse go to Tenth Avenue and Dyckman and walk south on the Lillian Goldman Walkway. Just before you get there, you'll pass by the restored Swindler Cove Park, a nice spot to stare at ducks or contemplate the river. If you decide to continue south on the walkway, the only way out is through the bridge that connects to 155th Street in Harlem.

On the campus of Yeshiva University, the unusual **Zysman Hall** was designed by Charles B. Meyers and blends Art-Deco and Moorish styles. Today, the building is home to Yeshiva's High School for Boys. If you feel the need to stock up on kosher goodies, now is the time. Cross the street for a full selection of delis, restaurants, and bodegas that carry them.

There isn't a ginormous selection of bars but don't leave the neighborhood just yet. **The Monkey Room** is ideal for game nights or late-night drinks. Quaff craft beer to your heart's content at **Buddha Beer Bar**. For a good neighborhood spot, try **Locksmith Wine Bar**.

In case of empty picnic baskets, visitors to Fort Tryon can go to **New Leaf Restaurant**, an upscale restaurant in a historic building within the park. Find great Indian cuisine at **Kismat**. Enjoy a real Caribbean meal at **La Casa Del Mofongo** or go Venezuelan at **Cachapas Y Mas**. The Mexican food can't be beat at **Tacos El Paisa**. For perfect falafel make your way to **Golan Heights**.

Map 24

Fort George / Fort Tryon

○ Landmarks

- **The Cloisters** •
99 Margaret Corbin Dr [Ft Tryon Pl]
212-923-3700
The Met's storehouse of medieval art. Great herb garden, nice views.
- **Fort Tryon Park** •
W 181st St & Hudson River Greenway
A totally beautiful and scenic park on New York's north edge.
- **Peter Jay Sharp Boathouse** •
Swindler Cove Park
See the West Bronx by boat.
- **Yeshiva University Zysman Hall** •
2540 Amsterdam Ave [W 186th St]
Interesting Byzantine-style building.

Coffee

- **Cafe Buunni** • 213 Pinehurst Ave [W 187th St]
212-568-8700
Espresso drinks and Ethiopian foods.
- **Dunkin' Donuts** •
1599 St Nicholas Ave [W 190th St]
212-568-1039
Decent coffee served in gigantic Styrofoam cups.

Nightlife

- **Buddha Beer Bar** •
4476 Broadway [W 191st St]
646-861-2595
Nice set of taps and Korean/Mexi fusion worth the trip.
- **Locksmith Wine & Burger Bar** •
4463 Broadway [W 192nd St]
212-304-9463
Friendly spot to grab a glass of wine or beer.
- **Monkey Room** •
589 Fort Washington Ave [W 187th St]
212-543-9888
Tiny like a capuchin.

🍴 Restaurants

- **809 Bar & Grill** • 112 Dyckman St [Nagle Ave]
212-304-3800 • $$$
Dominican grilled meat-a-thon.
- **Cachapas Y Mas** • 107 Dyckman St [Post Ave]
212-304-2224 • $
Fried Latin tastiness in corn and meat form.
- **Golan Heights** •
2553 Amsterdam Ave [W 187th St]
212-795-7842 • $
Tasty Israeli falafel and shawarma. Popular for lunch.
- **Kismat** •
603 Fort Washington Ave [W 187th St]
212-795-8633 • $$
Throw your taste buds a surprise party.
- **La Casa Del Mofongo** •
1447 St Nicholas Ave [W 182nd St]
212-740-1200 • $$
The obvious: have the mofongo.
- **New Leaf Restaurant & Bar** •
1 Margaret Corbin Dr [Henry Hudson Pkwy]
212-568-5323 • $$$$
Uptown haven for a fancier dinner or brunch.
- **Tacos El Paisa** •
1548 St Nicholas Ave [W 188th St]
917-521-0972 • $
Fantastic hole-in-the-wall Mexican.

Fort George / Fort Tryon

This area is home to one-of-a-kind shops like **Gideon's Bakery**, for kosher sweets, and **Food Palace**, for caviar and other Russian goodies. Buy your furry friend a treat and a makeover at **Critter Outfitter**. Get gourmet edibles at **Frank's Market** or enjoy a rhyme by buying wine from **Vines on Pine**.

Shopping

- **Apex Supply Co.** •
  4580 Broadway [W 196th St]
  212-304-0808
  Where eggshell is considered a color
- **Associated Supermarkets** •
  592 Fort Washington Ave [W 187th St]
  212-543-0721
  No-frills market way cheaper than your local bodega.
- **Century Hardware** •
  4309 Broadway [W 184th St]
  212-927-9000
  Experts in nuts and bolts.
- **The Cloisters Museum Store** •
  99 Margaret Corbin Dr [Fort Tryon Park]
  212-650-2277
  Dark Age trinkets.
- **Fine Fare Supermarkets** •
  1617 St Nicholas Ave [W 191st St]
  212-543-3008
  Decent supermarket. "Fine" may be stretching it.

- **Foot Locker** • 146 Dyckman St [Sherman Ave]
  212-544-8613
  No lockers. But lots of sneakers.
- **Frank's Gourmet Market** •
  807 W 187th St [Fort Washington Ave]
  212-795-2929
  Gourmet meats, cheeses, and groceries. A neighborhood institution.
- **JP Discount Liquors** •
  377 Audubon Ave [W 184th St]
  212-740-4027
  Who doesn't like cheaper liquor?
- **Metropolitan Museum of Art Bookshop–Cloisters Branch** •
  799 Fort Washington Ave [Margaret Corbin Dr]
  212-650-2277
  Specialty—art books.
- **NHS Hardware** •
  1539 St Nicholas Ave [W 187th St]
  212-927-3549
  Get into the DIY spirit.
- **Vines on Pine** •
  814 W 187th St [Pinehurst Ave]
  212-923-0584
  One-of-a-kind selections.

Map 25 · **Inwood**

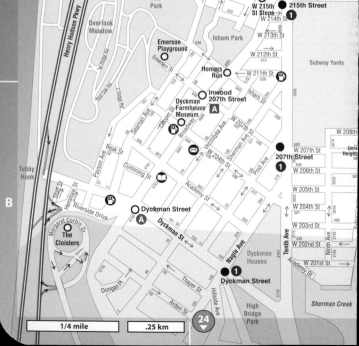

Neighborhood Overview

Located on the northernmost tip of the island, the hilly neighborhood of Inwood has something for everyone. And at a moment when there are so few places left in Manhattan where you can get affordable housing and fit all your belongings in something bigger than a shoebox, the 'hood is a solid alternative for those considering abandoning the island for one of the outer boroughs.

West of Broadway offers views, pathways, quiet streets, and artsy cafés. Parking is tricky, but possible—worst-case scenario is parking in one of the many lots around the area, which are still an affordable option. Rents west of Broadway can be higher because of the aforementioned perks and because it's right next to Inwood Hill Park, which is arguably the best neighborhood resource. The grass might be greener on this side of Broadway, but the predominantly Dominican area east of Broadway has even cheaper housing alternatives. That, and you'll find the air is filled with free *bachata*, especially during the summer.

Speaking of **Inwood Hill Park**, its 160 acres of greenspace stretch along the Hudson from Dyckman Street to the northern tip of the island. The park is home to last remaining natural forest in Manhattan, affording one the opportunity to brag about hiking through real woods without leaving the city. Take your kids (or nephews or nieces) to **Emerson Playground** on a sunny day, let your dog play with its kinfolk at **Homer's Run** or use one of several outdoor tennis courts. The **Inwood Greenmarket** happens rain or shine Saturdays at the foot of Inwood Hill Park.

That little house on the hill at 204th Street that looks out of place among the low-slung apartment buildings along Broadway is the **Dyckman Farmhouse** (c. 1784). Originally part of several hundred acres of farmland owned by a family with roots stretching back to New York's Dutch beginnings, today it's a stark visual reminder of just how much the city has evolved. On weekends say hello (or *hola*) to the seniors sitting on the benches by the farmhouse's garden.

The **Henry Hudson Bridge** connects Manhattan and The Bronx via a two-level, seven-lane structure. With thousands of vehicles crossing back and forth each day, drivers and passengers can take a minute to admire the lavish engineering efforts, views of the Hudson River, and the Harlem Ship Canal below. And speaking of channels, channel your inner Rocky by climbing the **West 215th Steps**. All 111 of them (yep, we counted). On the way up note Park Terrace East to see a few rare species: Actual houses with driveways.

Well, if you refuse to take the 1 or A trains south for more exciting options, then dive into **Piper's Kilt** for a perfect pint of Guinness and a burger. **Inwood Local** has many brews on tap and a fun neighborhood feel. For some vino, hit up **Corcho** for a glass and some tapas.

Get brunch at **Garden Cafe**. Go calorie crazy at **Elsa La Reina del Chicharron** with the best pork rinds in town. Sushi lovers go to **Mama Sushi** and Italian aficionados go to **Il Sole**. Practice your Spanish at **Mamajuana Cafe** and be artsy at **Indian Road Cafe**.

O Landmarks

- **Dyckman Farmhouse Museum** •
4881 Broadway [W 204th St]
212-304-9422
Oldest farmhouse in Manhattan, now restored as a museum.
- **Emerson Playground** •
Seaman Ave & Isham St
Kids (and adults) love playing around on the iron wolf.
- **Henry Hudson Bridge** • Henry Hudson Pkwy
Affords a nice view from the Inwood Hill Park side.
- **Homer's Run** • Isham St [W 211th St]
Where dogs par-tay.
- **Inwood Hill Park** • Dyckman St & Payson Ave
The last natural forest and salt marsh in Manhattan!
- **West 215th Street Steps** •
W 215th St & Park Terrace E
Elevation of sidewalk requires steps. Now get a move on it!

Coffee

- **Beans & Vines** • 4799 Broadway [Academy St]
646-928-0209
Cozy coffee shop and wine bar serving food.
- **Dunkin' Donuts** •
4942 Broadway [W 207th St]
212-544-0453
Decent coffee served in gigantic Styrofoam cups.
- **Indian Road Cafe** • 600 W 218th St [Indian Rd]
212-942-7451
Friendly neighborhood café.

Farmers Markets

- **Inwood Greenmarket** •
Seaman Ave & Isham St
Sat 8 am–3 pm, Year Round

Nightlife

- **Corcho** • 227 Dyckman St [Seaman Ave]
212-300-5700
Cozy spot to sip and nibble; happy hour and wine classes a bonus.
- **Inwood Local** • 4957 Broadway [W 207th St]
212-544-8900
Beer garden, wine bar, and sports pub with a side of tasty grub.
- **Post Billiards Café** • 154 Post Ave [W 207th St]
212-569-1840
When you need to shoot pool way way uptown.

Shopping isn't exactly Inwood's forte but **El Nuevo Azteca** does have a huge selection of typical/junk Mexican foods. Order a fresh-rolled cigar to go at **Q Cigars**, take that old couch for an upholstery makeover to **The Victorian House** or relieve your sweet tooth fix at **Carrot Top Pastries**.

 Restaurants

- **Capitol Restaurant** •
4933 Broadway [W 207th St]
212-942-5090 • $$
Nice neighborhood diner.
- **El Lina** • 500 W 207th St [10th Ave]
212-567-5031 • $
Satisfying though tiny Dominican diner.
- **Elsa La Reina Del Chicharron** •
4840 Broadway [W 204th St]
212-304-1070 • $
It's worth the coronary bypass.
- **Garden Café** • 4961 Broadway [Isham St]
212 544 9480 • $$
Homestyle brunch for less than 10 bucks.
- **Grandpa's Brick Oven Pizza** •
4973 Broadway [Isham St]
212-304-1185 • $$
Personal brick oven pies and catering
- **Guadalupe** • 597 W 207th St [Broadway]
212-304-1083 • $$
High class Mexican.
- **Il Sole** • 233 Dyckman St [Seaman Ave]
212 544 0406 • $$
Neighborhood Italian.
- **Junior's Tacos** • 253 Sherman Ave [Isham St]
212-942-7202 • $
Low budget, high taste.
- **Mamasushi** • 237 Dyckman St [Seaman Ave]
212 567 2150 • $
As good as uptown sushi gets.
- **Mamajuana Cafe** •
247 Dyckman St [Seaman Ave]
212-304-1217 • $$$
Tasty Nuevo Latino cuisine.
- **Papasito** • 223 Dyckman St [Broadway]
212-544-0001 • $$
Margaritas, music, and Mexican food.
- **Pizza Haven** • 4942 Broadway [W 207th St]
212-569-3720 • $
They bring-a the pizza.
- **Yummy Thai** • 4959 Broadway [Isham St]
917-529-0812 • $$
Affordable and reliable, especially for take-out and delivery.

Shopping

- **Carrot Top Pastries** •
5025 Broadway [W 214th St]
212-569-1532
Top carrot cake, muffins, chocolate cake, rugalach, and more.
- **El Nuevo Azteca** • 3861 10th Ave [W 206th St]
212-567-6028
For the Mexican junkfood junky.
- **Gopher Broke** • 4926 Broadway [W 204th St]
917-692-7749
All I want for Xmas is a piece of forest.
- **Inwood Paint & Hardware** •
165 Sherman Ave [W 204th St]
212-569-6002
High security locks and more.
- **Portes Cigars** • 5009 Broadway [W 214th St]
212-544-9623
Fresh out of the hand cigars.
- **Richie's Cleaners and Tailors** •
4915 Broadway [W 204th St]
212-304-0289
Trust the R. man.
- **Tread Bike Shop** •
250 Dyckman St [Broadway]
212-544-7055
Where to fix your bike after riding through Inwood Hill Park.
- **V.I.M.** • 565 W 207th St [Vermilyea Ave]
212-942-7478
Street wear—jeans, sneakers, tops—for all.
- **The Victorian House** •
4961 Broadway [W 207th St]
212-304-0202
Upholstery sanctuary.

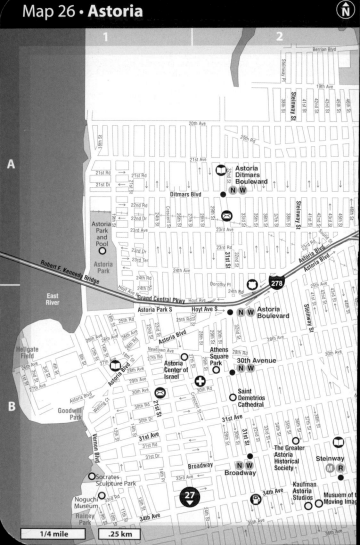

Neighborhood Overview

Despite the influx of young people, Astoria holds onto its diversity tooth and nail, and thank goodness. North Africans on Steinway Street, Greeks and Italians in northern Astoria, Brazilians and Bangladeshis in the south and east, and Croatians, Serbians, Bosnians, Mexicans, Japanese, and so many others (including an expanding LGBT community and seemingly most of New York's young standup comics) call this neighborhood home.

Astoria is roughly split in two parts. The blocks south of the Grand Central tend to be filled with low-slung, well-appointed apartment buildings, providing tons of decent rentals within 20 minutes from Midtown. 30th Avenue in particular is packed with great restaurants and nightlife. There are more single—and two-family homes on the other side of the Grand Central, which gives that part of Astoria more of a neighborhood feel. Ditmars Boulevard is the main street north of the Grand Central, and its storefronts are filling in as a secondary destination for great restaurants. You'll find that many retail establishments have branches both north and south of the Grand Central.

Before the subway's arrival in 1917, Astoria was made up of several small communities, including Ravenswood, Dutch Kills, Steinway, and Old Astoria Village. The folks at **The Greater Astoria Historical Society** are dedicated to documenting the area's rich history as a farming and manufacturing center. Among the many ornate neighborhood houses of worship are the **Astoria Center of Israel**, founded in 1925 and recently added to the National and State Registers of Historic Places, and **Saint Demetrios Cathedral**, spiritual center of the Greek Orthodox community.

With its reasonable rents and proximity to Manhattan, Astoria, and Western Queens in general, has a thriving arts scene. Movies have been made here since the days of silent films, and the revitalized **Kaufman Astoria Studios** is the city's main film and TV studio complex. Just down the street from Kaufman Astoria is the **Museum of the Moving Image**, which recently underwent a major expansion, resulting in a sleek new building by architect Thomas Leeser. Sculpture buffs should also check out the **Noguchi Museum**. Just across the street is the **Socrates Sculpture Park**, located on the East River waterfront, open year-round with rotating contemporary outdoor exhibits plus international film screenings in the summer.

Not many green spaces exist in Astoria, but the neighborhood is blessed with **Astoria Park** and its massive WPA-era Olympic-sized pool, one of 11 such pools that were opened across the city in 1936. It hosted the Olympic swimming trials that summer for the U.S. swim and diving teams. Although the city no longer allows diving boards in parks, Astoria Park's diving pool and its intriguing towers are slated to become part of an outdoor venue. The park also has many (underutilized!) tennis courts and a large running track, along with great views of Manhattan and the Robert F. Kennedy Bridge and the Hell Gate Bridge, the approaches for both of which cross through the park. Elsewhere, the vest-pocket **Athens Square Park** is a nod to Astoria's Greek roots, and features a mini-amphitheater and a sculpture donated by the mayor of Athens.

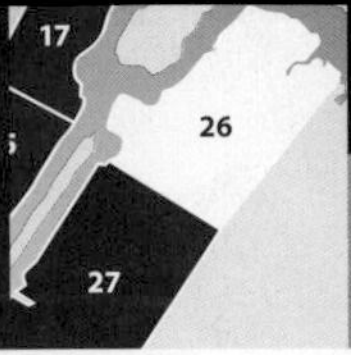

Map 26

17

26

27

Astoria

o Landmarks

- **Astoria Center of Israel** • 27-35 Crescent St
718-278-2680
Beautiful Louis Pierre Rigal murals grace the sanctuary.
- **Astoria Park and Pool** • 19th St & 23rd Dr
718-626-8621
60 acres of waterfront parkland and an awesome pool.
- **Athens Square** • 30th Ave & 30th St
You'll love it as much as the kids.
- **Greater Astoria Historical Society** •
35-20 Broadway
718-278-0700
Preserving the past and future of Astoria.
- **Kaufman Astoria Studios** • 34-12 36th St
718-392-5600
US's largest studio outside of LA, and just as historic.
- **Museum of the Moving Image** •
36-01 35th Ave
718-777-6888
Fantastic interactive film/TV museum, with screenings of classic films.
- **The Noguchi Museum** • 9-01 33rd Rd
718-204-7088
Noguchi's converted factory studio with representative works and beautiful garden.
- **Saint Demetrios Cathedral** • 30-11 30th Dr
718-728-1718
The main Greek Orthodox church in Astoria.
- **Socrates Sculpture Park** • 32-01 Vernon Blvd
718-956-1819
Cool, gritty sculpture park with events and films.

Coffee

- **60 Beans Coffee & Tea** • 36-02 Ditmars Blvd
347-967-3994
Part of the first wave of Astoria's third-wave coffee shops.
- **Astoria Coffee** • 30-04 30th St
Sleek, friendly café with ecumenical roasting approach.
- **Egyptian Coffee Shop** • 25-09 Steinway St
718-777-5517
Smoke hookah, sip strong coffee, watch Al-Jazeera.
- **Kinship Coffee Cooperative** •
30-05 Steinway St
Third-wave-cold-brew-pour-over-latte-hearted loveliness.
- **OK Cafe** • 22-04 33rd St
718-440-8789
Cozy artisanal coffee shop on the way to the train.

Farmers Markets

- **Astoria Greenmarket** • 31st Ave & 14th St
212-788-7476
Wednesdays, July–Nov, 8 am–3 pm

Nightlife

- **Albatross Bar** • 36-19 24th Ave
718-204-9707
Gay dive bar with a raucous karaoke night
- **Astor Room** • 35-11 35th Ave
347-983-6491
Mahogany bar in the original Paramount Studio dinner club.
- **Astoria Craft** • 18-01 26th Rd
718-278-4300
Cocktails/above-average beer selection/food on river side of 21st Street.
- **Astoria Tavern** • 33-16 23rd Ave
347-813-4954
Platonic ideal of Astoria Irish bar.

Map 26

There's something for everyone, from Irish bars like **Cronin & Phelan** and the **Irish Rover** to artisanal cocktails at **Sweet Afton** to wines by the glass at **Crescent & Vine** and **DiWine**. **The Queens Kickshaw** stays open late serving craft beer and live music, and **SingleCut** has a great taproom. **The Sparrow** is a go-to north of the Grand Central, and the **Bohemian Hall & Beer Garden** is always a jam-packed summertime favorite.

- **Bohemian Hall & Beer Garden** •
  29-19 24th Ave
  718-274-4925
  Over 100 years old; room for 500 in the garden.
- **The Bonnie** • 29-12 23rd Ave
  718-274-2105
  Heady cocktail lounge/gastropub from folks behind Sweet Afton.
- **Monika's Café Bar** • 32-90 36th St
  718-204-5273
  Funky place for coffee or cocktails serving Mediterranean food.
- **Crescent & Vine** • 25-03 Ditmars Blvd
  718-204-4774
  Lovely little wine bar, with good beers to boot.
- **Cronin & Phelan** • 38-14 Broadway
  718 545-0999
  Open mic, live music, and karaoke! Irish you'd buy me another ale.
- **Daly's Pub** • 31-86 31st St
  718-606-2561
  Another Irish pub, but featuring live music from local artists.
- **Diamond Dogs** • 34-04 31st Ave
  929-522-0061
  Rotating craft cocktails by way of Bowie.
- **The Ditty** • 35-03 Ditmars Blvd
  Good cocktails and beer selection + excellent low-key vibe.
- **DiWine** • 41-15 31st Ave
  718-777-1355
  Another Astoria wine bar, another bad pun.
- **Dominie's** • 34-07 30th Ave
  Rare Astoria bar without televisions.
- **Fatty's Café** • 45-17 28th Ave
  718-267-7071
  Latin-infused grub with nice outdoor option.
- **Gastroteca** • 33-02 34th Ave
  718-729-9080
  Wine, cocktails, excellent specials.
- **Gilbey's** • 32-01 Broadway
  718-545-8567
  The local yokels and cheap brews will have you saying, "Gib me's another beer."

- **Icon** • 31-84 33rd St
  347-808-7592
  Gay bar/lounge with mixed crowd.
- **Irish Rover** • 37-18 28th Ave
  718-278-9372
  A well-loved hangout with live music, quiz nights, and Irish aparta.
- **Judy & Punch** • 34-08 30th Ave
  718-626-3101
  Friendly mixological spot also featuring many craft beers on tap.
- **The Let Love Inn** • 27-20 23rd Ave
  718-777-5683
  Good cocktails and no TVs from folks behind Sparrow.
- **McCann's Pub & Grill** • 36-15 Ditmars Blvd
  718-278-2621
  Bustling Irish sports bar that attracts the young, the loud, and the thirsty.
- **Q.E.D.** • 27-16 23rd Ave
  347 451-3873
  Safe space for comedy, crafting, and game nights.
- **The Quays** • 45-02 30th Ave
  718-204-8435
  Guinness, live music, and about that dart league…
- **Sekend Sun** • 32-11 Broadway
  917-832-6414
  Smart cocktails from people who own Williamsburg's Ba'sik.
- **Sissy McGinty's** • 25-67 Steinway St
  718-545-4286
  Typical Irish pub, nuff' said.
- **The Sparrow Tavern** • 24-01 29th St
  718-606-2260
  A hipster outpost from the folks who brought us Tupelo.
- **Sunswick 35/35** • 35-02 35th St
  718-752-0620
  Convenient to Museum of the Moving Image; dozens of beers on tap.
- **Sweet Afton** • 30-09 34th St
  718-777-2570
  Salvaged wood, comfort food, fancy drinks. Sweet.

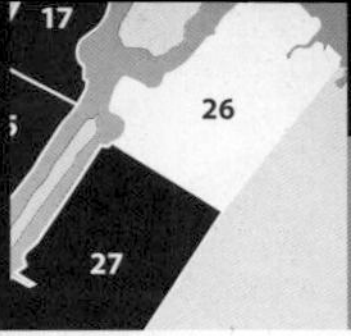

Map 26

26
17
27

Astoria

🍴 Restaurants

- **Agnanti Meze** • 19-06 Ditmars Blvd
  718-545-4554 • $$
  Wonderful Greek/Cypriot cuisine just across
  from Astoria Park.
- **Aliada** • 29-19 Broadway
  718-932-2240 • $$
  Excellent Cypriot with deservedly famous
  lamb chops.
- **Artichoke Basille's Pizza** • 22-56 31st St
  718-215-8100 • $$
  The gut-busting artichoke slice comes to
  Astoria.
- **Bareburger** • 23-21 31st Ave
  718-777-7011 • $$
  Organic burgers and sides. Try the elk or bison!
- **Basil Brick Oven Pizza** • 28-17 Astoria Blvd
  718-204-1205 • $$
  Elegant ingredients and great crust.
- **BZ Grill** • 27-02 Astoria Blvd
  718-932-7858 • $$
  Fantastic gyros, kebabs, and souvlaki.
- **Cevabdzinica Sarajevo** • 37-18 34th Ave
  718-752-9528 • $$
  Bosnian diner grub.
- **Christos Steak House** • 41-08 23rd Ave
  718-777-8400 • $$$$$
  Excellent Greek-inflected steakhouse.
- **Crave Astoria** • 28-55 36th St
  718-726-4976 • $$
  Greek stoner food that will please the entire
  family.
- **De Mole II** • 42-20 30th Ave
  718-777-1655 • $$$
  Fresh Mexican in bistro setting after Sunnyside
  original.
- **Djerdan Burek** • 34-04 31st Ave
  718-721-2694 • $$
  Bureks and other Eastern European delights.
- **Elias Corner** • 24-02 31st St
  718-932-1510 • $$
  No menu, just pick your fish from the counter.
- **Enthaice** • 33-20 31st Ave
  718-932-1111 • $$$
  Haute-Thai cuisine & cocktails; forgive the
  word play.
- **Favela** • 33-18 28th Ave
  718-545-8250 • $$$
  Hearty Brazilian food. Think meat, and piles
  of it.
- **Gregory's 26 Corner Taverna** •
  26-02 23rd Ave
  718-777-5511 • $$$
  Highly recommended low-key Greek taverna.
- **HinoMaru Ramen** • 33-18 Ditmars Blvd
  718-777-0228 • $$
  Authenticated ramen shop on Ditmars;
  "kaedama" gets you more!
- **Il Bambino** • 34-08 31st Ave
  718-626-0087 • $
  Paninis, tapas, and other light Italian/
  Mediterranean grub.
- **JJ's** • 37-05 31st Ave
  718-626-8888 • $$
  Sushi-French fusion.
- **Jujube Tree** • 35-02 30th Ave
  718-545-1888 • $$
  Vegan Asian fusion with fun fake meat.
- **Kabab Café** • 25-12 Steinway St
  718-728-9858 • $$
  Haute Egyptian cooked to order by friendly
  chef-owner, Ali.
- **Koliba Restaurant** • 31-11 23rd Ave
  718-626-0430 • $$$
  Nice Czech option north of the Grand Central.
- **Kondo** • 29-13 Broadway
  347-617-1236 • $$$$
  Japanese that transcends the tempura-
  California roll industrial complex.
- **La Rioja** • 33-05 Broadway
  718-932-0101 • $$
  Lots of tapas, plus Spanish groceries in the
  back.
- **Los Amigos Mexican Restaurant** •
  22-73 31st St
  718-726-8708 • $$
  Cheap, reliable, easy-going Mexican joint with
  generous portions.
- **Loukoumi** • 45-07 Ditmars Blvd
  718-626-3200 • $$$
  Excellent Greek taverna off the beaten path
  down Ditmars.

Sure, there are plenty of Greek restaurants (**Agnanti** and **Taverna Kyclades** are local faves), but why stop there? Visit **Vesta** for good, cheap Italian food and wine, **Djerdan** for Bosnia's best, and **Favela** for a taste of Rio. **Tufino** has some of the best pizza in the city, minus the waits. Meanwhile, **Queens Comfort** hits a pitch-perfect rec room vibe while the tiny **Pao & Cha Cha** serves up inspired Venezuelan-Asian fusion.

- **Maizol Mexican Cuisine & Tequila Bar** •
  32-07 34th Ave
  718-406-9431 • $$$
  Fun Mexican with cocktails to match.
- **Mar's** • 34 21 34th Ave
  718-685-2480 • $$$
  Oysters I good cocktails.
- **Max Bratwurst und Bier** • 47-02 30th Ave
  718-777-1635 • $$
  German-style beer hall/sports bar.
- **Milkflower** • 34-12 31st Ave
  718-204-1300 • $$
  Reclaimed wood fired pizza.
- **Mojave** • 22-36 31st St
  718 545 4100 • $$$
  Fun place for margaritas and nachos
- **Mokja** • 35-19 Broadway
  718-721-0654 • $$$
  Stylish all-purpose Korean.
- **Mombar** • 25-22 Steinway St
  718-726-2356 • $$
  Egyptian by Kabab Café Ali's brother in a
  beautiful setting.
- **Ornella Trattoria Italiana** • 29-17 23rd Ave
  718-777-9477 • $$
  Inspired experimental Italian trattoria with
  great pizza.
- **Ovelia** • 34-01 30th Ave
  718-721 7217 • $$$
  Not your yiayia's tzatziki, or her brunch.
- **Pachanga Patterson** • 33-17 31st Ave
  718-554-0525 • $$$
  Haute taqueria from the folks that brought
  you Vesta.
- **Pao & Cha Cha** • 23-03 Astoria Blvd
  646-494 6770 • $$
  Rare Chinese-Venezuelan fusion.
- **Petey's Burger** • 30-17 30th Ave
  718-267-6300 • $
  It's like an In-N-Out cover band; fills a need.
- **The Pomeroy** • 36-12 Ditmars Blvd
  718-721-1579 • $$
  Haute-fried food with carefully crafted
  cocktails.

- **Pye Boat Noodle** • 35-13 Broadway
  718-685-2329 • $$
  Thai beyond the usual pad thai staples.
- **Queens Comfort** • 40-09 30th Ave
  718-728-2350 • $$$
  Haute comfort cuisine in rec room atmosphere.
  (BYOB a plus!)
- **Rizzo's Pizza** • 30-13 Steinway St
  718-721-9862 • $
  Yummy thin-crust square pies.
- **Sabry's Seafood** • 24-25 Steinway St
  718-721-9010 • $$
  Great Egyptian seafood.
- **Sac's Place** • 25-41 Broadway
  718-204-5002 • $$
  Coal oven pizza brilliance.
- **Santord's** • 31-13 Broadway
  718-932-9569 • $$
  Family diner remodeled and spiffed up by
  the kids
- **Seva Indian Cuisine** • 30-07 34th St
  718-626-4440 • $$
  Go to Indian in a neighborhood without many
  South Asian options.
- **The Shady Lady** • 34-19 30th Ave
  718-440-9081 • $$$
  Inspired and slightly off-key bistro you want
  to root for.
- **Snowdonia** • 34-55 32nd St
  347-730-5783 • $$$
  Gastropub open late.
- **Stamatis** • 29-09 23rd Ave
  718-932-8596 • $$$
  Basic Astoria Greek, octopus and other grilled
  fish recommended.
- **SugarFreak** • 37-11 30th Ave
  718-606-1900 • $$$
  Authenticated Lousiana/Cajunesque cuisine
  on 30th Ave restaurant row.
- **Taverna Kyclades** • 33-07 Ditmars Blvd
  718-545-8666 • $$-$$$
  Consistent, homey Greek seafood; worth
  the wait.

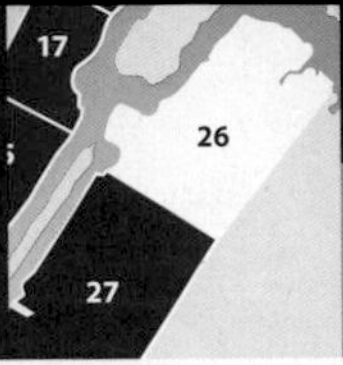

Map 26

Astoria

• **Telly's Taverna** • 28-13 23rd Ave
718-728-9056 • $$
Creative specials and bang-up Greek classics.

• **The Thirsty Koala** • 35-12 Ditmars Blvd
718-626-5430 •
You may have to Google "eschalot"; not so for
"kangaroo."

• **Trattoria L'Incontro** • 21-76 31st St
718-721-3532 • $$$$$
One of the city's best Italian restaurants.
Seriously.

• **Tufino Pizzeria** • 36-08 Ditmars Blvd
718-278-4800 • $$
Big-boy, big-time Neopolitan from a custom-
built oven.

• **Vesta** • 21-02 30th Ave
718-545-5550 • $$$
Italian heaven in Greek haven.

• **Vite Vinosteria** • 31-05 34th St
718-278-8483 • $$$
Great Italian wine and food from Manhattan
restaurant veterans.

• **Watawa** • 33-10 Ditmars Blvd
718-545-9596 • $$$
Best-of-Ditmars destination sushi.

• **William Hallett** • 36-10 30th Ave
718-269-3443 • $$$$
Equal parts cocktails, food, and ambiance.

• **Yaar Indian Restaurant** • 22-55 31st St
718-721-0205 • $$
Solid Indian cuisine from folks behind Seva.

• **Zenon Taverna** • 34-10 31st Ave
718-956-0133 • $$
Cypriot taverna with some of the best meze
in town.

🛍 Shopping

• **Adega Wine & Spirits** • 31-25 Ditmars Blvd
718-545-2525
Nicely curated and well-appointed liquor
store.

• **Artopolis Bakery** • 23-18 31st St
718-728-8484
Delicious Greek desserts, especially the
baklava pie.

• **Astoria Bier and Cheese** • 34-14 Broadway
718-545-5588
The Craft cheesemonger and beermonger
Astoria's been waiting for.

• **Astoria Bookshop** • 31-29 31st St
718-278-2665
Curated selection and community events.

• **Astoria Park Wine & Spirits** • 28-07 24th Ave
718-606-1142
Curated selection with good prices;
convenient to Astoria Park.

• **Astoria Wine & Spirits** • 34-12 Broadway
718-545-9463
New wine store, featuring frequent tastings.

• **The Bagel House** • 38-11 Ditmars Blvd
718-726-1869
Good old-school bagels.

• **Belief** • 24-01 29th St
917-832-6491
Astoria's only boutique skate shop.

• **Bike Stop** • 37-19 28th Ave
718-278-2453
Bike store on north end of Astoria.

• **Brass Owl** • 36-19 Ditmars Blvd
347-848-0905
Stylish boutique selling shoes, jewelry and
gifts.

• **Brooklyn Bagel & Coffee Company** •
35-05 Broadway
718-204-0141
Forgive the geographic confusion and enjoy
the wacky cream cheeses.

• **Brooklyn Bagel & Coffee Company** •
35-09 Ditmars Blvd
718-932-8280
The neighborhood's best bagels.

• **Brooklyn Bagel & Coffee Company** •
36-14 30th Ave
718-777-1121
Also good coffee, fresh OJ, and signature
sandwiches.

• **Buffalo Exchange** • 29-16 Ditmars Blvd
718-274-2054
The recycled clothing chain's first Queens
store.

• **Butcher Bar** • 37-08 30th Ave
718-606-8140
Organic, natural butcher with barbecue to eat
in or take home.

• **Cassinelli Food Products, Inc.** •
31-12 23rd Ave
718-274-4881
All kinds of fresh pasta, but go before 2 pm.

• **Ditmars Thrift Shop** • 31-20 Ditmars Blvd
718-545-2529
Awesome cheap finds for clothing, winter
coats, and housewares.

• **Euro Market** • 30-42 31st St
718-545-5569
Best of Eurofoods.

Titan Foods, Parrot Coffee, and EuroMarket offer the best of Europe, and FamilyMarket has everything Japanese, including bento boxes. Astoria Bier and Cheese fills a craft beer and cheese niche. Find that special vintage clothing item at Loveday 31 and reward yourself with sweets from La Guli, Martha's or Artopolis.

- **Family Market** • 29-15 Broadway
718-956-7925
Japanese convenience store, and resource center for the neighborhood Japanese.
- **Fresh Start** • 29-13 23rd Ave
718-204-7868
Organic/natural market for most of your needs, plus prepared foods.
- **Grand Wine & Liquor** • 30-05 31st St
718-728-2520
One of the best in the borough, crazy international offerings.
- **HiFi Records & Cafe** • 23-19 Steinway St
718-606-1474
Great indie record store and café; browse, listen, and buy.
- **Inside Astoria** • 28-07 Ditmars Blvd
718-956-4000
Chock full of interesting things to buy-frames, jewelry, books, gifts, housewares.
- **International Meat Market** • 36-12 30th Ave
718 626-6656
The Citarella of Astoria.
- **K&T Quality Meats** • 37-11 Broadway
718-726-3301
Everyday butcher specializing in Greek & Italian cuts of meat.
- **La Guli Pastry Shop** • 29-15 Ditmars Blvd
718-728-5612
Old-school Italian pastry shop. A neighborhood institution.
- **Lockwood Shop** • 32-15 33rd St
718-626-6030
Lifestyle shop run by Astoria boosters; good events and extras.
- **Loveday 31 Vintage** • 33-06 31st Ave
718-728-4057
Hip new and vintage clothes.
- **Martha's Country Bakery** •
36-21 Ditmars Blvd
718-545-9737
Best pound cake around, and everything else is good too.
- **Mediterranean Foods** • 22-78 35th St
718-728-0266
Great spot for Mediterranean-imported groceries.
- **New York City Bagel & Coffee House** •
29-08 23rd Ave
718-728-9500
With a nice emphasis on good coffee drinks.
- **Omega Wines & Spirits** • 23-18 31st St
718-728-0056
Great selection of Greek wines.

- **Parrot Coffee** • 31-12 Ditmars Blvd
718-545-7920
Gourmet European food, mostly Eastern Europe, plus fresh roasted coffee.
- **Raising Astoria** • 26-11 23rd Ave
718-440-9444
One stop shopping for baby/maternity consignment, classes, and workshops.
- **Rosario's Deli** • 22-55 31st St
718-728-2920
Italian specialty foods, great sandwiches, and pizza, too.
- **Rose & Joe's Italian Bakery** • 22-40 31st St
718-721-9422
Fresh cannolis made to order.
- **Sal, Kris, and Charlie Deli** • 33-12 23rd Ave
718-278-9240
They don't call them the "sandwich kings of Astoria" for nothing.
- **Silver Age Comics** • 22-55 31st St
718 721-9691
Comics.
- **SingleCut Beersmiths** • 19-33 37th St
718-606-0788
Queens' first brewery in decades; visit tap room for growlers.
- **Titan Foods** • 25-56 31st St
718-626-7771
The Zabar's of Astoria.
- **Tony's Bicycles** • 33-01 23rd Ave
718-278 3355
Bike store north of the Grand Central.
- **Trade Fair** • 30-08 30th Ave
718-728-9484
Phenomenal selection of international foods; best Trade Fair around.
- **Triboro Beverage** • 41-08 Astoria Blvd S
718-278-0620
Probably the best beer selection in the city.
- **United Brothers Fruit Markets** •
32-24 30th Ave
718-932-9876
Great 24-hour fruit/vegetable market.

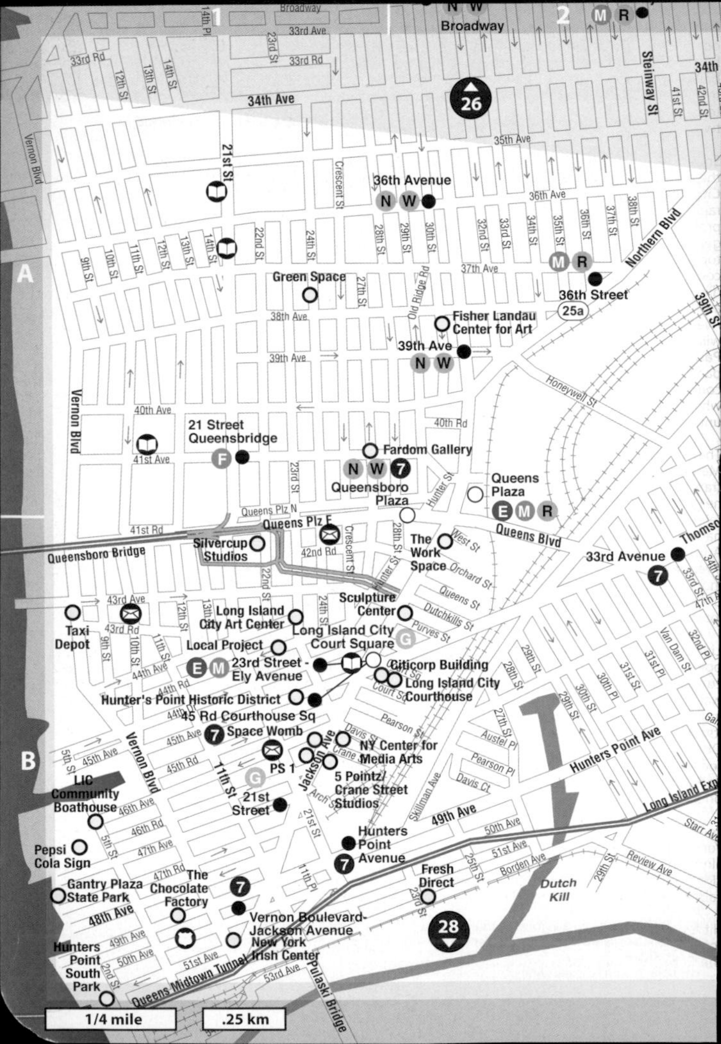

Map 27 · **Long Island City**

Broadway

N W
Broadway

M R

14th Pl
33rd Ave
33rd Rd

33rd Rd
12th St
13th St

34th Ave

Steinway St

34th

26

Vernon Blvd
9th St
11th St

21st St

13th St
22nd St
24th St

Crescent St

35th Ave

36th Ave

41st St
42nd St

Northern Blvd

N W
36th Avenue

28th St
29th St
30th St

37th Ave

31st St
33rd St
34th St
35th St
37th St
38th St

M R
36th Street
25a

A

38th Ave

Green Space

27th St

Old Bottle Way

Fisher Landau
Center for Art

39th St

39th Ave

39th Ave

N W

Honeywell St

40th Ave

41st St

21 Street
Queensbridge

F

23rd St

Fardom Gallery

N W 7
Queensboro
Plaza

Queens
Plaza

E M R
Queens Blvd

Queens Plz E

Queens Plz E

41st Rd

Queensboro Bridge

Silvercup
Studios

42nd Rd

Crescent St

Hunter St

West St

The
Work
Space

Orchard St

33rd Avenue

7

Thomson

Taxi
Depot

43rd Rd

12th St

21st St

Long Island
City Art Center

Local Project

E M

43rd Ave

44th Dr

Dutchkills St

Purves St

Sculpture
Center

G

Long Island City
Court Square

Citicorp Building

Long Island City
Courthouse

Van Dam St

27th St

29th St

30th St

31st St

32nd St

23rd Street -
Ely Avenue

Hunter's Point Historic District

45 Rd Courthouse Sq

Court Sq

Pearson St

Hunters Point Ave

B

Vernon Blvd

44th Rd
45th Ave

7
Space Womb

Jackson Ave

Davis St

Pearson Pl

NY Center for
Media Arts

Davis Ct

49th Ave

Long Island Exp

LIC
Community
Boathouse

46th Ave

PS 1

Crane St

5 Pointz/
Crane Street
Studios

Skillman Ave

Pepsi
Cola Sign

47th Rd

11th St

21st
Street

Hunters
Point
Avenue

Gantry Plaza
State Park

48th Ave

The
Chocolate
Factory

7

7

Vernon Boulevard-
Jackson Avenue
New York
Irish Center

Fresh
Direct

50th St

Borden Ave

51st Ave

Review Ave

Dutch
Kill

28

Hunters
Point
South
Park

49th Ave

51st Ave

Queens Midtown Tunnel

Pulaski Bridge

1/4 mile

.25 km

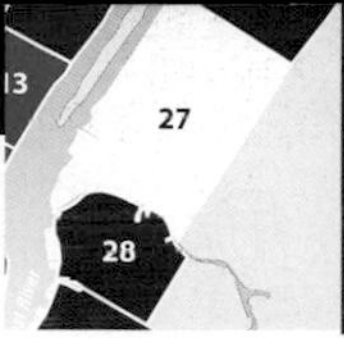

Neighborhood Overview

Map 27

Long Island City has some excellent waterfront features, but it's also one of Queens' most developed, Manhattanish neighborhoods, plus when the 7 train is acting up, it turns a 5-minute ride between boroughs into a commuting nightmare. LIC's technical boundaries stretch from Newtown Creek to the south to roughly 34th Avenue to the north, bordering Astoria, but LIC has two distinct areas separated by Queens Plaza.

South of Queens Plaza beyond the **Citigroup Building**, which until recently was the only large tower in the area (still the tallest building on Long Island, though perhaps not for long), Beaux arts **Long Island City Courthouse** and **Hunter's Point Historic District** lies genuine Hunter's Point, which has grown rapidly thanks to rezoning that allowed Battery Park City like high rises along the waterfront. The young professional influx brought new stores and restaurants to Vernon Boulevard. Sushi, that leading gentrifying indicator, shows the evolution: until relatively recently Hunter's Point had no sushi at all, but today there are several sushi joints, not to mention a handful of comfort food spots and even a full-time comedy club. Even the **New York Irish Center** arrived, providing a community center for the city's Irish diaspora. **Gantry Plaza State Park** along the waterfront is hands-down the best view of Manhattan anywhere, and it has grown along with the neighborhood; all the way up to Anable Basin near 46th Avenue. South of Gantry Plaza State Park the city has started work on Hunters Point South, a project that will bring thousands of middle-income units to the waterfront. The city-owned **Hunters Point South Park** completes the ribbon of waterfront open space along the East River; the park offers the requisite panoramic Midtown skyline vista along with well-maintained recreational facilities and a lovely concession attached to the water taxi dock. Also along the waterfront is the **LIC Community Boathouse**, which heralds the triumphant reuse of the city's waterways; just keep your kayak out of Newtown Creek until the EPA is finished there.

The area around Queens Plaza has seen much new development. Expensive condos with great Manhattan views now surround Queensboro Plaza, the first stop in Queens for the N and Q trains and a transfer point for the 7 train out to Flushing. Also north of Queens Plaza lies the vestigial Dutch Kills neighborhood, which looks much like Astoria (so much so that you are forgiven in advance for simply referring to it as Astoria), and Queensbridge Houses, one of the largest public housing projects in the nation. Onetime home to artists like Marley Marl's Juice Crew and Nas, Queensbridge is to hip-hop as Addisleigh Park is to jazz. Linked to Midtown via one or two stops, the area between 37th and 41st Avenues north of Queens Plaza has seen a (literal) rise in mid-range hotels slowly squeezing out light industry while providing an inexpensive and convenient option for visitors. Meanwhile, the area south of Queens Plaza is filling up quickly with luxury condos and rentals. The Citigroup Building is looking a lot less lonely these days.

Light industry sprang up in LIC after the Queensboro Bridge (or 59th Street Bridge, depending on your point of view) opened in 1909 and thrived until the middle of the century, though parts of the area are currently designated an Industrial Business Zone by the city. The iconic **Pepsi-Cola Sign** along the waterfront is a vestige of LIC's industrial past preserved for all Beekman Place to see. Many of LIC's industrial buildings were repurposed for studio space in the 1970s and 1980s, giving the neighborhood its artistic reputation that survives today. **MoMA PS1**, housed in a historic school building, dates to 1976. Other museums and galleries followed, including the **Noguchi Museum** (1985), **Fisher Landau Center for Art** (1991) and **SculptureCenter** (2001). Smaller galleries, performance spaces, and collectives such as **Flux Factory**, **Dorsky Gallery**, **Local Project**, and **The Chocolate Factory** thrive even as real estate prices have risen.

Long Island City is about location, location, location — both in terms of real estate and as a hub of New York City's film and television industry. **Silvercup Studios** uses the former Silvercup Bakery building along the East River, and what was once a sleepy industrial area best suited for taxi companies is now clogged with film crews for on-location shoots. The two are combined at **Taxi Depot**, whose vintage cabs parked out front are not for hacks but rather film crews needing props.

Hit **Anable Basin Sailing Bar & Grill** for outdoor waterfront drinks or indulge in mixology at **Dutch Kills**. Join the locals at **LIC Bar** and **Dominie's Hoek**. Try the beer selection at **Alewife**. Both **The Creek and the Cave** and **Laughing Devil** offer top-notch comedy.

Map 27

13
27
28

Long Island City

O Landmarks

- **The Chocolate Factory** • 5-49 49th Ave
  718-482-7069
  Performance space for experimental theater.
- **Citicorp Building** • 1 Court Sq
  This 48-story structure is the tallest New York
  building outside of Manhattan.
- **Fisher Landau Center for Art** • 38-27 30th St
  718-937-0727
  Temporary exhibits plus a world-class
  permanent collection of contemporary art.
- **Fresh Direct** • 23-30 Borden Ave
  718-433-0982
  This is where all those cardboard boxes come
  from.
- **Gantry Plaza State Park** • 4-9 47th Road
  718-786-6385
  Waterfront park and piers with breathtaking
  skyline views.
- **Green Space** • 37-24 24th St
  718-956-3037
  Dance company sublets professional rehearsal
  space sublets to artists.
- **Hunters Point Historic District** •
  21st St & 45th Ave
  Well-preserved homes from LIC's first heyday
  in the late 1800s.
- **Hunters Point South Park** •
  Center Blvd & 50th Ave
  10 acres of prime parkland along the East
  River.
- **LIC Art Center** • 44-02 23rd St
  Theaters, galleries, and studios in former LIC
  factory building.
- **LIC Community Boathouse** • 46-01 5th St
  Launch kayaks from here, explore the
  waterfront like never before.
- **Long Island City Courthouse** •
  25-10 Court Sq
  718-298-1000
  Built in 1876 and rebuilt in 1904, an
  architectural gem.
- **MoMA PS1** • 22-25 Jackson Ave
  718-784-2084
  MoMA's contemporary art space, w/ dance
  parties every summer Saturday.

- **New York Irish Center** • 10-40 Jackson Ave
  718-482-0909
  Bingo nights for the tri-state Irish community.
- **Pepsi-Cola Sign** • 47th Ave & Center Blvd
  Iconic sign atop the Pepsi Bottling Company
  building saved here.
- **Queensbridge Park** • Vernon Blvd & 41st Ave
  Park for the people under the Queensboro
  Bridge.
- **SculptureCenter** • 44-19 Purves St
  718-361-1750
  An artist-run nonprofit and gallery supporting
  experimental sculpture since 1928.
- **Silvercup Studios** • 42-22 22nd St
  718-906-2000
  Former bakery is now a busy film and
  television studio.
- **Taxi Depot** • 43-01 Vernon Blvd
  718-784-4737
  Check out the vintage cabs parked out in
  front.

Coffee

- **Communitea** • 11-18 46th Rd
  718-729-7708
  Coffee, tea, and café food.
- **The Mill** • 44-61 11th St
  718-843-6455
  Coffee, tea, and fun baked goods.
- **Sweetleaf** • 10-93 Jackson Ave
  917-832-6726
  Stumptown coffee and tasty homemade
  sweets.

O Farmers Markets

- **Long Island City Youthmarket** •
  Hunters Point South Park
  Saturdays, May–Sept
- **Socrates Sculpture Park Greenmarket** •
  Vernon Blvd & Broadway
  212-788-7476
  Saturdays, July–Nov, 8 am–3 pm

Standbys like **Manducatis**, **Bella Via**, and **Tournesol**all chug along.
Casa Enrique's offerings are inspired by the cuisine of the Mexican
state of Chiapas, **Corner Bistro** serves West Village-style burgers, and
John Brown Smokehouse is the current neighborhood go-to for
barbecue. **Mu Ramen**'s broth blows people's minds.

☿ Nightlife

- **Alewife** • 5-14 51st Ave
  718-937-7494
  Dozens of beers on tap on LIC side street.
- **Anable Basin Sailing Bar & Grill** • 4 40
  44th Dr
  646-207-1333
  Outdoor spot along East River with direct view
  of Midtown.
- **The Baroness** • 41-26 Crescent St
  718-784-5065
  High-concept wine and beer joint close to
  Queens Plaza.
- **Bierocracy** • 12-23 Jackson Ave
  718-361-9333
  Beer hall with old-world flair.
- **BLVD** • 47-20 Center Blvd
  718-440-8520
  Wine bar/small plates in tall building near
  Gantry Park.
- **The Creek and The Cave** • 10-93 Jackson Ave
  718-706-8783
  Subterranean lounge with awesome comedy
  nights.
- **Domaine Bar a Vins** • 50-04 Vernon Blvd
  718-784-2350
  Great new wine bar from the people who
  brought you Tournesol, with oysters to boot.
- **Dominie's Hoek** • 48 17 Vernon Blvd
  718-706-6531
  No-frills bar with backyard patio and live
  music.

- **Dutch Kills** • 27-24 Jackson Ave
  718-383-2724
  Old time saloon decor and a classic cocktail
  menu.
- **LIC Bar** • 45-58 Vernon Blvd
  718-786-5400
  Vintage New York saloon with serene backyard
  BBQ patio and photo booth.
- **Penthouse 808 at the Ravel Hotel** •
  8 08 Queens Plaza S
  718-289-6118
  Former hotsheet now swank hotel, still under
  the Queensboro Bridge though.
- **PJ Leahy's** • 30-02 Vernon Blvd
  718-472-5131
  Sports bar. Aka WP Dick Whistle's and HB
  Hanratty's.
- **Rest-au-Rant** • 30-01 35th Ave
  718-729-9009
  Wine, beer, cheese, and various smallplates.
- **Studio Square** • 35-33 36th St
  718-383-1001
  Huge, new-school beer garden with plenty of
  space for groups.
- **Veronica's Bar** • 34-04 36th Ave
  718 729 9744
  Formerly old-school, with new ownership…

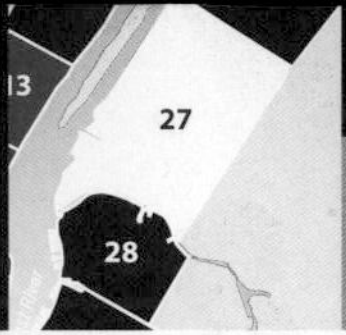

Map 27

13 27 28

Long Island City

🍴Restaurants

- **5 Star Punjabi Diner** • 13-05 43rd Ave
718-784-7444 • $$
Indian diner/cabbie hangout/banquet hall.
- **Arepas Cafe** • 33-07 36th Ave
718-937-3835 • $$
Sabor Venezolano!
- **Bella Via** • 47-46 Vernon Blvd
718-361-7510 • $$
Wonderful modern Italian dishes and brick-oven pizza.
- **Blend** • 47-04 Vernon Blvd
718-729-2800 • $$
Sleek Cuban-fusion spot.
- **Cafe Henri** • 10-10 50th Ave
718-383-9315 • $$
Low-key French bistro.
- **Cafe Ole** • 38-09 36th Ave
718-349-7777 • $$
Spanish, paella, etc. sprucing up 36th Avenue.
- **Cafe Triskell** • 33-04 36th Ave
718-472-0612 • $$
Cash-only French-style bistro on 36th Avenue.
- **Casa Enrique** • 5-48 49th Ave
347-448-6040 • $$$
Mexican cuisine from Chiapas via Bar Henry folks.
- **Chela & Garnacha** • 33-09 36th Ave
917-832-6876 • $$
Charming brick-and-mortar outpost of Mexico Blvd food truck.
- **Coffeed** • 37-18 Northern Blvd
718-606-1299 • $
Locally sourced coffeehouse with Brooklyn Grange-supplied food.
- **Corner Bistro** • 47-18 Vernon Blvd
718-606-6500 • $
Legendary Village burger mainstay's LIC outpost.
- **Court Square Diner** • 45-30 23rd St
718-392-1222 • $
Reliable grub available 24 hours.

- **Crescent Grill** • 38-40 Crescent St
718-729-4040 • $$$
Stylish farm-to-table cuisine.
- **Cyclo** • 5-51 47th Ave
718-786-8309 • $$
Vietnamese pho and banh mi from the folks behind Tuk Tuk.
- **Dorian Café** • 10-01 50th Ave
718-937-1120 • $
Cozy neighborhood diner, excellent turkey club.
- **Gaw Gai Thai Express** • 23-06 Jackson Ave
718-706-0999 • $
Tuk Tuk's express lunch service near Court Square.
- **John Brown Smokehouse** • 10-43 44th Dr
347-617-1120 • $$
Kansas City-style barbecue just off the E train.
- **LIC Landing** • 52-10 Center Blvd
$$
COFFEED's contribution to the Hunter's Point waterfront; spectacular views.
- **LIC Market** • 21-52 44th Dr
718-361-0013 • $$
Handsome space with seasonal dishes and wine bar.
- **M. Wells Dinette** • 22-25 Jackson Ave
718-786-1800 • $$
Kind of like if Matthew Barney ran a museum café.
- **M. Wells Steakhouse** • 43-15 Crescent St
718-786-9060 • $$$$
More boffo dishes from strange animal parts at this hipster meat palace.
- **Manducatis** • 13-27 Jackson Ave
718-729-4602 • $$$
Classic Italian cuisine expertly prepared; a beloved neighborhood institution.
- **Manetta's** • 10-76 Jackson Ave
718-786-6171 • $$
Above-average brick oven pizza and good house-made pastas.
- **Mu Ramen** • 12-09 Jackson Ave
917-868-8903 • $$
Big-league ramen with crazy attention to broth detail.

Get your custom-built axe at **Sadowsky Guitars**. Go to **Hunter's Point Wines & Spirits** for a carefully curated selection and great guidance. Quality and prices are both elevated at **Food Cellar**, which is the cost of doing business here. And **Just Things** is a quirky amalgamation of thrift, junk, and antique store that we hope never ever leaves.

• Petey's Burger • 46-46 Vernon Blvd
718-937-4040 • $
It's like an In-N-Out cover band; fills a need.

• Shi • 47-20 Center Blvd
347-242-2450 • $$
The view is LIC. The decor is Soho. The diners are Murray Hill.

• Skinny's Cantina • 47-05 Center Blvd
718-806-1068 • $$$
Upscale Mexican comfort food.

• Tournesol • 50-12 Vernon Blvd
718-472-4355 • $$$
Cozy French bistro, a neighborhood gem.

• Tuk Tuk • 49-06 Vernon Blvd
718-472-5597 • $$
Hip space. Good Thai food.

🛍 Shopping

• Artbook @ MoMA PS1 • 22-25 Jackson Ave
718-433-1088
Fabulous selection of art books.

• Astoria Seafood • 37-10 33rd St
718-392-2680
Top notch seafood in unsuspecting location.

• Blue Streak Wine & Spirits • 4720 Center Blvd
718-706-9463
Wine and booze from around the globe.

• C-Town • 44-65 21st St
718-361-7471
Your basic no-frills, comparatively inexpensive New York supermarket.

• Court Square Wine & Spirits •
24-20 Jackson Ave
718-707-9911
Excellent selection and prices.

• Duane Reade • 47-02 5th St
718-472-3600
Good for toilet paper, nail polish remover, and Us Weekly.

• Foodcellar & Co. Market • 4-85 47th Rd
718-606-9786
Like Whole Foods, but not.

• Greenmarket • 48th Ave & Vernon Blvd
212-788-7476
Local farmers and bakers, every Saturday except in winter.

• Hunter's Point Wines & Spirits •
47-07 Vernon Blvd
718-472-9463
Trust the owner to recommend great wines from $5 to $50. Also a well-edited liquor selection.

• Just Things • 47-28 Vernon Blvd
917-558-4869
Quirky amalgamation of thrift store, junk store, and antique store.

• Matted • 46-36 Vernon Blvd
718-786-8660
Picture framing plus an assortment of artsy tchotckes.

• Rio Bonito Market • 32-15 36th Ave
718-706-7272
Brazilian-focused specialty store.

• Sadowsky Guitars • 21-07 41st Ave
718-433-1990
Custom-made guitars and basses since 1979.

• Spokesman Cycles • 49-04 Vernon Blvd
718-433-0150
Great bike store on Vernon Blvd.

• Vernon Blvd Pharmacy • 48-15 Vernon Blvd
718-361-7390
Local pharmacy gives you the attention the chains don't.

• Vernon Wine & Liquor • 50-06 Vernon Blvd
718-784-5096
Use when you need cheap prosecco for the party.

• Western Beef • 36-20 Steinway St
718-389-7770
Stock up on cheap meat.

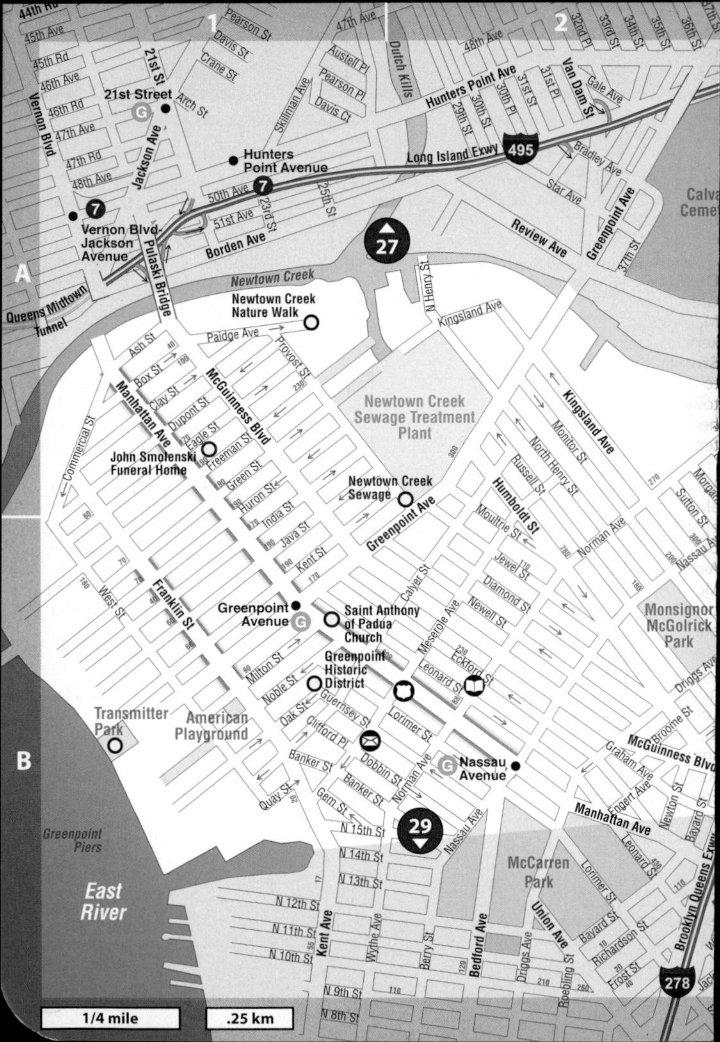

Map 28 · **Greenpoint**

N

44th Rd
Pearson St
Davis St
47th Ave
48th Ave

Crane St
Austell Pl
Pearson Pl

45th Rd
46th Ave
21st St
Arch St
Stilwell Ave
Davis Ct

Dutch Kills
Hunters Point Ave
29th St
31st St
30th St
Van Dam St

46th Rd
47th Ave
21st Street
G

31st Pl
33rd Pl
34th St
35th St
36th St
Gale Ave

47th Rd
48th Ave
Jackson Ave
Long Island Exwy **495**
Bradley Ave
Star Ave

Greenpoint Ave
Calvary
Ceme

Hunters Point Avenue
7

Vernon Blvd
Jackson Avenue
Vernon Blvd
50th Ave
51st Ave
23rd St
25th St
Review Ave

37th Ave

Borden Ave
Pulaski Bridge
Newtown Creek

Queens Midtown Tunnel

▲ **27**

St Adams St
Kingsland Ave

Newtown Creek Nature Walk
Paidge Ave
Provost St

Ash St
Box St
Clay St
Manhattan Ave
McGuinness Blvd
Dupont St
Commercial St

Kingsland Ave
Monitor St
North Henry St
Russell St

Newtown Creek Sewage Treatment Plant

John Smolenski Funeral Home
Eagle St
Freeman St
Green St

Newtown Creek Sewage

Humboldt St
Moultrie St
Norman Ave

278

Sutton St

Huron St
India St
Java St
Kent St

Greenpoint Ave
Greenpoint Ave

Jewel St
Diamond St
Newell St

Nassau

Franklin St
West St

Greenpoint Avenue
G
Saint Anthony of Padua Church

Calyer St

Meserole Ave
Eckford St
Leonard St

Monsignor McGolrick Park

Greenpoint Historic District
Milton St
Noble St

278

Transmitter Park

American Playground
Oak St
Clifford Pl
Guernsey St
Lorimer St

McGuinness Blvd
Graham Ave

B

Quay St
Banker St
Banker St
Dobbin St
Norman Ave
Gem St
Nassau Ave
G
Nassau Avenue

Manhattan Ave
Leonard

Greenpoint Piers

▼ **29**
N 15th St
N 14th St
N 13th St
Nassau Ave

McCarren Park

Lorimer St
Bayard St
Frost St
Richardson St

East River

Kent Ave
Wythe Ave
N 12th St
N 11th St
N 10th St
Berry St

Union Ave

Brooklyn Queens Exwy

N 9th St
N 8th St
Bedford Ave
Driggs Ave
Roebling St
278

| 1/4 mile | .25 km |

Neighborhood Overview

Map 28

10
28
7
29

The northernmost neighborhood in Brooklyn, Greenpoint has multiple personality disorder. It's strongly Polish (hence the mouth-watering bakeries and butcher shops) and solidly trendy. As the name suggests, parts are indeed green, but it's also home to one of America's filthiest waterways.

As longtime hub for shipping and manufacturing, Greenpoint sits at the nexus of Newtown Creek and the East River. Newtown Creek is infamous for the 1950 oil spill more than twice the size of Exxon Valdez; now an EPA Superfund site, remediation will continue for years. On a brighter note, Newtown Creek's quarter-mile **Nature Walk** is a valiant attempt to spruce things up, and the tree-lined **Greenpoint Historical District** (originally home to local industrial workers) is still in excellent shape. Greenpoint is also the proud owner of the verdant oasis known as **McGolrick Park**. Manhattan Avenue Park (at the northern dead-end of that thoroughfare) is a well-kept, tiny gem with several cool sculptures. Also check out the impressive **Eagle Street Rooftop Farm**, support their efforts by buying fresh greens (give your regards to the rabbits and chickens). And **Transmitter Park**, the former home of WNYC's radio towers at the end of Greenpoint Avenue, is a rare spot of green along the waterfront; head to the end of the zig-zagging pier for a respite from the heat of the city—it's like ten degrees cooler out in the middle of the East River.

Manhattan Avenue is the neighborhood's main artery (buses and the G train run along it). Mass is held at the stunning **Saint Anthony of Padua Church** and your everyday needs are met along the way—fruit & vegetable stands, taco restaurants, bars and the like. Franklin Street is a relaxing antidote to the grimy bustle of Manhattan Avenue, with galleries, boutiques and various high-concept entities. East of McGuinness Boulevard you'll find various cheap bars, liquor stores, restaurants, Polish bakeries and a few real, respectable coffee shops, including Hannah Horvath's employers, **Café Grumpy**.

One exciting aspect of Greenpoint (though not for locals with cars) is the frequent number of movie and television productions filmed here. It's close to Manhattan and Long Island City (where a number of studios are based) and can stand in for a green, industrial, or cozy neighborhood setting. *Flight of the Conchords* shot their French song video in McGolrick Park. *30 Rock* filmed in front of a dollar store on Manhattan Avenue. Recent productions have included *The Bounty Hunter*, *Date Night*, *Boardwalk Empire*, and *Girls*. If you keep your ears open at a bar, you may even hear someone who worked on a shoot giving the lowdown on which star is a bitch or which guy played the diva and spent the entire shoot moaning about a recent breakup. Ah, New York.

Barflies of every stripe can find something to suit their tastes, from sports bars (**Red Star**) to cocktail lounges (**Manhattan Inn**). **PencilFactory** and **Black Rabbit** are excellent standbys on Greenpoint Avenue and NFT staffers can be found at the **Palace Cafe**.

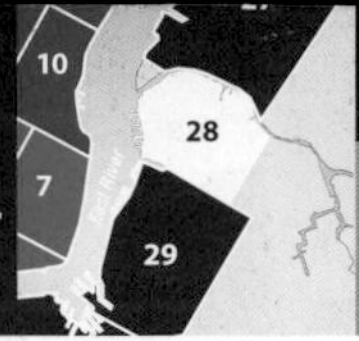

Map 28 · **Greenpoint**

⭘ Landmarks

- **Greenpoint Historic District** ·
  Oak St & Guernsey St
  Charming rowhouses that were built for
  workers of early merchants.
- **John Smolenski Funeral Home** ·
  1044 Manhattan Ave [Freeman St]
  718-389-4170
  1920s landmark with one of Greenpoint's
  beautiful clocks.
- **Newtown Creek Nature Walk** ·
  Provost St & Paidge Ave
  Great views of the sewage plant!
- **Newtown Creek Wastewater
  Treatment Plant** ·
  Greenpoint Ave & Provost St
  Take a moment to contemplate all of the
  famous and beautiful peoples' crap floating
  around in here.
- **Saint Anthony of Padua Church** ·
  862 Manhattan Ave [Milton St]
  718-383-3339
  Beautiful church sticking out like a healthy
  thumb on congested avenue.
- **Transmitter Park** ·
  West St b/n Kent St & Greenpoint Ave
  Greenpoint's waterfront park; former home of
  WNYC transmitter towers.

Coffee

- **Ashbox** · 1154 Manhattan Ave [Ash St]
  718-389-3222
  Cool shop on the very north tip of Greenpoint.
- **Café Grumpy** ·
  193 Meserole Ave [Diamond St]
  718-349-7623
  The finest coffee house in Brooklyn now has its
  own roastery.
- **Café Riviera** · 830 Manhattan Ave [Noble St]
  718-383-8450
  Delicious baked-goods and such.
- **Crema BK** · 182 Driggs Ave [Diamond St]
  347-457-5363
  Cold-brewed in Brooklyn.

- **Konditori** · 687 Manhattan Ave [Norman Ave]
  347-223-4837
  Cozy/packed mini-chain of Swedish
  coffeehouses.
- **Uro Café** · 277 Driggs Ave [Leonard St]
  718-599-1230
  Best espresso south of Greenpoint Ave.
- **Van Leeuwen Ice Cream** ·
  632 Manhattan Ave [Nassau Ave]
  718-701-1630
  Excellent coffee to go with your coffee ice
  cream.
- **Variety Coffee & Tea** ·
  145 Driggs Ave [Russell St]
  347-689-3790
  Nice coffee shop with views of McGolrick Park.

🍅 Farmers Markets

- **Eagle Street Rooftop Farm** ·
  44 Eagle St [West St]
  Sunday, 1 pm–4pm during growing season.

🍸 Nightlife

- **Achilles Heel** · 180 West St [Green St]
  347-987-3666
  Worn, hip local bar way over by the docks.
- **Black Rabbit** · 91 Greenpoint Ave [Franklin St]
  718-349-1595
  Fantastic fireplace, delicious mini-burgers.
  Trivia night is packed.
- **The Diamond** · 43 Franklin St [Calyer St]
  718-383-5030
  Wine, massive beer selection, and
  shuffleboard.
- **Dirck the Norseman** · 7 N 15th St [Franklin St]
  718-389-2940
  Excellent brewed-on-site beer with German
  food as a bonus. Great space, too.
- **Enid's** · 560 Manhattan Ave [Driggs Ave]
  718-349-3859
  Greenpoint's finest hipster stand-by.

A Greenpoint visit must include a meal at a cheap and hearty Polish restaurant, like **Christina's**. Afterwards, get a Polish pastry at **Café Riviera** or have some caffeine in the adorable backyard of **Champion Coffee**. One of the best brunches in the city is at **Cafecito Bogota**, so come hungry.

• **Europa** • 98 Meserole Ave [Manhattan Ave]
917-826-1119
Strobe light extravaganza.

The Habitat • 988 Manhattan Ave [Huron St]
718-383-5615
Featuring waffle fries and "zero attitude."

The Manhattan Inn •
632 Manhattan Ave [Nassau Ave]
718-383-0885
Dark bar, pricey but delicious food, piano man in back.

Northern Territory •
12 Franklin St [Meserole Ave]
347-609-4065
Leafy rooftop bar with expansive view, get the Territory's Tea

One Stop Beer Shop •
134 Kingsland Ave [Beadel St]
718-599-0128
Craft beer and artisanal food, of course.

Palace Café • 206 Nassau Ave [Russell St]
718-383-9848
Heavy jukebox and stiff drinks. Metal lives!

Pencil Factory Bar •
142 Franklin St [Greenpoint Ave]
718-609-5858
Great beer; great vibe. Perfectly understated.

Pit Stop Bar •
152 Meserole Ave [McGuinness Blvd]
718-383-0981
Buy a couple scratch-offs and experience blue collar Brooklyn.

Shayz Lounge • 130 Franklin St [Milton St]
718-389-3888
Irish pub in a sea of Polish.

Spritzenhaus • 33 Nassau Ave [Dobbin St]
347-987-4632
Predictably packed beer garden in Greenpoint.

TBD Bar • 224 Franklin St [Green St]
718-349-6727
Backyard "beer garden" is tops on nice days.

Tommy's Tavern •
1041 Manhattan Ave [Freeman St]
718-383-9699
Super-dive with live music on weekends.

Torst • 615 Manhattan Ave [Nassau Ave]
718-389-6034
Not just a beer bar, a fancy beer bar with Danish accents.

Warsaw • 261 Driggs Ave [Eckford St]
718-387-0505
Brooklyn's best concert venue.

🍴 Restaurants

• **Acapulco Deli & Restaurant** •
1116 Manhattan Ave [Clay St]
718-349-0429 • $
Authentic Mexican. Includes homemade chips and telenovelas at full volume.

• **Amarin Café** •
617 Manhattan Ave [Nassau Ave]
718-349-2788 • $
Good, cheap Thai food.

• **Amber Steak House** •
119 Nassau Ave [Eckford St]
718-389-3757 • $$$$
Porterhouse for two and Crestor to go.

• **Anella** • 222 Franklin St [Green St]
718-389-8100 • $$
Seasonal Italian, beautifully simple, bread baked in flowerpots

• **Ashbox** • 1154 Manhattan Ave [Ash St]
718-389-3222 • $
Japanese-influenced café fare at the mouth of Newton Creek.

• **The Bounty** •
131 Greenpoint Ave [Manhattan Ave]
347-689-3325 • $$$
Perfectly-executed seafood, nice back garden.

• **Brooklyn Ice Cream Factory** •
97 Commercial St [Box St]
718-349-2506 • $
As yummy as the DUMBO shop, without the lines.

• **Cafecito Bogota** •
1015 Manhattan Ave [Green St]
718-569-0077 • $$
Authentic and amazing Colombian cuisine.

• **Calexico Carne Asada** •
645 Manhattan Ave [Bedford Ave]
347-763-2129 • $
Polish tacos? The tasty Mexi food truck settles down in Greenpoint.

• **Christina's** • 853 Manhattan Ave [Noble St]
718-383-4382 • $
Traditional Polish food, cheap breakfasts!

• **Delilah's Steaks** •
55 McGuinness Blvd [Engert Ave]
347-689-4409 • $$
The kind with the word "cheese" in front, silly.

• **Dirck the Norseman** • 7 N 15th St [Franklin St]
718-389-2940 • $$
Craft brewery with killer German plates—schnitzel, roast, etc.

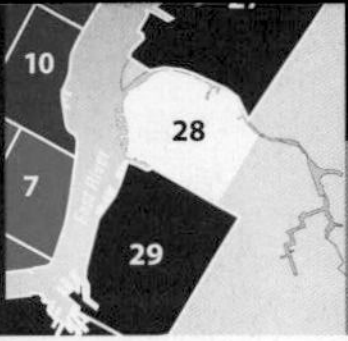

Map 28

Greenpoint

- **El Born** • 651 Manhattan Ave [Nassau Ave]
347-844-9299 • $$$
Spanish/tapas with some nice surprises.
- **Enid's** • 560 Manhattan Ave [Driggs Ave]
718-349-3859 • $$
Popular brunch on weekends; also dinner
weeknights.
- **Erb** • 681 Manhattan Ave [Norman Ave]
718-349-8215 • $$
Terrific Thai; try the curry noodles.
- **Esme** • 999 Manhattan Ave [Huron St]
718-383-0999 • $$$
Just love, no squalor. Or, capaccio & cocktails.
- **Five Leaves** • 18 Bedford Ave [Nassau Ave]
718-383-5345 • $$$
Heath Ledger's post-mortem restaurant is
cooler than you.
- **Fornino** • 849 Manhattan Ave [Noble St]
718-389-5300 • $$
Brick oven 'za wedged in between Polish food
heaven.
- **Glasserie** • 95 Commercial St [Manhattan Ave]
718-389-0640 • $$$
Light-filled Mediterranean with luscious side
dishes.
- **God Bless Deli** •
818 Manhattan Ave [Calyer St]
718-349-0605 • $
The only 24-hour joint in the 'hood. Cheap
sandwiches and burgers.
- **Greenpoint Fish & Lobster Co.** •
114 Nassau Ave [Eckford St]
718-389-0400 • $$$
Fresh oysters, cold Narragansetts, and a hot
'nabe spot.
- **Karczma** •
136 Greenpoint Ave [Manhattan Ave]
718-349-1744 • $$
Homestyle Polish, rightly popular among
locals, rustic interior.
- **Kestane Kebab** • 110 Nassau Ave [Eckford St]
718-349-8601 • $
Refuel your party tank around the clock for
cheap.
- **Kyoto Sushi** • 161 Nassau Ave [Diamond St]
718-383-8882 • $$
Best sushi in Greenpoint; dine in for the sake
and after-dinner Dum Dums.

- **Le Fond** • 105 Norman Ave [Leonard St]
718-389-6859 • $$$
Can't get into Five Leaves? No problemo, eat
here.
- **Lobster Joint** • 1073 Manhattan Ave [Eagle St]
718-389-8990 • $$$
What the world needs: more lobster rolls. And
bloody marys.
- **Lomzynianka** •
646 Manhattan Ave [Nassau Ave]
718-389-9439 • $
Get your kitschy Polish fix dirt cheap.
- **Manhattan Three Decker** •
695 Manhattan Ave [Norman Ave]
718-389-6664 • $$
Greek and American fare.
- **Ott** • 970 Manhattan Ave [India St]
718-609-2416 • $$
Another excellent Thai choice on Manhattan
Ave.
- **Paulie Gee's** • 60 Greenpoint Ave [West St]
347-987-3747 • $$
Top brick-oven 'za right by the river. Nice.
- **Peter Pan Doughnuts** •
727 Manhattan Ave [Norman Ave]
718-389-3676 • $
Polish girls in smocks serving tasty donuts.
- **Raizes** • 139 Nassau Ave [McGuinness Blvd]
718-389-0088 • $$$
Portuguese meat-on-a-stick with some
surprises.
- **Sapporo Ichiban** •
622 Manhattan Ave [Nassau Ave]
718-389-9712 • $$
Fresh sushi, friendly service.
- **Selamat Pagi** • 152 Driggs Ave [Humboldt St]
718-701-4333 • $$$
Indonesian goodness very near Polish
goodness.

Greenpoint

Map 28

Hit the (sausage) links at **Steve's Meat Market**. Visit **Old Hollywood** for vintage; refurbished is in style at **Alter Women**. The fabulously junky second-hand shop **The Thing** is more affordable than **Luddite**. Vinyl junkies browse the bins at **Permanent Records**. Shop **Eastern District** for that which is artisanal and Brooklyn based. **Wedel** sells imported chocolates, and **New Warsaw Bakery**, **Charlotte Patisserie**, and **Jaslowiczanka** have baked goods. **Word**'s an English-language independent bookstore.

🛍 Shopping

- **Alter Men** • 140 Franklin St [Greenpoint Ave]
  718-349-0203
  Nice selection of vintage and hard-to-find labels.
- **Bellocq Tea Atelier** • 104 West St [Kent St]
  347-463-9231
  Exquisite tea sold per ounce, look hard for the sign.
- **Brooklyn Craft Company** •
  61 Greenpoint Ave [Franklin St]
  646-201-4049
  Girly DIY classes to while away the crafternoon…
- **Brouwerij Lane** •
  78 Greenpoint Ave [Franklin St]
  347-529-6133
  For beer junkies. Global bottles or pour-your-own growlers.
- **Charlotte Patisserie** •
  596 Manhattan Ave [Driggs Ave]
  718-383-8313
  Polish-run dessert and coffee shop, delicious French-style pastries.
- **Cracovia Liquors** • 150 Nassau Ave [Newell St]
  718-383-2010
  Easiest place to spot a bum in Greenpoint. Open late.
- **Dandelion Wine** • 153 Franklin St [Java St]
  347-689-4303
  Knowledgeable staff and frequent wine tastings—double win!
- **Eastern District** •
  1053 Manhattan Ave [Freeman St]
  718-349-1432
  Cheese and beer shop with tons of Brooklyn brands.
- **Fox & Fawn Vintage** •
  570 Manhattan Ave [Driggs Ave]
  718-349-9510
  Same great vintage store, new location. Hips (arms and legs) don't lie.
- **The Garden** • 921 Manhattan Ave [Kent St]
  718-389-6448
  Awe-inspiring natural foods selection.
- **Jaslowiczanka Bakery** •
  163 Nassau Ave [Diamond St]
  718-389-0263
  Polish bakery with tempting layer cakes and babkas.

- **Luddite** • 201 Franklin St [Freeman St]
  718-387-3450
  Beautifully curated antiques and curios.
- **Maria's Deli** • 136 Meserole Ave [Eckford St]
  718-383-9063
  One of many Polish bodegas. Pickle soup & mayonnaise salads!
- **The One Well** •
  165 Greenpoint Ave [Leonard St]
  347-889-6792
  Cheery, girlie gift shop, emphasis on the girlie.
- **Ovenly** • 31 Greenpoint Ave [West St]
  347-689-3608
  Growing bakery serving sweet and salty treats.
- **Pentatonic Guitars & Music** •
  139 Franklin St [Java St]
  347-599-2576
  Guitars, basses, ukuleles, banjos, mandolins, gear, and repairs.
- **Permanent Records** •
  181 Franklin St [Huron St]
  718-383-4083
  Stellar selection of new and used vinyl, friendly service.
- **Pop's Popular Clothing** •
  7 Franklin St [Meserole Ave]
  718-349-7677
  Work clothes & boots for blue-collar authenticity.
- **Rzeszowska Bakery** •
  948 Manhattan Ave [Java St]
  718-383-8142
  Authentic Polish bakery; mobbed around holidays you were unaware of.
- **Sun Hee Farm** •
  886 Manhattan Ave [Greenpoint Ave]
  718-349-5965
  Ridiculously cheap fruits and veggies.
- **The Thing** • 1001 Manhattan Ave [Huron St]
  718-349-8234
  Unusual second-hand store offers thousands of used LPs.
- **WORD** • 126 Franklin St [Milton St]
  718-383-0096
  Literary fiction, non-fiction, and kids' books.

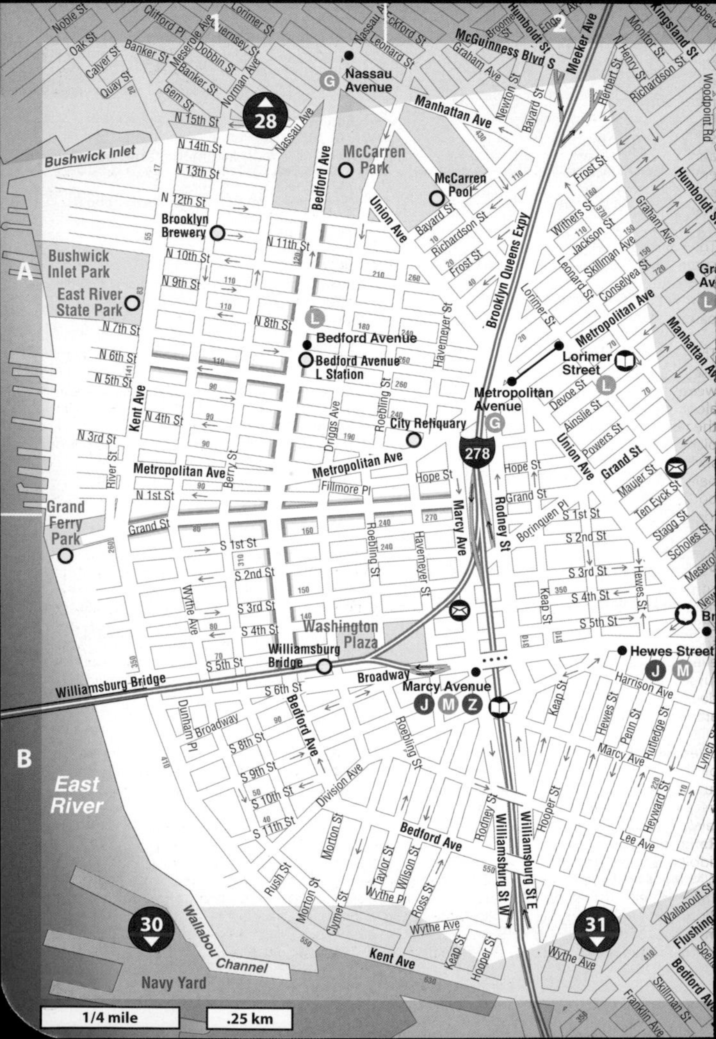

Map 29 • **Williamsburg**

Noble St
Clifford Pl
Guernsey St
Nassau Ave
Leonard St
McGuinness Blvd S
Graham Ave
Meeker Ave
Kingsland Ave
Monitor St
N Henry St
Richardson St
Woodpoint Rd

Oak St
Banker St
Dobbin St
Norman Ave

Calyer St
Meserole Ave

Quay St
Gem St
N 15th St

G **Nassau Avenue**

Manhattan Ave

Bayard St

Bushwick Inlet

Bedford Ave

N 14th St
N 13th St

McCarren Park

Frost St

Jackson St
Skillman Ave
Graham Ave
Humboldt St

N 12th St

McCarren Pool

Richardson St

Conselyea St

Brooklyn Brewery

N 11th St

Union Ave

Bayard St
Frost St

Leonard St
Skillman Ave

Grand Ave L

A

N 10th St
N 9th St

Bushwick Inlet Park

East River State Park

N 7th St

Havemeyer St

Brooklyn Queens Expy

Lorimer St

Metropolitan Avenue L

Manhattan Ave

N 6th St
N 5th St

Kent Ave

N 8th St

L **Bedford Avenue**

Bedford Avenue L Station

Lorimer Street L

Devoe St
Ainslie St
Powers St

Metropolitan Avenue G

Union Ave

Mauger St

Grand St

N 4th St
N 3rd St

Wythe Ave

River St

Berry St

Driggs Ave

Roebling St

City Reliquary

278

Hope St

Grand St

Ten Eyck St

Stagg St
Scholes St
Meserole

N 1st St

Metropolitan Ave

Metropolitan Ave

Fillmore Pl

Borinquen Pl

S 1st St

Grand Ferry Park

Grand St

S 1st St
S 2nd St

Rodney St

S 2nd St
S 3rd St

Keap St

Bro

B

East River

Wythe Ave

S 3rd St

S 4th St

Havemeyer St

S 4th St
S 5th St

Hewes Street J M

Washington Plaza

140

Harrison Ave

S 5th St

Williamsburg Bridge

Broadway

Marcy Avenue J M Z

Marcy Ave

Hewes St
Penn St

Williamsburg Bridge

S 6th St

Bedford Ave

Roebling St

Williamsburg St E

Lynch St
Heyward St

S 8th St

Broadway

S 9th St

Division Ave

S 10th St

Marcy Ave

Lee Ave

S 11th St

Bedford Ave

Rodney St

Wilson St
Ross St
Wythe Pl

Rush St
Clymer St

Taylor St

Wallabout

Lynch St
Heyward St

30 ▼

Wallabou Channel

Kent Ave

Hooper St
Keap St

Wythe Ave

Williamsburg St W

31 ▼

Navy Yard

Flushing
Bedford Av
Franklin Av

| 1/4 mile | .25 km |

You've probably already made up your mind about Williamsburg, but let's be honest, there is always something that brings you back to this hipsturbia on the river. Are the throngs of younguns "struggling" to make rent eight times the national median obnoxious? Sure. Is your mind blown by three-hour waits at ineffectually staffed no-reservation restaurants that sell "appetizers" like "bread and butter"? Whose isn't? But do a handful of blocks around Bedford and North 7th have enough excellent restaurants, unique shops, live music, bowling alleys, enviable parks, real bookstores, and *record stores* for God's sake to make the rest of us schmos salivate at what our own neighborhoods can't possibly offer? Sadly, yes. Which is when you find yourself squeezing onto the L or the B62 with everyone else who knows the same to be true.

The hulking steel towers of the **Williamsburg Bridge** (1903), long before the L came to be, connected the working class neighborhoods of Brooklyn with jobs in Manhattan. Before the bridge there was the Grand Street Ferry, which departed from the end of Grand Street. That spot is now taken up by the scrappy and pleasant **Grand Ferry Park**, which was one of the few parcels of waterfront open to the public during the area's industrial heyday.

The East River of today bears the fruit of Bloomberg-era rezoning in the form of gleaming high-rise rentals and condos and a manicured waterfront. **East River State Park**, reclaimed from the weeds and still slightly rustic around the edges, is a sunny, sometimes a little too sunny, spot along the river. On summer weekends, the park hosts all manner of fairs and events. Even after the tents and tables are gone, however, East River State Park is definitely worth a weekly trip; the picnic tables at the river's edge are one of the best spots in Brooklyn to gawk at that gorgeous skyline and a killer sunset. A few blocks away is **Brooklyn Brewery**. Brooklyn branded long before Brooklyn was a brand, only a small portion of its beer is actually brewed on site (the bottles, for example, come from Utica), though this spiritual home has anchored Williamsburg's identity since the late 1990s.

Just down the street from Brooklyn Brewery at the northern end of Williamsburg sits **McCarren Park**, with its 35 acres of ball fields, dog runs, and gardens where residents of every stripe convene when the sun is out. Although not the nicest looking park in the city, or even the neighborhood, there's an anarchic spirit to the park that's hard to resist, from the infantilizing children's games being played by aging cool hunters to the pick-up softball, basketball, and soccer on dirt patches and concrete fields to the steady stream of low-key craft-film-food-music events that fill up the weekend docket during the summer; it's a park that is well used and not fussed over, unlike some of the bigger, newer, "nicer" parks. **McCarren Pool**, shuttered for decades, reopened as an actual pool and recreation center in 2012, and as such is a state-of-the-art year-round facility.

Stretching south from McCarren Park is Bedford Avenue, Williamsburg's main thoroughfare, full of shops, bars, boutiques, and activity. The **Bedford Avenue L station** at North 7th Street functions as a sort of millennial wave pool, casting shoals of young people into the hip thick as frequently as communications-based train control can allow. Williamsburg's excesses ease the farther south and east you move from here. Along Metropolitan Avenue to the south is **City Reliquary**, a clever little (literally little) museum filled with New York City artifacts and historical exhibits, and a great way to connect with pre-gentrified Williamsburg. The south side of Williamsburg, especially south of Broadway, where stately **Peter Luger** has served steak since 1887, is one of the city's largest and most established Hasidic neighborhoods. During the Bloomberg era the issue of bike lanes along Bedford Avenue became controversial when members of the Hasidic community objected to the idea of supposedly scantily clad (or at least less clad than they're used to) cyclists riding through their neighborhood.

O Landmarks

- **Bedford L Train Station** •
Bedford St & N 7th St
Williamsburg's epicenter.
- **Brooklyn Brewery** • 79 N 11th St [Wythe Ave]
718-486-7422
Connect with your beer by witnessing its birth;
free samples also encourage closeness.
- **City Reliquary** •
370 Metropolitan Ave [Havemeyer St]
718-782-4842
Artifacts from New York's vast and rich history.
- **East River State Park** • Kent Ave & N 9th St
Swath of waterfront greenspace, Williamsburg
style.
- **Grand Ferry Park** • Grand St & River St
Ferry is gone. Park remains.
- **McCarren Park** • Bedford Ave & N 12th St
Hipsters, Poles, and athletes unite!
- **McCarren Park Pool** • Lorimer St & Bayard St
718-965-6580
Massive WPA-era pool and recreation center.
- **Williamsburg Bridge** • Driggs St & S 5th St
Bridge of the chosen people—Jews and well-
off hipsters.

Coffee

- **Black Brick** • 300 Bedford Ave [S 1st St]
718-384-0075
Cool exposed-brick-and-distressed-wood
coffee hangout.
- **Black Star Bakery** •
595 Metropolitan Ave [Lorimer St]
718-782-0060
Oslo coffee and good croissants, too.
- **Blue Bottle Coffee** • 160 Berry St [N 4th St]
718-387-4160
Bay Area masters with the long lines for pour
overs.
- **Devocion** • 69 Grand St [Wythe Ave]
718-285-6180
Williamsburg via Colombia; emphasis on
sourcing and fair trade.
- **Gimme Coffee** • 495 Lorimer St [Powers St]
718-388-7771
Coffee genius from Ithaca comes to Brooklyn.
- **Konditori** • 167 N 7th St [Bedford Ave]
347-529-4803
Cozy/packed mini-chain of Swedish
coffeehouses.
- **MatchaBar** • 93 Wythe Ave [N 10th St]
718-599-0015
Home of the Iced Vanilla Almond Matcha
Latte.
- **Momofuku Milk Bar** •
382 Metropolitan Ave [Havemeyer St]
347-577-9504
Coffee and a bunch of other weird stuff.
- **Oslo** • 133 Roebling St [N 4th St]
718-782-0332
Flagship store; coffee with attention to detail.
- **Sweetleaf** • 135 Kent Ave [N 6th St]
347-725-4862
LIC-based West Coast bean importers share
space with Realtor.
- **Toby's Estate** • 125 N 6th St [Berry St]
347-457-6155
Australian artisanal coffee powerhouse's first
US shop.

Williamsburg

Map 29

The legendary **Knitting Factory**, relocated from TriBeCa, symbolizes the shift away from Manhattan in the New York City music scene, joining **Music Hall** and **Pete's Candy Store** in a target-rich environment. Even **Brooklyn Bowl** has a stage. After the show, head to **Spuyten-Duyvil** or **Radegast** for beers, **The Richardson** for a proper cocktail, or **Barcade** for 8-bit goodness.

Farmers Markets

- **Greenpoint/McCarren Park Greenmarket** •
  Union Ave & N 12th St [Driggs Ave]
  Saturday, 8 am–3 pm, year-round.
- **Williamsburg Greenmarket** • Broadway &
  Havemeyer St
  Thursday, 8 am–4 pm, July–Nov.

Nightlife

- **The Abbey** • 536 Driggs Ave [N 8th St]
  718-599-4400
  Great jukebox and staff.
- **Alligator Lounge** •
  600 Metropolitan Ave [Lorimer St]
  718-599-4440
  Ignore the decor, and enjoy the free brick oven
  pizza with your beer.
- **Ba'sik** • 323 Graham Ave [Devoe St]
  347-889-7597
  Awesome cocktails this far East? Don't tell
  them over in 11249.
- **Barcade** • 388 Union Ave [Powers St]
  718-302-6464
  Paradise for '80s console champions and craft-
  beer guzzlers.
- **Bembe** • 81 S 6th St [Berry St]
  718-387-5389
  Hookahville.
- **Berry Park** • 4 Berry St [N 14th St]
  718-782-2829
  Williamburg's best rooftop: great beer and
  plenty of skyline.
- **Black Bear Bar** • 70 N 6th St [Wythe Ave]
  917-538-8399
  Bar in front, music in the back.
- **Burnside** • 506 Grand St [Lorimer St]
  347-889-7793
  Midwestern-themed bar complete with brats
  and cheese curds.
- **Charleston** • 174 Bedford Ave [N 7th St]
  718-599-9599
  Still going.
- **Clem's** • 264 Grand St [Roebling St]
  718-387-9617
  Classic narrow bar + drink specials = a
  neighborhood staple.
- **D.O.C.** • 83 N 7th St [Wythe Ave]
  718-963-1925
  All-Italian wine list with upscale finger food.
- **Dram** • 177 S 4th St [Driggs Ave]
  718-486-3726
  NYC's best cocktails that nobody knows about.
- **Duff's Brooklyn** • 168 Marcy Ave [Broadway]
  718-599-2092
  Heavy metal basement dive in the J train
  shadow.
- **East River Bar** • 97 S 6th St [Berry St]
  718-302-0511
  Fun interior, patio, and live music.

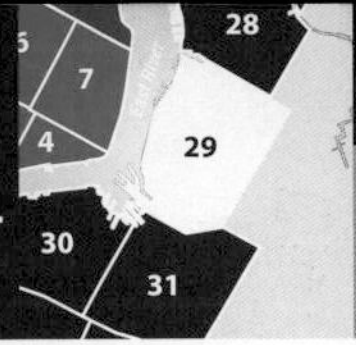

Map 29

Williamsburg

- **The Gibson** • 108 Bedford Ave [N 11th St]
718-387-6296
Quiet, classy Williamsburg bar.
- **Greenpoint Tavern** •
188 Bedford Ave [N 7th St]
718-384-9539
Cheap beer in Styrofoam cups.
- **Hotel Delmano** • 82 Berry St [N 9th St]
718-387-1945
Classic cocktails. Great date spot.
- **Huckleberry Bar** • 588 Grand St [Lorimer St]
718-218-8555
Solid cocktails, nice garden out back.
- **The Ides Bar at Wythe Hotel** •
80 Wythe Ave [N 11th St]
718-460-8004
Ridiculous city views (in a good way) for a
chicster crowd.
- **Iona** • 180 Grand St [Bedford Ave]
718-384-5008
Plenty of choices on tap.
- **Jr. and Son** •
575 Metropolitan Ave [Lorimer St]
Unabashedly hipster free.
- **Knitting Factory Brooklyn** •
361 Metropolitan Ave [Havemeyer St]
347-529-6696
Fifth-carbon of its former greatness.
- **Larry Lawrence Bar** •
295 Grand St [Havemeyer St]
718-218-7866
Laid-back bar with a lovely loft for smokers.
- **The Levee** • 212 Berry St [Metropolitan Ave]
718-218-8787
Formerly Cokies, now a laid-back vibe with
free cheese balls.
- **Maison Premiere** •
298 Bedford Ave [Grand St]
347-335-0446
Cocktails and oysters, New Orleans-style.
- **Mugs Ale House** • 125 Bedford Ave [N 10th St]
718-486-8232
Surprisingly good food, great beer selection,
cheap.
- **Music Hall of Williamsburg** •
66 N 6th St [Kent Ave]
212-260-4700
Brooklyn's Bowery Ballroom; national acts.
- **Nitehawk Cinema** •
136 Metropolitan Ave [Berry St]
718-384-3980
Dinner, cocktails, and craft beer while you
watch indie flicks.
- **Pete's Candy Store** •
709 Lorimer St [Richardson St]
718-302-3770

Live music, trivia nights, awesome back room,
and Scrabble.
- **Post Office** • 188 Havemeyer St [S 4th St]
Get some cocktails and some perfectly-
executed steak tartare.
- **R Bar** • 451 Meeker Ave [Graham Ave]
718-486-6116
Locals call it "our bar."
- **Radegast Hall & Biergarten** •
113 N 3rd St [Berry St]
718-963-3973
German beer hall with retractable roof. Only in
Williamsburg.
- **The Richardson** •
451 Graham Ave [Richardson St]
718-389-0839
Proper cocktails and small plates served in the
BQE's shadow.
- **The Shanty** • 79 Richardson St [Leonard St]
718-412-0874
Tasting room of local distillers, packed with
all stars.
- **Spuyten Duyvil** •
359 Metropolitan Ave [Havemeyer St]
718-963-4140
Join the Belgian beer cult.
- **This n' That** • 108 N 6th St [Berry St]
718-599-5959
Lively gay bar with dancing and raunchy drag
queens.
- **Trophy Bar** • 351 Broadway [Keap St]
347-227-8515
Cool little bar under the elevated. Beware
"skanks and thieves."
- **Turkey's Nest Tavern** •
94 Bedford Ave [N 12th St]
718-384-9774
Best dive in Williamsburg.
- **Union Pool** • 484 Union Ave [Skillman Ave]
718-609-0484
Good starting point—or finishing point.
- **The Woods** • 48 S 4th St [Wythe Ave]
Spacious non-hipster bar plus burgers, bacon,
and tacos in back.
- **Wythe Hotel** • 80 Wythe Ave [N 11th St]
718-460-8000
Home to rooftop bar The Ides, and hip
restaurant Reynard.

Williamsburg

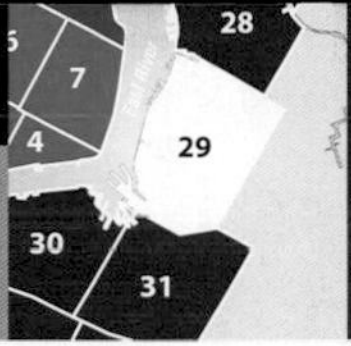

For low-key, go for hipster fusion at **Snacky**. That said, don't miss the dressed-up American spots: **Walter Foods**, **Rye**, and the more casual **DuMont**. For brunch (and believe us, we hesitate recommending brunch to anyone), **Pates et Traditions** has mouth-watering crepes. Carnivores must pay respects to **Fette Sau** and **Peter Luger**. If Luger didn't empty your bank account, **Zenkichi** is another special dining experience.

🍴 Restaurants

- **Acqua Santa** • 556 Driggs Ave [N 7th St]
  718-384-9695 • $$
  Bistro Italian—amazing patio.
- **Anna Maria Pizza** • 179 Bedford Ave [N 7th St]
  718-599-4550 • $
  A must after late night drinking.
- **Aurora** • 70 Grand St [Wythe Ave]
  718-388-5100 • $$$
  Warm, friendly rustic Italian. Just about perfect.
- **Baci & Abbracci** • 204 Grand St [Driggs Ave]
  718-599-6599 • $$
  Old-world Italian in a modern setting.
- **Bakeri** • 150 Wythe Ave [N 8th St]
  718-388-8037 • $$
  Adorably Amish decor and hipster vibe. Excellent baked goods.
- **Bamonte's** • 32 Withers St [Union Ave]
  718-384-8831 • $$
  Historic Italian joint; mediocre food but a great space.
- **Daoburg** • 614 Manhattan Ave
  718-349-0011 • $$$
  Delicious fusion, wings to die for.
- **Bozu** • 296 Grand St [Havemeyer Ave]
  718-384-7770 • $$
  Amazing Japanese tapas and sushi bombs.
- **BrisketTown** • 359 Bedford Ave [S 4th St]
  718-701-0909 • $$$
  Southside BBQ that's a perfect lunch fix.
- **Caracas Arepa Bar** •
  291 Grand St [Roebling St]
  718-218-6050 • $$
  Arepas are to pupusas as crepes are to dosas.
- **Cerveceria Havemeyer** •
  149 Havemeyer St [S 2nd St]
  718-599-5799 • $$
  Delish Mex and you know, those drinks that start with "M."
- **Chimu** • 482 Union Ave [Conselyea St]
  718-383-0045 • $$$
  Hopping Peruvian with giant drinks and fun vibe.

- **The Commodore** •
  366 Metropolitan Ave [Havemeyer]
  718-218-7632 • $
  Southern hipster cuisine. Good and cheap.
- **Counting Room** • 44 Berry St [N 11th St]
  718-599-1860 •
  Gorgeous space. Great wine. Fine food.
- **Delaware and Hudson** •
  135 N 5th St [Bedford Ave]
  718-218-8191 • $$$
  Farm-to-table goodness and crab cakes hollandaise for brunch.
- **DeStefano's Steak House** •
  89 Conselyea St [Leonard St]
  718-384-2836 • $$$$
  Fun old school steakhouse.
- **Diner** • 85 Broadway [Berry St]
  718-486-3077 • $$
  Amazing simple food like you've never tasted—never disappoints.
- **Dokebi** • 199 Grand St [Driggs Ave]
  718-782-1424 • $$$
  Cook your own Korean BBQ with tabletop hibachis.
- **DuMont Burger** • 314 Bedford Ave [S 1st St]
  718-384-6127 • $$
  The mini burger is even better proportioned than the original.
- **Egg** • 135 N 5th St [Bedford Ave]
  718-302-5151 • $$
  Organic breakfast and free range burgers.
- **El Almacen** • 557 Driggs Ave [N 7th St]
  718-218-7284 • $$$
  Buzzy Latin American. Give it a shot.
- **Evil Olive Pizza Bar** • 198 Union Ave [5th St]
  718-387-0707 • $$
  New York-style slices, bar in the back.
- **Extra Fancy** •
  302 Metropolitan Ave [Roebling St]
  347-422-0939 • $$$
  Extra good, extra pricey...extra everything, really.
- **Fat Goose** • 125 Wythe Ave [N 8th St]
  718-963-2200 • $$$
  Locavore deliciousness a block up from East River State Park.

Map 29

Map 29

Williamsburg

• **Fette Sau** •
354 Metropolitan Ave [Roebling St]
718-963-3404 • $$
Enjoy pounds of meat and casks of beer in a
former auto-body repair shop.
• **Frost Restaurant** • 193 Frost St [Graham Ave]
718-389-3347 • $$
Piles of parm and a nightcap of 'buca.
• **The Grand Bar & Grill** • 647 Grand St
[Manhattan Ave]
718-782-4726 • $$$
Raw bar, burgers, and cocktails. A perfect plan.
• **The Heyward** •
258 Wythe Ave [Metropolitan Ave]
718-384-1990 • $$$
The cuisine of Southernlandia.
• **Jerry's Pizza** • 649 Grand St [Manhattan Ave]
718-384-7680 • $
Slices, heroes, and garlic knots.
• **Juliette** • 135 N 5th St [Bedford Ave]
718-388-9222 • $$
Northside bistro with rooftop deck.
• **Kellogg's Diner** •
518 Metropolitan Ave [Union Ave]
718-782-4502 • $
The ultimate diner/deli.
• **La Locanda** • 432 Graham Ave [Withers St]
718-349-7800 • $$
Fried calamari, chicken parm, and so forth.
• **La Piazzetta** • 442 Graham Ave [Frost St]
718-349-1627 • $$$
Family-style restaurant with Northern and
Southern Italian dishes.
• **La Superior** • 295 Berry St [S 2nd St]
718-388-5988 • $$
Authentic Mexican street food.
• **Le Barricou** • 533 Grand St [Union Ave]
718-782-7372 • $$
Everyone's all about the bouillabaisse.
• **Lilia** • 567 Union Ave [N 10th St]
718-576-3095 • $$$
Sunny upscale Italian in repurposed auto
body shop.

• **Llama Inn** • 50 Withers St [Meeker Ave]
718-387-3434 • $$$
Elegant Peruvian, undoing ceviche/roasted
chicken tropes.
• **Lodge** • 318 Grand St [Havemeyer St]
718-486-9400 • $$$
Great space. The Adirondacks in Brooklyn.
• **Lorimer Market** •
620 Lorimer St [Skillman Ave]
718-389-2691 • $
Boffo Italian sandwiches.
• **Mable's Smokehouse & Banquet Hall** •
44 Berry St [N 12th St]
718-218-6655 • $$
Totally decent BBQ in hipster ambiance
(babies at the bar!).
• **Marlow & Sons** • 81 Broadway [Berry St]
718-384-1441 • $$$
Oysters and beer, old timey-like—go for
Happy Hour.
• **Meadowsweet** • 149 Broadway [Bedford Ave]
718-384-0673 • $$$$
Postmodern American in the old Dressler
space. Nice.
• **Mexico 2000** • 367 Broadway [Keap St]
718-782-3797 • $
Inner-bodega taco counter replete with
Mexican soap operas.
• **Moto** • 394 Broadway [Hooper St]
718-599-6895 • $$
Triangular nook with horseshoe bar and
comfort food.
• **Northside Bakery** •
149 N 8th St [Bedford Ave]
718-782-2700 • $
Best Polish bakery this side of Greenpoint/
Williamsburg. Perfect chocolate croissants.
• **Nuovo Fiore** • 284 Grand St [Roebling St]
718-782-8222 • $$
Rustic, delicious Italian at best-bargain-in-
Williamsburg prices.

Map 29

The Federal Bar is an import from LA featuring high-concept comfort cuisine. **Lilia** has been wowing diners with its elegant Italian in a former auto-body shop. Meanwhile, **Llama Inn** highlights Peruvian food's true culinary qualities, and features the sort of haute deliciousness you might find in Miraflores. And **MP Taverna** is Michael Psilakis' fantastic rendition of a classic Greek taverna.

- **Okonomi** • 150 Ainslie St [Lorimer St]
718-302-0598 • $$$
Photo-worthy bite-sized Japanese, with brekkie...
- **Onomea** • 84 Havemeyer St [Havemeyer St]
347-844-9559 • $$
Hawaiian cuisine lands in Williamsburg. Go for the poke.
- **Pates et Traditions** •
52 Havemeyer St [N 6th St]
718-302-1878 • $$
Divine savory crepes, honestly worth the wait for brunch.
- **Peter Luger Steak House** •
178 Broadway [Driggs Ave]
718-387-7400 • $$$$$
Best steak, potatoes, and spinach in this solar system.
- **Pies 'N' Thighs** • 166 S 4th St [Driggs]
347-529-6090 • $$
Comfortable, Southern-style where the chicken biscuits reign supreme.
- **PT** • 331 Bedford Ave [S 3rd St]
718-388-7438 • $$
D.O.C.'s sophisticated older brother.
- **Reunion** • 544 Union Ave [Frost St]
718-599-3670 • $$
Two shakshukas and then back to bed for us.
- **Reynard** • 80 Wythe Ave [N 11th St]
718-460-8004 • $$$
The Wythe Hotel's in house resto. It's all good here.
- **Roebling Tea Room** •
143 Roebling St [Metropolitan Ave]
718-963-0760 • $$$
Fancy tea eatery.
- **Sal's Pizzeria** • 544 Lorimer St [Devoe St]
718-388-6838 • $$
Calzones, slices, heroes, and pastas.
- **Santa Salsa** • 594 Union Ave [Richardson St]
347-683-2605 • $$
Venezuelan hot dogs, parillas, and more.

- **Sea** • 114 N 6th St [Berry St]
718-384-8850 • $$
Outshines its Manhattan counterpart.
- **Snacky** • 187 Grand St [Bedford Ave]
718 486 4848 • $
Kitschy.
- **St Anselm** •
355 Metropolitan Ave [Havemeyer St]
718-384-5054 • $$$
We have no reservations about this sizzling steak spot.
- **Sweetwater** • 105 N 6th St [Berry St]
718 963 0608 • $$
Just a cozy bar with nice bistro food.
- **Tabare** • 221 S 1st St [Roebling]
347-335-0187 • $$
Authentic Uruguayan food serving delicious family recipes.
- **Taj Kabab & Curry** • 568 Grand St [Lorimer St]
718-782-1722 • $$
Cheap takeout and delivery.
- **Teddy's Bar and Grill** • 96 Berry St [N 8th St]
718-384-9787 • $
Best bar food ever. Hipster and Polish locals unite.
- **Traif** • 229 S 4th St [Havemeyer St]
347-844-9578 • $$$
Small plates brilliance under the Williamsburg Bridge. Go.
- **Walter Foods** • 253 Grand St [Roebling St]
718-387-8783 • $$$
Spiffed up American classics in a warmly lit bistro.
- **Yola's Café** •
524 Metropolitan Ave [Union Ave]
718-486-0757 • $
Terrific, authentic Mexican in a claustrophobic atmosphere.
- **Zenkichi** • 77 N 6th St [Wythe Ave]
718-388-8985 • $$
Amazing izakaya suitable for a tryst.

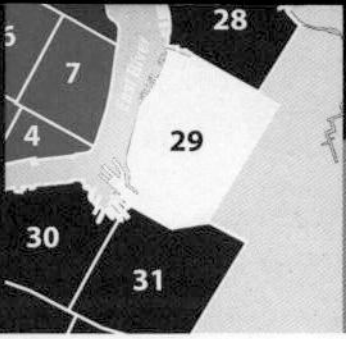

Map 29

28
7
4
29
30
31

Williamsburg

🛍 Shopping

- **10 Ft. Single by Stella Dallas** •
285 N 6th St [Meeker Ave]
718-486-9482
Dress up like you're in *Dazed & Confused 2*.
- **A&G Merch** • 111 N 6th St [Berry St]
718-388-1779
A collection of utilitarian objects ranging from
couches to candles.
- **Academy Records Annex** •
85 Oak St [Franklin St]
718-218-8200
Bins and bins of new and used LPs.
- **Amarcord Vintage Fashion** •
223 Bedford Ave [N 4th St]
718-963-4001
Well-edited vintage goodies, many pieces
direct from Europe.
- **Artists & Fleas** • 70 N 7th St [Wythe Ave]
Market for quirky jewelry, accessories, vintage,
housewares.
- **Beacon's Closet** • 88 N 11th St [Wythe Ave]
718-486-0816
Rad resale with lots of gems.
- **Bedford Cheese Shop** •
229 Bedford Ave [N 5th St]
718-599-7588
Best cheese selection in the borough.
- **Beer Street** • 413 Graham Ave [Withers St]
347-294-0495
Rotating taps, growlers, bottles, & more at
Williamsburg's craft beer store.
- **BQE Wine & Liquors** •
504 Meeker Ave [Humboldt St]
718-389-3833
Good selection, cheap.

- **The Brooklyn Kitchen** •
100 Frost St [Manhattan Ave]
718-389-2982
Awesome butcher shop and gourmet cooking
supplies next to the BQE.
- **Brooklyn Winery** • 213 N 8th St [Driggs Ave]
347-763-1506
Craft your own barrel of wine from crushing
the grapes to bottling.
- **Buffalo Exchange** • 504 Driggs Ave [N 9th St]
718-384-6901
Recycled clothing chain's first NYC store.
- **Catbird** • 219 Bedford Ave [N 5th St]
718-599-3457
Unique clothing and jewelry from up-and-
coming designers.
- **Crest True Value Hardware** •
558 Metropolitan Ave [Lorimer St]
718-388-9521
Arty hardware store, believe it or not.
- **Desert Island** •
540 Metropolitan Ave [Union Ave]
718-388-5087
Comics, visual arts books, zines, and
consignment finds.
- **Earwax Records** • 167 N 9th St [Bedford Ave]
718-486-3771
Record store with all the indie classics.
- **Emily's Pork Store** •
426 Graham Ave [Withers St]
718-383-7216
Broccoli rabe sausage is their specialty.
- **Fuego 718** • 249 Grand St [Roebling St]
718-302-2913
Handcrafted gifts made with passion from
Mexico, Peru, Italy…

Beacon's Closet and Buffalo Exchange require some stamina, but they're worth it; Amarcord's nicely edited vintage selection is the antidote. Vinyl collectors geek out within blocks of the Bedford stop at Academy, Rough Trade, and Earwax, while foodsters find gadgets at Whisk and Brooklyn Kitchen. Marlow & Daughters's locally sourced, quality (i.e.. expensive) meat is paired with helpful advice.

- **Idlewild Books** • 218 Bedford Ave [N 5th St]
  212-414-8888
  Extensive foreign language offerings and language classes.
- **KCDC Skateshop** • 252 Wythe Ave [N 3rd St]
  718-387-9006
  Shop and gallery featuring locally designed gear.
- **Marlow & Daughters** • 95 Broadway [Berry St]
  718-388-5700
  Gorgeous (yes, expensive) cuts for the discerning carnivore.
- **Mast Bros Chocolate** • 111 N 3rd St [Berry St]
  718-388-2625
  Artisan chocolatiers that begat peak Brooklyn.
- **Monk Vintage** • 496 Driggs Ave [N 9th St]
  718-384-6665
  Young and fun selection of vintage clothes, shoes, accessories.
- **The Natural Wine Company** •
  211 N 11th St [Roebling St]
  646-397-9463
  Smart staff and excellent selection of sustainably produced, tasty wines.
- **Open Air Modern** •
  489 Lorimer St [Nassau Ave]
  718-383-6465
  Old and rare books and furniture.
- **Rough Trade** • 64 N 9th St [Kent Ave]
  718-388-4111
  NYC outpost of famous London record store; many live events.

- **Savino's Quality Pasta** •
  111 Conselyea St [Manhattan Ave]
  718-388-2038
  Homemade ravioli.
- **SlapBack** • 490 Metropolitan Ave [Rodney St]
  347-227-7133
  Indulge your inner Jayne Mansfield.
- **Smorgasburg** • N 7th St & Kent Ave
  Massive Saturday food fest. Sunglasses mandatory.
- **Spoonbill & Sugartown** •
  218 Bedford Ave [N 5th St]
  718-387-7322
  Art, architecture, design, philosophy, and literature. New and used.
- **Sprout Home** • 44 Grand St [Kent Ave]
  718-388-4440
  Contemporary home and garden store.
- **Treehouse** • 430 Graham Ave [Frost St]
  718 482 8733
  Quirky, one-of-a-kind clothing and jewelry.
- **Uva Wines & Spirits** •
  199 Bedford Ave [N 5th St]
  718-963-3939
  The staff knows and loves their small, meticulous selection.
- **Whisk** • 231 Bedford Ave [N 4th St]
  718-218-7230
  Kitchen boutique stocked with basic gear and beyond.

Three 'nabes for the price of one! Or is that three 'nabes for the price of ten? Yes, Brooklyn Heights really is that expensive, but there's a reason: it's one of the most sublimely beautiful neighborhoods in all of New York, with jaw-dropping city views along the **Brooklyn Heights Promenade**, two friendly retail strips on Montague and Henry Streets, views of the iconic **Brooklyn Bridge**, and perhaps the city's best stock of brownstones and clapboard homes, especially around the "fruit street" area of Orange, Cranberry, and Pineapple, but even heading all the way south along Henry and Hicks Streets until the neighborhood ends at busy Atlantic Avenue.

By the time one hits Court Street heading east from Brooklyn Heights, however, you can chuck the sublime right out the window. The borough's central nervous system, Downtown Brooklyn, features several courthouses (you'll learn your way around when Kings County jury duty calls), **Brooklyn Borough Hall**, **Metrotech Center** (encompassing the **New York City College of Technology**, a large Marriott hotel, **Polytechnic Institute of New York University**, and a convenient **TKTS Booth**), Brooklyn Law School, the **Fulton Street Mall**, jam-packed daily with lunchtime shoppers, and finally, a warren of subways that can take you to any other point in New York City. Speaking of which, don't miss the **New York Transit Museum**, a fascinating look at how our underground web of trains came to be—and not just for aficionados.

DUMBO ("Down Under the Manhattan Bridge Overpass," the acronym appropriated from Walt Disney since the late 1970s), the third neighborhood in this trilogy, has followed the warehouse-turned-artist-studio-turned-expensive-condo route. Like Brooklyn Heights, DUMBO features killer views of downtown Manhattan, just closer to the waterfront. Retail in DUMBO, will be forever limited, and many shops close early (by New York standards). As DUMBO truly only has one subway stop (the York Street F), it can get a little desolate, especially late at night. And while this all sounds like a quiet, idyllic little neighborhood, there's only one problem: the *constant* rumble of the B, D, N, and Q trains overhead on the **Manhattan Bridge**. Thank goodness for double pane windows.

For true peace and quiet, you'll have to head east about five blocks from DUMBO to check out one of our favorite micro-neighborhoods, **Vinegar Hill**. Literally only three blocks wide and two blocks long, Vinegar Hill is bordered by a power plant to the north, the **Navy Yard** to the east, the Farragut Houses to the south, and DUMBO to the west. Inside its cobblestoned streets are a vestige of 19th-century Navy housing and an ex-retail strip along Hudson Street.

And then there's **Brooklyn Bridge Park**, stretching 1.3 miles along the East River waterfront from Atlantic Avenue to the south all the way past Manhattan Bridge to the north. Comprising six repurposed shipping piers, the former Empire-Fulton Ferry State Park, two Civil War-era historic buildings, and various city-owned open spaces along the waterfront, the 85-acre site combines active and passive recreation with the stunning backdrop of the Brooklyn and Manhattan Bridges, Lower Manhattan, and the New York Harbor beyond.

By 8 p.m., teeming Downtown Brooklyn is a ghost town; you'll either need to head north to DUMBO or west to the Heights to wet your whistle. In DUMBO check out bustling **Galapagos Art Space** after a performance at brilliant **St. Ann's Warehouse**. In the Heights, **Henry Street Ale House** is a good complement to catching a flick at cozy **Heights Cinema**.

O Landmarks

- **Brooklyn Borough Hall** •
209 Joralemon St [Cadman Plz W]
718-802-3700
Built in the 1840s, this Greek Revival landmark
was once employed as the official City Hall of
Brooklyn.
- **Brooklyn Bridge** • Adams St & East River
If you haven't walked over it at least twice yet,
you're not cool.
- **Brooklyn Bridge Park** •
Old Fulton St & Furman St
718-222-9939
Waterfront park with stellar views and many
active recreational amenities.
- **Brooklyn Heights Promenade** •
Montague St & Pierrepont Pl
The best place to really see Manhattan. It's the
view that's in all the movies.
- **Brooklyn Historical Society** •
128 Pierrepont St [Clinton St]
718-222-4111
Want to really learn about Brooklyn? Go here.
- **Brooklyn Ice Cream Factory** •
1 Water St [Old Fulton St]
718-246-3963
Expensive, old-fashioned ice cream beneath
the bridge.
- **The Brooklyn Tabernacle** •
17 Smith St [Livingston St]
718-290-2000
Home of the award-winning Brooklyn
Tabernacle Choir.
- **Fulton Street Mall** • Fulton St & Flatbush Ave
The shopping experience, Brooklyn style. Hot
sneakers can be had for a song.
- **Jetsons Building** • 110 York St [Jay St]
View this sculptural roof from the Manhattan
Bridge at night when it's lit with colored lights.
- **Junior's Restaurant** •
386 Flatbush Avenue Ext [DeKalb Ave]
718-852-5257
For the only cheesecake worth its curds and
whey.

- **Manhattan Bridge** •
Flatbush Avenue Ext & Nassau St
Connecting Brooklyn to that other borough.
- **MetroTech Center** •
16-acre commercial/governmental/
educational/cultural entity in Downtown
Brooklyn.
- **New York Transit Museum** •
130 Livingston St [Boerum St]
718-694-1600
Ride vintage subway cars through formerly
abandoned tunnels? Yes, please!
- **Vinegar Hill** • Water St & Hudson Ave
NYC's coolest micro-neighborhood. Promise.

Coffee

- **Absolute Coffee** • 327 Atlantic Ave [Hoyt St]
718-522-0969
Absolutely perfect for an Atlantic Ave. pit stop.
- **Almondine Bakery** • 85 Water St [Main St]
718-797-5026
Grab a cup and check out the view.
- **Brooklyn Roasting Company** •
25 Jay St [John St]
718-855-1000
DUMBO roasters; international focus.
- **Cranberry's** • 48 Henry St [Cranberry St]
718-624-3500
Long-serving BH coffee stop.
- **Iris Café** • 20 Columbia Pl [Joralemon St]
718-722-7395
Very tiny. Very Brooklyn.
- **Tazza** • 311 Henry St [Atlantic Ave]
718-243-0487
Coffee, tea, baked goods, sammiches. And
wine.
- **Two For the Pot** • 200 Clinton St [Atlantic Ave]
718-855-8173
Coffee, tea, and British imports as well.

Farmers Markets

- **Brooklyn Borough Hall Greenmarket** •
Court St & Montague St
Tues, Thurs & Sat, 8 am–6 pm, year-round.

Map 30

Our favorite places here are mostly in the "special occasion" category due to price: the Heights' cozy gastropub **Jack the Horse**, game-oriented old-school **Henry's End**, and the superb **Vinegar Hill House**. Otherwise, get great pizza at **Juliana's**, grab fast food on **Fulton Street Mall**, or hit classic **Junior's** for hangover food.

🍸 Nightlife

- **68 Jay Street Bar** • 68 Jay St [Front St]
  718-260-8207
  Arty local bar.
- **Grand Army** • 336 State St [Hoyt St]
  718-422-7867
  Cocktails and oysters, do we need anything else really?
- **Henry Street Ale House** •
  62 Henry St [Cranberry St]
  718-522-4801
  Cozy, dark space with good selections on tap.
- **Jack the Horse Tavern** •
  66 Hicks St [Cranberry St]
  718-852-5084
  Outstanding upscale pub/New American cuisine, great feel.
- **Le Boudoir** • 135 Atlantic Ave [Hoyt St]
  347-227-8337
  Marie Antoinette-themed cocktail lounge underneath Chez Moi.
- **O'Keefe's Bar & Grill** •
  62 Court St [Livingston St]
  718-855-8751
  Sports bar (large Mets following). Surprisingly decent food.
- **St Ann's Warehouse** • 45 Water St
  718-254-8779
  Be careful not to cut yourself on the edginess.

🍴 Restaurants

- **AlMar** • 111 Front St [Washington St]
  718-855-5288 • $$$
  Cavernous, friendly, communal-table Italian in DUMBO. Go to hang.
- **Bijan's** • 81 Hoyt St [Atlantic Ave]
  718-855-5574 • $$$
  Lamb burgers and rosemary chicken. It's good.
- **Chef's Table at Brooklyn Fare** •
  200 Schermerhorn St [Hoyt St]
  718-243-0050 • $$$$$
  When you get a seat, give it to us.
- **Chez Moi** • 135 Atlantic Ave [Henry St]
  347-227-8337 • $$$$
  Even more French on Atlantic Avenue. We love it.

- **Colonie** • 127 Atlantic Ave [Henry St]
  718-855-7500 • $$$$
  Hip to be square. Oysters, cocktails, and much more.
- **Dellarocco's of Brooklyn** •
  214 Hicks St [Montague St]
  718-858 1010 • $$
  Perfectly good brick oven tucked away on Hicks. Nice.
- **Fascati Pizza** • 80 Henry St [Orange St]
  718-237-1278 • $
  Excellent slice pizza.
- **Five Guys** • 138 Montague St [Henry St]
  718-797-9380 • $
  Burger joint with tasty fries and free peanuts while you wait.
- **Forno Rosso** • 327 Gold St [Flatbush Ave]
  718-451-3800 • $$$
  Chic industrial space with perfect brick-oven pizzas.
- **Gallito's Kitchen** • 110 Montague St [Henry St]
  718-855-4791 • $$$
  Good Mexican, especially for Montague Street.
- **Ganso** • 25 Bond St [Livingston St]
  718-403-0900 • $$
  Perfect ramen tucked away just north of Atlantic.
- **Grimaldi's** • 1 Front St [Cadman Plaza W]
  718-858 4300 • $$
  Excellent, respected, arguably among the best NYC pizza joints.
- **Hale & Hearty Soup** • 32 Court St [Remsen St]
  718-596-5600 • $$
  Super soups.
- **Heights Café** • 84 Montague St [Hicks St]
  718-625-5555 • $$$
  Decent dining near the Promenade.
- **Henry's End** • 44 Henry St [Cranberry St]
  718-834-1776 • $$$
  Inventive, game-oriented menu.
- **Hill Country Chicken** •
  345 Adams St [Willoughby St]
  718-885-4609 • $
  Fried chicken and BBQ goodness close to the courts.
- **Iris Café** • 20 Columbia Pl [Joralemon St]
  718-722-7395 • $$$
  Trending: avocado toast and housemade ricotta.

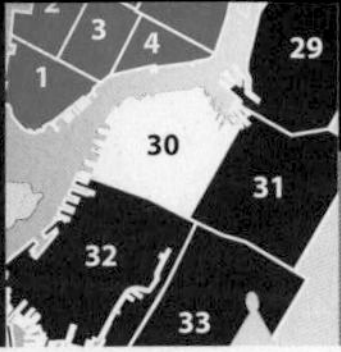

Map 30 • Brooklyn Heights/DUMBO/Downtown

• **Iron Chef House** • 92 Clark St [Monroe Pl]
718-858-8517 • $$
Dependable sushi and cozy atmosphere.
• **Jack the Horse Tavern** •
66 Hicks St [Cranberry St]
718-852-5084 • $$$$
Outstanding upscale pub/New American cuisine, great feel.
• **Juliana's Pizza** • 19 Old Fulton St [Front St]
718-596-6700 • $$
Patsy makes his triumphant return to original Grimaldi's space.
• **Junior's Restaurant** •
386 Flatbush Avenue Ext [DeKalb Ave]
718-852-5257 • $
American with huge portions. Cheesecake.
• **Lantern Thai** • 101 Montague St [Hicks St]
718-237-2594 • $$
Mediocre Thai. The Montague curse.
• **Luzzo's BK** • 145 Atlantic Ave [Henry St]
718-855-6400 • $$$
East Village Italian pizza masters say hello to Brooklyn.
• **Miso** • 40 Main St [Front St]
718-858-8388 • $$$
Japanese fusion cuisine.
• **Noodle Pudding** • 38 Henry St [Middagh St]
718-625-3737 • $$
Northern Italian fare.

• **Park Plaza Restaurant** •
220 Cadman Plaza W [Clark St]
718-596-5900 • $
NFT-approved neighborhood diner.
• **Queen Restaurant** •
84 Court St [Livingston St]
718-596-5955 • $$$$
Good white-tablecloth, bow-tied waiter Italian joint.
• **The River Café** • 1 Water St [Old Fulton St]
718-522-5200 • $$$$$
Great view, but overrated.
• **Shake Shack** • 409 Fulton St [Boerum Pl]
718-307-7590 • $
The empire comes to Brooklyn.
• **Shake Shack** • 1 Old Fulton St [Water St]
347-435-2676 • $$
Danny Meyer's burgers, conveniently located near Brooklyn Bridge Park.
• **Superfine** • 126 Front St [Pearl St]
718-243-9005 • $$
Mediterranean-inspired menu, bi-level bar, local art and music. NFT pick.
• **Sushi Gallery** • 71 Clark St [Henry St]
718-222-0308 • $$
Sushi Express, reasonable prices.
• **Teresa's Restaurant** •
80 Montague St [Hicks St]
718-797-3996 • $
Polish-American comfort food. Come hungry.
• **Vinegar Hill House** •
72 Hudson Ave [Water St]
718-522-1018 • $$$
Excellent wood fired meats and veggies served in old-timey setting.

Need something, anything, quick and cheap? The **Fulton Street Mall** area is your answer, with a **Macy's** and tons of discount shops. In DUMBO, you can get great books at **powerHouse**, chocolate at **Jacques Torres**, and pastries at **Almondine**. In the Heights, browse women's clothing at **Tango** on Montague.

🛍 Shopping

- **Barnes & Noble** • 106 Court St [State St]
  718-246-4996
  Chain bookstore.
- **Bridge Fresh** • 68 Jay St [Water St]
  718-488-1993
  Organic grocer.
- **Brooklyn Historical Society** •
  128 Pierrepont St [Clinton St]
  718-222-4111
  Fun gift shop with all manner of Brooklyn-themed merch.
- **Brooklyn Ice Cream Factory** •
  1 Water St [Old Fulton St]
  718-246-3963
  Get your ice cream fix on the Brooklyn waterfront.
- **Cranberry's** • 48 Henry St [Cranberry St]
  718-624-3500
  Oldtime deli/grocery of rationally-priced comestibles.
- **Egg Baby** • 72 Jay St [Water St]
  347-356-4097
  Clothes for mommy and baby.
- **Grumpy Bert** • 82 Bond St [State St]
  347-855-4849
  Gift-toy-print-zine apparel boutique.
- **Halcyon** • 57 Pearl St [Water St]
  718-260-9299
  Vinyl for DJ fanatics.
- **Heights Prime Meats** • 59 Clark St [Henry St]
  718-237-0133
  Butcher.
- **Housing Works Thrift Shop** •
  122 Montague St [Henry St]
  718-237-0521
  Our favorite thrift store.
- **Jacques Torres Chocolate** •
  66 Water St [Main St]
  718-875-1269
  The Platonic ideal of chocolate.
- **Lassen & Hennigs** •
  114 Montague St [Henry St]
  718-875-6272
  Specialty foods and deli.

- **Macy's** • 422 Fulton St [Hoyt St]
  718-875-7200
  Less crazed than Herald Square by about 1700%.
- **Modell's Sporting Goods** •
  360 Fulton Mall [Red Hook Ln]
  718-866-1021
  Sports. Sports. Sports. Get your Cyclones stuff here!
- **Montague Wine & Spirits** •
  78 Montague St [Hicks St]
  718-254-9422
  Consistently good wine store in Brooklyn Heights.
- **One Girl Cookies** • 33 Main St [Water St]
  347-338-1268
  Delicious treats via Cobble Hill.
- **Peas & Pickles** • 55 Washington St [Front St]
  718-488-8336
  DUMBO's first grocery.
- **powerHouse Arena** • 37 Main St [Water St]
  718-666-3049
  One of our favorite gallery/bookstores.
- **Recycle-A-Bicycle** • 35 Pearl St [Plymouth St]
  718-858-2972
  Bikes to the ceiling.
- **Super Runners Shop** • 123 Court St [State St]
  718-858-8550
  Running sneaks and the like.
- **Tango** • 145 Montague St [Henry St]
  718-625-7518
  Indie lover the clothes here. 'Nuff said.
- **TKTS Booth** • 1 Metrotech Ctr [Jay St]
  212-912-9770
  Shhh…don't tell anyone there's one in Brooklyn!
- **Trunk** • 68 Jay St [Front St]
  718-522-6488
  Awesome dresses and accessories, run by independent local designers.
- **Waterfront Wines & Spirits** •
  360 Furman St [Joralemon St]
  718-246-5101
  Well curated selection; stop before visiting friends for dinner.
- **West Elm** • 75 Front St [Main St]
  718-875-7757
  Cool home decor at reasonable prices.

Map 31 • **Fort Greene / Clinton Hill**

Neighborhood Overview

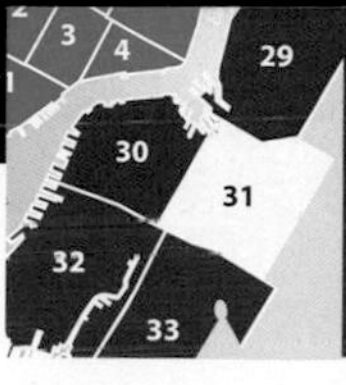

Map 31

Fort Greene could be the perfect outer borough neighborhood: the population is diverse, it's close to Manhattan, it's got a stellar park, tons of restaurants, a farmer's market, the hippest swap meet on the planet, beautiful tree-and brownstone-lined streets, historic buildings, subway and LIRR access, and a world-class performing arts center. Unfortunately, many people already know this, so rents are increasingly high, but the area still retains a homey, community vibe.

Fort Greene's landmarks run the gamut from religious to cultural to economic to civic to military. Check out the Underground Railroad murals at the **Lafayette Avenue Presbyterian Church**. In addition to templing Masons, the **Brooklyn Masonic Temple** also hosts indie concerts. The **Brooklyn Academy of Music** (BAM) has two live performance spaces, movie theaters, a café (which hosts free shows), plus the "Next Wave" festival of dance, opera, music, and theater. (Also, the Mark Morris Dance Center is just down the block.) The **Williamsburg Savings Bank Building** is one of the tallest structures in Brooklyn and has now been converted to condos. The **Brooklyn Navy Yard** now houses businesses as well as **Steiner Studios**. Shoppers and those who need the soul-sucking DMV flock to the hulking, commercial **Atlantic Terminal Mall**, which sits above a massive **Long Island Railroad Station**.

On weekends, hilly **Fort Greene Park** is rollicking with a **farmer's market**, playgrounds, cricket, soccer, and local community groups. Just a few blocks away, **Brooklyn Flea** is a major shopping (and eating!) destination, complete with tons of Etsy-type crafts, vendors, and enough food to fill up a year's worth of blog entries.

But that's only half the story, because Fort Greene's "sister" neighborhood, Clinton Hill, has a lot going for it, namely a proximity to the amenities of Fort Greene with fewer crowds. Clinton Hill hosts bucolic **St. Joseph's College** and the **Pratt Institute**, whose grounds are home to both sculpture art and a **Power Plant**. Several historic churches also dot the Clinton Hill landscape, which is filled with beautiful brownstones as well as some massive single-family homes on Washington Street.

Clinton Hill is home to an African community that has set up a number of restaurants and shops in the neighborhood, and it's also home to a whole row of artist's studios on Lexington Avenue. And film shoots—that peculiar New York City metric of neighborhood self-worth—are a regular occurrence in Clinton Hill. As if that weren't enough, you know Clinton Hill has clearly arrived when local coffee/food nexus **Choice Market** had its BLT profiled by Food Network.

Frank's, **Alibi**, and **Stonehome** are all great places to grab a drink before or after a movie at **BAM Rose Cinemas** or a performance at the **Masonic Hall**. **Hanson Dry** focuses on cocktails. Farther afield, **The Fulton Grand** is a nice option.

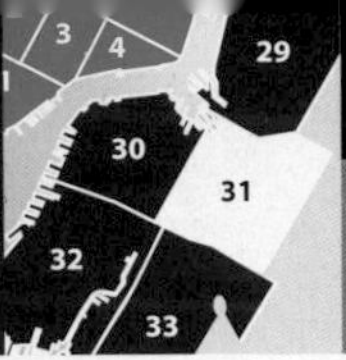

Map 31

Fort Greene / Clinton Hill

O Landmarks

- **Brooklyn Academy of Music (BAM)** •
30 Lafayette Ave [Ashland Pl]
718-636-4100
America's oldest continuously operating
performing arts center. Never dull.
- **Brooklyn Masonic Temple** •
317 Clermont Ave [Lafayette Ave]
718-638-1256
Its vestrymen have included Robert E. Lee and
Thomas J. (Stonewall) Jackson.
- **Brooklyn Navy Yard** •
Flushing Ave & Clinton Ave
718-907-5900
Nation's first navy yard employed 70,000
people during WWII. Today, it houses a diverse
range of businesses.
- **Fort Greene Park** •
Willoughby Ave & Washington Park
718-222-1461
Liquor store proximity is a plus on a warm
afternoon when you visit this welcome chunk
of green.
- **Lafayette Avenue Presbyterian Church** •
85 S Oxford St [Lafayette Ave]
718-625-7515
Nationally known church with performing
arts; former Underground Railroad stop.
- **Long Island Rail Road Atlantic Terminal** •
Flatbush Ave & Hanson Pl
718-217-5477
A low red-brick building hosting more than 20
million passengers annually. A total craphole.
- **Pratt Institute Steam Turbine Power Plant** •
200 Willoughby Ave [Hall St]
This authentic steam generator gets fired up
a few times a year to impress the parents. Cool.
- **Prison Ship Martyrs' Monument** •
Fort Greene Park
Crypt holds remains of thousands of
Revolutionary War-era prisoners.
- **Steiner Studios** •
15 Washington Ave [Flushing Ave]
718-858-1600
Film studio in the Brooklyn Navy Yard.
- **Williamsburgh Savings Bank Building** •
1 Hanson Pl [Ashland Pl]
Still the tallest building in the borough and
when you're lost, a sight for sore eyes.

Coffee

- **Bedford Hill** • 343 Franklin Ave [Greene Ave]
718-636-7650
Coffee, plus beer and egg sammiches.
- **Bittersweet** • 180 Dekalb Ave [Carlton Ave]
718-852-2556
Line-out-the-door coffee on weekend
mornings.
- **Greene Grape Annex** •
753 Fulton St [S Portland Ave]
718-858-4791
Bright, busy, super-quiet, with alcohol, too.
- **Hungry Ghost** • 781 Fulton St [S Oxford St]
718-797-3595
Perfect coffee and a few fun noshes.
- **Marcy & Myrtle Cafe** •
574 Marcy [Myrtle Ave]
917-648-7800
Small coffee shop with pastries and a cool
design.
- **Outpost** • 1014 Fulton St [Downing St]
718-636-1260
Important Fulton-area coffee shop.
- **Red Lantern Bicycles** •
345 Myrtle Ave [Adelphi St]
347-889-5338
Coffee shop, bicycle shop, a tad loud though.
- **Smooch** • 264 Carlton Ave [Dekalb Ave]
718-624-4075
Coffee, tea, and vegetarian noshes.
- **Tripp & Cooper Cafe** •
80 Dekalb Ave [Rockwell Pl]
718-596-3070
Coffee for the LIU crowd.

Farmers Markets

- **Fort Greene Park Greenmarket** •
Dekalb Ave & Washington Park
Saturday, 8 am–4 pm., year-round, southeast
corner of park.

Map 31

It's all here, folks: Italian (**Locanda** and **Scopello**), French (**Chez Oskar**), BBQ (**Smoke Joint**), tapas (**Olea**), hip (**General Greene** and **No. 7**), Middle Eastern (**Black Iris**), Mexican (**Castro**), burgers (**67 Burger**), and a reliable greasy spoon diner (**Mike's Coffee Shop**). Full yet?

🍸Nightlife

- **The Alibi** • 242 Dekalb Ave [Vanderbilt Ave]
718-783-8519
Real deal neighborhood bar.
- **Bar Olivino** • 899 Fulton St [Vanderbilt Ave]
718-857-7952
Companion wine bar to Olivino Wines.
- **Brooklyn Masonic Temple** •
317 Clermont Ave [Lafayette Ave]
718-638-1256
Masons + Indie Rock = smiles all around.
- **Brooklyn Public House** •
247 Dekalb Ave [Vanderbilt Ave]
347-227-8976
Lots of beers, with food, open 'till 2 am.
Perfect.
- **Der Schwarze Kolner** •
710 Fulton St [S Oxford St]
347-841-4495
German beer hall, w/ food. Ft. Greene now
almost perfect.
- **Dick & Jane's Bar** •
266 Adelphi St [Dekalb Ave]
347-227-8021
A very, very cool speakeasy hidden behind
four garage doors. Sssshhhh…
- **The Emerson** • 561 Myrtle Ave [Emerson Pl]
347-763-1310
Good pub for Pratt students and locals.
- **Frank's Cocktail Lounge** •
660 Fulton St [S Elliott Pl]
718-625-9339
When you need to get funky.
- **The Fulton Grand** •
1011 Fulton St [Grand Ave]
718-399-2240
Well appointed, good beer and whiskey
selection.
- **Hanson Dry** • 925 Fulton St [Waverly Ave]
Good cocktails.
- **One Last Shag** •
348 Franklin Ave [Lexington Ave]
718-398-2472
Great locals bar with patio, free grill, and
Guinness on tap.
- **Project Parlor** • 742 Myrtle Ave [Sanford St]
347-497-0550
Cozy bar with surprisingly huge backyard in
shabby environs.
- **Rustik Tavern** • 471 Dekalb Ave [Kent Ave]
347-406-9700
Neighborhood tap draws cozy clientele.

🍴Restaurants

- **67 Burger** • 67 Lafayette Ave [S Elliott Pl]
718-797-7150 • $$
Super-cool stop for a quick bite before your
movie at BAM.
- **Baguetteaboudit!** •
270 Vanderbilt Ave [DeKalb Ave]
718-622-8333 • $$
Great breakfast and sandwiches, say hi to
Keith.
- **Baron's** • 564 Dekalb Ave [Spencer Ct]
718-230-7100 • $$$
Burgers, cocktails, and perfect brunchtime
breakfast sandwiches.
- **Bati** • 747 Fulton St [S Portland Ave]
718-797-9696 • $$
Friendly (aren't they all?) Ft. Greene Ethiopian.
Good pre-BAM option.
- **Berlyn** • 25 Lafayette Ave [Ashland Pl]
718-222-5800 • $$$
De rigueur pre-BAM schnitzel performances.
- **Black Iris** • 228 Dekalb Ave [Clermont Ave]
718-852-9800 • $$
Middle Eastern; good lamb, terrible chicken,
excellent Zataar bread.
- **Black Swan** •
1048 Bedford Ave [Lafayette Ave]
718-783-4744 • $$$
Great pub, long menu, late-night bites …
about perfect.
- **Caffe E Vino** • 112 Dekalb Ave [St Felix St]
718-855-6222 • $$$
Friendly Italian across from Brooklyn Hospital.
- **Castro's** • 511 Myrtle Ave [Grand Ave]
718-398-1459 • $$
Burritos delivered con cervezas, if you like.
- **Chez Oskar** • 211 Dekalb Ave [Adelphi St]
718-852-6250 • $$$
French cuisine in a good neighborhood bistro.
- **Choice Market** •
318 Lafayette Ave [Grand Ave]
718-230-5234 • $
Excellent sandwiches, baked goods, burgers,
etc. served w/ maddening slowness.
- **Colonia Verde** • 219 Dekalb Ave [Adelphi St]
347-689-4287 • $$$$
Latin American flavors and 3 great dining
spaces. Nice.

Map 31

Fort Greene / Clinton Hill

- **Dolores Deli Grocery** •
173 Park Ave [Adelphi St]
718-246-9707 • $
Dominican delicacies (roast pork, goat, etc.) for $3.50. Awesome.
- **Dough** • 305 Franklin Ave [Lafayette Ave]
347-533-7544 • $
The perfect coffee partner: amazing doughnuts!
- **Emily** • 919 Fulton St [Clinton Ave]
347-844-9588 • $$$
Delicious pizza, and, well, who cares about anything else?
- **Fancy Nancy** •
1038 Bedford Ave [Lafayette Ave]
347-350-7289 • $$$
Tater tots. And duck wings. And more tater tots.
- **The Finch** • 212 Greene Ave [Grand Ave]
718-218-4444 • $$$$
Absolutely delicious in a warm, romantic setting.
- **Five Spot Soul Food** •
459 Myrtle Ave [Washington Ave]
718-852-0202 • $$$
Hoppin' soul food joint w/ live entertainment.
- **The General Greene** •
229 Dekalb Ave [Clermont Ave]
718-222-1510 • $$
Two words: candied bacon.
- **Gentleman Farmer** •
378 Myrtle Ave [Clermont Ave]
929-295-0784 • $$$
Top French on Myrtle. Imported all the way from Manhattan.
- **Humo Smokehouse** •
336 Myrtle Ave [Carlton Ave]
347-689-9631 • $$$
Go for the pork belly. A rule for life, really.
- **Il Porto** • 37 Washington Ave [Flushing Ave]
718-624-2965 • $$
Cute Italian/pizzeria in front of the Navy Yard.
- **Locanda Vini & Olii** •
129 Gates Ave [Cambridge Pl]
718-622-9202 • $$$$$
Rustic but pricey neighborhood Italian. Marvelous decor.
- **Madiba** • 195 Dekalb Ave [Carlton Ave]
718-855-9190 • $$$
South African—Bunny Chow, need we say more? Shebeen with live music.

- **Marietta** • 285 Grand Ave [Lafayette Ave]
718-638-9500 • $$$$
Haute-Southern cuisine plus good cocktails.
- **Mekelburg's** • 293 Grand Ave [Clifton Pl]
718-399-2337 • $$$
Great craft beers and nice little bites to go along with 'em.
- **Mike's Coffee Shop** •
328 Dekalb Ave [St James Pl]
718-857-1462 • $
Classic diner option.
- **MOLOKO** • 705 Myrtle Ave [Walworth St]
718-596-3624 • $$$
Double cheeseburgers and oh, yeah, a root salad.
- **National** • 723 Fulton St [Fort Greene Pl]
718-522-3510 • $$
Best Thai in Fort Greene, easily.
- **No. 7** • 7 Greene Ave [Fulton St]
718-522-6370 • $$$
Hip killer postmodern goodness in Ft. Greene.
- **Olea** • 171 Lafayette Ave [Adelphi St]
718-643-7003 • $$
Friendly, buzzing neighborhood tapas/Mediterranean. Get the bronzino.
- **Prospect** • 773 Fulton St [S Oxford St]
718-596-6826 • $$$
Top-end goodness comes to Fulton Street.
- **Putnam's Pub & Cooker** •
419 Myrtle Ave [Clinton Ave]
347-799-2382 • $$$
Buzzing bar, oysters, burgers, mussels, two levels, outdoor seating…we love it.
- **Roman's** • 243 Dekalb Ave [Vanderbilt Ave]
718-622-5300 • $$$
Postmodern Italian buzzes in Fort Greene. Recommended.
- **Scopello** • 63 Lafayette Ave [S Elliott Pl]
718-852-1100 • $$
Sicilian chic in stylish surroundings. Get the octopus.
- **The Smoke Joint** •
87 S Elliot Pl [Lafayette Ave]
718-797-1011 • $$
Spend the $16 and get the short rib. Thank us later.

Hit either **Greene Grape Provisions** or **Choice Greene** for gourmet groceries to go with that nice bottle of wine from **Olivino**, **Gnarly Vines**, or **Thirst**. Pick up books at **Greenlight Books**, mid-century antiques at **Yu Interiors**, and everything else at **Target**. Watch for the occasional artsy bazaar outside of BAM.

- **Speedy Romeo** • 376 Classon Ave [Greene St]
718-230-0061 • $$
Bizzarro pizzas, good grilled meats, and a killer Caesar salad.
- **Tilda All Day** • 930 Fulton St [St James Pl]
718-622-4300 • $$
Food-forward cafe; graphically neat.
- **Umi Nom** • 433 Dekalb Ave [Classon Ave]
718-789-8806 • $$
Filipino heavy Asian fusion done right
- **Walter's** • 166 Dekalb Ave [Cumberland St]
718-488-7800 • $$
Hip oysters, meats, and fish steps from Ft. Greene Park.
- **Zaytoons** • 472 Myrtle Ave [Washington Ave]
718-623-5522 • $$
Above-average Middle Eastern's second outpost. Get the chicken.

🛍 Shopping

- **Atlantic Terminal Mall** •
Atlantic Ave & Flatbush Ave
718 834 3400
And then there's Target.
- **Bicycle Station** • 171 Park Ave [Adelphi St]
718-638-0300
Laid-back store convenient to points east and west.
- **Blick Art Materials** •
536 Myrtle Ave [Grand Ave]
718-789-0308
Cavernous art store servicing Pratt students & local artists.
- **Brooklyn Flea** •
176 Lafayette Ave [Clermont Ave]
Already-famous flea market with rotating vendors & killer food.
- **Choice Greene** • 214 Greene Ave [Grand Ave]
718-230-1243
Cheese, game, produce. The gentrification of Fort Greene is complete.
- **Gnarly Vines** • 350 Myrtle Ave [Carlton Ave]
718-797-3183
Cool Myrtle wine merchant.

- **Green in BKLYN** •
432 Myrtle Ave [Clinton Ave]
718-855-4383
One-stop shop to help you live an eco-friendly lifestyle.
- **The Greene Grape** •
765 Fulton St [S Oxford St]
718-797-9463
Ft. Greene wine nexus.
- **Greene Grape Provisions** •
753 Fulton St [S Portland Ave]
718-233-2700
Excellent gourmet meat-cheese-fish trifecta.
- **Greenlight Bookstore** •
686 Fulton St [S Portland Ave]
718-246-0200
Ft. Greene's newest and immediately best bookstore.
- **Hardware 2.0** • 860 Atlantic Ave [Clinton Ave]
347-663-4603
Best music in a hardware store you'll ever hear.
- **Malchijah Hats** •
942 Atlantic Ave [St James Pl]
718-643-3269
Beautiful and unique hats.
- **Olivino Wines** • 905 Fulton St [Clinton Ave]
718-857-7952
Micro-sized wine shop.
- **Out of the Closet** •
475 Atlantic Ave [Nevins St]
718-637-2955
Thrift shop with clothing, furniture, pharmacy, and free HIV testing.
- **Red Lantern Bicycles** •
345 Myrtle Ave [Adelphi St]
347-889-5338
Coffee shop, bicycle shop, a tad loud though.
- **Target** • 139 Flatbush Ave [Atlantic Ave]
718-290-1109
The everything store. Seriously.
- **Thirst Wine Merchants** •
187 Dekalb Ave [Carlton Ave]
718-596-7643
Brilliant wine and alcohol selection, plus bar.
- **Yu Interiors** • 15 Greene Ave [Cumberland St]
718-237-5878
Modern furniture, bags, and candles.

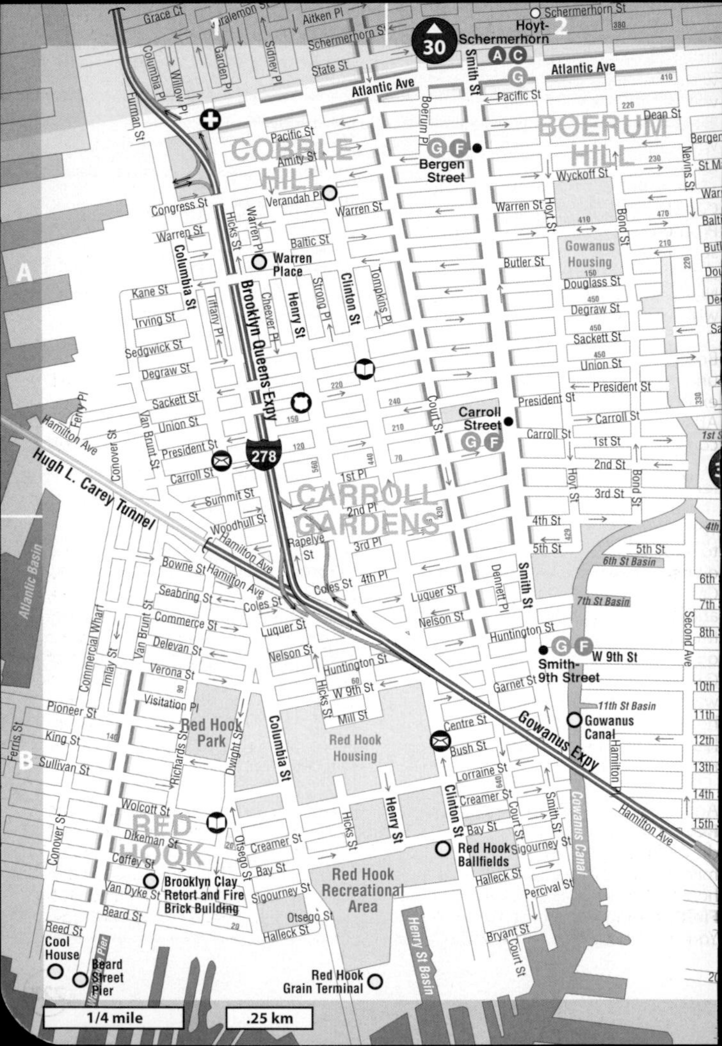

Map 32 • BoCoCa / Red Hook

Map 32 • BoCoCa / Red Hook

Grace Ct
Jeralemon St
Aitken Pl
Schermerhorn St
Schermerhorn St
Hoyt-Schermerhorn
State St
30
Atlantic Ave
A C
G
Atlantic Ave

COBBLE HILL
Pacific St
Amity St
Verandah Pl
Warren St
G F
Bergen Street
BOERUM HILL
Wyckoff St
Dean St

Congress St
Warren St
Warren St
Baltic St
Warren Place
Butler St
Gowanus Housing
Douglass St

Kane St
Irving St
Sedgwick St
Degraw St
Sackett St
Union St
President St

Henry St
Clinton St
Tompkins Pl
Strong Pl
Degraw St
Sackett St
Union St
President St
Carroll St

Brooklyn Queens Expy

CARROLL GARDENS
Summit St
Woodhull St
Hamilton Ave
Rapelye
278
Carroll Street
G F
1st St
2nd St
3rd St
4th St
5th St
6th St Basin

Hugh L. Carey Tunnel

Bowne St
Seabring St
Commerce St
Delavan St
Verona St
Coles St
Luquer St
Nelson St
Huntington St
W 9th St
Garnet St
7th St Basin

Smith-9th Street
G F
W 9th St

Atlantic Basin
Commercial Wharf
Pioneer St
King St
Sullivan St
Visitation Pl
Red Hook Park
Red Hook Housing
11th St Basin
Gowanus Canal
Centre St
Bush St
Lorraine St
Creamer St
13th St
14th St
15th St

RED HOOK
Conover St
Wolcott St
Dikeman St
Coffey St
Van Dyke St
Beard St
Brooklyn Clay Retort and Fire Brick Building
Creamer St
Bay St
Sigourney St
Halleck St
Red Hook Ballfields
Red Hook Recreational Area
Henry St Basin

Reed St
Cool House
Beard Street Pier
Halleck St
Otsego St
Red Hook Grain Terminal
Bryant St

1/4 mile   .25 km

Neighborhood Overview

Map 32

Sorry for the "BoCoCa" thing, but we just can't fit "Boerum Hill / Cobble Hill / Carroll Gardens" along with "Red Hook" on the header bar. Crusty oldtimers will say "I remember when this area was just called 'South Brooklyn.'" Well, Mr. Crusty Oldtimer, this is what happens when neighborhoods age, become economically stable, and are ravaged by hungry real estate agents.

Cobble Hill is like the bastard child of Brooklyn Heights—waterfront without the Promenade, nice-but-not-stunning brownstones, and slightly less convenient subway access. That said, Cobble Hill's dining, shopping, and nightlife are far and away superior to the Heights. Plus, it has one of the quaintest small parks in all of New York—if you've ever seen **Cobble Hill Park** right after a snowfall, you'll know what we're talking about.

Boerum Hill, immortalized in Jonathan Lethem's *The Fortress of Solitude*, has an unusual floor plan in that it's much wider east-west than north-south; Boerum Hill extends east all the way to 4th Avenue, and encompasses more retail along the Atlantic Avenue corridor, as well as Smith Street's northern half. Boerum Hill has come a long way, as evidenced by Smith Street's high commercial rents (say goodbye to porn video, furniture rental, and dollar stores) and the ongoing renovation of many brownstones.

The image of Carroll Gardens is of hard-working immigrant Italian families tending to wide brownstones with those unusual garden frontages. Now many of these owners are either condo-izing or selling outright to Manhattanites who flock to Carroll Gardens for its schools, amenities, a 20-minute subway ride to Manhattan, and huge retail options on lower Court and Smith Streets. There are still old-school Italian shops and eateries that hold their own against the influx of hip restaurants on lower Court Street and the design shops of Smith Street. Somewhere east of Carroll Gardens lies/flows the **Gowanus Canal**, the notorious gonorrhea-breeding waterway/polluted vestigial nightmare that is home to various and sundry household refuse and alleged mafia dumping ground. All that aside, things are looking up for this low-lying stretch of "South Brooklyn," what with new remediation technologies and even a Whole Foods on 3rd Avenue.

And then there's Red Hook. Isolated, peppered with derelict industrial sites (re: the **Red Hook Grain Terminal**), and lacking high-quality housing, Red Hook still draws folks to the other side of the BQE. Even with the closest subway stop over a mile away, **Fairway** and **IKEA** have chosen to make Red Hook their Brooklyn home. Elsewhere, the vibrant sports-and-food-stall scene at the **Red Hook Ball Fields** during summer is not to be missed, and did we mention the view of New York Bay from **Louis J Valentino Park**? It rocks.

30
31
32
33
Prospe

O Landmarks

- **Beard Street Pier** • Van Brunt St & Reed St
  Historic 19th century warehouses, now a cluster of shops and offices.
- **Brooklyn Clay Retort and Fire Brick Works** •
  76 Van Dyke St [Richards St]
  Red Hook's first official Landmark building dates to the mid-19th century.
- **Cobble Hill Park** • Clinton St & Verandah Pl
  One of the cutest parks in all of New York.
- **Cool House** • 26 Reed St [Van Brunt St]
  One of the coolest single-family dwellings in the city.
- **Gowanus Canal** • Smith St & 9th St
  Brooklyn's answer to the Seine.
- **Louis Valentino Jr Park and Pier** •
  Coffey St & Ferris St
  Escape gentrification-industrial complex with perfect view Statue of Liberty.
- **Red Hook Ball Fields** • Clinton St & Bay St
  Watch futbol and eat Central American street food every Saturday from spring through fall.
- **Red Hook Grain Terminal** •
  Columbia St & Halleck St
  Visit this abandoned grain elevator just to wonder what it's doing there.
- **Warren Place** • Warren Pl [Warren St]
  Public housing from the 1870s.

Coffee

- **The Black Flamingo** •
  168 Borinquen Pl
  Hippest spot in the 'hook for java.
- **Black Gold** • 461 Court St [Luquer St]
  347-227-8227
  Coffee, records, antiques, baked goods. All they're missing is cheese.
- **Blue Bottle Coffee** • 85 Dean St [Smith St]
  Bay Area masters with the long lines for pour overs.
- **D'Amico Foods** • 309 Court St [Degraw St]
  718-875-5403
  The neighborhood spot for fresh beans.
- **Henry's Local** • 570 Henry St [1st Pl]
  718-522-3508
  Very chill, quiet cafe with baked goods.
- **Konditori** • 114 Smith St [Pacific St]
  347-721-3738
  Cozy/packed mini-chain of Swedish coffeehouses.
- **Momofuku Milk Bar** • 360 Smith St [2nd Pl]
  347-577-9504
  Coffee and a bunch of other weird stuff.

O Farmers Markets

- **Carroll Gardens** • Smith St & Carroll St
  Sunday, 8 am–3 pm, year-round.

BoCoCa / Red Hook

Each of the 'nabes here have their stalwarts. In Boerum Hill, it's classic **Brooklyn Inn** or the jukebox at **The Boat**. Cobble Hill has several good places on Atlantic (**Floyd**, **Montero's**, **Last Exit**), or stick with old-tyme cocktails at **Henry Public**. In Carroll Gardens, it's **Gowanus Yacht Club** in summer and **Brooklyn Social** in winter, and in Red Hook, **Bait and Tackle** and **Fort Defiance** compete with classic dive **Sunny's**.

Nightlife

- **61 Local** • 61 Bergen St [Smith St]
  718-875-1150
  Spacious bar with a wide, local craft beer selection.
- **Abilene** • 442 Court St [3rd Pl]
  718-522-6900
  Cozy and unpretentious. Drink specials galore.
- **Bar Great Harry** • 280 Smith St [Sackett St]
  718-222-1103
  There's a blog devoted to the draft beer section.
- **Black Mountain Wine House** •
  415 Union St [Hoyt St]
  718-522-4340
  Try the Lebanese wine!
- **Boat Bar** • 175 Smith St [Wyckoff St]
  718-254-0607
  Dank, dark, and friendly. Nice tunes to boot.
- **Botanica** • 220 Conover St [Coffey St]
  347-225-0148
  Classy looking joint.
- **The Brazen Head** • 228 Atlantic Ave [Court St]
  718-488-0430
  Cask ale, mixed crowd
- **The Brooklyn Inn** • 148 Hoyt St [Bergen St]
  718-522-2525
  When you're feeling nostalgic.
- **Brooklyn Social** • 335 Smith St [Carroll St]
  718-858-7758
  Old boy's lounge revamped. Cocktails still the same. NFT Pick.
- **Building on Bond** • 112 Bond St [Pacific St]
  347-853-8687
  Coffee by day, alcohol by night. Perfect.
- **Clover Club** • 210 Smith St [Baltic St]
  718-855-7939
  Charming den of cocktails and conversation.
- **Cody's American Bar & Grill** •
  154 Court St [Dean St]
  718-852-6115
  Great sports bar. Seriously.
- **Floyd** • 131 Atlantic Ave [Henry St]
  718-858-5810
  Indoor bocce ball court!
- **Fort Defiance** • 365 Van Brunt St [Dikeman St]
  347-453-6672
  Great cocktails, great beer, great pork chop.

- **Gowanus Yacht Club** •
  323 Smith St [President St]
  718-246-1321
  Dogs, burgers, and beer. Love it.
- **Henry Public** • 329 Henry St [Atlantic Ave]
  718-852-8630
  From thou that brought us Brooklyn Social.
- **Hollow Nickel** • 494 Atlantic Ave [Nevins St]
  347-236-3417
  Fried pickles, BLTs, and burgers for the Barclays crowd.
- **home/made** • 293 Van Brunt St [Pioneer St]
  347-223-4135
  Wine-soaked and king on the Red Hook waterfront.
- **Jalopy Tavern** •
  315 Columbia St [Hamilton Ave]
  718-395-3214
  Live music from rockabilly to out jazz; banjos in the window.
- **Last Exit** • 136 Atlantic Ave [Henry St]
  718-222-9198
  Still trying to win trivia night. $10 pails of PBR.
- **Montero's Bar and Grill** •
  73 Atlantic Ave [Hicks St]
  718-624-9799
  A taste of what things used to be like.
- **Other Half Brewing** •
  195 Centre St [Hamilton Ave]
  347-987-3527
  Elegant/bold brews sold in cans or from tasting room
- **Rocky Sullivan's** • 34 Van Dyke St [Dwight St]
  718-246-8050
  The Sixpoint portfolio is on tap—a Red Hook must.
- **Roebling Inn** • 97 Atlantic Ave [Hicks St]
  718-488-0040
  Good vibe at this sister tavern of the Brooklyn Inn.
- **Sunny's** • 253 Conover St [Reed St]
  718-625-8211
  No longer pay-what-you-wish, but still cheap and good.

30 31 32 33

Prospe

Map 32

Map 32

30 31
32
33
Prospect

BoCoCa / Red Hook

🍴Restaurants

- **Alma** • 187 Columbia St [Degraw St]
718-643-5400 • $$$
Top NYC Mexican with great views of lower
Manhattan.
- **Atlantic Chip Shop** •
129 Atlantic Ave [Henry St]
718-855-7775 • $$
Heart attack on a plate.
- **Avlee** • 349 Smith St [Carroll St]
718-855-5125 • $$$
Good Greek that you don't have to schlep to
Astoria for.
- **Bacchus** • 409 Atlantic Ave [Bond St]
718-852-1572 • $$$
Low key neighborhood Frenchy bistro.
- **Bar Bruno** • 520 Henry St [Union St]
347-763-0850 • $$$
Mexican gastropub just off the main drag in
Carroll Gardens.
- **Bar Tabac** • 128 Smith St [Dean St]
718-923-0918 • $$$
Open late; fabulous frites, burgers, et al.
- **Battersby** • 255 Smith St [Degraw St]
718-852-8321 • $$$$$
Upscale joint in tiny space. Let us know if you
get in.
- **Bedouin Tent** • 405 Atlantic Ave [Bond St]
718-852-5555 • $
Two words: lamb sandwich. No, four: best
lamb sandwich ever.
- **Brooklyn Crab** • 24 Reed St [Van Brunt St]
718-643-2722 • $$$$
3 floors of delish seafood with a view of New
York Bay. We love it, except for weekends.
- **Brooklyn Farmacy & Soda Fountain** •
513 Henry St [Sackett St]
718-522-6260 • $
A blast from the past. Homemade sodas and
shakes.

- **Buddy's Burrito & Taco Bar** •
260 Court St [Baltic St]
718-488-8695 • $
Fast, cheap, and out-of-control huge burritos.
- **Buttermilk Channel** •
524 Court St [Huntington St]
718-852-8490 • $$$
Oysters, sausages, fried chicken, waffles,
burgers, ahhh.
- **Café Luluc** • 214 Smith St [Butler St]
718-625-3815 • $$$
Friendly French bistro.
- **Carroll Gardens Classic Diner** •
155 Smith St [Bergen St]
718-403-9940 • $$
Good diner food with 24-hour delivery—
Crucial for survival.
- **Chance** • 223 Smith St [Butler St]
718-242-1515 • $$$$
Upscale Asian fusion—recommended.
- **Char No. 4** • 196 Smith St [Baltic St]
718-643-2106 • $$
Worship (and eat) at this temple of whisky
and bourbon.
- **Chocolate Room** • 269 Court St [Douglass St]
718-246-2600 • $
Guess what's here?
- **Court Street Grocers** •
485 Court St [Nelson St]
718-722-7229 • $$
Killer breakfast sandwiches and yes! Taylor
Pork Roll.
- **DeFonte's Sandwich Shop** •
379 Columbia St [Luquer St]
718-625-8052 • $
Crazy-ass Italian hero shop.
- **Dosa Royale** • 316 Court St [Degraw St]
718-576-3800 • $$
Servicable dosa joint satisfies the craving.

BoCoCa / Red Hook

Map 32

There's more good food here than in some entire states, trust us, from Michelin-noted **Ki Sushi**, **Saul**, and **The Grocery** to brick-oven goodness at **Lucali** (we're still waiting for a table), loud Thai at **Joya**, fried chicken at **Buttermilk Channel**, seasonal Italian at **Frankies 457**, Central European comfort food at **Karloff**, Middle Eastern haven **Bedouin Tent**, late-night French at **Bar Tabac**, or rooftop Mexican at **Alma**.

- **Dover** • 412 Court St [1st Pl]
347-987-3545 • $$$$
Top-end dining from the Battersby folks.
- **Fatoosh** • 330 Hicks St [Atlantic Ave]
718-243-0500 • $
Nicely priced Middle Eastern Food.
- **Ferdinando's Focacceria** •
151 Union St [Hicks St]
718-855-1545 • $
Sicilian specialties you won't find anywhere else! Get the panelle special.
- **Fragole Ristorante** • 394 Court St [Carroll St]
718-522-7133 • $$
Fresh and cozy Italian. An absolute gem.
- **Frankie's 457** • 457 Court St [Luquer St]
718 403-0033 • $$
Fantastic meatballs. Cool space. Killer brunch.
- **French Louie** • 320 Atlantic Ave [Smith St]
718-935-1200 • $$$
Friendly French on Atlantic. More is better.
- **The Good Fork** • 391 Van Brunt St [Coffey St]
718-643 6636 • $$$
Yep. It's good. VERY good.
- **The Grocery** • 288 Smith St [Sackett St]
718-596-3335 • $$$$
Magnificent. Reservations recommended.
- **Hanco's** • 135 Smith St [Dean St]
718 858 6010 • $
Bánh mì for people who won't trek to Sunset Park.
- **Hibino** • 333 Henry St [Pacific St]
718-260 8052 • $$
Highly regarded Cobble Hill sushi.
- **Hometown Bar-B-Que** •
454 Van Brunt St [Reed St]
347-294-4644 • $$
Grab some 'cue while the significant other shops for groceries at Fairway.
- **Joya Thai** • 215 Court St [Warren St]
718-222-3484 • $$
Excellent, inexpensive, but super-noisy Thai.
- **Karloff** • 254 Court St [Kane St]
347-689-4279 • $$
Eastern European classics, won't bust your gut, plus ice cream!

- **Kevin's** • 277 Van Brunt St [Visitation Pl]
718-596-8335 • $$
Eggs Chesapeake. Mmmm
- **Ki Sushi** • 122 Smith St [Dean St]
718-935-0575 • $$
Affordable sushi in sleek surroundings; Michelin starred.
- **La Cigogne** • 213 Union St [Henry St]
718-858-5641 • $$$
Stylish Alsatian food on Union.
- **Layla Jones** • 214 Court St [Warren St]
718-624-2361 • $
The best pizza delivery in the hood.
- **Le Petit Café** • 502 Court St [Nelson St]
718-596-7060 • $$
Good bistro food—check out the garden.
- **Libertador** • 400 Henry St [Baltic St]
347 689-3122 • $$$
Mixed grill for two and call us in the morning.
- **Lucali** • 575 Henry St [Carroll St]
718 858-4086 • $$
One man makes every perfect pizza by hand. Be prepared to wait.
- **Mazzat** • 208 Columbia St [Sackett St]
718-852-1652 • $$
Donut-style falafel will make you a believer.
- **Mile End** • 97 Hoyt St [Atlantic Ave]
718-852-7510 • $$
Jewish deli, Montreal-style. Two words: smoked meat.
- **Monte's** • 451 Carroll St [3rd Ave]
718-852-7800 • $$$
Pizza and pasta since 1906, updated for the new millennium.
- **Petite Crevette** • 144 Union St [Hicks St]
718-855-2632 • $$$
Tucked-away French hard by the BQE.
- **Pizza Moto** • 338 Hamilton Ave [Clinton St]
718-834-6686 • $$$
Artisanal pizza made in a 100-year-old-plus oven.

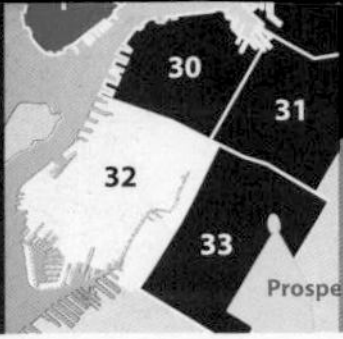

Map 32

BoCoCa / Red Hook

30
31
32
33
Prospe

- **Pok Pok NY** • 117 Columbia St [Kane St]
718-923-9322 • $$$
Killer Thai with spicy wings straight from the
Godhead.
- **Prime Meats** • 465 Court St [Luquer St]
718-254-0327 • $$$
German delights like wurst and sauerbraten
take center stage.
- **Rucola** • 190 Dean St [Bond St]
718-576-3209 • $$$
Rustic neighborhood Northern Italian. Just a
great vibe.
- **Saul** • 200 Eastern Pkwy [Washington Ave]
718-935-9844 • $$$
Romantical and delicioso.
- **Sottocasa Pizzeria** •
298 Atlantic Ave [Smith St]
718-852-8758 • $
Top pizza on Atlantic, with great Italian beer
selection.
- **Tripoli** • 156 Atlantic Ave [Clinton St]
718-596-5800 • $$
A Lebanese standby since 1973 is great for a
party, with meze platters and BYOB.
- **Uglyduckling** • 166 Smith St [Wyckoff St]
718-451-3825 • $$
Chicken 'n waffles, burgers, brunch, and lots
of taps.
- **Yemen Café** • 176 Atlantic Ave [Clinton St]
718-834-9533 • $
More good Yemeni food, because you can
never have too much lamb.
- **Yemen Cuisine** • 145 Court St [Atlantic Ave]
718-624-9325 • $$
Don't let the decor (or lack thereof) keep you
out, go and eat amazing lamb.
- **Zaytoons** • 283 Smith St [Sackett St]
718-875-1880 • $$
Excellent Middle Eastern pizzas and kebabs.

🛍 Shopping

- **Article&** • 198 Smith St [Baltic St]
718-852-3620
Designer duds and accessories. Who needs
the LES?
- **Baked** • 359 Van Brunt St [Dikeman St]
718-222-0345
Death by dessert.
- **Bien Cuit** • 120 Smith St [Pacific St]
718-852-0200
Stand-out breads and pastries.
- **BookCourt** • 163 Court St [Dean St]
718-875-3677
Classic Cobble Hill bookstore w/ great
readings, selection, etc.
- **Botanica El Phoenix** •
224 Columbia St [Union St]
718-422-0300
Santeria accessories, religious candles, icons,
books.
- **By Brooklyn** • 261 Smith St [Degraw St]
718-643-0606
Dedicated to stuff made in the borough of
Kings.
- **Caputo's Fine Foods** • 460 Court St [3rd Pl]
718-855-8852
Italian gourmet specialties. The real deal.
- **City Foundry** • 365 Atlantic Ave [Hoyt St]
718-923-1786
If you can afford it your place will be in a
magazine.
- **Clayworks on Columbia** •
195 Columbia St [Degraw St]
718-694-9540
Unique, practical pottery and classes for all
levels.

BoCoCa / Red Hook

Map 32

You can find anything on Atlantic, Smith, or Court Streets, especially food: **Sahadi's, Staubitz, D'Amico's, Caputo's, Fish Tales, Smith & Vine,** and **Stinky** are all great. Treat yourself at **Swallow** or **Article &. Clayworks on Columbia**'s housewares are made by local artists. **GRDN** has lush plants, **Idlewild Books** is the spot for travel books, and all manner of kitchenware can be found at **A Cook's Companion.**

• **D'Amico Foods** • 309 Court St [Degraw St]
718-875-5403
The best coffee in the 'hood, if not the city.

• **Erie Basin** • 388 Van Brunt St [Dikeman St]
718-554-6147
Jewelry and stuff from the 19th and early 20th century.

• **Eva Gentry Consignment** •
371 Atlantic Ave [Hoyt St]
718-522-3522
Fashionista consignment emporium.

• **Exit 9** • 127 Smith St [Dean St]
718-422-7720
Quirky gifts

• **Fairway** • 480 Van Brunt St [Reed St]
718-694-6868
Best grocery store in Brooklyn. By far.

• **Fish Tales** • 191 Court St [Wyckoff St]
718-246-1346
The place for expensive, but fresh, fish.

• **G. Esposito & Sons** •
357 Court St [President St]
718-875-6863
Sopressata and sausages direct from the Godhead.

• **Gowanus Nursery** • 9 Carroll St [Van Brunt St]
718-852-3116
Make your garden happen in a not-so-green 'hood.

• **GRDN** • 103 Hoyt St [Pacific St]
718-797-3628
Great store...if you're lucky enough to have a garden.

• **Hard Soul Boutique** •
418 Atlantic Ave [Bond St]
718-625-2838
Fierce jewelry, recording studio founded by Strafe ("Set It Off").

• **Heights Chateau Wines** •
123 Atlantic Ave [Henry St]
718-330-0963
Consistently good store straddling Brooklyn Heights & Cobble Hill.

• **Idlewild Books** • 249 Warren St [Court St]
718-403-9600
Extensive foreign language offerings and language classes.

• **IKEA** • 1 Beard St [Otsego St]
718 246-4532
Everything you need for your 312-sq ft apt.

• **Malko Karkanni Bros.** •
174 Atlantic Ave [Clinton St]
718-834-0845
Cashew Baklava makes you believe again.

• **Mazzola Bakery** • 192 Union St [Henry St]
718 643 1719
Top bakery in CG. Get the lard bread.

• **One Girl Cookies** • 68 Dean St [Smith St]
212-675-4996
Custom cookies in Cobble Hill.

• **Red Hook Lobster Pound** •
284 Van Brunt St [Visitation Pl]
718-858-7650
Mmmmm...fresh gorgeous lobsters.

• **Sahadi's** • 187 Atlantic Ave [Court St]
718-624-4550
Totally brilliant Middle Eastern supermarket—olives, cheese, bread, etc.

• **Smith & Vine** • 268 Smith St [Douglass St]
718 243 2864
If NFT owned a liquor store, this would be it.

• **Staubitz Market** • 222 Court St [Baltic St]
718 624 0014
Top NYC butcher.

• **Stinky** • 215 Smith St [Butler St]
718-596-2873
I get it! It's a cheese store!

• **Swallow** • 361 Smith St [2nd St]
718-222-8201
An exquisite selection of glass, jewelry, and books.

• **Trader Joe's** • 130 Court St [Court St]
718-246-8460
The line moves pretty fast, really.

Neighborhood Overview

Map 33

Park Slope is an easy target. Power moms use their strollers as battering rams, stylish dads use the hippest bars and bistros as daycare centers, and the children, *the children*, they are born into this vicious cycle. But you know what? The Slope isn't just a haven for wealthy breeders and toiling serfs at the **Park Slope Food Co-op**. It's also got some amazing restaurants and shops, incredible brownstones, and the only park in the city that truly rivals Central Park.

The park they're referring to at the top of the slope is **Prospect Park**, Frederick Law Olmsted and Calvert Vaux's Brooklyn masterpiece. The ultimate design was executed piecemeal in the 1860s and 1870s, delayed in part by the Civil War. People, not all of whom from Brooklyn, claim that Prospect Park was the quintessence of Olmsted and Vaux park design, eclipsing a certain little vestpocket nicety that stretches for 50-some-odd blocks in the middle of Manhattan island. Whatever the one upmanship, the man-made landscape is a pretty nice amenity to have in your backyard. Its charms include its historic bridges and walks, the largest swath of forest in the borough, remarkable summer concerts, a zoo, and last but certainly not least, the rare opportunity to grill in a city park. The Beaux-Arts arch and neoclassical columns around **Grand Army Plaza** were added toward the end of the 19th century. Across from Grand Army Plaza is the fantastic main branch of the **Brooklyn Public Library**.

Park Slope is nineteenth-century brownstone architecture at its best. The rows of houses all have distinct touches on their stoops and facades; idyllic and photo ready. It seems every other block has a soaring limestone church, lending skyline of regal steeples. But that brings us to the modern side: The number of cool shops, restaurants, and bars on 5th Avenue, 7th Avenue, and Flatbush Avenue is simply astounding. (If you look at these three streets on a map, it forms Pi, which clearly means something.) There is so much retail on these streets that you'd think there wouldn't be room for any more, but the action has spread to 4th Avenue and now even 3rd Avenue, near the appalling **Gowanus Canal**, now an EPA Superfund site thanks to decades of factory sediment, coal-tar, heavy metals, paint, sewage, and waste-fed algae.

And the wave of development is expanding ever outward. The world-class **Barclays Center** arena is just the first phase of the fledgling and controversial redevelopment set to take place above the train tracks of the Atlantic Yards. Sports arenas aside, Vanderbilt and Washington Avenues in Prospect Heights have been bustling commercial strips for years now. And with its many lovely and relatively rare three-story brownstones, we expect at least four kids in every Prospect Heights brownstone by the end of the next decade. Meanwhile, on the southeastern end of the Slope is Windsor Terrace, a longtime Irish enclave scrunched between Prospect Park and the Prospect Expressway that has attracted a new wave of young renters who can't afford the Slope but still enjoy prime park access and a mini-retail strip along Prospect Park West. Now if they could only reroute those infernal aviation machines flying into La Guardia to, uh, somewhere else, we could actually enjoy a backyard barbecue once in a while.

O Landmarks

• **Bailey Fountain** •
Grand Army Plaza [Flatbush Ave]
With sculpted figures of Neptune, Triton and
attendants (some said to represent Wisdom
and Felicity), the power eminating from this
fountain could supply the Justice League.

• **Barclays Center** •
620 Atlantic Ave [Flatbush Ave]
917-618-6700
World-class arena in the heart of Brooklyn.

• **Brooklyn Museum** •
200 Eastern Pkwy [Washington Ave]
718-638-5000
Breathtakingly beautiful building, excellent
collection.

• **Brooklyn Public Library** •
10 Grand Army Plaza [Grand Ave]
718-230-2100
Fabulous Art Deco temple to knowledge.

• **The Co-Cathedral of St. Joseph** •
856 Pacific St [Underhill Ave]
718-638-1071
Check out this stunning just-renovated interior
of this 1912 cathedral. Wow.

• **Grand Army Plaza** • Flatbush Ave & Plaza St
Site of John H. Duncan's Soldiers' and Sailors'
Memorial Arch.

• **New York Puppet Library** •
Grand Army Plaza [Soliders and Sailors Arch]
The Memorial Arch at Grand Army Plaza has a
funky theatre at the top. A must-see (Summer
Saturdays only).

• **Park Slope Food Co-op** •
782 Union St [7th Ave]
718-622-0560
These farm-fresh veggies will do for those in
search of their peck of dirt. Rinse.

• **Prospect Park** •
Prospect Park W & Flatbush Ave
718-965-8951
Olmsted & Vaux's true masterpiece.

Coffee

• **Café Grumpy** • 383 7th Ave [12th St]
718-499-4404
Gourmet java comes to strollerland.

• **Cafe Martin** • 355 5th Ave [4th St]
347-261-6836
Necessary pit stop in the center 'Slope for java.

• **Café Regular** • 318 11th St [5th Ave]
718-768-4170
Café with exceptional aesthetics.

• **Café Regular du Nord** •
158 Berkeley Pl [7th Ave]
718-783-0673
Almost more lifestyle than café.

• **Colson Patisserie** • 374 9th St [6th Ave]
718-965-6400
French pastries and fancy lunches.

• **Crop to Cup** • 541 3rd Ave [14th St]
347-599-0053
Good Gowanus spot w/ outdoor space.

• **Elk Cafe** •
154 Prospect Park Southwest [Vanderbilt St]
718-853-5500
Perfect spot for coffee across from Prospect
Park.

• **Gorilla Coffee** • 97 5th Ave [Park Pl]
718-230-3244
Milk, two sugars, and a shot of hipness.

• **Gorilla Coffee** • 472 Bergen St [Flatbush Ave]
Works directly with in-country producers.

• **Hungry Ghost** • 253 Flatbush Ave [6th Ave]
718-483-8666
Perfect coffee and a few fun noshes.

• **Joyce Bakeshop** • 646 Vanderbilt Ave [Park Pl]
718-623-7470
Prospect Heights goodness.

• **Konditori** • 186 5th Ave [Berkeley Pl]
347-384-2028
Cozy/packed mini-chain of Swedish
coffeehouses.

Gourmet cocktails and beers have been sprouting up everywhere at spots like **Union Hall**, or support your local dive at **Freddy's**. Since the untimely demise of Southpaw, **The Bell House** is the place for rock shows and other events (Moth StorySlams!), but **Barbes** has a fabulous mix of world music jammed into its tiny back room space.

- **Konditori** •
696 Washington Ave [St Marks Ave]
347-689-8471
Specialized "Konditori" roasting process and Swedish treats.
- **Kos Kaffe** • 251 5th Ave [Garfield Pl]
718-768-6868
Bright white space with good salads, too.
- **Lincoln Station** •
409 Lincoln Pl [Washington Ave]
718-399-2211
Coffee, sandwiches, and, most importantly, fried chicken.
- **Penny House Cafe** •
732 Washington Ave [Prospect Pl]
347-240-7281
Yet another great option for coffee on Washington
- **Postmark Café** • 326 6th St [5th Ave]
718-768-2613
Cozy coffee shop w/ chess, too!
- **Root Hill Cafe** • 262 4th Ave [Carroll St]
718-797-0100
A bit of calm on traffic-choked 4th Ave.
- **Sit & Wonder** •
688 Washington Ave [St Marks Ave]
718-622-0299
Good hangover sandwiches and Stumptown Coffee.

🎶 Farmers Markets

- **Bartel-Pritchard Square Greenmarket** •
Prospect Park W & 15th St
Wednesday, 8 a.m.–3 p.m., May–Nov.
- **Grand Army Plaza Greenmarket** •
Flatbush Ave & Eastern Pkwy
Saturday, 8 am–4 pm, year-round.
- **Park Slope Farmers Market** • 5th Ave & 4th St
Sunday, 11 am.–5 pm, year-round.
- **Windsor Terrace – PS 154 Greenmarket** •
Prospect Park W & 16th St
Sunday, 9 am–3 pm., May–Dec.

🍸 Nightlife

- **4th Avenue Pub** • 76 4th Ave [Bergen St]
718 643-2273
1. Toss darts. 2. Drink fine draft beer. 3. Repeat
- **Bar Reis** • 375 5th Ave [6th St]
718-207-7874
Disarmingly charming when you sit on the terrace.
- **Bar Sepia** • 234 Underhill Ave [Lincoln Pl]
718-399-6680
Neighborhood fave.
- **Bar Toto** • 411 11th St [6th Ave]
718-768-4698
Great bar food.
- **Barbes** • 376 9th St [6th Ave]
347-422-0248
Smart-looking space with eclectic entertainment. Recommended.
- **The Bell House** • 149 7th St [3rd Ave]
718-643-6510
Huge Gowanus live music venue + front bar; stellar.
- **Black Horse Pub** • 568 5th Ave [16th St]
718-788-1975
Where to watch footy.
- **Brookvin** • 381 7th Ave [12th St]
718-768-9463
Wine. Cheese. Ambience.
- **Buttermilk Bar** • 577 5th Ave [16th St]
718 788-6297
A solid more-than dive.
- **Canal Bar** • 270 3rd Ave [President St]
718-246-0011
Dive near the Gowanus, but not into it.
- **Cherry Tree Bar** • 65 4th Ave [Bergen St]
718-399-1353
Rowdy Irish pub with a stately backyard.
- **Commonwealth** • 497 5th Ave [12th St]
718-768-2040
So many beers, so little time.
- **Double Windsor** •
210 Prospect Park West [16th St]
347 725-3479
Good food. Great beer.
- **Excelsior** • 390 5th Ave [6th St]
718-832-1599
Decent bar with mixed gay crowd.
- **Farrell's** • 215 Prospect Park West [16th St]
718-788-8779
No frills neighborhood bar with styrofoam cups.

Map 33

Park Slope/Prospect Heights/Windsor Terrace

- **Freddy's Bar and Backroom** •
627 5th Ave [18th St]
718-768-0131
It lives again! And with great avant-jazz bookings, too.
- **The Gate** • 321 5th Ave [3rd St]
718-768-4329
Large outdoor area. Twenty beers on tap.
- **Ginger's** • 363 5th Ave [5th St]
718-788-0924
Nice and casual for center Slope.
- **Hank's Saloon** • 46 3rd Ave [Atlantic Ave]
347-227-8495
Sweaty, hillbilly-esque.
- **littlefield** • 622 Degraw St [4th Ave]
718-855-3388
Eco-friendly performance space: music, film, art. Sweet.
- **Loki Lounge** • 304 5th Ave [2nd St]
718-965-9600
Darts and billiards tone down the classic wood bar. Good music.
- **Lucky 13 Saloon** • 644 Sackett St
718-596-0666
Park Slope's only punk/metal dive bar.
- **Pacific Standard** • 82 4th Ave [St Marks Pl]
718-858-1951
Drinking and board games most certainly mix.
- **Park Slope Ale House** • 356 6th Ave [5th St]
718-788-1756
Good pub grub and beer selection.
- **The Sackett** • 661 Sackett St [4th Ave]
718-622-0437
Hidden on a side street. Cozy spot for a cocktail.

- **Soda Bar** • 629 Vanderbilt Ave [Prospect Pl]
718-230-8393
Nice summer drinkin' spot. NFT pick.
- **Tooker Alley** •
793 Washington Ave [Lincoln Pl]
347-955-4743
Good cocktail spot.
- **Union Hall** • 702 Union St [5th Ave]
718-638-4400
Quirky spot for indie shows and stuffed birds.
- **The Vanderbilt** •
570 Vanderbilt Ave [Bergen St]
718-623-0570
Specialty cocktails with free open-kitchen entertainment.
- **Washington Commons** •
748 Washington Ave [Park Pl]
718-230-3666
Rotating beer selection, late happy hour, and a great outdoor space.
- **The Way Station** •
683 Washington Ave [Prospect Pl]
347-627-4949
Steampunk bar with Doctor Who's TARDIS and screenings. Lovin' babe.
- **Weather Up** • 589 Vanderbilt Ave [Dean St]
Pricey cocktails are justified by very cool ambience.
- **Wolf & Deer** • 74 5th Ave [St Marks Ave]
718-398-3181
Wine bar and small plates pre-Barclays.
- **Woodwork** • 583 Vanderbilt Ave [Dean St]
718-857-5777
Brooklyn's World Cup headquarters.

Where to begin? There's the Italian at **Al Di La**, slow-food at **Applewood**, Portuguese/Italian at **Convivium Osteria**, and killer pizza at **Franny's**. Branch out with Colombian at **Bogota**, Ethiopian at **Ghenet**, and Australian at **Sheep Station**. Then there are the classic diners **Tom's** and **The Usual**, the creative seasonal at **Rose Water**, and of course **Blue Ribbon**.

🍴 Restaurants

12th Street Bar and Grill •
1123 8th Ave [11th St]
718-965-9526 • $$$
Great New American, burgers, beers, brunch...
we can't say enough.

7th Avenue Donuts • 324 7th Ave [9th St]
718-768-3410 • $
Dirt-cheap dinery goodness.

al di la Trattoria • 248 5th Ave [Carroll St]
718-783-4565 • $$$
Chandelier & brick-walled Italian. Super.

Alchemy • 56 5th Ave [Bergen St]
718-636-4385 • $$$
Slick pub grub near Barclays Center. Check
it out.

Amorina • 624 Vanderbilt Ave [Prospect Pl]
718-230-3030 • $$$
Watch your perfect pizza get made with sea
salt and love.

Applewood • 501 11th St [7th Ave]
718-788-1810 • $$$
Elegant, cheerful slow food.

Beet Thai II • 344 7th Ave [10th St]
718-832-2338 • $$$
Romantic ambiance for sumptuous Thai.

Bella Gioia • 209 4th Ave [Union St]
347-223-4176 • $$$
Sicilian small plates and a good brunch.

Blue Ribbon Brooklyn • 280 5th Ave [1st St]
718-840-0404 • $$$$
Brooklyn outpost of brilliant late-night
Manhattan eatery.

Bogota Latin Bistro •
141 5th Ave [St Johns Pl]
718-230-3805 • $$$
Stylish South- and Central-American
restaurant.

Bonnie's Grill • 278 5th Ave [1st St]
718-369-9527 • $$
Habit-forming contemporary diner.

Bricolage • 162 5th Ave [Degraw St]
718-230-1835 • $$$
Buzzy Vietnamese with delish crispy rolls.

Café Steinhof • 422 7th Ave [14th St]
718-369-7776 • $$
Austrian comfort food at this South Slope
mainstay.

Carnem Prime Steakhouse •
318 5th Ave [3rd St]
718-499-5600 • $$$
Steaks, mussels, octopus, burgers—all good.

Cheryl's Global Soul •
236 Underhill Ave [Lincoln Pl]
347-529-2855 • $$
Modern, international menu emphasizing
comfort.

The Chocolate Room • 82 5th Ave [Warren St]
718-783-2900 • $
Chocolate-infused desserts in an inviting
location.

Coco Roco • 392 5th Ave [6th St]
718-965-3376 • $$
Inexpensive Peruvian.

Convivium Osteria • 68 5th Ave [St Marks Pl]
718-857-1833 • $$$$
Delicious Italian with a Portugese influence.
Rustic, warm setting.

Cooklyn • 659 Vanderbilt Ave [Park Pl]
347-915-0721 • $$$
Duck spaghetti and octopus on Vanderbilt.
Nice one.

Cousin John's Café and Bakery •
70 7th Ave [Lincoln Pl]
718-622-7333 • $
Casual breakfast and lunch.

Dinosaur Bar-B-Que • 604 Union St [4th Ave]
347-429-7030 • $$$
Syracuse BBQ empire.

Elora's • 272 Prospect Park West [17th St]
718-788-6190 • $$
Spanish, Mexican, and margaritas, oh my!

Flatbush Farm • 76 St Marks Ave [6th Ave]
718-622-3276 • $$
Local, seasonal, and delish.

Fletcher's Brooklyn Barbecue •
433 3rd Ave [7th St]
347-763-2680 • $$$
Fair-trade high-concept barbecue.

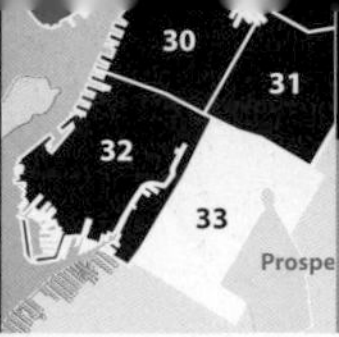

Map 33

Park Slope/Prospect Heights/Windsor Terrace

- **Fonda** • 434 7th Ave [14th St]
  718-369-3144 • $$$
  Neighborhood Mexican beloved by all.
- **Four & Twenty Blackbirds** •
  439 3rd Ave [8th St]
  718-499 2917 • $$
  Seasonal pies (and other treats) baked fresh daily. Delicious goodness!
- **Franny's** • 348 Flatbush Ave [Sterling Pl]
  718-230-0221 • $$
  Brilliant pizza, drop-dead fresh, NFT fave.
- **Geido** • 331 Flatbush Ave [7th Ave]
  718-638-8866 • $
  Get stuffed to the gills.
- **Gen Restaurant** •
  659 Washington Ave [St Marks Ave]
  718-398-3550 • $$$
  Delicious, fresh Japanese cuisine and laid-back service.
- **Ghenet Brooklyn** • 348 Douglass St [4th Ave]
  718-230-4475 • $$
  Top NYC Ethiopian, hands-down.
- **Hanco's** • 350 7th Ave [10th St]
  718-499-8081 • $
  Banh mi and bubble tea hotspot.
- **The Islands** • 803 Washington Ave [Lincoln Pl]
  718-398-3575 • $$
  Tasty Caribbean; get the jerk chicken.
- **James** • 605 Carlton Ave [St. Marks Ave]
  718-942-4255 • $$
  Steamed zucchini blossoms and peekytoe crab, served under chandeliers.
- **Java Indonesian Rijsttafel** •
  455 7th Ave [16th St]
  718-832-4583 • $$
  Mom-and-pop Indonesian, natch!
- **Johnny Mack's** • 1114 8th Ave [11th St]
  718-832-7961 • $$
  Neighborhood bar and grill with sidewalk seating.
- **Jpan Sushi** • 287 5th Ave [1st St]
  718-788-2880 • $$$
  Excellent, inventive special rolls; weird space.
- **Kinara** • 473 5th Ave [11th St]
  718-499-3777 • $$
  Large selection of vegetarian and non-vegetarian Indian dishes.

- **Krupa Grocery** •
  231 Prospect Park West [Windsor Pl]
  718-709-7098 • $$$
  Salt cod croquettes and plenty of alcohol.
- **Le P'tit Paris Bistro** •
  256 Prospect Park West [Prospect Ave]
  718-369-3590 • $$$
  French onion soup, mussels, escargot—essentially, the basics.
- **Littleneck** • 288 3rd Ave [Carroll St]
  718-522-1921 • $$$
  Hip oysters and seafood steps from the pastoral Gowanus.
- **Lobo** • 188 5th Ave [Sackett St]
  718-636-8886 • $$
  Guilty pleasure Tex-Mex, not Mexican, plenty of tequila.
- **Luke's Lobster** • 237 5th Ave [Carroll St]
  347-457-6855 • $$$
  Maine-style seafood rolls without the six-hour drive.
- **Milk Bar** • 620 Vanderbilt Ave [Prospect Pl]
  718-230-0844 • $$
  Australian-inflected cafe; unrelated to Chang empire.
- **Mitchell's Soul Food** •
  617 Vanderbilt Ave [St Marks Ave]
  718-789-3212 • $
  Seedy, cheap soul food.
- **Moim** • 206 Garfield Pl [7th Ave]
  718-499-8092 • $$
  Innovative Korean in a swanky setting.
- **Nana** • 155 5th Ave [Lincoln Pl]
  718-230-3749 • $$
  Absolutely delicious Pan-Asian.
- **Ogliastro** • 784 Washington Ave [Sterling Pl]
  718-789-3700 • $$$
  An A-one pizza joint on Washington Ave.
- **Olivier Bistro** • 469 4th Ave [11th St]
  718-768-6600 • $$$
  Steak frites and a good brunch on, yes, 4th Ave.
- **Palo Santo** • 652 Union St [4th Ave]
  718-636-6311 • $$$
  South American elegance for date night.

The Pines is four-star dining out on the Gowanus side of the neighborhood. **Flatbush Farm** hits the requisite local-seasonal notes. Go to **Bar Chuko** for buzzy izakaya-style Japanese. Also, don't miss the warm and eclectic **Stone Park Cafe** and the burgers at **Bonnie's Grill**.

- **Pino's La Forchetta** • 181 7th Ave [2nd St]
  718-965-4020 • $
  Pizza heavyweight on the Slope.
- **Puerto Viejo** • 564 Grand Ave [Dean St]
  718-398-3758 • $$
  Perfect. Hands-down top NYC Dominican.
  Eat it all
- **Rachel's Taqueria** • 408 5th Ave [7th St]
  718-788-1137 • $
  Serviceable California-style Mexican
- **Rhythm & Booze** •
  1674 10th Ave [Prospect Ave]
  718-788-9699 • $$
  A survivor of the pre-boom 'Slope. Eat a
  burger.
- **Rose Water** • 787 Union St [6th Ave]
  718-783-3800 • $$
  Intimate, airy Mediterranean.
- **Runner & Stone** • 285 3rd Ave [Carroll St]
  718-576-3360 • $$$
  Coffee, bakery, brunch, and dinner, all good.
- **Santa Fe Grill** • 62 7th Ave [Lincoln Pl]
  718-636-0279 • $$
  Dinner? Chips, salsa, and icy piñas!
- **Scalino** • 347 7th Ave [10th St]
  718-840-5738 • $$
  Fresh Italian food mama would approve of.
- **Scottadito Osteria Toscana** •
  788 Union St [7th Ave]
  718-636-4800 • $$$
  Rustic Tuscan, with wallet friendly prix fixe
  specials.
- **Shake Shack** • 170 Flatbush Ave [5th Ave]
  347 442-7711 • $$
  Danny Meyer's pitch-perfect burgers, across
  from Barclays Center.
- **Sidecar** • 560 5th Ave [15th St]
  718-369-0077 • $$
  Yummy comfort dining with equally
  comforting cocktails.
- **Smiling Pizzeria** • 323 7th Ave [9th St]
  718-788-2137 • $
  Good quick happy slices.

- **Song** • 295 5th Ave [2nd St]
  718-965-1108 • $
  Essential, tasty Thai in a pinch.
- **Sotto Voce** • 225 7th Ave [4th St]
  718-369-9322 • $$
  Italian cuisine with better brunch options
- **Stone Park Cafe** • 324 5th Ave [3rd St]
  718-369-0082 • $$$$
  Definitely a contender for best Park Slope
  dining.
- **Talde** • 369 7th Ave [11th St]
  347-916-0031 • $$$$
  Fusion to die for. Worth a trip.
- **Taro Sushi** • 244 Flatbush Ave [St Marks Ave]
  718-398-5420 • $$
  Top sushi, cozy seating. Lunch specials
  available Monday through Saturday.
- **Tom's** • 782 Washington Ave [Sterling Pl]
  718-636-9738 • $$
  Old-school mom-and-pop diner since 1936. A
  cholesterol love affair.
- **Tomato N Basil** • 226 4th Ave [Union St]
  718-596-8855 • $
  Good 4th Avenue option; close to subway.
- **The V-Spot** • 156 5th Ave [Degraw St]
  718-928-8778 • $$
  Loads of "meat" options, good for the veggie
  initiate.
- **Wangs** • 671 Union St [4th Ave]
  718-636-6390 • $$
  We are wooed by Wangs' wings.
- **White Tiger** • 661 Vanderbilt Ave [Bergen St]
  718-552-2272 • $$$
  Korean cocktails and small plates. Therefore,
  delicious.
- **Windsor Café** •
  220 Prospect Park West [16th St]
  718-788-9700 • $$
  American diner with something for everyone.

Map 33 Park Slope/Prospect Heights/Windsor Terrac

⚲ Shopping

- **A Cheng** • 466 Bergen St
718-783-2826
Modern classic women's clothing.
- **Beacon's Closet** • 92 5th Ave [Warren St]
718-230-1630
Rad resale with lots of gems.
- **Big Nose Full Body** • 382 7th Ave [11th St]
718-369-4030
Interesting, diverse rotating stock of wine.
- **Bitter & Esters** •
700 Washington Ave [St Mark's Ave]
917-596-7261
Homebrew kits and supplies in Prospect Heights.
- **Bklyn Larder** • 228 Flatbush Ave [Bergen St]
718-783-1250
Take home a taste of Franny's every night.
- **Blue Apron Foods** • 814 Union St [7th Ave]
718-230-3180
Euro-style cheese, charcuterie, and imported goodies.
- **Blue Marble Ice Cream** •
186 Underhill Ave [St Johns Pl]
718-399-6926
Delicious even in February.
- **Blue Sky Bakery** • 53 5th Ave [St Marks Ave]
718-783-4123
Moist muffins full of fresh fruit.
- **Brooklyn Industries** • 206 5th Ave [Union St]
718-789-2764
Brooklyn-centric T-shirts, sweatshirts, coats, and bags.
- **Brooklyn Museum** •
200 Eastern Pkwy [Washington Ave]
718-638-5000
Usual art-related offerings plus fun Brooklyn-made items.
- **Brooklyn Superhero Supply Co.** •
372 5th Ave [5th St]
718-499-9884
Capes, treasure maps, and bottled special powers. Also, McSweeney's publications.
- **The Clay Pot** • 162 7th Ave [Garfield Pl]
718-788-6564
Hand-crafted gifts, jewelry.
- **Community Book Store** •
143 7th Ave [Garfield Pl]
718-783-3075
General books.
- **Dixon's Bicycle Shop** • 792 Union St [7th Ave]
718-636-0067
Classic, friendly, family-owned bike shop.
- **DUB Pies** • 211 Prospect Park W [16th St]
718-788 2448
Aussie/Kiwi-style meat pies.
- **Fermented Grapes Wines & Spirits** •
651 Vanderbilt Ave [Prospect Pl]
718-230-3216
Diverse, affordable selection of wines & spirits in Prospect Heights.
- **Fifth Avenue Record & Tape Center** •
439 5th Ave [9th St]
718-499-8483
Unassuming locale for surprising finds.

For food (and beer), try **Bierkraft**, **Bklyn Larder**, **Blue Apron**, **Blue Marble**, **Russo's**, and **United Meat**. Check out gift/jewelry stores like **The Clay Pot** and **Razur**. **Beacon's Closet** is still a clothing destination. **Dixon's** is a classic bike shop, and get your capes and lasers at **Brooklyn Superhero Supply**. If you dare enter the machine, value awaits at the fishbowl that is the **Park Slope Food Co-op**.

• **Flirt** • 586 5th Ave [Park Pl]
929-367-8248
Indie fashion, local designers, and custom bridal.

• **Gurele** • 886 Pacific St [Underhill Ave]
718-857-2522
West African flavored clothing, with a music club in the back!

• **Hiho Batik** • 184 5th Ave [Sackett St]
718-622-4446
Batik clothing and do-it-yourself classes.

• **Housing Works Thrift Shop** •
244 5th Ave [Carroll St]
718-636-2271
Used books, shabby chic home decor, and vintage designer ware.

• **JackRabbit Sports** • 151 7th Ave [Garfield Pl]
718-636-9000
Mecca for runners, swimmers, and cyclists.

• **Midtown Florist & Greenhouse** •
565 Atlantic Ave [Hanson Pl]
718-237-1500
Fully stocked with plants and gardening supplies.

• **The Pie Shop** • 211 Prospect Park W [16th St]
718-788-2448
Handmade meat pies from Down Under.

• **Pink Olive Boutique** • 167 5th Ave
718-398-2016
Whimsical gifts for kids.

• **Prospect Wine Shop** • 322 7th Ave [8th St]
718-768-1232
Well-edited and gets the job done.

• **Red, White and Bubbly** •
211 5th Ave [Union St]
718-636-9463
Helpful staff with no attitude.

• **Ride Brooklyn** • 468 Bergen St [5th Ave]
347-599-1340
Friendly and helpful bike store.

• **Russo's Fresh Mozzarella & Pasta** •
363 7th Ave [11th St]
718-369-2874
Homemade pasta and sauce. Yum.

• **Slope Cellars** • 436 7th Ave [15th St]
718-369-7307
Helpful staff and wine club loyalty card.

• **Sterling Grapes & Grains** •
115 5th Ave [Sterling Pl]
718-789-9521
Known around the 'hood for good prices.

• **Terrace Books** •
242 Prospect Park W [Prospect Ave]
718-788-3475
Used & new.

• **Trailer Park** • 77 Sterling Pl [6th Ave]
718-623-2170
Unique and handcrafted furnishings.

• **United Meat Market** •
219 Prospect Park West [16th St]
718-768-7227
Butchered sheep flesh never tasted so good.

• **Unnameable Books** •
600 Vanderbilt Ave [St Marks Ave]
718-789-1534
General new and used.

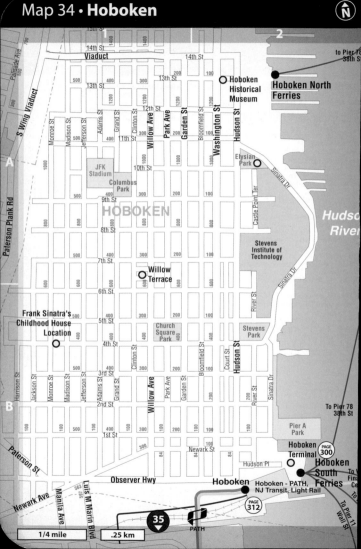

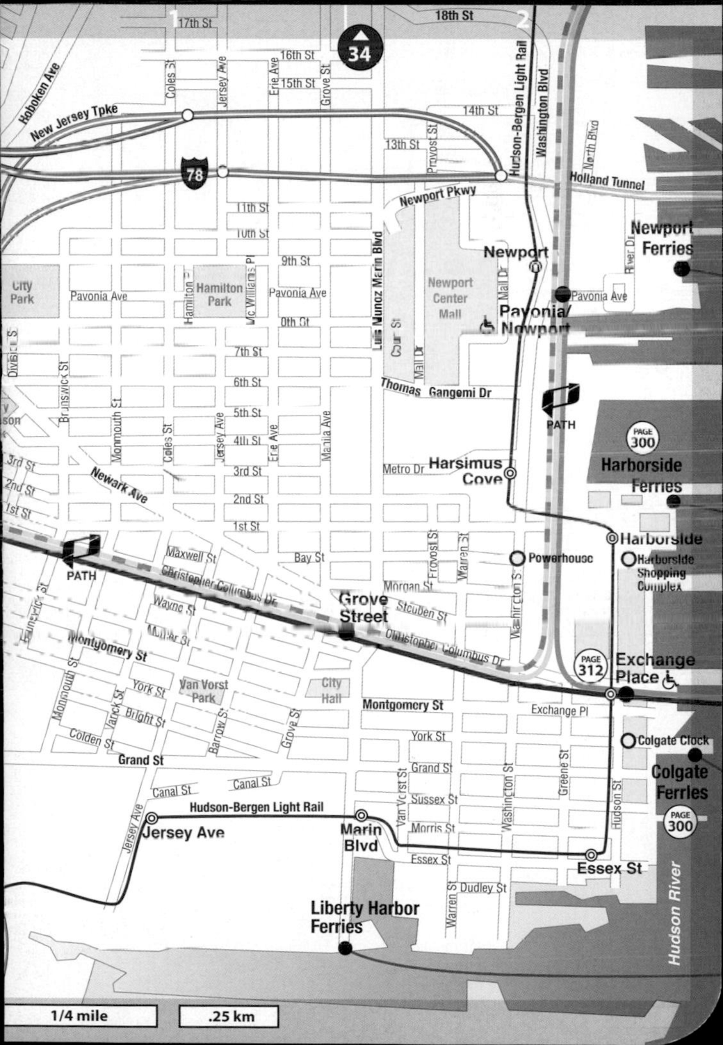

Map 35 · **Jersey City**

Ⓝ

17th St
18th St
16th St
15th St
Coles St
Jersey Ave
Erie St
Grove St
Hoboken Ave
New Jersey Tpke
14th St
Provost St
Washington Blvd
Hudson-Bergen Light Rail
34
2

13th St

I-78

Newport Pkwy
11th St
10th St
9th St
Pavonia Ave
Hamilton Park
McWilliams Pl
Luis Munoz Marin Blvd
Coles St
Mall Dr
Newport Center Mall
North Blvd

Holland Tunnel

Newport
Pavonia Ave
Newport Ferries

City Park
Pavonia Ave

8th St
7th St
6th St
5th St
4th St
3rd St
Erie Ave
Jersey Ave
Manila Ave
Brunswick St
Monmouth St
Division St
Thomas Gangemi Dr

Pavonia/ Newport
PATH

Metro Dr
Harsimus Cove

PAGE 300
Harborside Ferries

2nd St
1st St
Newark Ave
Bay St
Maxwell Pl
Morgan St
Steuben St
Warren St
Erie St
Provost St

○ Powerhouse
● Harborside Shopping Complex
● **Harborside**

PATH
Christopher Columbus Dr
Wayne St
M.L.K. Dr
Grove Street
Christopher Columbus Dr

Washington St

PAGE 312
● **Exchange Place**

Montgomery St
York St
Bright St
Jersey Ave
Van Vorst Park
Grove St
City Hall
Montgomery St
Exchange Pl

Colden St
Grand St
York St
Grand St
Sussex St
Van Vorst St
Washington St
Greene St
Hudson St

● Colgate Clock
Colgate Ferries

Canal St
Canal St
Hudson-Bergen Light Rail
Jersey Ave
Jersey Ave
Barrow St
Monmouth St
Varick St

Morris St
Marin Blvd
Essex St
Essex St
PAGE 300

Dudley St
Warren St
Liberty Harbor Ferries

Hudson River

| 1/4 mile | | .25 km | |

Don't be afraid of the Boogie Down Bronx. Decades of entrenched poverty and poor urban planning once frayed many neighborhoods, but the borough today is no longer the burning wreck your parents warned you about years ago.

Communities

Belmont's Arthur Avenue (3) is still an authentic Little Italy even though many businesses now belong to Albanians. Woodlawn (9) is home to many Irish immigrants and it's got the pubs to prove it. With 15,372 units, towering Co-op City (13) is rightly called a city within the city; it even has its own mall! The Mott Haven (14) and Longwood (15) historic districts boast beautiful homes, but "The Hub" (16) features the grand architecture of the past conveniently filled with the discount shopping of today. For antiques, visit the cobblestone corridor of Bruckner Boulevard (17) at Alexander Avenue. Some of the city's grandest homes sit in the wooded environs of Riverdale (4), while City Island (12) resembles nothing so much as a New England fishing village crossed with a New Jersey suburb.

Culture

The New York Botanical Garden (8) and the Bronx Zoo (10) are justly famous, well worth whatever effort it may take to get there. For a beautiful view of the Hudson and the Palisades beyond, choose the botanical garden and historic estate Wave Hill (5) or the quirky Hall of Fame for Great Americans (2) featuring 98 bronze busts of notable citizens in a grand outdoor colonnade. Explore your inner Goth at historic Woodlawn Cemetery (7) or Poe Cottage (18), the American poet's final home. Bronx Museum focuses on 20th- and 21st-century art by African, Asian, and Latin American artists, and it's completely free (and open late on Fridays).

Sports

New Yankee Stadium (1) is not so new anymore, and Old Yankee Stadium is a distant memory, except for its field, which has been preserved across the street. Get the cheapest ticket you can find and just spend the game walking around the concourses, which have the best views of the field. Van Cortlandt Park (6) offers playgrounds, ballfields, tennis and basketball courts, hiking trails, stables for horseback riding, and one of golf's classic courses, "Vanny."

Nature

The restoration of the Bronx River (19) coincides with the improvement of green spaces throughout the borough. Pelham Bay Park (11) is the city's largest at 2,764 acres, offering many recreational opportunities in addition to the Thomas Pell Wildlife Sanctuary, two nature centers, and immensely popular Orchard Beach.

Food

Belmont:
  Dominick's, 2335 Arthur Ave, 718-733-2807. Famous old-school Italian-American where there are no menus and no set prices.

- Full Moon, 602 East 187th St, 718-584-3451—Wonderful pizza and calzones.
- Roberto's Restaurant, 603 Crescent Ave, 718-733-9503. Classic fare; it's that good.
- Trattoria Zero Otto Nove, 2357 Arthur Ave, 718-220-1027. Best high-end pizza in the borough at Roberto sister restaurant.
- Arthur Avenue Retail Market, 2344 Arthur Ave. Get all the right ingredients for home-cooked Italian meals.

City Island:
- Johnny's Reef, 2 City Island Ave, 718-885-2086. Local favorite for fresh inexpensive seafood.

Riverdale:
- An Beal Bocht, 445 West 238th St, 718-884-7127. Café/bar/coffee shop hangout for the hip, young, and Irish
- S &S Cheesecake, 222 West 238th St, 718-549-3888. Forget Junior's, this is the city's best.

University Heights:
- Eba Ya Yio, 2364 Jerome Ave, 718-563-6061. Hearty Ghanaian meals

Concourse Village:
- Feeding Tree, 892 Gerard Ave, 718-293-5025. Delicious Jamaican food close to Yankee Stadium.

Kingsbridge:
- El Economico, 5589 Broadway, 718-796-4851. Homestyle Puerto Rican meals.

Bedford Park:
- Com Tam Ninh Kieu, 2641 Jerome Ave, 718-365-2680. Best Vietnamese in the Bronx; order the pho.

Pelham Bay:
Louie & Ernie's, 1300 Crosby Ave, 718-829-6230. Thin-crust casual pizza that rivals best in the borough.

Parkchester:
- Taqueria Tlaxcalli, 2103 Starling Ave, 347-851-3085. Authentic Mexican dishes.

Landmarks

1 Yankee Stadium
2 Hall of Fame for Great Americans
3 Arthur Avenue
4 Riverdale
5 Wave Hill
6 Van Cortlandt Park
7 Woodlawn Cemetery
8 New York Botanical Garden
9 Woodlawn
10 Bronx Zoo
11 Pelham Bay Park
12 City Island
13 Co-op City
14 Mott Haven
15 Longwood
16 The Hub
17 Bruckner Boulevard
18 Poe Cottage
19 Bronx River
20 Bronx Museum of the Arts

Outer Boroughs · **Brooklyn**

The Great Mistake of 1898, Brooklyn is no longer its own city, but that little technicality hasn't kept the Borough of Kings down. As Manhattan becomes prohibitively expensive and middle-Americanized, Brooklyn's popularity is at an all-time high. Scores of recent college grads, immigrants, ex-Manhattanites, and even celebrities are calling Brooklyn home, whether in a row of brownstones, a pre-war house, or a brand-new loft. Along with the residential boom, Brooklyn has firmly arrived as a cultural and entertainment mecca, and it boasts some of the hottest bars, astounding cultural diversity, and stellar parks. Atlantic Yards is now a reality after much protest, but Brooklyn won't let go of its unique character that easily.

Communities

As the largest borough by population (over 2.5 million!), Brooklyn holds a special place as one of the nation's most remarkable urban areas. As many as one in four people can trace their roots here! In Brooklyn, you can find pretty much any type of community—for better or worse. As gentrification marches deeper into Brooklyn, the borough is changing fast. Neighborhoods most likely to see their first baby boutiques open soon include Red Hook, East Williamsburg, Prospect-Lefferts Gardens, and Crown Heights.

The first thing you notice when looking at Brooklyn on a map is the sheer size of it. Yet much of Brooklyn is largely unknown to most New Yorkers. Yes, Brooklyn Heights, Williamsburg, and Park Slope are nice communities that are fun to explore. However, if you've never ventured further out into Brooklyn than the obligatory trip to Coney Island you're missing some fantastic neighborhoods. For instance, Bay Ridge (4) has beautiful single-family homes along its western edge, a killer view of the Verrazano Bridge, and a host of excellent shops and restaurants. Dyker Heights (6) is composed of almost all single-family homes, many of which go all-out with Christmas light displays during the holiday season. Brighton Beach (8) continues to be a haven for many Russian expatriates. The quiet, tree-lined streets of both Ocean Parkway (10) and Midwood (11) can make one forget all about the hustle and bustle of downtown Brooklyn, or downtown anywhere else for that matter. Finally, Bedford-Stuyvesant (12) has a host of cool public buildings, fun eateries, and beautiful brownstones.

Sports

No, the Dodgers are never coming back. This is still hard for many older Brooklynites to accept and accounts for much of the nostalgia that is still associated with the borough. If you can get beyond the fact that Ebbets Field is now a giant concrete housing complex, then you will enjoy spending a fine summer evening watching the Cyclones at Coney Island (7). But really, Brooklynites need to get over it: The Barclays Center (15) already captured one major professional sports team (the Nets) and soon another will begin playing there (the Islanders). Elsewhere, Kensington Stables in Prospect Park (1) provides lessons for wannabe equestrians.

Attractions

Coney Island's (7) redevelopment is well underway but has left untouched the Cyclone, the Wonder Wheel, Nathan's, Totonno's pizza, movies at the Coney Island Museum, the beach, the freaks, and The Warriors. Close by is the Aquarium (13). Nature trails, parked blimps, views of the water, scenic marinas, live events and overnight camping all make historical Floyd Bennett Field (9) a worthwhile trip. For more beautiful views, you can check out Owl's Point Park (3) in Bay Ridge, on the parking lot underneath the Verrazano Narrows Bridge (5) (located right off the Shore Parkway). The Verrazano might not be New York's most beautiful bridge, but it's hands-down the most awe-inspiring. Both Green-Wood Cemetery (2) and Prospect Park (1) provide enough greenery to keep you happy until you get to Yosemite. Finally, Brooklyn Heights (14) is the most beautiful residential neighborhood in all of New York. Don't believe us? Go stand on the corner of Willow and Orange Streets and find out for yourself.

Food

Here are some restaurants in some of the outlying areas of Brooklyn:
Bay Ridge: **Casablanca Restaurant**, 484 77th St, 718-748-2077—Highly recommended Moroccan
Midwood: **DiFara's Pizzeria**, E 15th St & Ave J, 718-258-1367—Dirty, cheap, and fresh as hell.
Sunset Park: **Nyonya**, 5223 Eighth Ave, 718-633-0808—Good quality Malaysian.
Sheepshead Bay: **Russian Bath of NY**, 1200 Gravesend Neck Rd, 718-332-1676—Delicious Russian food after a schvitz.

Landmarks

1 Prospect Park	6 Dyker Heights	10 Midwood
2 Green-Wood Cemetery	7 Coney Island	12 Bedford-Stuyvesant
3 Owl's Point Park	8 Brighton Beach	13 New York Aquarium
4 Bay Ridge	9 Floyd Bennett Field	14 Brooklyn Heights
5 Verrazano-Narrows Bridge	10 Ocean Parkway	15 Barclays Center

The most diverse borough in the city, people from all over have been "discovering" Queens for years, making it home to some of the city's best ethnic restaurants and neighborhoods. Flushing's Chinatown is rivaling Manhattan's as the center of New York's Chinese community. Queens also has some of the city's best open spaces with everything from forestland to surfing beaches. And at a time when Brooklyn real estate prices push higher and higher toward Manhattan extremes, Queens is a great alternative for those who are willing to explore a little.

Communities

From the stately Tudor homes of Forest Hills Gardens (28) to the hip-hop beat of Jamaica Avenue (11), Queens has it all. Eastern Queens tends toward suburbia, while the communities along the borough's southern border often include active industrial districts. All things Asian can be found in Flushing (20), the city's largest Chinatown. Sunnyside (21) and Woodside (22) are home to Irish and Mexican immigrants alike, making it easy to find a proper pint and a fabulous taco on the same block. Jackson Heights (10) 74th Street is Little India, while (one block over) 82nd St packed with South and Central American businesses. Corona (23) blends old-school Italian-American delis with Latino dance clubs. Elmhurst (24) has attracted Asian, Southeast Asian, and South American immigrants to set up shop on its crowded streets. Island Broad Channel (12) feels like a sleepy village, while the Rockaways (13) offer the only surfing beaches in the city.

Culture

Fans of contemporary art have long known P.S. 1 (4) is the place to be, especially during its summer weekend WarmUp parties. Then head over to the Sculpture Center (31), to see what new exhibit they've cooked up for us. The Noguchi Museum (3), dedicated to the work of the Japanese-American sculptor, and neighboring Socrates Sculpture Park (2), a waterfront space with changing exhibitions, attract visitors from far beyond the five boroughs. The Fisher Landau Center for Art (25) features a world-class collection of modern art (and is free, to boot). Movie buffs should look for repertory screenings at the Museum of the Moving Image (5). The delightfully kitschy Louis Armstrong House (26) is a must-see for jazz lovers. In Flushing Meadows Corona Park, the New York Hall of Science (8) beckons the geeky kid in all of us with its hands-on exhibits while the Queens Museum of Art's (9) scale model of the entire city will wow even the most jaded New Yorkers.

Sports

In 2009, the Mets inaugurated a brand new place to make memories of exquisite disappointment, Citi Field, just in time for the team's ownership and its corporate sponsor to lose proverbial shirts. The U.S. Open takes place right across the street at the Billie Jean King National Tennis Center (7). Check out girls gone wild when our local ladies, The Queens of Pain, compete in the Gotham Girls Roller Derby league. See the ponies and fritter away your hard-earned cash at the Aqueduct Racetrack (14). Hitch a ride to Rockaway Beach (13) for swimming and surfing or paddle out in a kayak on loan from the Long Island City Community Boathouse (27). Astoria Pool (1) is the city's largest with room for 3,000 swimmers. For bowling, all night Whitestone Lanes (18) is the place to go.

Nature

Gantry Plaza State Park's (29) spacious piers attract strollers and urban fishermen alike with panoramic views of the Manhattan skyline, and a major park expansion will eventually connect the waterfront from Anable Basin to the north all the way down to Newtown Creek. The Jamaica Bay Wildlife Refuge (15) in Gateway National Recreation Area is internationally known for bird-watching. Queens Botanical Garden is a peaceful refuge with its own bee hives out in Flushing. Fort Tilden is becoming more popular, but it's still one of New York's prettiest, natural, non-commercial beaches. Flushing Meadows Corona Park (30) is designed for active recreation, but Alley Pond Park (16) and Forest Park (17) have wooded trails perfect for wandering.

Food

Entire books have been written on where to eat in Queens, so these are just a handful of suggestions:
Corona: **Leo's Latticini** (a.k.a. Mama's), 46-02 104th St, 718-898-6069—Insanely good Italian sandwiches that pair with dessert from the **Lemon Ice King**, 52-02 108th Street, 718-699-5133, just a few blocks away.
Rego Park: **Cheburechnaya**, 92-09 63rd Dr, 718-897-9080—grilled meats are the specialty at this Kosher Uzbek gem.
Sunnyside: **De Mole**, 45-02 48th Ave, 718-392-2161— Fresh, simply prepared Mexican food in bistro setting.
Bayside: **Uncle Jack's**, 39-40 Bell Blvd, 718-229-1100—Mayor Bloomberg's favorite steakhouse serves up fine flesh.
Flushing: **Spicy and Tasty**, 39 07 Prince Street, 718-359-1601—The name of this Sichuan place is entirely accurate.
Woodside: **Sripraphai**, 64-13 39th Ave, 718-899-9599—Easily the best Thai food in the city; **La Flor**, 53-02 Roosevelt Ave, 718-426-8023—Fantastic neighborhood café with Mexican-inflected dishes.

Landmarks

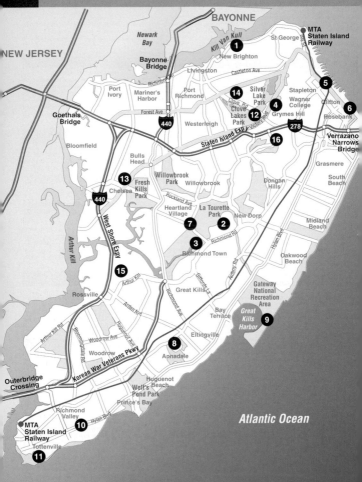

Staten Island, of thee we sing! Don't let the sight of jabronis with fake tans and gelled hair hold you back from exploring, lest you miss out on heaps of excellent pizza, the wild flower meadows at Mount Loretto, the windows on the past at Historic Richmond Town, the small town charm of minor league baseball at St. George, and the striking design of the Chinese Scholars' Garden at Snug Harbor. It's high time you pulled your head out of your borough and hitched a ride on the ferry, if only to eat at one of SI's "holy trinity" of pizzerias.

Culture

1 Snug Harbor Cultural Center, 1000 Richmond Ter, 718-448-2500. A former sailors' home transformed to a waterfront arts complex, Snug Harbor's 83 acres into to classrooms, studio spaces, performance venues, galleries, live museums, and a truly noteworthy botanical garden. Call to learn about cultural events and exhibits on site.

2 Jacques Marchais Museum of Tibetan Art, 338 Lighthouse Ave, 718-987-3500. A world-class collection of Tibetan art, courtesy of former art collector Edna Coblentz, who had the surprising French pseudonym Jacques Marchais.

3 Historic Richmond Town, 441 Clarke Ave, 718-351-1611. Get back to old-timey times visiting restored homes from the 17th to the 19th centuries, most populated by costumed guides. Great for kids and adults who want to learn how to churn butter/forge metal.

4 Wagner College, 1 Campus Rd, 718-390-3100. Wagner's tranquil hilltop location rewards visitors with beautiful views of the serene surroundings, but its best feature is the planetarium.

5 Staten Island Village Hall, 111 Canal St. Last remaining village hall building in Staten Island, a reminder of the borough's rural past.

6 Alice Austen House, 2 Hylan Blvd, 718-816-4506. Alice Austen was an early twentieth-century amateur photographer, and now she's got a museum and a ferry boat named after her. Go figure. Some of her 8,000 images are on view at her house, which has a great view of lower New York Harbor.

Nature

7 Staten Island Greenbelt, 200 Nevada Ave, 718-667-2165. This 2,800 acre swath of land (comprising several distinct parks) in the center of the island contains a golf course, a hospital, a scout camp, several graveyards, and plenty of wooded areas that remain relatively undeveloped and can be accessed only by walking trails. A good starting point is High Rock Park. Panoramic views abound.

8 Blue Heron Park, 222 Poillon Ave, 718-967-3542. This quiet, 236 acre park has a fantastic Nature Center and plenty of ponds, wetlands, and streams to explore. Noted for bird-watching, hence the name.

9 Great Kills Park, 718-987-6790. Part of the Gateway National Recreation Area, Great Kills boasts clean beaches, a marina, and a nature preserve.

10 Mount Loretto Unique Area, 6450 Hylan Blvd, 718-482-7287. Flourishing wetlands, grasslands, and beaches all rolled into one serenely beautiful waterfront park. Mysterious sculptures dot the beach.

11 Conference House Park, 7455 Hylan Blvd, 718-984-6046. The historic house is worth a look, but watching the sunset from the restored waterfront pavilion is a must. You'll also find NYC's very own "South Pole" on the beach here.

12 Clove Lakes Park, Clove Rd and Victory Blvd, 311. Who needs Central Park? Check out these romantic rowboats on the lake in season.

13 Freshkills Park, off Route 440. Former landfill, now a park. Sorta. They're working on it over the next 30 years. Free tours by appointment.

Other

14 110/120 Longfellow Road. Celebrate one of the greatest American films without having to schlep to Sicily. This address is where the Corleone family held court in The Godfather.

15 Ship Graveyard, at Arthur Kill Rd and Rossville Ave. These ships of the damned make a perfect backdrop for Goth photo shoots.

16 Staten Island Zoo, 614 Broadway, 718-442-3100. Kids will go wild here, near the stunning Clove Lakes Park. Be sure to bring them to the vampire bat feedings.

Food

Tompkinsville:
New Asha, 322 Victory Blvd, 718-420-0649. Great Sri Lankan food on the cheap. Spicy!
Port Richmond:
Denino's, 524 Port Richmond Ave, 718-442-9401. Some of the best pizza in town.
Dongan Hills:
Lee's Tavern, 60 Hancock St, 718-667-9749. Great bar with great pizza—get the fresh mozzarella.
Grant City:
Nunzio's, 2155 Hylan Blvd, 718-667-9647. More great pizza. Notice a theme here?
Tottenville:
Egger's Ice Cream Parlor, 7437 Amboy Rd, 718-605-9335. Old time ice cream and sweets. Kids love it
Killmeyer's Old Bavaria Inn, 4254 Arthur Kill Rd, 718-984-1202. Historic German beer garden and eats. JA¥!
Castleton Corners
Joe & Pat's, 1758 Victory Blvd, 718-981-0887. Completing SI's "Holy Trinity" of pizza.
West Brighton:
Nurnberger Bierhaus, 817 Castleton Ave, 718-816-7461. German beer and food.
St. George:
Pier 76 Italian Restaurant, 76 Bay Street, 718-447-7437, What Joe & Pat begat; walking distance to ferry.

Driving In / Through Staten Island

To visit Staten Island, one must either drive/take a bus/take a cab over the Verrazano Bridge (it is ruinously expensive toll) from Bay Ridge, Brooklyn, or catch the ferry from Lower Manhattan. If you elect to do the latter, you'll find myriad buses departing from the St. George side of the ferry as well as the terminal of the Staten Island Railway, ready to whisk you all the way down to Tottenville and back with one swipe of the Metrocard. To reach New Jersey via Staten Island, take the Verrazano to the Staten Island Expressway (Route 278) to Route 440 to the Outerbridge Crossing, and you're nearly halfway to Princeton on the Jersey shore. However…the Staten Island Expressway often gets jammed. Two scenic, though not really quicker, alternatives: one, take Hylan Boulevard all the way south to almost the southwest tip of Staten Island, and then cut up to the Outerbridge Crossing; two, take Richmond Terrace around the north shore and cross to New Jersey at the Goethals Bridge. Remember, neither is really faster, but at least you'll be moving.

General Information

Battery Park City Authority:
212-417-2000 or www.batteryparkcity.org

Battery Park City Parks Conservancy:
212-267-9700 or www.bpcparks.org

Overview

Welcome to Battery Park City—a master-planned community reminiscent of Pleasantville. Originally the brainchild of Nelson Rockefeller, this urban experiment transformed a WTC construction landfill into a 92-acre planned enclave on the southwestern tip of Manhattan. As space in Manhattan continues to disappear into the stratosphere (literally, the only way to build is up), the idea of BPC requires a doubletake. It's about making public spaces (about 30% of those 92 acres) work within private entities. Imagine taking Central Park, cutting it up, and saying, "Here, your neighborhood can have a chunk of it, and that street down there, and that street over there, too." Admit it: walking among private, commercial spaces day in and day out is enough to make anyone claustrophobic (thank you, Financial District). In BPC you walk through spacious parks with weird statues and brick pavers all on your way to work, the grocery store, the gym, or the movie theater. BPC will have you asking: "What's outside Battery Park City?"

Those looking for all-night eateries and party spots should pass it up, but if you've got kids this is the place for you. Many NY families—roughly 25,000 people—occupy the 40% of BPC that's dedicated residential space, including a future-forward "green" building, the Solaire. Robert F. Wagner Jr. and Rector are good choices for a picnic; The Esplanade or South Cove to walk along the Hudson; Nelson A. Rockefeller to play Frisbee; North Cove to park your yacht; and Teardrop Park for the kids. People of all ages have welcomed the ever-popular Shake Shack (the cheapest meal in the neighborhood), live music at the World Financial Center, and Manhattan's first green LEED-certified branch library.

Seeing: Amazing sculptures by Bourgeois, Otterness, Puryear, Dine, and Cragg. Inspired architecture: Stuyvesant High School, Siah Armajani's Tribeca Bridge, Kevin Roche's Museum of Jewish Heritage, Caesar Pelli's Winter Garden, and the World Financial Center. If you like things nice, neat, and compartmentalized, this 'hood is for you.

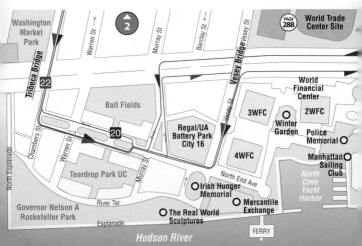

O Landmarks

- **The Irish Hunger Memorial** ·
  Vesey St & North End Ave
- **Manhattan Sailing Club** ·
  Liberty St & S End Ave
- **Mercantile Exchange** ·
  1 North End Ave [Vesey St]
- **Museum of Jewish Heritage** ·
  36 Battery Pl [Little West St]
- **Police Memorial** · Liberty St & South End Ave
- **The Skyscraper Museum** ·
  39 Battery Pl [Little West St]
- **Tom Otterness's The Real World Sculptures** ·
  Rockefeller Park
- **Winter Garden** · 37 Vesey St [Church St]

Movie Theaters

- **Regal Battery Park Stadium 11** ·
  102 North End Ave [Vesey St]

Restaurants

- **Amada** · 250 Vesey St [West St]
- **Black Seed** · 200 Vesey St [West St]
- **Blue Smoke** · 255 Vesey St [North End Ave]
- **El Vez** · 259 Vesey St [North End Ave]
- **Gigino at Wagner Park** ·
  20 Battery Pl [Washington St]
- **Le District** · 225 Liberty St [South End Ave]
- **Mighty Quinn's** ·
  225 Liberty St [South End Ave]
- **North End Grill** ·
  104 North End Ave [Murray St]
- **P.J. Clarke's on the Hudson** ·
  4 World Financial Ctr [Vesey St]
- **Picasso Pizza** · 303 South End Ave [Albany St]
- **Shake Shack** · 215 Murray St [North End Ave]
- **Umami Burger** ·
  225 Liberty St [South End Ave]

General Information

Central Park Conservancy: 212-310-6600
Website: www.centralparknyc.org
@CentralParkNYC

Overview

Taking a stroll through Central Park is something that tourists and residents can always agree on. This world-class sanctuary is a huge, peaceful lush oasis in the concrete jungle, and who hasn't skipped therapy once or twice in favor of clearing your mind the old-fashioned way, by taking a long walk in the park? On any given day, you'll see people disco roller skating, playing jazz, juggling, walking their dogs, running, making out, meditating, playing softball, whining through soccer practice, getting married, picnicking, and playing chess.

Designed by Frederick Law Olmsted and Calvert Vaux in the 1850s, Central Park has a diverse mix of attractions. The **Central Park Conservancy** (www.centralparknyc.org) leads walking tours, and you can always hail a horse-drawn carriage or bike taxi for a ride through the park if you want to look like a true tourist.

Practicalities

Central Park is easily accessible by subway, since the A, C, B, D, N, R, Q, 1, 2 and 3 trains all circle the park. Parking along CPW is harder, so try side streets. Unless you're heading to the park for a big concert, a softball game, or Shakespeare in the Park, walking or hanging out (especially alone!) in the park at night is not recommended.

Nature

Central Park is the place to see and be seen, for birds, actually; 230 species can be spotted and The Ramble (27) is a good place to stake out. There are an amazing number of both plant and animal species that inhabit the park, including the creatures housed at the zoo (4 & 8). Some people forage for edible plants throughout the park, perhaps out of curiosity, though officials tend to discourage this practice. A good source of information on all of the park's flora and fauna is NYC schoolteacher Leslie Day's book, *Field Guide to the Natural World of New York City*.

Architecture & Sculpture

Central Park was designed to thrill visitors at every turn. The Bethesda Fountain (11), designed by Emma Stebbins, is one of the main attractions of the park. Don't miss the view of Turtle Pond from Belvedere Castle (16). The Arsenal (5) is a wonderful ivy-clad building that houses the Parks Department headquarters. The original Greensward plan for Central Park is located in the Arsenal's third-floor conference room—if there isn't a meeting going on, you might be able to sneak a peek. Two of the most notable sculptures in the park are Alice in Wonderland (15) and the Obelisk (19). Oh, and one other tiny point of interest… the Metropolitan Museum of Art (24) also happens to be in the park.

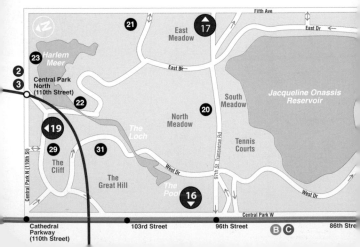

Open Spaces

New Yorkers covet space. Since they rarely get it in their apartments, they rely on large open areas such as the Great Lawn (26), and Sheep Meadow (28). The Ramble (27) is stocked with trees and is great for hiking around—just use common sense after dark. When it snows, you can find great sledding on Cedar Hill (30), which is otherwise perfect for picnicking and sunbathing.

Performance

In warmer weather, Central Park is a microcosm of the great cultural attractions New York has to offer. The Delacorte Theater (18) is the home of **Shakespeare in the Park**, a New York tradition begun by famous director Joseph Papp. Summerstage (9) is the city's best outdoor concert venue for all types of music, including killer rock shows. Free opera and classical concerts happen all summer long on the Great Lawn (26). Or just enjoy a sing-along with some dude with an acoustic guitar for as long you can stand it at the homely memorial to John Lennon at Strawberry Fields (10).

Sports

Rollerblading and roller skating are still popular, as is jogging, especially around the reservoir (1.57 mi). The Great Lawn (26) boasts well-maintained softball fields. Central Park has 30 tennis courts (if you make a reservation, you can walk right on to the clay court with tennis shoes only—212-280-0205), fishing at Harlem Meer, gondola rides and boat rentals at the Loeb Boathouse (13), model boat rentals at the Conservatory Water (14), chess and checkers at the Chess & Checkers House (25), two ice skating rinks (1 & 22), croquet and lawn bowling just north of Sheep Meadow (28), and basketball courts at the North Meadow Rec Center (20). You will also see volleyball, basketball, skateboarding, bicycling, and many pick-up soccer, frisbee, football, and kill-the-carrier games to join. During heavy snows, bust out your snowboard, cross-country skis, or homemade sled. Finally, Central Park is where the NYC Marathon ends each year.

Landmarks

1 Wollman Rink
2 Carousel
3 The Dairy
4 Central Park Zoo
5 The Arsenal
6 Tavern on the Green
7 Roller Skating Rink
8 Children's Zoo
9 Summerstage

10 Strawberry Fields
11 Bethesda Fountain
12 Bow Bridge
13 Loeb Boathouse
14 Model Boat Racing
15 Alice in Wonderland
16 Belvedere Castle
17 Shakespeare Gardens
18 Delacorte Theater

19 The Obelisk
20 North Meadow Recreation Center
21 Conservatory Garden
22 Lasker Rink
23 Dana Discovery Center
24 Metropolitan Museum of Art

25 Chess & Checkers House
26 The Great Lawn
27 The Ramble
28 Sheep Meadow
29 The Cliff
30 Cedar Hill
31 The Great Hill

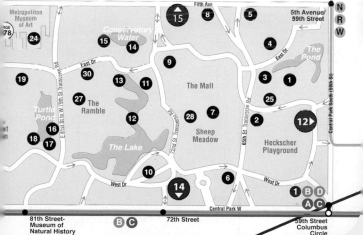

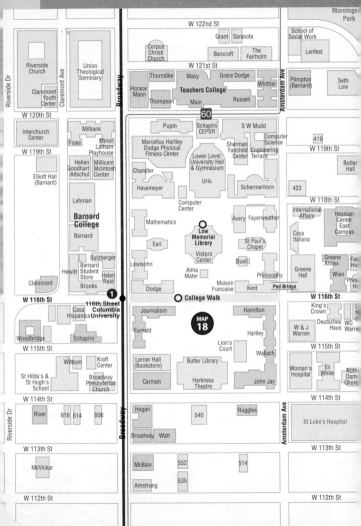

Morningside Park

W 122nd St

Grant | Sarasota

School of Social Work

Corpus Christi Church

Bancroft | The Fairholm

Lenfest

W 121st St

Riverside Church

Union Theological Seminary

Thorndike | Macy | Grace Dodge

Whittier

Plimpton (Barnard)

Seth Low

Horace Mann

Teachers College

Claremont Youth Center

Thompson | Main | Russell

W 120th St

60

Interchurch Center

Milbank

Pupin | Schapiro CEPSR | S W Mudd

Computer Science

419

Fiske | Minor Latham Playhouse

Marcellus Hartley Dodge Physical Fitness Center

Sherman Fairchild Center

Engineering Terrace

W 119th St

Hellen Goodhart Altschul | Millicent McIntosh Center

Lower Level: University Hall & Gymnasium

Butler Hall

Elliott Hall (Barnard)

Chandler

Uris

Havemeyer | Schermerhorn

423

Lehman

W 118th St

Barnard College

Computer Center

Avery | Fayerweather

International Affairs

Heyman Center East Campus

Barnard

Mathematics

Low Memorial Library

Casa Italiana

Earl

St Paul's Chapel

Greene Annex

Fac Ho

Sulzberger

Vistors Center

Buell

Wien

Pres Ho

Hewitt | Barnard Student Store | Helen Reid

Lewisohn

Alma Mater

Greene Hall

Philosophy

Claremont

Brooks

Dodge

Maison Francaise | Kent | Ped Bridge

W 116th St

1 116th Street **Columbia University**

College Walk

King's Crown

Casa Hispanica

Journalism

Hamilton

W & J Warren

Deutsches Haus

WC Warre

Woodbridge | Schapiro

Furnald

MAP 18

Hartley

W 115th St

St Hilda's & St Hugh's School

Watson | Kraft Center

Lion's Court

Wallach

Woman's Hospital

Eli White

Notr Dam Chur

River | 616 | 614 | 606

Lerner Hall (Bookstore)

Butler Library

Harkness Theatre

John Jay

Broadway Presbyterian Church

Carman

W 114th St

Hogan

540

Ruggles

St Luke's Hospital

McVickar

Broadway | Watt

W 113th St

McBain | 552 | 514

Amstrong | 535

W 112th St

Riverside Dr · Claremont Ave · Broadway · Amsterdam Ave

General Information

NFT Map: 18
Morningside Heights: 2960 Broadway & 116th St
Medical Center: 601 W 168th St
Phone: 212-854-1754
Website: www.columbia.edu or @Columbia
Students Enrolled: 29,250 (2013)
Endowment: $8.2 billion (2013)

Overview

Yearning for those carefree days spent debating nihilism in the quad and wearing pajamas in public? Look no further than a quick trip to the Ivy League haven of Columbia University.

Unlike the other collegiate institutions that pepper Manhattan's real estate, Columbia actually has a campus. The main campus, located in Morningside Heights, spans six blocks between Broadway and Amsterdam. Most of the undergraduate classes are held here, along with several of the graduate schools. Other graduate schools, including the Law School and School of International and Public Affairs, are close by on Amsterdam Avenue. The main libraries, Miller Theater, and St. Paul's Chapel are also located on the Morningside Heights campus. You can even get your intramural fix on a few fields for Frisbee-throwing and pick up soccer games.

Founded in 1754 as King's College, Columbia University is one of the country's most prestigious academic institutions. The university is well known for its core curriculum, a program of requirements that gives students an introduction to the most influential works in literature, philosophy, science, and other disciplines. It also prepares them for the rigors of those pesky dinner parties.

After residing in two different downtown locations, Columbia moved to its present campus (designed by McKim, Mead, and White) in 1897. Low Library remains the focal point of the campus as does the Alma Mater statue front—a landmark that continues to inspire student superstitions (find the hidden owl and you might be the next valedictorian!) thanks to a thwarted plot to blow it up by the radical Weather Underground in the 60s. Students use the stairs in front of the library on sunny days, eating lunch and chatting with classmates. Columbia even has its own spooky network of underground tunnels (third largest in the world) that date back to the old Morningside mental asylum and were utilized by students and police during the 1968 strike.

Town-gown relations in Morningside Heights are quite controversial. While Columbia students show local businesses the money, the university continues to relentlessly buy up property and expand into the community, to the chagrin of many New Yorkers city-wide. The most famous of these struggles came in response to Columbia's plans to build a gymnasium in Morningside Park. Contentious proposals, approved in 2009, for a 17-acre expansion into Manhattanville (the area north of 125th Street) by 2030 still cause tension and fear of evictions, and the debate between the university and old-time residents continues.

Columbia's medical school is the second oldest in the nation, and the world's first academic medical center. The school is affiliated with the Columbia-Presbyterian Medical Center in Washington Heights and encompasses the graduate schools of medicine, dentistry, nursing, and public health. Columbia is the only Ivy League university with a journalism school, which was founded by the bequest of Joseph Pulitzer in 1912. (The prize is administered there.) The school is also affiliated with Barnard College, Jewish Theological Seminary, Teachers College, and Union Theological Seminary.

Numerous movies have been filmed on or around the campus, including Ghostbusters, Hannah and Her Sisters, and various iterations of Spiderman.

Notable alums and faculty include artists James Cagney, Art Garfunkel, Georgia O'Keeffe, Rodgers and Hammerstein, Paul Robeson, and Twyla Tharp; critic Lionel Trilling; baseball player Lou Gehrig; and writers Isaac Asimov, Joseph Heller, Carson McCullers, Eudora Welty, Zora Neale Hurston, and Herman Wouk. Business alumni include Warren Buffet, Alfred Knopf, Joseph Pulitzer, and Milton Friedman, while government officials Madeline Albright, Dwight Eisenhower, Alexander Hamilton, Robert Moses, Franklin Delano Roosevelt, and Teddy Roosevelt all graced the university's classrooms. In the field of law, Benjamin Cardozo, Ruth Bader Ginsburg, Charles Evans Hughes, and John Jay called Columbia home, and Stephen Jay Gould, Margaret Mead, and Benjamin Spock make the list of notable science alumni.

Tuition

Undergraduate tuition is approximately $50,000 per year plus room, board, books, illegal substances, therapy for your inferiority/superiority complex, etc. We suggest shacking up with your Aunt Agatha on the Upper West Side for the duration.

Sports

The Columbia Marching Band plays "Roar, Lion, Roar" after every touchdown, but their moments remain tragically roarless most of the time. The Lions almost set the record for straight losses when a major college football team when they dropped 44 consecutive games between 1983 and 1988. Success has continued to elude the team. The hapless program even inspired a pennant on the local HBO affiliate. The Lions play their mostly Ivy League opponents at Lawrence A. Wien Stadium (Baker Field), located way up at the top of Manhattan.

Columbia excels in other sports including crew, fencing, golf, tennis, and sailing (silver spoon not included). The university is represented by 29 men's and women's teams in the NCAA Division I. It also has the oldest wrestling team in the country.

Culture on Campus

The ire evoked by its controversial immigration speech, when students stormed the stage, pales when compared to Columbia's 2007 invitation to Iranian president Mahmoud Ahmadinejad to participate in a debate. Good or bad, it created much hype and put the campus in the spotlight for a day or two. Columbia does, however, feature plenty of other less volatile dance, film, music, theater, lectures, readings, and talks. Venues include the Macy Gallery at the Teacher's College, which exhibits works by a variety of artists, including faculty and children's artwork; the fabulous Miller Theatre at 2960 Broadway, which primarily features musical performances and lectures; the student-run Postcrypt Art Gallery in the basement of St. Paul's Chapel; the Theatre of the Riverside Church for theatrical performances from their top-rated graduate program; and the Wallach Art Gallery on the 8th floor of Schermerhorn Hall, featuring art and architecture exhibits. Check the website for a calendar of events. And bring your rubber bullets, just in case.

Phone Numbers

Morningside Campus: 212-854-1754
Medical Center: 212-305-CUMC (2862)
Visitors Center: 212-854-4900
Office of Communications and Public Affairs: 212-854-5573
Office of Alumni and Development: 212-851-7800
Public Safety: 212-854-2797, 212-854-5555 (emergency)
Library Information: 212-854-7309

Overview

East River Park is a thin slice of land sandwiched between the FDR Drive and the East River, and running from Montgomery Street up to 12th Street. Built in the late 1930s as part of the FDR Drive, the park's sporting facilities are some of the best Manhattan has to offer. The East River Esplanade welcomes runners, rollerbladers, dog-walkers, and those who just want to enjoy up-close views of the Williamsburg Bridge and across to Brooklyn. Long-term plans call for waterfront parkland from The Battery to Harlem, and in fact East River Park is part of an overall plan to someday create one continuous green stretch from Maine to Florida, known as the **East Coast Greenway**.

Attractions

The park comes alive in the summer and on weekends, when hundreds of families barbecue in the areas between the athletic fields, blaring music and eating to their hearts' content. Others take leisurely strolls or jogs along the East River Esplanade, which offers dramatic views of the river and Brooklyn. Many have turned the park's unused areas into unofficial dog runs, places for pick-up games of ultimate Frisbee or soccer, and sunbathing areas. And aside from bathing beauties, you'll even find fishermen waiting patiently for striped bass (not that we have to tell you, but nothing caught in the East River should be eaten—while the water quality has improved dramatically, it's still full of pollutants).

Sports

The sports facilities at East River Park have undergone heavy reconstruction. The park now includes facilities for football, softball, basketball, soccer, tennis, and even cricket. Thankfully, many of the fields have been resurfaced with a resilient synthetic turf—a smart move given the amount of use the park gets by all the different sports leagues.

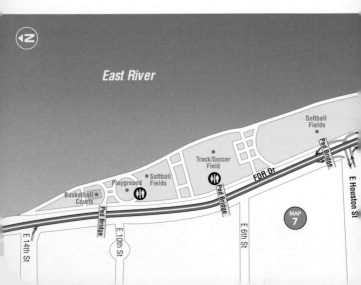

Facilities

There are three bathroom facilities located in the park—one at the tennis courts, one at the soccer/track field, and one up in the northern part of the park by the playground. The reconstruction has provided East River Park with new benches, game tables, seal sprinklers for the kids, and new water fountains. Aside from the occasional guy with a cart full of cold drinks, there are no food or drink options close by. Your best bet is to arrive at the park with any supplies you might need—if that's too difficult, try a bodega on Avenue D.

Esoterica

Built in 1941, the Corlears Hook Pavilion was the original home of Joseph Papp's Shakespeare in the Park. However, it closed in 1973, and has never quite returned to its glory days. Plans for the fancy $9.9 million amphitheater/restaurant that was to replace the sad-looking, abandoned, graffiti-covered Corlears Hook Pavilion band shell have been canned.

A less ambitious reconstruction took place in 2001, however, and with new seating, a renovated band shell, and a good scrubbing, the facility is currently open for use.

How to Get There

Two FDR Drive exits will get you very close to East River Park—the Houston Street exit and the Grand Street exit. Technically, cars are not allowed in the park. There is some parking available at the extreme south end of the park by Jackson Street off the access road, but it's hard to get to and poorly marked. Plan to find street parking just west of the FDR and cross over on a footbridge.

If you are taking the subway, you'd better have your hiking boots on—the fact that the closest subways (them J, M, Z, F at Delancey/Essex St and the L at First Ave) are so far away (at least four avenue blocks) is one of the reasons East River Park has stayed mainly a neighborhood park. Fortunately, if you're into buses, the M22, M21, M14 and M8 get you pretty close. Regardless of the bus or subway lines, you will have to cross one of the five pedestrian bridges that traverse the FDR Drive, unless you approach via the East River Esplanade.

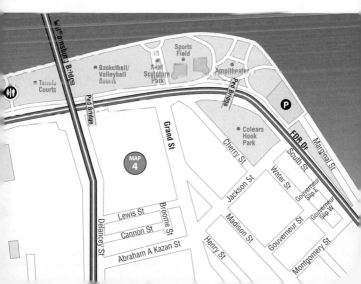

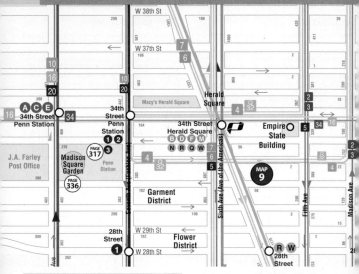

General Information

NFT Map:	9
Address:	350 Fifth Ave (& 34th St)
Phone:	212-736-3100
Website:	www.esbnyc.com
	@EmpireStateBldg
Observatory Hours:	Open daily 365 days a year

8 am–2 am. Last elevators
go up at 1:15 am
Observatory Admission: $27 for adults, $21 for kids,
$24 for seniors, $50 if you want to be a show off
and cut in front of everyone to the front of the line
(we're not lying with this one, folks…our society is
indeed morally bankrupt).

Overview

There may not be a gorilla climbing it, but if you
don't already know the "World's Most Famous Office
Building," the jig is up, Mac. Put down the NFT and
back away slooowly. You're not a true Manhattanite;
you're not even a well-researched tourist. So, folks,
how did the giant end up perching on our block?
In 1930, at the hands of raw men compounding
raw material day after day, four-and-a-half stories
were erected per week. Those ravaged from the
Depression and eager to put their minds to work
built the 1,500-foot structure in just 14 months, way

ahead of schedule. We used to make stuff in thi
country. Quickly.

A year later, it served as an ambassador to visitine
dignitaries like Queen Elizabeth and, years late
your Aunt Elizabeth. These days it is one of New Yor
City's (and the world's) most famous landmarks
Movies have been shot there. Big shots work there
Wherever you are in Manhattan (and sometime
Brooklyn or Queens), it's there to orient you. An
you can take plenty of snapshots from the reason
you-go-there observation deck on the 86th floor. N
trick questions asked. Some New Yorkers think it
hip to have never been to the Empire State Building
These people are nuts. Whether you choose to g
during the day or at night, it's a totally different bu
amazing experience either way.

The Lights

As far away as downtown and all the way uptowr
the lights of the Empire State Building soar abov
the clouds, signifying an international holiday anc
or an interminable disease. On the 86th floor, a ma
with binoculars and a direct line to the lightin
engineers waits. His raison d'être? Close-flying flock
of birds. One phone call, and the lights go out, le
the poor suckers smash their beaks and plunge t
their death from the mesmerizing lights. True story

Lighting Schedule (for updates/changes, check www.esbnyc.com)

■■■ January • Martin Luther King, Jr. Day
■□■ January • March of Dimes
■■■ January–February • Lunar New Year
■■■ February 14 • Valentine's Day
■□■ February • President's Day
■■■ February • Westminster Kennel Club
■■□ February • Swisspeaks Festival for Switzerland
■■■ February • World Cup Archery Championship
■■■ March 17 • St. Patrick's Day
■■□ March • Greek Independence Day
■■■ March • Equal Parents Day/ Children's Rights
■■□ March • Wales/St. David's Day
■■■ March • Oscar Week in NYC
■■■ March • Colon Cancer Awareness
■■□ March • Red Cross Month
■□□ March–April • Spring/Easter Week
■■■ April • Earth Day
■■■ April • Child Abuse Prevention
■■□ April • National Osteoporosis Society
■■■ April • Rain Forest Day
□□■ April • Israel Independence Day
■■□ April • Dutch Queen's Day
■□■ April • Tartan Day
■■□ May • Muscular Dystrophy
□□■ May • Armed Forces Day
■□■ May • Memorial Day
■■■ May • Police Memorial Day
■■□ May • Fire Department Memorial Day
■■■ May • Haitian Culture Awareness
■■■ June 14 • Flag Day
■□■ June • Portugal Day
■ ■ June • NYC Triathlon
■■□ June • Stonewall Anniversary/ Gay Pride
◄□■ July 4 • Independence Day
■□■ July • Bahamas Independence Day
□□■ July • Bastille Day
□□■ July • Peru Independence
■■■ July • Columbia Heritage & Independence
■■■ August • US Open

■■■ August • Jamaica Independence Day
■□■ August • India Independence Day
■■□ August • Pakistan Independence Day
■□■ September • Mexico Independence Day
■□■ September • Labor Day
■■■ September • Brazil Independence Day
■■■ September • Pulaski Day
■■■ September • Race for the Cure
■□■ September • Switzerland admitted to the UN
■■■ September • Qatar Independence
■□■ September • Fleet Week/Support our Servicemen and Servicewomen/ Memorial for 9/11
■■■ September • Feast of San Gennaro
■■□ October • Breast Cancer Awareness
■■■ October • German Reunification Day
■□■ October • Columbus Day
□□■ October 24 • United Nations Day
■■■ October • Big Apple Circus
■■□ October • Pennant/World Series win for the Yankees
■■■ October • Pennant/World Series win for the Mets [Ha!]
■■■ October • NY Knicks Opening Day
■■□ October–November • Autumn
■■□ October • Walk to End Domestic Violence
■■■ November • NYC Marathon
■□■ November • Veterans' Day
■■□ November • Alzheimer's Awareness
■□■ December • First night of Hanukkah
■■■ December • "Day Without Art/Night Without Lights"/AIDS Awareness
■■■ December–January 7 (with interruptions) • Holiday Season

General Information

NFT Maps: 5 & 8
Website: www.thehighline.org or @highlinenyc

Overview

Built on top of a disused portion of elevated freight train tracks, The High Line is at once both an escape from the chaos of the city's streets and a celebration of Manhattan's West Side, especially its architecture. The first section between Gansevoort Street and West 20th Street opened in 2009 and was an instant success, proving that open space could be hip and stylish, and causing the city tax assessor's heart to race at the thought of all the surrounding property that suddenly deserved a second look. Section 2, which opened in June 2011, doubled the length of the park up to 30th Street. Section 4, completed in 2014, follows the elevated track to its end at 34th Street.

The rail line was built in the 1930s as part of the West Side Improvement project that eliminated dangerous at-grade railroad crossings and alleviated terrible traffic along Manhattan's West Side. The same project expanded Riverside Park on the Upper West Side. As trucking became more efficient, train traffic on the rail line slowed. By 1980 the entire line shut down and quickly fell into disrepair. Many wanted to demolish the line, which was prohibitively expensive, but a grassroots group, Friends of the High Line, slowly built support that became a groundswell, thanks in part to a mayoral administration that didn't mind investing in high-end development. The final cost of sections 1 and 2 was $152.3 million, including $112 million from the city, $20 million from the federal government and nearly $50 million in privately raised funds.

The High Line is open from 7 am to 10 pm daily (7 pm during winter and 11 pm during summer). The entire thing is wheelchair accessible although there are limited access points along the way. Dogs and bicycles are strictly prohibited, though there are bike racks at street level at various access points. Closest subway access is the A, C, and E along Eighth Avenue or the 1 along Seventh Avenue. The M11, M14, M23 and M34 buses also travel toward the park.

The park has several environmentally friendly touches. The flora planted along the High Line is representative of the region's native ecology. Half of the plants are native to North America and 30% are native to the Northeast, making the park a natural home to birds and butterflies. The park also absorbs and uses rainwater that would otherwise be finding its way into gutters. Although the philosophy is low impact, the High Line has had a decidedly high impact on the surrounding neighborhood. In addition to providing an aesthetically pleasing path from the Meatpacking District north into the heart of Chelsea's art galleries, the High Line has attracted people and businesses to a part of the city that was perhaps better known for its untz-untz dance clubs and Scores. The High Line has been a catalyst for both architectural and cultural development in the area, including The Whitney's new home in the Meatpacking District.

Take a quick survey of the architecture by simply looking up. **The Standard**, which straddles the High Line just south of 14th Street, sports a posh restaurant as well as a beer garden, both directly underneath the High Line. Two other stunning architectural gems visible from the High Line (looking down) are Frank Gehry's first commercial office building in New York, Barry Diller's **IAC Building**, and Jean Nouvel's **100 Eleventh Avenue** condo building right across the street. The IAC is one of the most wonderfully luminescent buildings in all of New York, and Nouvel's facade of hundreds of differently sized panes of glass became an instant classic. Of course, the work on the High Line itself, by architects Diller Scofidio + Renfro and landscape architects James Corner Field Operations, is simply amazing. The 10th Avenue Square area, with amphitheater-style seating and a living-room-window view of the northbound traffic of Tenth Avenue, is a favorite as well as a perfect place for a picnic (hit up the nearby Chelsea Market food vendors).

While weekend days during summer on the High Line is already a madhouse, we recommend an early-morning or evening stroll during spring and fall. The cityscape views at night are stunning; early morning is quiet and generally cool, until the sun moves above the skyscrapers to the east of the park. Really, there is no bad time to visit the High Line. The views will be great no matter what time of day it is.

Great food options abound nearby, including hip **Cookshop (Map 8)**, French haven **La Lunchonette (Map 8)**, neighborhood standby **Red Cat (Map 8)**, Jean-Georges Vongerichten's **Spice Market (Map 5)**, and warm Italian **Bottino (Map 8)**. Want cheaper fare? Hit greasy spoon **Hector's (Map 5)** or wait for one of the gourmet trucks to pull up around the corner from the Gansevoort stairs, or go DIY by buying food at **Chelsea Market (Map 8)**. On the High Line itself, look out for stands selling artisanal popsicles, ice cream, tacos and coffee.

At night, you can hang around to rock out at **The Highline Ballroom (Map 8)**, or drink at pubs **The Half King (Map 8)**, **Brass Monkey (Map 5)**, or The Standard's **Biergarten (Map 5)**, or, better yet, walk the streets of the West 20s in search of gallery openings (read: free wine and cheese). No matter how you slice it, a visit to the High Line will only make you happier. We promise.

Parks & Places · **Hudson River Park**

General Information

Hudson River
Park Trust: 212-627-2020
www.hudsonriverpark.org
www.friendsofhudsonriverpark.org
Twitter: @HudsonRiverPark

Overview

It's up for debate whether Hudson River Park is a beacon for downtown joggers or a Bermuda triangle that pilots should fly away from. In a matter of months, this western stretch of green torpedoed into infamy when two planes and a helicopter crash-landed off the banks of the park. Most famously, the U.S. Airways "Miracle on the Hudson" skidded to a safe water landing in early 2009. Seven months later, a helicopter and a small plane collided in nearly the same spot and killed nine people.

Of course, we'd rather talk about the park's safer aerial acrobatics, like the trapezes and half-pipes that define this 550-acre, $330 million park development along the south and southwest coastline of Manhattan, stretching from Battery Place to West 59th Street.

As part of the New York State Significant Coastal Fish and Wildlife Habitat, 400 acres of the total 550 thrive as estuarine sanctuary. This means the 70 fish species (there are fish in the Hudson?) and 30 bird species on the waterfront won't go belly up or beak down with all the marine preservation. Thanks to this effort, you'll be able to enjoy the winter flounder, white perch, owls, hawks, and songbirds for generations to come. (That's fantastic! Bob, tell them what else they've won...) What downtown, nature-loving, organic-eating savers of the planet have won is in what they've lost. As a mandate, office buildings, hotels, casino gambling boats, and manufacturing plants are prohibited from the HRP, as are residences (sorry, no water-front property next to your yacht) and jet skis (better to leave them in the Caymans). Check out the *Intrepid* aircraft carrier/sea-air space museum, especially during Fleet Week each year (usually the week of Memorial Day, in May). You'll get to see teeming Navy personnel and much more modern vessels, some of which absolutely dwarf the *Intrepid* itself. A sight not to be missed.

Art

HRP takes its culture cue from the surrounding downtown art scene of TriBeCa, SoHo, and Chelsea. Perhaps you saw one of Merce Cunningham Dance Company's final performances before they shut down. Or maybe you were waiting in line to see *Ashes and Snow*, Gregory Colbert's rendition of the interaction between animals and humans took form in the temporary Nomadic Museum on Pier 54. Or maybe you checked out Malcolm Cochran's *Private Passage* on Clinton Cove (55th–57th St). Similar to your late-night antics, you peered into a gigantic wine bottle. There from portholes carved on the sides, you could see the interior of the stateroom of the Queen Mary. Or, hearkening back to an early time, the *Shadow of the Lusitania*. Justen Ladda recreated the shadow of the famous ship on the south side of Pier 54 (also home to reconstructed historic ships, not just their shadows), its original docking place, with glass and planters. Jutting out where Pier 49 used to sit is one of the park's more sombre exhibits, the New York City AIDS memorial. Dedicated on World AIDS Day in 2008 after 14 years of fundraising and planning, the 42-foot-long memorial is both a striking accomplishment and a sober nod to those whose lives have been lost to the disease. A more permanent piece in HRP: *Salinity Gradient* in TriBeCa. Paver stones spanning 2000 feet take the shape of Hudson marine creatures. Striped bass included. Not impressed? HRP Trust hired different designers for each segment of the five-mile park, with only the esplanade and waterfront railing as universal pieces. Check out the landscape design of each segment.

Attractions

Season-specific events are held year-round at HRP. During the summer, experience fight-night basics on Pier 84 for Rumble on the River with live blood splattering with each KO. Sundays in the summer host MoonDances on Pier 84 with free dance lessons before live New York bands play Wednesday and Fridays in the summer boast River Flicks on Pier 54 and Pier 84 with throwback films like *The Goonies*. Pier of Fear is mainly a Halloween party for the kiddies, but if you're still down with dressing up as the Scream guy, hey, no one will stop you. An estuarium (dedicated to the science of the river) and a TriBeCa dog run, among other projects, are next on the list of improvements for HRP.

Sports

Think of sports in terms of piers. You already know about ritzy Chelsea Piers, but soon enough "Pier 40" or "Pier 63" will also become vernacular to sports freaks. And there are far less expensive piers beyond CP. Most crucial to athletic-minded souls, a five-mile running/biking/blading path that threads through the piers. It's a miniature divided highway—smooth, simple, and super crowded during peak times (early evening and weekends). You'll find sunbathing lawns throughout (the most sport some will ever do). Pier 40: three and a half ball fields. Area south of Houston: three tennis courts. Mini-golf. Batting cages. Skateboard park. Beach volleyball. Trapeze lessons. Pier 40, CP, Pier 63, Pier 96: free kayaking. Those are the highlights; for more that's up your particular sports alley, check out the website.

How to Get There

Hmmm. How to most efficiently make your way through all the concrete to the shoreline? The 1 and A, C, E between Chambers and 59th Streets will get you the closest. Go west 'til you hit water. You're there.

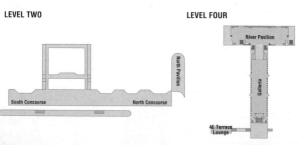

LEVEL ONE

Special Events Hall

Exhibition Halls

1E 1D 1C 1B 1A

LEVEL THREE

3E 3D 3B 3A

LEVEL TWO

South Concourse

North Concourse

North Pavilion

LEVEL FOUR

River Pavilion

Galleria

4E Terrace Lounge

General Information

NFT Map:	8
Address:	655 W 34th St
Website:	www.javitscenter.com
	@javitscenter
Phone Number:	212-216-2000

Overview

This massive 2.1 million square-foot glass-and-steel behemoth of a convention hall next to the Hudson River was officially built to house big trade shows, conventions and expositions, but clearly its true purpose is to annoy anyone who has to go there. Located between 34th and 38th Streets, the James Ingo Freed design has been sitting in the middle of nowhere since 1986. Although it generates well over $1 billion of business for New York, dissatisfaction with the convention center has brewed for a number of years, with complaints ranging from the aesthetic (big ugly box) to the practical (lack of space). Various plans have been proposed over the years to expand the center up or over the adjoining west side rail yards, and overhaul the building's facade. The Javits even got dragged into the Jets stadium fiasco, but seems to have emerged with some concrete progress towards a revamping: in late-2006, ground was broken on an expansion that would more than double the size of the Center. The election of a new governor, Eliot Spitzer, and subsequent resignation of said governor due to prostitution allegations resulted in a re-evaluation of the plans. When discovered that most of the $1.6 billion budget would go towards fixing—not expanding—the project was essentially nixed. Meanwhile, somewhere along the way someone even got the idea to demolish Javits completely, replacing it with a larger version out at the Aqueduct Racetrack near JFK in Queens. In the meantime, a less ambitious and somewhat less-expensive $465 million renovation added 110,000 square feet of space to the north, connected via level two, and various (environmentally) friendly features.

What is most important to know about the Javits, and most other convention centers in the world, is that they are essentially soulless, dehumanizing spaces with crappy bathrooms, horrific food, nowhere to sit, and filled (generally) with absolutely slimy, soulless, moronic sales and marketing people; it just depends on which industry is in town that moment as to what exact breed you're getting. Even the presence of sweet sports cars (i.e. the Auto Show each Easter week) can't overcome a feeling, after spending even two hours in this convention center, of an absolute black nihilism. Surely someone's come up with something better? Perhaps all trade shows should simply be outdoors in Southern California in the spring—at least, that's our vote. Wait, was that out loud?

All that said, the extension of the 7 train to 11th Avenue and 34th Street should help make the 'ol glass eyesore seem a little more connected to civilization (or at least the rest of Midtown). And plans are in place for a third phase of the nearby High Line that will terminate at Javits' southern edge at West 34th Street. Easier to get to and a more pleasant overall experience—all this in spite of itself (sounds about right).

The main exhibition halls are on the first and third levels. Levels one and three also have ATMs. Go to level two for coffee, newsstands, and transportation. The lounges are on the fourth level.

Food

The food at the Javits Center is, of course, rapaciously expensive, and, if you're exhibiting, usually sold out by mid-afternoon. There are food courts on levels one and three that serve typical food court fare: pizza, deli sandwiches, juices & smoothies, and the requisite mall-style Asian and panini tare. As an alternative, look for people handing out Chinese food menus and have them deliver to your booth. (And yes, they take credit cards. And yes, it's bad Chinese food.)

How to Get There—
Mass Transit

Until the extension of 7 train, there was no direct subway access to the center. The next closest subway stop is 34th Street/Penn Station, a good four- to five-block hike away. The M42 and M34 buses travel crosstown on 42nd Street and 34th Street, respectively, connecting with subway stops along the center. Both bus routes drop you off right outside the center.

There are also numerous shuttle buses that run to various participating hotels and other locales free of charge for convention goers. Schedules and routes vary for each convention, so ask at the information desk on the first floor.

From New Jersey, the NY Waterway operates ferries from Weehawken that ships you across the Hudson River to 39th Street and Twelfth Avenue in under 10 minutes, dropping you just one block from the Javits Center. The ferries leave every 15–30 minutes during peak hours. Call 1-800-53-FERRY or go to www.nywaterway.com for a schedule and more information.

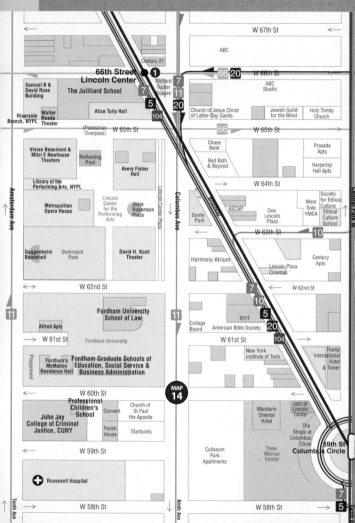

General Information

NFT Map:	14
Website:	www.lincolncenter.org
	@LincolnCenter
General Info:	212-875-5000
Guided Tours:	212-875-5350
CenterCharge:	212-721-6500

Venues

Alice Tully Hall:	212-671-4050
Avery Fisher Hall	212-875-5030
David H. Koch Theater:	212-870-5570
Walter Reade Theater:	212-875-5610

Organizations

The Chamber Music Society:	212-875-5775
Film Society of Lincoln Center:	212-875-5367
Jazz at Lincoln Center:	212 258 9000
The Julliard School:	212-799-5000
Lincoln Center Theater:	212-362-7600
The Metropolitan Opera House:	212-362-6000
New York City Ballet:	212-496-0600
New York Philharmonic:	212-875-5656
New York Public Library for the Performing Arts:	917-275-6975

Overview

Lincoln Center is the largest performing arts center in the world, which means it's a beloved icon, but it's also guilty of some cultural Disneyfication. It sets the gold standard, but it also needs to make money, which it does by presenting the same venerable artists performing the same standard works, geared toward an aging, wealthy, elitist audience. However, that shouldn't stop you from seeing the Met Opera, hearing the New York Philharmonic, and taking a photo by the fountain at least once in your life. Go ahead, wear jeans to the ballet, in the name of the people!

In 2012 LC completed a massive $1.2 billion renovation, which included a much-needed facelift (inside and out) for Alice Tully Hall and the addition of a lawn-covered café, among other worthy attractions. Don't miss out on discount tickets at the new Atrium, one small step toward lowering LC's snob factor. (But not for long, as LC now hosts Mercedes-Benz Fashion Week.) Jazz at Lincoln Center, opened in 2004, benefits from having Wynton Marsalis as its artistic director; the trumpet deus has done wonders for promoting jazz education. That said, JALC embodies the same disparity as the rest of LC: it's an esteemed heavyweight in the jazz world, but it caters to the 1%, despite jazz having been conceived as accessible music for regular folks like you and me.

Who Lives Where

A mecca of tulle, tin, and strings, Lincoln Center houses companies upon troupes upon societies. Matching the performing group to the building means you won't end up watching *Swan Lake* when you should be listening to Mozart. The most confusing part about Lincoln Center is that "Lincoln Center Theater" is actually two theaters—the Vivian Beaumont and the Mitzi E. Newhouse theaters. Jazz at Lincoln Center moved into the Frederick P. Rose Hall in the Time Warner Center.

American Ballet Theater—Metropolitan Opera House
Chamber Music Society—Alice Tully Hall
Film Society of Lincoln Center—Walter Reade Theater
Jazz at Lincoln Center—Frederick P. Rose Hall
Julliard Orchestra & Symphony—Alice Tully Hall
Metropolitan Opera Company—Metropolitan Opera House
Lincoln Center Theater—Vivian Beaumont Theater and Mitzi E. Newhouse Theater
Mostly Mozart Festival—Avery Fisher Hall
New York City Ballet—David H. Koch Theater
New York Philharmonic—Avery Fisher Hall
School of American Ballet—Samuel B. and David Rose Building

Columbus Circle

The crazy-making subterranean Whole Foods in the Time Warner Center is probably the reason most trek over to Columbus Circle, but don't miss the intriguing Museum of Arts and Design, which opened up on the south side of the circle in 2008 following an expensive and controversial renovation of 2 Columbus Circle. Check out its sublime permanent collection, excellent temporary exhibits, and cool design shop. As for the Time Warner Center, the shops therein cohere into something resembling a mall, a Manhattan rarity, though one with a great view of Central Park. Elsewhere there is the Mandarin Oriental Hotel, featuring 18,000-count sheets on which your out-of-town guests will not sleep unless they own a small kingdom. Ditto for eating at Thomas Keller's Per Se ($300-plus per person, not including wine), though his Bouchon Bakery is more within reach. See also the uptown outpost of TriBeCa's cool Landmarc restaurant. The Trump International Hotel and Tower rises up across the street, next to the riff on the Unisphere; Nougatine, of Jean-Georges fame, is its premier lunch spot...ahh...the other reason you go to Columbus Circle.

How to Get There

Lincoln Center is right off Broadway and only a few blocks north of Columbus Circle, which makes getting there easy. The closest subway is the 66th Street 1 stop, which has an exit right on the edge of the center. It's also an easy walk from the trains that roll into Columbus Circle. If you prefer above-ground transportation, the M5, M7, M10, M11, M20, M66, and M104 bus lines all stop within one block of Lincoln Center. There is also a parking lot underneath the complex.

1. 31 Union Sq. W.
   Residence Hall
2. Albert and Vera List Academic Center
   6 E. 16th St.
3. 8 E. 16th St. / 79 Fifth Ave.
4. 25 E. 13th St.
5. 65 Fifth Ave.
6. 80 Fifth Ave.
7. Fanton Hall/Welcome Center
   72 Fifth Ave.
8. Arnhold Hall
   55 W. 13th St.
9. 118 W. 13th St.
   Residence Hall
10. 2 W. 13th St.
11. 70 Fifth Ave.
12. 68 Fifth Ave.
13. Shelia C. Johnson Design Center
    66 Fifth Ave.
14. Loeb Hall
    135 E. 12th St.
15. Alvin Johnson/
    J.M. Kaplan Building
    66 W. 12th St.
16. Eugene Lang College
    65 W. 11th St.
17. 64 W. 11th St.
18. 5 W. 8th St.
    Marlton House

General Information

NFT Maps: 5 & 6
Welcome Center: 72 Fifth Ave (at 13th St)
Phone: 212-229-5600
Website: www.newschool.edu
                   @TheNewSchool
Enrollment: 10,340 (2012)
Endowment: $205 million (2012)

Overview

The New School, formerly The New School for Social Research, is a legendary progressive university located in and around Greenwich Village, housing seven major divisions, a world-renowned think tank and the backdrop for Project Runway. Founded in 1919 as a refuge for intellectual nonconformists (including historian Charles Beard, philosopher John Dewey, and several former Columbia professors), The New School credits its philosophy to the fusing of American intellectual rigor and European critical thought.

The university annually enrolls 10,000 students within seven undergraduate and graduate divisions, including Parsons The New School for Design, The New School for Public Engagement, Eugene Lang College The New School for Liberal Arts, Mannes College The New School for Music, The New School for Drama, The New School for Social Research, and The New School for Jazz and Contemporary Music.

The current New School for Social Research, formerly the Graduate Faculty of Political and Social Science, formerly the University in Exile was a division founded as a haven for dismissed teachers from totalitarian regimes in Europe. Original members included psychologist Erich Fromm and political philosopher Leo Strauss. Quite a lineage with which more recent graduates as Sufjan Stevens and Marc Jacobs have to contend.

Tuition

Tuition for undergraduates can exceed $40,000 per year plus nearly $14,000 to share an apartment with two or three other students. Yes, that's over $1,650 per month to share a living space for the school year (not the full calendar year). See website for detailed division-by-division tuition information.

Culture on Campus

Parsons is always showcasing something or other, from student shows to MoMA-presented conferences to fine arts lectures. The John L. Tischman Auditorium is the egg-shaped art deco venue for the masses. The quad courtyard, between buildings on 12th and 13th Streets, is the closest thing to a college campus. Otherwise, there's the city.

Transportation

All the subways that Union Square has to offer: N, Q, R, 4, 5, 6, and the L. See also the F and M trains along Sixth Avenue.

General Phone Numbers

Admission and Financial
Aid Information . . . . 212-229-5150 or 800-292-3040
Alumni Relations: 212-229-5662
Campus Security: 212-229-7001

Academic Phone Numbers

Parsons The New School for Design 212-229-8900
Eugene Lang College The New School
for Liberal Arts 212-229-5665
The New School for Social Research 212-229-5700
The New School for Public Engagement . . . 212-229-5615
Mannes College The New School
for Music 212-580-0210
The New School for Drama 212-229-5859
The New School for Jazz and
Contemporary Music 212-229-5896

1. Carlyle Court
2. Coral Towers
3. Thirteenth St Residence Hall
4. 145 Fourth Avenue
5. University Hall
6. Palladium Hall
7. 113 University Place
8. 838 Broadway
9. 7 E 12th Street
10. Casa Italiana Zerilli-Marimò
11. Founder's Hall
12. Third Avenue North Residence Hall
13. Rubin Residence Hall
14. Bronfman Center
15. Brittany Residence Hall
16. Lillian Vernon Creative Writers House

17. Alumni Hall
18. Barney Building
19. 13 University Place
20. Cantor Film Center
21. 10 Astor Place
22. Deutches Haus
23. Glucksman Ireland House
24. Institute of French Studies/ La Maison Française
25. Weinstein Residence Hall
26. Straus Institute
27. 19 Washington Sq. North
28. One-Half Fifth Avenue
29. 1-6 Washington Square North
   - School of Social Work
   - Graduate School of Arts and Science
30. Rufus D Smith Hall
31. Seventh Street Residence
32. 111, 113A Second Avenue

33. Silver Center Block
   - Silver Center for Arts and Science
   - Waverly Building
   - Brown Building
   - Grey Art Gallery
34. Kimball Block
   - Kimball Hall
   - Torch Club
   - Copy Central
   - 285 Mercer Street

35. Broadway Block
   - 715 Broadway
   - 719 Broadway
   - 719 Broadway
   - 1 Washington P
   - 3 Washington P
   - 5 Washington P
36. NYU Health Center College of Nursin
37. 411 Lafayette Str

38. 48 Cooper Square
39. Hayden Residence Hall
40. Education Block
   - Pless Hall
   - Pless Annex
   - NYU Bookstore
   - East Building
   - Faye's @ the Square
   - Goddard Hall
41. Student Services Block
   - 25 West Fourth Street
   - Public Safety
   - 242 Greene Street
   - 14A Washington Place
   - 19 West Fourth Street
   - 8 Washington Place
   - 10 Washington Place
42. Meyer Block
   - Meyer Hall
   - Psychology Building
43. Provincetown Playhouse
   - Wilf Hall
44. Vanderbilt Hall
45. Judson Block
   - Kevorkian Center
   - Skirball Department
   - King Juan Carlos I Center
   - Furman Hall

46. 58 Washington Square South
47. Kimmel Center for University Life
   - Skirball Center for the Performing Arts
48. Bobst Library
49. Schwartz Plaza
50. Shimkin Hall
   - Gould Welcome Center
51. Kaufman Management Center
52. Tisch Hall
53. Courant Institute
54. Silk Building
55. Housing
56. D'Agostino Hall
57. 561 La Guardia Place
58. Mercer Street Residence

59. 530 La Guardia Place
60. Mail Services
61. Off Campus Housing
62. 665 Broadway
63. Second Street Residence Hall
64. University Plaza
65. Silver Towers
66. Coles Sports and Recreation Center
67. 194, 196 Mercer Street
68. Puck Building
   - Wagner Graduate School of Public Service

General Information

NFT Map:	6
Phone:	212-998-1212
Website:	www.nyu.edu or @nyuniversity
Enrollment:	44,599 (2013)
Endowment:	$3.1 billion (2013)

Overview

Founded in 1831, one of the nation's largest private universities sprawls throughout Manhattan, though its most recognizable buildings border Washington Square. Total enrollment hovers around 45,000, about half of whom are undergrads, many of whom will flood the city with their artistic product upon graduation, as if there wasn't enough competition for young artists here.

The expansion of NYU during recent years has not been welcomed by local residents. Some Village folks blame NYU's sprawl for higher rents and diminished neighborhood character. On the other hand, the students are a great boon to area businesses, the Washington Square campus is one of the city's largest private employers (this in a sector that enjoyed great growth even despite the country's recent economic downturn), and—to the ostensible point of many of the university's detractors—many historical buildings, such as the row houses on Washington Square, are owned and kept in good condition by the university.

NYU comprises 14 colleges, schools, and divisions, including the well-regarded Stern School of Business, the School of Law, and the Tisch School of Arts. It also has a school of Continuing and Professional Studies, with offerings in publishing, real estate, and just about every other city-centric industry you could imagine. Oh, and somehow they have the only Chick-fil-A this side of Paramus.

Tuition

If you squint, tuition for undergraduates runs around $50,000, plus $15,000 for room and board. Presented without comment.

Sports

NYU isn't big on athletics. They don't have a football team—where would they play anyway? It does have a number of other sports teams, however, and its fencing teams are highly competitive, with a long list of Olympians. The school competes in Division III and its mascot is the Bobcat, although all of their teams are nicknamed the Violets. The reason for this is explainable but by no means awe-inspiring. "Violets" comes from the cute purple flowers that grew in Washington Square Park. Preferring a more robust identity, in the early 1980s the school turned to the Bobcat, inspired by—no kidding—its novel new computerized Bobst Library Catalog system dubbed "BobCat." Somewhere Albert Gallatin was all like, "SMH," but it stuck and here we are today…

Culture on Campus

The Grey Art Gallery usually have something cool (www.nyu.edu/greyart), and the Skirball Center for the Performing Arts hosts live performances (nyuskirball.org). Still, NYU doesn't host nearly as many events as decent liberal arts schools in the middle of nowhere. But then again, why would they? NYU is in Greenwich Village, surrounded by some of the world's best rock and jazz clubs, and on the same island as 700+ art galleries, thousands of restaurants, and tons of revival and new cinema. This is both the blessing and the curse of NYU—no true "campus," but situated in the middle of the greatest cultural square mileage in the world.

Transportation

NYU runs its own campus transportation service for students, faculty, staff, and alumni with school ID cards. They run 7 am to 12 midnight weekdays and 10 am to 12 midnight weekends. During fall and spring session, free overnight Safe Ride Van Service is available to and from NYU facilities. NYU also has its own bike share program. Unlike Citibike, it's free and users can have bikes for the entire day.

General Phone Numbers

Gould Welcome Center	212-998-4550
Office of Financial Aid	212-998-4444
University Development and Alumni Relations	212-998-6900
Bobst Library Information	212-998-2500
Main Bookstore	212-998-4667

Bronx Kill

Bronx Shore Fields

PAGE
242

Bronx

RFK Bridge

10

Parks 5 Boro
Complex   9

RFK Bridge

Golf
Center   1

Discus
Thrower

Picnic
Area

**Randall's
Island**

Sunken Meadows
Fields

Paladino Ave

E 120th St

E 119th St

E 118th St

MAP
20

Harlem
River
Event
Area

2
Icahn
Stadium

Tennis
Center

8

FDNY
Fire Academy

7

Manhattan

E 116th St

Pleasant Ave

FDR Dr

E 114th St

278

Shand Rd

Nature
Center

**East
River**

Harlem River

Roosevelt Dr

Manhattan
Psychiatric
Center

6   Wards Island
Treatment
Plant

**Wards
Island**

Central Fields

Hell Gate Bridge

3

5

Kantor
Fields

Children's Playground

Sunken
Garden Fields

Picnic
Area

E 103 St Footbridge

4

Hell Gate
Fields

Wards
Meadow
Fields

East River Fields

RFK Bridge

Hell Gate

Que

General Information

Randall's Island Park Alliance: 212-830-7722

Website: www.randallsisland.org or @randallsisland

Overview

If landfills, minimal food options, and a treacherous mix of the Harlem and East Rivers called "Hell Gate" don't entice you over the RFK Bridge, you probably have good instincts. But put Randall's & Wards Islands' sullied past aside, and its 480 acres of open space just across the bridge will surprise you, not only its abundant recreational facilities but also the large concerts, art fairs and various festivals that set up shop each summer.

The islands, which were actually once two separate features since connected by landfill, were once home to hospitals and various social outreach facilities. In the 1930s the site began to transition to its current use as a public park and recreational hub. Over the years the island's Downing Stadium hosted concerts starring the likes of Duke Ellington and Jimi Hendrix. Jesse Owens competed there in Olympic trials, and Soccer great Pele played there with the Cosmos in the 1970s.

As with many of the city's ambitious 1930s-era projects, by the 1980s Randall's Island fell into disrepair, but since 1999 it has undergone a huge overhaul, and now it again boasts some of the city's top recreational amenities. The Randall's Island Park Alliance public-private conservancy now operates the greenspace and keeps progress humming. The foundation kicked off the park's renovation by replacing Downing Stadium with the state-of-the-art Icahn Track & Field Stadium, opened in 2005. Since then, they've restored dozens of ballfields, marshes, and wetlands, and built new waterfront bike and pedestrian paths. Some ideas have not come to pass: in 2007, local activists put the kibosh on a grand plan to build a fancy suburban-style water park.

No matter what, we hope future plans bring in more food facilities. Currently, the only culinary options are a smattering of food trucks near the Icahn Stadium and the golf center's snack bar. One suggestion: make a Whole Foods/Fairway/Zabar pit stop before enjoying a chill weekend afternoon in the park.

How to Get There

By Car: Take the RFK Bridge, exit left to Randall's Island. While you do have to pay the MTA's hefty toll to get on the island, rest assured that it's free to leave!

By Subway/Bus: From Manhattan: take the 4, 5, 6 train to 125th Street, then transfer on the corner of 125th Street and Lexington Avenue for the M35 bus to Randall's Island. There's a bus about every 15-20 minutes during the day.

By Foot: A pedestrian footbridge at 103rd Street was built by Robert Moses in the '50s to provide Harlem residents access to the recreational facilities of the parks after then-City Council President Newbold Morris criticized the lack of facilities in Harlem. The bridge is open to pedestrians and cyclists 24/7.

Facilities

1 Randall's Island Golf Center; 212-427-5609; The golf center on Randall's Island features a year-round driving range with heated stalls along with grass tees and an area to practice your short game (complete with sand bunkers). See also their 36 holes of mini-golf, nine batting cages, snack bar, and beer garden. Shuttle service is available weekends year-round and weekdays in season ($12 round trip).

2 Icahn Track & Field Stadium; Named for financier Carl Icahn (who contributed $10 million for naming rights), the 5,000-seat stadium is the only state-of-the-art outdoor track and field venue in New York City with a 400-meter running track and a regulation-size soccer field.

3 Supportive Employment Center

4 Charles H. Gay Shelter Care Center for Men

5 Odyssey House Drug Rehab Center/Mabon Building

6 DEP Water Pollution Control Plant

7 Fire Department Training Center; the NYC Fire Academy is located on 27 acres of landfill on the east side of Randall's Island. In an effort to keep the city's bravest in shape, the academy utilizes 68 acres of parkland for physical fitness programs. The ultra-cool training facility includes 11 Universal Studios-like buildings for simulations training, a 200,000 gallon water supply tank, gasoline and diesel fuel pumps, and a 300-car parking lot. In addition, the New York Transit Authority installed tracks and subway cars for learning and developing techniques to battle subway fires and other emergencies. They're clearly missing an opportunity here…

8 Sportime Tennis Center; 212-427-6150; 20 year-round courts, including courts heated for winter use, a training facility and café.

9 Robert Moses Building; perhaps a few urban planning students have made a pilgrimage here, the one-time home of Moses' power-consolidating Triborough Bridge and Tunnel Authority.

10 NYPD; they launch cool-looking police boats from here.

General Information

Website: riversideparknyc.org
Phone: 212-870-3070

Overview

Riverside Park, stretching from 59th Street to 155th Street along the Hudson River on Manhattan's West Side, is the place where Upper West Siders go to find a little bit of rest and respite in the one of the most crowded neighborhoods in the country. The park also serves as a vital link between Upper Manhattan and Midtown for bicyclists and joggers along the water's edge, and there are ample recreational opportunities all along the way. Oh, and the views to the west across the Hudson from the vistas above are just magnificent.

The park developed in stages. The initial plans, from 72nd to 125th Streets, were conceived in the 1870s by Frederick Law Olmsted, co-designer of Central and Prospect Parks. Those designs were implemented piecemeal into the early part of the 20th century; the garden pathways and vistas along Riverside Drive are part of the original Olmsted plans. In the 1930s the Parks Department under the leadership of so-called master builder Robert Moses undertook a massive expansion of the park when the Henry Hudson Parkway was built along the waterfront and recreational facilities were added, along with the 79th Street Marina and Rotunda. In 1980, the park was designated an official scenic landmark by the City Landmarks Commission; it is one of only a handful of scenic landmarks in the city. The new millennium saw further expansion south of 72nd Street to 59th Street.

Sights & Sounds

The thin path between the Henry Hudson Parkway and the water's edge between 100th and 125th Streets is home to dozens of cherry trees, gifts of the Japanese government from 1909, and from the same batch as were planted in D.C.'s Tidal Basin. In spring the pink flowers are stunning. Speaking of trees, the American Elms along Riverside Drive are a relatively rare living example of a species that has been nearly decimated by disease over the years. Many films and television shows are shot in Riverside Park, but head to the garden at 91st Street to see where Tom Hanks finally met Meg Ryan in You've Got Mail. The Soldiers' and Sailors' Monument at 89th Street is the site of the city's annual Memorial Day commemoration. At 122nd Street is the punchline to the old Groucho Marx joke: technically, no one is buried in Grant's Tomb, as the 18th President and his wife lay in rest in two sarcophagi above ground. And if you thought you had a good deal on rent, check out the lucky few who get to dock their houseboats at the 79th Street Boat Basin. But will Zabar's deliver?

Recreation

In the early part of the 20th century park systems across the country began focusing less on passive recreation in favor of active recreation. Part of the Westside Improvement Project that covered the train tracks and built the Henry Hudson Parkway also added recreation facilities on the land below bluffs. Today Riverside Park has ballfields, basketball, tennis, volleyball and handball courts, and even kayak launches. It's safe to say that Olmsted probably never expected dog runs dotting his park

Practicalities

Take the 1, 2, 3 train to any stop between Columbus Circle and 157th and it's just a short walk west to Riverside Park. The M72 bus gets you closest to Riverside Park South and the M5 bus runs up and down Riverside Drive, right at the edge of the park.

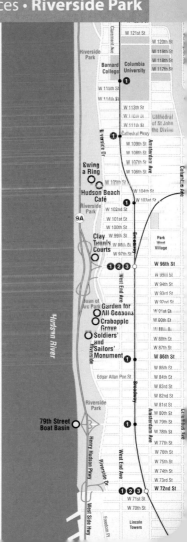

STREET LEVEL

CONCOURSE LEVEL

General Information

NFT Map:	12
Phone:	212-332-6868
Website:	www.rockefellercenter.com
	@rockcenternyc
Rink Phone:	212-332-7655
Rink Website:	www.therinkatrockcenter.com
NBC Tour	
Phone:	212-664-3700
Top of	
the Rock:	www.topoftherocknyc.com

Overview

Perhaps you've been blinded five streets away by 25,000 Swarovski crystals. Or maybe you've glimpsed a gargantuan King Kong of a tree shooting seventy feet in the air and wondered how on earth such vegetation could grow in concrete. Regardless, you fall for antics, arrive in bewilderment at Rockefeller Center, and stay for the ice skating rink, services at St. Patrick's, and the Rockettes at Radio City Music Hall. When there's not a huge pine tree to distract you, you'll note that the Rockefeller Center occupies three square blocks with a slew of retail, dining, and office facilities. Midtown corporate just ain't the same without its magic.

The massive Rockefeller Center complex was begun at the height of the Great Depression and reflects the Art Deco architecture of the era. It opened in 1933 and it's notable that most of the iconic Rockefeller Center attractions and features actually date back to those early years: the tree tradition began in 1931, the Rainbow Room opened for business in 1934, the wintertime rink first welcomed skaters in 1936, and Radio City Music Hall and its Rockettes date back to the early days. NBC has been headquartered at 30 Rockefeller Plaza (i.e., "30 Rock") since the very beginning; when you go, you'll recognize the Today show exterior immediately, and *Saturday Night Live*, *The Tonight Show Starring Jimmy Fallon* and *Late Night with Seth Meyers* all take place in the NBC studios on the lower floors of the 30 Rock. NBC offers tours of its facilities; call or visit online for more information.

The Top of the Rock Observation Deck has jaw-dropping, 360-degree views of the skyline from atop 30 Rock. In some ways it's a better view than that from the Empire State Building, if only because it features a great view of the Empire State Building. Top of the Rock is open daily 8 am–12 am (last elevator 11 pm). Tickets are timed entry and cost $27. Guided tours of Rockefeller Center are offered daily throughout the day and combined Top of the Rock/Tour tickets are available.

Where to Eat

How hungry are you? Rock Center isn't a prime dining destination, but you won't starve if you find yourself in the area. For cheaper fare, try places down in the Concourse. You'll pay for the view if you eat overlooking the skating rink. For coffee, there is an outpost of Blue Bottle on the Concourse level. The Magnolia Bakery on 49th and Sixth is one of two architectural holdouts that refused to sell to the Rockefellers. Many restaurants in Rockefeller Center are open on Saturdays, but aside from the "nice" restaurants, only a few open their doors on Sundays.

Where to Shop

Much of the Rockefeller Center roster could be at a mall nearly anywhere, but there are some fun standouts in the crowd. **FDNY Fire Zone** (50 Rockefeller Plaza) features both interactive fire safety exhibits and official FDNY merch. **La Maison Du Chocolat** (30 Rockefeller Plaza) sells high-end French chocolate and boffo hot chocolate. **Posman Books** (30 Rockefeller Plaza) is a family-owned independent bookstore. **Teuscher Chocolates** (620 Fifth Ave) are Swiss chocolates in the truest sense: they're flown in from Switzerland.

The Rink

To practice your double loop: The rink opens Columbus Day weekend and closes in April to make way for the Rink Bar. Skating hours are 8:30 am–12 am daily. Rates are $27 for each 90-minute session plus $12 skate rental. Season passes are available. If it all seems a little pricey, keep in mind that only 150 skaters are allowed on the rink at one time, making for a more intimate experience. And that setting, duh.

Overview

Once upon a time, Roosevelt Island was much like the rest of New York—populated by criminals, the sick, and the mentally ill. The difference was that they were the residents of the island's various mental institutions, hospitals, and jails, but these days this slender tract of land between Manhattan and Queens has become prime real estate for families and UN officials.

The 147-acre island, formerly known as "Welfare Island" because of its population of outcasts and the poor, was renamed for Franklin D. Roosevelt in 1973, when the island began changing its image. The first residential housing complex opened in 1975. Some of the old "monuments" remain, including the Smallpox Hospital and the Blackwell House (one of the oldest farmhouses in the city), while the Octagon Building, formerly a 19th-century mental hospital known for its deplorable conditions, has been turned into luxury condos (so yes, you're still in New York). Four Freedoms Park, which dusts off a decades-old design by the architect Louis I. Kahn, is a focal point for the southern tip of the island; the putting green-length grass and severe white granite isn't exactly welcoming, but you certainly can't beat that view of East Midtown.

The island's northern tip is a popular destination for fishermen with iron gullets. It's also the home of a lighthouse designed by James Renwick, Jr., of St. Patrick's Cathedral fame. The two rehab/convalescent hospitals on the island don't offer emergency services, so if you're in need of medical attention right away, you're out of luck. The island's main drag, Main Street (where did they come up with the name?), resembles a cement-block college campus circa 1968. Just south, closer to the tram, is a more recent stretch of development that fetches top dollar. Two of these buildings are residences for Memorial Sloan-Kettering Cancer Center and Rockefeller and Cornell University employees.

Perhaps the best way to experience the island is to spend a little while on the local shuttle bus that runs the length of the island. You'll see a wonderful mix of folks, some crazy characters, and have a chance to grill the friendly bus drivers about all things Roosevelt Island. Trust us.

How to Get There

Roosevelt Island can be reached by the train, but it's much more fun to take the tram. Plus, your out-of-town friends will love that this is the tram Tobey Maguire saved as Spiderman in the first movie. You can board it with a Metrocard (including an unlimited!) at 60th Street and Second Avenue in Manhattan—look for the big hulking mass drifting through the sky. It takes 4 minutes to cross and runs every 15 minutes (every 7 minutes during rush hour) 6 am–2 am, Sunday through Thursday, and 'til 3:30 am on Fridays and Saturdays. To get there by car, take the Queensboro Ed Koch Bridge and follow signs for the 21st Street-North exit. Go north on 21st Street and make a left on 36th Avenue. Go west on 36th Avenue and cross over the red Roosevelt Island Bridge. There is limited reliable street parking on Roosevelt Island; hit the Motorgate Plaza garage at the end of the bridge at Main Street instead.

O Landmarks

- **Blackwell House** · 591 Main St [River Rd]
- **Blackwell's Lighthouse** ·
  North tip of Roosevelt Island
- **Chapel of the Good Shepherd** ·
  546 Main St [West Rd]
- **Four Freedoms Park** ·
  1 FDR Four Freedoms Park
- **Smallpox Hospital** ·
  South tip of Roosevelt Island
- **Tramway** · 346 Main St [West Rd]

Restaurants

- **Riverwalk Bar & Grill** · 425 Main St

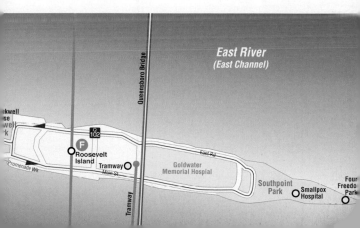

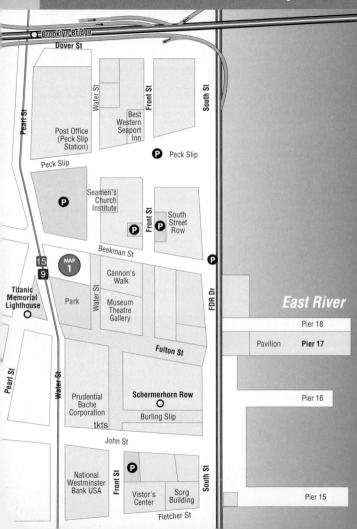

General Information

NFT Maps:	1 & 3
Phone:	212-732-8257
Website:	www.southstreetseaport.com
	@TheSeaport

Overview

For years New York's modus operandi has been something along the lines of build, tear down, build bigger, tear down again, and build even bigger until it's the biggest, bestest, most badass thing in the Western Hemisphere. Or something like that. Which is what makes the South Street Seaport such an odd and endearing spot in Lower Manhattan. The old tymey tyme historic ships and intact nineteenth-century buildings take you back to New York's mercantile/shipping past. If you squint, you just might make out Walt Whitman ducking a roving band of Dead Rabbits. Or maybe those are just a few preteens goofing while their folks settle up at the TKTS booth. Same-same.

Indeed, time was you could be forgiven if you assumed South Street Seaport was just a mall and a cobblestoned pedestrian mallful of chain stores. After Superstorm Sandy, however, the area has undergone quite a physical and spiritual change. Today the Seaport has been rebranded as a spot for container ship pop-ups, artisanal vendors from Brooklyn and a space for live events. Even the bad old mall is scheduled for a major renovation.

Part of the impetus for change has come from the Howard Hughes Corporation, which has plans to make up what had become a sleepy and, honestly, somewhat stale part of Lower Manhattan. The museum and its picturesque tall ships had been struggling financially for years, the bland shops along Schermerhorn Row amounted to a lesser Faneuil Hall Marketplace, and the less said about that strange Pier 17 mall the better. It remains to be seen whether the plans for a giant tower and multi-screen mixed-use fantasia survive first contact, but the ball is definitely rolling. And if they can do something wonderful with the former Fulton Fish Market, which has been waiting for a permanent repurposing since it closed in 2005, then it will all be for the best.

For the time being, the area deserves all the support it can get. For years, our favorite stop is friendly and crowded **Nelson Blue**, with its crisp, clean New Zealand cuisine. It can get crowded early evenings with Wall Streeters, but off-times and weekends it's a perfect respite from walking the pavement. **UteiShi**, right across the street, does excellent sushi rolls, while **Barbalu**'s owners proved stronger than the storm. A gourmet cuppa joe can be sipped at **Jack's Stir Brew** or have a glass of wine at **Bin 20** before indulging in succulent steaks at **Mark Joseph**. And then there are those great old-old school places that remain awesome—don't miss brunch at 19th-century spot **Bridge Café** and drinks at former fishmonger hangout **Paris Café**. And **Pasanella** is a great wine store.

The South Street Historic District is at a crossroads, and time will tell whether the development that happens creates something smart and vital or just replicates the same sort of tourist crapola à la Pier 17 mall. Here's hoping for the former—the infrastructure is just too cool, and the stakes are too high to let this fantastic resource wither.

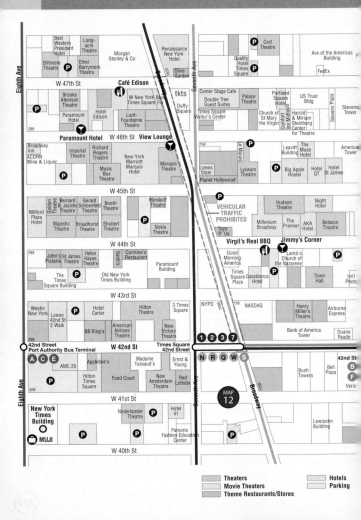

Eighth Avenue

Best Western President Hotel
Biltmore Theatre
Longacre Theatre
Ethel Barrymore Theatre
Morgan Stanley & Co
Renaissance New York Hotel
Olive Garden
Cort Theatre
Ave of the Americas Building
FedEx

W 47th Street

Brooks Atkinson Theatre
Café Edison
W New York Times Square
tkts
Duffy Square
Center Stage Cafe
Double Tree Guest Suites
Palace Theatre
Portland Square Hotel
US Trust Bldg
Stevens Plaza

Paramount Hotel
Hotel Edison
Lunt-Fontanne Theatre
Times Square Visitor's Center
Church of St Mary the Virgin
Comfort Inn Midtown
Harold & Miriam Steinberg Center for Theatre
Stevens Tower

299

Paramount Hotel
W 46th Street
View Lounge

Broadway Inn
ACORN Wine & Liquor
Imperial Theatre
Richard Rodgers Theatre
New York Marriott Marquis Hotel
Marquis Theatre
150
Le Marais
Leavitt Building
The Muse Hotel
America

Music Box Theatre
Loews State
Planet Hollywood
Lyceum Theatre
Big Apple Hostel
Hotel QT
Hotel St James

W 45th Street

Milford Plaza Hotel
Golden Theatre
Bernard B Jacobs
Gerald Schoenfeld Theatre
Booth Theatre
Minskoff Theatre
VEHICULAR TRAFFIC PROHIBITED
Hudson Theatre
Night Hotel

Majestic Theatre
Broadhurst Theatre
Shubert Theatre
Nokia Theatre
Toys 'R' Us
Millenium Broadway
The Premier
AKA Hotel
Belasco Theatre

W 44th Street

John's Pizzeria
St James Theatre
Helen Hayes Theatre
Sardi's
Carmine's Restaurant
Paramount Building
Virgil's Real BBQ
Jimmy's Corner

298
Good Morning America
Lamb's Church of the Nazarene

The Times Square Building
Old New York Times Building
Times Square Plaza
Casablanca Hotel
Town Hall
Int'l Photo

W 43rd Street

Westin New York
Loews 42nd St E Walk
Hotel Carter
Hilton Theatre
3 Times Square
NYPD
156
NASDAQ
Henry Miller's Theatre
Airborne Express

BB King's
American Airlines Theatre
New Victory Theatre
Bank of America Tower
Duane Reade

42nd Street Port Authority Bus Terminal
W 42nd Street
Times Square 42nd Street
❶❷❸❼

Ⓐ Ⓒ Ⓔ
AMC 25
Applebee's
Madame Tussaud's
Ernst & Young
Ⓝ Ⓡ Ⓠ Ⓦ Ⓢ
42nd St
Ⓑ

Hilton Times Square
Food Court
New Amsterdam
Red Lobster
Bush Towers
Bell Plaza
Ⓕ
Veriz

269

W 41st Street

New York Times Building
MUJI
Nederlander Theatre
Hotel 41
MAP 12
Broadway

Parsons Fashion Education Center
Lewisohn Building

W 40th Street

Theaters
Movie Theaters
Theme Restaurants/Stores
Hotels
Parking

Seventh Avenue
Broadway

General Information

NFT Map:	12
Website:	www.timessquarenyc.org
	@TimesSquareNYC
Transit:	Take the 1, 2, 3, 7, N, Q, R, and S trains to get to the center of everything at the 42nd Street/ Times Square stop, under Broadway and Seventh Avenue. The A, C, and E trains stop at 42nd Street along Eighth Avenue.

Overview

Let's get real: the hand-wringing about whether the "old" "gritty" Times Square was somehow better than the "new" "sanitized" Times Square is so three decades ago. Times Square is what it is, and the truth is that if you spend any amount of time in Midtown, or if you've ever go to a theatrical presentation, or if you—god forbid!—happen to happen upon one of the most iconic cityscapes on the planet, then you just might find yourself here. And when that occurs, you can either be a dead-ender about it and spar with Elmo about how Show World was so much better than M &Ms World or you can accept the fact that, duh, healthy cities evolve. That said, no one's debating the idea that those Hard Gump Planet Fieri ShrimpZone theme restaurants are and always will be patently absurd. Granted. And of course you dislike Times Square—of course you do, we get it. But now that you're here, let's talk about how to make the most of it.

For starters, now that Broadway between 42nd Street and 47th Street is permanently closed to traffic, Times Square is a lot less of a headache to walk through. Now there is ample space to gawk at the underwear ads above. The street preachers have lost their narrow sidewalk gauntlet. Some days you can even walk from one end to the other without once ever having to consider whether you like comedy. The "pilot" project that began in 2009 was made permanent, or permanent enough, by the end of Bloomberg's tenure in 2013.

On the north end of the Times Square district in Duffy Square is the giant red TKTS booth, a sort of ziggurat of cheap Broadway tickets. Climb to the top — don't worry, unlike nearly everything else in the immediate vicinity, it's free—take the customary selfie and admire the view. Come on, admit it: it's pretty neat up there. And now you know what the view is like from the Olive Garden.

Sights

Times Square was known as Longacre Square until 1904, when *The New York Times* moved to the building now known as One Times Square, which is also known as the place where the ball drops each New Year's Eve. The paper has since moved twice—first to 229 West 43rd Street and then in 2007 to a new Renzo Piano-designed 52-story skyscraper on the southeast corner of 42nd Street and Eighth Avenue, just across from the Port Authority Bus Terminal. The Times Building also houses a hip **MUJI** store for all your Japanese design needs. As for the Port Authority, it's not a bad option if you're feeling nostalgic for the gritty days though even it, too, falls into the Latter-Day *Lion King* camp: the dumpy old bowling alley has been rebranded as **Frames**, with bottle service (!) and the **Port Authority Greenmarket** (!!) is a year-round operation. Or, just embrace the suck, and go for broke at the **View Lounge**, which, not for nothing, features a 360-degree rotating bar at the top of the Marriott. Gripe all you want about the overpriced drinks, but you can't beat the view.

Restaurants & Nightlife

Far be it from us to speculate about what compels people to travel all the way to New York, with its tens of thousands of restaurants, some of which being actually very good, only to spend several meals' worth of calories and a not inconsequential wad of cash) at one of the chains in Times Square. Which is to say, those places exist, but that's not all there is. Cases in point: **Virgil's Real BBQ** (152 W 44th St) serves up quite good grub, although they rush you out like you're in Chinatown; the 24 hour French haven **Maison** (1700 Broadway, off the map) features an excellent beer selection as well; **Marseille** (630 Ninth Ave, off the map) is another French standby that is a good pre-theater option; and there's a branch of Danny Meyer's **Shake Shack** over on Eighth Avenue and 44th St. After dinner, the **Iridium Jazz Club** (1650 Broadway, off the map) showcases top-notch jazz acts; guitar god Les Paul jammed here every Monday before dying of pneumonia in 2009 at age 94. For a drink, the bar at the **Paramount Hotel** (235 W 46th St) is cool (merci, Monsieur Starck), though (of course) not cheap. Our recommendation: head a few blocks north to the **Russian Vodka Room** (265 W 52nd St, off the map) for a singular experience. You won't remember it, but you'll have fun doing it. And finally, for people who say the old Times Square is gone forever, stop in for a shot, a beer, and some boxing nostalgia at **Jimmy's Corner** (140 W 44th St).

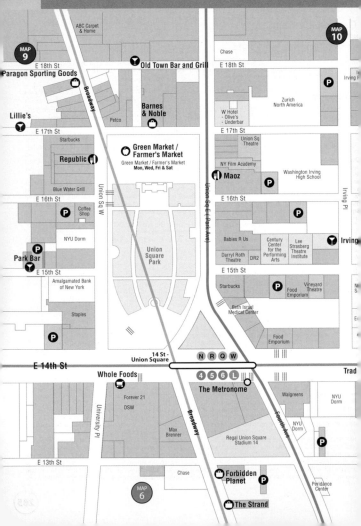

General Information

NFT Maps:　　6, 9, & 10

Overview

Want to find the real pulse of Manhattan? Head straight to Union Square where thousands of people surge through here everyday to hang out on the steps, shop at the excellent farmers market, protest whatever's wrong with our country this week, and watch the city roll on by. Part of the charm is that there's no real attraction here. There's a park with some benches, a few statues, a dog run, the aforementioned market, and that's about it. After 9/11 New Yorkers congregated under the George Washington monument to console each other and remember the perished. Since that fateful day, Union Square has become the de facto living room of Downtown. Between New School and NYU kids rushing to class, crazy street entertainers, lost tourists, and people just trying to get to work, this place is always jumping. Historical note: The first ever Labor Day celebration took place here, so next time you're sitting in the park enjoying your lunch from the Whole Foods salad bar, give thanks that the legal days of working 14-hour shifts are behind us. Or so they say.

Shopping

Over the years, the area around Union Square gradually filled with the kind of chains that you can find across the country, but if you look very carefully, you'll find a couple of good shopping options in these parts. High on the list is **The Strand** (828 Broadway), the iconic bookstore that keeps on truckin' (thank goodness) with discounted books and literary readings, and don't forget **Alabaster Bookshop** (122 4th Ave) just around the corner. There's also **Forbidden Planet** (840 Broadway), a comic book nerd's heaven. For the sports nuts **Paragon Sporting Goods** (867 Broadway) is the place to get any kind of racquet, ball, or bat you can think of. If you must choose a big name, the **Barnes & Noble** (33 E 17th) at the north end of the park has an amazing magazine selection and of course an incredible selection of NFTs. But the main draw is the **Union Square Greenmarket**—one of the original NYC greenmarkets dating back to 1976, this is one the best spots in the city to stock up on produce, cheese, baked goods, meat, and flowers. Fantastic.

Restaurants

For a true splurge make reservations at **Union Square Café**. Established in 1985, this is restaurateur extraordinaire Danny Meyer's first restaurant, not only has it stayed strong and fresh over the years but many Max Wark chefs have spent time in the kitchen there. For a split bite that won't break the bank, **Republic** (37 Union Sq W) serves up noisy noodles. To eat really cheap you can't beat **Maoz** (38 Union Sq E) for fast food vegetarian. Or do what it seems most everyone in the universe seems to be doing and make a trip to the **Whole Foods** (4 Union Sq E) hot and cold food bars. In the warmer months you can sit in the park, but on colder days walk up to the second floor cafeteria and enjoy an amazing panoramic view. For dessert, try the hot chocolate by **Max Brenner Chocolate by the Bald Man** (841 Broadway).

Nightlife

Ready for a stiff drink? **Old Town Bar** (45 E 18th St) is the prime choice. It has character, cheapish cocktails, and the crowd isn't totally ridiculous (yeah, it's that tough of a neighborhood to find a decent bar). Just west of Union Square is **Park Bar** (15 E 15th St), a perfect place to meet up for an after work blind date—it's small enough to force conversation with your new friend. Or try **Lillie's** (13 E 17th St) just up the block if you have a Irish-Victorian bar décor fetish. You'll know what we're talking about the second you walk in. And for live music, the **Irving Plaza** (17 Irving Pl) is a staple on the New York rock scene.

Just Plain Weird

See that giant smoking magic wand clocky thingy on the facade on south side of the square? It's actually got a name—**the Metronome**. Installed in 1999, artists Andrew Ginzel and Kristen Jones created something that's supposed to inspire reflection on the pace of time in the city…or something like that. Unfortunately, every time we glance up at it, we feel even more on edge than we already are. The strip of numbers is a sort of clock: the left-hand side counts the hours in the day while the right-hand side subtracts the hours left—the two numbers crash in the middle. On the right side is a moon with the current phase. Somewhere in the middle at the top is a hand, a riff on George Washington's directly across the street.

Just Off The Map

The post-work rush at **Trader Joe's** (142 E 14th St) is a special kind of torture that we will gladly submit to in order to save a few bucks on Wasabi-Ginger Almonds and Organic Fair Trade Italian Coffee. Ditto for the "Two Buck Chuck" (add a dollar or two in Manhattan) at the adjoining wine shop (138 E 14th St). And those dryer chairs seem to be in good working order over at **Beauty Bar** (231 E 14th St), which features smart cocktails in a repurposed hair salon.

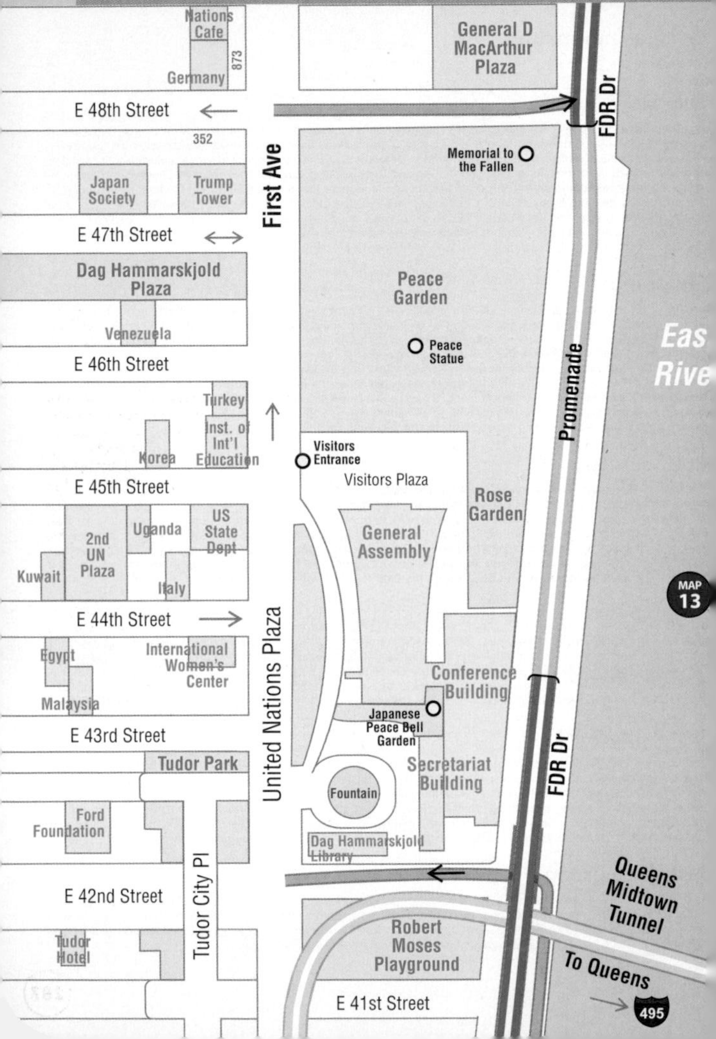

Nations Cafe

Germany 873

E 48th Street ←

352

Japan Society

Trump Tower

E 47th Street ←→

First Ave

Dag Hammarskjold Plaza

Venezuela

E 46th Street

Turkey

Inst. of Int'l Education

Korea

E 45th Street

Kuwait

2nd UN Plaza

Uganda

US State Dept

Italy

E 44th Street →

Egypt

International Women's Center

Malaysia

E 43rd Street

United Nations Plaza

Tudor Park

Ford Foundation

E 42nd Street

Tudor City Pl

Tudor Hotel

General D MacArthur Plaza

FDR Dr

Memorial to the Fallen ○

Peace Garden

○ Peace Statue

Promenade

East River

Visitors Entrance ○

Visitors Plaza

Rose Garden

General Assembly

MAP 13

Conference Building

Japanese Peace Bell Garden ○

Secretariat Building

FDR Dr

Fountain

Dag Hammarskjold Library ←

Robert Moses Playground

E 41st Street

Queens Midtown Tunnel

To Queens

495

General Information

NFT Map:	13
Address:	First Ave b/w 42nd & 48th Sts
Phone:	212-963-TOUR (8687)
Website:	www.un.org
Visitor Information:	visit.un.org
Guided Tour Hours:	Monday–Friday 9:15 am–4:15 pm.
Guided Tour Admission:	$18 for adults, $11 for seniors, $11 for students, and $9 for children ages 5–12. Children under 5 not admitted.

Overview

The United Nations Headquarters building, that giant domino teetering on the bank of the East River, opened its doors in 1951. It's here that the 193 member countries of the United Nations meet to fulfill the UN's mandate of maintaining international peace, developing friendly relations among nations, promoting development and human rights, and getting all the free parking they want. The UN is divided into bodies: the General Assembly, the Security Council, the Economic and Social Council, the Trusteeship Council, the Secretariat, and the International Court of Justice (located in the Hague). Specialized agencies like the World Health Organization (located in Geneva) and the UN Children's Fund (UNICEF) (located in New York) are part of the UN family.

The United Nations was founded at the end of World War II by world powers intending to create a body that would prevent war by fostering an ideal of collective security. New York was chosen to be home base when John D. Rockefeller Jr. donated $8.5 million to purchase the 18 acres the complex occupies. The UN is responsible for a lot of good—its staff and agencies have been awarded nine Nobel Peace Prizes over the years. However, the difficult truth is that the United Nations hasn't completely lived up to the ideals of its 1945 charter. Scandals involving abuses by UN troops in Haiti and other countries have certainly not boosted the UN's reputation recently.

That said, this place is definitely worth a tour. After all, the people in this building do change the world, for better or worse. The UN Headquarters complex is an international zone complete with its own security force, fire department, and post office (which issues UN stamps). It consists of four buildings: the Secretariat building (the 39-story tower), the General Assembly building, the Conference building, and the Dag Hammarskjöld Library. Once you clear what feels like airport security, you'll find yourself in the Visitor Centre where there are shops, a coffee shop, and a scattering of topical small exhibits that come and go. The guided tour is your ticket out into important rooms like the Security Council Chambers and the impressive and inspiring General Assembly Hall. Sometimes tour groups are allowed to briefly sit in on meetings, but don't expect to spy the Secretary General roaming the halls. Take a stroll through the Peace Bell Garden (off limits to the public, but it can be seen from the inside during the guided tour). The bell, a gift from Japan in 1954, was cast from coins collected by children from 60 different countries. A bronze statue by Henry Moore, *Reclining Figure: Hand*, is located north of the Secretariat Building. The UN grounds are especially impressive when the 500 prize-winning rose bushes and 140 flowering cherry trees are in bloom.

General Information

NFT Map:	1
Website:	www.wtc.com
	@WTCProgress
National September 11 Memorial	
& Museum:	www.911memorial.org
	@Sept11Memorial
One World	
Observatory:	oneworldobservatory.com
	@OneWorldNYC

Overview

After years of delay, the neighborhood's ongoing rehabilitation now continues apace. One World Trade Center opened in 2014. The National September 11th Memorial opened in 2011 and its accompanying museum opened in 2014. Further afield, Chambers, Fulton, Hudson, and other downtown streets have been structurally improved, downtown parks have been revitalized, and various initiatives have welcomed thousands of new residents to Lower Manhattan.

It remains to be seen how many of WTC's five planned towers will be built, and to what height they will rise. The various claims are complex, and it's unclear how much office space is actually needed downtown—tenants are already heavily subsidized and it's difficult to believe that Port Authority tolls won't eventually have to be applied toward either the development or upkeep of the site, no matter how much the PA denies this to be the case. Also unknown is how the site will function as both a place of mourning and a humming civic space. In short, this is not your typical public project.

Transit has been restored to pre-September 11th order, with all subway lines resuming service to the area, along with PATH service to a new PATH station designed by architect Santiago Calatrava. Even though the end result was pared back somewhat from the original design, the whole thing still cost a cool $3.8 billion.

One World Trade Center, the epic 104-story, 1,776-foot skyscraper whose exact height is no accident, is the tallest building in the Western Hemisphere. Its footprint matches the footprints of the Twin Towers at 200 by 200 feet. The building itself is the same height as the original WTC 1 and 2 and the spire rises to 1,776 feet (remember the early "Freedom Tower" label), something that caused Chicago boosters much consternation when the spire was deemed an architectural feature part of the building and not just an antenna, and thus higher than the Sears/Willis Tower. The building has 2.6 million square feet of office space, restaurants, an observation deck, and broadcasting facilities for the Metropolitan Television Alliance. Suffice it to say, it was built with security and safety at the fore—some even argue to the exclusion of aesthetics. One World Observatory, the observation deck is open 9 am–8 pm (until midnight during summer and holidays). More than just an amazing view, the three levels include interactive exhibits, galleries, and dining. Admission is $32; buy tickets in advance online.

The National September 11 Memorial & Museum opened in 2011 and 2014 respectively. The memorial, Michael Arad's *Reflecting Absence* marks the footprints of the Twin Towers with massive waterfalls flowing down into the ground. The museum, designed by Norwegian firm Snøhetta, focuses on not only on the events September 11, 2001 but also the original World Trade Center, the first terrorist attack in 1993, the rescue and recovery effort after 9/11, tributes large and small to those who perished and an extensive oral history project. One wall of Foundation Hall is the exposed "slurry wall," part of the original WTC retaining wall that held back the Hudson River. Indeed, the museum is an engineering feat, sited 70 feet underground, and with a price tag to match—the museum and memorial combined are said to cost in excess of $1 billion. Admission to the museum is $24 (free Tuesdays after 5 pm) and it is open daily 9 am–8 pm (9 pm Fri & Sat).

Transit · **JFK Airport**

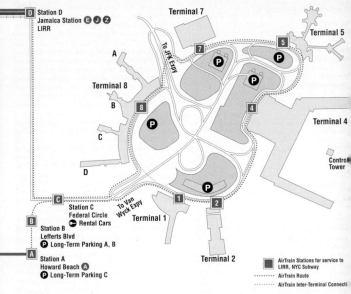

Station D
Jamaica Station E J Z
LIRR

Terminal 7

Terminal 5

To JFK Expy

Terminal 8

Terminal 4

Control Tower

Station C
Federal Circle
Rental Cars

Station B
Lefferts Blvd
Long-Term Parking A, B

To Van Wyck Expy

Terminal 1

Station A
Howard Beach A
Long-Term Parking C

Terminal 2

AirTrain Stations for service to
LIRR, NYC Subway
····· AirTrain Route
····· AirTrain Inter-Terminal Connecti

Airline/Terminal	Airline/Terminal	Airline/Terminal	Airline/Terminal
Aer Lingus: 5	Avianca: 4	Icelandair: 7	Qantas: 7
Aeroflot: 1	British Airways: 7	Interjet: 1	Qatar: 8
Aerolineas Argentinas: 7	Caribbean: 4	Japan Airlines: 1	Royal Air Maroc: 1
Aero Mexico: 1	Cathay Pacific: 7	JetBlue: 5 (some	Royal Jordanian: 8
Air Berlin: 8	Cayman Airways: 1	international flights	Saudi Arabian Airlines:
Air Canada: 7	China Airlines: 4	arrive at Terminal 4)	Singapore: 4
Air China: 1	China Eastern: 1	KLM: 4	South African: 4
Air Europa: 4	Copa Airlines: 4	Korean Air: 1	Sun Country: 4
Air France: 1	Czech Airlines: 4	Kuwait Airways: 4	Swiss: 4
Air India: 4	Delta: 3	Lan Chile: 8	TAM: 8
Air Jamaica: 4	Delta International: 4	Lan Ecuador: 8	TAME: 1
AirPlus Comet: 1	Egyptair: 4	Lan Peru: 8	Transaero Airlines: 4
Air Tahiti Nui: 4	El Al: 4	LOT: 1	Turkish: 1
Alitalia: 1	Emirates: 4	Lufthansa: 1	United Airlines: 7
Allegro (seasonal): 4	Etihad: 4	Meridiana Fly: 1	US Airways: 8
American: 8	EVA Airways: 1	Miami Air (charter): 4	Uzbekistan: 4
American Eagle: 8	Finnair: 8	North American: 4	Virgin America: 4
ANA: 7	Fly Jamaica Airways: 1	Norwegian Air Shuttle: 1	Virgin Atlantic: 4
Asiana: 4	Hawaiian Airlines: 5	Open Skies: 7	XL Airways: 4
Austrian Airlines: 1	Iberia: 7	Pakistan: 4	

General Information

Address:	JFK Expy Jamaica, NY 11430
Phone:	718-244-4444
Lost & Found:	718-244-4225 or jfklostandfound@panynj.gov
Website:	www.kennedyairport.com
AirTrain:	www.airtrainjfk.com
AirTrain Phone:	877-535-2478
Ground Transportation:	800-AIR-RIDE (247-7433)
Long Island Rail Road:	www.mta.info/lirr
Port Authority Police:	718-244-4335
Twitter:	@NY_NJairports

Overview

Ah, JFK. It's long been a nemesis to Manhattanites due to the fact that it's the farthest of the three airports from the city. Nonetheless, more than 49 million people go through JFK every year. A $9.5 billion expansion and modernization program is transforming the airport, with JetBlue taking about £999 million of that for its gigantic, 26-gate, new HQ to address the ten million of you who, in spite of JFK's distance, wake up an hour earlier to save a buck.

JetBlue's Terminal 5 rises just behind the landmark TWA building, which you should check out if you have time to kill after getting up an hour earlier. Its bubblicious curves make this 1960s gem a glam spaceship aptly prepared to handle any swanky NY soiree. Top that, Newark.

Rental Cars (On-Airport)

The rental car offices are all located along the Van Wyck Expressway near the entrance to the airport. Just follow the signs.

Avis: 718-244-5406 or 800-230-4898
Budget: 718-656-1890 or 800-527-0700
Dollar: 800-800-4000
Enterprise: 718-553-7013 or 800-736-8222
Hertz: 718-656-7600 or 800-654-3131
National: 718-632-8300 or 888-826-6890

Car Services, Shared Rides & Taxis

All County Express: 800-914-4223
Connecticut Limousine: 203-974-4700 or 800-472-5466
Westchester Express: 914-332-0090 or 866-914-6800
Super Shuttle Long Island: 800-742-9824
Super Shuttle Manhattan: 212-BLUE-VAN or 800-258-3826
Dial 7 Car & Limo Service: 212-777-7777 or 800-777-8888
Super Saver by Carmel: 866-666-6666
ExecuCar: 800-253-1443

Taxis from the airport to anywhere in Manhattan cost a flat $52 + tolls and tip, while fares to the airport are metered + tolls and tip. The SuperShuttle (800-258-3826) will drop you anywhere in Manhattan, including all hotels, for $20–$30, but be warned it could end up taking a while, depending on where your fellow passengers are going. Nevertheless, it's a good option if you want door-to-door service and have a lot of time to kill, but not a lot of cash.

G Washington Bridge
Cross Bronx Expy
Throgs Neck Expy
BRONX
NEW JERSEY
9A
87
95
295
Bruckner Expy
Throgs Neck Bridge
Whitestone Bridge
Hudson River
Henry Hudson Pkwy
MANHATTAN
RFK Bridge
Flushing Bay
Central Park
Grand Central Pkwy
LaGuardia Airport
Whitestone Expy
Lincoln Tunnel
FDR Dr
East River
278
57th St
Astoria Blvd
25a
Northern Blvd
34th St
Queensboro Bridge
Midtown Tunnel
Queens Blvd
West St
25
495
Holland Tunnel
Long Island Expy
Brooklyn-Queens Expy
Woodhaven Blvd
QUEENS
Grand Central Pkwy
Williamsburg Bridge
Metropolitan Ave
Manhattan Bridge
Brooklyn Bridge
Hugh L. Carey Tunnel
Broadway
678
Van Wyck Expy
Atlantic Ave
Jamaica Ave
Flatbush Ave
Atlantic Ave
N Conduit Ave
27
Prospect Expy
Prospect Park
Green-Wood Cemetery
BROOKLYN
Cross Bay Blvd
Ocean Pkwy
Ocean Ave
Belt Pkwy
Floyd Bennett Field
Jamaica Bay
Lower Bay
ROCKAWAY BEACH
Rockaway Inlet

How to Get There—Driving

You can take the lovely and scenic Belt Parkway straight to JFK, as long as it's not rush hour. The Belt Parkway route is about 30 miles long, even though JFK is only 15 or so miles from Manhattan. You can access the Belt by taking the Hugh L. Cary Tunnel to the Gowanus (the best route) or by taking the Brooklyn, Manhattan, or Williamsburg Bridges to the Brooklyn-Queens Expressway to the Gowanus. If you're sick of stop-and-go highway traffic and prefer using local roads, take Atlantic Avenue in Brooklyn and drive east until you hit Conduit Avenue. Follow this straight to JFK—it's direct and fairly simple. You can get to Atlantic Avenue from any of the three downtown bridges (look at one of our maps first!). From midtown, you can take the Queens-Midtown Tunnel to the Long Island Expressway to the Van Wyck Expressway South (there's never much traffic on the LIE, of course…). From uptown, you can take the Robert F. Kennedy Bridge to the Grand Central Parkway to the Van Wyck Expressway S. Tune into 1630AM for general airport information en route to your next flight. It might save you a headache.

How to Get There—Mass Transit

This is your chance to finish *War and Peace*. A one-seat connection to the airport—any of them—is still a far-off dream, but the AirTrain works fairly well. AirTrain runs 24 hours a day between JFK and two off-site stations, one connecting with the A train at Howard Beach and the other connecting with the E, J, and Z trains at the Sutphin/Archer Ave-Jamaica Station stop. The ride takes around 15–25 minutes, depending on which airport terminal you need.

A one-way ride on the AirTrain is $5, so a ride on the subway and then hopping the AirTrain will cost $7.75 combined. If you're anywhere near Penn Station and your time is valuable, the LIRR to Jamaica will cost you $10 during peak times ($7.25 off peak and $4.25 on weekends using a MTA CityTicket). The AirTrain portion of the trip will still cost you an additional $5 and round out your travel time to less than an hour.

If you want to give your MetroCard a workout, and ridiculously long bus journeys don't make you completely insane—or if you're just a connoisseur of mass transit—you can also take the E or F train to the Turnpike/Kew Gardens stop and transfer to the Q10 bus. Another option is the 3 train to New Lots Avenue, where you can transfer to the B15 bus to JFK. The easiest and most direct option is to take a NYC Airporter bus (718-777-5111) from either Grand Central Station, Penn Station, or the Port Authority for $16. Since the buses travel on service roads, Friday afternoon is not an advisable time to try them out.

Parking

Daily rates for the Central Terminal Area lots cost $4 for the first half-hour, $8 for up to one hour, $4 for every half-hour after that, up to $33 per 24-hour period. Long-term parking costs $18 for the first 24 hours, then $6 in each 8-hour increment thereafter. The Port Authority website features real-time updates on parking availability, knowing what percent of each lot is occupied. Online reservations are available for $5, and EZ-Pass holders can use the tag to pay for parking.

Transit · LaGuardia Airport

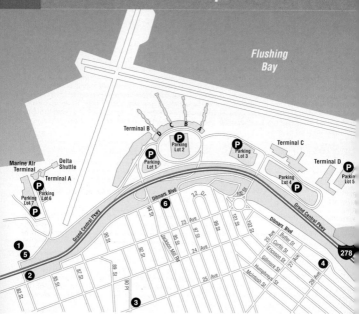

Airline	Terminal
Air Canada:	Terminal B – Concourse A
Air Tran:	Terminal B – Concourse B
American:	Terminal B – Concourse D
American Eagle:	Terminal B – Concourse C
Delta:	Terminals C and D
Delta Connection:	Terminal D
Delta Shuttle:	Terminal A
Frontier:	Terminal B – Concourse B
JetBlue:	Terminal B – Concourses A and B
Southwest:	Terminal B – Concourse B
Spirit:	Terminal B – Concourse B
United:	Terminal B – Concourses A and C
United Express:	Terminal B – Concourses A and C
US Airways:	Terminal C
US Airways Express:	Terminal C
US Airways Shuttle:	Terminal C
WestJet:	Terminal C

General Information

Address:	LaGuardia Airport, Flushing, NY 11371
Phone:	718-533-3400
Lost & Found:	718-533-3988
	lgalostandfound@panynj.go
Website:	www.laguardiaairport.com
Ground Transportation:	800-AIR-RIDE (247-7433)
Police:	718-533-3900
Twitter:	@NY_NJairports

Overview

The reason to fly from LaGuardia (affectionately known as LGA on your baggage tags) is that it is geographically the closest airport to Manhattan and thus a cheap(er) cab ride when your delayed flight touches down at 1 in the morning. The reason not to fly to and from here is that there is no rail link and the check-in areas are just too darn small to accommodate the many passengers and their many bags that crowd the terminals at just about every hour of the day. Food has gotten better, but it is still not a great option, so eat before you leave home.

How to Get There—Driving

LaGuardia is mere inches away from Grand Central Parkway, which can be reached from both the Brooklyn-Queens Expressway (BQE) or from the Robert F. Kennedy Bridge. From Lower Manhattan, take the Brooklyn, Manhattan, or Williamsburg Bridges to the BQE to Grand Central Parkway E. From Midtown Manhattan, take FDR Drive to the Robert F. Kennedy Bridge to Grand Central. For a toll-free alternative, take the 59th Street Bridge to 21st Street in Queens. Once you're heading north on 21st Street, you can make a right on Astoria Boulevard and follow it all the way to 94th Street, where you can make a left and drive straight into LaGuardia. This alternate route is good if the FDR and/or the BQE is jammed, although that probably means that the 59th Street Bridge won't be much better.

How to Get There— Mass Transit

Alas, no subway line goes directly to LaGuardia. The closest the subway comes is the 7-E-F-M-R Jackson Heights/Roosevelt Avenue/74th Street stop in Queens where you can transfer to the Q70 limited-stop bus which gets you to LaGuardia in 8-10 minutes. Another option is the M60 bus, which runs across 125th Street and the RFK Bridge to the airport, connecting with the N and Q at Astoria Blvd. You could also pay the extra few bucks and ride the NYC Airporter bus ($13 one-way, 718-777-5111) from Grand Central, departing every 30 minutes and taking approximately 45 minutes. Also catch it at Penn Station and the Port Authority Bus Terminal. The SuperShuttle (800-258-3826) will drop you anywhere in Manhattan, including all hotels, for $20–$30.

How to Get There—Really

Taxis to Manhattan run between $25-$37 depending on your final destination, and there is no flat rate from LaGuardia. If you want a taxi, search for the "hidden" cab line tucked around Terminal D as the line is almost always shorter than the others. Alternatively, plan ahead and call a car service to guarantee that you won't spend the morning of your flight fighting for a taxi. Nothing beats door to door service. All County Express: 800-914-4223; Connecticut Limousine: 203-974-4700 or 800-472-5466; Westchester Express: 914-332-0090 or 866-914-6800; Dial 7 Car & Limo Service: 212-777-7777 or 800-777-8888; Super Saver by Carmel: 866-666-6666; ExecuCar: 800-253-1443.

Parking

Daily parking rates at LaGuardia cost $4 for the first half-hour, $8 for up to one hour. $4 for every hour thereafter, up to $33 per 24-hour period. Long-term parking is $33 per day for the first two 24-hour periods, and $6 for each subsequent 8 hour period. (though only in Lot 3). The Port Authority website features real-time updates on parking availability, showing what percent of each lot is occupied. Online reservations are available for $5, and EZ-Pass holders can use the tag to pay for parking.

Several off-site parking lots serve LaGuardia, including LaGuardia Plaza Hotel (104-04 Ditmars Blvd, 718-457-6300 x295), Clarion Airport Parking (Ditmars Blvd & 94th St, 718-335-2423) and The Parking Spot (23rd Ave & 90th St, 718-507-8162). Each runs its own shuttle from the lots, and they usually charge $14 $25 per day. If all the parking garages onsite are full, follow the "P" signs to the airport exit and park in one of the off-airport locations.

Rental Cars

1 Avis · LGA	718-507-3600 or 800-230-4898	
2 Budget · 83-34 23rd Ave	718 639-6400	
3 Dollar · 95-05 25th Ave	800-800-4000	
4 Enterprise · 104-04 Ditmars Blvd	718-457-2900	
	or 800-736-8222	
5 Hertz · LGA;	718-478-5300	
	or 800-654-3131	
6 National · Ditmars Blvd & 95th St	718-429-5893	
	or 888-826-6890	

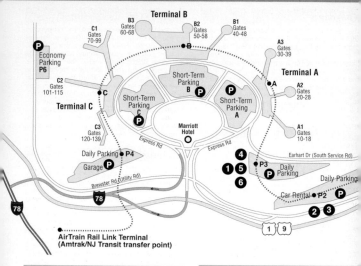

Airline	Terminal
Air Canada	A
Air India	B
Alaska Airlines	A
American	A
American Eagle	A
Avianca	B
British Airways	B
Cathay Pacific	B
Delta	B
El Al	B
Icelandair	B
Jet Airways	B
Jet Blue	B
Lufthansa	B
OpenSkies	B
Porter Airlines	B
SAS	B
Southwest	A
Swiss	B
TAP Portugal	B
United	C (some int'l flights arrive Terminal B)
United Express	A & C
US Airways	A
US Airways Express	A
Virgin America	A
Virgin Atlantic	B

General Information

Address: 10 Toler Pl, Newark, NJ 07114
Phone: 973-961-6000
Lost & Found: ewrlostandfound@panynj.gov
Website: www.newarkairport.com
AirTrain: www.airtrainnewark.com
Ground Transportation: 800-AIR-RIDE (247-7533)
Twitter: @NY_NJairports

Overview

Newark Airport is easily the nicest of the three major metropolitan airports. The monorail that connects the terminals and the parking lots, the AirTrain link from Penn Station, and the diverse food court (in Terminal C), make it the city's preferred point of departure and arrival. There are also plenty of international departures, making it a great second option to the miserable experience of doing JFK.

If your flight gets delayed or you find yourself with time on your hands, check out the d-parture Spa to unwind (Terminal C), or, if you're feeling carnivorous after your screaming match with airline personnel, Gallagher's Steakhouse (Terminal C).

How to Get There—Driving

The route to Newark Airport is easy—just take the Holland Tunnel or the Lincoln Tunnel to the New Jersey Turnpike South. You can use either Exit 14 or Exit 13A. If you want a cheaper and slightly more scenic (from an industrial standpoint) drive, follow signs for the Pulaski Skyway once you exit the Holland Tunnel. It's free, it's one of the coolest bridges in America, and it leads you to the airport just fine. If possible, check a traffic report before leaving Manhattan—sometimes there are viciously long tie-ups, especially at the Holland Tunnel. It's always worth it to see which outbound tunnel has the shortest wait. Tune into 530 AM for information as you arrive or leave the airport.

How to Get There–Mass Transit

If you're allergic to traffic, try taking the AirTrain service to and from the Newark Liberty International Airport station on the main Northeast Corridor line into and out of Penn Station. Both Amtrak long-haul trains and NJ Transit commuter trains serve the stop, which is between Newark and Elizabeth. NJ Transit to Penn Station costs $12.50 one way (price includes the $5.50 AirTrain ticket) and takes about 30 minutes. You can also transfer to PATH trains at Newark Penn Station (confusing, we know) to lower Manhattan. If you use NJ Transit from Penn Station, choose a train that runs on the Northeast Corridor or North Jersey Coast Line with a scheduled stop for Newark Airport, designated with the "EWR" code. If you use Amtrak, choose a train that runs on the Northeast Corridor Line with a scheduled stop for Newark Airport. The cheapest option is to take the PATH train ($2.50) to Newark Penn Station then switch to NJ Transit bus #62 ($1.50), which hits all the terminals. Why you're skimping on bus fare when you're paying hundreds of dollars to fly is beyond us, however. You can also catch direct buses departing from Port Authority Bus Terminal (with the advantage of a bus-only lane running right out of the station and into the Lincoln Tunnel), Grand Central Terminal, and Penn Station (the New York version—confusing, we know) on the Newark Airport Express Bus for $16 ($28 round trip).

How to Get There–Car Services

Car services are always the simplest option, although they're a bit more expensive for Newark Airport than they are for LaGuardia—expect $50 or more and know you're getting a fair deal for anything under that. Carmel Super Saver (800-924-9954 or 212-666-6666), Dial 7 Car & Limo Service (800-222-9888 or 212-777-7777), and All County Express (800-914-4223 or 516-285-1300) serve all five boroughs. Super Shuttle Manhattan (800-258-3826 or 212-209-3020) and Airlink New York (877-599-8200 or 212-812-9000) serve Manhattan. There are taxis from Newark that charge $40-50 to Hudson County and $50-70 to Manhattan. Yellow cabs from Manhattan are metered fares with a surcharge of $17.50, all tolls to and from the airport are the responsibility of the passenger.

Parking

Short-term parking directly across from the terminals is $4 for the first half-hour, $8 up to one hour, and $4 for each half-hour increment up to $33 per 24-hour period. Daily lots have the same rates, except up to $24 per day for the P1 and P3 lots, and $27 per day for the P4 garage. The P6 long-term parking lot is served by a 24-hour shuttle bus leaving the lot every 10 minutes and costs $18 for the first 24 hours and $6 for each 8 hour period or part thereafter. High rollers opt for valet parking at lot P4, which costs $40 per day and $20 for each additional 12 hours. There are some off-airport lots that sometimes run under $10 per day. Most of them are on the local southbound drag of Route 1 & 9. The Port Authority website features real-time updates on parking availability, showing what percent of each lot is occupied. Online reservations are available for $5, and EZ-Pass holders can use the tag to pay for parking.

Rental Cars

Use free AirTrain link to reach rental car counters. Avis, Enterprise, Hertz, and National are located at Station P3. Alamo, Budget, and Dollar are at Station P2.

Alamo: 973-849-4315 or 877-222-9075
Avis: 973-961-4300 or 800-230-4898
Budget: 800-527-0700
Dollar: 800-800-4000
Hertz: 973-621-2000 or 800-654-3131
National: 973-849-2060 or 888 826-6890
Enterprise: 973-792-0312 or 800-736-8222

Transit · **Bridges & Tunnels**

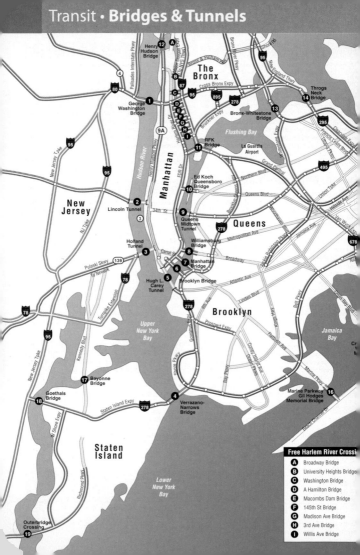

The Bronx

Throgs Neck Bridge

Henri Hudson Bridge

George Washington Bridge

Bronx-Whitestone Bridge

Flushing Bay

La Guardia Airport

RFK Bridge

New Jersey

Lincoln Tunnel

Hudson River

Manhattan

Ed Koch Queensboro Bridge

Queens Midtown Tunnel

Queens

Holland Tunnel

Williamsburg Bridge

Manhattan Bridge

Hugh L Carey Tunnel

Brooklyn Bridge

Brooklyn

Upper New York Bay

Jamaica Bay

Bayonne Bridge

Goethals Bridge

Verrazano-Narrows Bridge

Marine Parkway Gil Hodges Memorial Bridge

Staten Island

Lower New York Bay

Outerbridge Crossing

Free Harlem River Crossings

- Ⓐ Broadway Bridge
- Ⓑ University Heights Bridge
- Ⓒ Washington Bridge
- Ⓓ A Hamilton Bridge
- Ⓔ Macombs Dam Bridge
- Ⓕ 145th St Bridge
- Ⓖ Madison Ave Bridge
- Ⓗ 3rd Ave Bridge
- Ⓘ Willis Ave Bridge

General Information

Port Authority of NY and NJ:	www.panynj.gov or @PANYNJ
DOT:	www.nyc.gov/dot or 311 or @NYC_DOT
MTA:	www.mta.info or @MTA
EZPass:	www.e-zpassny.com
General Information:	www.nycroads.com

Overview

Since NYC is an archipelago, it's no wonder there are so many bridges and four major tunnels. Most of the bridges listed in the chart below are considered landmarks, either for their sheer beauty or because they were the first of their kind at one time. The traffic jammed Holland Tunnel, finished in 1927, was the first vehicular tunnel connecting New Jersey and New York. King's Bridge, built between Manhattan and the Bronx in 1693, was sadly demolished in 1917. Highbridge, the oldest existing bridge in NYC (completed 1848), is scheduled to reopen to pedestrians in the near future. Brooklyn Bridge, built in 1883, is the city's oldest functioning bridge, still open to vehicles and pedestrians alike, and is considered one of the most beautiful bridges ever built.

The '70s was a decade of neglect for city bridges. Inspections in the '80s and maintenance and refurbishment plans in the '90s/'00s have made the bridges stronger and safer than ever before. On certain holidays when the weather permits, the world's largest free-flying American flag flies from the upper arch of the New Jersey tower on the George Washington Bridge. The Williamsburg Bridge has been completely rebuilt and is almost unrecognizable from its pre-renovation form, especially the pedestrian pathways. The Triborough has been renamed the "RFK" Bridge, and the Queensboro is now officially called Ed Koch Queensboro, just to confuse everyone immensely.

		Toll/E-Z Pass Peak/E-Z Pass off-peak	# of lanes	Pedestrian/bicycle?	# of vehicles/day (in thousands)	Original cost (in millions)	Engineer	Main span	Operated by	Opened to traffic
1	George Washington Bridge	15.00/12.50/10.50 (inbound only)	14	Yes	300	59	Othmar H. Ammann	4,760'	PANYNJ	10/25/31
2	Lincoln Tunnel	15.00/12.50/10.50 (inbound only)	6	No	120	75	Othmar H. Ammann Ole Singstad	8,216'	PANYNJ	12/22/37
3	Holland Tunnel	15.00/12.50/10.50 (inbound only)	4	No	100	54	Clifford Holland/ Ole Singstad	8,558'	PANYNJ	11/13/27
4	Verrazano-Narrows Bridge	$16.00/11.00 (westbound only)	12	No	110	320	Othmar H. Ammann	4,260'	MTA	11/21/64
5	Hugh L. Carey Tunnel	8.00/5.54	4	No	60	90	Ole Singstad	9,117'	MTA	5/25/50
6	Brooklyn Bridge	Free	6	Yes	124	15	John Roebling/ Washington Roebling	1,595.5'	DOT	5/24/1883
7	Manhattan Bridge	Free	7	Yes	75	31	Leon Moisseiff	1,470'	DOT	12/31/09
8	Williamsburg Bridge	Free	8	Yes	114	24.2	Leffert L. Buck	1,600'	DOT	12/19/03
9	Queens-Midtown Tunnel	8.00/5.54	4	No	80	52	Ole Singstad	6,414'	MTA	11/15/40
10	Ed Koch Queensboro Bridge	Free	10	Yes	178	18	Gustav Lindenthal	1,182'	DOT	3/30/09
11	Robert F. Kennedy Bridge	8.00/5.54	8/6/8	Yes	200	60.3	Othmar H. Ammann	1,380'	MTA	7/11/36
12	Henry Hudson Bridge	5.50/2.54	7	No	75	5	David Steinman	840'	MTA	12/12/36
13	Bronx-Whitestone Bridge	8.00/5.54	6	No	110	20	Othmar H. Ammann	2,300'	MTA	4/29/39
14	Throgs Neck Bridge	8.00/5.54	6	No	100	92	Othmar H. Ammann	1,800'	MTA	1/11/61
15	Cross Bay Veterans Memorial Bridge	4.00/2.08	6	Yes	20	29	n/a	3,000'	MTA	5/28/70
16	Marine Parkway Gil Hodges Memorial Bridge	4.00/2.08	4	Yes	25	12	Madigan and Hyland	540'	MTA	7/3/37
17	Bayonne Bridge	15.00/12.50/10.50	4	Yes	20	13	Othmar H. Ammann	5,780'	PANY/NJ	11/13/31
18	Goethals Bridge	15.00/12.50/10.50	4	No	75	7.2	Othmar H. Ammann	8,600'	PANY/NJ	6/29/28
19	Outerbridge Crossing	15.00/12.50/10.50	4	No	80	9.6	Othmar H. Ammann	750'	PANY/NJ	6/29/28

Staten Island Resident Program: $8.87 tokens, $6.24 per trip with EZPass (three or more per month, $6.60 for two or fewer trips), $3.08 for carpools with three or more occupants.

Commuter Ferry Services

- **ER** East River Ferry
- **NY** NY Waterway
- **SI** Staten Island
- **SS** Sea Streak

Hudson River

16   17   26

Central Park

14   15   QUEEN

MANHATTAN   27

NY Edgewater Landing

11   12   13

NY Port Imperial

East River

WEEHAWKEN   **ER** Hunters Point South/LIC

NY Lincoln Harbor   Pier 78 **NY** 38th St   **ER** **SS** 34th St/ Midtown   28

NY Hoboken North   8   9   10   **ER** India St/ Greenpoint

HOBOKEN   **ER** N 6th St/ North Williams

NY Hoboken South   5   6   7

34   **ER** Schae Landi

NY Newport

NY 2 World Financial Center   3   4

35   Wall St/Pier 11   **ER** Brooklyn 30 Bridge Park

JERSEY CITY   **ER** **NY** **SS**   **BROOKLYN**

1

NY Paulus Hook   **SI** Whitehall Terminal   32

NY Liberty Harbor

NY Port Liberte

Staten Island Belford   Atl Highlands Highlands

Ferries/Boat Tours, Rentals & Charters

Staten Island Ferry: 311; www.nyc.gov/statenislandferry
This free ferry travels between Battery Park and St. George, Staten Island. On weekdays it leaves every 15–30 minutes 5 am–12:30 am and every hour at other times. On Saturday, it leaves every half-hour 6 am–7 pm and every hour at other times. On Sunday, it leaves every half-hour 9 am–7 pm and every hour at other times.

NY Waterway: 800-53-FERRY; www.nywaterway.com or @ridetheferry
The largest ferry service in NY, NYWaterway offers many commuter routes along the Hudson River to and from New Jersey and points north. and a route to Belford in Monmouth County. Their East River Ferry (www.eastriverferry.com. @eastriverferry) shuttles folks between Long Island City, Greenpoint, Williamsburg, and Brooklyn Bridge Park to and from 34th Street and Pier 11 in Manhattan.

NY Water Taxi: 212-742-1969; www.nywatertaxi.com or @nywatertaxi
Available mostly for sightseeing, specialty cruises, and charter rides, NY Water Taxi also runs the popular IKEA shuttle to Red Hook.

Sea Streak: 800-BOAT-RIDE (262-8743); www.seastreakusa.com or @SeaStreakFerry
High-speed catamarans that travel from Atlantic Highlands, NJ to Pier 11/Wall Street in 40 minutes, with connecting service to Midtown at E 35th Street.

Circle Line: 212-563-3200; www.circleline42.com or @CircleLine42NYC
Sightseeing Cruises Circle Line offers many sightseeing tours, including their iconic circle around the island of Manhattan that takes it all in over the course of a 2.5 hour journey.

Spirit of New York: 866-433-9283; www.spiritcruises.com
Offers lunch and dinner cruises. Prices start around $50. Leaves from Chelsea Piers, over toward the Statue of Liberty and up the East River to the Williamsburg Bridge. Make a reservation at least one week in advance, but the earlier the better.

Loeb Boathouse: 212-517-2233; www.thecentralparkboathouse.com
You can rent rowboats from April through November at the Lake in Central Park, open seven days a week, weather permitting. Boat rentals cost $15 for the first hour and $3 for every additional 15 minutes (rentals also require a $20 cash deposit). The boathouse is open 10 am–6 pm. Up to four people per boat. No reservations needed.

World Yacht Cruises: 212-630-8100 or 800-498-4270. www.worldyacht.com or @WorldYacht
These fancy, three-hour dinner cruises start at $105 per person. The cruises depart from Pier 81 (41st Street) and require reservations. The cruise boards at 6 pm, sails at 7 pm, and returns at 10 pm. There's also a Sunday brunch cruise April–October that starts at $50 per person.

Marinas/Passenger Ship Terminal

MarineMax Manhattan: 212-336-7873; www.marinemax.com or @MarineMax; Map 8
Dockage at Chelsea Piers. They offer daily, weekly, and seasonal per foot rates (there's always a waiting list).

West 79th St Boat Basin: 212-496-2105; Map 14
This city-operated dock is filled with long-term houseboat residents. It's located at W 79th Street and the Hudson River in Riverside Park.

Dyckman Marina: 212-496-2105; Map 25
Transient dockage on the Hudson River at 348 Dyckman Street

Manhattan Cruise Terminal: 212-246-5450; www.nycruise.com; Map 11
If Love Boat re-runs aren't enough and you decide to go on a cruise yourself, you'll leave from the Manhattan Cruise Terminal. W 55th Avenue. Take the West Side Highway to Piers 88-92.

North Cove Yacht Harbor: 212-786-1200; www.thenorthcove.com; Battery Park City
A very, very fancy place to park your yacht in Battery Park City.

Helicopter Services

Helicopter Flight Services: 212-355-0801; www.heliny.com; Map 3, 8
For a minimum of $149, you can hop on a helicopter at the Downtown Manhattan Heliport at Pier 6 on the East River on weekdays or on weekends and spend 15 minutes gazing down on Manhattan. Reservations are recommended, and there's a minimum of two passengers per flight.

Liberty Helicopter Tours: 212-967-6464; www.libertyhelicopters.com or @LibertyHelicop; Map 3, 8
Leaves from the Downtown Manhattan Heliport at Pier 6 on the East River (9 am–6:30 pm). Prices start at $150. Minimum of four passengers per flight.

General Information

E-ZPass Information: www.e-zpassny.com
Radio Station Traffic
Updates: 1010 WINS on the 1s for a five-
borough focus and 880 on the 8s
for a suburban focus
NYCDOT: www.nyc.gov/dot
@NYC_DOT
NYS DMV: 212-645-5550
718-966-6155
dmv.ny.gov
@nysdmv

Real-Time NYC
Traffic Cameras: nyctmc.org

Driving in Manhattan

Avoid it. Why drive when you can see the city so well on foot or by bus? (We don't count the subway as seeing the city, but rather as a cultural experience in and of itself.) We know that sometimes you just have to drive in the city, so we've made you a list of essentials.

· Great auto insurance that doesn't care if the guy who hit you doesn't have insurance and doesn't speak any English.
· Thick skin on driver, passengers, and car. Needed for the fender benders and screamed profanity from the cabbies that are ticked anyone but cabbies are on the road.
· Anti-anxiety medication to counteract cardiac arrest-inducing "almost" accidents.
· NFT. But we know you would never leave home without it.
· E-ZPass. Saves time and lives. Maybe not lives, but definitely time and some money.
· New York State license plates. Even pedestrians will curse you out if you represent anywhere other than the Empire State, especially NJ or CT or Texas.
· A tiny car that can fit into a spot slightly larger than a postage stamp or tons of cash for parking garages.
· Patience with pedestrians—they own the streets of New York. Well, co-own them with the cabbies, sanitation trucks, cops, and fire engines.

The following are some tips that we've picked up over the years:

Hudson River Crossings

In the Bridge or Tunnel battle, the Bridge almost always wins. The George Washington Bridge is by far the best Hudson River crossing. It's got more lanes and better access than either tunnel with a fantastic view to boot. If you're going anywhere in the country that's north of central New Jersey, take it. However, inbound traffic on the George can back up for hours in the morning because they don't have enough toll booth operators to handle all those nuts who don't have E-ZPass. The Lincoln Tunnel is decent inbound, but check 1010 AM (WINS) if you have the chance. Avoid the Lincoln like the plague during evening rush hour (starts at about 3:30 pm). If you have to take the Holland Tunnel outbound, try the Broome Street approach, but don't even bother between 5 and 7 pm on weekdays.

East River Crossings

Brooklyn
Pearl Street to the Brooklyn Bridge is the least-known approach. Only the Williamsburg Bridge has direct access (i.e. no traffic lights) to the northbound BQE in Brooklyn, and only the Brooklyn Bridge has direct access to the FDR Drive in Manhattan. Again, listen to the radio if you can, but all three bridges can be disastrous as they seem to be constantly under construction (or, in a fabulous new twist, having one lane closed by the NYPD for some unknown reason). The Williamsburg is by far the best free route into North Brooklyn, but make sure to take the outer roadway to keep your options open in case the BQE is jammed. Your best option to go anywhere else in Brooklyn is usually the Brooklyn-Battery Tunnel, which can be reached from the FDR as well as the West Side Highway. Fun fact: The water you pass was so dirty in the '50s that it used to catch fire. The tunnel is not free, but if you followed our instructions you've got E-ZPass anyway. The bridges from south to north can be remembered as B-M-W, but they are not as cool as the cars that share this world.

Queens
There are three options for crossing into Queens by car. The Queens-Midtown Tunnel is usually miserable, since it feeds directly onto the parking lot known as the Long Island Expressway. The 59th Street Bridge (otherwise known as the Ed Koch Queensboro) is the only free crossing to Queens. The best approach to it is First Avenue to 57th Street (after that, follow the signs) or to 59th Street if you want to jump on the outer roadway that saves a ton of time and only precludes easy access to Northern Boulevard. If you're in Queens and want to go downtown in Manhattan, you can take the lower level of the 59th Street Bridge since it will feed directly onto Second Avenue, which of course goes downtown. The Robert F. Kennedy Bridge (née Triborough) is usually the best option (especially if you're going to LaGuardia, Shea, Astoria for Greek, or Flushing for dim sum). The FDR to the RFK is good except for rush hour—then try Third Avenue to 124th Street.

Harlem River Crossings

The RFK will get you to the Bronx in pretty good shape, especially if you are heading east on the Bruckner toward I-95 or the Hutchinson (which will take you to eastern Westchester and Connecticut). To get to Yankee Stadium, take the Willis or the Macomb's Dam (which are both free). When you feel comfortable maneuvering the tight turns approaching the Willis, use it for all travel to Westchester and Connecticut in order to save toll money. The Henry Hudson Bridge will take you up to western Westchester along the Hudson. It wins the fast and pretty prize for its beautiful surroundings. The Cross-Bronx Expressway will take years off your life. Avoid it at all costs.

Manhattan's "Highways"

There are two so-called highways in Manhattan—the Harlem River Drive/FDR Drive/East River Drive (which prohibits commercial vehicles) and the Henry Hudson Parkway/West Side Highway/Joe DiMaggio Highway. The main advantage of the FDR is that it has no traffic lights, while the West Side Highway has lights from Battery Park up through 57th Street. The main disadvantages of the FDR are (1) the potholes and (2) the narrow lanes. If there's been a lot of rain, both highways will flood, so you're out of luck (but the FDR floods first). Although the West Side Highway can fly, we would rather look at Brooklyn and Queens than Jersey, so the FDR wins.

Driving Uptown

The 96th Street transverse across Central Park is usually the best one, although if there's been a lot of rain, it will flood. If you're driving on the west side, Riverside Drive is the best route, followed next by West End Avenue. People drive like morons on Broadway, and Columbus jams up in the mid 60s before Lincoln Center and the mid 40s before the Lincoln Tunnel but it's still the best way to get all the way downtown without changing avenues. Amsterdam is a good uptown route if you can get to it. For the east side, you can take Fifth Avenue downtown to about 65th Street, whereupon you should bail out and cut over to Park Avenue for the rest of the trip. Do NOT drive on Fifth Avenue below 65th Street within a month of Christmas, and check the parade schedules before attempting it on weekends throughout the year. The 96th Street entrance to the FDR screws up First and Third Avenues going north and the 59th Street Bridge screws up Lexington and Second Avenues going downtown. Getting stuck in 59th Street Bridge traffic is one of the most frustrating things in the universe because there is absolutely no way out of it.

Driving in Midtown

Good luck! Sometimes Sixth (northbound) or Seventh (southbound) is best because everyone's trying to get out of Manhattan, jamming up the west side (via the Lincoln Tunnel) and the east side (via the 59th Street Bridge and the Queens-Midtown Tunnel). Friday nights at 9:30 pm can be a breeze, but from 10 pm to midnight, you're screwed as shows let out. The "interior" of the city is the last place to get jammed up – it's surprisingly quiet at 8 am. At 10 am, however, it's a parking lot. Those who plan to drive in Midtown on weekends from about March–October should check parade schedules for Fifth AND Sixth Avenues.

The demarcation of several "THRU Streets" running east-west in Midtown has been with the city permanently since 2004 and when people don't openly flout the no-turn signs, the system works pretty well. See "THRU Streets" section for more information.

Driving in the Village

People get confused walking in the Village, so you can imagine how challenging driving can be in the maze of one ways and short streets. Beware. If you're coming into the Village from the northwest, 14th Street is the safest crosstown route heading east. However, going west, take 13th Street. Houston Street has the great benefit of direct access to FDR Drive, both getting onto it and coming off of it. If you want to get to Houston Street from the Holland Tunnel, take Hudson Street to King Street to the Avenue of the Americas to Houston Street (this is the only efficient way to get to the Village from the Holland Tunnel). First Avenue is good going north and Fifth Avenue is good going south. Washington Street is the only way to make any headway southbound and Hudson Street is the only way to make any headway northbound in the West Village.

Driving Downtown

Don't do it unless you have to. Western TriBeCa is okay and so is the Lower East Side—try not to "turn in" to SoHo, Chinatown, or the Civic Center. Canal Street is a complete mess during the day (avoid it), since on its western end, everyone is trying to get to the Holland Tunnel, and on its eastern end, everyone is mistakenly driving over the Manhattan Bridge (your only other option when heading east on Canal is to turn right on Bowery!). Watch the potholes!

DMV Locations in Manhattan

If you're going to the DMV to get your first NY license (including drivers with other states' licenses), you'll need extensive documentation of your identity. The offices have a long list of accepted documents, but your best bet is a US passport and a Social Security card. If you don't have these things, birth certificates from the US, foreign passports, and various INS documents will be okay under certain conditions. Do not be surprised if you are turned away the first time. This trip requires great amounts of patience. Plan on spending three to six hours here. This is not a lunch-hour errand. That said, there is an online reservation system that takes some of the stress out of the whole endeavor, and do yourself a favor and check online if you might be able to transact business from home.

Greenwich Street Office
11 Greenwich St
New York, NY 10004
(Cross Streets Battery Park Pl & Morris St)
M–F 8:30 am–1 pm

Harlem Office
159 E 125th St, #1011
New York, NY 10035
(Lexington and Third)
M, T, W & F 8:30 am–4 pm, Thursday 10 am–6 pm

Herald Square Office
1293-1311 Broadway, 8th Fl
New York, NY 10001
(Between W 33 & W 34th Sts)
Handles out-of-state license exchange.
M–F 8 am–6 pm

Manhattan
License X-Press Office
300 W 34th St
New York, NY 10001
(Between Eighth & Ninth Aves)
Service limited to license and registration renewals and surrendering your license plate. You can't get your snowmobile or boat license here, and they do not do out-of-state exchanges. Oh, and no permit renewals.
M–F 8:30 am–4 pm

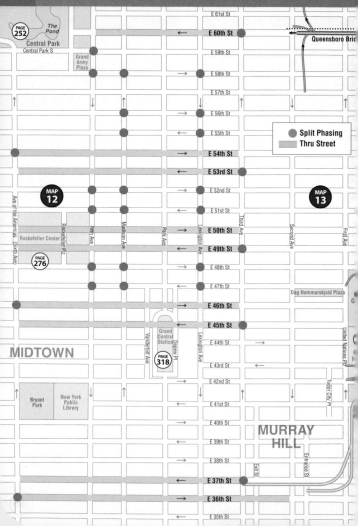

General Information

NFT Maps:	12 & 13
DOT:	311, www.nyc.gov/dot
	@NYC_DOT

Overview

In the tradition of "don't block the box" and other traffic solutions (such as randomly arresting political protesters), the city adopted "THRU Streets," in Midtown in 2004. The plan was implemented on some crosstown streets in Midtown in order to reduce travel times, relieve congestion, and provide a safer environment for pedestrians and cyclists. They are still working on cleaning up the exhaust fume issue for those concerned about said environment. On certain streets, cars are not allowed to make turns between Sixth and Third Avenues (with the exception of Park Avenue). The regulations are in effect between 10 am and 6 pm on weekdays. The affected streets are:

36th & 37th Streets

45th & 46th Streets

49th & 50th Streets

53rd & 54th Streets

60th Street (between Third and Fifth Avenues)

The above streets are easily identifiable by big, purple "THRU Streets" signs. With everything that's going on in midtown Manhattan though, you'd be forgiven for missing a sign (by us, not by the NYPD). If you happen to unwittingly find yourself on a THRU Street and can't escape on Park Avenue, you're going to have to suck it up until you get to Sixth Avenue or Third Avenue, depending on the direction you're heading. If you attempt to turn before the designated avenue, you'll find yourself with an insanely expensive ticket. Of course, if you're trying to drive crosstown, it's in your best interests to take one of these streets.

Both sides of almost every non-THRU Street in this grid have been stuck with "No Standing Except Trucks Loading and Unloading" regulations, supposedly creating up to 150 spaces for truck loading (if you were ever stuck behind a truck in morning rush hour on a THRU Street in 2004, you would rejoice at this news). Additionally, one side of each non-THRU street has been "daylighted" for 80–100 feet in advance of the intersection. We are not exactly sure how they came up with the term "daylighted," but the DOT tells us it allows space for turning vehicles. DOT studies showed that THRU Streets worked—initial studies showed travel times falling by 25% (as people decided to emigrate to New Zealand) and vehicle speeds increasing by an average of 33% (from 4 mph to 5.3 mph). The THRU Streets combined carried 4,854 vehicles per hour (up from 4,187), an average of 74 additional vehicles per hour.

Split Signal Phasing

"Split signal phasing" is just a fancy term for red lights for left- or right-hand turns, allowing pedestrians to cross the street without having to worry about vehicles turning in their path. This is in place at about 40 non-THRU Street intersections in this same grid. Of course, this system assumes that both pedestrians and drivers follow the rules of the road. In spite of the disregard that most New Yorkers display for crossing signals, the number of pedestrian accidents in the eight-month trial period compared to the eight months prior to implementation) fell from 81 to 74. The number of cycling accidents fell from 30 to 17. Accidents not related to pedestrians or bikes fell from 168 to 102.

Now if the DOT and NYPD could get traffic to flow smoothly onto bridges and into tunnels, they might actually be onto something…

Information

Department of
Transportation (DOT):   311
        www.nyc.gov/dot
        @NYC_DOT
Parking Violations Help Line: 311
Dept of Finance TTY
Hearing-Impaired: 212-504-4115
Department of Finance
Parking Ticket Info: www.nyc.gov/html/dof/html/
        parking/parking.shtml
DOT Alternate Side Parking
Info: www.nyc.gov/dot/asprules
        @NYCASP

Standing, Stopping and Parking Rules

In "No Stopping" areas, you can't wait in your car, drop off passengers, or load/unload.

In "No Standing" areas, you can't wait in your car or load/unload, but you can drop off passengers.

In "No Parking" areas, you can't wait in your car or drop off passengers, but you can load/unload.

NYC also has a "no idling" law, so when you're doing one of the three illegal things mentioned above, shut your car off, so at least you only get one ticket, not two!

Parking Meter Zones

On holidays when street cleaning rules are suspended (see calendar), the "no parking" cleaning regulations for metered parking are also suspended. You can park in these spots but have to pay the meters. Also, metered spots are still subject to rules not suspended on holidays (see below). On MLH (major legal holidays), meter rules are suspended (so no need to feed the meter).

Meters

Instead of old-fashioned individual meters, NYC relies on muni-meters that let you purchase time-stamped slips which you stick in your windshield to show you paid. These machines accept coins, parking cards, and credit cards. In the case of a non-functional muni-meter, a one-hour time limit applies. Sundays are free.

The DOT sells parking cards that come in $20, $50, and $100 denominations and can be used in muni-meters, municipal parking lots, and some single space meters (look for a yellow decal). The cards can be purchased through the DOT website (www.nyc.gov/dot), or by going to the Staten Island Ferry Terminal or one of the two City Stores.

Signs

New York City Traffic Rules state that one parking sign per block is sufficient notification. Check the entire block and read all signs carefully before you park. Then read them again.

If there is more than one sign posted for the same area, the more restrictive sign takes effect (of course). If a sign is missing on a block, the remaining posted regulations are the ones in effect.

The Blue Zone

The Blue Zone is a "No Parking" (Mon–Fri, 7 am–7 pm) area in Lower Manhattan. Its perimeter has been designated with blue paint; however, there are no individual "Blue Zone" signs posted. Any other signs posted in that area supersede Blue Zone regulations. Confused yet?

General

• All of NYC was designated a Tow Away Zone under the State's Vehicle & Traffic Law and the NYC Traffic Rules. This means that any vehicle parked or operated illegally, or with missing or expired registration or inspection stickers, may, and probably will, be towed.

• On major legal holidays, stopping, standing, and parking are permitted except in areas where stopping, standing, and parking rules are in effect seven days a week (for example, "No Standing Anytime").

• It is illegal to park in a spot where SCR are in effect, even if the street cleaner has already passed. If you sit in your car, the metermaid will usually let you stay

• Double-parking of passenger vehicles is illegal at all times. Including street-cleaning days, regardless of location, purpose, or duration. Everyone, of course, does this anyway. If everyone is double parked on a certain block during street cleaning, the NYPD probably is not ticketing. However, leave your phone number in the window in case the person you blocked in feels vindictive and demand that a cop write you a ticket.

• It is illegal to park within 15 feet of either side of a fire hydrant. The painted curbs at hydrant locations do not indicate where you can park. Isn't New York great? Metermaids will tell you that each cement block on the sidewalk is five feet, so make sure you are three cement blocks from the hydrant (2.5 will not do).

• If you think you're parked legally in Manhattan, you're probably not, so go and read the signs again.

• Cops will now just write you parking tickets and mail them to you if you are parked in a bus stop, so you won't even know it's happening unless you're very alert.

• There is now clearly an all-out effort to harass everyone who is insane enough to drive and/or park during the day in downtown Manhattan. Beware.

Tow Pounds

Manhattan

Pier 76 at W 38th St & Twelfth Ave
Open 24 hours: Monday 7 am–Monday 5 am
212-971-0771 or 212-971-0772

Bronx

745 E 141st St b/w Bruckner Expy & East River
Open Monday–Friday 8 am–10 pm and
Saturday 8 am–3 pm; closed Sunday
718-585-1385 or 718-585-1391

Brooklyn

Brooklyn Navy Yard; corner of Sands St & Navy St
Open Monday–Friday 8 am–10 pm and
Saturday 8 am–3 pm; closed Sunday
718-237-3300

Queens

31-22 College Point Boulevard, Flushing
Open Monday–Friday 8 am–10 pm and
Saturday 8 am–3 pm; closed Sunday
718-359-6200

Find out if your car was towed (and not stolen or disintegrated) by contacting your local police precinct or online via NYCServ: nycserv.nyc.gov/NYCServWeb/NYCSERVMain.

Once you've discovered that your car has indeed been towed, your next challenge is to find out which borough it's been towed to. This depends on who exactly towed your car—the NYPD, the Marshall, etc. Don't assume that since your car was parked in Manhattan that they will tow it to Manhattan—always call first.

So you've located your car, now come the particulars: If you own said towed car, you're required to present your license, registration, insurance, and payment of your fine before you can collect the impounded vehicle. If you are not the owner of the car you can usually get it back with all of the above, if your last name matches the registration (i.e. the car belongs to a relative or spouse), otherwise, you'll need a notarized letter with the owner's signature authorizing you to take the car. The tow fee is $185, plus $20 for each day it's in the pound. If they've put a boot on it instead, it's still $185. You can pay with cash, credit or debit card, certified check or money order. We recommend bringing a wad of cash and a long Russian novel for this experience. The longest waiting times are around noon and the late afternoon hours.

Transit · **LIRR**

General Information

In New York State	call 511
All inquiries (24/7)	say "Long Island Rail Road"
From Outside New York State:	877-690-5116
International Callers:	212-878-7000
Schedule Information (24/7)	Say "Schedules"
Fare Information (24/7)	Say "Fares"
Mail & Ride (M-F, 7:30 am-5 pm)	Say "Mail and Ride"
Group Travel and Getaways (M-F, 8 am-4 pm)	Say "Group Travel"
Lost & Found (M-F, 6 am-10 pm)	Say "Lost & Found"
Refunds (M-F, 8 am-4 pm)	Say "More Options"
	then "Ticket Refunds"
Ticket Machine Assistance	Say "More Options"
(M-F, 6:30 am-3:30 pm)	then "Ticket Machines"
Hamptons Reserve Service (May-Sept)	Say "More Options"
	then "Hamptons Reserve"
MTA Police:	212-878-1001
Website:	www.mta.info/lirr
Twitter:	@LIRR

Overview

The Long Island Railroad is the busiest railroad in North America. It has eleven lines with 124 stations stretching from Penn Station in midtown Manhattan, to the eastern tip of Long Island, Montauk Point. Over 80 million people ride the LIRR every year. If you are going anywhere on Long Island and you don't have a car, the LIRR is your best bet. Don't be surprised if the feeling of being in a seedy bar creeps over you during evening rush—those middle-aged business men like their beer en route. Despite a recent movement to ban the sale of alcohol on LIRR station platforms and trains, for now, it's still legal to get your buzz on.

If you're not a regular LIRR user, you might find yourself taking the train to Citi Field for a Mets game (Port Washington Branch), Long Beach for some summer

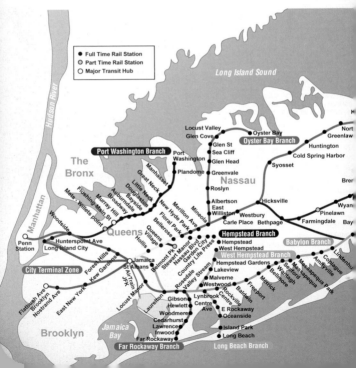

surfing (Long Beach Branch), or to Jamaica to transfer to the AirTrain to JFK (tip—the subway is cheaper). For the truly adventurous, take the LIRR all the way out to the Hamptons beach house you are visiting for the weekend (Hamptons Reserve seating is available during the summer for passengers taking eight or more trips). Bring a book as it is a long ride.

Fares and Schedules

Fares and schedules can be obtained by calling one of the general information lines, depending on your area. They can also be found on the LIRR website. Make sure to buy your ticket before you get on the train at a ticket window or at one of the ticket vending machines in the station. Otherwise it'll cost you an extra $5.75 or $6.50 depending on your destination. As it is a commuter railroad, the LIRR offers weekly and monthly passes, as well as ten-trip packages for on – or off-peak hours. The LIRR's CityTicket

program offers discounted one-way tickets for $4 within the five boroughs during weekends.

Pets on the LIRR

Trained service animals accompanying passengers with disabilities are permitted on LIRR trains. Other small pets are allowed on trains, but they must be confined to closed, ventilated containers.

Bikes on the LIRR

You need a permit ($5) to take your bicycle onto the Long Island Railroad. Pick one up at a ticket window or online at the LIRR website.

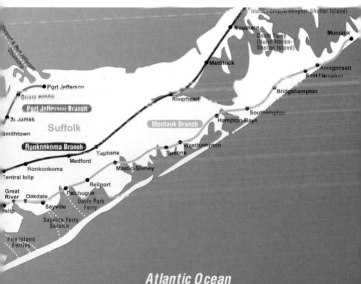

Key

Rail Station

Wheelchair or ADA Accessible station

Major transit hub — Rail Station

Connecting rail service

© 2004 Metropolitan Transportation Authority
Design: Michael Hertz Associates, NYC

Amtrak to Albany

Poughkeepsie

HUDSON LINE

DUTCHESS

Wassaic
Tenmile River
Dover Plains

New Hamburg

Harlem Valley–Wingdale
Appalachian Trail

HARLEM LINE

Pawling

Beacon

Breakneck Ridge
Cold Spring

Patterson

PUTNAM

Garrison

NEW YORK
CONNECTICUT

LITCHFIELD

Waterbury
Branch

Waterbury

Naugatuck

NEW
HAVEN

Beacon Falls
Seymour

Manitou

Southeast
Brewster

Danbury
Branch

Danbury

FAIRFIELD

Ansonia

Derby–Shelton

Peekskill

Croton Falls
Purdy's

Bethel

New Haven–
Union Station

Cortlandt

WESTCHESTER

Golden's Bridge
Katonah

Redding

Hudson River

Croton–Harmon

Bedford Hills
Mount Kisco

Branchville

Ossining

Chappaqua

Cannondale
Wilton

Milford

Scarborough

Pleasantville

New Canaan
Branch

NEW HAVEN LINE

Stratford

Philipse
Manor

Hawthorne
Mt Pleasant

NEW YORK
CONNECTICUT

New Canaan

Merritt 7

Bridgeport

Fairfield

Tarrytown

Valhalla

Talmadge Hill

Westport

Southport

Port Jefferson
Steamboat Co.

Irvington
Ardsley-on-
Hudson

North White Plains
White Plains

Springdale
Glenbrook

Green's Farms

Dobbs Ferry

Hartsdale

Stamford

East Norwalk
South Norwalk

Greystone

Scarsdale

Old Greenwich

Darien
Noroton Heights

Glenwood

Crestwood
Tuckahoe

Riverside
Cos Cob

Yonkers
Mt
Vernon West

Bronxville

Rye
Port Chester, NY
Greenwich, CT

Ludlow

Fleetwood

Mamaroneck

Long Island Sound

Wakefield

New Rochelle

Larchmont

Riverdale
Spuyten
Duyvil

Pelham

Mt Vernon East

Woodlawn

Williams Bridge
Botanical Garden

Marble Hill
University Hts
Morris Hts

Fordham
Tremont

Yankees–
E 153 St

Melrose

THE BRONX

NASSAU

Harlem–125 St

**NEW
YORK**

Grand
Central
Terminal

QUEENS

Penn
Station

PATH

BROOKLYN

General Information

In New York State	call 511
All inquiries	say "Metro-North Railroad"
From Connecticut:	877-690-5114
From Outside New York State.	877-690-5116
International Callers:	212-878-7000
Schedule Information (24/7):	Say "Schedules"
Fare Information (24/7):	Say "Fares"
Mail & Ride (M-F, 6:30 am-5 pm)	Say "More Options" then "Mail and Ride"
Group Sales (M-F, 8:30 am-5 pm):	Say "More Options" then "Group Sales"
Lost & Found (M-F, 6 am-10 pm):	Say "More Options" then "Lost & Found"
Ticket Machine Assistance (24/7):	Say "More Options" then "Ticket Machines"
MTA Police: 2	12-878-1001
Website:	www.mta.info/mnr
Twitter:	@MetroNorth

Overview

Metro-North is an extremely accessible and efficient railroad with three of its main lines (Hudson, Harlem, and New Haven) originating in Grand Central Station in Manhattan (42nd St & Park Ave). Those three lines east of the Hudson River, along with two lines west of the Hudson River that operate out of Hoboken, NJ (operated by NJ Transit; not shown on map), form the Metro-North commuter railroad system in the US. Approximately 250,000 commuters use the tri-state Metro-North service each day for travel between New Jersey, New York, and Connecticut. Metro-North rail lines cover roughly 2,700 square miles of territory. The best thing about Metro-North is that it lands you at Grand Central Station, one of the city's finest pieces of architecture. On weekdays, sneak into the land of platforms via the North Passage, accessible at 47th & 48th Streets. At least for now, it's still legal to have an after work drink on Metro-North. During happy hour (starting somewhere around 3 pm), hit the bar car or buy your booze in advance on the platform at Grand Central. It might make you feel better about being a wage slave. But beware of having too happy of an hour as the bathrooms can be stinky and not all cars have them.

Fares and Schedules

Fare information is available on Metro-North's extraordinarily detailed website (along with in-depth information on each station, full timetables, and excellent maps) or at Grand Central Station. The cost of a ticket to ride varies depending on your destination so you should probably check the website before setting out. Buy advance tickets on MTA's WebTicket site for the cheapest fares. If you wait until you're on the train to pay, it'll cost you an extra $5.75–$6.50. Monthly and weekly rail passes are also available for commuters. Daily commuters save 50% on fares when they purchase a monthly travel pass.

Hours

Train frequency depends on your destination and the time of day that you're traveling. On weekdays, peak-period trains east of the Hudson River run every 20–30 minutes; off-peak trains run every 30–60 minutes; and weekend trains run hourly. Hours of operation are approximately 4 am to 3:40 am. First trains arrive at Grand Central at 5:30 am and the last ones leave at 2 am. Don't miss the last train out as they leave on time and wait for no one.

Bikes on Board

If you're planning on taking your two-wheeler onboard, you'll need to apply for a bicycle permit first. An application form can be found on the Metro-North website at http://mta.info/mnr/html/mnrbikepermit.htm. The $5 lifetime permit fee and application can either be mailed into the MTA, or processed right away at ticket booths and on board trains.

Common sense rules for taking bikes on board include: no bikes on escalators, no riding on the platform, and board the train after other passengers have boarded. Unfortunately there are restrictions on bicycles during peak travel times. Bicycles are not allowed on trains departing from Grand Central Terminal 4 pm–8 pm and connecting trains. In addition, bikes are not allowed on trains leaving from Grand Central between 5:30 am–9 am, 3 pm–3:59 pm, and 8:01–8:15 pm. Bikes are not permitted on trains arriving at Grand Central 5 am–10 am and connecting trains. Bicycles are subject to expanded restrictions around major holidays, including major Jewish holidays, and Fridays before long weekends. No bicycles are allowed on New Year's Eve, New Year's Day, St. Patrick's Day, Mother's Day, Eve of Rosh Hashanah, Eve of Yom Kippur, Eve of Thanksgiving, Thanksgiving Day, Christmas Eve and Christmas Day. There's a limit of two bikes per carriage, and four bikes per train on weekdays, and eight on the weekends. Unfortunately the same limitations are not imposed on passengers with 4 Vera Bradley overnight bags heading off to the country house, but that is another story.

Riders of folding bikes do not require a permit and do not have to comply with the above rules, provided that the bike is folded at all times at stations and on trains.

Pets

Only seeing-eye dogs and small pets, if restrained or confined, are allowed aboard the trains.

One-Day Getaways

Metro-North offers "One-Day Getaway" packages on its website. Packages include reduced rail fare and discounted entry to destinations along MNR lines including Bruce Museum, Dia:Beacon, Hudson River Museum/Andrus Planetarium, Maritime Aquarium at Norwalk, Mohegan Sun Casino, New York Botanical Garden, and Wave Hill. Tickets are available at Metro-North ticket offices or full-service ticket vending machines. The MTA website also suggests one-day hiking and biking excursions.

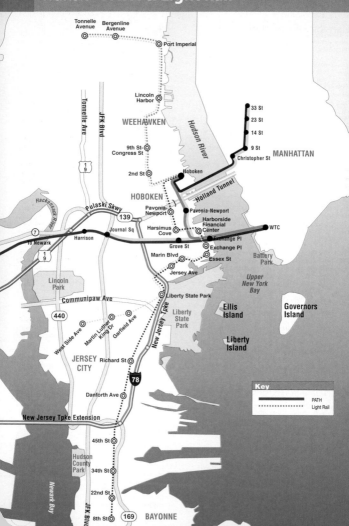

Transit • PATH & Light Rail

PATH Train

General Information
Phone: 800-234-7284
Police/
Lost & Found: 201-216-6078
Website: www.panynj.gov/path
Twitter: @PATHTrain

Overview

The PATH (Port Authority Trans-Hudson Corp.) is an excellent small rail system that services Newark, Jersey City, Hoboken, and Manhattan. There are a few basic lines that run directly between 33rd Street (Herald Square) in Manhattan & Hoboken, 33rd Street & Jersey City, and Newark & the WTC. Transfers between the lines are available at most stations. The PATH can be quite useful for commuters on the west side of Manhattan when the subway isn't running, say, due to a sick passenger or mysterious police investigation. Additionally, you can catch the PATH to Newark and then either jump in a cheap cab or take New Jersey Transit one stop to Newark Airport.

Check the front or the sides of incoming trains to determine their destination. Don't assume that if a Journal Square train just passed through, the next train is going to Hoboken. Often there will be two Journal Square trains in a row, followed by two Hoboken trains. During the weekend, PATH service can be excruciatingly slow and confusing, and is best endeavored with a seasoned rider

Fares

The PATH costs $2.50 one-way. Regular riders can purchase 10-trip, 20-trip, and 40-trip SmartLink cards, which reduce the fare per journey to $1.90. The fare for seniors (65+) is $1 per ride. You can also use pay-per-ride MTA MetroCards for easy transition between the PATH and NYC subway.

Hours

The PATH runs 24/7 (although a modified service operates between 11pm–6am, M–F, and 7:30pm–9 am, Sat, Sun, & holidays). Daytime service is pretty consistent, but the night schedule for the PATH is a bit confusing, so make sure to look at the map. You may be waiting underground for up to 35 minutes. During off hours the train runs on the same track through the tunnel. This allows for maintenance to be completed on the unused track.

Hudson-Bergen Light Rail

General Information
Phone: 973-275-5555
Website: www.njtransit.com
Twitter: @NJTRANSIT

Overview

Even though it's called the Hudson-Bergen Light Rail system (HBLR, operated by NJ Transit), it actually only serves Hudson county. Bergen County residents are still waiting for their long promised connection. The HBLR has brought about some exciting changes (a.k.a. "gentrification") in Jersey City, though Bayonne remains (for the moment) totally, well, Bayonne. Currently there are 24 stops in the system, including service to Jersey City, Hoboken, Weehawken, and Union City.

Fares

The Light Rail is $2.10 per trip; reduced fare is $1.05. Ten-trip tickets are $21, monthly passes cost $64. Unless you have a monthly pass, you need to validate your ticket before boarding at a Ticket Validating Machine (TVM). Once validated, tickets are only valid for 90 minutes, so don't buy too far in advance. The trains and stations have random fare inspection and the fine for fare evasion is up to $100.

Hours

Light rail service operates between 5 am and 1:20 am. Times are approximate, check the website for exact schedules on each line.

Bikes on Board

Bikes are allowed (no permit or fee required) on board during off-peak times—weekdays from 9:30 am to 4 pm and 7 pm to 6 am, and all day Saturday, Sunday, and NJ state holidays. Bicycles have to be accompanied on the low-floor vestibule section of each rail car.

Pets

Small pets are allowed, as long as they're confined to a carry container. Service animals are permitted at all times.

Transit · NJ Transit

General Information

Address: 1 Penn Plz E Newark, NJ 07105
Phone: 973-275-5555
Suspicious
activity: 888-TIPS-NJT
Lost and
Found: Call main number
Website: www.njtransit.com
Twitter: @NJTRANSIT

Overview

With a service area of over 5,000 square miles, NJ Transit (just "NJ," thank you) is one of the largest transit systems in the country. And yet, sandwiched between New York and Philadelphia, and a feeder into both city's transportation systems, you can't blame NJ Transit for feeling a little slighted. And when you think about it there's a point there; an incredibly large proportion of those urban workforces are utterly dependent on a commuter system that relies on a handful of underground links with Manhattan and a few bridges into Philly. All of which is to say, let's hear it for NJ Transit, for all they do to get us in and out of two major cities day in and day out, as well as moving folks around the Garden State itself.

That said, are the rails prone to power loss and broken switches? Sure. And did someone or something screw pooches when they or it left much of its rolling stock in a flood plain during Superstorm Sandy? Well, yes. And does the Pascack Valley Line seem to just creep along, which can be problematic when you're trying to make a transfer before reaching the Big Apple? Absolutely. And do you wonder who exactly thought it was a good idea to dub Secaucus Junction "Frank R. Lautenberg Station at Secaucus Junction" long before the Senator passed away? No question. But for all that, the trains are usually clean (and immune to the weirdness that seems to plague the LIRR), and there's nothing better than relaxing on one of their brand spanking new Bombardier MultiLevel Coach cars while your boys wait in traffic at one of the three uneasy Hudson River automobile crossings. And don't forget NJ Transit's convenient and efficient bus lines connecting areas not served by the train lines.

That's right, when you're cruising into the departure lounge at Newark an hour early because your Northeast Corridor line train got you to the airport in just 30 minutes from Midtown, just know who to thank: the good folks at NJ Transit. And when you're settling into your lower-level seat at the Izod Center to check out the latest WWE tour event, remember who took you there—and who's going home with you. That's right: NJ Transit.

Secaucus Junction Station

By way of a history lesson, before the three-level hub with the senatorially laden moniker at Secaucus was built, two major lines crossed but never met, as existential as that sounds. Fourteen years and $450 million later, hundreds of thousands of commuters found relief by being able to connect in Secaucus, without having to travel all the way to Hoboken. That and the super-badass New Jersey Turnpike "Exit 15X" was created from literally nothing. Goya Foods and The Children's Place have their corporate headquarters in Secaucus, and Robert John Burck, otherwise known as Times Square's Naked Cowboy, makes his home in Secaucus. Oh, and if you want to be a huge smartass, know that Secaucus Junction is technically not actually a junction.

For riders, Secaucus Junction is just an 8-minute ride from Penn Station, and connects ten of NJ Transit's 11 rail lines, while offering service to Newark Airport, downtown Newark, Trenton, and the Jersey Shore.

Fares and Schedules

Fares and schedules can be obtained at Hoboken, Newark, Penn Station, on NJ Transit's website, or by calling NJ Transit. If you wait to pay until you're on the train and you board from a station that has an available ticket agent or open ticket machine, you'll pay an extra five bucks for the privilege. NJ Transit also offers discounted monthly, weekly, weekend, and ten trip tickets for regular commuters. Tickets are valid until used and have no expiration date.

Pets

Only seeing-eye dogs and small pets in carry-on containers are allowed aboard the trains and buses.

Bikes

The short answer is that in general, you can take your bicycle on board a NJ Transit train only during off-peak hours and during all hours on the weekends. The nitty gritty is this: bicycles are permitted on all trains except inbound trains that end in Hoboken, Newark or New York between 6 am and 10 am weekdays, outbound trains that originate in Hoboken, Newark or New York between 4 pm and 7 pm weekdays, and on weekend trains along the Northeast Corridor, North Jersey Coast Line and Morristown Line trains terminating in New York between 9 am and 12 pm and trains originating in New York between 5 pm and 8 pm. If confused, look on the timetables for trains designated by a bicycle symbol. Bikes are not allowed on board most holidays, or the Fridays prior to any holiday weekend; however, a folding frame bicycle can be taken on board at any time. Most NJ Transit buses participate in the "Rack 'n' Roll" program, which allows you to load your bike right on to the front of the bus.

Overview

Phone: 800-USA-RAIL (872-7245)
Website: www.amtrak.com
Twitter: @Amtrak

General Information

Amtrak is our national train system, and while it's not particularly punctual or affordable, it will take you to many major northeastern cities in half a day or less. Spending a few hours on Amtrak also makes you want to move to Europe where France is now running trains at 357 mph (as opposed to 35 mph in the US). We exaggerate. But seriously, if you plan a trip at the last minute and miss the requisite advance on buying airline tickets or want to bring liquids with you when checking baggage, you might want to shop Amtrak's fares. Bonus: Amtrak allows you to talk on cell phones in most cars and has plugs for laptop computers at your seat.

Amtrak was created by the federal government in 1971. Today, Amtrak services 500+ stations in 46 states (Alaska, Hawaii, South Dakota, and Wyoming sadly do not have the pleasure of being serviced by Amtrak, as much as Joe Biden would like to commit funding toward a trans-Pacific high-speed link). While not being as advanced as the Eurail system, Amtrak does serve over 30 million passengers a year, employs 20,000 people, still has the same decor it did in the early 1970s, and provides "contract-commuter services" for several state and regional rail lines.

Red Caps (station agents) are very helpful, especially for passengers traveling with children and strollers. The only problem is finding an available one!

Amtrak in New York

In New York City, Amtrak runs out of Pennsylvania Station, an eyesore currently located underneath Madison Square Garden. We treat the station like our annoying little brother, calling it Penn for short and avoiding it when we can. But don't despair—chances are the city you'll wind up in will have a very nice station, and, if all goes well, so will we, once the front half of the Farley Post Office is converted to a "new" Penn Station. Warning: If you hop in a cab to get to Amtrak, specify that you want to be dropped off at Eighth Avenue and 33rd Street in order to avoid LIRR and Madison Square Garden foot traffic. Don't let the cabbie argue with you, especially if you have luggage. He is just trying to make his life easier.

Popular Destinations

Many New Yorkers use Amtrak to get to Boston, Philadelphia, or Washington DC. Of course, these are the New Yorkers who are traveling on an expense account or fear the Chinatown bus service. Amtrak also runs a line up to Montreal and through western New York state (making stops in Buffalo, Rochester, Albany, etc.). Check Amtrak's website for a complete listing of all Amtrak stations.

Going to Boston

Amtrak usually runs about two dozen trains daily to Boston. One-way fares cost approximately $70–$200, and the trip, which ends at South Station in downtown Boston, takes about four-and-a-half hours door-to-door. For over $100 you can ride the high speed Acela ("acceleration" and "excellence" combined into one word, though perhaps "expensive" would have been more appropriate) and complete the journey in three to three-and-a-half hours—if there are not track problems.

Going to Philadelphia

Dozens of Amtrak trains pass through Philadelphia every day. One-way tickets start from about $50–$55 on a regular Amtrak train; if you're really in a hurry, Acela service starts around $100, which will get you there in an hour or so. The cheapest rail option to Philly is actually to take NJ Transit to Trenton and then hook up with Eastern Pennsylvania's excellent SEPTA service—this will take longer, but will cost you approximately $25. Some commuters take this EVERY day. Thank your lucky stars you're probably not one of them.

Going to Washington DC

(Subtitle: *How Much is Your Time Worth?*)
Amtrak runs dozens of trains daily to DC and the prices vary dramatically. The cheapest trains cost around $85 one-way and take between three and four hours. The Acela service costs at the cheapest $150 one-way, and delivers you to our nation's capital in less than three hours (sometimes). Worth it? Only you can say. Depending on what time of day you travel, you may be better off taking the cheaper train when the Acela will only save you 30 minutes.

A Note About Fares

While the prices quoted above for Boston, Philly, and DC destinations tend to remain fairly consistent, fare rates to other destinations, such as Cleveland, Chicago, etc., can vary depending on how far in advance you book your seat. For "rail sales" and other discounts, check www.amtrak. com. Military IDs will save you a bundle, so use them if you have them. Occasionally (or rarely), Amtrak frequently offers discounts that can be found on their website—hunt around.

Baggage Check (Amtrak Passengers)

A maximum of two items may be checked up to thirty minutes before departure. Two additional bags may be checked for a fee of $20 each (two carry-on items allowed). No electronic equipment, plastic bags, or paper bags may be checked. See the "Baggage Policy" section of the website for details.

General Information

NFT Map:	9
Address:	Seventh Ave & 33rd St
General Information (Amtrak):	800-872-7245
NJ Transit:	Tracks 1–12
Amtrak:	Tracks 5–16
LIRR:	Tracks 13–21
MTA Subway Stops:	1, 2, 3 (Seventh Avenue side) and A, C, E (Eighth Avenue side)
NYCT Bus Lines:	M34, M20, M7, M4, Q32
Train Lines:	LIRR, Amtrak, NJ Transit
LGA/JFK Airport Bus Service:	www.nycairporter.com, 718-777-5111 or 855-269-7747
Penn Station Map:	www.njtransit.com/pdf/nypenn_map.prlf
Unofficial Guide to New York Penn Station:	jasonglbbs.com/pennstation

Overview

Penn Station, designed by McKim, Mead & White (New York's greatest Beaux-Arts architectural firm), is a treasure, filled with light and...oh wait, that's the one that was torn down. Penn Station is essentially a basement, complete with well-weathered leather chairs, unidentifiable dust particles, and high-cholesterol snack food. Its claim to fame is that it is the busiest Amtrak station in the country. If the government gods are with us, the plan to convert the current half of the Farley Post Office (also designed by McKim, Mead & White) that used to an above-ground, light-filled station will come to fruition. With bureaucracy at hand, we aren't holding our collective breath. Until then, Penn Station will go on servicing 600,000 people per day in the rat's maze under Madison Square Garden.

Penn Station serves Amtrak, the LIRR, and NJ Transit. Amtrak, which is surely the worst national train system of any first-world country, administers the station. How is it that the Europeans have bullet trains and it still takes three or more hours to get from NYC to DC? While we're hoping the new station proposal will come through, will it help the crazed LIRR commuters struggling to squish down stairwells to catch the 6:05 to Ronkonkoma? We can only hope.

Riders traveling through Penn Station should pre-pack snacks. The fast food joints are just too tempting. Donuts and ice cream and KFC, oh my! Leave yourself time to pick up some magazines and a bottle of water for your train trip. It may turn out to be longer than you think

The plus side to Penn is that it's easy to get to from just about anywhere in the city via subway or bus. If you are just too ritzy to take the MTA (or you have an abundance of baggage), have your cab driver drop you off anywhere surrounding the station except for Seventh Avenue—it is constantly jammed with tour buses and cabs trying to drop off desperately late passengers.

Temporary Parcel/Baggage Check

The only facility for storing parcels and baggage in Penn Station is at the Baggage Check on the Amtrak level (to the left of the ticket counter). There are no locker facilities at Penn Station. The Baggage Check is open from 5:15 am until 10 pm and costs $ per item for each 24-hour period.

Terminal Shops

Food & Drink (Upper Level)
Auntie Anne's Pretzels
Chickpea
CocoMoka Cafe
Don Pepi Pizza & Deli
Haagen Dazs
Labooz's
KFC
Krispy Kreme
Moe's Southwest Grill
Nathan's
Penn Sushi
Pizza Hut
Planet Smoothie
Primo! Cappuccino
Soup Stop
Taco Bell
Tasti D-Lite
TGI Friday's
Tim Horton
Zaro's Bread Basket

Food & Drink (Lower Level)
Au Bon Pain
Auntie Anne's Pretzels
Caruso Pizza
Carvel
Central Market
Charley's Grilled Subs
Chickpea
Cinnabon
Colombo Yogurt
Don Pepi Express
European Cafe
Frankie's Dogs on the Go
Hot & Crusty
Jamba Juice
KFC
Knot Just Pretzels
Le Bon Café
McDonalds
Moe's Southwest Grill
Nathan's
Pizza Hut
Planet Smoothie

Riese Restaurant
Rose Pasta & Pizza
Starbucks
Subway
Taco Bell
TGI Friday's
Tim Horton
Tracks Raw Bar & Grill

Shopping & Services (Upper Level)
Book Corner
Drago Shoe Shine/Repair
Duane Reade
Elegance
GNC
Hudson News
New York New York
Perfumania
Soleman Shoe Repair
Petal Pusher
Tiecoon
Verizon Wireless

Shopping & Services (Lower Level)
Carlton Cards
Duane Reade
Expert Shoe Repair
Fresh Flowers
GNC
Hudson News
Kmart
Penn Books
Penn Station Bookstore
Penn Wine & Spirits
Petal Pusher
Puff 'n Stuff
Soleman Shoe Repair

Banking/ATM (Upper Level)
Chase Bank
Wells Fargo

Banking/ATM (Lower Level)
Bank of America
HSBC

317

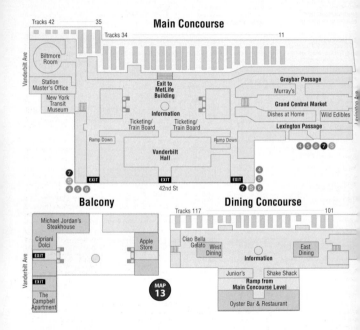

Main Concourse

Tracks 42   35

Tracks 34   11

Vanderbilt Ave

Biltmore Room

Station Master's Office

New York Transit Museum

Exit to MetLife Building

Information

Ticketing/ Train Board

Ticketing/ Train Board

Ramp Down

Ramp Down

Vanderbilt Hall

Graybar Passage

Murray's

Grand Central Market

Dishes at Home   Wild Edibles

Lexington Passage

Lexington Ave

④⑤⑥⑦Ⓢ

④
⑤
⑥

⑦
Ⓢ

④⑤⑥

EXIT   EXIT   EXIT

⑦Ⓢⓢⓢ

42nd St

Balcony

Dining Concourse

Tracks 117   101

Vanderbilt Ave

Michael Jordan's Steakhouse

Cipriani Dolci

EXIT

Apple Store

EXIT

The Campbell Apartment

MAP 13

Ciao Bella Gelato   West Dining

Information

East Dining

Junior's   Shake Shack

Ramp from Main Concourse Level

Oyster Bar & Restaurant

General Information

NFT Map:	13
Address:	42nd St & Park Ave
General Information:	212-340-2583
Lost and Found:	212-340-2555
Website:	www.grandcentralterminal.com
Twitter:	@GrandCentralNYC
Metro-North:	mta.info/mnr or @MetroNorth
MTA Subway Stops:	4, 5, 6, 7, Shuttle to Times Square
MTA Bus Lines:	M1, M2, M3, M4, M5, M101, M102, M103, M42
Newark Airport Express:	www.newarkairportexpress.com, 877-8-NEWARK
GA/JFK Airport Bus Service:	www.nycairporter.com, 718-777-5111 or 855-269-2247

Overview

Grand Central Terminal, designed in the Beaux-Arts style by Warren & Wetmore, is by far the most beautiful of Manhattan's major terminals, and it is considered one of the most stunning terminals in the world. Its convenient location in the heart of Midtown and its refurbishments only add to its appeal. The only downside is that the station will only get you on a train as far north as Dutchess County or as far east as New Haven via Metro-North—in order to head to the Island or Jersey, you'll have to hoof it over to GCT's architecturally ugly stepsister Penn Station.

If you ever find yourself underestimating the importance of the Grand Central renovations (begun in 1996 with continued work and maintenance today), just take a peek at the ceiling toward the Vanderbilt Avenue side—the small patch of black shows how dirty the ceiling was previously (and, believe us, it was really dirty...). In 2013 Grand Central celebrated its 100th anniversary, marked by a comprehensive exhibit in Vanderbilt Hall. The exhibit, worth checking out, survives online at www.gchistory.com.

Sometime in the next 75 or 100 years, the multi-gazillion-dollar East Side Access project will connect the Long Island Rail Road to Grand Central via the new tunnel under 63rd Street, adding an eight-track terminal and concourse below Grand Central.

Amenities

Diners have any number of choices including Michael Jordan's The Steak House N.YC. or Cipriani Dolci for nice views overlooking the main concourse or the food court on the lower level (perfect for commuters or those intent on saving a few bucks). As food courts go, the lower level food court isn't half bad; if you squint, it's like a curated selection of NYC mainstays: gelato from Ciao Bella, cheesesteaks from Junior's, and Shake Shack for burgers (lower concourse open Monday–Saturday 7 am to 9 pm, Sunday 11 am to 6 pm). After hitting the raw stuff at Oyster Bar, go right outside its entrance to hear a strange audio anomaly: If you and a friend stand in opposite corners and whisper, you'll be able to hear each other clearly. Alternatively, folks looking to hit the sauce may do so in 1920s grandeur in The Campbell Apartment near the Vanderbilt Avenue entrance, or for a non-edible treat, grab an iPad for your train ride at the shiny Apple Store on the east balcony overlooking the main concourse. One of the more fun spots to shop at in Grand Central is the New York Transit Museum Gallery Annex and Store, a satellite branch of the MTA's excellent Transit Museum in Downtown Brooklyn. The annex features a gallery with changing exhibits and the gift shop has some great gift ideas.

Grand Central Market, located between the east passages of the terminal as you head out toward Lexington Avenue, is a true big-boy market featuring various purveyors of high-quality foodstuffs. Build your own bread-meat-cheese extravaganza here, or take home fresh fish or meat to cook at home later on. Our favorite vendors include Wild Edibles, Dishes at Home and a Midtown branch of the best cheese shop in NYC—Murray's. Market open weekdays 7 am to 9 pm, Saturday 10 am to 7 pm, and Sunday 11 am to 6 pm.

Tours

The Municipal Arts Society runs a 75-minute tour of Grand Central guided by MAS docents. Tours depart daily at 12:30 pm. Tickets cost $20 ($15 reduced) at the tour window on the main concourse. Visit www.mas.org/tours for more information. Grand Central also offers a headset audio tour ($8) daily from 9 am to 6 pm, and an app version of the tour ($4.99) via the website for visitors who want to wander on their own (myorpheo.com/official-grand-central-tour).

General Information

NFT Map:	11
Address:	625 Eighth Ave at 41st St
General Information:	212-502-2200
Website:	www.panynj.gov/bus-terminals/port-authority-bus-terminal.html
Subway:	A, C, E, 42nd St/Port Authority or 1, 2, 3, 7, N, R, Q, S to Times Square
NYCT Bus:	M42, M34A, M20, M11, M104
Newark Airport Express:	www.newarkairportexpress.com, 877-8-NEWARK
JGA/JFK Airport Bus Service:	www.nycairporter.com, 718-777-5111 or 855-269-2247

Overview

Devised as a solution to New York City's horrendous bus congestion, the Port Authority Bus Terminal was completed in 1950. The colossal structure consolidated midtown Manhattan's eight, separate, interstate bus stations into one convenient drop-off and pick-up point. Back in the day the Port Authority held the title of "largest bus terminal in the world," but for now we'll have to be content with merely the biggest depot in the United States. The Port Authority is located on the north and south sides of W 41st Street (b/w Eighth Ave & Ninth Ave) in a neighborhood that real estate agents haven't yet graced with an official name. How about Greyhound Gardens?

There are plenty of things to do should you find that you've got some time to kill here. Send a postcard from the post office, donate blood at the blood bank on the main floor, use the refurbished bathrooms, roll a few strikes and enjoy a cocktail at Frames bowling lounge, chug a couple of decent brews at mini-chain Heartland Brewery, or shop the Greenmarket on Thursdays. There are also many souvenir carts, newsstands, and on-the-go restaurants, as well as a statue of beloved bus driver Ralph Kramden located outside of the south wing. The grungiest area of the terminal is the lower bus level, which is dirty and exhaust-filled, best visited just a few minutes before you need to board your bus.

If you can, avoid interstate bus rides from the Port Authority on the busiest travel days of the year. The lines are long, the people are cranky, and some of the larger bus companies hire anyone who shows up with a valid bus operator's license and their very own bus (apparently, easier to obtain than you might think). The odds of having a disastrous trip skyrocket when the driver is unfamiliar with th usual itinerary.

On Easter Sunday, Christmas Eve, or Thanksgiving, one can see all the angst-ridden sons and daughters of suburban New Jersey parents joyfully waiting in cramped, disgusting corridors for that nauseating bus ride back to Leonia or Morristown or Plainfield or wherever. A fascinating sight.

Terminal Shops

Subway Level
Green Trees
Hudson News
Au Bon Pain
Hudson News
Music Explosion

Main Floor
Au Bon Pain
Auntie Anne's
Blank SL8 Pop-Up Store
Bolton's
Casa Java
Deli Plus
Duane Reade
GNC
Jamba Juice
Heartland Brewery
Hudson News
Hudson News Business
  Center
Marrella Men's Hair Stylist
NY Blood Center
Radio Shack
Strawberry
US Postal Service
Villa Pizza

Second Floor
Australian Homemade
Bank of America
Book Corner
Café Metro
Cinnabon/Carvel
Drago Shoe Repair
Frames
Hudson News
Jay's Hallmark
Jewel Box
Lotto
McAnn's Pub
Mrs Fields Cookies
Munchy's Gourmet
Sak's Florist

Bus Lines

Academy (201-420-7000, www.academybus.com): Northeastern US and Florida
Adirondack Pine Hill New York Trailways (800-858-8555, www.trailwaysny.com): New York State and nearby Canadian destinations
Bieber (800-243-2374, www.biebertourways.com): Eastern Pennsylvania
Community (Coach USA) (800-877-1888, www.coachusa.com/community): Morris and Essex Counties (NJ)
Community Lines (201-309-0006): Hudson County (NJ)
DeCamp (800-631-1281, www.decamp.com): Northern New Jersey
Greyhound (800-231-2222, www.greyhound.com): US and Canada
Lakeland (973-366-0600, www.lakelandbus.com): Northern New Jersey
Martz Trailways (800-233-8604, www.martztrailways.com): New York, New Jersey, Pennsylvania
Megabus (877-462-6342, www.megabus.com): US and Canada
NJ TRANSIT (973-275-5555, www.njtransit.com): New Jersey commuter
Olympia (Coach USA) (877-894-9155, www.coachusa.com): Newark Airport Express
Peter Pan (800-343-9999, www.peterpanbus.com): Mid-Atlantic US and New England
Rockland (Coach USA) (201-263-1254, www.coachusa.com): Rockland County (NY) and Northern New Jersey
Shortline (Coach USA) (800-631-8405, www.coachusa.com): Upstate NY, Colleges, Orange, Rockland, Sullivan, Bergen and Pike Counties, Woodbury Common Premium Outlets
Suburban (Coach USA) (800-222-0492, www.coachusa.com): Mercer, Middlesex, and Somerset Counties (NJ)
Susquehanna Trailways (800-692-6314, www.susquehannabus.com): Susquehanna River Valley, PA
Trans-Bridge Lines (610-868-6001, www.transbridgelines.com): Lehigh Valley, PA

General Information

NFT Map:	23
Address:	4211 Broadway at 178th St
Phone:	800-221-9903 or 212-564-8484
Website:	www.panynj.gov/bus-terminals/ george-washington-bridge-bus-station.html
Subway:	A to 175th St or 1 or A to 181st St
Buses:	M4, M5, M98, M100, Bx3, Bx7, Bx11, Bx13, Bx35, Bx36

Overview

The George Washington Bridge Bus Station opened in 1963 to consolidate bus operations in the Washington Heights section of Manhattan. Italian architect Pier Luigi Nervi designed the facility and its striking roof consisting of 26 reinforced concrete triangle sections. The design is a great living example of 1960s architecture, and the reinforced concrete material is typical of Nervi's work. This was his first US project, after designing many well-known structures in Italy including the 1960 Olympic Stadium in Rome.

With easy access to the George Washington Bridge, the station connects Upper Manhattan with Northern New Jersey, and is served by several private carriers along with NJ Transit. A passageway connects with the 175th Street station of the A train (open 5 am to 1 am). Sitting directly atop the Trans-Manhattan Expressway (otherwise known as I-95), the views of the George Washington Bridge are pretty spectacular, and worth checking out even if you're not catching the bus to Hackensack.

For years the station's 30,000 square feet of retail space sat underutilized, but change is coming slowly. A $183 million rehabilitation is underway to modernize the facility and expand retail opportunities, including a 120,000-square-foot "MarketPlace" (no room for spaces) that will feature a gym, supermarket and Marshall's department store. Part of us hopes it will never lose its "lived-in" charm, but really, any place with pigeons routinely wandering around indoors can never be too sanitized.

Bus Companies

- Air Brook
  (800-800-1990, www.airbrook.com): Casino shuttle to Atlantic City

- New Jersey Transit
  (973-275-5555, www.njtransit.com): To 60th St Bergenfield, Bogota, Cliffside Park, Coytesville, Dumont, Edgewater (including Edgewater Commons Mall), Englewood, Englewood Cliffs West Englewood, Fair Lawn (including the Radburn section), Fairview, Fort Lee, Glen Rock, Guttenberg, Hackensack (including NJ Bus Transfer), Hoboken, North Hackensack (Riverside Square), Irvington, Jersey City, Kearney, Leonia, Maywood, Newark, North Bergen, Paramus (including the Bergen Mall and Garden State Plaza), Paterson (including Broadway Terminal), Ridgewood, Rochelle Park, Teaneck (including Glenpointe and Holy Name Hospital), Union City, Weehawken, and West New York.

- Rockland Coaches (Coach USA)
  (908-354-3330, www.coachusa.com/rockland) To Alpine, Bergenfield, Central Nyack, Closter, Congers, Coytesville, Cresskill, Demarest, Dumont, Emerson, Englewood, Englewood Cliffs, Fort Lee, Grandview, Harrington Park, Haverstraw, Haworth, Hillsdale, Leonia, Linwood Park, Montvale, Nanuet, New City, New Milford, Northvale, Norwood, Nyack, Old Tappan, Oradell, Palisades, Palisades Park, Park Ridge, Pearl River, Piermont, Rivervale, Rockland Lake, Rockleigh, Sparkill, Spring Valley, Stony Point, Tappan, Tenafly, Upper Nyack, Valley Cottage, West Englewood, Westwood, Woodcliff Lake

- Shortline (Coach USA)
  (800-631-8405, www.coachusa.com/shortline) Express service to Montgomery, Washingtonville, Monroe, Central Valley and Ridgewood, NJ

Overview

High-speed rail is efficient, fast, sleek and…decades away. Which is where low cost, bare-bones intercity bus travel comes in. No, it's not particularly glamorous, especially when you're fumbling with quarters in front of a vending machine at a rest stop along Interstate 91, but it's cheap. Real cheap. Like cheaper than a cab to LaGuardia cheap. Cheaper than a fancy downtown cocktail cheap. Cheaper than an outerborough cocktail cheap. Like $10 cheap. $20 cheap. Even at $30, you're practically saving money sitting quietly on a bus to Boston or DC. No, this is no 300 kilometer-per-hour bullet train. But that *is* a VHS tape of look *Who's Talking Too*, so what do you want?

There was a moment in time, starting around the late 1990s, when low-cost intercity coach travel was referred to as the "Chinatown Bus." The chartered buses catered to an Asian clientele, traveling between Chinatowns along the Northeast Corridor. The lines had no need for advertising, overhead, or—most importantly—gates at bus stations. Travelers bought tickets on the sidewalk and boarded buses on street corners. They'd play choppy movies, subtitled in various Chinese dialects. Soon budget travelers began noticing and it wasn't long before the buses revolutionized short-haul travel—the fledgling Acela high-speed train was in an entirely different league, money-wise, and shuttle plane service between Northeastern cities was often not as fast, especially when taking into account post-9/11 security protocols and traffic to and from airports.

The early days of the Chinatown Bus were a hoot. Often trips were perfectly fine. Sometimes they seemed a little too efficient; three hours from Boston is great—except on a Chinatown bus. Other times, odds were high that you experienced at least one problem during the course of your trip including, but not limited to, poor customer service, unmarked bus stops, late departures, less than ideal bus conditions, and loogie-hucking and/or spitting from other passengers. Then there were the cancellations without warning, breakdowns, fires, broken bathrooms, fragrant bathrooms or no bathrooms at all, uncoupled luggage, drop-offs on the side of the road near the highway because bus companies didn't have permission to deliver passengers to central transportation hubs, and (alleged) organized crime links. We exaggerate. But only slightly. And still none of that deterred folks from using the buses. Again, the prices were just too good.

Before long, legacy bus carriers like Greyhound and railways began noticing, and rather than trying to beat the Chinatown companies, they joined them, creating low-cost carriers like Megabus and BoltBus that mimicked the style and pricing of Chinatown buses. Of course, innovation ruffles feathers, and eventually neighborhoods tired of rolling bags clogging up the sidewalks. Concessions ensued, but for the time being a detente exists; the prices are just too good. The free wi-fi isn't too bad either.

After years of accidents, including a particularly gruesome March 2011 accident along I-95 that killed 15 people, the feds began cracking down on the carriers, shutting down many, including Fung Wah, one of the original lines. Of the organizations that remained, something miraculous happened: prices have stayed relatively low while oversight and regulation have increased. So now at least you can ride with some peace of mind. What were you saying about high-speed what?

Bus Companies

- Lucky Star Bus Transportation
  (888-881-0887 or 617-269-5468, www.luckystarbus.com): To Boston 13 times daily 7 am–9 pm. From 55-59 Chrystie St to South Station: one-way $20

- Washington Deluxe
  (866-BUS-NY-DC, www.washny.com). To Washington multiple times a day; From 36th St & Seventh Ave. Additional departures from Delancey & Allen Sts, and Empire Blvd and Bedford Ave in Crown Heights, Brooklyn to Dupont Circle and Union Station in DC. Schedule varies by day of the week, so it's recommended that you check the website for info. $26-$35 one-way.

- Eastern Travel
  (212-244-6132, www.easternshuttle.com): To Washington DC, Baltimore, Rockville, MD, and Richmond, VA; From Allen St/Canal St and 34th St/Seventh Ave.

- Yo! Bus
  (855-66YOBUS, yobus.com): To Boston and Philadelphia, joint venture of Greyhound and Peter Pan, tickets as low as $10; buses leave from East Broadway and Division St.

- Vamoose
  (212-695-6766, www.vamoosebus.com): To Bethesda, MD, Arlington, VA and Lorton, VA; stops at 30th St and Seventh Ave.

- Megabus
  (us.megabus.com): To destinations across US; departure from 34th St and Eleventh Ave, arrival at 28th St and Seventh Ave.

- BoltBus
  (877-265-8287, www.boltbus.com): To Boston, Philadelphia, Baltimore, DC area; special $1 early fares; stops at 33rd St and Eleventh Ave.

- TripperBus
  (877-826-3874, www.tripperbus.com): To Bethesda, MD and Arlington, VA; stops at 31st St and Eighth Ave.

General Information

Bicycle Defense Fund:	www.bicycledefensefund.org
Bike Blog NYC:	www.bikeblognyc.com or @bikeblognyc
Bike New York, Five Borough Bike Tour:	www.bikenewyork.org or @bikenewyork
Century Road Club Association (CRCA):	www.crca.net or @crca
Department of City Planning:	www.nyc.gov/html/dcp/html/transportation/td_projectbicycle.shtml
Department of Parks & Recreation:	www.nycgovparks.org
Department of Transportation:	www.nyc.gov/html/dot/html/bicyclists/bicyclists.shtml
Fast & Fabulous Lesbian & Gay Bike Club:	www.fastnfab.org
Five Boro Bicycle Club:	www.5bbc.org or @5BBC
League of American Bicyclists:	www.bikeleague.org or @BikeLeague
New York Bicycle Coalition:	www.nybc.net or @BikeNYBC
NYC Bike Share:	www.citibikenyc.com or @CitibikeNYC
New York Cycle Club:	www.nycc.org or @NYCycleClub
Recycle-A-Bicycle:	www.recycleabicycle.org or @RAB_NYC
Streetsblog NYC:	www.streetsblog.org or @StreetsblogNYC
Time's Up! Bicycle Advocacy Group:	www.times-up.org or @nyctimesup
Transportation Alternatives:	www.transalt.org or @transalt

Overview

While not for the faint of heart, biking around Manhattan can be one of the most efficient and exhilarating forms of transportation. The advocacy group Transportation Alternatives estimates that over 200,000 New Yorkers hop on a bike each day. Manhattan is relatively flat, and the fitness and environmental advantages of using people power are incontrovertible. However, there are also some downsides, including, but not limited to: psychotic cab drivers, buses, traffic, pedestrians, pavement with potholes, glass, debris, and poor air quality. For years now biking has enjoyed the support of the city: many new miles of bike lanes have been added, and there has been an effort to create well-protected lanes whenever possible including in Times Square, Eighth and Ninth Avenues in Chelsea, and Second and Third Avenues in the East Village. These tend to be the safest places to ride, though they often get blocked by parked or standing cars. Central Park is a great place to ride, as is the Greenway along the Hudson River from Battery Park all the way up to the GWB (it's actually a 32-mile loop around the island). East River Park is another nice destination for recreational riding, as well as skating. The most exciting cycling news in recent years is the launch of the Citi Bike bike share program, designed for quick trips around town.

A word about protecting your investment: bikes have to be locked up on the street and are always at risk of being stolen. Unfortunately, bike racks can be hard to come by in NYC, so you may need to get creative on where to park. Always lock them to immovable objects and don't skimp on a cheap bike lock. With over 40,000 bikes a year stolen in NYC, the extra cost for a top-of-the-line bike lock is worth it.

Now that we've got your attention, let's review some of the various rules and regulations pertaining to biking. First, remember that with great power comes great responsibility: bicyclists not only have all the rights of motor vehicles but they are also subject to all the same basic rules, including obeying all traffic signals, signage and pavement markings. Just as you can't drive a car on the sidewalk, neither are you allowed to ride on the sidewalk. And just as you can't drive a car into a park, remember that bicycle riding is prohibited in parks, except along designated bike paths. Some less-known rules: you can use either side of a one-way roadway; deliverymen must wear apparel with the name of their place of business when riding; when riding, you can't wear more than one earphone, feet must be on pedals; and riders must keep hands on the handlebars, and at least one hand when carrying packages. Also keep in mind the rules of equipment: a white headlight and red taillight are mandatory from dusk to dawn, and both bells and reflectors are required. Here's another thing: hand signals are mandatory. Children bring a whole other set of considerations: children under one year are not allowed on bikes, even in a Baby Bjorn; children ages one through five must wear a helmet and sit in an appropriate carrier. Children five through 13 must wear an approved helmet. Oh, and for Pete's sake, don't be a Jerk.

Crossing the Bridges by Bike

Brooklyn Bridge

Separate bicycle and pedestrian lanes run down the center of the bridge, with the bicycle lane on the north side and the pedestrian lane on the south. Cyclists should beware of wayfaring tourists taking photographs. The bridge is quite level and, aside from the tourists and planks, fairly easy to traverse.

Brooklyn Access: Stairs to Cadman Plz E and Prospect St, ramp to Johnson & Adams Sts
Manhattan Access: Park Row and Centre St, across from City Hall Park

Manhattan Bridge

The last of the Brooklyn crossings to be outfitted with decent pedestrian and bike paths, the Manhattan Bridge bike and pedestrian paths are on separate sides of the bridge. The walking path is on the south side, and the bike path is on the north side of the bridge. The major drawback to walking across the Manhattan Bridge is that you have to climb a steep set of stairs on the Brooklyn side (not the best conditions for lugging around a stroller or suitcase). Fortunately, the bike path on the north side of the bridge is ramped on both approaches. However, be careful on Jay Street when accessing the bridge in Brooklyn due to the dangerous, fast-moving traffic.

Brooklyn Access: Jay St & Sands St
Manhattan Access: Bike Lane–Canal St & Forsyth St
Pedestrian Lane–Bowery, just south of Canal St

Williamsburg Bridge

The Williamsburg Bridge has the widest pedestrian/bike path of the three bridges to Brooklyn. The path on the north side, shared by cyclists and pedestrians, is 12 feet wide. The southern path, at eight feet wide, is also shared by bikers and walkers. Now that both sides of the bridge are always open to pedestrians and bikes, this is one of the best ways to get to and from Brooklyn. As a bonus fitness feature, the steep gradient on both the Manhattan and Brooklyn sides of the bridge gives bikers and pedestrians a good workout.

Brooklyn Access: North Entrance–Driggs Ave, right by the Washington Plz
South Entrance–Bedford Ave b/w S 5th & S 6th Sts
Manhattan Access: Delancey St & Clinton St/Suffolk St

George Washington Bridge
Bikers get marginalized by the pedestrians on this crossway to New Jersey. The north walkway is for pedestrians only, and the south side is shared by pedestrians and bikers. Cyclists had to fight to keep their right to even bike on this one walkway, as city officials wanted to institute a "walk your bike across" rule to avoid bicycle/pedestrian accidents during construction. The bikers won the battle but are warned to "exercise extra caution" when passing pedestrians.

Manhattan Access: W 178th St & Fort Washington Ave
New Jersey Access: Hudson Ter in Fort Lee

Robert F. Kennedy Bridge
Biking is officially prohibited on this two-mile span that connects the Bronx, Queens, and Manhattan. Unofficially, people ride between the boroughs and over to Wards Island all the time. The bike path is quite narrow, compared to the paths on other bridges, and the lighting at night is mediocre at best. The tight path sees less pedestrian/cycling traffic than other bridges, which, paired with the insufficient lighting, gives the span a rather ominous feeling after dark. If you're worried about safety, or keen on obeying the laws, the 103rd Street footbridge provides an alternative way to reach Wards Island sans car. This pedestrian pass is open only during the warmer months, and then only during daylight hours.

Bronx Access: 133rd St & Cypress Ave
Manhattan Access: Ramps—124/126th Sts & First Ave Stairs–Second Ave and 124/126 Sts
Queens Access: 26th St & Hoyt Ave (beware of extremely steep stairs).

Ed Koch Queensboro Bridge
The north outer roadway of the Ed Koch Queensboro Bridge is open exclusively to bikers, 24/7, except for the day of the New York Marathon. More than 2,500 cyclists and pedestrians per day traverse the bridge. Bikers complain about safety issues on the Manhattan side of the bridge: With no direct connection from Manhattan onto the bridge's West Side, bikers are forced into an awkward five-block detour to get to Second Avenue, where they can finally access the bridge.

Manhattan Entrance: 60th St, b/w First Ave & Second Ave
Queens Entrance: Queens Plz & Crescent St

Citi Bike Bike Share

The membership-only Citi Bike bike sharing program began in 2013. Designed for short jaunts around town, annual memberships cost $155 and entitle the user to unlimited trips of up to 45 minutes. One-day and 7-day "Access Passes" for unlimited trips up to 30 minutes are available for $9.95 and $25, respectively. Trips exceeding the time limit incur steep overage charges; much like ZipCar, the program is not intended to function as a bike rental. Bike stations are located in Manhattan south of 86th Street, in Western Brooklyn north of Fulton Street, and Long Island City in Queens (in Brooklyn and Queens, picture a chunk of land bounded by Brooklyn Bridge Park to the west, Fulton Park in Bed-Stuy to the east, and the Queensboro Bridge to the north). The bikes themselves are functional three-speed machines, with easily adjustable seats, bells and LED safety lights, and multiple logos of main sponsor Citibank, which pledged more than $40 million to start the program. For more information, visit citibikenyc.com.

Bike Sales and Rentals

Gotham Bikes • 112 West Broadway • 212-732-2453 • Map 2
Metro Bicycles • 75 Varick St • 212-334-8000 • Map 2
Bike Works • 106 Ridge St • 212-388-1077 • Map 4
Chari & Co. • 175 Stanton St • 212-475-0102 • Map 4
Dah Bike Shop • 134 Division St • 212-925-0155 • Map 4

Frank's Bike Shop · 533 Grand St · 212-533-6332 · Map 4
Waterfront Bike Shop · 391 West St · 212-414-2453 · Map 5
Bfold · 224 E 13th St · 212-529-7247 · Map 6
Bicycle Habitat · 244 Lafayette St · 212-431-3315 · Map 6
NYC Velo · 64 2nd Ave · 212-253-7771 · Map 6
Landmark Bicycles · 43 Ave A · 212-674-2343 · Map 7
Recycle-A-Bicycle · 75 Ave C · 212-475-1655 · Map 7
Bike and Roll · 557 12th Ave · 212-260-0400 · Map 8
City Bicycles · 315 W 38th St · 212-563-3373 · Map 8
Enoch's Bike Shop · 480 10th Ave · 212-582-0620 · Map 8
Chelsea Bicycles · 130 W 26th St · 212-727-7278 · Map 9
Metro Bicycles · 546 Avenue of the Americas · 212-255-5100 · Map 9
Paragon Sporting Goods · 867 Broadway · 212-255-8889 · Map 9
Sid's Bikes · 151 W 19th St · 212-989-1060 · Map 9
Spokesman Cycles · 34 Irving Pl · 212-995-0450 · Map 10
Liberty Bicycles · 846 9th Ave · 212-757-2418 · Map 11
Metro Bicycles · 653 10th Ave · 212-581-4500 · Map 11
Conrad's Bike Shop · 25 Tudor City Pl · 212-697-6966 · Map 13
Bicycle Renaissance · 430 Columbus Ave · 212-724-2350 · Map 14
Eddie's Bicycles · 480 Amsterdam Ave · 212-580-2011 · Map 14
Toga Bikes · 110 West End Ave · 212-799-9625 · Map 14
Jeff's Bicycles NYC 1400 · 3rd Ave · 212-794-2929 · Map 15
NYCeWheels · 1603 York Ave · 800-692-3943 · Map 15
Pedal Pusher Bike Shop · 1306 2nd Ave · 212-288-5592 · Map 15
Champion Bicycles · 896 Amsterdam Ave · 212-662-2690 · Map 16
Innovation Bike Shop · 105 W 106th St · 212-678-7130 · Map 16
Metro Bicycles · 231 W 96th St · 212-663-7531 · Map 16
Danny's Cycles · 1690 2nd Ave · 212-722-2201 · Map 17
Metro Bicycles · 1311 Lexington Ave · 212-427-4450 · Map 17
ModSquad Cycles · 2119 Frederick Douglass Blvd · 212-865-5050 · Map 19
Heavy Metal Bike Shop · 2016 3rd Ave · 212-410-1144 · Map 20
Junior Bicycle Shop · 1820 Amsterdam Ave · 212-690-6511 · Map 21
Victor's Bike Repair · 4125 Broadway · 212-740-5137 · Map 23
Tread Bike Shop · 250 Dyckman St · 212-544-7055 · Map 25

Bikes and Mass Transit

You can take your bike on trains and some buses—just make sure it's not during rush hour and you are courteous to other passengers. The subway requires you to carry your bike down staircases, use the service gate instead of the turnstile, and board at the very front or back end of the train. To ride the commuter railroads with your bike, you may need to purchase a bike permit. For appropriate contact information, see transportation pages.

Amtrak: Train with baggage car required
LIRR: $5 permit required
Metro-North: $5 permit required
New Jersey Transit: No permit required
PATH: No permit required
New York Water Taxi: As space allows; no fee or permit required
NY Waterway: $1.25 surcharge
Staten Island Ferry: Enter at lower level
Bus companies: Call individual companies

Sports • Chelsea Piers

General Information

NFT Map:	8
Address:	23rd Street & Hudson River Park
Phone:	212-336-6666
Website:	www.chelseapiers.com
Twitter:	@ChelseaPiersNYC

Overview

Opened in 1910 as a popular port for trans-Atlantic ships, Chelsea Piers found itself neglected and deteriorating by the 1960s. In 1992, Roland W. Betts (fraternity brother of George W. Bush) began the plan to renovate and refurbish the piers as a gargantuan 28-acre sports and entertainment center. In 1995, Chelsea Piers re-opened its doors to the public at a final cost of $120 million—all private money. The only help from the state was a very generous 49-year lease. By 1998, Chelsea Piers was the third most popular attraction in New York City, after Times Square.

How to Get There

Unless you live in Chelsea, it's a real pain to get to the Piers. The closest subway is the C or E to 23rd Street and Eighth Avenue, and then it's still a three-avenue block hike there. If you're lucky, you can hop a M23 bus on 23rd Street and expedite the last leg of your journey. L train commuters should get off at the Eighth Avenue stop and take the M14D bus across to the West Side Highway where you'll be dropped off at 18th Street. There are two Citi Bike stations near Chelsea Piers: 22nd Street and 10th Avenue and 18th Street and 11th Avenue.

If you drive, entering from the south can be a little tricky. It's pretty well signed, so keep your eyes peeled. Basically, you exit right at Eleventh Avenue and 22nd Street, turn left onto 24th Street, and then make a left onto the West Side Highway. Enter Chelsea Piers the same way you would if you were approaching from the north. Parking costs $16 for the first hour, $21 for two, $25 for three on up to $60 for eight ($10 for each additional hour thereafter). Street parking in the West 20s is an excellent alternative in the evenings after 6 pm.

Facilities

Chelsea Piers is amazing. There are swimming pools, ice skating rinks, a bowling alley, spa, restaurants, shops, batting cages—you name it. So, what's the catch? Well it's gonna cost ya. Like Manhattan rents, only investment bankers can afford this place.

1 **The Golf Club at Chelsea Piers** • 212-336-6400. Aside from potentially long wait times, the 250-yard driving range with 52 heated stalls and automated ball-feed (no buckets or bending over!) is pretty awesome. $25 buys you 90 balls (peak) or 147 balls (off-peak). If you don't bring your own, club hire is $4/one club, $6/two, $7/three, or $12/ten. Before 6 pm on weekdays, you can whack all the balls you want for $25 between 6:30 and 9 am.

2 **Bowlmor** • 212-835-2695 or www.bowlmor.com. Schmancy 40-lane bowling alley equipped with video games, bar, and private eight-lane bowling suite.

3 **'wichcraft** • 212-780-0577 or wichcraftnyc.com. Handcrafted sandwiches, soups, salads, and sweets.

4 **Paul Labrecque Salon & Spa** • 212-988-7186. Hair, skin, nails, and massage services to get you ready for the court, pitch, or pool.

5 **The Sports Center** • 212-336-6000. A very expensive monster health club with a 10,000-square-foot climbing wall, a quarter-mile track, a swimming pool and enough fitness equipment for a small army in training. If you have to ask how much the membership is, you can't afford it.

6 **Sky Rink** • 212-336-6100. Two 24/7 ice rinks mainly used for classes, training, and bar mitzvahs.

7 **Pier Sixty & The Lighthouse** • 212-336-6144 or piersixty.com. 10,000-square-foot event space for private gatherings catered by Abigail Kirsch.

8 **The Field House** • 212-336-6500. The Field House is an 80,000-square-foot building with a 23-foot climbing wall, a gymnastics training center, four batting cages, two basketball courts, and two indoor soccer fields.

9 **Spirit Cruise** • 866-433-9283 or www.spiritofnewyork.com. Ships run out of Chelsea Piers. Dinner cruises start at around $80/person, and if you're having a big function, you can rent the entire boat.

Unfortunately, but not surprisingly, there are no golf courses on the island of Manhattan. Thankfully, there are two driving ranges where you can at least smack the ball around until you can get to a real course, as well as a golf simulator at Chelsea Piers that lets you play a full round "at" various popular courses (Pebble Beach, St. Andrews, etc.). NYC has a number of private and public courses throughout the outer boroughs and Westchester; however, they don't even come close to satisfying the area's huge demand for courses. The **Trump Golf Links at Ferry Point** in the Bronx is a world-class course with amazing views of the East River, Whitestone Bridge and Manhattan skyline.

Golf Courses

	Borough	Address	Phone	Par	Fee
Mosholu Golf Course	Bronx	3700 Jerome Ave	718-655-9164	18 holes, par 30	Weekend $27.00 for non residents $74.75 for residents; weekdays $15.25 for 18 holes before 1 pm, $33.00 for non-residents and $29.00 for residents for 18 holes after 1 pm
Pelham/Split Rock Golf	Bronx	870 Shore Rd	718-885-1258	18 holes, par 71	Weekend fees $17.75/early, twilight/$39.50 morning and afternoon - weekday fees $16.75-$28, non-residents add $8.
Trump Golf Links at Ferry Point	Bronx	500 Hutchinson River Pkwy	718-414-1555	18 holes	$141 weekdays/$169 weekends (NYC residents)
Van Cortlandt Golf Course	Bronx	Van Cortlandt Pk S & Bailey Ave	718-543-1395	18 holes, par 70	9 holes early for $18 M F, 19.25 weekends; $39-$43 for 18 holes after 12, $21-$25 for Twilight on weekday weekend $38 $42 after 12, $24 twilight
Marine Park Golf Club	Brooklyn	2880 Flatbush Ave	718-338-7149	18 holes, par 72	Weekend fees $19.25/early for 9 holes, afternoon–weekday fees $18-$38, non residents add $8
Dyker Beach Golf Course	Brooklyn	86th St & Seventh Ave	718-836-9722	18 holes, Par 71	Weekend fees $17/early, twilight/$38 morning and afternoon; weekday fees $16-$27, non-residents add $8
Golf Simulator	New York	Chelsea Piers Golf Club	212-336-6400		$45/hour (see previous Chelsea Piers page)
LaTourette Golf Course	Staten Island	1001 Richmond Hill Rd	718-351-1889	18 holes, par 72	M–F/$16.75-$28; weekend $17.75/early, twilight; $39.50/ morning and afternoon; non-resident add $8.
Silver Lake Golf Course	Staten Island	915 Victory Blvd	718-442-4653	18 holes, par 69	Weekend $22.00/early for 9 holes; 18 holes (before 12:00 pm) $33.00; twilight (adjusted seasonally) $25.00; Weekday (Reservation Fee Included); Early Morning (9 holes) $23.25; 18 holes (before 12:00 pm) $51.00; 18 holes (at or after 12:00 pm) $42.00; Twilight $28.00 plus $8 non resident fee
South Shore Golf Course	Staten Island	200 Huguenot Ave	718-984-0101	18 holes, par 72	Please see Silver Lake Golf Course rates also apply
Clearview Golf Course	Queens	202-12 Willets Point Blvd	718-229-2570	18 holes, par 18	Please see Silver Lake Golf Course rates also apply
Douglaston Golf Course	Queens	63-20 Marathon Pkwy, Douglaston	718-224-6566	18 holes, par 67	Please see Silver Lake Golf Course rates also apply
Forest Park Golf Course	Queens	101 Forest Park Dr, Woodhaven	718-296-0999	18 holes, par 70	Please see Silver Lake Golf Course rates also apply
Kissena Park Golf Course	Queens	164-15 Booth Memorial Ave	718-939-4594	18 holes, Par 64	Weekend fees $17.75/early, twilight/$39.50 morning and afternoon–weekday fees $16.75-$28, non-residents add $8.

Driving Ranges

		Address	Phone	Fee
Brooklyn Sports Center	Brooklyn	3200 Flatbush Ave	718-253-6816	$10 for 150 balls, $12 for 285 balls
Chelsea Piers: Pier 59	Manhattan	Pier 59	212-336-6400	$20 for 118 balls, $30 for 186 balls
Randall's Island Golf	Manhattan	1 Randalls Is Rd	212-427-5689	$12 for 119 balls
Center Golden Bear	Queens	232-01 Northern Blvd	718-225-9187	$10 for large bucket, $7.50 for small bucket

For swimming pools in Manhattan, you pretty much have two options: pay exorbitant gym fees or health club fees in order to use the private swimming facilities, or wait until the summer to share the city's free outdoor pools with openly urinating summer camp attendees. OK, so it's not that bad! Some YMCAs and YWCAs have nice indoor pools, and their fees are reasonable. And several of the same New York public recreation centers that have outdoor pools (and some that do not) have indoor pools for year-round swimming. Though plenty of kids use the pools, there are dedicated adult swim hours in the mornings, at lunch time, and in the evenings (pee-free if you get there early). Just don't forget to follow each pool's admittance ritual, strange as it may seem—the locker room attendants generally rule with an iron fist. And if you can wait the obligatory 30 minutes, there's an authentic local food court near the standout public pool in Red Hook (155 Bay St, Brooklyn).

Then there's the Hudson. Yes, we're serious. There are about eight races in the Hudson each year, and the water quality is tested before each race. New York City also has some great beaches for swimming, including Coney Island, Manhattan Beach, and the Rockaways. If you prefer your swimming area enclosed, check out the pool options in Manhattan.

Pools

	Address	Phone	Type	Fees	Map
92nd Street Y	1395 Lexington Ave	212-415-5700	Indoor	$30/day or $100/day	17
Asphalt Green	555 E 90th St	212-369-8890	Indoor	$25/day	17
Asser Levy Recreation Center	E 23rd St & Asser Levy Pl	212-447-2020	Indoor, Outdoor, Outdoor free, Indoor $75/year	10
Athletic and Swim Club	787 7th Ave	212-265-3490	Indoor	Call for fees	12
Bally Toal Fitness	139 W 32nd St	212-465-1750	Indoor	$25/day	9
Chelsea Piers Sports Center	19th St & Hudson River Park	212-336-6000	Indoor	Call for fees	8
Chelsea Recreation Center	430 W 25th St	212-255-3705	Indoor	$100/year for adults, free for children	8
Equinox Sports Club New York	160 Columbus Ave	212-362-6800	Indoor	$188/month	14
Frederick Douglass	Amsterdam Ave & W 100 St	212-316-3241	Outdoor - Summer months		16
Gertrude Ederle Pool	533 W 59th St	212-397-3159	Indoor	$75/year	11
Gravity Fitness Center at Le Parker Meridien	119 W 56th St	212-708-7340	Indoor	$50/day	12
Harlem YMCA	180 W 135th St	212-281-4100	Indoor	$30/day or $88/month	19
Jackie Robinson Pool	85 Bradhurst Ave	212-234-9606	Outdoor - Summer months	Free	21
John Jay	E 77th St & Cherokee Pl	212-794-6566	Outdoor - Summer months	Free	15
Lasker Pool	110th St & Lenox Ave	212-534-7639	Outdoor - Summer months	Free	19
Lenox Hill Neighborhood House	331 E 70th St	212-744-5022	Indoor	Call for fees	15
Manhattan Plaza Health Club	482 W 43rd St	212-563-7001	Indoor - Summer months	$35/day	11
Marcus Garvey Pool	18 Mt Morris Park W	212-410-2818	Outdoor - Summer months	Free	19
New York Health & Racquet Club	39 Whitehall St	212-269-9800	Indoor	$50/day or $99/month	1
New York Health & Racquet Club	62 Cooper Sq	212-904-0400	Indoor	$50/day or $99/month	6
New York Health & Racquet Club	24 E 13th St	212-924-4600	Indoor	$50/day or $99/month	6
New York Health & Racquet Club	20 E 50th St	212-593-1500	Indoor	$50/day or $99/month	12
New York Health & Racquet Club	110 W 56th St	212-541-7200	Indoor	$50/day or $99/month	12
New York Health & Racquet Club	132 E 45th St	212-986-3100	Indoor	$50/day or $99/month	13
New York Health & Racquet Club	1433 York Ave	212-737-6666	Indoor	$50/day or $99/month	15
New York Sports Club	614 2nd Ave	212-213-5999	Indoor	$25/day	10
New York Sports Club	1601 Broadway	212-977-8880	Indoor	$25/day	12
New York Sports Club	75 West End Ave	212-265-8200	Indoor	$16/day	14
New York Sports Club	1637 3rd Ave	212-987-7200	Indoor	$25/day	17
ONE UN New York	1 United Nations Plaza	212-702-5016	Indoor	$30/day or $88/month	13
Recreation Center 54 Pool	348 E 54th St	212-754-5411	Indoor	$75/year	13
Riverbank State Park	679 Riverside Dr	212-694-3600	Indoor - Summer months	$2/day	21
Thomas Jefferson Park	2180 1st Ave	212-860-1383	Outdoor - Summer months	Free	20
Tompkins Square Mini Pool	500 E 9th St	212-387-7685	Outdoor - Summer months	Free	7
Tony Dapolito Recreation Center	1 Clarkson St	212-242-5228	Indoor, Outdoor	$75/year	5
Vanderbilt YMCA	224 E 47th St	212-756-9600	Indoor	$30/day or $88/month	13

330

General Information

Parks Permit Office:	212-360-8131
Website:	www.nycgovparks.org/permits/tennis-permits
Permit Locations:	The Arsenal, 830 Fifth Ave & 64th St
(Manhattan)	Paragon Sporting Goods Store, 867 Broadway & 18th St

Overview

There are more tennis courts on the island of Manhattan than you might think, although getting to them may be a bit more than you bargained for. Most of the public courts in Manhattan are either smack in the middle of Central Park or are on the edges of the city—such as **Hudson River Park (Map 5)**, **East River Park (Map 7)** and **Riverside Park (Map 16)**. These courts in particular can make for some pretty windy playing conditions.

Getting a Permit

The Parks tennis season starts on the first Saturday of April and ends on the Sunday before Thanksgiving. Permits are good for use until the end of the season at all public courts in all boroughs, and are good for one hour of singles or two hours of doubles play. Fees are: Adults (18–61 yrs), $200; Juniors (17 yrs and under), $10; Senior Citizen (62 yrs and over), $20; Single-play tickets $15. Permits can be acquired in person at the Parks Department headquarters Central Park or Paragon Sporting Goods or online via the Parks website or by mail (applications can be found online). Renewals are accepted in person, by mail or via the website, except if originally purchased at Paragon.

Tennis

Tennis	Address	Phone	Type/ # of Cts./Surface	Map
East River Park	East River Park at Broome St	212-533-0656	12 hardcourts, lessons	4
Jerome S. Coles Sports Center	181 Mercer St	212-998-2045	Schools, 9 courts, Rubber	6
Midtown Tennis Club	341 Eighth Ave	212-989-8572	Private, 5 courts, Har-Tru	8
Manhattan Plaza Racquet Club	450 W 43rd St	212-594-0554	Private, 5 courts, Cushioned Hard	11
Millennium UN Plaza Hotel Gym	2nd Ave & 44th St	212-758-1234	Private, 1 court, Supreme	13
ONE UN New York	1 United Nations Plaza	212-702-5016	Private, 1 hardcourt	13
The River Club	447 E 52nd St	212-751-0100	Private, 2 courts, Clay	13
Town Tennis Club	430 E 56th St	212-752-4059	Private, 2 courts, Clay, Hard	13
Vanderbilt Tennis Club	15 Vanderbilt Ave, 3rd Fl	212-687-3841	Private, 2 courts, Hard	13
Rockefeller University	1230 York Ave	212-327-8000	Schools, 1 court, Hard	15
Sutton East Tennis Club	488 E 60th St	212-751-3452	Private, 8 courts, Clay, Available Oct–April.	15
Central Park Tennis Center	93rd St near West Dr	212-280-0205	Public, Outdoor, 26 Fast-Dry, 4 Hard	16
Riverside Park	Riverside Dr & W 96th St	212-469-2006	Public, Outdoor, 10 courts, Clay	16
PS 146 Ann M Short	421 E 106th St	n/a	Schools, 3 courts, Hard	17
Tower Tennis Courts	1725 York Ave	212-860-2464	Private, 2 courts, Hard	17
PS 125 Ralph Bunche	425 W 123rd St	n/a	Schools, 3 courts, Hard	18
Riverside Park	W 119th St & Riverside Dr	212-978-0277	10 hardcourts, lessons	18
Riverbank State Park	W 145th St & Riverside Dr	212-694-3600	Public, Outdoor, 1 court, Hard	21
Frederick Johnson Playground	W 151st St & Seventh Ave	212-234-9609	Public, Outdoor, 8 courts, Hard	22
Fort Washington Park	Hudson River & 170th St	212-304-2322	Public, Outdoor, 10 courts, Hard	23
Dick Savitt Tennis Center	575 W 218th St	212-942-7100	Private, 6 courts, Hard	25
Inwood Hill Park	207th St & Seaman Ave	212-304-2381	Public, Outdoor, 9 courts, Hard	25
Roosevelt Island Racquet Club	281 Main St	212-935-0250	Private, 12 courts, Clay	RI
Sportime at Randall's Island	East & Harlem Rivers	212-860-1827	Public, Outdoor, 11 courts, Hard	RWI
Sportime at Randall's Island	Randall's Island Park	212-427-6150	Public/Private, 5 indoor hardcourts, 5 indoor/outdoor hardcourts, 10 indoor/outdoor clay courts, lessons	RWI

Billiards Overview

Whether you're looking for a new hobby or need a new atmosphere in which to booze (that isn't your 300 sq. ft. apartment) a good pool-hall is a great way to get the job done. Or perhaps you simply enjoy a hearty game of 8-ball, and it's as simple as that; in any case, an eclectic mix of options dot the island of Manhattan.

	Address	Phone	Map	Fee
Tropical 128	128 Elizabeth St	212-925-8219	3	$5.50–$6.50 per hour per player
Fat Cat	75 Christopher St	212-675-6056	5	$5.75–10.25 per person per hour
Amsterdam Billiards Club	110 E 11th St	212-995-1314	6	$17 per hour for two players
Slate Restaurant Bar & Billiards	54 W 21st St	212-989-0096	9	$17 per hour for two players
Society Billiards + Bar	298 Mulberry St	212-925-3753	9	$17/hour two players
Eastside Billiards	163 E 86th St	212-831-7665	17	
Post Billiards Café	154 Post Ave	212-569-1840	25	

Bowling Overview

If you want to go bowling in Manhattan, you have four solid options. Keep in mind that there's just about no way to bowl cheaply, so if you're struggling to keep a positive balance in your bank account, you may want to find another activity or head out to New Jersey.

At **Frames (Map 12)** you can pay per game or per lane. Connected to the Port Authority (remember this in case you have a long wait for a bus), Frames has 30 lanes, a full bar and pub menu, and two game-rooms, with a new dance floor and lounge on the way. You can even make online reservations. At Chelsea Piers, you'll find **Bowlmor (Map 8)**. The high-end bowling alley also offers laser tag and a ropes obstacle course. Not cheap but they do feature all-you-can-bowl specials on slow nights.

Finally, for the world's ultimate (hipster) bowling experience, head to **The Gutter (Map 29)** in Brooklyn—the borough's first new bowling alley in over fifty years. It's like a Stroh's ad from the 1980s (except the beer is fancier). It doesn't get any better than bowling on beautiful, old-school lanes and drinking tasty microbrews with your buddies.

But The Gutter now has some serious competition, as sprawling **Brooklyn Bowl (Map 29)** has opened two blocks away. Featuring food by Blue Ribbon and live bands many nights, it's already become another great bowling option—and again far better than anything in Manhattan.

Manhattan	Address	Phone	Map	Fees
Bowlmor	Pier 60	212-835-2695	8	If you have to ask…
Lucky Strike Lanes	624 W 42nd St	646-829-0170	11	$25 per lane per 1/2 hour, $4 shoes.
Bowlmor	222 W 44th St	212-680-0012	12	If you have to ask…
Frames	550 9th Ave	212-268-6909	12	M–F before 5pm, $7/game; All other times, $10.50/game; $6 shoes

Brooklyn	Address	Phone	Fees
Brooklyn Bowl	61 Wythe Ave	718-963-3369	$25 per lane per 1/2 hour, $3.50 shoes
The Gutter	200 N 14th St	718-387-3585	$6–$7/game/person, $2 for shoes
Melody Lanes	461 37th St	718-832-2695	$5.50–$7.00 per game, $3.50 shoes
Shell Lanes	1 Bouck Ct	718-336-6700	$3.25–$5.25 per game, $3.50 shoes
Strike 10 Lanes	6161 Strickland Ave	718-763-3333	$6.00–$8.00, $4.25 shoes

Queens	Address	Phone	Fees
AMF 34th Avenue Lanes	69-10 34th Ave	718-651-0440	$4–$6 per game, $4.75 for shoes
Astoria Bowl	19-45 49th St	718-274-1910	$4/game and $4/shoes, $6/game on the weekends
Cozy Bowl	98-18 Rockaway Blvd	718-843-5553	$3/game/person, $2.50 shoes, $6/game/person, $3.50/shoes on Fri, Sat and Sun!
Jib Lanes	67-19 Parsons Blvd	718-591-0600	$3.75 per game $3.50 for shoes, $4.75 per game on the weekends
Whitestone Lanes	30-05 Whitestone Expy	718-353-6300	$4.50–$7.50 per game, $4.50 shoes

General Information

Address:	620 Atlantic Avenue, Brooklyn NY 11217
Website:	barclayscenter.com or @barclayscenter
Nets:	www.nba.com/nets or @BrooklynNets
Islanders:	www.newyorkislanders.com
	or @NYIslanders
Tickets:	877-77-BKTIX

Overview

Barclays Center, the home of the Brooklyn Nets and New York Islanders, opened in 2012 as part of the controversial $4.9 billion Atlantic Yards redevelopment project that decked over LIRR tracks and focused everyone's attention on controversial eminent domain issues, for a while there at least, until Barbra, Jay-Z, and Deron Williams redirected again.

The original architectural design was created by Frank Gehry, the king of urban revitalization, but it was horrendously expensive, especially following the 2008 financial collapse, so the firm of Ellerbe Becket took over. The scaled-down plans proved to be horrendously uninspiring, eliciting negative comparisons to an airplane hangar and/or the downtown Indianapolis arena where the NBA's Pacers play (also designed by Ellerbe Becket). In the end, expectations were lowered just enough to make the final product look kind of cool: the brown weathered steel exterior evokes the site's industrial past and pays slight tribute to the brownstone materials in the surrounding neighborhoods. In addition, the height is not overwhelming; the structure almost fits snugly into the Flatbush Avenue streetscape. The triangular public space at the intersection of Flatbush and Atlantic is visually appealing: the new subway entrance features a living planted roof and the arena's exterior structure, along with its oculus sky opening (don't worry, we had to look up that word too) and mesmerizing LED screen is—yikes—almost kind of elegant. As arenas go, it's pretty nice looking. And it's about 59 times more appealing looking than the Atlantic Center Mall, if you want to know the truth.

The Brooklyn Nets began playing at the arena for the 2012–13 season after moving from New Jersey. The NHL's New York Islanders began skating at Barclays Center for the 2015–16 season after leaving Nassau Coliseum (elsewhere on Long Island) where they had played since their founding in 1972. The arena has hosted college basketball almost since it opened, including the Barclays Center Classic, an early season eight-team tournament. For those who don't dig basketball, the concerts (accommodating 19,000 fans) have been big time: Barbra Streisand, Jay Z (who owned a small stake in the Nets before becoming a sports agent), Billy Joel, not to mention the MTV Video Music Awards, which were broadcast from Barclays Center.

How to Get There—Driving

Parking is so limited that Barclays Center practically demands that you use public transport, but if you must, you can reserve a spot at the center (should there be any available, having a suitehelper helps), find a nearby garage, or scour for street parking.

How to Get There—Mass Transit

Part of the draw of Barclays Center is its proximity to Brooklyn's largest transportation hub. The 2, 3, 4, 5, B, D, N, Q and R trains all service the arena, and you can also take the to Lafayette Avenue or the to Fulton Street. The LIRR stops at Atlantic Terminal, just across the street from the arena. In addition, eleven bus lines stop right outside or nearby.

How to Get Tickets

To avoid exorbitant Ticketmaster charges, the American Express Box Office (yes, even the freakin' box office has naming rights attached to it) is open Monday–Saturday 12 pm–6 pm (Saturday 4 pm). Despite being a box office, they will not sell tickets to events on the first day tickets are offered to the public.

LOWER
MEZZANINE
UPPER

General Information

Address: 25 Lafayette St Newark, NJ 07102
Website: www.prucenter.com or @PruCenter
NJ Devils: devils.nhl.com or @NHLDevils
Seton Hall: www.shupirates.com or @SHUAthletics
Box Office: 973-757-6600
Ticketmaster: 800-745-3000 or www.ticketmaster.com

Overview

The $380 million Prudential Center (or "The Rock" to the media and fans) opened in downtown Newark in 2007 and immediately became a prime destination for major league sports and top-notch live music. With a capacity of 17,000-plus and all the bells and whistles of the modern sports going experience, the Prudential Center is the full-time home for the NHL's New Jersey Devils and the Big East basketball's Seton Hall Pirates. The Rock is hands down a billion times better than the cold and charmless Izod Center which is sitting in the middle of the Meadowlands all alone and empty except for the occasional Doo Wop or Megadeth concert (no joke)—its future is now as murky as a bucketful of Meadowlands swamp water.

How to Get There—Driving

Follow NJ Turnpike southbound and take Exit 15W onto I-280 westbound. Turn right on Exit 15A towards Route 21 southbound. Turn right onto Rector Street. Turn left onto Broad Street southbound. Continue on Broad Street to Lafayette Street and make a left. Prudential Center will be on your left hand side. There is lots of parking, but traffic can still be unpredictable. Always allow more time than you think you'll need. Highways surrounding the arena include 280, 78, NJ Turnpike, 1 & 9, 21, 22, Garden State Parkway, 80 and NJ 3.

How to Get There—Mass Transit

No need to get on a bus anymore at Port Authority, thank goodness, for Devils games. Just take NJ Transit to Broad Street Station, then switch to Newark Light Rail to Newark Penn Station, which is only two blocks west of the Prudential Center. Even easier is taking the PATH train to Newark Penn Station. The arena is only a short walk away. Call or check the website for more details.

How to Get Tickets

The box office is open Monday to Friday from 11 am to ? pm and is closed Saturday and Sunday, unless there is an event. To purchase tickets without going to the box office, call Ticketmaster at 800-745-3000, or visit their website. Or try TicketsNow (www.ticketsnow.com) or StubHub (stubhub.com) the day of the game to find some good deals.

General Information

Address:	One MetLife Stadium Dr
	East Rutherford, NJ 07073
Phone:	201-559 1500
Website:	www.metlifestadium.com
	or @MLStadium
Giants:	www.giants.com or @Giants
Jets:	www.newyorkjets.com or @nyjets
Box Office:	201-559-1300
Ticketmaster:	www.ticketmaster.com or 800-745-3000

Overview

The $1.6 billion MetLife Stadium is a state-of-the-art facility that hosts 20 NFL games a season—the most of any NFL stadium—as well as the biggest of big name concerts. In February 2014 it became the first cold-weather outdoor stadium to host a Super Bowl (though interestingly it wasn't the coldest temperature ever for a Super Bowl game). The stadium is home to both the New York Jets and New York Giants; the changeover from week to week to give the facility home team touches is fascinating in and of itself. Even the team shop switches from one to another. So that $1.6 billion is put to good use. Did we mention that New Jersey taxpayers are still paying off bonds from the old Giants Stadium, which was demolished in 2010?

How to Get There—Driving

MetLife Stadium is only five miles from the Lincoln Tunnel (closer to Midtown than Citi Field), but leave early if you want to get to the game on time—remember that the Giants and the Jets are a) sold out for every game and b) have tons of fans from both Long Island and the five boroughs. You can take the Lincoln Tunnel to Route 3W to Route 120 N, or you can try either the Holland Tunnel to the New Jersey Turnpike N to Exit 16W or the George Washington Bridge to the New Jersey Turnpike S to Exit 16W. Accessing the stadium from both Exit 16W allows direct access to parking areas. Parking costs $30 for most events except NFL games where all cars must have pre-paid parking permits only.

How to Get There—Mass Transit

On game days NJ Transit now runs trains directly to the stadium (Meadowlands Sports Complex) from Secaucus Junction for events over 50,000. Round-trip tickets are $4.50 and travel time is 10 minutes. Train service begins three hours before the start of a major event or football game. After events, trains will depart frequently from the Meadowlands for up to two hours. Metro-North runs trains directly to Secaucus Junction for selected games.

How to Get Tickets

In general, scalpers and friends are the only options for Jets and the Giants games. Try the resale sites if you're dying to attend a game. The box office is open Monday–Friday 11 am to 5 pm.

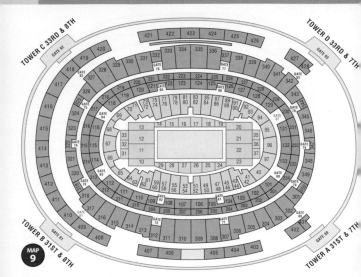

General Information

NFT Map: 9
Address: 4 Pennsylvania Plz New York, NY 10001
Phone: 212-465-6741
Website: www.thegarden.com or @TheGarden
Knicks: www.nba.com/knicks or @nyknicks
Liberty: www.nyliberty.com or @nyliberty
Rangers: rangers.nhl.com or @NYRangers
Ticketmaster: www.ticketmaster.com or 800-745-3000

Overview

Once resembling the Doge's Palace in Venice (c.1900), the since-relocated Altoid 'tween Seventh and Eighth Avenues atop Penn Station remains one of the legendary venues in sport, becoming so almost solely by way of the sport of boxing. Now, for good and ill, "The World's Most Famous Arena" houses the NBA's Knicks (catch Spike Lee and various supermodels courtside), NHL's Rangers, The Liberty of the WNBA, St. John's University's Red Storm, as well as concerts, tennis tournaments, dog shows, political conventions, and, for those of you with 2+ years of graduate school, monster truck rallies and "professional" wrestling. There's also The Theater at Madison Square

Garden for more intimate shows. Check out MSG's website for a full calendar of events. A $1 billion (!) renovation completed in 2013 upgraded nearly everything and added two bridges running parallel to the floor that provide a unique view from way, way high above.

How to Get There—Mass Transit

MSG is right above Penn Station, which makes getting there very easy. You can take the A, C, E and 1, 2, 3 lines to 34th Street and Penn Station, or the N, Q, R, B, D and PATH lines to 34th Street and 6th Avenue. The Long Island Rail Road also runs right into Penn Station.

How to Get Tickets

Box Office open Monday–Saturday 10 am–6 pm. Try Ticketmaster or the resale sites for single-game seats for the Knicks and the Rangers. The ubiquitous ticket scalpers surrounding the Garden are a good last resort for when your rich out-of-town friends breeze in to see a game. Liberty tickets (and tickets for other events) are usually available through Ticketmaster. First day of concert ticket sales are via Ticketmaster only.

General Information

Address:	123-01 Roosevelt Ave Flushing NY, 11368
Citi Field Box Office:	718 507 TIXX
Website:	www.mets.com or @Mets
Mets Clubhouse Shops:	11 W 42nd St & Roosevelt Field Mall, Garden City, LI

Overview

Shea Stadium, the Mets longtime former home, is all but a very distant memory, except for some rousing Billy Joel concerts (email the end there that they sometimes replay on PBS late at night. And although most find Citi Field appealing enough, its debut coincided with the worldwide economic downturn and a particularly brutal period in the Mets history—connected in more ways than you'd think. The ballpark's corporate sponsorship was questioned and mocked after Citigroup received a government bailout; renaming the stadium "Debits Field" was one of the more inspired reactions. Then came news that the Mets ownership had been investing with Ponzi pro Bernie Madoff; the team's finances took a, er, real hit, and management began paring its payroll. Thus began a vicious cycle of high ticket prices and mediocre seasons; sort of like the economy itself, come to think of it...

All of that aside—and it's a lot to put aside!— Citi Field is actually a pretty nice ballpark. Fans enter through The Jackie Robinson Rotunda, getting a little lesson on civil rights as they read the inspiring quotes etched in the façade and pose for pictures next to Robert Indiana's sculpture of the number 42. The food options are strong, from Danny Meyer's Shake Shack (beware multi-inning lines) to the Italian sandwiches courtesy Mama's of Corona. Beer options rise above the typical Crud Light—head to the outfield beyond the scoreboard for expanded tap and bottle options.

So much about Citi Field seems to be a response to the old Shea Stadium. Where the old sprawling multi-use facility sometimes seemed cavernous, Citi Field strives for an intimate experience—the only problem is that sightlines are often blocked, even in the high roller seats behind the dugouts. Speaking of which, tickets are expensive—after all, they have to pay for the privately financed $800 million-plus stadium somehow—but the resale market is robust and the Mets tier ticket prices so that a weeknight game against a lousy team can be a pretty good deal (even if you have no view of the left field corner). Oh, and a bit of advice: steer clear of section 538—yes, the seats are cheap, but that out-of-town scoreboard works hard to block your view from the upper reaches.

How to Get Tickets

You can order Mets tickets by phone through the Mets' box office, on the Internet through the Mets' website, or at the Mets Clubhouse Shops (11 West 42nd St, the Manhattan Mall, and Hoosevelt Field Mall in Garden City). StubHub (www.stubhub.com) is a good option to scoop up unwanted tickets at reduced prices and there are StubHub kiosks located just outside the entrance to Citi Field.

How to Get There—Driving

Yeah. Good luck trying to make the first pitch on a weekday night. But if you must, take the Robert F. Kennedy Bridge to the Grand Central Parkway; the Midtown Tunnel to the Long Island Expressway to the Grand Central; or the Brooklyn-Queens Expressway to the LIE to the Grand Central. If you want to try and avoid the highways, get yourself over to Astoria Boulevard in Queens, make a right on 108th Street, then a left onto Roosevelt Avenue. Parking is absurdly expensive, but if you're willing to walk 15-20 minutes there is free street parking in the Corona neighborhoods surrounding Citi Field.

How to Get There—Mass Transit

The 7 train runs straight to Citi Field, and the MTA frequently offers special express trains that make limited stops between Citi Field and Times Square, making it by far the easiest way to get to the stadium. The E, F, M and R trains connect with the 7 at 74th Street-Roosevelt Avenue. The other option from Midtown is the Port Washington LIRR from Penn Station, which stops at Citi Field on game days. Seastreak (seastreakusa.com/mets.aspx or 800-BOATRIDE) runs ferries from Highlands, NJ for selected games; see website for details.

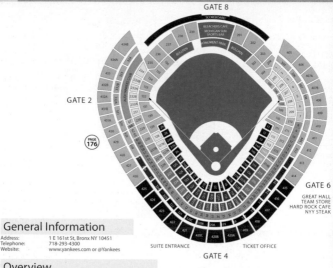

General Information

Address: 1 E 161st St, Bronx NY 10451
Telephone: 718-293-4300
Website: www.yankees.com or @Yankees

Overview

When a city or a team builds a new stadium they usually take the opportunity to come in with something bold and fresh. When the Yankees opened their new stadium in 2009 about 85 years in the old place, it was striking how similar it looked to the old version. And that was by design: after all, as they say, if it ain't broke, spend $1.5 billion to basically replicate it across the street. Architecturally, the exterior and the iconic frieze at the top of the upper decks are just about exactly the same. That said, there are some key changes—the concourses are wide and airy, the concessions are better (the Lobel's Sliced Steak Sandwich Cart is far and away our favorite), the 59-by-101-foot HD LED scoreboard is boffo-redonkulous, and the open-plan lower level allows you to catch a glimpse of the action from the area behind the expensive seats. That's the good. The not so good includes but is not limited to: seats cost more and seem farther away from the field of play, the place doesn't get as loud anymore, there is a stupid wire that runs across your field of vision on the first and third base lines from the upper levels, you have to pay extra to get into the schmancy outfield bar, you can't get into other places without a fancy seat, half the fancy seats go unused so there is all this empty space where all the best seats are, there are major unconscionable blind spots in the bleachers where that schmancy outfield bar juts out— we could go on. One thing that's the same: you still can't bring a bag into the place, which is just asinine if you're coming from work.

If you've never done it, make sure you check out Monument Park at least once. A sort of hall of fame for Yankees players, Monument Park sits just beyond the center field wall. The bronze plaques immortalize the great players—and there have been many of them over the years—who made the franchise one of the most successful in all of sports. And then there's the way oversized tribute to George Steinbrenner, the cantankerous owner who rescued the team from irrelevance when he led an ownership group to purchase the floundering team from CBS in 1972 for about $10 million. When Steinbrenner died in 2010, the Yankees were worth $1.6 billion. Situated dead center, Steinbrenner's plaque is about five times the size of any other, including those to Mantle and DiMaggio—both of which dutifully flank The Boss. Monument Park is open until 45 minutes before the start of a game. Follow signs from the main entrance.

Yankee Stadium has hosted several non-baseball events: concerts like Metallica, Jay-Z and Justin Timberlake, European soccer, college football, and several NHL outdoor games. It is also the home of the New York City FC (www.nycfc.com or @NYCFC), the city's MLS franchise. The field layout for NYCFC games is slightly odd, with one end of the pitch roughly along the

first base foul line and the other end somewhere near the left field wall, meaning that a lot of the seats can seem removed from the action; check the seat map before you buy tickets. And then there's the monumental task of sodding the infield (and removing the pitcher's mound) for each game. This is no dirt and grass early season Raiders game at Oakland Coliseum, that's for sure. All that aside, soccer in Yankee Stadium is a blast, and (sorry Red Bulls) having a hometown team to root for is a, er, kick.

How to Get There—Driving

Driving to Yankee Stadium from Manhattan isn't as bad as you might think. Your best bet is to take the Willis Avenue Bridge from either First Avenue or FDR Drive and get on the Major Deegan for about one mile until you spot the stadium exit. From the Upper West Side, follow Broadway up to 155th Street and use the Macombs Dam Bridge to cross over the river to the stadium (thus avoiding crosstown traffic). Parking (in contrast to ticket prices) is cheap, especially at lots a few blocks away from the stadium.

How to Get There—Mass Transit

Getting to the stadium by subway is easy. The 4 and D and the B (on weekdays) all run express to the stadium, and you can easily hook up with those lines at several junctions in Manhattan. A dedicated Metro-North train (Yankees–E 153rd Street) brings folks from Grand Central on the Hudson line in under 15 minutes. Seastreak (seastreakusa.com/yankees.aspx or 800-BOATRIDE) runs ferries from Highlands, NJ for selected games; see website for details.

How to Get Tickets

You can purchase tickets by phone through Ticketmaster, at the box office or the Yankee store, or online through either Ticketmaster or the Yankees website. StubHub is a good option to grab unwanted tickets, especially when the team is underperforming. And of course the illegal scalpers who are all over the damned place.

Beyond the obvious crowd-pleasers, New York City landmarks are super-subjective. One person's favorite cobblestoned alley is some developer's idea of prime real estate. Bits of old New York disappear to differing amounts of fanfare and make room for whatever it is we'll be romanticizing in the future. Ain't that the circle of life? The landmarks discussed are highly idiosyncratic choices, and this list is by no means complete or even logical, but we've included an array of places, from world famous to little known, all worth visiting.

Coolest Skyscrapers

Most visitors to New York go to the top of the **Empire State Building (Map 9)**, but it's far more familiar to New Yorkers from afar—as a directional guide, or as a tip-off to obscure holidays (orange & white means it's time to celebrate ASPCA Day again!). If it's class you're looking for, the **Chrysler Building (Map 13)** has it in spades. Unfortunately, this means that only the "classiest" are admitted to the top floors. Other midtown highlights include the **Citicorp Center (Map 13)**, a building that breaks out of the boxy tower form, and the **GE Building (Map 12)**, one of the steepest-looking skyscrapers in the city. More neck-craning excitement can be found in the financial district, including the **Woolworth Building (Map 3)**, the **American International Building (Map 1)** at 70 Pine Street (with private spire rooms accessible only to the connected), **40 Wall Street (Map 1)**, the **Bankers Trust Company Building (Map 1)**, and **20 Exchange Place (Map 1)**. For a fine example of blending old, new, and eco-friendly architecture styles, check out the stunning **Hearst Tower (Map 12)**.

Best Bridges

The **Brooklyn Bridge (Map 3)** is undoubtedly the best bridge in New York—aesthetically, historically, and practically; you can walk or bike across on a wooden sidewalk high above the traffic. It's also worth walking across the **George Washington Bridge (Map 23)**, though it takes more time than you'd expect (trust us). The **Henry Hudson Bridge (Map 25)** expresses the tranquility of that part of the island—view it from Inwood Hill Park to see its graceful span over Spuyten Duyvil.

Great Architecture

The Beaux Arts interior of **Grand Central Terminal (Map 13)** is full of soaring arches and skylights. Head to SoHo to see the **Little Singer Building (Map 6)** and other gorgeous cast-iron structures. You can find intricately carved faces and creatures on the tenement facades on the Lower East Side. **The Flatiron (Map 9)**, once among the tallest buildings in the city, remains one of the most distinctive. The **Lever House (Map 13)** and the **Seagram Building (Map 13)** redefined corporate architecture and are great examples of Modernism. Take the **Ferry to Ellis Island (Map 1)**, devoted solely to the immigrant experience, features domed ceilings and Guastavino tiled arches. The **Guggenheim (Map 17)** is one of New York's most unique and distinctive buildings (apparently there's some art inside, too). The **Cathedral of St. John the Divine (Map 18)** has a very medieval vibe and is the world's largest unfinished cathedral—a much cooler destination than the eternally crowded **St. Patrick's Cathedral (Map 12)**.

Great Public Buildings

Once upon a time, the city felt that public buildings should inspire civic pride through great architecture. Head downtown to view **City Hall (Map 3)** (1812), **Tweed Courthouse (Map 3)** (1881), **Jefferson Market Courthouse (Map 5)** (1877—now a library), the **Municipal Building (Map 3)** (1914), and a host of other courthouses built in the early 20th century. The **Old Police Headquarters (Map 3)**, now a posh condo, would be a more celebrated building if it wasn't located on a little-trafficked block of Centre Street in Little Italy/Chinatown. And what are the chances a firehouse built today would have the same charm as the **Great Jones Firehouse (Map 6)**? If the guys are around outside, they're happy to let you in to look around.

Outdoor Spaces

Central Park obviously. **Madison Square Park (Map 9)** is not as well known as many other central city parks, but it's home to the Shake Shack, where you can grab a burger, a shake, and a bit of peace and quiet on the grass. Newly renovated **Washington Square Park (Map 6)** has re-opened its gates to the NYU students, street performers, tourists, and pot dealers that love to gather there. There's all kinds of interesting folk around **Tompkins Square Park (Map 7)**, which makes it ideal for people watching. In addition to **Union Square (Map 9)** housing a bunch of great statues (Gandhi, Washington, Lincoln), it also hosts an amazing farmers market (Mon, Wed, Fri, and Sat) and is close to great shopping. You can dream all you want about having a picnic at **Gramercy Park (Map 10)**, but until you score a coveted key (or become friends with Julia Roberts), you'll have to admire the greenery from the sidewalk like the rest of us. **Bryant Park (Map 12)** attracts a chi-chi lunch crowd (it's a Wi-Fi hotspot) and hosts movies in the summer. Next door, people lounge on the **New York Public Library (Map 12)** steps and reminisce about their favorite scene from Ghostbusters, no doubt. **Rockefeller Center (Map 12)** tends to get overrun by tourists, but it's still deserving of a visit, especially to view the Art Deco styling. **The Cloisters (Map 24)** and **Inwood Hill Park (Map 25)** are great uptown escapes. Thanks to Stuyvesant Street's diagonal path, **St. Mark's-in-the-Bowery (Map 6)** gets a nice little corner of land in front for a park, which gives a hint of its rural past. Mountainous **Marcus Garvey Park (Map 19)** in Harlem is a good destination on Sundays when the famous drum circle is in full effect.

Lowbrow Landmarks

The **Chinatown Ice Cream Factory (Map 3)** is worth a slog through Chinatown crowds on a hot day. Just around the corner is **Doyers Street (Map 3)**, which retains the slight air of danger from its gang war past. **CBGB's (Map 6)** is gone, but punk spirit survives (somewhat) on the nearby street corner known as **Joey Ramone Place (Map 6)**. If you're into old-time debauchery, there are tons of classic and historic New York bars including the **Bridge Café (Map 1)**, **McSorley's (Map 6)**, Pete's Tavern **(Map 10)**, the **White Horse Tavern (Map 5)**, **Chumley's (Map 5)**, the **Ear Inn (Map 5)**, and **Old Town Bar (Map 9)**.

Overrated Landmarks

Even the most cynical New Yorker would have to admit that **Times Square (Map 12)** is a unique place, but the truth is that it's no fun to compete in the same scrum as visitors in search of grub at the Bump Wump Shrimp Garden, or whatever it's called. **South Street Seaport (Map 1)** is a marvelous setting in search of an identity. And note the lawyerly language behind **Madison Square Garden**'s **(Map 9)** bold "world's most famous arena" claim—as many a dictator has known firsthand, fame doesn't always equal greatness; aside from a few shining moments, the teams there usually stink, and the architecture is mostly banal. The worst part is that the gorgeous old Penn Station was torn down to make room for it. You can see pictures of the old station when you walk through the new **Penn Station (Map 9)**, which is famous not for its totally drab and depressing environs, but because of the sheer volume of traffic it handles. The **Cross-Bronx Expressway (Map 23)** deserves a mention here just because it's probably the worst highway, like, ever.

Underrated Landmarks

Many of these get overlooked because they are uptown. **Grant's Tomb (Map 18)** was once one of New York's most famous attractions, but these days it's mostly a destination for history buffs. The **City College (Map 21)** campus is quite beautiful, even though a few newer buildings would things up. Farther north, **Sylvan Terrace (Map 23)** and the **Morris-Jumel Mansion (Map 23)**, a unique block of small row houses and a revolutionary war era house, offer a truer glimpse of old New York than the Seaport or Fraunces Tavern. Memorialized in a beloved children's book, a visit to The **Little Red Lighthouse (Map 23)** will make you feel like you're on the coast of Maine and not actually standing under the George Washington Bridge.

General Information • Media

Television

1 NY1 (Time Warner Cable 24-Hour News) www.ny1.com
1 FIOS1 (Verizon FIOS 24-Hour News) www.fios1news.com
2 WCBS (CBS) newyork.cbslocal.com
4 WNBC (NBC) www.nbcnewyork.com
5 WNYW (FOX) www.myfoxny.com
7 WABC (ABC) abclocal.go.com/wabc
9 WWOR (My9) www.my9nj.com
11 WPIX (PIX11/CW) pix11.com
12 News12 (Cablevision 24-Hour News) www.news12.com
13 WNET (PBS) www.thirteen.org
21 WLIW (PBS—Long Island) www.wliw.org
25 WNYE (NYCTV/NYC Media) www.nyc.gov/media
31 WPXN (Ion) iontelevision.com
41 WXTV (Univision) univision.univision.com
47 WNJU (Telemundo) www.telemundo47.com
48 WRNN (RNN) www.rnntv.com
49 WEDW (PBS—Connecticut) www.cpbn.org
55 WLNY (CBS affiliate)
newyork.cbslocal.com/station/wlny
63 WMBC (Ethnic/Religious) www.wmbctv.com

AM Stations

570 WMCA Religious
620 WSNR Russian
660 WFAN Sports Talk and Giants/Devils/Nets/Yankees
710 WOR Talk/News/New York Mets
770 WABC Conservative Talk
820 WNYC Public Radio; NPR Affiliate
880 WCBS News
930 WPAT Multi-Cultural (NJ)
970 WNYM Salem Radio Network; Conservative Talk
and College Sports
1010 WINS News
1050 WEPN ESPN Deportes; Spanish Language Sports Talk
and Jets/Mets
1100 WHLI Easy Listening/Standards
1130 WBBR Bloomberg Radio
1160 WVNJ Talk and Brokered Programming
1190 WLIB Gospel
1230 WFAS News/Talk/Iona Basketball
1240 WGBB Mandarin Chinese Language
1280 WADO Spanish Language Talk/Sports/Sports
Broadcasts
1330 WWRV Spanish Language Christian
1380 WKDM Chinese and Spanish Language
Brokered Programming
1430 WNSW Spanish Language Christian
1460 WVOX Variety; Westchester Focus
1480 WZRC Cantonese Chinese Language
1520 WTHE Gospel
1530 WJDM Spanish Language Christian
1560 WQEW Radio Disney
1600 WWRL Spanish Language
1660 WWRU Korean Language

FM Stations

88.1 WCWP College (LIU-Post)
88.3 WBGO Jazz (NJ)
88.7 WRHU College (Hofstra University)
88.9 WSIA College (College of Staten Island)
89.1 WFDU College (Fairleigh Dickinson University)
89.1 WNYU College (NYU)
89.5 WSOU College/Rock (Seton Hall University)
89.9 WKCR College/Jazz (Columbia University)
90.3 WKRB College (Kingsborough Community College)
90.3 WHCR College (City College of New York)
90.3 WHPC College (Nassau Community College)
90.7 WFUV Adult Alternative (Fordham University)
91.1 WFMU Free-form! (NJ)
91.5 WNYE NYC Radio
92.3 WNOW Top 40
92.7 WQBU Spanish Language
93.1 WPAT Spanish Language

93.5 WVIP Caribbean
93.9 WNYC Public Radio; NPR Affiliate
94.7 WNSH Country
95.5 WPLJ Hot Adult Contemporary
96.3 WXNY Spanish Language
96.7 WKLV Contemporary Christian
97.1 WQHT Hot 97; Mainstream Urban
97.9 WSKQ La Mega; Spanish Language
98.3 WKJY Adult Contemporary
98.7 WEPN ESPN New York; Sports Talk and New York Jets
99.3 WBAI Listener Supported Variety
100.3 WHTZ (Z-100) Top 40 Contemporary Hit Radio
100.7 WHUD Adult Contemporary
101.1 WCBS Oldies
101.9 WFAN Sports Talk and Giants/Devils/Nets/Yankees
102.7 WWFS Hot Adult Contemporary
103.5 WKTU Rhythmic Contemporary
103.9 WFAS Adult Contemporary
104.3 WAXQ Classic Rock
105.1 WWPR Power 105.1; Urban Contemporary
105.5 WDHA Rock (NJ)
105.9 WQXR Classical
106.7 WLTW Adult Contemporary
107.1 WWHB Adult Alternative
107.5 WBLS Urban Adult Contemporary

Print Media

AM New York (240 W 35th St, 9th Floor, 646-293-9499, www.amny.
com): Free daily; pick it up at the subway but please dispose of
properly so as to prevent track fires.
Brooklyn Paper (1 Metrotech Ctr, Ste 1001, 718-260-2500,
brooklynpaper.com): Brooklyn's hometown weekly with in-depth
brunch and kickball coverage.
Daily News (4 New York Plaza, 212-210-2100. www.nydailynews.
com). Daily tabloid; rival of the Post. Good sports.
El Diario (1 Metrotech Ctr, 18th Floor, Brooklyn, 212-807-4600,
www.eldiariony.com): Daily; America's oldest Spanish-language
newspaper.
The L magazine (1 Metrotech Ctr, 18th Floor, Ste B, Brooklyn, 718-
596-3462, www.thelmagazine.com): Free bi-weekly with arts and
events focus.
Metro New York (120 Broadway, 6th Flr, 212-457-7790, www.metro.
us/newyork): Free daily; pick it up at the subway but please
dispose of properly so as to prevent track fires.
Newsday (235 Pinelawn Rd, Melville, 800-630-7220, www.
newsday.com): Daily based in Long Island.
New York Magazine (75 Varick St, 212-508-0700, nymag.com): New
York City-focused news, arts, culture bi-weekly with emphasis on
cloying trend pieces.
New York Review of Books (435 Hudson St, 3rd Floor, 212-757-8070,
www.nybooks.com): Bi-weekly intellectual lit review.
New York Observer (321 W 44th St, 6th Floor, 212-755-2400,
observer.com): Weekly that seeks influence by focusing on rich
people problems.
New York Post (1211 Avenue of the Americas, 212-930-8000,
nypost.com): Daily tabloid with infuriating and irresistible
coverage and iconic headlines.
The New York Times (620 Eighth Ave, 212-556-1234, nytimes.com):
Daily; former "Grey Lady," now with Clairol treatments.
The New Yorker (4 Times Square, 212-286-5400, www.newyorker.
com): Weekly with intellectualish analysis; often subscribed,
seldom finished.
Staten Island Advance (950 Fingerboard Rd, Staten Island, 718-
981-1234, www.silive.com/advance): Richmond County's
hometown daily; pronounce it "ADD-vance" to sound in-the-
know.
Time Out New York (475 Tenth Ave, 12th Fl, 646-432-3000, www.
timeout.com/newyork): Comprehensive weekly guide to goings-
on in the city with crazy-making "Top 5, 10, 15, 20" lists.
The Village Voice (80 Maiden Ln, Ste 2105, 212-475-3333, www.
villagevoice.com): Ur alternative weekly trying to rehab from
skanky ad addiction.
Wall Street Journal (1211 Avenue of the Americas,
212-416-2000, www.wsj.com): Financial news with
expanded local coverage.

January

Winter Antiques Show: Park Ave Armory at 67th St; Selections from all over the country.
Three Kings Day Parade: El Museo del Barrio; Features a cast of hundreds from all over the city dressed as kings or animals—camels, sheep, and donkeys (early Jan).
New York Boat Show: Jacob Javits Convention Center; Don't go expecting a test drive (early Jan).
Lunar New Year: Chinatown; Features dragons, performers, and parades.
NYC Winter Jazzfest: Greenwich Village; A full weekend of jazz at multiple Village venues.

February

Empire State Building Run-Up: Empire State Building; Run until the 86th floor (0.2 miles) or heart seizure.
Westminster Dog Show: Madison Square Garden; Fancy canines who know more about grooming than most of you deadbeats.
Fashion Week: Lincoln Center; Twice yearly week-long celeb-studded event.

March

The Art Show: Park Ave Armory at 67th St; Art fair organized by Art Dealers Association of America to benefit charity.
St Patrick's Day Parade: Fifth Avenue; Hoochless LIRR holiday, gays need not apply (March 17).
Orchid Show: New York Botanical Garden; Yearly festival with changing themes.
Whitney Biennial: Whitney Museum; Whitney's most important American art, every other year (March–June).
Greek Independence Day Parade: Fifth Avenue; Floats and bands representing area Greek Orthodox churches and Greek federations and organizations (Late March).
The Armory Show: West Side Piers; Brilliant best-of-galleries show.
New Directors/New Films: MoMA/Lincoln Center; Film festival featuring new films by emerging directors.
Pier Antique Show: Pier 94; Look at old things you can't afford.

April

Macy's Flower Show: Broadway and 34th St; Flowers and leather-clad vixens. Okay, just flowers really.
Easter Parade: Fifth Avenue; Starts at 11 am, get there early with your Easter bonnet (Easter Sunday).
New York Antiquarian Book Fair: Park Ave Armory at 67th St; Dealers exhibiting rare books, maps, manuscripts, illuminated manuscripts, and various ephemera.
New York International Auto Show: Jacob Javits Convention Center; Traffic jam.
Tribeca Film Festival: Various Lower Manhattan locations; Festival includes film screenings, panels, lectures, discussion groups, and concerts.
Affordable Art Fair: Midtown; Prices from $100 to no more than $10,000; worth a look if you're buying.
New York City Ballet Spring Season: Lincoln Center; Features new and classical ballet (April–June).

May

Outsider Art Fair: Chelsea; Art in many forms of media from an international set.
The Great Five Boro Bike Tour: The single worst day of the year to use the BQE (first Sunday in May).
Ninth Avenue International Food Festival: Ninth Ave from 42nd to 57th Sts.
Fleet Week: USS Intrepid; Around Memorial Day weekend—Hello, Sailor!
New York AIDS Walk: Central Park; 10K walk whose proceeds go toward finding a cure.
Lower East Side Festival of the Arts: Theater for the New City, 155 First Ave; Celebrating Beatniks and Pop Art (last weekend in May).
Cherry Blossom Festival: Brooklyn Botanic Garden; Flowering trees and Japanese cultural events (late April–early May).
Martin Luther King, Jr/369th Regiment Parade: Fifth Avenue; Celebration of equal rights (third Sunday in May).

June

Puerto Rican Day Parade: Fifth Avenue; Puerto Rican pride (second Sunday in June).
Metropolitan Opera Summer Recital Series: Various locations throughout five boroughs; Free performances through June and July.
Museum Mile Festival: Fifth Avenue; Free admission and block party from 82nd–105th Sts.
NYC Pride: March from Midtown to Christopher St; Commemorates the 1969 Stonewall riots (last Sunday in June).
Blue Note Jazz Festival: Various locations; All kinds of jazz.
Mermaid Parade: Coney Island; Showcase of sea-creatures and freaks/celebration of Coney Island.
Feast of St Anthony of Padua: Little Italy; Patron saint of expectant mothers, Portugal, seekers of lost articles, shipwrecks, Tigua Indians, and travel hostesses, among other things (Saturday before summer solstice).
Central Park SummerStage: Central Park, Free concerts, but get there very, VERY early. (June–August).
Bryant Park Summer Film Festival: Sixth Ave at 42nd St; Free films Monday evenings (June–August).
Midsummer Night Swing: Lincoln Center; Live performances with free dance lessons (June–July).
Big Apple Barbecue Block Party: Madison Sq Park; Endless smoked meats from country's top smokers.
American Crafts Festival: Lincoln Center; Celebrating quilts and such.
Village Voice 4Knots Music Festival: South Street Seaport; Free outdoor show featuring renowned and emerging indie artists.
Howl Festival: Tompkins Square Park; Spirit of Alan Ginsberg lives on in multi-day East Village festival.

July

Macy's Fireworks Display: East River; Independence Day's literal highlight (July 4).
Washington Square Music Festival: W 4th St at LaGuardia Pl; Open-air concert Tuesdays in July.
New York Philharmonic Concerts in the Parks: Various locations throughout five boroughs; Varied programs.
Summergarden: MoMA; Free classical concerts July Sundays in sculpture garden.
Celebrate Brooklyn!: Prospect Park Bandshell; Nine weeks of free outdoor film, music, dance, and theater events (July–August).
Mostly Mozart: Lincoln Center; The name says it all (July–August).
Shakespeare in the Park: Delacorte Theater in Central Park; Every summer two free outsized outside plays with boldface names bring long lunch hour lines for evening shows.
PS1 Warm Up: MoMA PS1, Long Island City; Sweaty DJ-dance-installations every Saturday afternoon (late June–Labor Day).

August

Harlem Week: Harlem; Music and community events last all month long.
Hong Kong Dragon Boat Festival: Flushing Meadows Park Lake, Queens; Wimpy canoes need not apply.
New York International Fringe Festival: Various locations; 200 companies, 16 days, more than 20 venues, 1,200 performances—and your friends expect you to show up to all of them.
US Open: USTA National Tennis Center, Flushing; Final Grand Slam event of the year (August–September).
Lincoln Center Out of Doors: Lincoln Center; Free outdoor performances throughout the month.

September

Brooklyn Book Festival: Two of Brooklyn's favorite things--books and Brooklyn.
West Indian American Day Carnival: Eastern Parkway from Utica to Grand Army Plaza, Brooklyn; Children's parade on Saturday, adult's parade on Labor Day (Labor Day Weekend).
Richmond County Fair: Historic Richmondtown, Staten Island; Best agricultural competitions (Labor Day).
Fashion Week: Lincoln Center; Twice yearly week-long celeb-studded event.
Feast of San Gennaro: Little Italy; Plenty of greasy street food.
Atlantic Antic: Brooklyn Heights; Multicultural street fair.
DUMBO Art Festival: DUMBO, Brooklyn; Hundreds of artists exhibiting in front of stunning bridge-skyline backdrop.

October

New York Film Festival: Lincoln Center; Features film premieres (early October).
Autumn Crafts Festival: Lincoln Center; Celebrating quilts and such.
Columbus Day Parade: Fifth Avenue; Celebrating the second person to discover America (Columbus Day).
Halloween Parade: West Village; Brings a new meaning to costumed event (October 31).
Halloween Dog Parade: East Village; Cute dogs, terrible puns.
Blessing of the Animals: St John the Divine, Morningside Heights; Where to take your gecko.
Big Apple Circus: Lincoln Center; Step right up (October–January)!
Hispanic Day Parade: Fifth Ave b/w 44th and 86th Sts; A celebration of Latin America's rich heritage (mid-October).
Open House NY: Various locations, all boroughs; Insider access to architecture and design landmarks (early October).
NY Comic Con: Jacob Javits Center; Comic enthusiasts convene at the nerd mecca.

November

New York City Marathon: Verrazano Bridge to Central Park; 26 miles of NYC air (first Sunday of November).
Veteran's Day Parade: Fifth Ave from 26th St to 56th St; Opening service at Eternal Light Memorial in Madison Square Park.
Macy's Thanksgiving Day Parade: Central Park West at 77th St to Macy's in Herald Square; Giant balloons with Santa bringing up the rear.
The Nutcracker Suite: Lincoln Center; Balanchine's ballet is a Christmas tradition (November–December).
Christmas Spectacular: Radio City Music Hall; Rockettes' mesmerizing legs steal show from Santa and little people (November–January).
Origami Christmas Tree: Museum of Natural History; Hopefully not decorated with candles (Nov–Jan).
Pier Antique Show: Pier 94; Look at old things you can't afford.

December

Christmas Tree Lighting Ceremony: Rockefeller Center; Most enchanting spot in the city, if you don't mind sharing it with about a million others.
Menorah Lighting: Fifth Avenue & 59th St; Just the world's biggest menorah, that's what.
John Lennon Anniversary Vigil: Strawberry Fields, Central Park; Every December 8 crowds gather to remember the singer/songwriter on the anniversary of his death.
Holiday Window Displays: Saks Fifth Avenue, Macy's, Lord & Taylor, etc.; A New York tradition.
Alvin Ailey American Dance Theater: New York City Center; Winter season lasts all month long.
Messiah Sing-In: Lincoln Center; For once—just this once—it's OK to sing along. Don't blow it.
New Year's Eve Ball Drop: Times Square; Welcome the new year with a freezing mob (December 31).
New Year's Eve Fireworks: Central Park; Hot cider and food available (December 31).
New Year's Eve Midnight Run: Central Park; Never too soon to start with the resolutions (four miles).

Useful Phone Numbers

Emergencies: 911
General City Information: 311
MTA Hotline 511
City Board of Elections: vote.nyc.ny.us or 212-487-5400
Con Edison: 800-752-6633
Time Warner Cable: 212-358-0900 (Manhattan); 718-358-0900 (Queens/Brooklyn); 718-816-8686 (Staten Island)
Cablevision: 718-860-3514
Verizon: 800-837-4966

Bathrooms

When nature calls, New York can make your life excruciatingly difficult. The city-sponsored public bathroom offerings, including dodgy subway restrooms and the sporadic experimentation with self-cleaning super porta-potties, leave a lot to be desired. Your best bet, especially in an emergency, remains bathrooms in stores and other buildings that are open to the public.

The three most popular bathroom choices for needy New Yorkers (and visitors) are Barnes & Noble, Starbucks, and any kind of fast food chain. Barnes & Noble bathrooms are essentially open to everyone (as long as you're willing to walk past countless shelves of books during your navigation to the restrooms). They're usually clean enough, but sometimes you'll find yourself waiting in line during the evening and weekends. Although Starbucks bathrooms are more prevalent, they tend to be more closely guarded (in some places you have to ask for a key) and not as clean as you'd like. Fast food restrooms are similarly unhygienic, but easy to use inconspicuously without needing to purchase anything.

For a nice interactive map of bathrooms in NYC (including hours and even ratings), try the Bathroom Diaries at www.thebathroomdiaries.com or—if you use a smart phone—any of a number of apps designed to help you avoid a ticket for peeing in the street. If you're busting to go and there's no Barnes & Noble, Starbucks, or fast food joint in sight, consider the following options:

Public buildings: Libraries, train stations (Grand Central, Penn Station) and shopping areas (e.g., South Street Seaport, World Financial Center, Manhattan Mall, The Shops at Columbus Circle).
Department stores: Macy's, Bloomingdale's, Saks, etc.
Other stores: Old Navy, Bed Bath & Beyond, FAO Schwarz, The Strand, etc.
Supermarkets: Whole Foods is a sure bet; with garden-variety Pathmark, Food Emporium, D'Agostino, Gristedes, Key Food, etc. you'll probably have to ask, because those are usually way in the back among the employee lockers.

Diners: In every neighborhood, and usually busy enough so that if you simply stride in and head towards the back (since that's where the bathroom is most of the time anyway) WITHOUT stopping, they probably won't notice. Works for us, usually.
Bars: Good option at night when most other places are closed; head straight back; can get raunchy toward closing time.
Parks: Nothing beats a stainless steel "mirror" and a transient bathing in the sink. That said, things aren't always what they used to be—newly renovated parks sometimes have very nice facilities and the public private Bryant Park bathroom is among the nicest in Midtown (and stocked with fresh flowers, to boot).
Hotels: Midtown hotels are basically public buildings, for all intents and purposes; lobbies also good for a quick rest.
Times Square Visitors Center: 1560 Broadway.
Subways: At ends of lines, in major transit hubs and same stops between; raunchy, not for the timid.

Websites

theboweryboys.blogspot.com or @BoweryBoys: NYC history.
ny.curbed.com or @CurbedNY: For those who obsess over building permits.
www.eatingintranslation.com or @EIT: One guy eats his way through NYC.
ny.eater.com or @EaterNY: Restaurant gossip galore.
www.forgotten-ny.com or @ForgottenNY: Fascinating look at the relics of New York's past.
www.gothamgazette.com or @GothamGazette: NYC policy and politics website.
www.gothamist.com or @Gothamist: Blog detailing various daily news and goings-on in the city.
newyork.craigslist.org: Classified site that single handedly put print media out of business.
www.notfortourists.com or @notfortourists: The ultimate NYC website.
www.nyc.gov or @nyc311: New York City government resources.
www.nyc-grid.com or @paulsahner: Photo blog of NYC, block by block.
www.nycgo.com or @nycgo: The official NYC tourism site.
www.overheardinnewyork.com: Repository of great overheard snippets.
www.scoutingny.com or @nycscout: The city from point of view of a film scout.
www.theskint.com or @theskint: Free and cheap worthwhile events listed daily.
www.vanishingnewyork.blogspot.com or @jeremoss: Chronicling lost or nearly lost old-timey time spots.

New York Timeline — a timeline of significant events in New York history (by no means complete)

1524: Giovanni de Verrazano enters the New York harbor.
1609: Henry Hudson explores what is now called the Hudson River.
1626: The Dutch purchase Manhattan and New Amsterdam is founded.
1647: Peter Stuyvesant becomes Director General of New Amsterdam.
1664: The British capture the colony and rename it "New York".
1754: King's College/Columbia founded.
1776: British drive colonial army from New York and hold it for the duration of the war.
1776: Fire destroys a third of the city.
1789: Washington takes the Oath of Office as the first President of the United States.
1801: Alexander Hamilton founds the New-York Evening Post, still published today as the New York Post.
1811: The Commissioners Plan dictates a grid plan for the streets of New York.
1812: City Hall completed.
1825: Completion of the Erie Canal connects New York City commerce to the Great Lakes.
1835: New York Herald publishes its first edition.
1835: Great Fire destroys 600 buildings and kills 30 New Yorkers.
1854: First Tammany Hall-supported mayor Fernando Woods elected.
1859: Central Park opens.
1863: The Draft Riots terrorize New York for three days.
1868: Prospect Park opens.
1871: Thomas Nast cartoons and New York Times exposes lead to the end of the Tweed Ring.
1880: The population of Manhattan reaches over 1 million.
1883: Brooklyn Bridge opens.
1886: The Statue of Liberty is dedicated, inspires first ticker tape parade.
1888: The Blizzard of '88 incapacitates the city for two weeks.
1892: Ellis Island opens; 16 million immigrants will pass through in the next 32 years.
1897: Steeplechase Park opens, first large amusement park in Coney Island.
1898: The City of Greater New York is founded when the five boroughs are merged.
1904: General Slocum disaster kills 1,021.
1904: The subway opens.
1906: First New Year's celebration in Times Square.
1911: Triangle Shirtwaist Fire kills 146, impels work safety movement.
1920: A TNT-packed horse cart explodes on Wall Street, killing 30; the crime goes unsolved.
1923: The Yankees win their first World Championship.
1929: Stock market crashes, signaling the beginning of the Great Depression.
1929: The Chrysler Building is completed.
1930: The Empire State Building is built, then tallest in the world.
1927: The Holland Tunnel opens, making it the world's longest underwater tunnel.
1931: The George Washington Bridge is completed.
1933: Fiorello LaGuardia elected mayor.
1934: Robert Moses becomes Parks Commissioner.
1939: The city's first airport, LaGuardia, opens.
1950: United Nations opens.
1955: Dodgers win the World Series; they move to LA two years later.
1963: Pennsylvania Station is demolished to the dismay of many; preservation efforts gain steam.
1964: The Verrazano-Narrows Bridge is built, at the time the world's longest suspension bridge.
1965: Malcolm X assassinated in the Audubon Ballroom.
1965: Blackout strands hundreds of thousands during rush hour.
1969: The Stonewall Rebellion marks beginning of the gay rights movement.
1969: The Miracle Mets win the World Series.
1970: Knicks win their first championship.
1970: First New York City Marathon takes place.
1971: World Trade Center opens.
1975: Ford to City: Drop Dead.
1977: Thousands arrested for various mischief during a city-wide blackout.
1981: First NYC AIDS death begins a decade of tragedy.
1977: Ed Koch elected mayor to the first of three terms.
1987: Black Monday—stock market plunges.
1993: Giuliani elected mayor.
1993: A bomb explodes in the parking garage of the World Trade Center, killing 5.
1994: Rangers win the Stanley Cup after a 40-year drought.
2000: NFT publishes its first edition.
2001: The World Trade Center is destroyed in a terrorist attack; New Yorkers vow to rebuild.
2003: Blackout becomes best party in NYC history.
2003: Tokens are no longer accepted in subway turnstiles.
2006: Ground is broken on the WTC memorial.
2007: Construction begins (again) on the Second Avenue subway line.
2009: Bloomberg purchases a third term.
2012: 1 WTC is once again tallest in NYC.
2012: Superstorm Sandy ravages Zone A, altering New Yorkers' relationship with the waterfront.
2014: NYC hosts Super Bowl XLVIII, first outdoor cold-weather city game in history.

Essential New York Songs

"Sidewalks of New York"—Various, written by James Blake and Charles Lawlor, 1894

"Give My Regards to Broadway"—Various, written by George Cohan, 1904

"I'll Take Manhattan"—Various, written by Rodgers and Hart, 1925

"Puttin' on the Ritz"—Various, written by Irving Berlin, 1929

"42nd Street"—Various, written by Al Dubin and Harry Warren, 1932

"Take the A Train"—Duke Ellington, 1940

"Autumn in New York"—Frank Sinatra, 1947

"Spanish Harlem"—Ben E. King, 1961

"Car 54 Where Are You?"—Nat Hiken and John Strauss, 1961

"On Broadway"—Various, written by Weil/Mann/Leiber/ Stoller, 1962

"Talkin' New York"—Bob Dylan, 1962

"Up on the Roof"—The Drifters, 1963

"59th Street Bridge Song"—Simon and Garfunkel, 1966

"I'm Waiting for My Man"—Velvet Underground, 1967

"Brooklyn Roads"—Neil Diamond, 1968

"Crosstown Traffic"—Jimi Hendrix, 1969

"Personality Crisis"— The New York Dolls, 1973

"New York State of Mind"—Billy Joel, 1976

"53rd and 3rd"—The Ramones, 1977

"Shattered"—Rolling Stones, 1978

"New York, New York"—Frank Sinatra, 1979

"Life During Wartime"—Talking Heads, 1979

"New York New York"—Grandmaster Flash and the Furious 5, 1984

"No Sleep Til Brooklyn"—Beastie Boys, 1987

"Christmas in Hollis"—Run-D.M.C., 1987

"New York"—U2, 2000

"I've Got New York"—The 6ths, 2000

"New York, New York"—Ryan Adams, 2001

"The Empty Page"—Sonic Youth, 2002

"New York"—Ja Rule f. Fat Joe, Jadakiss, 2004

"Empire State of Mind"—Jay-Z, 2009

"Welcome to New York"—Taylor Swift, 2014

Essential New York Movies

The Crowd (1928)
42nd Street (1933)
King Kong (1933)
Pride of the Yankees (1942)
Arsenic and Old Lace (1944)
Miracle on 34th Street (1947)
On the Town (1949)
On the Waterfront (1954)
The Blackboard Jungle (1955)
An Affair to Remember (1957)
The Apartment (1960)
Breakfast at Tiffany's (1961)
West Side Story (1961)
Barefoot in the Park (1967)
John & Mary (1969)
Midnight Cowboy (1969)
French Connection (1970)
The Out of Towners (1970)
Shaft (1971)
Mean Streets (1973)
Serpico (1973)

Godfather II (1974)
The Taking of Pelham One Two Three (1974)
Dog Day Afternoon (1975)
Taxi Driver (1976)
Saturday Night Fever (1977)
Superman (1978)
Manhattan (1979)
The Warriors (1979)
Fame (1980)
Escape From New York (1981)
Nighthawks (1981)
Ghostbusters (1984)
The Muppets Take Manhattan (1984)
After Hours (1985)
Crocodile Dundee (1986)
Wall Street (1987)
Moonstruck (1987)
Big (1988)
Bright Lights, Big City (1988)
Working Girl (1988)

Do the Right Thing (1989)
Last Exit to Brooklyn (1989)
When Harry Met Sally (1989)
A Bronx Tale (1993)
Kids (1995)
Men in Black (1997)
Bringing Out the Dead (1999)
The Royal Tenenbaums (2001)
Gangs of New York (2002)
Spider-Man (2002)
25th Hour (2002)
The Interpreter (2005)
Inside Man (2006)
The Devil Wears Prada (2006)
American Gangster (2007)
Enchanted (2007)
Sex and the City (2008)
New York I Love You (2009)
Whatever Works (2009)
The Wolf of Wall Street (2013)

Essential New York Books

A Tree Grows in Brooklyn by Betty Smith; coming-of-age story set in the slums of Brooklyn.

The Alienist by Caleb Carr; great portrait of late-19th century New York complete with serial killer, detective, and Teddy Roosevelt.

The Bonfire of the Vanities by Tom Wolfe; money, class, and politics undo a wealthy bond trader.

Bright Lights, Big City by Jay McInerney; 1980s yuppie and the temptations of the city.

Catcher in the Rye by J. D. Salinger; classic portrayal of teenage angst.

The Death and Life of Great American Cities by Jane Jacobs; influential exposition on what matters in making cities work.

The Encyclopedia of New York City by Kenneth T. Jackson, ed.; huge and definitive reference work.

Gotham: A History of New York City to 1898 by Edwin G. Burrows and Mike Wallace; authoritative history of New York.

The Epic of New York City by Edward Robb Ellis; super-readable chapter-by-chapter compendium of hits and highlights of NYC history.

The Fuck-Up by Arsenie Nersesian; scraping by in the East Village of the '80s.

Here is New York by E. B. White; reflections on the city.

House of Mirth by Edith Wharton; climbing the social ladder in upper-class, late 19th-century NY.

Knickerbocker's History of New York by Washington Irving; very early (1809) whimsical "history" of NY.

Manchild in the Promised Land by Claude Brown; autobiographical tale of growing up in Harlem.

The Power Broker by Robert Caro; lengthy biography of 20th century municipal titan Robert Moses, you'll never look at the city the same way after reading it.

The Recognitions by William Gaddis; ever thought New Yorkers were phony? They are.

Washington Square by Henry James; love and marriage in upper-middle-class 1880s NY.

The Cricket in Times Square by George Selden; classic children's book.

This Is New York by Miroslav Sasek; charming children's book from 1960; great gift idea.

The Best of the Best

With all the culture the city has to offer, finding activities to amuse children is easy enough. From fencing classes to the funnest parks, our guide will provide you with great ideas for entertaining your little ones.

Neatest Time-Honored Tradition
There are carousels in all five boroughs; the Central Park Carousel (www.centralparknyc.org) is a vintage carousel featuring Coney Island-style hand-carved horses dating to 1908. Jane's Carousel on the DUMBO waterfront in Brooklyn Bridge Park (www.brooklynbridgepark.org) dates from 1922 and is housed in a striking all-glass pavilion.

Coolest Rainy Day Activity
The Children's Museum of the Arts (103 Charlton St, 212-274-0986 or cmany.org) offers activities for wee ones as young as 10 months, because its never too early to find out whether your child might be the next Picasso. Budding painters can use the open art studio; dramatic ones stage productions in the performing arts gallery; those who must touch everything delight in the creative play stations.

Sweetest Place to Get a Cavity
Jacques Torres (350 Hudson St, 212-414-2462 or www. mrchocolate.com) where kids can watch cocoa beans turn into chocolate bars in the glass-encased factory emporium. As if you needed another reason: Torres makes chocolate-covered Cheerios, and a host of other fun concoctions.

Best Spots for Sledding
Central Park's Pilgrim Hill and Cedar Hill (centralparknyc.org). Kids pray for a snow day for the chance to try out this slick slope. BYO sled or toboggan.

Funnest Park
Pier 51 Play Area (Hudson River Park, Pier 51 at Gansevoort St, www.hudsonriverpark.org) With a beautiful view of the Hudson River, the park features several sprinklers, a winding '"canal,"' and a boat-themed area complete with prow, mast, and captain's wheel.

No Tears Hair Cuts
Jennifer Bilek's Get Coiffed (917-548-3643 or www.getcoiffed. com) offers professional in-home services, eliminating the fear of the unknown. She also offers '"glamour parties"' for girls ages 5–12.

Best Halloween Costume Shopping
Halloween Adventure (104 Fourth Ave, 212-673-4546 or www. newyorkcostumes.com) is the city's costume emporium that has every disguise you can possibly imagine, along with wigs, make-up supplies, and magic tricks to complete any child's dress-up fantasy. Open year-round.

Best Place for Sunday Brunch
There a billion places to take the kids to get pancakes and eggs on Sunday mornings, so why not try something totally different—dim sum in Chinatown! The kids will be entertained as carts of dumplings, pork buns, and unidentified foods constantly roll on by for non-stop eating fun.

Rainy Day Activities

American Museum of Natural History
(Central Park West at 79th St, 212-769-5100 or www.amnh. org) Fantastic for kids of all ages, with something to suit every child's interest. From the larger-than-life dinosaur fossils and the realistic animal dioramas to the out-of-this-world Hayden Planetarium, all attention will be kept. The hands-on exhibits in the Discovery Room and the IMAX theater are also worth a visit.

Bowlmor Lanes
(Chelsea Piers, and Midtown, www.bowlmor.com) Great bowling alley with a retro decor that kids will love. Bumpers are available to cut down on those pesky gutter balls. Children are welcome every day before 5 pm and all day Sunday—a popular birthday spot.

Brooklyn Children's Museum
(145 Brooklyn Ave, 718-735-4400 or www.brooklynkids.org) The world's first museum for children (opened in 1899) engages kids in educational hands-on activities and exhibits.

Staten Island Children's Museum
(1000 Richmond Ter, 718-273-2060 or sichildrensmuseum.org) Offers plenty of hands-on opportunities for kids to explore everything from pirate ships to the rainforest. There's also an outdoor play space (weather permitting).

Children's Museum of Manhattan
(212 W 83rd St, 212-721-1234 or cmom.org) As soon as you arrive at the museum, sign up for some of the day's activities. While you're waiting, check out the exhibits, which are fun for all ages.

Intrepid Sea, Air & Space Museum
(Pier 86, 46th St & 12th Ave, 212-245-0072 or www. intrepidmuseum.org) Tour the Growler, a real submarine that was once a top-secret missile command center, or take a virtual trip on one of the simulator rides. After you've taken a look at the authentic aircraft on deck—including space shuttle *Enterprise*—visit the museum of the Intrepid to see an extensive model airplane collection and a Cockpit Challenge flight video game for those aspiring pilots.

Little Shop of Crafts
(711 Amsterdam Ave, 212-531-2723 or littleshopny.com) Great space to bead/paint. Stop by for hours.

Lower East Side Tenement Museum
(103 Orchard St, 212-982-8420 or www.tenement.org) The museum offers insight into immigrant life in the late 19th and early 20th centuries by taking groups on tours of an historic tenement building on the Lower East Side. One tour called '"Visit the Confino Living Room"' is led by '"Victoria Confino,"' a young girl dressed in authentic costume who teaches children about the lives of immigrants in the early 1900s. A great place to take your kids if they haven't already been there on a school field trip.

The Metropolitan Museum of Art
(1000 Fifth Ave, 212-535-7710 or www.metmuseum.org) A great museum to explore with audio guides designed specifically for children. From the armor exhibits to the Egyptian Wing, the museum offers art exhibits from all historical periods.

The Noguchi Museum
(9-01 33rd Rd at Vernon Blvd, Long Island City, 718-204-7088 or www.noguchi.org) This museum showcasing the works of Japanese-American artist Isamu Noguchi offers interesting tours and hands-on workshops for toddlers to teens. The fees are nominal, but you must register beforehand.

The Museum of Modern Art
(11 W 53rd St, 212-708-9400 or www.moma.org) Besides the kid-friendly audio guides that help make this renowned museum enjoyable for tykes, MoMA has a lot of exciting weekend family programs that get kids talking about art and film. Lots of fun hands-on programs too. Registration is a must—these programs book up fast.

Outdoor and Educational

Central Park Zoo
(64th St and Fifth Ave, 212-439-6500 or www.centralparkzoo. com) Houses more than 1,400 animals, including some

endangered species. Exhibits run the gamut, from the Arctic habitat of penguins to the steamy tropical Rain Forest Pavilion. The Tisch Children's Zoo nearby is more suited for the younger crowd with its smaller, cuddlier animals.

Fort Washington Park
(W 155 St to Dyckman St along the Hudson River, 212-304-2365 or www.nycgovparks.org) The Urban Park Rangers periodically open Jeffrey's Hook Lighthouse to tours. The lighthouse, popularized in the book *The Little Red Lighthouse*, is located at the base of the George Washington Bridge. The lighthouse affords some spectacular views—better than anything they'd see from atop Dad's shoulders.

Historic Richmond Town
(441 Clarke Ave, Staten Island, 718-351-1611 or www.historicrichmondtown.org) A 100 acre complex with over 40 points of interest and a museum that covers three centuries of the history of Staten Island. People dressed in authentic period garb lead demonstrations and tours.

New York Botanical Garden
(Bronx River Parkway at Fordham Road, Bronx, 718-817-8700 or www.nybg.org) 250 acres and 50 different indoor and outdoor gardens and plant exhibits to explore. The Children's Adventure Garden changes each season, and kids can get down and dirty in the Family Garden. Keen young botanists can join the Children's Gardening Program and get their own plot to care for.

Classes

With all of their after-school classes and camps, the children of New York City are some of the most well-rounded and programmed in the country. Help them beef up their college applications with some fancy extracurriculars. It's never too early.

92nd Street Y
(1395 Lexington Ave, 212-415-5500 or www.92y.org) The center provides children of all ages with tons of activities, ranging from music lessons and chess to flamenco and yoga. 92nd St is known as "the Y to beat all Ys."

Abrons Arts Center
(466 Grand St, 212-598-0400 or www.abronsartscenter.org) A program of the Henry Street Settlement, the Arts Center offers classes and workshops for children of all ages in music, dance, theater, and visual arts.

Archikids
(472 16th St, Brooklyn, 718-768-6123 or www.archikids.org) Programs that inspire kids about architecture.

The Art Farm
(419 E 91st St, 212-410-3117 or www.theartfarms.org) Ecological and animal programs by way of the Hamptons for all ages.

Asphalt Green
(555 E 90th St, 212-369-8890 or www.asphaltgreen.org) Swimming and diving lessons, gymnastics, team sports, and art classes. They've got it all for kids one and up.

Berry School
(155 Bank St, 212-255-1685 or perryschool.com) Enrichment programs for kids ages 4 months to 13 years.

Church Street School for Music and Art
(74 Warren St, 212-571-7290 or www.churchstreetschool.org) This community arts center offers a variety of classes in music and art involving several different media, along with private lessons and courses for parents and children.

Dieu Donné
(315 W 36th St, 212-226-0573 or dieudonne.org) Workshops and papermaking offered for children ages seven and up.

Greenwich House Music School
(46 Barrow St, 212-242-4770 or www.greenwichhouse.org) Group classes and private lessons in music and ballet for children of all ages.

Hamilton Fish Recreation Center
(128 Pitt St, 212-387-7687 or www.nycgovparks.org) The center offers free swimming lessons in two outdoor pools along with free after-school programs with classes like astronomy and photography.

Hi Art!
(227 W 29th St, Studio 4R, 212-209-1552 or www.hiartkids.com) For children ages 2-12, the classes focus on the exploration of art in museums and galleries in the city and giving kids the freedom to develop what they've seen into new concepts in a spacious studio setting.

Institute of Culinary Education
(50 W 23rd St, 800-522-4610 or recreational.ice.edu) Hands-on cooking classes.

Irish Arts Center
(553 W 51st St, 212-757-3318 or www.irishartscenter.org) Introductory Irish step dancing classes for children five and up.

The Jewish Community Center in Manhattan
(334 Amsterdam Ave, 646-505-4444 or www.jccmanhattan.org) The center offers swimming lessons, team sports, courses in arts and cooking, and summer programs. There's even a rooftop playground.

Kids at Art
(1412 Second Ave, 212-410-9780 or www.kidsatartnyc.com) Art program that focuses on the basics in a non-competitive environment for kids ages 2-11.

Marshall Chess Club
(23 W 10th St, 212-477-3716 or www.marshallchessclub.org) Membership to the club offers access to weekend chess classes, summer camp, and tournaments for children ages five and up.

Tannen's Magic
(45 W 34th St, Ste 608, 212-929-4500 or www.tannens.com) Ask about private and group lessons. Their week long summer sleep-away camp (www.tannensmagiccamp.com) is also very popular.

The Techno Team
(160 Columbus Ave, 212-501-1425 or thetechnoteam.com) Computer technology classes for children ages 3-12.

Trapeze School
(Locations in Lower Manhattan and Long Island City 212-242-8769 or newyork.trapezeschool.com) Kids ages six and up can learn how to fly through the air with the greatest of ease.

Babysitting/Nanny Services

The Babysitters' Guild
60 E 42nd St, Ste 912; 212-682-0227 or babysittersguild.com)

Barnard Babysitting Agency
(49 Claremont Ave; 212-854-2035 or barnardbabysitting.com)

Pinch Sitters (212-260-6005 or www.nypinchsitters.com)

Useful Websites

Mommy Poppins
mommypoppins.com or @mommypoppins

New York Magazine Family Guide
nymag.com/urban/guides/family
(dated but a lot still applies)

349

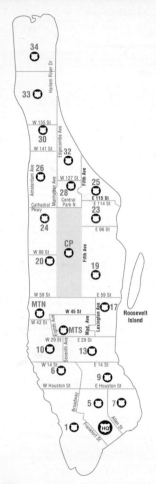

Important Phone Numbers

All Emergencies: 911
Non-Emergencies: 311
NYPD Switchboard: 646-610-5000
Terrorism Hot Line: 888-NYC-SAFE
Sex Crimes Report Line: 212-267-RAPE
Crime Stoppers: 800-577-TIPS
Crime Stoppers (Spanish): 888-57-PISTA
Crime Victims Hotline: 212-577-7777
Cop Shot: 800-COP-SHOT
Missing Persons Case Status: 212-694-7781
Operation Gun Stop: 866-GUN-STOP
Organized Crime Control Bureau: 888-374-DRUG
Civilian Complaint Review Board: 311 or www.nyc.gov/ccrb
Website: www.nyc.gov/nypd
Twitter: @NYPDnews

Statistics

	2013	2011	2009	2007	2005
Uniformed Personnel	34,413	33,777	35,641	35,548	35,489
Murders	335	515	471	496	539
Rapes	1,378	1,420	1,205	1,351	1,858
Robberies	19,128	19,717	18,601	21,809	24,722
Felony Assaults	20,297	18,482	13,773	17,493	17,750
Burglaries	17,429	18,720	19,430	21,762	24,117
Grand Larcenies	45,368	38,501	39,580	44,924	48,243
Grand Larcenies (Cars)	7,400	9,314	10,670	13,174	18,246

Precinct

Precinct		Phone	Map
1st Precinct	16 Ericsson Pl	212-334-0611	2
5th Precinct	19 Elizabeth St	212-334-0711	3
7th Precinct	19 Pitt St	212-477-7311	4
6th Precinct	233 W 10th St	212-741-4811	5
9th Precinct	130 Avenue C	212-477-7811	7
Midtown South	357 W 35th St	212-239-9811	8
10th Precinct	230 W 20th St	212-741-8211	9
13th Precinct	230 E 21st St	212-477-7411	10
Mid-Town North	306 W 54th St	212-760-8400	11
17th Precinct	167 E 51st St	212-826-3211	13
20th Precinct	120 W 82nd St	212-580-6411	14
19th Precinct	153 E 67th St	212-452-0600	15
24th Precinct	151 W 100th St	212-678-1811	16
23rd Precinct	162 E 102nd St	212-860-6411	17
26th Precinct	520 W 126th St	212-678-1311	18
28th Precinct	2271 8th Ave	212-678-1611	19
32nd Precinct	250 W 135th St	212-690-6311	19
25th Precinct	120 E 119th St	212-860-6511	20
30th Precinct	451 W 151st St	212-690-8811	21
33rd Precinct	2207 Amsterdam Ave	212-927-3200	23
34th Precinct	4295 Broadway	212-927-9711	24
Central Park Precinct	W 86th St & Transverse Rd	212-570-4820	CP

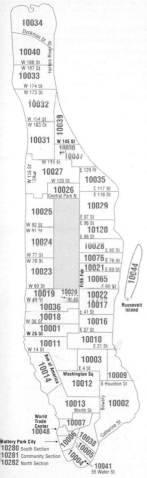

Branch	Address	Phone	Map
Battery Park Retail	15 Rector St	212-330-5151	1
Hanover Finance	1 Hanover St	212-425-5875	1
Peck Slip	1 Peck Slip	212-964-1054	1
Whitehall Retail	1 Whitehall St	212-330-5151	1
Canal Street	350 Canal St	212-925-3378	2
Church Street	90 Church St	212-330-5001	2
Chinatown	6 Doyers St	212-267-3510	3
Federal Plaza	26 Federal Plaza	212-608-2420	3
Knickerbocker	128 East Broadway	212-608-3598	4
Pitt Station	185 Clinton St	212-254-9270	4
Village	201 Varick St	212-645-0327	6
West Village	527 Hudson St	212 909-5084	5
Cooper	93 Fourth Ave	212-254-1390	6
Patchin	70 W 10th St	212-475-2534	6
Peter Stuyvesant	432 E 14th St	212-677-2112	7
Tompkins Square	244 E 3rd St	212-673-6415	7
James A Farley	421 Eighth Ave	212-330-2902	8
London Terrace	234 Tenth Ave	800-275-8777	8
Port Authority	309 W 15th St	212-645-0331	8
Greeley Square	39 W 31st St	212-244-7055	9
Midtown	223 W 38th St	212-819-9604	9
Old Chelsea	217 W 18th St	212-675-0548	9
Madison Square	149 E 23rd St	212-673-3771	10
Murray Hill Finance	115 E 34th St	212-689-1124	10
Radio City	322 W 52nd St	212-265-3672	11
Times Square	340 W 42nd St	212-502-0421	11
Port Authority Convenience	625 8th Ave	646-472-0501	11
Bryant	23 W 43rd St	212-279-5960	12
Rockefeller Center	610 Fifth Ave	212-265-3054	12
Dag Hammarskjold	884 Second Ave	800-275-8777	13
Franklin D Roosevelt	909 Third Ave	800-275-8777	13
Grand Central Station	450 Lexington Ave	212-330-5722	13
United Nations	405 F 42nd St	212-963-7353	13
Ansonia	178 Columbus Ave	212-362-1697	14
Columbus Circle	27 W 60th St	212-265-7858	14
Planetarium	127 W 83rd St	212-873-5609	14
Cherokee	1483 York Ave	212-517-8361	15
Gracie	229 E 85th St	212-988-6680	15
Lenox Hill	217 E 70th St	212-330-5561	15
Cathedral	215 W 104th St	212-662-0355	16
Park West	693 Columbus Ave	800-275-8777	16
Yorkville	1617 Third Ave	212-369-2747	17
Columbia University	534 W 112th St	800-275-8777	18
Manhattanville	365 W 125th St	212-662-1540	18
Morningside	232 W 116th St	800-275-8777	19
Hellgate	153 E 110th St	212-860-1896	20
Triborough	167 E 124th St	212-534-0381	20
Hamilton Grange	521 W 146th St	212-281-1538	21
Fort Washington	556 W 158th St	212-923-1763	21
College Station	217 W 140th St	212-283-7096	22
Colonial Park	99 Macombs Pl	212-368-9849	22
Lincolnton	2266 Fifth Ave	212-281-9781	22
Audubon	511 W 165th St	212-568-2387	23
Washington Bridge	555 W 180th St	212-568-2690	23
Fort George	4558 Broadway	212-942-5266	24
Inwood Post Office	90 Vermilyea Ave	212-567-7821	25
Roosevelt Island	694 Main St	800-275-8777	RI

If you have to get to a hospital (especially in an emergency), it's best to go to the closest one. However, as a quick reference, the following is a list of the largest hospitals by neighborhood, complete with the name of its corresponding map. But no matter which hospital you drag yourself into, for heaven's sake make sure you have your insurance card.

Lower Manhattan: NYU Downtown Hospital · William & Beekman Sts, just south of the Brooklyn Bridge · [Map 3]

East Village: Beth Israel Medical Center · 14th St & Broadway/Union Square · [Map 10]

Murray Hill: Bellevue Hospital Center · First Ave & 27th St [Map 10] ; NYU College of Dentistry · First Ave & 24th St [Map 10]

Hell's Kitchen/Upper West Side: St Luke's Roosevelt Hospital · 10th Ave & 58th St [Map 11]

East Side: NewYork-Presbyterian · York Ave & 68th St [Map 15]; Lenox Hill Hospital · Lexington Ave & 77th St [Map 15]; Mt Sinai Medical Center · Madison Ave & 101st St [Map 17]

Columbia/Morningside Heights: St Luke's Hospital Center · Amsterdam Ave & 114th St [Map 18]

Farther Uptown: Columbia Presbyterian Medical Center · 168th St & Broadway [Map 23]

If you have a condition that isn't immediately threatening, certain hospitals in New York specialize and excel in specific areas of medicine:

Cancer: Memorial Sloan-Kettering

Birthing Center/Labor & Delivery: St Luke's Roosevelt

Digestive Disorders: Mt Sinai

Dentistry: NYU College of Dentistry

Ear, Nose, and Throat: Mt Sinai

Eyes: New York Eye and Ear Infirmary

Geriatrics: Mt Sinai, NewYork-Presbyterian

Heart: NewYork-Presbyterian

Hormonal Disorders: NewYork-Presbyterian

Kidney Disease: NewYork-Presbyterian

Mental Health: Bellevue

Neurology: NewYork-Presbyterian, NYU Medical Center

Orthopedics: Hospital for Special Surgery, NewYork Presbyterian

Pediatrics: Children's Hospital of NewYork-Presbyterian

Psychiatry: NewYork-Presbyterian, NYU Medical Center

Rheumatology: Hospital for Special Surgery, Hospital for Joint Diseases Orthopedic Institute, NYU Medical Center

Emergency Rooms	Address	Phone	Map
Bellevue Hospital Center	462 First Ave	212-562-1000	10
Beth Israel Medical Center	281 First Ave	212-420-2000	10
Harlem Hospital Center	506 Lenox Ave	212-939-1000	22
Hospital for Joint Diseases	301 E 17th St	212-598-6000	10
Lenox Hill Hospital	110 E 77th St	212-434-2000	15
Metropolitan Hospital Center	1901 First Ave	212-423-6262	17
Mount Sinai Medical Center	1190 Fifth Ave	212-241-6500	17
New York Downtown Hospital	170 William St	212-312-5000	1
New York Eye & Ear Infirmary	310 E 14th St	212-979-4000	6
NewYork-Presbyterian–Weill Cornell Medical Center	525 E 68th St	212-746-5454	15
New York-Presbyterian Hospital Allen Pavilion	5141 Broadway	212-932-4000	25
New York-Presbyterian Hospital/Columbia University Medical Center	622 W 168th St	212-305-2500	23
North General Hospital	1879 Madison Ave	212-423-4000	20
NYU Langone Medical Center	550 First Ave	212-263-7300	10
St Luke's Hospital	1111 Amsterdam Ave	212-523-4000	18
St Luke's Roosevelt Hospital Center	1000 Tenth Ave	212-523-4000	11
VA NY Harbor Healthcare System - Manhattan Campus	423 E 23rd St	212-686-7500	10
Wilzig Hospital	355 Grand St	201-309-1090	35

Other Hospitals	Address	Phone	Map
Beth Israel—Phillips Ambulatory Care Center	10 Union Sq E	212-844-8000	10
Coler Goldwater–Coler Campus	1 Main St	212-848-6000	RI
Coler Goldwater–Goldwater Campus	1 Main St	212-318-8000	RI
Gouverneur Healthcare Services	227 Madison St	212-238-7000	4
Gracie Square Hospital	420 E 76th St	212-988-4400	15
Hospital for Special Surgery	535 E 70 St	212-606-1000	15
Manhattan Eye, Ear & Throat	210 E 64th St	212-838-9200	15
Memorial Sloan-Kettering Cancer Center	1275 York Ave	212-639-2000	15
Renaissance Health Care Network Diagnostic and Treatment Center	215 W 125th St	212-932-6500	18

Beginner's mistake: Walk into the "main branch" of the New York Public Library at Bryant Park, and ask how to check out books. Trust us; it's happened. Recognizable for its reclining stone lions, *Patience* and *Fortitude*, the famous building is a research library with non-circulating materials that you can peruse in the iconic reading room. In 2008, the Children's Center, a circulating children's library, moved to this location and now you can check out kids books here, too. If you want to read *War and Peace* or *50 Shades of Da Vinci Pray Love*, it's best to go to your local branch (there are 80 of them spread out through Manhattan, The Bronx and Staten Island). Note: Holds take a very long time to fill, at least a week and a half. If the book you need is only a 20-minute subway ride away, and you need the book now, invest the time and the subway fare.

The main branch of the **New York Public Library (Map 12)** (renamed the Schwarzman Building in 2008 for billionaire donor Stephen A. Schwarzman) is one of Manhattan's architectural treasures. Designed by Carrère and Hastings and opened to the public in 1911, the building was one of the Beaux-Arts firm's most famous commissions. The main branch has several special collections and services, such as the Humanities and Social Sciences Library, the Map Division, Exhibition galleries, and divisions dedicated to various ethnic groups. The main branch contains 88 miles of shelves and has more than 10,000 current periodicals from almost 150 countries. Research libraries require an ACCESS card which you can apply for at the library and which allows you to request materials in any of the reading rooms. Card sign-up can be slow, so be patient, and it never hurts to bring along multiple kinds of ID, or a piece of mail if you're a new NYC resident.

If it's reference material you're after, there are specialized research libraries to help: The **Schomburg Center for Research in Black Culture (Map 22)** is the nation's foremost source on African-American history. The **Library for the Performing Arts (Map 14)** contains the Theatre on Film and Tape Archive, featuring taped performances of many Broadway shows. There's also the **Andrew Heiskell Braille and Talking Book Library (Map 9)**, designed to be barrier-free. The library contains large collections of special format materials and audio equipment for listening to recorded books and magazines. You can check out the full system online at www.nypl.org.

Library	Address	Phone	Map
115th Street	203 W 115th St	212-666-9393	19
125th St	224 E 125th St	212-534-5050	20
58th St	127 E 58th St	212-759-7358	13
67th st	328 E 67th St	212-734-1717	15
96th Street	112 F 96th St	212-289-0000	17
Aguilar	174 E 110th St	212-534-2930	20
Andrew Heiskell Braille & Talking Book Library	40 W 20th St	212-206-5400	9
Bloomingdale	150 W 100th St	212-222-8030	16
Chatham Square	3v East Broadway	212-964-0396	3
Columbus	742 Tenth Ave	212-586-5098	11
Countee Cullen	104 W 136th St	212-491-2070	22
Early Childhood Resource & Information Center	455 5th Ave	917-275-6975	12
Epiphany	228 E 23rd St	212-679-2645	10
Fort Washington	535 W 179th St	212-927-3533	23
Frick Art Reference Library	10 F 71st St	212-547-0641	15
George Bruce	518 W 125th St	212-662-9727	18
Grand Central Branch	135 E 46th St	212-621-0670	13
Hamilton Fish Park	415 E Houston St	212-388-1930	7
Hamilton Grange	503 W 145th St	212-926-2147	21
Harlem	9 W 124th St	212-348-5620	19
Hudson Park	66 Leroy St	212-243-6876	5
Inwood	4790 Broadway	212-942-2445	25
Jefferson Market	425 Sixth Ave	212-243-4334	5
Kips Bay	446 Third Ave	212-683-2520	10
Macomb's Bridge	2650 Adam Clayton Powell Jr Blvd	212-281-4900	22
Mid-Manhattan Library	455 Fifth Ave	917-275-6975	12
Morningside Heights Library	2900 Broadway	212-864-2530	18
Muhlenberg	209 W 23rd St	212-924-1585	9
Mulberry Street	10 Jersey St	212-966-3424	6
National Archives	201 Varick St	212-401-1620	5
New Amsterdam	9 Murray St	212-732-8186	3
New York Academy of Medicine Library	1216 Fifth Ave	212-822-7200	17
New York Public Library for the Performing Arts	40 Lincoln Center Plz	212-870-1630	14
New York Society Library	53 E 79th St	212-288-6900	15
Ottendorfer	135 Second Ave	212-674-0947	6
Riverside	127 Amsterdam Ave	212-870-1810	14
Roosevelt Island	524 Main St	212-308-6243	RI
Schomburg Center for Research	515 Malcolm X Blvd	212-491-2200	22
Science, Industry, and Business Library	188 Madison Ave	212-592-7000	9
Seward Park	192 East Broadway	212-477-6770	4
St Agnes	444 Amsterdam Ave	212-877-4380	14
Stephen A. Schwarzman Building	42nd St & Fifth Ave	212-340-0849	12
Terence Cardinal Cooke-Cathedral	560 Lexington Ave	212-752-3824	13
Tompkins Square	331 E 10th St	212-228-4747	7
Washington Heights	1000 St Nicholas Ave	212-923-6054	23
Webster	1465 York Ave	212-288-5049	15
Yorkville	222 E 79th St	212-744-5824	15

Very few places, anywhere, rival New York when it comes to quality gay living. Gay men can get almost anything they want, any time of day, with many businesses catering specifically to gay clientele. Bars remain the backbone of the social scene: some, like **Industry (Map 11)**, focus on a chic atmosphere, while places like **The Phoenix (Map 7)** and **9th Avenue Saloon (Map 11)** are friendly dive bars. You can sing your face off on karaoke nights at **Pieces (Map 5)**, get into trouble at **The Cock (Map 6)**, and dance with the locals at **The Ritz (Map 11)** or with bridge-and-tunnel types at **XL (Map 11)**.

There are more lesbian bars and parties than ever in New York City, so all you have to do is decide what night, which neighborhood and how you'll snag a girl! Although you'll find quality drinks, music, and women at **Henrietta Hudson (Map 5)**, the notorious and intolerable bathroom line might discourage those lesbians who actually have a bladder. Lovergirl (www. lovergirlnyc.com) puts on Saturday night dance parties while **Cubbyhole (Map 5)** promises a homey atmosphere and friendly crowd. In Brooklyn, chill on the patio at **Ginger's (Map 33)**.

Websites

newyork.gaycities.com: New York section of comprehensive LGBT-focused travel site.

www.gayyellowpages.com: Gayellow Pages for gay/ lesbian-owned and gay/lesbian-friendly businesses in the US and Canada.

Publications

Gay City News: Bi-weekly newspaper for lesbian and gay New Yorkers including current local and national news items. (www.gaycitynews.com or @GayCityNews).

Get Out!: Weekly with emphasis on goings on about town (getoutmag.com or @GetOutMag).

Next Magazine: Weekly magazine that includes frisky nightlife listings, film reviews, feature articles, and more. (www.nextmagazine.com or @NextMagazineNY).

Bookshops

Bluestockings: Lesbian/radical bookstore and activist center with regular readings and a fair-trade café. (172 Allen St, 212-777-6028, www.bluestockings.com or @ bluestockings).

Health Centers and Support Organizations

Callen-Lorde Community Health Center: Health care and services for the LGBT community (356 W 18th St, 212-271-7200, www.callen-lorde.org or @CallenLorde).

GMHC: Founded in 1981, Gay Men's Health Crisis is dedicated to AIDS awareness and support for those living with HIV (446 W 33rd St, 212-367-1000, www.gmhc.org or @GMHC).

The Lesbian, Gay, Bisexual & Transgender Community Center: The largest LGBT multi-service organization on the East Coast. (208 W 13th, 212-620-7310, www. gaycenter.org).

GLBT National Help Center: Switchboard for referrals, advice, and counseling (888-843-4564, www.glnh.org or @glbtNatlHelpCtr).

Identity House: Offers LGBTQ peer counseling services, short-term therapy and/or referrals, groups, and workshops (208 W 13th St, 212-243-8181, www. identityhouse.org).

Lambda Legal: Legal foundation securing civil rights for the entire LGBT population (120 Wall St, 19th Flr, 212 809-8585, www.lambdalegal.org, or @LambdaLegal).

National Gay & Lesbian Task Force: National organization building LGBT political power and de-marginalizing LGBT issues. (80 Maiden Ln, Ste 1504, 212-604-9830, www.thetaskforce.org or @TheTaskForce).

New York City Anti-Violence Project: 24-hour crisis support line for violence against LGTBH communities (212-714-1141, www.avp.org or @antiviolence).

PFLAG: Parents, Families, and Friends of Lesbians and Gays working together to raise awareness of LGBT youth and adults (130 E 25th St, Ste M1, 646-240-4288, www. pflagnyc.org or @pflagnyc).

Immigration Equality: Advocates for changing US policy on immigration of permanent partners (40 Exchange Pl, Ste 1300, 212-714-2904, immigrationequality.org or @IEquality).

GLAAD (Gay and Lesbian Alliance Against Defamation): The are the folks who go to bat for you in the media. (104 W 29th St, 4th Flr, 212-629-3322, www. glaad.org or @glaad).

OUTdancing @ Stepping Out Studios: The first LGBT partner dance program in the US. (37 W 26th St, 9th Flr 646-742-9400, www.steppingoutstudios.com).

LGBT Connections Night at Leo Bar: Each third Friday of the month, Asia Society partners with various LGBT professional organizations; free exhibition tours included (725 Park Ave, 212-327-9352, www.asiasociety.org).

Positive Alliance: Organizes weekly Friday social mixer and party for HIV+ gay men, their friends and supporters at The Ritz (369 W 46th St, 2nd Flr); also provides regular email newsletter with links to resources and news updates (@PozAlliance).

Annual Events

Pride Week: Usually the last full week in June (212-807 7433, www.nycpride.org or @NYCPride).

NewFest: NY's Premier LGBT Film Festival: Showcase of international gay and lesbian films, July (646-290-8136 newfest.org or @NewFestNYC).

It's good to be a dog in New York. NYC's pooches are among the world's most pampered: they celebrate birthdays, don expensive sweaters, and prance down Fifth Avenue in weather-appropriate gear. Even for those of us who can't afford to dress our pups in Burberry raincoats, there are ways to spoil our canine companions. NYC is full of dog runs—both formal and informal—scattered throughout the city's parks and neighborhood community spaces. Good thing too, as the fine for having a dog off-leash can run upward of $100, and park officials are vigilant. While the city takes no active role in the management of the dog runs, it provides space to the community groups who do. These community groups are always eager for help (volunteer time or financial contributions) and many post volunteer information on park bulletin boards. It can take many years and several thousand dollars to build a dog run in New York. NYC boasts dozens of dog runs, but that doesn't seem like very much when you consider that there are more than a million pooches in the five boroughs. Each dog run is different. It's good to know, for example, that Riverside Park at 87th Street has a fountain and hose to keep dogs cool in the summer. Formal runs are probably the safest bet for pets, as most are enclosed and maintained. For safety reasons, choke or pronged collars are forbidden, and identification and rabies tags should remain on the flat collar. Most runs prohibit dogs in heat, aggressive dogs, and dogs without up-to-date shots. For more information about dog runs in city parks, see www.nycgovparks.org/facilities/dogareas

There are no dog runs in Central Park, but before 9 am the park is full of people walking their dogs off-leash. While this is a strict no-no the rest of the day (and punishable by hefty fines), park officials tolerate the practice as long as dogs maintain a low profile, and are leashed immediately at 9 am. Check out www.centralparknyc.org for more info and check in with Central Park Paws, an initiative of the Central Park Conservancy to connect with dog owners about responsible ways to enjoy the park.

While there are too many dog runs to create a complete list, these are some of the best-established ones.

P.S. 234 (300 Greenwich St at Chambers St, Map 2): Private run/membership required.

Fish Bridge Park (Dover and Pearl Sts, Map 3): Concrete-surfaced run; features water hose, wading pool, and lock box with newspapers.

Coleman Oval Park (Pike & Monroe Sts, Map 4): Under the Manhattan Bridge.

West Village D.O.G. Run (Little W 12th St between Washington St and 10th Ave, www.wvdog.org, Map 5): Features benches, water hose, and drink bowl; membership required.

Washington Square Park (MacDougal St at W 4th St, Map 6): Located in the southwest corner of the park, this is a large, gravel-surfaced run with many spectators, popular and gets very crowded, but is well-maintained nonetheless.

Mercer-Houston Dog Run (Mercer St at Houston St, mercerhoustondogrun.org, Map 6): Private run with a membership; benefits include running water and a plastic wading pool for your dog to splash in.

Union Square (Broadway at 17th St, Map 6): Crushed stone surface.

Tompkins Square Park (Avenue B at 10th St, www.tompkinssquaredogrun.com, Map 7): NYC's first dog run opened in 1990; this community-centered run offers lots of shade, benches, and running water—but be aware, toys, frisbees, balls, and dogs in heat are prohibited.

Thomas Smith Triangle (11th Ave at 23rd St, Map 8): Concrete-surfaced run.

Chelsea Waterside Park (11th Ave at 22nd St, Map 8):

Madison Square Park (Madison Ave at 25th St, Map 10): Medium-sized run with gravel surface and plenty of trees.

DeWitt Clinton Park (11th Ave at 52nd & 54th Sts, Map 11): Two small concrete-surfaced runs.

Astro's Hell's Kitchen Neighborhood Dog Run (W 39th St at 10th Ave, astrosdogrun.org, Map 11): A private dog run featuring chairs, umbrellas, fenced garden, and woodchip surface.

East River Esplanade (East River at 63rd St, Map 13): Concrete dog run by the river.

Peter Detmold Park (Beekman Pl at 51st St, Map 13): Large well-maintained run with cement and dirt surfaces and many trees.

Robert Moses Park (First Ave and 42nd St, Map 13): Concrete surface.

Theodore Roosevelt Park (Central Park W at W 81st St, Map 14): Gravel surface.

Riverside Park (Riverside Dr at 72nd St, Map 14)

Carl Schurz Park (East End Ave at 85th–86th Sts, Map 15, 17): Medium-sized enclosed run with pebbled surface and separate space for small dogs; this run has benches and shady trees, and running water is available in the bathrooms.

Riverside Park (Riverside Dr at 87th St, Map 16): Medium-sized run with gravel surface.

Riverside Park (Riverside Dr at 105th-106th Sts, Map 16): Medium-sized run with gravel surface.

Morningside Park (Morningside Ave b/w 114th & 119th Sts, Map 18).

Thomas Jefferson Park (E 112th St at First Ave, Map 20): Wood chip surface.

J. Hood Wright Park (Haven Ave at W 173rd St, Map 23): An enclosed dirt-surfaced run.

Fort Tryon Park/Sir William's Dog Run (Margaret Corbin Dr, Washington Heights, Map 24):

Inwood Hill Dog Run (Dyckman St and Payson Ave, Map 25): Gravel surface.

Kowsky Plaza Dog Run (Gateway Plaza, Battery Park City): Located near the marina, this area has small hills for your dog to run on, as well as a small fountain and bathing pool.

Battery Park City (Along River Ter between Park Pl W and Murray St): Concrete-surfaced run with a view of the river.

If you're reading this you're probably not a tourist, and if you're not a tourist you probably don't need a hotel. However, chances are good that at some point your obnoxious friend or relative from out of state will suddenly come a-knockin', bearing news of their long-awaited arrival to the big city. "So I thought I'd stay at your place," they will suggest casually, displaying their complete ignorance of the number of square feet in an average New York apartment—and simultaneously realizing your greatest fear of playing host to someone you greatly dislike. Or there's the possibility that your place is infested with mice, bed bugs, or pigeons and you need to escape, pronto. Or maybe you're just looking for a romantic (or slightly less than romantic) getaway without leaving the city. Whatever the case, be assured that there is a seemingly endless array of possibilities to suit all your overnight desires and needs.

Obviously, your options run from dirt cheap (well, by New York standards) to disgustingly, offensively expensive. For those with tons of extra cash, either call us or check out some of the elite luxury chains—The **Ritz Carlton** (cheaper to stay at the one in **Battery Park** than **Central Park (Map 12)**), The **Four Seasons (Map 12)** at E 57th St, **The W at Union Square (Map 10)**, **Times Square (Map 12)**, **E 39th St (Map 10)**, and **Lexington Ave at 49th St (Map 13)**, **Le Parker Meridien (Map 12)**, **The Peninsula (Map 12)**, **The St. Regis(Map 12)**, and The **Mandarin-Oriental (Map 11)**.

Those hotels that are more unique to Manhattan include: the **Lowell (Map 15)**, a fortress of pretentiousness nestled beside Central Park, which successfully captures the feel of a snobby, high-class gentleman's club. For a similar feeling, only with a heavy dose of Renaissance Italy and a design dating back to 1882, check into The **New York Palace (Map 12)**. If you prefer more modern surroundings, the swank-tastic **Bryant Park Hotel (Map 12)** (once the landmark Radiator building before it was transformed) is a favorite amongst entertainment and fashion industry folks. Similarly, The **Regency (Map 15)**, nicknamed "Hollywood East" in the 1960s, is a must for all celeb-stalkers hangers-on alike. Meanwhile, The **Algonquin (Map 12)** offers complimentary delivery of the New Yorker, as if to suggest that they cater to a more literary crowd (maybe in the 1920s, but whether or not that's the case today is up for debate). If you're feeling fabulous, there's **The Muse Hotel (Map 12)**, located in the heart of Times Square, mere steps away from the bright lights of Broadway. If you're more comfortable with the old-money folks (or if you're a nostalgic member of the nouveau-riche), check out the apartment-size rooms at **The Carlyle (Map 15)**. Be a bit easier on your wallet and get a room at **The Excelsior Hotel (Map 14)**—it may be a tad less indulgent, but get over it, you're still right on Central Park. Yet more affordable and not an ounce less attractive is **The Hudson (Map 11)**, a chic boutique hotel from Ian Schrager. Then there's **The Shoreham (Map 12)**, which offers complimentary champagne at the front desk (so it's definitely worth a shot to pose as a guest) in addition to a fantastically retro bar, that looks like it's straight out of *A Clockwork Orange*. If you are gay or have a gay relative or friend coming to visit, consider **The Out NYC**

(Map 11), a sleek resort hotel catering to a LGBT clientele that bills itself as New York's first "straight-friendly" hotel. Last but certainly not least, one can always stay at the world-famous **Waldorf Astoria (Map 13)**, where unrivaled service and a lavish renovation more than justify the cost of staying (at least for the 1% and those who edging close to that elite coterie).

There are additional high-end options downtown, perfect for nights of drunken bar-hopping or cool European friends with deep but chic pockets. The sexier of these hotels include: **The Hotel Gansevoort (Map 5)**, a sleek tower of luxury, located steps away from the Meatpacking District—New York's very own version of Miami Beach! Nearby, you'll find **The Maritime Hotel (Map 8)**, which does a great impression of a cruise ship, replete with porthole-shaped windows and La Bottega, an Italian restaurant with a massive outdoor patio that feels like the deck of a Carnival liner. In trendy SoHo, you'll find **The Mercer Hotel (Map 6)**, **60 Thompson (Map 6)**, and **The SoHo Grand (Map 2)** (there's also its sister, **The Tribeca Grand (Map 2)**, farther south)—which vary ever-so-slightly in degrees of coolness, depending on your demands. A little ways north, next to Gramercy Park, you'll find **The Inn at Irving Place (Map 10)**—things are a tad less modern at this upscale bed and breakfast (it consists of two restored 19th-century townhouses), but the Cibar Lounge, the rock and fashion royalty, and the lack of any visible signage outside are sure to validate your inner yearning to hip. Speaking of which, there are a few new boutique hotels on the Bowery to make all your rock star dreams come true. **The Bowery Hotel (Map 6)** was the first to make its mark on this former stretch of skid row. The Lobby Bar is worth checking

out even if you can't afford a room. Up the street the semi-sleek **Cooper Square Hotel (Map 6)** is competing for models and I-Bankers expense accounts. Check out how they squeezed the fancy hotel in between two existing tenement buildings. And not too far away is the super fancy **Crosby Street Hotel (Map 6)**, another of those cool hotels we'll never be able to afford. One thing we can afford is a stroll down the High Line to crane our necks at the exhibitionists who often can be spotted cavorting in the floor-to-ceiling windows of **The Standard (Map 5)** which, er, straddles the airborne park. Guests are reminded by staff that their rooms will be highly visible and they should be careful, which of course prompts many to be careful to show off as much as they can for onlookers.

But speaking of money and thrills we can't afford, let's get real: most of us can't begin to afford such luxuries as those outlined above. We live in a city where pay is kinda flat (or at least flatter than expenses), there's a rent affordability crisis unlike anything in NYC history, and the only reason you really need a hotel is because as much as you might love Aunt Edna from Des Moines and want to spend time with her during her fortnight in the city, you don't want to step on her as she sleeps on the floor of your studio apartment when you stumble home after last call. For these real-world occasions, rest assured there are a few hotels in the city where real people can actually afford to stay. Some of these include **The Gershwin Hotel (Map 9)**, **Herald Square Hotel (Map 9)**, **The Hotel at Times Square (Map 12)**, **Red Roof Inn (Map 9)**, **Second Home on Second Avenue (Map 6)**, and **The Chelsea Savoy (Map 9)**—all solid, safe choices.

More mid-range options include: **Hotel Thirty Thirty (Map 9)**, **The Abingdon Guest House (Map 5)**, **The Roger Williams Hotel (Map 9)**, **Portland Square Hotel (Map 12)**, **Comfort Inn (Map 9)**, **Clarion Hotel (Map 10)**, and **The New Yorker Hotel (Map 8)**. Whatever you do, never book your family, friends, or self into a hotel that you don't know or haven't scouted, no matter how appealing the cost—if it seems too good to be true, it may well be. Some of the lowest-priced "hotels" in town appear on some leading hotel booking sites, and they can be really scary. Some are in unsavory neighborhoods, or are in old buildings and barely qualify as hotels. You may arrive and find that someone's suitcases are already in your room, or that there's no heat or hot water, or that the room feels more like a homeless shelter than a hotel. (Yup, this actually happens. Even to seasoned New Yorkers like us, when we get too enamored of a would-be bargain.) And let's not mention the bedbug threat. Suffice it to say, always always always go with a brand you trust, or check it out beforehand in person or online. That's the only way to be sure you or your out-of-town visitors won't end up with the most unwelcome kind of New York story.

No matter what range of hotel you are looking to book, and for whatever reason, note that rates are generally highest during the holiday season and the summer, and lowest during the off season. Other specific events, like Fashion Week or the UN General Assembly, can cause the price of hotel rooms to increase markedly. Regardless of time of year, sometimes you'll get a better deal if you book well in advance, and sometimes you can score an awesome find by booking at the very last minute on a site like **Hotwire.com**. And sometimes you're just out of luck—rates are ballpark and they are subject to change up until you have the reservation. If you find yourself in a bind and you need to get a room for yourself or someone else, also try some of the other aggregator sites: **Hotels.com**, **Priceline**, **Hotwire**, **Travelocity**, **Kayak**, **Expedia**, or even individual company websites. You can also call a hotel directly to ask if they have any specials. Be aware that not all hotels have a star rating and sometimes those that do aren't accurate. The quoted rates will give you an idea of the quality being offered. The bottom line is, like most things in New York, while you have plenty of options, few of them are cheap—but with serendipity and creativity, you may be the lucky one who gets the bargain.

Hotel	Address	Phone	Rate $	Map
Soho Grand Hotel	310 W Broadway	212-965-3000	$$$$$	2
Tribeca Grand Hotel	2 6th Ave	212-519-6600	$$$$$	2
Hotel Gansevoort	18 9th Ave	212-206-6700	$$$$$	5
The Standard	848 Washington St	212-645-4646	$$$$$	5
Crosby Street Hotel	79 Crosby St	800-337-4685	$$$$$	6
The Bowery Hotel	335 Bowery	212-505-9100	$$$$	6
The Mercer	147 Mercer St	212 966-6060	$$$$$	6
Sixty SoHo	60 Thompson St	212-431-0400	$$$$	6
New Yorker Hotel	481 8th Ave	212 244-0719	$$$$	8
The Maritime Hotel	363 W 16th St	212-242-4300	$$$$	11
Burl Roof Inn	8 W 32nd St	212-643-7100	$$	9
Roger Williams Hotel	131 Madison Ave	212-448-7000	$$$$	9
Chelsea Savoy Hotel	204 W 23rd St	212-929-9353	$$	9
Comfort Inn Chelsea	18 W 25th St	212-645-3990	$$	9
The Evelyn	7 E 27th St	212-545-8000	$	9
Herald Square Hotel	19 W 31st St	212-279-4017	$$	9
Martha Washington	29 E 29th St	212-689-1900	$$	9
Inn at Irving Place	56 Irving Pl	212-533-4600	$$$$	10
Clarion Hotel Park Avenue	429 Park Ave S	212-532-4860	$$$	10
The Court	130 E 39th St	212-685-1100	$$$$$	10
The Tuscany	120 E 39th St	212 686 1600	$$$$	10
W New York Union Square	201 Park Ave S	212-253-9119	$$$$$	10
Ritz-Carlton New York Battery Park	2 West St	212-344-0800	$$$$$	BPC
Hudson Hotel	356 W 58th St	212-554-6000	$$$$	11
Mandarin Oriental New York	80 Columbus Cir	212-805-8800	$$$$$	11
The Out NYC	510 W 42nd St	212-947-2999	$$$$	11
W New York Times Square	1567 Broadway	212-930-7400	$$$$$	12
Four Seasons Hotel	57 E 57th St	212-758-5700	$$$$$	12
New York Palace Hotel	455 Madison Ave	212-888-7000	$$$$$	12
Le Parker Meridien	119 W 56th St	212-245-5000	$$$$$	12
Algonquin Hotel	59 W 44th St	212-840-6800	$$$$	12
Shoreham Hotel	33 W 55th St	212-247-6700	$$$$	12
The Peninsula New York	700 5th Ave	212-956-2888	$$$$$	12
St Regis	2 E 55th St	212-753-4500	$$$$$	12
The Hotel at Times Square	59 W 46th St	212-719-2300	$$$	12
The Muse	130 W 46th St	212-485-2400	$$$$	12
Ritz Carlton Central Park	50 Central Park S	212-308-9100	$$$$$	12
W New York	541 Lexington Ave	212-755-1200	$$$$$	13
Waldorf Astoria	301 Park Ave	212-355-3000	$$$	13
Excelsior Hotel	45 W 81st St	212-362-9200	$$$	14
Carlyle Hotel	35 E 76th St	212-744-1600	$$$$$	15
Lowell Hotel	28 E 63rd St	212-838-1400	$$$$$	15
Regency Hotel	540 Park Ave	212-759-4100	$$$$$	15

Sure, eating out in New York can be a competitive sport, sometimes a contact sport. However, once you're equipped with enough information about New York's 25,000 restaurant choices, the rewards are limitless, and we can confirm that this is one of the best damn towns on Earth to eat in. Certainly you could take advantage of the city's gourmet grocery stores and make fabulous meals at home, but compare your Citarella grocery bill to the check at Westville and you'll be eating out more often. But not to worry, we can always help you find the perfect place. Whether you're looking for a restaurant with a rare 28 from Zagat, or you refuse to let that D health rating get between you and good food (re: Kosher delis and Chinatown basements), you'll never have to settle.

Eating Old

Since New York City is a perpetual culinary hotspot featuring tons of celebrity chefs (and Top Chef contestants who packed their knives and went), it's easy to get wrapped up in trendy food that looks more like a Rorschach test than dinner. Some experimental restaurants are remarkably on the cutting edge, but when you're not in the mood for aerated olive-chocolate foie gras (Wylie Dufresne, we're looking at you), you can rely on the Big Apple's longstanding heavyweights. They've relaxed the tie and jacket rule, but you can still rub elbows with the who's who at the posh **21 Club** (circa 1929, Map 12); dine on New American cuisine at the 200-plus-year-old Bridge Café, the oldest business in the city, older than Chase Manhattan (circa 1794, Map 1); slurp fresh-shucked oysters and enjoy amazing desserts under the vaulted, tiled ceiling at Grand Central Station's **Oyster Bar** (circa 1913, Map 13); sample more oysters and one of the best burgers in existence at the venerable Midtown watering hole **P.J. Clarke's** (circa 1884, Map 13); order the sturgeon scrambled with eggs, onions, and a bialy on the side at **Barney Greengrass** (circa 1908, Map 16); feast like old-world royalty at The Russian Tea Room (circa 1927, Map 12); or expand your culinary horizons with calf's spleen and cheese on a roll at **Ferdinando's Focacceria** (circa 1904, Map 32).

Eating Cheap

New York has always had options for us broke folks, and the economic collapse (still hanging on, isn't it?) didn't hurt those options either. At **Shake Shack** (Maps 9, 11, 14, 17, 30, 33, Battery Park City), you can still grab a Shack Burger for under $5 or a Shack Stack (twice the goods) for under $10. Ethnic food has always been a great friend to eaters on a budget. For the city's most

succulent soup dumplings, head to **Shanghai Café (Map 3)**. For brilliant Middle Eastern go to **Hummus Place (Map 7)**, **Gazala Place (Map 11)**, or **Taïm (Map 5)** for some of the best falafel on the planet. For Mexican check out the taquería at The Corner a.k.a. **La Esquina (Map 6)** or head out to Bushwick's factory-restaurant **Tortillería Los Hermanos (Map 10)**. The Indian lunch buffet at **Tiffin Wallah (Map 10)** is less than ten bucks and veggie friendly to boot. **Papaya King (Map 17)** has kept hot dog lovers grinning since 1932. For a gigantic plate of Puerto Rican food under ten dollars, sit at the counter of **La Taza De Oro (Map 8)**. For a cheap breakfast that even celebs appreciate, **La Bonbonniere (Map 5)** can't be beat. And many of us can't survive a day without the staples of NYC Jewish eats: bagels and knishes. For bagels, go with perennial winner **Ess-a-Bagel (Map 10, 13)** or try our favorites: **Kossar's Bialys (Map 4)**, **Absolute Bagels (Map 16)**, or the original **Tal Bagels (Map 13, 16, 17)**. For knishes, nothing beats the **Yonah Schimmel Knish Bakery (Map 6)**. Since the NFT office began in Chinatown and we're always broke (free advice: don't go into publishing), we are certified experts on eating cheap in this part of town. At **Nice Green Bo (Map 3)** get the scallion pancakes, at **Food Shing/Food Sing 88 (Map 3)** get the beef noodle soup, at **Fuleen (Map 3)** get the shrimp with chili sauce, and for Malaysian order the stingray (!) at **Sanur (Map 3)**.

Eating Hip

Eating hip usually involves the food of the moment (kale chips and artisanal popsicles) beautiful people (who couldn't possibly eat another bite of that amuse-bouche), and some kind of exclusivity (unpublished phone numbers and hidden entrances). Although, with this little hiccup in our economic stability, even the hippest places have had to let the dirty, burger-eating plebeians through their doors. That being said, the ultimate in cool dining is, of course, **Rao's (Map 20)**—or so we hear. But unless you're the Mayor, the Governor, or Woody Allen, you probably won't be getting a reservation anytime soon. If you can find the unmarked basement door of **Bobo (Map 5)**, you'll really impress your date. Head east to try the always crowded, no-reservations eatery **Freemans (Map 6)**, which hides itself at the end of an alleyway; do not miss the pork chops. For fans of Japanese izakayas, nothing is quite as fun as an evening at **En Brasserie (Map 5)**. Its gourmet menu brilliantly fuses homemade miso with duck, cod, tofu, and anything else you can think of. And the low lighting will make anyone look good. **Zenkichi (Map 29)** also has killer Japanese, and yes, it's behind a camouflaged front door, but both the food an ambiance are stellar, and it's a great date spot. David Chang's restaurant mini-empire is still on people's radars, so try **Momofuku Ko (Map 6)**. If the lines are too long at the Momofukus or you don't have friends that can afford to score a table at **The Spotted Pig (Map 5)**, try **Kuma Inn (Map 4)** on the Lower East Side. The small plates like Chinese sausage with Thai chili-lime sauce and pork wasabi dumplings are brilliant, it's BYO sake, and there's no secret phone number. If you don't mind waiting and your date isn't a vegetarian, grab a cocktail in the lobby of the slick Ace Hotel and get ready for a dinner you won't soon forget at **The Breslin (Map 9)**.

Eating Late

Some say New York never sleeps, and some (ahem, Madrid) insist that it does, but like any big city it depends on the neighborhood, so let us help you locate some options. **Kang Suh's (Map 9)** Korean barbecue runs all night, as well as a host of classic diners like **Odessa (Map 7)** and **Waverly Restaurant (Map 5)**. **Veselka (Map 6)** is the place for late-night Ukrainian soul food. You'll find cabbies chowing down past 3 am at **Lahore Deli (Map 6)**, **Big Arc Chicken (Map 9)**, or **99 Cents Fresh Pizza (Map 11, 13)**. **French Roast (Map 5, 14)** serves good croque monsieurs 24 hours, and that dessert you declined earlier in the evening. If you're near Chinatown at 3 a.m, let the wonton soup and barbecue duck at **Great NY Noodletown (Map 3)** soak up all that beer. And, of course, **Blue Ribbon (Map 6)** is still one of the best places to eat after midnight.

Eating Pizza

We don't care what Chicago says; we do pizza best! The coal oven spots top most lists: **Grimaldi's (Map 30)**, **Lombardi's (Map 6)**, **Luzzo's (Map 7)**, **John's Pizzeria (Map 5)**, and the original **Patsy's (Map 20)** in East Harlem. The coal oven enjoys extra cachet because it's illegal now, except in the aforementioned eateries where they were already in operation. However, the regular brick oven joints, such as **Franny's (Map 33)**, **Keste (Map 5)**, **Co (Map 8)** and **Lucali (Map 32)** are no slouches. For an upscale pie, try the exquisite creations at Mario Batali's **Otto (Map 6)**. Trying to find something edible near Wall Street? Check out **Adrienne's (Map 1)** delicious rectangle pies on Stone Street, or walk up to TriBeCa for a luscious Brussels-sprout-bacon-caramelized-onion pie at **Saluggi's (Map 2)**. For a classic Village scene complete with live jazz, check out **Arturo's (Map 6)** on Houston Street. The outer boroughs seriously represent here: **Louie & Ernie's** in The Bronx, **Tufino** in Queens **(Map 26)**, **Denino's** on Staten Island, and, of course, **Roberta's** and **Di**

Fara in Brooklyn. Pizza by the slice practically deserves its own category, but the highlights include **Patsy's (Map 20**, definitely the best slice in the city), **Artichoke Basille's Pizza (Map 6**, get the grandma slice), **Farinella (Map 15**, very unique), and **Joe's (Map 5**, classic NY Style).

Eating Ethnic

Spin a globe, blindly stick your finger onto a spot, and chances are you can find that cuisine on offer in New York. And an outstanding offering it will be. To wit:
Argentine: **Buenos Aires (Map 7)**
Austrian: **Edi & The Wolf (Map 7)**
Australian: **Tuck Shop (Map 6)** and **The Thirsty Koala (Map 26)**
Chinese: **Joe's Shanghai (Map 3)**, **Old Sichuan (Map 3)** and **Szechuan Gourmet (Map 9)**
Cuban: **Café Habana (Map 6)**
Dominican: **El Malecon (Map 16)** and **El Castillo de Jagua (Map 4)**
Egyptian: **Kabab Café (Map 26)**
Ethiopian: **Ghenet (Map 33)** and **Zoma (Map 19)**
German: **Heidelberg (Map 15)**, **Zum Schneider (Map 7)** and **Hallo Berlin (Map 11)**
Greek: **Kefi (Map 14)**, **Periyali (Map 9)** and **Pylos (Map 7)**
Indian: **Dawat (Map 13)**, **Banjara (Map 7)** and **Indian Tandoor Oven (Map 15)**
Italian: **Babbo (Map 6)**, **Felidia (Map 13)**, **Il Giglio (Map 2)**, **Sfoglia (Map 17)**, **Al Di La (Map 33)**, **I Trulli (Map 10)** and countless others
Japanese: **Nobu (Map 2)**, **Takahachi (Map 7)**, **Ki Sushi (Map 32)** and about 40 others
Jewish: **Sammy's Roumanian (Map 6)** and **B & H Dairy (Map 6)**
Korean: **Kang Suh (Map 9)** and **Seoul Garden (Map 9)**
Malaysian: **New Malaysia (Map 3)**
Mexican: **Alma (Map 32)** and **Mexico 2000 (Map 29)**
New Zealand: **Nelson Blue (Map 1)**
Pakistani: **Pakistan Tea House (Map 2)** and **Haandi (Map 10)**
Polish: **Christina's (Map 28)** and **Lomzynianka (Map 28)**
Russian: **The Russian Vodka Room (Map 12)** and **Russian Samovar (Map 12)**
Scandinavian: **Aquavit (Map 13)** and **Smörgås Chef (Map 1)**
South African: **Madiba (Map 31)**
Southern American: **Sylvia's (Map 19)** and **Cheryl's Global Soul (Map 33)**
Spanish: **Socarrat (Map 9)** and **Tia Pol (Map 8)**
Sri Lankan: **Sigiri (Map 7)**
Thai: **Pongsri Thai (Map 3)** and **Sripraphai (Queens)**
Turkish: **Turkish Kitchen (Map 10)**

Eating Meat

New York is home to arguably the world's best steakhouse, **Peter Luger (Map 29)**, but it's competitive at the top, and clawing at Luger's heels are: **Mark Joseph Steakhouse (Map 1)** and classics like **Sparks (Map 13)**, **Palm (Map 13)**, **Smith & Wollensky (Map 13)** and the **Strip House (Map 6)**. For the Brazilian-style "all you can eat meat fest," **Churrascaria Plataforma (Map 11)** does the trick. As for hamburgers, the rankings provide material for eternal debate: **Corner Bistro (Map 5, 26)**, **Burger Joint** at Le Parker Meridien **(Map 12)**, **J.G. Melon (Map 15)** and **Bonnie's Grill (Map 7)**, to name a few. Elsewhere, **Royale (Map 7)** compliments the perfect patty with stellar fixins for a song. Texans and Missourians alike can agree that New York has some damn good BBQ, even if we sometimes recruit our BBQ talent from down South: **Daisy May's (Map 11)**, **Hill Country (Map 9)**, **Dinosaur Bar-B-Que (Map 18)** and **Blue Smoke (Map 10, Battery Park City)** in Manhattan, and **Fette Sau (Map 29)** and **The Smoke Joint (Map 31)** in Brooklyn.

Eating Veggie

You could live your whole life here, never eat a shred of meat, and feast like a king every day (and probably live longer). Try the quality Indian fare at **Pongal (Map 10)** and, for high-end eats, **Franchia (Map 10)**, **Candle 79 (Map 15)**, and **Dirt Candy (Map 7)**. For those on a budget, try **Atlas Café (Map 7)** for a quick bite and **Angelica Kitchen (Map 6)** for something a step up. For a delicious macrobiotic meal including dessert, **Souen (Map 5, 6)** has yet to disappoint. For adventurous veggie heads, nothing beats **HanGawi (Map 9)**, consistently voted one of the best vegetarian and Korean restaurants in the city.

Eating Your Wallet

While we technically use the same currency as the rest of the country, it's actually worth about half as much here as elsewhere. Even the most frugal among us have spent 100 New York dollars on a night out and thought we got off easy—the damage can easily exceed $200 per person at a Michelin-starred restaurant. No doubt you're dying to try Eric Ripert's this and Daniel Boulud's that, but treat this like open bar at your holiday office party: Know your limit (financially, emotionally, morally), and try not to do anything you'll regret in the morning. If you can keep your food down after witnessing triple digits on your share of the tab, start on the slippery slope to gastronomically induced bankruptcy at the following restaurants, which rarely disappoint: **Babbo (Map 6)**, **Per Se (Map 11)**, **Gramercy Tavern (Map 9)**, **Le Bernardin (Map 12)**, **Bouley (Map 2)**, **Union Square Cafe (Map 9)**, **Craft (Map 9)**, **Aquavit (Map 13)** and **Spice Market (Map 5)**. And remember to manage your expectations: unless you fall in love with your server, the experience will probably not change your life. Although **Per Se (Map 11)** comes pretty damn close.

Our Favorite Restaurants

Consensus on this subject is always difficult, but with a group of New Yorkers opinionated enough to produce the NFT, we have to at least try and duke it out. We've historically granted the accolade to **Blue Ribbon (Map 6)**: it's open 'til 4 a.m., it's where the chefs of other restaurants go, it's got fondue, beef marrow, fried chicken, great liquor, a great vibe and great service. And it will always have that special place in our hearts and stomachs, but we also have to give a shout out to a few others: **Alma (Map 32)**, an out-of-the-way rooftop Mexican restaurant with stunning views and equally good tamales, mole, margaritas, and ambiance, **Sigiri (Map 7)**, a spicy Sri Lankan gem that's BYOB to boot; **Babbo (Map 6)**, because it's Babbo (call at least one month ahead); **Arturo's (Map 6)**, a classic, old-school pizza joint with live jazz, Greenwich Village locals and amazing coal-fired pizza and **Kuma Inn (Map 4)**, a hard-to-find Asian tapas restaurant that's cool and hip but also affordable, laid-back and mind-blowingly delicious.

If you ever get bored in New York City, you have only yourself to blame. When it comes to nightlife in particular, the only difficulty you'll have is in choosing amongst the seemingly infinite options for entertainment. You can just head out with your NFT and see where you end up, because many bars and venues open early and close late (can you say 4am?!). If you need a little more guidance, New York's top weeklies—*The Village Voice* and *Time Out New York*—offer tons of listings and round-ups of goings on about town, as do websites such as Flavorpill (www.flavorpill.com), **Brooklyn Vegan** (www. brooklynvegan.com), and **Oh My Rockness** (www. ohmyrockness.com). A favorite for usually cheap and off-beat picks is **The Skint** (www.theskint.com). For those of you who require more than your typical night out, **NonsenseNYC** (www.nonsensenyc.com) is an e-mail newsletter with a ton of dance parties, interactive art shows, guerrilla theater and other unusual events. Just a quick word of caution: don't forget to pace yourselves.

Dive Bars

There is no shortage of dumps in this city, so we've done our best to single out the darkest and the dirtiest. The oldest on our list is, of course, **McSorely's Old Ale House (Map 6)**, which has been in operation 1854, and looks it's straight out of *Gangs of New York*. Best experienced during the day and avoided like the plague on evenings and weekends (I mind checking out the place where Abe Lincoln drank and soaking in all that old-school barroom atmosphere. A popular choice among our staff is the oh-so-derelict **Milano's (Map 6)**. Tucked away on swiftly gentrifying Houston Street, it's been a funky refuge since 1880. In the East Village Lucy has been a fixture behind the bar at **Lucy's (Map 7)** for over three decades. Other downtown favorites include **Nancy Whiskey (Map 2)**, **Puffy's Tavern (Map 2)**, **Blue & Gold (Map 6)** and **Mona's (Map 7)**. In Midtown, **Jimmy's Corner (Map 12)** is the ultimate escape from Times Square tourist swarms, and the classic **Subway Inn (Map 15)** over on the east side. Near Port Authority keep New York City real by giving **Holland Bar (Map 11)** a few bucks in exchange for a beer. Uptown, we like **Reif's Tavern (Map 17)**, **Dublin House (Map 14)**, and **1020 Bar (Map 18)**. On the other side of the East River, check out **Turkey's Nest (Map 29)** and **Greenpoint Tavern (Map 29)** in Williamsburg and the Red Hook classic **Sunny's (Map 32)**. Finally, we offer drunken shout outs to true dives that are gone but never forgotten: Mars Bar, Max Fish, Holiday Cocktail Lounge, Milady's and so many more. If you're new to the city, Google them and see all the grime and grit you missed out on…

Great Beer Selections

It's a marvelous time to be a beer geek in New York City. The number of watering holes with mind-boggling craft beer lists grows every year, so we'll do your liver a favor and suggest a few of the best. If you're braving a bar crawl in Greenwich Village, heavily trodden **Peculier Pub (Map 6)** and **Blind Tiger Ale House (Map 5)** offer large and diverse selections, and **Vol de Nuit (Map 5)** has a huge list of Belgian beers. Going several steps further with the Trappist schtick, the East Village's **Burp Castle (Map 6)** has a fine array of Belgians, but use your inside voice or you'll be soundly shushed. Nearby **Jimmy's 43 (Map 6)** and **d.b.a. (Map 7)** are our neighborhood favorites in Alphabet City, **Zum Schneider (Map 7)** offers a slew of unique choices to wash down its German fare. In the Lower East Side, **Spitzer's Corner (Map 4)** is worth checking out early on a week night (good luck on a weekend). Beer shop **Good Beer (Map 7)** is a great place to order a flight of four beers or a growler to go, **Top Hops (Map 4)** offers a great selection of bottles and drafts, as well as a standing bar area, and **Randolph Beer (Map 3)** shines with—surprise, surprise—a great brew list. In Midtown your best bets are **Rattle n' Hum (Map 9)** or **Ginger Man (Map 9)**, which has an absolutely amazing selection with over 100 bottles and 60 taps. Chelsea has **Pony Bar (Map 11)** and **Valhalla (Map 11)** to get your horn fix. Our Uptown favorite is **Earl's Beer & Cheese (Map 17)**, which has a small space but excellent beer list.

If you're seeking good beer in Brooklyn, make Williamsburg your first stop. In fact, just head to easy, hi(pronunciation) **Spuyten Duyvil (Map 29)**, which has over 100 bottles and a rotating cask ale. From there, **Barcade (Map 29)** has an awesome synergy between its classic '80s arcade games and stellar beer list—our only complaint is that we can't drink and play Dig Dug at the same time. If you're a real beer nerd, you must go sipping at **Torst (Map 28)**, a sleek Danish-inspired taproom with incredible beers on draft. In Carroll Gardens, **Bar Great Harry (Map 32)** is not only a great hangout, but it also has tons of find beers to sample.

Outdoor Spaces

Outdoor space is a precious commodity in NYC, so couple it with booze and you've got the perfect destination for cooped-up city dwellers when the weather turns warm. Actually, you can find New Yorkers stubbornly holding court at outdoor venues in all sorts of weather short of electrical storms and sub-freezing temperatures, and they'll only retreat from those conditions when chased indoors by the staff. Although entry to many of the finest outdoor drinking dens requires supermodel looks or celebrity status, or at the very least a staggering tolerance for douchebags, there are plenty of options for the mere mortals among us. For example, the **Vu Bar (Map 9)** at the top of La Quinta Inn in Koreatown is a low-key establishment that'll let you in no matter what you wear or who you hang out with. For a little fancier but still accessible night out in the open air, try **Bookmarks (Map 12)**, the rooftop bar in the Library Hotel. For drinks with a view, check out **Berry Park (Map 29)** in Williamsburg, which looks out across the river toward Manhattan, or if you're hip enough to get in, glide up to **The Ides at Wythe Hotel (Map 29)** for a perfect Instagram skyline moment.

Our favorite places to enjoy a drink outside are in the many back patios that turn the darkest, funkiest watering holes into *bona fide* oases, no matter how small and concrete-laden they may be. Beer lovers congregate in the backyards at **d.b.a. (Map 7)** in the East Village and **Spuyten Duyvil (Map 29)** in Williamsburg, and the aptly named **Gowanus Yacht Club (Map 32)** remains our Carroll Gardens favorite. More outdoor drinking can be had at **Sweet & Vicious (Map 6)** for frozen margaritas in the Lower East Side, **The Park (Map 8)** in Chelsea, **The Heights Bar & Grill (Map 18)** in Morningside Heights, **The Gate (Map 33)** in Park Slope, and **Union Pool (Map 29)** in Williamsburg. In Long Island City, there's an excellent beer garden called **Studio Square (Map 27)**. Speaking of beer gardens, there's a seeming resurgence of these all-but-disappeared drinking venues, once popular with the central European immigrant set. Predictably packed results can be found at **La Birreria (Map 9)** or **Spritzenhaus (Map 29)**. But if you can only visit one, make it the 100-year-old **Bohemian Hall & Beer Garden (Map 26)** in Astoria. Snag a picnic table in the massive outdoor area with a gang of friends, and knock back frosty pitchers of pilsner just like they did in the old days (polka dancing optional).

Best Jukebox

Personal taste factors heavily in this category of course, but here is a condensed list of NFT picks. For Manhattan: **Ace Bar (Map 7)** (indie rock/punk), **Hi-Fi (Map 7)** (a huge and diverse selection), **7B (Horseshoe Bar) (Map 7)** (rock all the way), **WCOU Radio (Tile Bar) (Map 7)** (eclectic), **The Magician (Map 4)** (eclectic), **Rudy's Bar & Grill (Map 11)** (blues), **Welcome to the Johnsons (Map 4)** (indie rock/punk). For Brooklyn: **Boat Bar (Map 32)** (Carroll Gardens—indie rock), the **Brooklyn Social Club (Map 32)** (Carroll Gardens—country/soul) and **The Levee (Map 29)** (Williamsburg—good all around).

DJs and Dancing

New York's old cabaret laws make it tough to find free dance spots, but they do exist (albeit often with the velvet rope scenario that may deter the impatient). On the weekends, entry to the swankier clubs doesn't come without paying your dues in long lines and pricey cover charges. That's not our style. You'll find us dancing and hanging out at **Santos Party House (Map 3)** as well as **Le Poisson Rouge (Map 6)**. In and around Williamsburg, we suggest checking out the lively dance scene at **Bembe (Map 29)** or combine shaking your best move with a few frames at **Brooklyn Bowl (Map 29)**, which has frequent late-night DJ sets by the likes of Questlove.

Arts & Entertainment • **Nightlife**

Fancy Cocktails

In recent years mixology has practically become a religion in New York, and its temples of worship are conveniently clustered in the East Village. For starters, head to **Death & Company (Map 7)**, tell the knowledgeable servers what you like in a drink, and prepare to be converted. If wait lists aren't your thing (and there often is one) **The Summit Bar (Map 7)**, **Pouring Ribbons (Map 7)**, and bitters-focused **Amor y Amargo (Map 7)** are all solid options nearby. **Mayahuel (Map 6)**, located among 6th Street's within restaurants is practically a crash course in all things tequila and mezcal. If hardly-secret speakeasies are your thing, **PDT (Map 7)** is accessible through a telephone booth in deep-fried-dog haven **Crif Dogs** (reservations recommended). In the West Village, **Employees Only (Map 5)** is located behind a psychic's shop. And speaking of the West Village, be sure to check out **Little Branch (Map 5)** for live jazz and some of the strongest mixed drinks we've ever had the pleasure of meeting. **The Dead Rabbit (Map 1)** has brought a mixologist den to Wall Street in a historic building from the 1800's. Farther uptown, **Rye House (Map 9)** is our preferred after-work headquarters. In Midtown, the classy **The Campbell Apartment (Map 13)**, tucked inside Grand Central Terminal, is a must — especially if someone else is paying. **The Penrose (Map 15)** adds a touch of cocktail class to the Upper East Side. And for the fancier/cocktail dress set, for your opulent hotel bars, such as **Rose Bar (Map 10)** inside the Gramercy Park Hotel, **King Cole Bar (Map 12)** inside the St. Regis Hotel, or **Bemelmans Bar (Map 15)** inside the Carlyle Hotel. We're banking on our beverages to ease the pain of that tab.

Considering all the options in Manhattan, it's probably no surprise that Brooklyn has many bars offering just-as-high caliber cocktails, minus some of the crowds. Don't believe us? Head to **Dram (Map 29)**, **Hotel Delmano (Map 29)**, **Maison Premiere (Map 29)** or **Huckleberry Bar (Map 29)** in Williamsburg, or venture a little further east to **Ba'sik (Map 29)** or **The Richardson (Map 29)**. **Clover Club (Map 32)** is our favorite for mixed drinks in Cobble Hill, while **Hanson Dry (Map 31)** keeps Fort Greene residents buzzing with stellar drinks.

If you find yourself in Long Island City, Queens be sure to check out **Dutch Kills (Map 27)** and marvel at that custom-crafted ice that won't water down your drink no matter how slowly you savor it.

Wine Bars

Terroir (Map 2) has some funky wines and a friendly atmosphere despite the self-described "elitist wine bar" label. If it's date night, cozy up in the West Village at **Vin Sur Vingt (Map 5)** for a glass of Bordeaux. Go rustic-chic in at **Black Mountain Wine House (Map 32)** with a working fireplace and country lodge experience. In Brooklyn of course.

Music—Overview

New York caters to a wide array of tastes in everything, and music is no exception. From the indie rock venues of Brooklyn to the history-steeped jazz clubs in Greenwich Village to amateur night at the Apollo, your musical thirst can be quenched in every possible way.

Jazz, Folk, and Country

There are plenty of places to see jazz in the city, starting off with classic joints such as the **Village Vanguard (Map 5)** and **Birdland (Map 11)**. There's also the "Jazz at Lincoln Center" complex in the Time Warner Center on Columbus Circle which has three rooms: the 1,000-plus-seat, designed-for-jazz Rose Theater, the Allen Room, an amphitheater with a great view of the park, and the nightclub-esque Dizzy's Club Coca-Cola. For a smaller (and cheaper) jazz experience, try **Jazz Gallery (Map 9)** or **Arthur's Tavern (Map 5)** which always has a no cover charge policy. **The Nuyorican Poets Café (Map 7)** has frequent jazz performances. In Brooklyn, one of your best bets is the small back room at Park Slope's **Barbes (Map 33)**. Easily one of the best weekly jazz experiences is the Mingus Big Band's residency at **The Jazz Standard (Map 10)**. If you've never done it, do it—it's a truly great and unpredictable band that even surly Mr. Mingus (might) have been proud of. For folk & country, try **Hank's Saloon (Map 33)**, **Parkside Lounge (Map 7)** or **Jalopy (Map 32)**.

Rock and Pop

In case you've just moved back to NYC from, say, ten years in Mumbai, the rock scene is now firmly entrenched in Brooklyn. However, Manhattan's **Bowery Ballroom (Map 6)** remains the top live venue, with excellent sound and a good layout. Other notable spots this side of the East River include **Santos Party House (Map 3)**, **Webster Hall (Map 6)**, and the **Highline Ballroom (Map 8)**. **Irving Plaza (Map 10)**, **Terminal 5 (Map 11)**, and **Hammerstein Ballroom (Map 8)** aren't our favorites, but are worthwhile for the occasional top-notch acts. The best remaining small club in Manhattan is **Mercury Lounge (Map 7)**, which gets great bands right before they're ready to move up to Bowery Ballroom. As far as the rest of the Lower East Side, it helps if you like your clubs to be punky basements (**Cake Shop, Map 4**) or former bodegas (**Arlene Grocery, Map 4**). **Fat Baby (Map 4)**, and **Fontana's (Map 3)** all offer plenty of goings-on south of Houston Street as well.

When it comes to new talent, it's really the clubs in Brooklyn that shine. If you know your way around Bowery Ballroom, you'll feel right at home at Brooklyn's premiere venue, **Music Hall of Williamsburg (Map 29)**. Then there's **Trash Bar (Map 29)**, **Cameo Gallery (Map 29)**, **Pete's Candy Store (Map 29)**, **Brooklyn Bowl (Map 29)**… basically, the rocking never stops in Map 29. Maybe we'll even forgive **The Knitting Factory (Map 29)** for leaving Manhattan to move here. In Greenpoint, check out the **Warsaw (Map 28)** in the Polish National Home. We also love the **The Bell House (Map 33)** in Gowanus, **Brooklyn Masonic Temple (Map 31)** in Fort Greene and **Union Hall (Map 33)** in Park Slope.

Experimental

A number of venues in New York provide a place for experimental music to get exposure. **Experimental Intermedia (Map 3)** is fully dedicated to showcasing the avant-garde. John Zorn's performance space **The Stone (Map 7)**, takes an experimental approach in the venue's concept as well as its music, with a different artist acting as curator for an entire month and artists taking in 100% of the proceeds. **The Kitchen (Map 8)** features experimental music in addition to film, dance, and other art forms. **Le Poisson Rouge (Map 6)** has brought an exciting mix of different sounds back to the heart of Greenwich Village, and is one of our favorite spots. In Brooklyn, the experimental scene is cranking away, especially at **Issue Project Room's (Map 30)** space in Downtown Brooklyn and **Jalopy (Map 32)** in Carroll Gardens.

Everything Else

A few places run the gamut of musical genres; folksy artists one night, hot Latin tango the next, and a slew of comedy, spoken word, and other acts. **Joe's Pub (Map 6)** presents an excellent variety of popular styles and often hosts celebrated international musicians. Keep an eye on **BAMcafé (Map 31)** for a variety of great performers. For cabaret or piano bar, try **Don't Tell Mama (Map 11)**, **Duplex (Map 5)**, or **Brandy's (Map 15)**. For a more plush experience, try the **Café Carlyle (Map 15)**. But for top cabaret talent at affordable prices, go directly to **The Metropolitan Room (Map 9)**. If you're seeking some R &B or soul, check out the **Apollo Theater (Map 19)**, though they mostly get "oldies" acts. The Apollo's Amateur Night on Wednesday is your chance to see some up-and-comers. **The Pyramid Club (Map 7)** has open mic MC'ing nights. **Barbes (Map 33)** in Park Slope hosts a wide palette of "world music" (for lack of a better term), including Latin American, European, and traditional US styles, plus more experimental fare. For more sounds of the south, **SOB's (Map 5)** has live South American music and dancing and should definitely be experienced at least once. **Nublu (Map 7)** is always reliable for a fun and sweaty night, especially on Wednesdays when they feature Brazilian bands and DJs. For African music, check out **Barbes (Map 33)** on Wednesday nights with the Mandingo Ambassadors. And oh yeah—then there's all that classical music stuff, at places like **Carnegie Hall (Map 12)** and **Lincoln Center (Map 14)**—maybe you've heard of them?

For a price, you can buy anything here: a live octopus, a bag of Icelandic moss, a vintage accordion, a rolling ladder, a slap bracelet, a 3D printer, a Ferrari, a dozen cronut holes, that thing you jam into an orange to suck the juice out, *anything you want*. Even print books! While we occasionally lament the presence of chain stores, we'll challenge anyone to find a better city for shopping.

Clothing & Accessories

The Upper East Side is a classic destination for high fashion. Madison Avenue is the main artery in the 50s, 60s, and 70s, rounded out by Fifth Avenue and 57th Street. In this neighborhood you'll find **Chanel (Map 12)**, **Burberry (Map 12)**, **Tiffany & Co (Map 12)**, and other names of that ilk. For department stores, start with the original **Bloomingdale's (Map 15)**, which is close to those titans. **Saks Fifth Avenue (Map 12)**, **Henri Bendel (Map 12)**, **Barneys (Map 15)**, and **Bergdorf Goodman (Map 12)** if money's no object. We assume it *is* an object, so check out their intricate window displays for free; they're especially good around the holidays.

That being said, there are some bargains on the Upper East Side, too. **Bis Designer Resale (Map 15)** sells gently worn items from the likes of Hermes and Gucci at a fraction of the original price. **Housing Works Thrift Shop (Map 15)** typically has a great selection, and proceeds serve those affected by AIDS and homelessness. If you can deal with the crush of midtown tourists, look for sales at **Macy's (Map 9)**, or try **Century 21 (Map 1, 14)**.

These days, "vintage clothing" can mean "cute throwback" or "real period costume." The cute throwback t-shirts are at **Yellow Rat Bastard (Map 6)**, but serious applicants should investigate **What Goes Around Comes Around (Map 2)**. Our favorites overall: **Tokio 7 (Map 6)** in the East Village, **INA (Map 6)** in NoHo, **Edith Machinist (Map 4)** on the Lower East Side, **Monk Vintage (Map 29)** in Williamsburg, and for the especially fashion-forward, **Eva Gentry Consignment (Map 32)** in Boerum Hill. Devotees should attend the next Manhattan Vintage Clothing Show, where over 90 dealers sell their finery from the past century.

SoHo looks more and more like an outdoor mall, but it's still a great place to shop because of the variety and uber-high concentration. Beyond **Uniqlo (Map 6)** and **H &M (Map 6)**, there are countless huge names like **Marc Jacobs (Map 6)**, **Balenciaga (Map 6)**, and **Anna Sui (Map 6)**.

The West Village (and the Meatpacking District therein) is the spot for small, high-end boutiques. Some are a little more accessible like **Castor & Pollux (Map 5)**, and then others have $2,000 jeans. You can check out chic designs at **Stella McCartney (Map 5)**, **Alexander McQueen (Map 5)**, and department store **Jeffrey (Map 5)**, lampooned for its snobbery on Saturday Night Live (back when SNL kicked ass).

Flea Markets & Bazaars

For a classic, grungy, sprawling flea market, try **The Annex Markets (Map 11)** on 39th Street between Ninth and Tenth Avenues or **GreenFlea Market (Map 14)** on Columbus between 76th and 77th Streets. The more fashionable **Brooklyn Flea (Map 31)** dominates Fort Greene, Williamsburg, and Park Slope on the weekends with hundreds of hip vendors offering all things handcrafted: wood furniture, picture frames, sock monkeys, gold leaf necklaces, those rings made out of typewriter keys, you get the idea. **Artists & Fleas (Map 8, 29)** has a similar artsy feel in Williamsburg and inside Chelsea Market. The **Brooklyn Night Bazaar (Map 28)** in Greenpoint takes that model and adds food carts, booze, and live music, open Friday and Saturday nights until 1 a.m. **The Market NYC (Map 6)** on Bleecker Street between Thompson and Sullivan in Nolita features a refreshing group of young, local designers and their clothes, jewelry, collectibles, and other artwork.

Sports & Outdoors

Paragon Sporting Goods (Map 9) by Union Square isn't cheap, but it's a landmark and it's been there since 1908. **City Sports (Map 1, 12)** and **Modell's (Map 1, 3, 6, 9)** offer a broad range of affordable sports clothing, shoes, and athletic equipment. For cold weather and mountain gear, head to **Tent & Trails (Map 2)**, where you can also rent sleeping bags, tents, and packs.

Furniture

Done with IKEA and curb shopping on trash night? Get your credit card(s) ready for the stuff you can't afford at **West Elm (Map 30)**, **Room & Board (Map 6)**, and **BoConcept (Map 6)**. Have even more money to spend? Check out **Ligne Roset (Map 10)** in the Meatpacking District's brilliant **Vitra (Map 5)**. If vintage is your thing, head straight to Williamsburg's **Two Jakes (Map 29)** or check out a smaller shop like Fort Greene's **Yu Interiors (Map 31)**. Regular folks seeking solid pieces should look no further than the quality wood furniture at **Gothic Cabinet Craft (Map 28)** or **Scott Jordan Furniture (Map 5)**.

Housewares & Home Design

You'll lose hours of your life eyeing the exotic furnishings in **ABC Carpet & Home (Map 9)** just off Union Square. For those with shallower pockets, there's **Gracious Home (Map 8, 14, 15)** and any of **Muji's** half dozen Manhattan locations **(Map 3, 8, 9, 12)**. For paint, window dressings, and other home improvement supplies, try **Janovic (Map 11, 16)** or **Crest Hardware** in Williamsburg. Prepare for sensory overload if you take on the 35 showrooms at the **A &D Building (Map 13)**. Showrooms are open to the public, unlike at some smaller designshops nearby, which require business cards upon entry.

The adorable dinnerware at **Fishs Eddy (Map 9)** is a great alternative to mega-chains like Pottery Barn. **Zabar's (Map 14)** often-ignored second floor is a longtime favorite among the city's cooks. In Brooklyn, we love browsing for new toys and tools at **The Brooklyn Kitchen (Map 29)** and **A Cook's Companion (Map 32)**. Downtown, small but sublime **Global Table (Map 6)** has excellent, reasonably priced housewares, and **Lancelotti (Map 7)** is stuffed with colorful accessories.

Food

Three revered emporiums make the Upper West Side a culinary heaven: **Fairway (Map 14, 15, 18, 32)**, **Citarella (Map 5, 14, 15)**, and **Zabar's (Map 14)**—and then the Zabar's offshoot **Eli's Vinegar Factory (Map 17)** graces the Upper East Side. The much more affordable **Trader Joe's (Map 6, 9, 32)** is steadily multiplying, but the lines, *the lines*. **Essex Street Market (Map 4)** on the Lower East Side is a beloved institution filled with amazing meat, fish, produce, and cheese. **Grand Central Market (Map 13)** is equally good, located right in the eponymous station. **Chelsea Market (Map 8)**, housed in a National Biscuit Company factory complex, has excellent restaurants, bakeries, and food vendors (spoiler: it's not really a market).

For farm-to-table, the biggest player is the **Union Square Greenmarket (Map 9)**, which operates year-round on Mondays, Wednesdays, Fridays, and Saturdays, packed with talented chefs. The **Grand Army Plaza Greenmarket (Map 33)** in Brooklyn is also excellent and less claustrophobic than Union Square.

And now, imported foods. When it comes to Italian, Arthur Avenue in the Bronx is famed for its bakeries, butchers, and grocers, and don't forget Graham Avenue in East Williamsburg. The more centrally located **Di Palo Fine Foods (Map 3)** has regional Italian goodies and acclaimed fresh ricotta. Friendly **Despana (Map 3)** will satisfy all your Spanish desires, including $100-a-pound jamon iberico. **Sahadi's (Map 32)** has an impressive range of Middle Eastern specialties, and make time to visit their neighbors on Atlantic Avenue. For Indian and pan-Asian spices, teas, and groceries, try **Kalustyan's (Map 10)**. **New York Mart (Map 3)** is a solid one-stop for Chinese goods, and not just dehydrated scallops! There's even a destination for anglophiles, **Myers of Keswick (Map 5)**, and Aussies, **Tuck Shop (Map 6)**.

Cheese mongers? Among the best are **Murray's (Map 5)** in the West Village, **Lamarca Cheese Shop (Map 10)** in Gramercy, small but powerful **Stinky (Map 32)** in Carroll Gardens, and **Bedford Cheese Shop (Map 29)** in Williamsburg. If you're low on cash, **East Village Cheese (Map 6)** is your go-to. They don't give out free samples and the line is always long but it's one of the cheapest options in Manhattan by far. Then you'll need bread to go with your cheese, of course. Our favorites are **Sullivan Street Bakery (Map 11)**, **Grandaisy Bakery (Map 2, 14)**, and **Amy's Bread (Map 8, 11)**. For prosciutto to accompany the bread and cheese, hit **Faicco's Pork Store (Map 5)**, **Emily's Pork Store (Map 29)**, **G Esposito & Sons (Map 32)**, or **Choice Greene (Map 31)**.

Coffee is absolutely everywhere, so maybe there's no point in trying to pick a favorite, but we do enjoy the beans at **Porto Rico (Map 4, 5, 6)**, or **Colombe (Map 2, 6)** for an excellent step up. Tea drinkers (yes, there are many in this coffee-fueled town!) should consult the knowledgeable staff at **McNulty (Map 5)**, or connoisseurs can head to the exquisite **Bellocq (Map 28)**. For something harder, **Astor Wines & Spirits (Map 6)** is always reliable and affordable, but **BQE Wine & Liquors** can be even cheaper **(Map 29)**.

Art Supplies

You can't put a bird on it 'til you stock up on paint. Check out **Blick Art Materials (Map 6)**, convenient to both NYU and Cooper Union. You can find the best selection of paper at **New York Central Art Supply (Map 6)** on Third Avenue. **SoHo Art Materials (Map 2)** on Wooster Street is a small, traditional shop that sells super premium paints and brushes for fine artists. Don't forget to check out both **Sam Flax (Map 13)** and **A.I. Friedman (Map 9)** for graphic design supplies and portfolios. **Lee's Art Shop (Map 12)** is a fabulous resource; how it has survived midtown rents is anyone's guess. As for Williamsburg, **Artist & Craftsman (Map 29)** is a good bet for supplies. In Fort Greene, the **Pratt Store (Map 31)** is a combined art supply store and college bookstore.

Books

These beloved shops and their adorable cats are disappearing faster than anything else in the city, but thank goodness **The Strand (Map 6)** is still here with 18 miles of new and used books, and those tantalizing $2 carts outside. Right down the street is the smaller **Alabaster Bookshop (Map 6)**, then **Spoonbill & Sugartown (Map 29)** in Williamsburg is full of art and design books, and **Unnameable Books (Map 33)** in Prospect Heights is fun for browsing. **Idlewild (Map 9, 29, 32)** is mecca for travel guides and travel literature. The gift shop at the **Lower East Side Tenement Museum (Map 4)** is a great place to start digging into NYC history, as is **Freebird Books (Map 32)** above Red Hook.

Music Equipment & Instruments

Unfortunately, 48th Street is no longer Music Row, but **Roberto's Winds (Map 12)** still chugs along over on 46th. Our favorites for gigging rock bands include **Matt Umanov Guitars (Map 5)** for guitars and amps, **Rogue Music (Map 9)** for keyboards, and **Ludlow Guitars (Map 4)** for guitars and basses. Go see the jumble of world instruments hanging from the ceiling at **Music Inn (Map 6)**, which is among the last of a dying breed. Classical violinists and other civilized types should visit **Strings and Other Things (Map 14)**.

Music for Listening

CDs and cassettes are scarce these days, but vinyl is still supremely cool. We always love hip **Other Music (Map 6)** and avant garde **Downtown Music (Map 3)**. If you're into trolling through used bins, head to Bleecker Street's **Rebel Rebel (Map 5)** and **Bleecker Street Records (Map 5)**. Or head to one of North Brooklyn's many options, like **Earwax (Map 29)**, **Academy Annex (Map 29)**, or **Permanent Records (Map 28)**.

Electronics

If you can't remember what a regular 2D printer is and why should you?), go straight to the 3D photo booth at the **MakerBot Store (Map 7)**. B&H (Map 8) is the top destination for professionals and amateurs when it comes to photography, audio, and video, plus they have a decent selection of computers. Note that the hectic megastore is run by Orthodox Jews who strictly observe the Sabbath and holidays, so always check the hours online before heading over. For photographic equipment especially, remember the holy trinity of **B&H, Adorama, and K&M Camera (Map 3)**. B&H is the mothership, Adorama's great if you're nearby, and K&M is the only one open on Saturdays. Remember to flash that student ID if you've got it, as some art stores offer a discount. Audiophiles are wonderfully served by **Stereo Exchange (Map 6)** and the jaw-dropping **Sound by Singer (Map 9)**. For all things Mac, try **Tekserve (Map 9)**, the (other) Apple specialists.

Weird & Bizarre

First on the list is **Brooklyn Superhero Supply (Map 33)**, where your anti-gravity elixir and gold lamé sidekick cape are waiting. **Evolution (Map 6)** is mandatory for those with a dark side; think macabre biological jewelry, preserved scorpions, and bat skeletons. Equally bewitching is **Enchantments (Map 7)**, your incense-filled emporium for motherwort, frankincense tears, and all things wicca. Scribes and pen nerds, report to City Hall's **Fountain Pen Hospital (Map 3)**. And then you'll need the ultimate accessory for your library, so call the **Putnam Rolling Ladder Company (Map 6)**. Antique button collectors, check out the Upper East Side's **Tender Buttons (Map 15)**. **Western Spirit (Map 2)** is the city's only wild west themed store, selling not just Texan kitsch, but Lucchese boots and turquoise bolo ties. If you need authentic NYC memorabilia, whether it's a lucky NYPD horseshoe or a real taxi cab medallion, go directly to the **New York City Store (Map 3)**. Full disclosure, that medallion isn't actually usable—those can roll for over a million bucks.

Shopping Districts

In the age of internet shopping, these districts are fading out, so see them while you can. The Garment District (25th to 40th Streets, Fifth to Ninth Avenues) has fabrics, buttons, zippers, ribbons, sequins, and doo-dads of all sorts. The Diamond District (47th Street between Fifth and Sixth Avenues) is the world's largest market for the precious stone. The Flower District (28th Street between 6th and 7th Avenues) is right above the Perfume District (Broadway in the 20s and 30s). Bowery below Houston is chock full of restaurant supply stores, and Bowery below Delancey is the Lighting District.

Overview

If you want to see cutting-edge art, go to New York City's galleries. There are more than 500 galleries in the city, with artwork created in every conceivable medium (and of varying quality) on display. SoHo, Chelsea, DUMBO, and Williamsburg are the hot spots for gallery goers, but there are also many famous (and often more traditional) galleries and auction houses uptown, including **Christie's (Map 12)** and **Sotheby's (Map 15)**. With so much to choose from, there's almost always something that's at least *provocative*, if not actually *good*.

The scene at the upscale galleries is sometimes intimidating, especially if you look like you are on a budget. If you aren't interested in buying, they aren't interested in you being there. Some bigger galleries require appointments. Cut your teeth at smaller galleries; they aren't as scary. Also, put your name on the mailing lists. You'll get invites to openings so crowded that no one will try to pressure you into buying (and there's free wine). **The Armory Show** (www.thearmoryshow.com), an annual show of new art, is also a great way to see what the galleries have to offer without intimidation.

SoHo Area

It wasn't so long ago that there were hundreds of art galleries in SoHo. Now it has practically become an outdoor mall. However, there are still some permanent artworks in gallery spaces, such as Walter De Maria's excellent **The Broken Kilometer** (a Dia-sponsored space at 393 West Broadway), and his sublime **New York Earth Room (Map 6)**. A short jaunt down to TriBeCa will land you in LaMonte Young's awesome aural experience Dream House at the **MELA Foundation (Map 2)**. **Artists Space (Map 2)**, one of the first alternative art galleries in New York, is also in TriBeCa. The **HERE Arts Center (Map 5)** showcases a wide range of work and usually offers an exhibit or performance that warrants a visit. On the Lower East Side check out **Canada (Map 3)** for fun openings and **Envoy Gallery (Map 6)** for cutting edge photography and celebrity sightings.

Chelsea

The commercialization of SoHo has helped make Chelsea the center of the city's gallery scene. Our recommendation is to hit at least two streets—W 24th Street between Tenth and Eleventh Avenues, and W 22nd Street between Tenth and Eleventh Avenues. W 24th Street is anchored by the almost-always-brilliant **Gagosian Gallery (Map 8)** and also includes the **Luhring Augustine (Map 8)**, **Mary Boone (Map 12)**, **Barbara Gladstone (Map 8)**, **Marianne Boesky (Map 8)**, and **Matthew Marks (Map 8)** galleries. W 22nd favorites include and **Julie Saul (Map 8)**, **Leslie Tonkonow (Map 8)**, and **Yancey Richardson (Map 8)** galleries. Also, check out the famous "artist's" bookstore **Printed Matter (Map 8)**.

Other recommendations are the **Starrett-Lehigh Building (Map 8)**, not only for the art but also for the great pillars, windows, and converted freight elevators, **Pace Wildenstein (Map 8)**, and the **Jonathan LeVine Gallery (Map 8)**, which consistently features exciting artists.

Brooklyn

While the concentration of galleries in Brooklyn is nowhere near the same as in Chelsea, added together, there are well over a hundred in the borough now, with the three biggest areas being in DUMBO, Williamsburg, and Bushwick. Look for great events like Bushwick Open Studios and the DUMBO Arts Festival to get yourself oriented to Brooklyn's ever-growing art scene.

The New York City book scene has taken a sharp decline in terms of diversity in recent years, with many excellent bookshops—including Coliseum Books, A Different Light, Academy, A Photographer's Place, Rizzoli SoHo, Tower Books, Brentano's, Spring Street Books, and Shortwave—all going the way of the dodo. The remaining independent stores are now the last outposts before everything interesting or alternative disappears altogether. And some of NYC's richest cultural neighborhoods—such as the East Village and the Lower East Side—don't have enough bookstores to even come close to properly serving their populations. So we thought we'd take this opportunity to list some of our favorite remaining shops…

General New/Used

The **Strand (Map 6)** on Broadway, the largest and arguably most popular independent bookstore in town, boasts staggering range and depth in its offerings (and often the best prices around to boot). Whether you're interested in art tomes, rare first editions, foreign language texts, non-fiction works, or the latest bestseller, it's impossible to be disappointed. In SoHo, **McNally Jackson (Map 6)** might just be our favorite bookstore after The Strand. **St. Mark's Bookshop (Map 6)** anchors the border between the NYU crowd and the East Village hipster contingent and features an excellent selection of literary journals. **Argosy Book Store (Map 13)** on 59th Street is still a top destination for antiquarian books. Uptown, **Book Culture (Map 18)** serves the Columbia area well. With four locations around the city, the punchy **Shakespeare & Company (Maps 6, 10, 15)** is a local chain that somehow manages to maintain an aura of independence. In the West Village, **Three Lives and Co. (Map 5)** should be your destination. The **Barnes & Noble (Map 9)** in Union Square is their signature store and has a great feel. The **Housing Works Used Book Café (Map 6)** has a vintage coffeehouse feel and is one of our favorite bookstores—all of the profits go to help homeless New Yorkers living with HIV/AIDS.

Several neighborhoods in Brooklyn have great bookstores with lots of local (and well known!) author readings, such as **Spoonbill & Sugartown (Map 29)** in Williamsburg, **Word (Map 28)** in Greenpoint, **Greenlight Bookstore (Map 31)** in Fort Greene, and **BookCourt (Map 32)** in Cobble Hill. DUMBO's **powerHouse Arena (Map 30)** is a great destination for art books. In Queens, **Astoria Bookshop (Map 26)** is a welcoming, uncluttered space with good children's and NYC sections.

Small/Used

Fortunately there are still a lot of used bookstores tucked away all over the city. **Mercer Street Books (Map 6)** serves NYU and **East Village Books (Map 7)** takes care of the East Village, while on the Upper East Side both **Corner Bookstore (Map 17)** and **Crawford Doyle (Map 15)** keep it old-school. In Brooklyn, check out **Unnameable Books (Map 33)** for hyper-local poetry.

Travel

The city has some excellent travel book outlets, including the elegant **Complete Traveller Antiquarian Bookstore (Map 9)** and the wonderful **Idlewild Books (Map 9, 29, 32)**, which curates its collection by country where guidebooks, fiction, and travel writing all happily commingle for a unique way of browsing. So if you can't afford to travel, a trip here is the next best thing.

Art

Printed Matter (Map 8) houses one of the best collections of artists' books in the world and is highly recommended. The **New Museum Store (Map 6)** also offers a brilliant selection of both artists' and art books. If you aren't on a budget and have a new coffee table to fill, try **Ursus (Map 15)**. For handsome photography collections, check out **Dashwood Books (Map 6)** on super sleek Bond Street.

NYC/Government

The **City Store (Map 3)** in the Municipal Building is small but carries a solid selection (and is still the only store we've seen that sells old taxicab medallions). The **Civil Service Bookstore (Map 3)** has all the study guides you'll need when you want to change careers and start driving a bus. The **United Nations Bookshop (Map 13)** has a great range of international and governmental titles. The **New York Transit Museum Gallery Annex & Store (Map 13)** at Grand Central also has an excellent range of books on NYC.

Specialty

Books of Wonder (Map 9) in Chelsea has long been a downtown haven for children's books. For mysteries, **The Mysterious Bookshop (Map 2)** slakes the need for the whodunit. The **Drama Book Shop (Map 12)** is a great source for books on acting and the theater. **Bluestockings (Map 4)** is the epicenter for radical and feminist literature. Professional and amateur chefs turn to **Bonnie Slotnick (Map 5)** and **Kitchen Arts and Letters (Map 17)**. **La Casa Azul Bookstore (Map 17)** adds much needed lit cred to East Harlem, offering adult and kids books in Spanish and English, an art gallery, and a lovely backyard.

Readings

Anyone can *read* great authors, but New Yorkers have ample opportunities to meet them as well. The four-story **Barnes & Noble (Map 9)** in Union Square regularly hosts major writers. **Housing Works Used Book Café (Map 6)** also draws some big names. And **McNally Jackson (Map 6)** in Nolita is another spot known for hosting great author events. Nearly all bookstores present readings, even if irregularly; check a store's Web page for listings. Even bars have taken a literary turn for the better: **KGB Bar (Map 6)** features fiction, poetry, and nonfiction readings each week. In Brooklyn, **Pete's Candy Store (Map 29)** and its weekly reading series are a good bet for your weekly dose of literature.

Multiplexes abound in NYC, though of course you should brace yourself for far steeper ticket and concession prices than in the rest of the country (with the possible exception of LA). Dinner and a movie turns out to be a rather exorbitant affair, but hey, we don't live in the Big Apple because it's cheap. And whether you're looking for the latest box office hit, or a classic from the French New Wave, there's a theater to meet your needs.

If you're after a first-run Hollywood blockbuster, we highly recommend the **AMC Loews Kips Bay (Map 10)** in Murray Hill. It has spacious theaters with large screens, big sound, comfortable seats, plenty of aisle room, and most importantly, fewer people! The **AMC Loews Village (Map 6)** is gargantuan, too, but movies there sell out hours or days in advance on the weekends. An IMAX theater and a cheesy '30s movie palace decorating theme make **AMC Loews Lincoln Square (Map 14)** a great place to catch a huge film, and its ideal location offers loads of after-movie options. Another great choice is the **Regal Battery Park 16 (Battery Park City)**, but it's starting to get just as crowded as the Union Square location.

For independent or foreign films, the **Landmark Sunshine (Map 6)** has surpassed the **Angelika (Map 6)** as the superior downtown movie house. Don't get us wrong—the Angelika still presents great movies, but the tiny screens and constant subway rumble can sometimes make you wish you'd waited for the DVD. The **IFC Center (Map 5)** always shows great indie flicks. If you're looking for revivals, check the listings at the **Film Forum (Map 5)**, **BAM Rose Cinemas (Map 31)**, and the **MoMA (Map 12)**. Regular attendance at those three venues can provide an excellent education in cinema history. For the truly adventurous, there's **Anthology Film Archives (Map 6)**, which plays a repertory of forgotten classics, obscure international hits, and experimental American shorts. Finally, up in Harlem the tiny but terrific **Maysles Cinema (Map 19)** shows truly brilliant indie movies focusing on New York City. This may be the most unique movie going experience in Manhattan.

The most decadent and enjoyable movie experiences can be found at the theaters that feel the most "New York." Sadly, the Beekman Theatre immortalized in Woody Allen's Annie Hall was demolished in 2005 to make room for a new ward for Sloan-Kettering (it's hard to argue with a cancer hospital, but film buffs can't help but wish they'd found another space for their expansion). The **Ziegfeld (Map 12)** on 54th Street, a vestige from a time long past when movie theaters were real works of art, is so posh with its gilding and red velvet you'll feel like you're crossing the Atlantic on an expensive ocean liner; it also became relegated to the status of "event space" in 2016. That said, the **Paris Theatre (Map 12)** on 58th Street remains one of our favorites in the city, with the best balcony, hands down!

Seeing a movie in Brooklyn a significantly better experience these days. Our favorite is the jewel-box twin **Heights Cinema (Map 30)**. Also check out indie/blockbuster mashup **Cobble Hill Cinemas (Map 32)**, **BAM Rose Cinemas (Map 31)**, and food/drink **Nitehawk Cinema** in Williamsburg **(Map 29)**. In Astoria, talk back to the screen at the **UA Kaufman Astoria (Map 26)**, and talk back to an actual director at a screening at the **Museum of the Moving Image (Map 26)**.

Oh, and don't forget to purchase tickets in advance for crowded showtimes (opening weekends, holidays, or pretty much any night when you're trying to see a popular film). Both **Moviefone** (www.moviefone.com) and **Fandango** (www.fandango.com) work.

Manhattan

	Address	Phone	Map	
92nd Street Y	1395 Lexington Ave	212-415-5500	17	Community hub for film, theater, and interesting lectures.
AMC Empire 25	234 W 42nd St	212-398-2597	12	Buy tickets ahead. It's Times Square.
AMC Loews 19th Street East 6	890 Broadway	212-260-8173	9	Standard multiplex.
AMC Loews 34th Street 14	312 W 34th St	212-244-4556	8	The biggest and most comfortable of the Midtown multiplexes.
AMC Loews 84th Street 6	2310 Broadway	212-721-6023	14	Take the subway to Lincoln Square instead.
AMC Loews Kips Bay 15	570 2nd Ave	212-447-0638	10	This multiplex is starting to show its age.
AMC Loews Lincoln Square 13	1998 Broadway	212-336-5020	14	Classy Upper West Side multiplex with IMAX.
AMC Loews Orpheum 7	1538 Third Ave	212-876-2111	17	The Upper East Side's premier multiplex.
AMC Loews Village 7	66 Third Ave	212-982-2116	6	Good-sized multiplex that keeps Union Square crowds in check.
AMC Magic Johnson Harlem 9	2309 Frederick Douglass Blvd	212-665-6923	19	Owned by Magic. Best choice for Upper Manhattan.
American Museum of Natural History IMAX	200 Central Park West	212-769-5200	14	Rest your tired legs and learn something.
Angelika	18 W Houston St	212-995-2570	6	Higher profile indies play here first.
Anthology Film Archives	32 Second Ave	212-505-5181	6	Quirky retrospectives, revivals, and other rarities.
Asia Society	725 Park Ave	212-288-6400	15	Special country-themed programs every month.
Beekman Theatre	1271 Second Ave	212-585-4141	15	Another good choice owned by the folks behind the Paris.
Bow Tie Cinemas	260 W 23rd St	212-691-5519	9	Manhattan's big, comfy, and gay multiplex.
Bryant Park Summer Film Festival (outdoors)	Bryant Park, b/w 40th & 42nd Sts	212-512-5700	12	Groovy classics outdoors in sweltering summer heat.
Cinema Village	22 E 12th St	212-924-3363	6	Charming and tiny with exclusive documentaries and foreign films.

Arts & Entertainment • **Movie Theaters**

City Cinemas 1, 2, & 3	1001 Third Ave	212-753-6022	15	Ideal cure for Bloomingdale's hangover.
City Cinemas East 86th Street	210 E 86th St	212-744-1999	17	It wouldn't be our first choice.
Czech Center New York	321 E 73rd St	646-422-3399	15	Czech premieres and special events.
Film Forum	209 W Houston St	212-727-8110	5	Best place to pick up a film geek.
French Institute Alliance Francaise	22 E 60th St	212-355-6100	15	Frog-centric activities include movies, plays, talks and exhibits.
Guggenheim Museum	1071 Fifth Ave	212-423-3500	17	Special screenings in conjunction with current exhibitions.
IFC Center	323 Sixth Ave	212-924-7771	5	Great midnights, special events, and Manhattan exclusives.
Instituto Cervantes New York	211 E 49th St	212-308-7720	13	Spanish gems, but call to make sure there's subtitles.
Italian Academy	1161 Amsterdam Ave	212-854-2306	18	Fascinating film series at Columbia. Feel smart again.
Jewish Community Center in Manhattan	334 Amsterdam Ave	646-505-4444	14	Jewish premieres, previews, and festivals.
Landmark Theatres Sunshine Cinema	143 E Houston St	212-260-7289	6	High luxury indie film multiplex.
Leonard Nimoy Thalia at Symphony Space	2537 Broadway	212-864-5400	16	A different classic movie every week. Good variety.
Lincoln Plaza Cinemas	1886 Broadway	212-757-2280	14	Uptown version of the Angelika.
Maysles Cinema	343 Malcolm X Blvd	212-582-6050	19	Amazing indies and documentaries from local film makers.
MoMA	11 W 53rd St	212-708-9400	12	Arty programming changes every day.
New York Public Library Jefferson Market Branch	425 6th Ave	212-243-4334	5	Children's films on Tuesdays.
NYU Cantor Film Center	36 E 8th St	212-998-4100	6	Dirt cheap second-run blockbusters on Monday nights.
The Paley Center for Media	25 W 52nd St	212-621-6800	12	Formerly the Museum of Television & Radio.
Paris Theatre	4 W 58th St	212-688-3800	12	Art house equivalent of the Ziegfeld.
Quad Cinema	34 W 13th St	212-255-2243	6	Gay-themed world premieres and second run Hollywood releases.
Regal 64th and 2nd Avenue 3	1210 Second Ave	212-832-1671	15	Nice big theater with two ugly cousins.
Regal Battery Park Stadium 11	102 North End Ave	212 945 4370	BPC	Beautiful downtown multiplex. Getting too crowded.
Regal E-Walk Stadium 13	247 W 42nd St	212-840-7761	12	Across the street from the Empire, but not nearly as nice.
Regal Union Square Stadium 14	850 Broadway	212-253-6266	10	Extremely crowded but fairly comfortable.
The Scandinavia House	58 Park Ave	212-879-9779	10	Scandinavian movies. Bergman and beyond.
Tribeca Cinemas	54 Varick St	212-941-2001	2	Home base of De Niro's Tribeca Film Festival.
Village East Cinema	181 2nd Ave	212-529-6799	6	Half the theaters are gorgeous, half are dank pits.
Walter Reade Theater	144 W 65th St	212-875-5456	14	Amazing festivals and rare screenings.
Whitney Museum of American Art	99 Gansevoort St	212-570-3600	5	Artist retrospectives and lectures.
Ziegfeld Theatre	141 W 54th St	212-307-1862	12	Beloved NY classic with a gigantic screen. Don't miss.

Brooklyn

	Address	Phone	Map	
BAM Rose Cinemas	30 Lafayette Ave	718-636-4100	31	Great seating and mix of first run + revivals.
Brooklyn Heights Cinema	70 Henry St	718-596-5095	30	Intimate, classy, and just about perfect.
Cobble Hill Cinemas	265 Court St	718-596-9113	32	Great indie destination, though theaters are small.
Indie Screen	285 Kent Ave	347-512-6422	29	Dinner and an art house movie under one roof.
Nitehawk Cinema	136 Metropolitan Ave	718-384-3980	29	Dinner, cocktails and craft beer while you watch indie flicks.
Pavilion Movie Theatres	188 Prospect Park W	718-369-0838	33	Nice mix of stuff right across from Propsect Park.
Regal Court Street Stadium 12	108 Court St	718-246-8170	30	Audience-participation-friendly megaplex.
Rooftop Films	various locations	718-417-7362	n/a	Summer rooftop series—check website for locations!

Queens

	Address	Phone	Map	
Museum of the Moving Image	36-01 35th Ave	718-777-6888	26	Excellent alternative to blockbuster crap.
UA Kaufman Astoria Stadium 14 & RPX	35-30 38th St	718-786-1722	26	Standard blockbuster destination.

Make a resolution: Go to at least one museum in New York City every month. There are over 100 museums in the five boroughs, from the **Metropolitan Museum of Art (Map 15)** to the **Dyckman Farmhouse Museum (Map 25)**, an 18th-century relic in upper Manhattan. Many of these museums have special programs and lectures that are open to the public, as well as children's events and summer festivals. When you've found your favorite museums, look into membership. Benefits include free admission, guest passes, party invites, and a discount at the gift shop.

The famous Museum Mile comprises nine world-class museums along Fifth Avenue between 82nd Street and 105th Street, including the **Met (Map 15)**, and Frank Lloyd Wright's architectural masterpiece, the **Guggenheim (Map 17)**. **El Museo del Barrio (Map 17)**, devoted to early Latin American art, **The Museum of the City of New York (Map 17)**, the **Cooper-Hewitt National Design Museum (Map 17)** (housed in the Andrew Carnegie's Mansion), and the **Jewish Museum (Map 17)** are also along the mile.

See medieval European art at **The Cloisters (Map 25)** (also a famous picnic spot), exhibitions of up and coming African-American artists at the **Studio Museum in Harlem (Map 19)**, and **PS1 (Map 27)** for contemporary art. Take the kids to the **Brooklyn Children's Museum** or the **Children's Museum of Manhattan (Map 14)**. The **Lower East Side Tenement Museum (Map 4)** and the **Ellis Island Immigration Museum (Map 1)** will take you back to your roots, and the treasures of the Orient are on display at the **Asia Society (Map 15)**. Couch potatoes can meet their maker at the **The Paley Center for Media (Map 12)**, which features a massive collection of tens of thousands of television and radio programs and advertisements for your viewing pleasure. The **Brooklyn Museum (Map 33)** supplements its wide-ranging permanent collection with edgy exhibitions, performances, and other special events.

Just about every museum in the city is worth a visit. Other favorites include the **New Museum of Contemporary Art (Map 6)** (in its spiffy building on The Bowery), the **New-York Historical Society (Map 14)** (which focuses its exhibits on the birth of the city), the **New York Transit Museum (Map 30)**, the **Morgan Library (Map 9)** (with copies of Gutenberg's Bible on display), the **Museum of the Moving Image (Map 26)**, the **Museum of Sex (Map 9)**, and the **Queens Museum of Art** (check out the panorama of New York City). The **National September 11 Memorial Museum (Map 1)** aims to tell the definitive story of that day, relating the huge implications thereof, at the very spot it happened. The **Whitney Museum of American Art (Map 5)** showcases contemporary American artists and feature the celebrated Biennial in even-numbered years. Finally, the **Museum of Arts and Design (Map 12)**, on the southern edge of Columbus Circle, is a bold redesign of Edward Durrell Stone's quirky masterpiece for Huntington Hartford; the excellent permanent collection and diverting exhibitions, plus working artists-in-residence and a small lovely museum store, make the Museum a must-see.

Manhattan

	Address	Phone	Map
American Academy of Arts & Letters	633 W 155th St	212-368-5900	21
American Folk Art Museum	2 Lincoln Square	212-595-9533	12
American Institute of Graphic Arts	164 Fifth Ave	212-807-1990	9
American Irish Historical Society	991 5th Ave	212-288-2263	15
American Museum of Natural History	Central Park W at 79th St	212-769-5100	15
American Numismatic Society	75 Varick St	212-571-4470	2
Anthology Film Archives	32 Second Ave	212-505-5181	6
Arsenal Gallery	E 64th St & 5th Ave	212-360-8163	15
Asia Society & Museum	725 Park Ave	212-288-6400	15
Asian American Arts Centre	111 Norfolk St	212-233-2154	4
Children's Museum of Manhattan	212 W 83rd St	212-721-1223	14
Children's Museum of the Arts	103 Charlton St	212-274-0986	3
China Institute	125 E 65th St	212-744-8181	15
The Cloisters	99 Margaret Corbin Dr	212-923-3700	24
Cooper-Hewitt National Design Museum	2 E 91st St	212-849-8400	17
Czech Center	321 E 73rd St	646-422-3399	15
Discovery Times Square	226 W 44th St	866-987-9692	12
Dyckman Farmhouse Museum	4881 Broadway	212-304-9422	25
El Museo del Barrio	1230 Fifth Ave	212-831-7272	17

Ellis Island Immigration Museum	Ellis Island, via ferry at Battery Park	212 561 4500	1
Fraunces Tavern Museum	54 Pearl St	212-425-1778	1
Frick Collection	1 E 70th St	212-288-0700	15
Gracie Mansion	East End Ave at 88th St	212-570-4751	17
Grant's Tomb	W 122nd St & Riverside Dr	212-666-1640	18
Grey Art Gallery	100 Washington Sq E	212-998-6780	6
Guggenheim Museum	1071 Fifth Ave	212-423-3500	17
Hayden Planetarium	Central Park West & W 79th St	212-769-5100	14
Hispanic Society Museum	613 W 155th St	212-926-2234	21
International Center of Photography (ICP)	1133 Sixth Ave	212-857-0000	12
Intrepid Sea, Air and Space Museum	12th Ave & W 46th St	212-245-0072	11
Japan Society	333 E 47th St	212 832 1155	13
The Jewish Museum	1109 5th Ave	212-423-3200	17
Madame Tussauds NY	234 W 42nd St	866-841-3505	12
The Merchant's House Museum	29 E 4th St	212-777-1089	6
Metropolitan Museum of Art	1000 Fifth Ave	212-535-7710	15
Mmuseumm	4 Cortlandt Alley		3
Morgan Library	225 Madison Ave	212-685-0008	9
Morris Jumel Mansion	65 Jumel Ter	212 923 8008	23
Mount Vernon Hotel Museum and Garden	421 E 61st St	212-838-6878	15
Municipal Art Society	111 W 57th St	212-935-3960	12
Museum at Eldridge Street	12 Eldridge St	212-219-0888	3
Museum at the Fashion Institute of Technology	Seventh Ave & 27th St	212-217 4558	9
Museum of American Finance	48 Wall St	212-908-4110	1
Museum of American Illustration	128 E 63rd St	212-838-2560	15
Museum of Arts & Design	2 Columbus Circle	212-299 7777	12
The Museum of Biblical Art	1865 Broadway	212-408-1500	14
Museum of Chinese in America	215 Centre St	212-619-4785	3
Museum of the City of New York	1220 5th Ave	212-534-1672	17
Museum of Comic and Cartoon Art	128 E 63rd St	212-254-3511	15
Museum of Jewish Heritage	36 Battery Pl	646-437-4200	BPC
Museum of Modern Art (MoMA)	11 W 53rd St	212-708-9400	12
Museum of Sex	233 Fifth Ave	212-689-6337	9
National Academy Museum	1083 Fifth Ave	212-369-4880	17
National Museum of the American Indian	1 Bowling Green	212-514-3700	1
National Museum of Mathematics	11 E 26th St	212 542 0566	9
Neue Galerie	1048 Fifth Ave	212-628-6200	17
New Museum	235 Bowery	212-219-1222	6
New York City Fire Museum	278 Spring St	212-691-1303	5
New York City Police Museum	100 Old Slip	212-480-3100	1
New York Public Library for the Performing Arts	40 Lincoln Center Plaza	212-870-1600	14
The New York Public Library Humanities & Social Sciences Library	Fifth Ave & 42nd St	212-340-0849	12
New York Transit Museum Gallery Annex & Store	Grand Central Terminal, Main Concourse	212-878-0106	13
New-York Historical Society	170 Central Park W	212-873-3400	14
Nicholas Roerich Museum	319 W 107th St	212-864-7752	16
The Paley Center for Media	25 W 52nd St	212-621-6800	12
Rose Museum	154 W 57th St	212-247-7800	12
Rubin Museum of Art	150 W 17th St	212-620-5000	9
Scandinavia House	58 Park Ave	212-879-9779	10
Skyscraper Museum	39 Battery Pl	212-968-1961	BPC
South Street Seaport Museum	12 Fulton St	212-748-8600	1
Statue of Liberty Museum	Liberty Island, via ferry at Battery Park	212-363-3180	1
Studio Museum in Harlem	144 W 125th St	212-864-4500	19
Tenement Museum	108 Orchard St	212-431-0233	4
Tibet House	22 W 15th St	212-807-0563	9
Ukrainian Museum	222 E 6th St	212-228-0110	6
US Archives of American Art	300 Park Ave S	212-399-5015	10
Whitney Museum of American Art	99 Gansevoort St	212-570-3600	5
Yeshiva University Museum	15 W 16th St	212-294-8330	9

Brooklyn

	Address	Phone	Map
Brooklyn Children's Museum	145 Brooklyn Ave	718-735-4400	n/a
Brooklyn Historical Society	128 Pierrepont St	718-222-4111	30
Brooklyn Museum	200 Eastern Pkwy	718-638-5000	n/a
City Reliquary	370 Metropolitan Ave	718-782-4842	29
Coney Island Museum	1208 Surf Ave	718-372-5159	n/a
Harbor Defense Museum	230 Sheridan Loop	718-630-4349	n/a
Morbid Anatomy Museum	424 3rd Ave	347-799-1017	29
Museum of Contemporary African Diasporan Arts	80 Hanson Pl	718-230-0492	33
New York Aquarium	Surf Ave & W 8th St	718-265-3474	n/a
New York Transit Museum	130 Livingston St	718-694-1600	30
The Old Stone House	336 3rd St	718-768-3195	33
Toy Museum of NY	157 Montague St	718-243-0820	30
Waterfront Museum	290 Conover St	718-624-4719	32
Weeksville Heritage Center	1698 Bergen St	718-756-5250	n/a
Wyckoff Farmhouse Museum	5816 Clarendon Rd	718-629-5400	n/a

Queens

	Address	Phone	Map
Bowne House	37-01 Bowne St	718-359 0528	n/a
Fisher Landau Center for Art	38-27 30th St	718-937-0727	27
Godwin-Ternbach Museum	65-30 Kissena Blvd	718-997-4747	n/a
King Manor Museum	Jamaica Ave & 153rd St	718-206-0545	n/a
Kingsland Homestead	Weeping Beech Park, 143-35 37th Ave	718-939-0647	n/a
Louis Armstrong House Museum	34-56 107th St	718-478-8274	n/a
MoMa PS1	22 25 Jackson Ave	718-784-2084	27
Museum of the Moving Image	36-01 35th Ave	718-777-6888	26
New York Hall of Science	47-01 111th St	718-699-0005	n/a
The Noguchi Museum	9-01 33rd Rd	718-204-7088	27
Queens County Farm Museum	73-50 Little Neck Pkwy	718-347-3276	n/a
Queens Museum of Art	Flushing Meadows Corona Park	718-592-9700	n/a
Socrates Sculpture Park	32-01 Vernon Blvd	718-956-1819	26
Voelker Orth Museum	149 19 38th Ave	718-359-6227	n/a

The Bronx

	Address	Phone	Map
Bronx County Historical Society	3309 Bainbridge Ave	718-881-8900	n/a
Bronx Museum of the Arts	1040 Grand Concourse	718-681-6000	n/a

Staten Island

	Address	Phone	Map
Alice Austen House	2 Hylan Blvd	718-816-4506	n/a
Staten Island Museum	75 Stuyvesant Pl	718-727 1135	n/a

Metropolitan Museum of Art

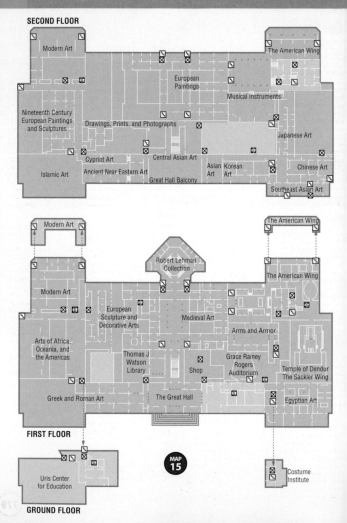

SECOND FLOOR

Modern Art

The American Wing

European Paintings

Musical Instruments

Nineteenth Century European Paintings and Sculptures

Drawings, Prints, and Photographs

Japanese Art

Cypriot Art

Central Asian Art

Chinese Art

Islamic Art

Ancient Near Eastern Art

Great Hall Balcony

Asian Art

Korean Art

Southeast Asian Art

FIRST FLOOR

Modern Art

The American Wing

Robert Lehman Collection

Modern Art

The American Wing

European Sculpture and Decorative Arts

Medieval Art

Arms and Armor

Arts of Africa, Oceania, and the Americas

Thomas J Watson Library

Shop

Grace Rainey Rogers Auditorium

Temple of Dendur The Sackler Wing

Greek and Roman Art

The Great Hall

Egyptian Art

MAP 15

GROUND FLOOR

Uris Center for Education

Costume Institute

Metropolitan Museum of Art

General Information

NFT Map: 15
Address: 1000 Fifth Ave at 82nd St
Phone: 212-535-7710
Website: www.metmuseum.org
@metmuseum
Hours: Sun–Thurs: 10 am–5:30 pm;
Fri & Sat: 10 am–9 pm;
closed Thanksgiving Day,
December 25, January 1,
and first Monday in May
Admission: A suggested $25 donation for adults,
$12 for students, and $17 for senior
citizens.

Overview

The Metropolitan Museum of Art is touted as the largest and most comprehensive museum in the Western hemisphere. Established by a group of American businessmen, artists, and thinkers back in 1870, the museum was created to preserve and stimulate appreciation for some of the greatest works of art in history.

In the first few years of its existence, the museum moved from its original location at 681 Fifth Avenue to the Douglas Mansion at 128 W 14th Street, and then finally to its current Central Park location in 1880.

Calvert Vaux and Jacob Wrey Mould designed the museum's Gothic Revival red-brick facade, which was later remodeled in 1926 into the grand, white-columned front entrance that you see today. Part of the original facade was left intact and can still be seen from the Robert Lehman Wing looking toward the European Sculpture and Decorative Arts galleries.

The Met's annual attendance reaches over 4 million visitors who flock to see the more than 2 million works of art housed in the museum's permanent collection. You could visit the museum many times and not see more than a small portion of the permanent collection. The vast paintings anthology had a modest beginning in 1870 with a small donation of 174 European paintings and has now swelled to include works spanning 5,000 years of world culture, from the prehistoric to the present and from every corner of the globe.

The Met is broken down into a series of smaller museums within each building. For instance, the American Wing contains the most complete accumulation of American paintings, sculpture, and decorative arts, including period rooms offering a look at domestic life throughout the nation's history. The Egyptian collection is the finest in the world outside of Cairo, while the Islamic art exhibition remains unparalleled, as does the mass of 2,500 European paintings and Impressionist and Post-Impressionist works. The permanent gallery of Islamic art underwent renovations in 2008, following the 10-15 year renovation of the Greek & Roman collection. The redesigned galleries display works that have been in storage for decades, assuring even the most frequent visitor something fresh to check out including the museum's newly restored, world-famous, non-gas-guzzling Etruscan chariot.

Other major collections include the arms and armor, Asian art, costumes, European sculpture and decorative arts, medieval and Renaissance art, musical instruments, drawings, prints, ancient antiquities from around the world, photography, and modern art. Add to this the many special exhibits and performances the Met offers throughout the year, and you have a world-class museum with Central Park as its backyard.

This is a massive museum and seating can be difficult to find during busy weekends. When you need a break from all of the culture, sit down for a snack in the American Wing Café or lunch in the cafeteria. Do a triple-dollar-sign splurge and eat in the Members Dining Room overlooking the park. In the summer climb up to the Roof Garden Café for a glass of wine and the most beautiful view of Central Park that your lack of money can buy.

The Greatest Hits

You can, of course, spend countless hours at the Met. Pick any style of art and chances are you will find a piece here. But if you're rushed for time, check out the sublime space that houses the Temple of Dendur in the Sackler Wing, the elegant Frank Lloyd Wright Room in the American Wing, the fabulous Tiffany Glass and Tiffany Mosaics, also in the American Wing, the choir screen in the Medieval Sculpture Hall, the Caravaggios and Goyas in the Renaissance Rooms the Picassos and Pollocks in Modern Art, and that huge canoe in Arts of Africa and Oceania. For a moment of tranquility, visit the beautiful Chinese Garden Court in the Asian galleries. When it's open, we highly recommend the Roof Garden, which has killer views of Central Park as a side dish to cocktails and conversation. When it's not, check out seasonal specials like the Christmas "Angel" Tree and Neapolitan Baroque Crèche, an annual favorite set up in front of the medieval choir screen.

How to Get There—Mass Transit

Subway
Take the 4, 5, 6 to the 86th Street stop and walk three blocks west to Fifth Avenue and four blocks south to 82nd Street.

Bus
Take the bus along Fifth Avenue (from uptown locations) to 82nd Street or along Madison Avenue (from downtown locations) to 83rd Street.

FIRST FLOOR

Ross Hall of Meteorites
Hall of Minerals
Columbus Avenue
Weston Pavilion
Human Origins
Kaufmann Theater
Linder Theater
Cafe 77
Northwest Coast Indians
Lefrak Imax Theater
Parking Garage
Special Exhibition Gallery 77
Discovery Room
Milstein Hall of Ocean Life
The Museum Shop
Sm Mammals
Hall of New York State Environment
North American Mammals
Rose Gallery
Rose Center for Earth and Space
West 77 Street
81St Entrance
North American Forests
Hall of Biodiversity
Theodore Roosevelt Memorial Hall
Gottesman Hall of Planet Earth
Central Park West
Exit

SECOND FLOOR

South American Peoples
Mexico and Central America
People Center
White Natural Science Center
Entrance
Birds of the World
African Peoples
Arthur Ross Terrace
Stout Hall of Asian Peoples
Akeley Gallery
Akeley Hall of African Mammals
Cosmic Pathwa
The Museum Shop
Big Bang
Scales of the Unive
Asian Mammals
Theodore Roosevelt Rotunda
The Butte Conserva
Main Entrance

THIRD FLOOR

Margaret Mead Hall of Pacific Peoples
Plains Indians
Eastern Woodlands Indians
Primates
Chapman Memorial Hall of North American Birds
NYS Mammals
NYC Birds
Special Exhibition Gallery 3
Akeley Hall of African Mammals
Hayden Planetarium Space Theater
Reptiles and Amphibians
Rose Center

FOURTH FLOOR

Research Library
Wallach Orientation Center
Vertebrate Origins
Saurischian Dinosaurs
Special Exhibition Gallery 4
Milstein Hall of Advanced Mammals
Primitive Mammals
Ornithischian Dinosaurs
Wallace Wing of Mammals & Their Extinct Relatives

MAP 14

General Information

NFT Map:	14
Address:	Central Park West at 79th Street
Phone:	212-769-5100
Website:	www.amnh.org
	@AMNH
Hours:	Daily, 10:00 am–5:45 pm; closed Thanksgiving Day & December 25
Admission:	Suggested general admission is $22 for adults, $12.50 for children (2–12), and $17 for senior citizens and students. Special exhibitions, IMAX movies, and the space show are extra; packages are available. Free to members.

Overview

Admit it. You secretly TiVo the Discovery Channel and the History Channel. You've even watched one—if not several—episodes of Star Trek. Something about African beetles, famous dead guys, and the unknown universe strokes your inner Einstein. Focus your microscope on this one, smarty-pants: the American Museum of Natural History, a paradise for geeks and aspiring geeks alike, not to mention good old nature lovers. And don't worry, your TV-watching secrets are safe with us.

Decades before anyone knew what an atom was, and when relativity was just a twinkle in Einstein's eye, Albert Smith Bickmore established the AMNH. Completed in 1869, the museum held its first exhibition in the Central Park Arsenal a few years later, garnering enough respect to acquire space along classy Central Park West. Architects Calvert Vaux and J. Wrey Mould designed the new, posh building on limited Benjamins and opened it to the public in 1877. Key additions followed: The Hayden Planetarium in 1935, the Theodore Roosevelt Memorial Hall and Rotunda in 1936, and the Rose Center for Earth and Space in 2000.

As Saturday morning museum-going ritual dictates, it's going to be painfully crowded. On those days, you dodge out-of-towners, eyes wide, mouths gaping. It's much the same on weekdays with rowdy school kids on field trips. How to avoid the Excedrin-necessitating atmosphere? Two words: permanent collection. The amazing series of wildlife dioramas even inspired an entire Hollywood movie (albeit not a great one, by adult standards). Don't expect to see any PETA supporters in these halls though.

When you can go at off hours, or if you feel you can brave the crowds, make a point of checking out the fascinating and often provocative special exhibits.

The Greatest Hits

Five floors of star-lovin', mammal-gazin', bird-watchin', fossil-fuelin' science await. Rain forest fever? Check out the Hall of Biodiversity. Didn't understand why that movie was called The Squid and The Whale? See the giant squid get his dimly lit comeuppance in the Milstein Hall of Ocean Life. Celebrity astrophysicist Neil deGrasse Tyson is the voice behind the Dark Universe space show. For more instant thrills, check out the gigantic meteorites at the Arthur Ross Hall of Meteorites, or the five story-tall dinosaur display in the Theodore Roosevelt Rotunda; it's the largest freestanding beast in the world. The AMNH also produces spectacular IMAX features, a great alternative to the museum's amazing but creepy taxidermy. The Hall of Gems houses the Star of India, the largest star sapphire in the world. Finally, for recreation of The Birds variety with less evil, visit The Butterfly Conservatory. Tropical butterflies flit all around you from, you guessed it, all over the world. It's enough to put TiVo on pause.

How to Get There—Mass Transit

Subway
Take the B or C to the 81st Street stop. Or take the 1 to 79th Street and walk two blocks east.

Bus
The M7, M10 and M11 all stop within a block of the museum. Take the M79 across Central Park if you are coming from the East Side.

Museum of Modern Art

General Information

NFT Map: 12
Address: 11 W 53rd St
Phone: 212-708-9400
Website: www.moma.org
                @MuseumModernArt
Hours: 10:30 am–5:30 pm (Fri until 8 pm);
                closed Thanksgiving and December 25
Admission: $25 for adults, $18 for seniors, $14
                for students; free to members and
                children under 16 accompanied by an
                adult

Overview

The Museum of Modern Art opened in 1929, back when impressionism and surrealism were truly modern art. Originally in the Heckscher Building at 730 Fifth Avenue, MoMA moved to its current address on West 53rd Street in 1932. What started out as a townhouse eventually expanded into an enormous space, with new buildings and additions in 1939 (including by Phillip L. Goodwin and Edward Durell Stone), 1953 (including a sculpture garden by Phillip Johnson), 1964 (another Johnson garden), and 1984 (by Cesar Pelli). During the summer of 2002, the museum closed its Manhattan location and moved temporarily to Sunnyside, Queens (MoMA's affiliate, MoMAPS1 remains a proud Queens institution). After a major expansion and renovation by Yoshio Taniguchi, MoMA reopened in September 2004.

After being re-Manhattanized, MoMA made waves when it became the first museum to break the $20 barrier—which sadly became all too common in the years since. If crowds on a typical Saturday afternoon are any indication, hefty entry fees are not keeping patrons away. Frequent flyers take note: If you plan to visit more than three times in a year, the yearly membership is the way to go. Plus, members get a 10% discount at MoMA stores, free tickets to all film screenings, and besides which, you're free to pop in whenever you want to see your favorite Picasso (or just use the restroom). For the best deal, visit the museum from 4–8 pm on Fridays when there is free admission—the crowds aren't as bad as you might think.

What to See

The fourth and fifth floors are where the big names reside—Johns, Pollock, Warhol (fourth floor), Braque, Cezanne, Dali, Duchamp, Ernst, Hopper, Kandinsky, Klee, Matisse, Miro, Monet, Picasso, Rosseau, Seurat, Van Gogh, and Wyeth (fifth floor). More recent works can be found in the contemporary gallery on the second floor. Special exhibitions are on the third and sixth floors. The surrealist collection is outstanding, but we've always suspected that MoMA has only a tiny fraction of its pop art on display. Well, you can't have everything…

Moving downstairs to the third floor, it's clear that the photography collection is, as always, one of the centerpieces of the museum and is highly recommended (although the Gursky pieces are actually dotted throughout the building). The architecture and design gallery showcases a range of cool consumer items, from chairs to cars to the first Mac computers, and is one of the most popular destinations in the museum.

Breakdown of the Space

Floor One: Lobby, Sculpture Garden, Museum Store, Restaurant

Floor Two: Contemporary Galleries, Media Gallery, Prints and Illustrated Books, Café

Floor Three: Architecture and Design, Drawing, Photography, Special Exhibitions

Floor Four: Painting and Sculpture II

Floor Five: Painting and Sculpture I, Café

Floor Six: Special Exhibitions

There are two theater levels below the first floor.

Amenities

Backpacks and large purses are not allowed in gallery spaces, and the free coat check can become messy when the check-in and check-out lines become intertwined. Leave large items (including laptops) at home. Bathrooms and water fountains are on all floors. We don't think that there are enough of them, and the bathrooms themselves are way too small to handle the crowds.

There are three places to get food in the museum, which has been elevated from the usual captive-audience fare by Danny Meyer's excellent Union Square Hospitality Group. Café 2, located on the second floor, offers a wide selection of small plates, sandwiches and panini, as well as above-average coffee drinks, beer and wine. Terrace 5 is a full-service establishment overlooking the beautiful sculpture garden, offers a la carte entrées and desserts, along with wine, cocktails, coffee, and tea. Both cafés open half an hour after the museum opens its doors and close half an hour before the museum closes.

The ultimate museum dining experience, The Modern (www.themodernyc.com) boasts three *New York Times* stars and one Michelin star. It has two main rooms—the Dining Room overlooking the sculpture garden, and a more casual Bar Room. An outdoor terrace is also made available when the weather permits. The Modern serves French and New American food and hubba-hubba tasting menus. The Modern is open beyond museum hours, with the Dining Room serving dinner until 10:30 pm Monday–Saturday. The Bar Room is open continuously 11:30 am–10:30 pm daily (9:30 pm Sundays). There's a separate street entrance to allow diners access to The Modern after the museum closes.

Theaters / Performing Arts

So long as there are adventurous artists putting on plays in abandoned storefronts and opportunistic real estate developers knocking down beautiful old theaters to put up hotels, the New York theater scene will always be adding a few venues here and deleting a few venues there. What remains constant is that on any given night there are at least dozens, and more often hundreds, of live theater performances to be seen. And the best ones are not always the most expensive.

Broadway (i.e., theaters in the Times Square vicinity that hold at least 500 people) still has the reputation of being the place to see American theater at its finest, but the peculiar fact of the matter is that there is more much money to be gained by appealing to the connoisseur. As a result, shows that are looked down on if not despised, by many lovers of the theater wind up selling out for years (Mamma Mia, anyone?), while more ambitious, artistically admired plays and musicals struggle to find an audience. Check out theater chat boards like BroadwayWorld.com and TalkinBroadway.com to see what the people who see everything have to say.

Nobody gets famous doing live theater anymore, so if you've never heard of the actor whose name is twinkling in lights chances are that person has the stage experience and in any chops to keep you enthralled for two and a half hours, unlike the big name celebrities who make their stage acting debuts in starring roles they're only sometimes somewhat prepared for. Of course, there are also the big-time actors with extensive stage credits who come back to Broadway regularly after becoming famous; you've got to admire anyone who willingly dives back into the grind of eight performances a week.

Many great performers work Off-Broadway (Manhattan theaters seating 100-499 people) where the writing and directing are actually more important than spectacle and scores made up of classic pop songs. Off-Off-Broadway (fewer than 100 seats) is a terrific grab bag of both beginners and seasoned pros doing material that is often unlikely to draw in masses. And tickets are pretty cheap, too.

TheaterMania.com keeps an extensive list of just about every show in New York, with direct links to the websites that sell tickets. Many shows offer a limited number of inexpensive standing room and/or same day rush tickets. A detailed directory of such offers can be found at TalkinBroadway.com.

Thousands of same day tickets for Broadway and Off-Broadway shows are sold for 20%-50% off at the TKTS booth in Times Square (long lines), at the South Street Seaport (shorter lines), in Downtown Brooklyn (which sells tickets to matinee performances a day in advance). They take cash, traveler's checks, and credit cards. Check for hours and to see what's been recently available at www. tdf.org. Don't expect to get a bargain for the top-selling hits, but most shows use this booth at some time or another. You can also download discount coupons at Playbill.com that you can use to get seats in advance.

The dirty little secret of New York theatre is that free tickets for high-quality shows are abundantly available through organizations that specialize in "dressing the house" for productions that depend more on word of mouth than expensive advertising costs. By paying a yearly membership fee to AudienceExtras.com or Play-by-Play. com, you can check your computer 24-hours a day for free tickets (there's a small per-ticket service charge) for a dozen or so Off-, Off-Off-, and sometimes Broadway shows available at the last minute. That dinky little play in some church basement that you went to on a whim might wind up being the next great American classic.

Keep an eye out for shows by these lesser-known companies:

The award-winning Classical Theatre of Harlem (www. classicaltheatreofharlem.org) has earned a reputation for mounting exciting, edgy revivals of classics from Shakespeare and Brecht, as well as solid productions from more recent greats such as August Wilson and Melvin Van Peebles. A multicultural company that frequently casts against racial type, they draw a youthful audience with imaginative interpretations.

The Mint Theatre Company (Map 11) (www.minttheater.org) specializes in reviving Broadway plays from the past they call "worthy, but neglected." In their tiny space you'll see forgotten comedies and dramas from the likes of A. A. Milne, Edith Wharton, and Thomas Wolfe played traditionally with sets and costumes that really make you feel like you're watching a production from over 50 years ago.

Musicals Tonight! does the same kind of thing with forgotten musicals only presenting them in low budget, but highly energized, staged readings. Nowadays most musicals revived on Broadway are revised and updated to the point where they lose their authenticity, but if you're in the mood to see what an Irving Berlin ragtime show from 1915 was really like, or if you want to see a Cole Porter tune from the '30s with all of the dated topical references that confused audiences even back then, Musicals Tonight! serves up the past as it really was written. And check for their special concerts where Broadway understudies sing songs from the roles they are currently covering. Shows take place at the Lion Theatre (Map 11).

Broadway insiders know that Monday nights, when most shows are dark, is often the hottest night of the week for entertainment. That's when performers use their night off to partake in benefits and special events. Consistently among the best are shows from Scott Siegel's Broadway By The Year series at Town Hall (Map 12) (www.thetownhall.org). Each one night concert is packed with theater and cabaret stars singing hits and obscurities introduced on Broadway in one selected year. Siegel also produces Broadway Unplugged at Town Hall, a concert of Broadway performers singing showtunes without amplification. The atmosphere is like a sports event, with the audience wildly cheering each naturally voiced solo.

Elsewhere, Pearl Theatre Company (www.pearltheatre.org) (Map 11) has been mounting kick-ass productions of classics by Shakespeare, Moliere, Sheridan, and the like since 1984. Horse Trade (www.horsetrade.info) produces a crazy assortment of readings, workshops, burlesque performances, and full-out productions in the East Village at venues like The Kraine Theater (Map 6). The multi-arts center HERE (Map 5) (www.here.org) not only houses two small theaters, but it also has an amazing gallery space and a cozy cafe/bar—perfect for pre- or post-show drinks. Located in a former school on First Avenue and 9th Street in the East Village, P.S. 122 (Map 7) (www.ps122.org) is a not-for-profit arts center serving New York City's dance and performance community. Shows rotate through on a regular basis, so check the website for the latest schedule. The outdoor Delacorte Theater (Map 15) in Central Park hosts performances only during the summer months. Tickets to the ridiculously popular and free Shakespeare in the Park performances are given away at 1 pm at the Delacorte and also at the Public Theater (Map 6) on the day of each performance. Hopefully, you enjoy camping because people line up for days in their tents and sleeping bags just to secure a ticket!

Just on the other side of the Manhattan Bridge in Brooklyn is the world famous Brooklyn Academy of Music (Map 31). A thriving urban arts center, BAM brings domestic and international performing arts and film to Brooklyn. The center is home to multiple venues of various sizes, including the Harvey Lichtenstein Theater (Map 31), Howard Gilman Opera House (Map 31), the Bam Rose Cinemas (Map 31), and the BAMcafe (Map 31), a restaurant and live music venue. Our favorite season is the Next Wave, an annual three-month celebration of cutting-edge dance, theater, music, and opera. As an alternative to BAM, St. Ann's Warehouse (Map 30) in DUMBO also produces exciting cutting-edge work.

Street Index

Street Index

Street Index

Street Index

Address Locator

Streets	Riverside	West End	Broadway	Amsterdam	Columbus	C.P.W.	Central Park
110-116	370-440		2800-2950	995-1120			
102-110	290-370	850-920	2675-2800	856-995	850-1021	419-500	
96-102	240-290	737-850	2554-2675	733-856	740-850	360-419	
90-96	180-240	620-737	2440-2554	620-733	621-740	300-360	
84-90	120-180	500-619	2321-2439	500-619	501-620	241-295	
78-84	60-120	380-499	2201-2320	380-499	381-500	239-241	
72-78	1-60	262-379	2081-2200	261-379	261-380	121-239	
66-72		122-261	1961-2079	140-260	141-260	65-115	
58-66		2-121	1791-1960	1-139	2-140	0-65	

Streets	12th Ave.	11th Ave.	Broadway	10th Ave.	9th Ave.	8th Ave.	7th Ave.	6th Ave.
52-58	710-850	741-854	1674-1791	772-889	782-907	870-992	798-921	1301-1419
46-52	600-710	625-740	1551-1673	654-770	662-781	735-869	701-797	1180-1297
40-46	480-600	503-624	1440-1550	538-653	432-662	620-734	560-701	1061-1178
34-40	360-480	405-502	Macy's-1439	430-537	431-432	480-619	442-559	1060-1061
28-34	240-360	282-404	1178-1282	314-429	314-431	362-479	322-442	815-1060
22-28	0-240	162-281	940-1177	210-313	198-313	236-361	210-321	696-814
14-22		26-161	842-940	58-209	44-197	80-235	64-209	5520-695
8-14			748-842	0-58	0-44	0-80	2-64	420-520
Houston-8			610-748					244-402

The address locator below is formatted north-south, from 116th Street to Houston Street. For east-west addresses, simply remember that Fifth Ave. is the dividing line—2 E 54th would be right off of Fifth, while 200 E 54th would be around Third Ave.

5th Ave.	Madison	Park	Lexington	3rd Ave.	2nd Ave.	1st Ave.	York	Streets
1280-1400	1630-1770	1489-1617	1766-1857	1981-2103	2109-2241	2175-2238		110-116
1209-1280	1500-1630	1350-1489	1612-1766	1820-1981	1990-2109	1975-2175		102-110
1148-1209	1379-1500	1236-1350	1486-1612	1709-1820	1854-1880	1855-1975		96-102
1090-1148	1254-1379	1120-1236	1361-1486	1601-1709	1736-1854	1740-1855	1700-end	90-96
1030-1089	1130-1250	1000-1114	1248-1355	1490-1602	1624-1739	1618-1735	1560-1700	84-90
970-1028	1012-1128	878-993	1120-1248	1374-1489	1498-1623	1495-1617	1477-1560	78-84
910-969	896-1006	760-877	1004-1116	1250-1373	1389-1497	1344-1494	1353-1477	72-78
850-907	772-872	640-755	900-993	1130-1249	1260-1363	1222-1343	1212-1353	66-72
755-849	621-771	476-639	722-886	972-1129	1101-1260	1063-1222	1100-1212	58-66

5th Ave.	Madison	Park	Lexington	3rd Ave.	2nd Ave.	1st Ave.	Avenue A	Streets
656-754	500-611	360-475	596-721	856-968	984-1101	945-1063		52-58
562-655	377-488	240-350	476-593	741-855	862-983	827-944		46-52
460-561	284-375	99-240	354-475	622-735	746-860	701-827		40-46
352-459	188-283	5-99	240-353	508-621	622-747	599-701		34-40
250-351	79-184	4-404	120-239	394-507	500-621	478-598		28-34
172-249	1-78	286-403	9-119	282-393	382-499	390-478		22-28
69-170	University	0-285	1-8	126-281	230-381	240-389		14-22
9-69	0-120			59-126	138-230	134-240	129-210	8-14
0-9				1-59	0-138	0-134	0-129	Houston - 8

NOT FOR TOURISTS
PUNCH LIST
NEW YORK CITY

EVENTS

☐ **Brooklyn Book Festival** .... Two of Brooklyn's favorite .... Downtown Brooklyn .... Brooklyn
things: Books and Brooklyn
(**mid-September**).

☐ **Shakespeare in the Park** .... Free out-sized outside .... Delacorte Theater, ... Manhattan
summertime plays with   Central Park
boldface names.

☐ **Mermaid Parade** .... Slap on your fins and celebrate .... Coney Island .... Brooklyn
summer (**late June**).

☐ **NYC Marathon** .... 26 miles of NYC air .... Citywide .... Citywide
(**first Sunday of November**).

☐ **Open House New York** .... Insider access to architecture and .... Various .... Citywide
design landmarks (**early October**).

SHINY & NEW

☐ **The Whitney** .... Always has something to talk .... 99 Gansevoort St .... Manhattan
about, now part of the
High Line-Industrial Complex.

☐ **One World Trade Center** .... At 1,776 feet, the tallest building ...... Vesey St .... Manhattan
in the Western Hemisphere.

☐ **Ridgewood** .... Queens charm and .... Ridgewood .... Queens
affordability meets Bushwick.

☐ **REI (Puck Building)** .... Outdoor gear superstore .... 295 Lafayette St .... Manhattan
in the Puck Building.

☐ **Food Halls (list)** .... Food courts go gourmet in .... Various .... Manhattan/
the city. Try Gotham West,   Brooklyn
Hudson Eats, Berg'n, or Eataly.

☐ **Four Freedoms Park** .... Posthumously built Louis Kahn .... Roosevelt Island .... Manhattan
design; FDR memorial and
stunning views.

☐ **Lincoln Center** .... High culture superblock .... 66th St and Broadway ..... Manhattan
retrofitted for a human dimension.

ENDANGERED SPECIES

☐ **Katz's** .... Classic New York pastrami; .... 205 E Houston St .... Manhattan
I'll have what she's having!

☐ **Gem Spa** .... Magazine stand that serves .... 131 2nd Ave .... Manhattan
fantastic egg creams.

☐ **Barbes** .... Smart-looking space with .... 376 9th St .... Brooklyn
eclectic entertainment.

☐ **Sunny's** .... No longer pay-what-you-wish .... 253 Conover St .... Brooklyn
but still cheap and good.

☐ **Crown Heights** .... Officially hot, just this .... Crown Heights .... Brooklyn
side of unaffordable.

☐ **Di Fara** .... Meticulously crafted .... 1424 Ave J .... Brooklyn
by hand since 1965.

☐ **Anthology Film** .... Jonas Mekas' dream come .... 32 2nd Ave .... Brooklyn
Archives to life—a monument to the
avant-garde in film.

☐ **Sammy's** .... An experience not to be missed .... 157 Chrystie St .... Manhattan
Roumanian Chopped liver which will
instantly kill you.

☐ **Economy Candy** .... Floor-to-ceiling candy madness .... 108 Rivington St .... Manhattan

REST IN PEACE

☐ **Pearl Paint** .... Mecca for artists, designers, and .... 308 Canal St .... Manhattan
people who just like art supplies.

☐ **Pearl River Mart** .... Chinese housewares and more. .... 477 Broadway .... Manhattan
Almost mind-numbling.

☐ **Mars Bar** .... The king of grungy bars sacrificed .... 25 E 1st St .... Manhattan
to the real estate gods.

☐ **wd~50** .... Michelin-starred gastronomical .... 50 Clinton St .... Manhattan
wonderworld sacrificed to the
real estate gods.

☐ **Winnie's** .... The best Chinese gangster .... 104 Bayard St .... Manhattan
karaoke dive in Lower Manhattan.

☐ **Stage Deli** .... Artery-clogging and ridiculously .... 834 Seventh Ave .... Manhattan
expensive but so, so missed.

☐ **Cafe Edison** .... Theater district mainstay for .... 228 W 47th St .... Manhattan
Jewish soul food sacrificed
to the gods of schmancy.

☐ **Williamsburg** .... Real Estate section ink-generating .... Williamsburg .... Brooklyn
hipsturbia. With a Duane Reade.

PUNCH LIST
Continued

CLASSICS

☐ **Cloisters** .... The Met's storehouse of .... Fort Tryon Park .... Manhattan
medieval art. Great herb
garden, nice views.

☐ **Brooklyn Bridge** .... The granddaddy of them all. .... Lower Manhattan- .... Manhattan
Walking toward Manhattan   Downtown Brooklyn   Brooklyn
at sunset is as good as it gets.

☐ **Recycle-A-Bicycle** .... Non-profit youth organization .... 75 Ave C .... Manhattan
refurbishing and selling used bikes.

☐ **West Village** .... Quaint beauty, great restaurants, ... West Village .... Manhattan
and top-notch/dollar shopping
with faint traces of bohemian past.

☐ **B & H Photo** .... Where everyone in North .... 420 Ninth Ave .... Manhattan
America buys their cameras
and film. Closed Saturdays.

☐ **Film Forum** .... Best place to pick up a film geek...... 209 W Houston St........... Manhattan

☐ **Coney Island** .... Classic New York summer: .... Coney Island .... Brooklyn
hot dog, coaster, sideshow, beach.

☐ **Dublin House** .... Great dingy UWS Irish pub. .... 225 W 79th St................ Manhattan

☐ **Di Palo Fine Foods** .... Delicacies from across Italy. .... 200 Grand St .... Manhattan
Excellent cheese.

☐ **Printed Matter** .... Astounding selection...................... 195 Tenth Ave .... Manhattan
of artist's books.

☐ **Village Vanguard** ...... Classic NYC jazz venue. .... 178 Seventh Ave So. .... Manhattan
Not to be missed.

HIDDEN GEMS

☐ **Alice Austen** .... Dedicated to the documentary.......... 2 Hylan Blvd .... Staten Island
House   photography and life of Alice Austen.

☐ **Wave Hill** .... The view of the Palisades is .... Independence Ave .... The Bronx
unbeatable.   and W 249th St

☐ **Green-Wood** .... Lots of winding paths and greenery . 500 25th St..................... Brooklyn
Cemetery   good for contemplation.

☐ **Weeksville Center** ..... Preserving the history of one of........ 158 Buffalo Ave .... Brooklyn
America's first free black communities.

☐ **Historic** .... Restored buildings from days of .... 441 Clarke Ave .... Staten Island
Richmond Town   yore, most populated by costumed guides.

USED TO BE COOL

☐ **Lower East Side** .... Soon the world will be one big .... Lower East Side .... Manhattan
12-story luxury building.

☐ **The High Line** .... A revelatory re-purposing; and .... West Village .... Manhattan
then everyone and everything
showed up.

☐ **Anything With** .... Do you even realize how many .... Citywide
Cupcakes goddamn calories are in
buttercream frosting?

GASTRONOMIC UNDERGROUND

☐ **Do or Dine** .... Definitely Do it. Bizarro small .... 1108 Bedford Ave .... Brooklyn
plates and back garden. Killer

☐ **Jungsik** .... White tablecloth multi-star Korean ... 2 Harrison St .... Manhattan
in former Chanterelle space.

☐ **St. Anselm** .... We have no reservations about .... 355 Metropolitan Ave .... Brooklyn
this sizzling steak spot.

☐ **M. Wells** .... More boffo dishes from strange .... 43-15 Crescent St .... Queens
Steakhouse animal parts at this hipster
meat palace.

☐ **Traif** .... Bacon-wrapped scallops at a .... 229 S 4th St .... Brooklyn
Saturday reception?
Go with your heart.

NEVER BEEN COOL

☐ **Javits Center** .... Glass-sheathed behemoth hosting ... 655 W 34th St .... Manhattan
various and sundry cons.

☐ **Macy's** .... There's a reason children on .... 151 W 34th St .... Manhattan
Santa's lap start to cry.

☐ **Port Authority** .... One day we'll rediscover the .... 625 Eighth Ave .... Manhattan
golden age of bus travel. Until then...

☐ **Penn Station** .... Makes commuters scream .... Eighth Ave .... Manhattan
and preservationists cry. and W 32nd St

☐ **Times Square** .... Can't there be a middle ground ...... Times Square .... Manhattan
between peep shows and
"retail experiences"?

☐ **Upper East Side** .... A place everyone's waiting to .... Upper East Side .... Manhattan
move out of. Alive or dead.